THE FILM
TILL NOW

Books by Paul Rotha

CELLULOID: THE FILM TODAY (1931)

DOCUMENTARY FILM
(1936, 1939, and with Richard Griffith and Sinclair Road, 1952, 1966)

MOVIE PARADE
(1936, and with Roger Manvell, 1950)

ROTHA ON THE FILM (1958)

WORLD OF PLENTY
(book of the film, 1945)

PORTRAIT OF A FLYING YORKSHIREMAN
(the letters of Eric Knight to Paul Rotha, 1952)

Editor of TELEVISION IN THE MAKING (1956)

Some Films by Paul Rotha

Feature

THE SILENT RAID (De Overval) (1963)
CAT AND MOUSE (1957)
NO RESTING PLACE (1950)

Documentary

THE LIFE OF ADOLF HITLER (1960–61)
CRADLE OF GENIUS (1958)
WORLD WITHOUT END (with Basil Wright) (1952–53)
THE WORLD IS RICH (1947–48)
A CITY SPEAKS (1946)
LAND OF PROMISE (1944–45)
WORLD OF PLENTY (1942–43)
THE FOURTH ESTATE (1939–40)
NEW WORLDS FOR OLD (1938)
THE FACE OF BRITAIN (1935)
SHIPYARD (1934)
CONTACT (1932–33) etc., etc.

Past Chairman of:
The British Film Academy, the Federation of
Documentary Film Units, Council Member of the
British Screenwriters Association.

Frontispiece: Paul Rotha editing "The Life of Adolf Hitler", Hamburg, 1960–61.

THE FILM TILL NOW

A SURVEY OF WORLD CINEMA

PAUL ROTHA

WITH AN ADDITIONAL SECTION BY

RICHARD GRIFFITH

SPRING BOOKS

Originally published 1930 by Jonathan Cape
Revised edition published 1949 by Vision Press Ltd, second impression 1951
Revised and enlarged edition 1960, second impression 1963
This edition published 1967 by
The Hamlyn Publishing Group Ltd
Hamlyn House · The Centre · Feltham · Middlesex
Second impression 1967
© Paul Rotha 1930, 1949, 1951, 1960, 1963, 1967
British Film Academy recommendation

Printed in Great Britain by
Fletcher & Son Ltd, Norwich
and bound by
Richard Clay (The Chaucer Press) Ltd, Bungay, Suffolk

CONTENTS

PAGE

PREFACE TO NEW EDITION   15

ACKNOWLEDGEMENTS   61

PART ONE
THE ACTUAL

I.	THE DEVELOPMENT OF THE FILM	67
II.	THE VARIOUS FORMS OF CINEMA	113
III.	THE AMERICAN FILM	126
IV.	THE AMERICAN FILM (*continued*)	148
V.	THE AMERICAN FILM (*concluded*)	189
VI.	THE SOVIET FILM	217
VII.	THE GERMAN FILM	252
VIII.	THE FRENCH FILM	293
IX.	THE BRITISH FILM	313
X.	FILMS FROM OTHER COUNTRIES	323

PART TWO
THE THEORETICAL

1.	THE AIM OF THE FILM IN GENERAL AND IN PARTICULAR	329
II.	THE PRECONCEPTION OF DRAMATIC CONTENT BY SCENARIO ORGANISATION	343
III.	THE METHODS OF EXPRESSION OF DRAMATIC CONTENT BY FILM CONSTRUCTION	360
	(I) THE PROCESS OF THE VISUAL CINEMA	361
	(II) THE VISUAL AND THE AUDIBLE CINEMA	403

CONTENTS
PART THREE
THE FILM SINCE THEN

	PAGE
INTRODUCTION	415
I. THE AMERICAN FILM 1929-48	428
(I) SUBJECT AND THEMES	428
(II) DIRECTORS, WRITERS AND PRODUCERS	469
(III) THREE INDEPENDENTS: CHAPLIN, DISNEY, FLAHERTY	509
II. THE EUROPEAN CINEMA 1929-48	526
(I) THE FRENCH FILM	526
(II) THE BRITISH FILM	544
(III) THE SOVIET FILM	561
(IV) THE GERMAN FILM	580
(V) THE ITALIAN FILM	595
(VI) FILMS FROM OTHER COUNTRIES	601

APPENDICES

	PAGE
I. THE PRODUCTION UNITS OF SOME OUTSTANDING FILMS	621
(I) FICTION FILMS	621
(II) DOCUMENTARY FILMS	674
(III) TRICK, CARTOON, PUPPET AND OTHER KINDS OF SPECIALISED AND EXPERIMENTAL FILMS	687
II. GLOSSARY. SOME TERMS USED IN THE FILM INDUSTRY	691
(I) TECHNICAL TERMS USED MAINLY IN PRODUCTION	691
(II) TERMS IN GENERAL USE IN THE TRADE AS A WHOLE	701
III. SELECTED BOOK LIST	706
(I) BRITISH AND AMERICAN	706
(II) FOREIGN	708
IV. EXTRACTS FROM A PROGRAMME PRINTED IN CONNECTION WITH A MEMORIAL PERFORMANCE HELD OF CARL MAYER'S WORK, SCALA THEATRE, LONDON, APRIL 13, 1947.	709

CONTENTS

EPILOGUE 1948–1958

INTRODUCTORY NOTE   721

COUNTRIES SURVEYED

    I   UNITED STATES   726

   II   UNITED KINGDOM   732

  III   FRANCE   737

   IV   ITALY   743

    V   SCANDINAVIA: SWEDEN, DENMARK, FINLAND, NORWAY 748

   VI   OTHER EUROPEAN COUNTRIES: WEST GERMANY,
        AUSTRIA, SPAIN, SWITZERLAND, NETHERLANDS,
        BELGIUM, GREECE, YUGOSLAVIA   750

  VII   SOVIET UNION   754

 VIII   EASTERN EUROPE: POLAND, EAST GERMANY,
        CZECHOSLOVAKIA, HUNGARY   756

   IX   BRITISH COMMONWEALTH: CANADA, AUSTRALIA,
        NEW ZEALAND, SOUTH AFRICA, CEYLON, GHANA,
        MALAYA, PAKISTAN, INDIA   761

    X   ASIA: JAPAN, CHINA   765

   XI   LATIN AMERICA: MEXICO, ARGENTINE, PUERTO
        RICO   769

CONCLUSION   771

POSTSCRIPT   775

INDEX   785

INDEX OF ILLUSTRATIONS
(The figures in italics refer to the plate numbers)

Paul Rotha editing *The Life of Adolf Hitler*,
a compilation film, Hamburg, 1960–61   *Frontispiece*

A Bout de Souffle (1959)	*189*
Age d'Or, L' (1930)	*86*
All Quiet on the Western Front (1929–30)	*80*
American Madness (1932)	*99*
Applause (1929)	*74*
Arsenal (1929)	*76*
Ashes and Diamonds (1958)	*188*
Atalante, L' (1934)	*111*
Atonement of Gösta Berling, The (1923)	*28*
Bataille du Rail, La (1944–45)	*156*
Battleship Potemkin (1925)	*47*
Be Big (c. 1931)	*96*
Bed and Sofa (1926)	*55*
Belle Equipe, La (1936)	*118*
Best Years of Our Lives (1946)	*165*
Bête Humaine, La (1938)	*130*
Bicycle Thieves (1948)	*175*
Big Parade, The (1925)	*43*
Birth of a Nation, The (1915)	*9*
Blackmail (1929)	*77*
Black Pirate, The (1926)	*51*
Blue Angel, The (1926)	*73*
Boomerang (1947)	*172*
Brief Encounter (1945)	*160*
Broken Blossoms (1919)	*12*
Cabinet of Dr. Caligari (1919)	*15*
Casque d'Or (1952)	*181*
Chapaev (1934)	*110*
Cigarette, La (1919)	*14*
Cinderella (1923)	*29*

9

INDEX OF ILLUSTRATIONS

Citizen Kane (1941)   *143*

City Streets (1931)   *91*

Condamné à Mort s'est Echappé, Un (1956)   *185*

Congress Dances (1931)   *94*

Covered Wagon, The (1923)   *31*

Cranes Are Flying, The (1957)   *186*

Crime Without Passion (1934)   *109*

Cripple Creek Barroom (1898)   *2*

Crossfire (1947)   *171*

Crowd, The (1927)   *59*

Day of Wrath, The (1944)   *151*

Dead End (1937)   *124*

Destiny (1921)   *19*

Diable au Corps, Le (1947)   *170*

Ditte Menneskebarn (1946)   *162*

Double Indemnity (1944)   *152*

Dracula (1922)   *27*

Dreigroschenoper, Die (1931)   *87*

Drifters (1929)   *8*

Dr. Strangelove (1963)   *198*

Emil and the Detectives (1931)   *90*

Enfants du Paradis, Les (1944)   *155*

En Rade (1927)   *7*

Extase (1933)   *105*

Fall of the House of Usher, The (1928)   *70*

Fires Were Started (1943)   *149*

Foolish Wives (1922)   *25*

Forbidden Paradise (1924)   *40*

Forty-Second Street (1933)   *106*

Four Horsemen of the Apocalypse (1920–21)   *18*

Fury (1936)   *119*

Gaslight (1940)   *138*

General Line, The (1926–29)   *58*

Ghost That Never Returns, The (1929)   *75*

Gold Rush, The (1925)   *45*

Golem, The (1920)   *16*

Gone With the Wind (1939)   *135*

Grande Illusion, La (1937)   *127*

INDEX OF ILLUSTRATIONS

Grandma's Boy (1922)	*22*
Grapes of Wrath, The (1940)	*136*
Great Beginning, The (1939)	*133*
Great Expectations (1946)	*164*
Greed (1923–24)	*35*
Hallelujah! (1929)	*78*
Hamlet (1963)	*199*
Henry V (1944)	*153*
Hippocampe, L' (1934)	*3*
Hiroshima Mon Amour (1959)	*190*
His Own Home Town (1918)	*11*
Hotel Imperial (1926)	*53*
Human Sparrows (1926)	*54*
I Am a Fugitive from a Chain Gang (1932)	*101*
Intolerance (1916)	*10*
Iron Horse, The (1924)	*39*
Italian Straw Hat, The (1927)	*64*
It Happened One Night (1934)	*108*
Jeux Interdits, Les (1952)	*182*
Jour se Lève, Le (1939)	*134*
Jules et Jim (1961)	*195*
Kameradschaft (1931)	*88*
Kean (1924)	*41*
Kermesse Héroïque, La (1935)	*113*
Lady Killer (1933)	*107*
Lady With the Little Dog, The (1960)	*193*
Land, The (1939–42)	*142*
Last Chance, The (1945)	*157*
Last Laugh, The (1924)	*37*
Late Matthew Pascal, The (1924)	*42*
Little Caesar (1930)	*81*
Little Foxes, The (1941)	*140*
Louisiana Story (1946–48)	*168*
Loves of Jeanne Ney, The (1927)	*61*
' M ' (1932)	*97*
Maedchen in Uniform (1931)	*89*
Maltese Falcon (1941)	*144*
Maternelle, La (1932)	*98*

11

Metropolis (1925–26)   *49*

Million, Le (1920)   *84*

Moana (1923–25)   *57*

Moby Dick (1930)   *82*

Modern Times (1936)   *116*

Monsieur Verdoux (1946–47)   *166*

Morocco (1930)   *83*

Mother (1926)   *56*

Mr. Deeds Goes to Town (1936)   *120*

Native Land (1942)   *145*

New Babylon (1929)   *72*

Nibelungen Saga : Siegfried (1923–24)   *36*

Night at the Opera (1935)   *115*

Night Mail (1936)   *122*

Nine Men (1943)   *150*

No Resting Place (1950)   *178*

North Sea (1938)   *131*

Odd Man Out (1947)   *173*

Oliver Twist (1947–48)   *174*

Olvidados, Los (1951)   *179*

Open City (1945)   *159*

Orphans of the Storm (1922)   *21*

Overlanders, The (1946)   *163*

Ox-Bow Incident, The (1943)   *148*

Paisan (1946)   *161*

Paris qui Dort (1923)   *34*

Passion de Jeanne d'Arc, La (1928)   *71*

Pather Panchali (1952–55)   *183*

Phantom Carriage, The (1919)   *13*

Posto, Il (1961)   *197*

Private Life of Henry VIII (1933)   *103*

Psycho (1960)   *192*

Public Enemy, The (1931)   *95*

Quai des Brûmes (1938)   *129*

Quatre Cent Coups, Les (1959)   *191*

Quick Millions (1931)   *92*

Rashomon (1950)   *177*

Red Desert, The (1964)   *200*

INDEX OF ILLUSTRATIONS

Rembrandt (1936)   121
Road to Life, The (1931)   93
Robin Hood (1923)   32
Sadie Thompson (1928)   66
Salome (1922)   26
Saturday Night, Sunday Morning (1960)   194
Scarface (1932)   100
Sept Châteaux de Diable, Les (1907)   1
Shape of Things to Come, The (1935)   4
She Done Him Wrong (1933)   104
Song of Ceylon, The (1934–35)   112
Sous les Toits de Paris (1929–30)   79
Spanish Earth (1937)   128
Star is Born, A (1937)   126
Stars Look Down, The (1939)   132
Steamboat Bill, Jr. (1928)   65
Stella Dallas (1925)   46
Storm Over Asia (1928)   67
Story of G.I. Joe, The (1945)   158
Street, The (1923)   30
Student of Prague, The (1926)   50
Sunrise (1927)   62
Target for Tonight (1941)   141
Terra Trema, La (1949)   176
Theodora Goes Wild (1937)   123
Thérèse Raquin (1937)   63
They Won't Forget (1937)   125
Tol'able David (1921)   20
Tom, Dick and Harry (1940)   139
Toni (1935)   114
Tower of Lies, The (1926)   52
Treasure of the Sierra Madre, The (1947)   169
Tumbleweeds (1925)   44
Turksib (1928)   68
Ugetsu Monogatari (1953)   184
Umberto D (1952)   180
Underworld (1927)   60
University of Life, The (1940)   137

INDEX OF ILLUSTRATIONS

Vanina (1922)   24
Vaudeville (1925)   48
Viridiana (1961)   196
Warning Shadows (1922)   23
Water Folk (Secrets of Nature) (1931)   5
Waxworks (1924)   38
Way Ahead, The (1943)   147
Way Down East (1920)   17
We From Kronstadt (1936)   117
Western Approaches (1944)   154
Westfront 1918 (1930)   85
Wild Boys of the Road (1933)   102
Wild Strawberries (1957)   187
Wind, The (1928)   69
Woman of Paris, A (1923)   33
World Is Rich, The (1946–47)   167
World of Plenty (1942–43)   146
Zéro de Conduite (1933)   6

PREFACE

It was with some misgivings that I decided to let this book be republished, although it had been often requested. When it was written in 1929, I had had about twelve months' practical work of film-making, having spent an excessive amount of my childhood and schooldays in cinemas. The first draft manuscript was about three times its published length, and perhaps the main thing in its favour was that it showed an enthusiasm for films. It also set down with fair accuracy a large amount of factual information not easily found elsewhere. It came about like this.

In 1928 I was employed first as an ' outside man ' (which meant hiring furniture and properties) and later as an assistant in the art-department in the biggest British film studio of the time. My youthful impetuosity led me to criticise the lack of creative opportunities in the studio where I worked, and within a few days I was out on the street with nothing in my pocket.[1] Many may now forget that 1929 saw the almost complete shut-down of British studios because of Hollywood's revolutionary change-over to the sound film. So, thwarted in my wish to be associated with making films I turned to the next best thing—writing about them. Mr. Jonathan Cape gave me the opportunity, for which I have always been grateful. Eighteen months later *The Film Till Now* appeared, to be received in general by a friendly Press with the exception of the Trade's own papers.

Naïvely I believed that its theories and facts would unlock the studio doors again to me. The opposite took place. I found employment still harder to get, until luckily I met Mr. John Grierson. He asked me to join his little unit at the Empire Marketing Board, where I worked for six months learning the rudiments of the documentary film method.

[1] *Film Weekly*, November 12, 1928.

15

Since then I have been occupied mainly in making films and helping others to make them. There has been little time for writing books. *The Film Till Now* should, of course, have been wholly re-written; but I wonder if it would have been fair to alter points of view held nearly twenty years ago? Finally it was decided to let the main body of the original text be reprinted as it stood, making only minor changes required for accuracy. Tempting as it was in places to modify an opinion, or add a new point of view, it has not been done. This is especially the case in regard to the Soviet chapter and with the early formative years of the American cinema. Prophecies about the dialogue film, largely disproved though they have been subsequently, must stand. I ask the reader's indulgence. I have, however, been unable to resist adding a number of new footnotes where I felt they were justified. Knowing that perhaps the most used section of the book has been the Appendix of Production Units of some Outstanding Films, this list has been revised, expanded and brought up-to-date. The same has been done for the Glossary of Technical Terms and the Book List. The volume has also been re-illustrated. Most of the stills are from well-known and important films but occasionally, as with *Lady Killer* or *Be Big*, one has been included because it represents a trend in film subjects or styles rather than the film from which it is taken.

To bring the survey as a whole up to 1948, I sought the help of my old friend in America, Mr. Richard Griffith, knowing that his approach to films is very close to mine. He was almost the first correspondent I had after the publication of the book in America in 1930, second only to the late Eric Knight, perhaps one of the best film critics we have ever had. Mr. Griffith now holds the important post of Executive-Director at the National Board of Review of Motion Pictures in New York. He is also Assistant Director of the Museum of Modern Art Film Library in the same city. He has thus a wide experience in film viewing both past and present. It should

1. LES SEPT CHATEAUX DE DIABLE, directed by ZECCA. [French, 1907]

2. CRIPPLE CREEK BARROOM, by EDISON. [American, 1898]

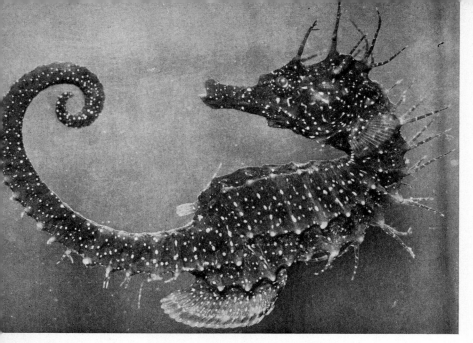

3. L'HIPPOCAMPE, directed by JEAN PAINLEVÉ.   [French, 1934]

4. THE SHAPE OF THINGS TO COME, directed by WILLIAM CAMERON MENZIES. [British, 1935]

be added that, from a practical point of view, he contributed to the making of certain wartime documentaries and cinemagazines for the U.S. Army, notably to the famous *Why We Fight* series under the supervision of Frank Capra. Griffith's additional section to this new edition, Part Three : *The Film Since Then*, to which he has written his own Introduction, carries my full support of his critical judgement and I take this opportunity of formally thanking him for his contribution. It should be remembered that he is writing from an American point of view. I must share occasional responsibility, however, where films have not been available to him, mainly in the non-American chapters, and where I have been fortunate enough to visit certain European countries since the war. Finally it should be added that he is writing briefly; to have surveyed the past eighteen years of films in detail would have meant a vast new book in itself.

*

A new edition, as the reader will have noted, permits an author to indulge in the luxury of a new Preface.

Films recollected in memory, says Richard Griffith, are apt to be biased by nostalgia. How right he is! When I was fortunate enough to spend some months at the Film Library in New York in 1937 and '38, I found that out only too well. On the other hand seeing old films again brings pleasant surprises; things you never saw and certainly implications which you were too inexperienced to observe. In general, however, films of the past usually live in our mind as being better than they really were, especially fiction films. Memory adds values to them that were never there. Yet, divorcing technique from viewpoint, one realises now how much one missed by not understanding fully a director's aim at the time, or not knowing the conditions under which a film was made, or the purpose indeed for which the film was made at all. That is why I greatly welcomed last year Dr. Siegfried Kracauer's book *From Caligari to Hitler* because it gave

a social, political and economic background to the early
German cinema that no one else to my knowledge had tried
to do. I wish that other writers (or perhaps Dr. Kracauer
himself?) could do the same thing for the films of other
countries; Griffith, I fancy, has done it briefly for the later
American cinema in this new edition, and Mr. Lewis
Jacobs also came near to this approach.[1]

Since the manuscript of this book was first written, I
have at least found out that the more you become involved
in making films the less you know about them. Sometimes
I have sat in a cutting-room with film draped round the
walls and overflowing the bins and realised just how little
one does know about the infinite possibilities of this
wonderful medium, with its magic property of joining
image to image and mixing sound with sound. Certainly
I would not again have the audacity to try and write a survey of the world's cinema now that I know not only how
difficult it is to make a film but how *much more difficult* it
is to find the economic conditions in which you can use
the medium with honesty and sincerity. It is always tragic
to me that a film-director must spend some three-quarters
of his time negotiating the ways and means to make the
film he wants to make and only a quarter in actually making
the film itself. To the director with something he thinks
it important to say the means of production are so hard
to come by that much creative time is spent in merely
getting access to the expensive materials of film
production.

These past thirty years have seen a steady concentration
of all means of film production in Western Europe and the
United States. With the possibility of making very large
returns both from a home-market and from audiences
overseas, the film industries of most countries have
now become more than ever before a matter of financial
investment and international trade bargaining at the highest
level. The film is no longer the happy-go-lucky investment of small-time *entrepreneurs*. It is gambling in public

[1] *The Rise of the American Film* (Harcourt Brace, 1939).

taste on the grand scale and has tended inevitably to be restricted to those controlling the other great international manufactures.

The screen's reflection of a people's character and ideals and traditions, its unlimited power to create goodwill and promote understanding, its unequalled importance as a medium for public communication are motives which have been largely overlooked in the scramble to monopolise this universal show-business. Governments, banks, insurance companies, electrical cartels and other holders of big capital guide the destiny of the motion picture medium rather than the creative artists who seek to use it as an outlet for their ideas and imaginations.

Almost the whole potential of the cinema as an instrument of public education has been neglected by the Industry's controllers in their pursuit of big returns. Little attempt, except in the field of documentary films, has as yet been made to use this powerful medium as a contribution to world thought. It has been characteristic of the Industry always to aim to produce its films for the largest possible number of people, and hence stand to gain the biggest revenue. Seldom have the serious social responsibilities attached to such an undertaking been recognised by the executives of the Industry. If the same disregard for responsibility were to obtain in the publishing or broadcasting worlds, public alarm would be at once expressed. The cinema has grown up as a cheap and convenient form of community amusement causing experiment in its artistic potentialities to be scarce and difficult to achieve. Only recently has it aroused the attention of educationalists and those concerned with social progress and moral welfare. Up till lately the interest of capitalist governments has been mainly confined to the film's commodity value and its vast yield in taxes. The showmen and promoters have been left to do what they liked with their adolescent Industry. To-day, they not illogically resent interference from the outside. The fact that the head of a Government department or a member of Parliament can have made himself knowledgeable about the complex internal affairs of the Industry has come as rather a shock.

But the making of sincere films by men who have something valuable and not necessarily unentertaining to say in the world has become a dim prospect when viewed in relation to the constant need to keep screen-space and studio-space filled, the call to save dollars, the spread of trade and what are hypocritically called ' ways of life ' by film exploitation, the need not only to relate box-office revenue to production cost but perhaps to adjust this picture to make money and that one to lose it in order to satisfy an accountant's balance-sheet. To produce a good fiction film to-day is often a matter of luck, or the stern insistence of a director having the guts and faith to stick by his intentions. When I see a *Crossfire,* a *Miracle* or an *Overlanders,* I give thanks to someone somewhere who has broken through the defences.

The three branches of the Industry—production, distribution and exhibition—once separate processes, have become so merged into big monopolies that the making of films by a handful of independent and sincerely creative film-makers has become something like an impossibility. Such freedom to produce can never return until exhibiting interests are wholly or at least partially divorced from production interests. Exhibitor control and influence over the making of films such as exists to some extent in Britain and certainly in America tend to lead to extreme caution, to resistance to new ideas, to obsession to believed proven box-office formulas, and to a general pandering to the lower instincts of the mass-audience. When you consider that the age level of this audience must be assessed at the lowest common denominator, the 'teen-age rule, by which exhibitors themselves view their own commodity, you can understand how this control paralyses adult creative initiative in production.[1]

---

[1] Thus it is difficult at first to understand the logic of the British Government setting up a Film Finance Corporation with £5 million to be invested in production at *the guidance of the distributors!*

But the public, dissatisfied as it might be, has automatically responded to the dynamic attraction of this new medium and is surely now ripe for special cinemas showing special types of films that will exploit the screen-medium to the full. More advanced in taste and knowledge than the exhibitors and distributors, it has no opportunity at present to sort itself out into discriminating levels. It has little resource except to stay away from cinemas. An American film-trade journal recently put the matter bluntly. After reporting a rival journal's comment that the Gallup Audience Research Survey stated that if all persons in the United States between the ages of 31 and 65 could be induced to go to the cinema once a week, then the increase in the box-office gross would amount to 800,000,000 dollars, the *Motion Picture Herald* remarked: ' The same Gallup sources a few weeks ago reported that the best customer of the screen was a person of nineteen years. That, as we have remarked before, is the age of eagerness, filled with urges and wishing and the hungry quest for experience—an order of vocational training for the business of living. After 31, and onward, the individual has had some experience, knows some of the answers, and the keen edge is off the appetites. . . . It would be *most unprofitable for the motion picture to seek out the genuinely mature instincts,* because in doing so the big hungry young audience would have no part of the stuff.' [1] These are the editorial words of a responsible journal of the American Motion Picture Industry. They are self-explanatory.[2]

To an exhibitor good entertainment means the attraction to his cinema of the largest number of people in his area. What methods of magnetism are used is irrelevant, although it is amazing what ingenuity is sometimes employed. Exhibitors are reluctant to show films that might encourage their audiences to think because—and this is the nub of the matter—a thoughtful audience would

[1] June 26, 1948. (My italics—P.R.)

[2] Relevant are the findings in regard to cinema-going in *Rising Twenty*, Pearl Jephcott (Faber & Faber, 1948).

endanger the blind cinema-going habit upon which the exhibitor depends for maintenance of his full houses. A questioning audience demanding a more mature standard of film programme would make an exhibitor's revenue far more speculative than up till now. I quote from the same American trade-journal: 'Once again may it be said that the motion picture theatre is not approached by its customers as a place of controversy, of consideration, of issues, of thinking—it is a place for feeling, for emotion, and for its millions those emotions are simple, and basic, never complex. The box-office people neither study nor think about pictures. They look at them. If they like them, they say so to friends and neighbours.'[1] Mr. Terry Ramsaye, the author of these quotations and the editor of the journal in question, may self-appoint himself to speak for America's millions of filmgoers, but I flatly refuse on evidence to accept this appraisal of the filmgoing public in other countries including Britain. If his thesis is valid, how does he account for the phenomenal box-office success of such films as *The Best Years of Our Lives, Crossfire* and *Gentleman's Agreement,* not only in Britain but in their country of origin?

It is this kind of sweeping assessment, so common among high film executives, of the ordinary man that explains such demonstrations of intolerance and bigotry as were witnessed at the Un-American Activities investigation on certain Hollywood personalities in Washington last November.[2] Opinions expressed at that sorry affair represent an attitude held by an influential section of the men who promote motion pictures and show them both in the United States and Britain.

This neurotic fear of losing their grip on the 'teen-age section of the public causes exhibitors and renters to oppose all showing of films other than for ephemeral amusement purposes, and especially to resist the development of the potentially-vast non-theatrical field. Following this is a

[1] November 1, 1947.

[2] *Vide, Hollywood on Trial,* Gordon Kahn, (Boni and Gaer, 1948).

natural hostility to the growth of film societies, one of the most encouraging signs of film appreciation in Great Britain to-day, in fact practically the only alternative to the commercial cinemas. This time I quote from the reliable British trade-journal *Kinematograph Weekly* and at some length, because it is important that the public should know that this point of view is held in the Industry: 'Film societies were the target for a slashing attack by the Kinematograph Renters Society Council last week which, accusing members of the movement of being ringleaders of the current-wide attacks on the Film Industry, decided to call a meeting with the Cinematograph Exhibitors Association to thrash out the whole position of these societies. Members said that film societies, which paid little for film hire, were so much on the increase that *they were creating a very grave threat to exhibitor interests* . . . The meeting then had a long debate on the merits and demerits of film culture, in which culture got the worse of the argument. It was said by a member that society members were the type of people who *never go to a normal kinema show*. The Industry would *never persuade them to adopt a regular kinema-going habit* by letting them have old films to see, which were far from representative of the modern type of film product. Another member said that the only type of film the societies booked was the " arty " type. *These people did absolutely no good to the Industry.* No one had anything to say in favour of the movement.' [1] It should be noted that the Kinematograph Renters Society is a national body representing all the leading and most of the small film distributors in the United Kingdom. It has representation on the Board of Governors of the British Film Institute, one of whose major objects is to encourage the growth of the film society movement!

Powerful Trade interests frequently denigrate and resent intelligent and honest film criticism. They obviously oppose civic or municipal cinemas, as was seen in their opposition to the Local Government Bill in which they were

[1] September 18, 1947. (My italics—P.R.)

unsuccessful. They obviously are disinclined to market a better type of film themselves and what is more try to prevent others from doing so. Their fear of film criticism amounts to a fixation. One moment they will ridicule all newspaper criticism except that which is mere gossip and valuable to them because it mentions star names and film titles; the next, when some critic exposes a spurious picture, the same voices will accuse him of failing totally to understand 'what the public wants'. In fact the film executive would like a film critic to be docile, unquestioning and obedient; in other words not a critic at all, merely a hack journalist susceptible to the fleshpots. Executives and publicity men are actually angry and hurt if a critic displays a mind of his own. Whenever intelligent, unwarped film criticism has appeared in the national Press or on the radio in Britain there has been a protest from the Industry. Cedric Belfrage, Alistair Cooke, and more recently Richard Winnington (quite the most important and sanest film critic of recent years) have all come in for denunciation. It is a healthy sign that in the last few years some British film critics have shown a certain unity in protecting their liberty and preserving their principles of free criticism. They have refused to be seduced into accepting the authoritarian directives of the Industry's executives and publicity men.

Fear of criticism is a sign of dishonesty of purpose, that is if it is dishonest to extort the maximum profit from a product irrespective of its social or aesthetic effect on the public, and to continue to aim that product deliberately at the less-developed side of public intelligence without regard to its effect? The producers, renters and exhibitors of this Industry would make no claim to be educators, social servants or uplifters of public taste. Why should they? They are businessmen, showmen and company promoters with maximum returns as their sole motive. Yet, and this is the whole dilemma of the cinema, they control the means of production and exhibition of the most persuasive and influential medium yet invented for mass-performance and absorption. As businessmen in capitalist or semi-capitalist societies they may defend their methods and principles; as citizens they cannot resent criticism of their lack of social responsibilities.

*

During the lobbying and propagandising that preceded the Parliamentary debates on the new Cinematograph Films Act of 1948, various proposals to solve the problem of separating exhibition from production were put forward. They ranged from complete nationalisation of the cinemas, as in Czechoslovakia, or the placing of cinemas under municipal management, as in Norway, to control over a proportion of the screen-space required by law for British films in each cinema. Most of these proposals, however, depended on the use of compulsory methods which in the fields of leisure and public education are not acceptable to all of us. The Act as it became law has done something to secure cinema-distribution for a limited number of independently-made films, but more important is a Committee of Enquiry into Exhibition to be appointed by the President of the Board of Trade. Of considerable long-range importance also is the recently-passed Local Government Act which empowers local authorities to run cinemas if there is evidence of a public demand but this will obviously take time to materialise.

Perhaps the most interesting proposal for immediate action was that for the formation of a fourth circuit of cinemas in Britain, a kind of B.B.C. Third Programme, under governmental or municipal control to guarantee an outlet not only for independently-produced British pictures of good quality but for films of all countries that attempt to use the screen more intelligently than it is used by the general run of circuit-controlled or independent cinemas.

The proposal was based on the recognition that, poor as is the quality of many feature films offered to the public, British audience attendances still remain higher than at the outbreak of the war, although the restrictions on other ways of spending increased earnings should be remembered.

It was accepted that to-day many people are apparently satisfied with the films already offered them, but suggested that there might be many others who would pay to see a better type of film if it was available, among them possibly many hundreds of thousands of people who do not go to the cinema at all or only occasionally. It was argued that a period in cinema exhibition may have been reached when it is possible to consider making certain kinds of film for certain specific types of audience among the great mass of people who make up the between twenty-five and thirty million paid attendances per week at British cinemas.

Almost all production companies to-day choose a subject, star and budget it in the hope that it will appeal to as many people as possible according to its circuit and other distribution. It has seldom been thought worthwhile to aim deliberately at certain sections of the public as in the case of publishing, broadcasting and the theatre, and to calculate production costs accordingly. Distribution and exhibition methods are not geared to such selection. The booking methods of the Industry are inflexibly organised on a basis of first-feature, second-feature, fill-ups and newsreel contracts; only rarely does a film get special methods of salesmanship and then only when a producer is strong enough to demand it. When it does, the success of this method of individual salesmanship amazes even the Industry itself.

There is also considerable need to investigate the make-up of cinema programmes themselves and to see if a more balanced selection of films might be to the public liking. The argument for and against the 'double-feature' programme has been heard endlessly. There is evidence that many people would prefer a single main feature film, supported by perhaps a documentary, a cartoon, a cine-magazine of *The March of Time* or *This Modern Age* type, with the inevitable newsreel. It should be remembered that the double-feature programme was instituted in America and Britain towards the end of the twenties only because there was a serious decline in cinema attendances due to the standardised type of picture coming off the Hollywood production belt. Exhibitors argued to themselves that to bring audiences back into the theatres, longer programmes must be provided on a ' more for your money ' theory. In the same way producers had tried earlier putting a popular star into more than one rôle in one film. (Gloria Swanson once played five parts in a single film thus giving her fans five times the value of their admission ticket.) At least one London cinema played a treble-feature programme for a time until the talking films brought back audiences with a rush.

If the single-feature programme was to be restored in a number of cinemas a greater opportunity would result to develop the variety of the supporting programme. Short-story films, animated cartoons, travel and scientific films, cinemagazines and documentaries of different kinds are fertile ground for the development of ideas, techniques and personalities, for experimental work which, if successful, would influence the whole scope of film-making. For many years supporting films have been sheer rubbish because exhibitors attach little importance to anything but the main picture. The revenue obtainable by supporting films has been so small as to make their manufacture highly speculative unless producers have resorted to sponsorship as have the documentary makers. One of the most progressive steps that could take place in the Industry would be the abolition of the double-feature bill and the substitution of a well-balanced programme. This would automatically rid us of that dubious import, the Hollywood ' B ' picture.

There is mounting evidence in Britain to-day, derived from the increasing formation of film societies,[1] from the attendances at the few specialist cinemas, from the success of non-theatrical distribution during and since the war, from the Press and from countless discussion groups and public meetings, that a certain section of the public would

[1] There are 148 general film societies in the United Kingdom (1948), and 42 scientific film societies.

support a much better quality type of film if there were the cinemas in which they could be exhibited. It is to this section of the public, very much larger than the Trade is aware of, that we could look for the initial returns on a better kind of picture, always provided that production costs are kept within the scope of its exhibition receipts. This is the type of distribution that would bring the impetus of new hope and faith to the creative makers of films who at present wear themselves out in the vain struggle for means of production.

Every city and town in the United Kingdom with a population of, say, more than fifty thousand inhabitants, and where there are four or more existing cinemas, should have at least one cinema set aside for such special films as are available or desirable. That cinema should be acquired either by outright purchase, or by renting for a trial period of five years. The number of these cinemas would vary in proportion with the population. In Manchester, for example, three might be the appropriate number; in London, twenty. Choice of cinema should be governed by suitability of site and seating capacity, seven hundred and fifty seats being a reasonable average. The cinemas thus selected would range over both existing circuit and independently-owned theatres, and should be placed either under the direct control of a Government Film Corporation or Board, or under the management of the municipality, but in either case their programme booking should be controlled by a central body. Programmes need not necessarily be restricted to a week's booking as is the general practice in the Trade, but should be permitted to run so long as public demand lasts. A minimum of five hundred such cinemas throughout the country should be the aim.

In addition to observing the normal opening hours in the locality, these cinemas should be made easily available at reasonable hire rates in the mornings and on Sundays for specialised performances to meet the increasing needs of municipalities, schools, universities, educational bodies of all kinds, cultural and scientific bodies, and the many other specialised groups that are using films more and more as part of their activities. The aim should be to build up each cinema into a kind of film centre, with a grip on every cultural activity of the medium including the housing of sub-standard libraries of educational films.

Thus the public would be able to absorb gradually a higher quality of entertainment than the ordinary commercial cinema provides, while leaving the latter free to cater to the mass-appeal. This proposal it is contended would cause the Trade to raise less objection to Government action than any proposals involving nationalisation or control over screen-time.

Some such project as this is the only solution I can see to curing a situation that leaves one twentieth of the film-going public frustrated and unsatisfied, and some of the best elements in film production impotent and unfulfilled.[1] Public taste in Britain in the past ten years has matured and is being met in the fields of art, music and literature. The same thing is happening in the cinema, and there is little the exhibitors and renters societies can do to prevent it.

*

Despite the inevitable process of commercialising the making of motion pictures by their manufacturing studios and the resultant organisation of technicians and other kinds of labour employed in production, the past eighteen years have seen certain notable developments in creative film-making which Mr. Griffith ably deals with later in this book. They have also been the subject of several considered works published since 1930, notably Mr. Lewis Jacobs' *Rise of the American Film* and Miss Iris Barry's translation of the French *History of Motion Pictures* by Bardèche and Brasillach. There are one or two trends of a general nature, however, upon which I feel impelled to comment.

[1] This proposal was contained in a private memorandum submitted to the President of the Board of Trade, December 12, 1945,

One of the most significant has been Hollywood's recent failure to fulfil its status of leadership. For the first time in motion picture history since the first World War, Hollywood's supremacy in world markets has been threatened. Not only have several countries imposed stiff restrictions on the import of American films, but they have also made considerable progress in their own production output. Britain is the outstanding example. The critical moment came when the British Government in August, 1947, imposed a seventy-five per cent. *ad valorem* tax on American pictures. In reply, the American production companies through their body the Motion Picture Association decided to cut off all supply of films to the United Kingdom, knowing well that re-issues of old films (on which the new tax was not payable) and new British films could not, after a while, keep open all the United Kingdom cinemas. Out of this situation, which continued in an atmosphere of tension for eight months, came the Anglo-American Film Agreement now signed for four years. It limits severely the proportion of money which American producers can take out of Britain from the earnings of their films, and lists various activities into which the remainder of their takings may be put. We are not concerned here with the details of the Agreement, reached on the highest political and trade levels; but had a compromise not been reached, Hollywood was undoubtedly faced with a complete reorganisation of its economy. The situation was again exacerbated when the quota of British feature films to be shown in British cinemas was fixed at forty-five per cent., thus lessening the playing-space of American films in Britain. Never before has Hollywood's domination of the world's screens been so seriously threatened.

How vital Washington regards its motion pictures in overseas markets was revealed in a document issued as far back as 1938 by the United States Department of Commerce and which deserves recall. Mr. Nathan D. Golden, Chief of the Motion Picture Division of the Bureau of Foreign and Domestic Commerce, contributed some revealing and presumably official views on the need for Hollywood to fight to maintain its lead in the world. To quote : ' In view of that fact, what action should be taken by our American companies in order to maintain a position of superiority over their competitors in the markets of the world? To what major measure can they to-day resort, with the object of checking trends which we must acknowledge to be adverse? What dynamic attraction or allurement can be exerted, of greater potency than the local appeal of a spectator's mother-tongue and his natural fondness for familiar scenes and ways of life? Plainly, before all else, we must emphasise to the utmost the *contrast in quality* between our good American pictures and the typical product of local producing industries abroad. We must make that contrast as vivid, as striking, as impressive, as it can possibly be made. Persistently and adroitly, we must make the foreign moviegoer acutely conscious that the American picture is a product of *decidedly superior* quality—of rich and varied artistry, of entertainment value unmatchable in the run-of-time output of our competitors abroad. We must make this " High-Quality" factor so universally recognised that local audiences abroad will have no desire to see inferior films that owe their existence simply to some Government legislation or subsidy.' That this could be done, Mr. Golden expressed no doubts in the final paragraph to his introduction : ' As we advance into the new year of 1939, the factors to be relied upon, in maintaining our position in foreign markets, may still be defined as the simple, basic elements of our unmatched scientific skill in motion picture production—our amazing capacity for devising new and really wonderful methods—our determination to achieve artistic and enthralling camera effects—the incomparable richness of our material facilities and resources—and our unequalled variety and range of every type of acting talent. Together these things spell *quality*—and it is quality that will continue to attract foreign audiences to American pictures.'

These modest sentiments were underlined in a foreword to the same document by Mr. N. H. Engle, Acting-Director of the Bureau of Foreign and Domestic Commerce: 'Not only are the foreign film markets important to American producers because of the amount of money earned abroad and remitted to this country—there is also the important factor of the influence which the pictures exert in familiarising foreign audiences with American ways of life, and stimulating the desire to own and use such garments, furnishings, utensils and scientific innovations as are depicted on the screen. The benefits derived by this country from a successful cultivation of the foreign motion picture markets are thus direct and indirect.' So the cat came out of the bag.

With such a clear definition of policy directives from Washington, we can imagine the shock of the British import tax in August, 1947; the comparative relief felt by Hollywood, Wall Street, and the commercial officials when the tax was repealed in April of this year and the new four-year agreement concluded; and their renewed anger when the high quota for British feature films in British cinemas became known. Unlike their predecessors, the British Labour Government has not been willing to bend the knee to Hollywood's Wall Street masters. Of interest to us here, moreover, over and above the trade aspects of these negotiations is the fact that nowhere in the United Kingdom, except among British exhibitors, was any great regret expressed that there would be a decrease in American pictures. The truth was that the Hollywood product since the war had in the main failed to live up to Mr. Golden's exhortation. Not that it lacked 'artistic and enthralling camera effects' but the themes and subjects were by and large completely out of step with what was going on in the world. In its hothouse of self-adulation and self-imitation Hollywood, remote from them, failed to sense the after-effects of a world-war. There were a small handful of exceptions, films such as *The Best Years of Our Lives, It's a Wonderful Life, Crossfire* and

5. WATER FOLK (SECRETS OF NATURE), directed by Percy Smith.   [British, 1931]

6. ZERO DE CONDUITE, directed by Jean Vigo.   [French, 1933]

7. EN RADE, directed by CAVALCANTI. CATHERINE HESSLING. [French, 1927]

8. DRIFTERS, directed by JOHN GRIERSON. [British, 1929]

Boomerang, but this was the work of isolated directors who had been in active touch with a world at war. Hollywood's dream-world of make-belief which lulled audiences into escapism in the twenties and thirties was way out of tune with the hard realities of post-war life.

It cannot be doubted that the British import tax was a clumsy gesture which if it had been kept would have inevitably led to a closing of many cinemas and hence probably to a smaller market for our home-produced films. At the same time, the challenge to Hollywood's supremacy over the motion picture screen was welcomed by many people who dislike imperialism in any form, and creative film-makers outside Hollywood were stimulated by this threat to its long-held dominance, including many people in Hollywood itself.

In forty years Hollywood has contributed to the world screens some very brilliant films. In the Appendix of Outstanding Films at the end of this book, out of one-hundred-and-ninety feature films listed, eighty-two are of Hollywood origin. But at the cost of how many deplorable ones? Hollywood has meant the perfection of a system of mechanics that has led to the stultification of its own creative instinct. Thousands of people who have worked there have been restricted and curbed by the machine that must perforce keep studio-space and screen-space fully occupied or else lose money. My interest now, as it was nearly twenty years back when this book first came to be written, is in the freedom for creative expression on the screen. Hollywood has come to hold back from the screen the work of men who want to say something freely about the world we live in and the people who make it up. By restrictive methods it has been made almost impossible for an independent film-maker of original ideas to exist in Hollywood unless he has immense personal financial backing. The cases of Chaplin and Howard Hughes are unique; Disney has toed the line since the early single-reel symphonies; Flaherty is not truly of Hollywood and has for nearly all his work

33

found finance elsewhere. The brave attempt after the war
by some of the most influential directors, such as Capra,
Ford, George Stevens and others, to exist as independent
units ended in compromise or failure. This industrial,
totalitarian state of affairs by which the major producing
groups control all policy is graphically revealed by Richard
Griffith in his subsequent chapters.

It is in pursuit of the ideology of mass-dominance over
producers on the one hand and over audiences on the
other (so bluntly expressed in the several quotations given
above), that Hollywood's executives have used billions of
feet of celluloid, occupied millions of hours of superbly
equipped studio-space—to do what? Entertain many
millions of people in many countries; yes. Provide
hundreds of thousands with employment; yes. Spread the
American 'way of life' across half the world; perhaps.
But in all this effort Hollywood films did little in the
thirties to make known those genuine American theories
which might have helped to stop another world war. Hollywood films did little to further the humanitarian uses of the
cinema. Hollywood was seldom concerned to use this
vast new medium, over which it had so tight a grip, to
raise the level of understanding among all peoples, as did
some of the films of other countries. No, Hollywood
must face the accusation of having deliberately kept
people from thinking, from asking questions, from
knowing how and what other people in other places were
doing, an aim so brilliantly and naïvely summed up by
remarks quoted above.

What constructive contribution, precisely, has Hollywood made to the conception of the United Nations since
the end of the war? How much goodwill and understanding and common sense could have been spread around
the world by Hollywood movies if their themes had been
chosen with that end in view? As one looked each week
at the current releases, and the list of product in the
making, hardly a film was in any way contributing to
bringing about a better world. Notably one excepts *The*

Best Years of Our Lives but Mr. William Wyler has been quoted in the *New Yorker* that he would not be permitted to make such a picture in Hollywood now, despite the film's phenomenal commercial success in Britain and the United States. Messrs. Adrian Scott and Edward Dmytryk, the makers of *Crossfire*, are to stand trial for ' contempt of Congress ', although I note that that did not deter Mr. Eric Johnston, spokesman of the American Film Industry, from accepting on RKO-Radio's behalf a humanitarian award for that picture.[1]

One reads to-day with pity that Hollywood, that ' fountain of intellect ', in its extremity is relying on audience surveys to say what subjects should be made and how.[2] Respect for the creative independence, imagination and liberty of the individual has sunk so low in the pursuit of the uniform mind. Hollywood now seems suicidally intent on making standardised pictures for standardised audiences in which individual thought and individual creation have no place. What an opportunity for other countries!

*

The British Film Industry has risen twice and fallen once since the dim days when I first wrote of its works in 1929. During the thirties, as is described at length later, it expanded and rose in a vast financial gamble. New studio plants were erected, money was poured into production, technicians and actors were brought from Hollywood and Europe at great expense, luxury pictures were embarked on, all in a few years; one company, not large or even important, went bankrupt and began a landslide from which British film finance has never fully recovered. The whole boom fizzled out quicker than it had begun. Studios were soon standing idle, and, alas, thousands of technicians unemployed. An artificially subsidised Industry completely failed to be indigenous.

In the early war years a remarkable recovery began.

[1] The *Cine-Technician*, Vol. 14, No. 70, January, 1948.
[2] Cf. footnote page 137.

Film-makers for the first time in British feature production found a genuine philosophic reason for making pictures. Just recently we have seen another boom in British films; more costly pictures this time, bigger salaries, bigger 'presentation' costs, the whole thing on a grandiose scale, with production-budgets often geared at expectations from the American market. I hope sincerely that Mr. Griffith's remarks about the reception of British films by United States's audiences and by American film exhibitors will fall on heedful ears.[1] He writes with first-hand knowledge, and I vouchsafe he has the interests of good film-making in Britain at heart.

The Rank Empire has, it is said, brought some degree of organisation into the chaos of British feature film production. Under Rank's auspices certain notable films have been made that have given many people a new faith in native film production. *Great Expectations* and *Odd Man Out* were culminations of a renaissance that began with *The Foreman Went to France, Millions Like Us* and *The Way Ahead*. During the war years a new honesty and integrity and freshness broke into British feature production, but the indications to-day are that these values have not been carried over into post-war. The realism and fidelity to life of the best of the wartime films have been replaced by an escape into romanticism and historical set-pieces. The familiar adaptation of successful novels and plays seems to have once again ousted the tendency during the war for stories to be written specially for the screen. We shall always, of course, have with us the temptation for producers to acquire for the screen books and plays that have achieved a public welcome. But if we look back at the outstanding works of the cinema, it is mainly the films which are wholly original in conception that have created film history: *Intolerance, Caligari, Nanook, Potemkin, The Last Laugh, A Nous la Liberté, Kameradschaft, The Public Enemy, Toni, The Way Ahead, The True Glory, Monsieur Verdoux* and

[1] *Vide,* pages 552, 553, 561.

Paisan—none was a transcription from another medium.

As pieces of artistry and craftsmanship, histrionic skill and studio brilliance, one may admire the deep-focussing, the colourings and the chiaroscuro of the *Hamlets* and the *Oliver Twists*, the *Ideal Husbands* and the *Red Shoes's*, while noting that they do not take British cinema forward in a fundamental sense. They are as claustrophobic as the early German studio creations.[1] For all their cunning use of camera magic they are theatrical and literary in conception. Despite all the opportunities of post-war human experience, Britain has yet to make a film that will measure up to the contemporary significance of a *Crossfire* or a *Paisan*. Despite all the freedom which Mr. Rank and his associates are said to have given to his group of film-makers, and I have no reason to doubt this,[2] have any of them since the war made a really important contribution to cinema which breaks new thematic ground, or is related seriously to life as lived to-day?

Leaving aside the problems of the major British production groups, Rank and Korda with their immediate futures so much dependent on the American market, the position of the would-be independent producer in Britain has been difficult. The Government has announced the setting up by legislation of a Film Finance Corporation with a life of five years and spending authority up to five million pounds. Although eventually it is said that the Corporation will deal direct with independent producers, initially the finance will be available to the producer only via distributors. Thus, presumably, the distributor will have to approve a producer's subject, and production details before the Corporation grants funds for the films to be made. It is too early to comment on this proposed arrangement, except perhaps to remind the reader of the remarks already expressed about distributors and their control over producton.[3] This official step is vitally important to the future

[1] *Vide,* pp. 255, 258.
[2] Cf. footnote page 554.
[3] *Vide,* pp. 20-22.

of the Industry because some producers and directors at present working with the big groups might decide to break away into independent producton. Faced with less chance than ever of getting revenue from the American market, the big producers may also consider a return to reasonably budgeted films about contemporary subjects, made by producers and directors and writers with something significant to say and an urge to say it, with a fair chance of honest distribution in the cinemas of the United Kingdom.

One thing in regard to British production is very clear : costs of all types of films have got to come down. They have been geared in the past few years to the belief that the abnormal box-office boom of the war years would continue. It has not. The increase in costs all round in the past eight years of production has been fantastic. All too often the expensive way has been adopted not because it has been the most efficient or the best but because it has been thought to impress executives whose sense of values is based on extravagance. We do not lack experienced technicians, directors and writers or skilled actors nearly so badly as we need producers with a first-hand knowledge of film-making gained from hard practical experience.

Criticism has also been levelled at the Trade Unions in Britain whose demand for wage increases and shorter working hours in the Film Industry have steadily been maintained since the early days of the war. It is probably correct to say that in relation to other industries, film technicians are better paid and some, no doubt, overpaid. On the other hand, technicians see absurdly vast salaries (agent-negotiated) paid to star-name actors and actresses, fantastic sums (also agent-negotiated) paid to authors for screen-rights of books and plays, and astronomical publicity and so-called presentation expenses. They remember, also, the sudden slumps in the past when almost all production stopped overnight. It is always the technician who suffers then, not the extravagant producer or the

' front office ' boys. Many British technicians recall the
years from 1937 up to the war; few of them were
employed then except in documentary production. Some
producers blame the introduction of the five-day week for
current slowness of production but, argue the Union
officials, the shorter week is welcomed by practical
experienced producers who work to a schedule. It is
opposed, they say, only by inefficient producers who do
not adhere to planned production and shelter behind a
pretence of ' artistic temperament '. Finally, says the
Union, it is always ready to discuss elasticity in its agree-
ments if it is genuinely related to a planned schedule, or
where a special subject demands relaxation of Union
demands. Nevertheless, some directors are said to feel that
the elaborate grading of technicians and the insistence on
minimum crews to do specific jobs tend not so much to
slow down production as to clog the spontaneous working
so often inseparable from creative production. It is just
not possible for a director to achieve that intimacy of
working and to obtain that closeness to his subject
demanded by film-making, if he is burdened with an
army-corps of technicians when a platoon would do.
Good film-directing must always remain a creative activity
no matter how much it depends on teams of people and
industrialised processes, except when the aim is the steady
manufacture of a standardised product for standardised
audiences.

The British Film Industry, despite its considerable
strides in the past eight years, is faced now with some
fundamental and very hard problems, economic, artistic,
and personal. At the same time it has in front of it an
opportunity such as it has never known before.

In Europe, apart from Britain, there has also been much
film activity. After the melodramatic though spasmodic
flowering of the French cinema in the middle and late
thirties and its enforced pyrotechnical sleeping-draft during
the Occupation, production in France has now become
almost paralysed as a result yet again of international trade

relations. Heavily over-taxed, short of materials and equipment, the French cinema has been ruthlessly sacrificed on the altar of dollar scarcity. Hollywood has long wanted to control the French market and virtually to suppress French production. It looks as if this is happening. American films, some ten and twelve years old, are flooding French cinemas as they have flooded ours. One's sympathy goes out to Grémillon, Clair, Autant-Lara, Carné, Clément, Rouquier and the other gifted French film-makers; their sense of frustration must be hard to bear.

Of the Soviet cinema in the thirties, in many ways a disappointment after the memorable films of the *Potemkin* to *Storm Over Asia* period, Griffith has his comments to make later. Here let me say only how regrettable it is that so little opportunity now comes our way to see even comparatively recent work by Pudovkin, Dovjenko, Donskoi and the others. We know that there is much film activity in the Soviet Union, but little of it has been given performance for us. Eisenstein's sudden death came as a shock to all lovers of the film, and at the Memorial Performance of his work in London, May 2nd last, organised by the Soviet Cultural Relations film section and the British Film Academy, it was possible to confirm again, if indeed confirmation were needed, the extent of his gift to the cinema. Let us hope that the immense stupidities and sometimes seemingly wilful misunderstandings on both sides that mark Russia's relations with ourselves will not continue to act as a barrier to the exchange of films between us. We need to see the work of the contemporary Soviet film-makers, if only because they have given so much to the screen in the past.

It is too early yet to make any satisfactory estimate of what may arise in the new German cinema, although from what we have seen it has lost none of the technical skill long associated with German production. The early thirties were memorable, of course, for *Kameradschaft*, *Westfront 1918* and *M*. The films made under the directives of Goebbels for Nazi purposes were mostly technically excellent. German films made during the war (some of which I was able to see in Prague in 1946) were dull and heavy in style. I except the overestimated *Baron Münchhausen* for its superb though mechanical trickwork. The new films of post-war Germany will be immensely revealing; they should reflect what chance there is of a new outlook in so far as a new outlook can be formed under Occupation. What we have seen up till now, notably *The Murderers are Among Us,* exhibit in an exaggerated form the national instinct for self-pity and morbidity.

In those countries where the film industries have been nationalised in the Soviet manner, a delicate process of balancing political aims with an expression of individual outlook can be observed. The Czechoslovak Film Industry, well equipped thanks to the German occupation, has made important technical strides as was seen at the Festival of Czechoslovak films held in London in 1947. The Yugoslavs and the Poles, short of equipment and experienced technicians, are grasping on to the documentary techniques because their films have so far been mostly about realistic themes. Much of interest may come from these new sources of production; at least they can be relied upon not to imitate the Hollywood method. In Sweden and Denmark, with their long traditions of sincere and poetic film-making, and in Switzerland, good work has been done despite the limiting factor of language. Here again the documentary method is coming to have influence on entertainment production.

But far away the most exciting films since the war have come from a small group of film-makers in Italy who, like the Russians in the mid-twenties and the British documentary movement in the thirties, have rediscovered the simple fact that imagination and inventiveness are worth all the technical paraphernalia of the luxury studios if you have something to say. With scanty film-stock and crude equipment, a handful of Italian films, of which *Paisan, Open City, The Miracle, Terra Firma, Four Steps in the Clouds* and *Under the Roman Sun* are among the most outstanding, have shown us again what vitality, sincerity and real skill mean in film-making. The deep passionate understanding of human beings, the sensitive camera observation found especially in Rossellini's films impel one to salute this fine Italian director, uninhibited by past traditions, as one of the most important figures in world cinema in recent years. His spontaneous method of working, his refusal to use a hard and fast script, above all his remarkable capacity for improvisation on the spot are reminiscent of cinema's earliest days. In Italy, he has many imitators but none so far shares his skill for shaping reality at first hand. Next to him, Visconti and Castellani reveal great talent and if left to develop their own futures they will undoubtedly create important work.

The serious danger which the new Italian cinema faces is from without. Companies from America and Britain with lire to spend have discovered Italy as a wonderful exterior location. An exploited Italian Film Industry for the benefit of Hollywood and London will surely try to sidetrack the fresh, unorthodox vitality of the new generation of Italian film-makers. It will spoil their writers, inhibit the enthusiasm of their technicians and make the methods of the Rossellinis impossible.

The desire to make films of this kind, films which not only demonstrate the real uses of the cinema but which contribute to world thought and world affairs, is not exclusively Italian. It exists in Britain especially, but is frustrated by difficulties of access to the means of production and distribution. The only alternative so far to speculative production or to a nationalised Film Industry is that pursued by the documentary film-makers in their discovery of sponsorship.

The past twenty years have seen developed, mainly in Great Britain, an economic basis for film-making alternative to the speculative investment of capital for profit return. As is well-known, the system of sponsorship of films by governments, municipalities, foundations, big national industries and others has been based on a realisation of the immense persuasive uses of the screen. That is to say it is the only method of financial film-backing that does not depend on substantial profits from the box-office. Let us be honest about this. Sponsorship has many dangers, not only the risk that the intentions of the sponsor may not always coincide with those of the film-maker, but also that the spending of money derived from public funds, as in the case of officially-sponsored films, can involve bureaucratic control. Such control can be as frustrating to initiative in the film-maker as the box-office demands of the commercial producer or the totalitarian directives of a nationalised industry.

Since the largest and longest-lived movement of sponsored production has taken place in Britain, I may be pardoned for examining in detail what some of its problems have been and still are. Documentary films may only occupy a small proportion of the world's total screen-space but their influence is wide. Their continuity of production over twenty unbroken years represents the only example of a planned policy in film-making over a sustained period that the cinema has yet known. If it is true, as some say, that British documentary has now reached a moment of standstill, even of decline, then at least it has behind it this record of twenty years of public service, twenty years of creative work, and twenty years of attempting to use the screen for more profound purposes than making profits and casually amusing people.

Since 1928 the growth of the British documentary movement has been related inseparably to the task of public information. In its pursuit of public service, it has avoided the normal cupidity of commercial production. Several hundred craftsmen and trained technicians have grown up in this tradition. This applies equally to the British Government's Crown Film Unit (which had its origins in the Empire Marketing Board and Post Office Film Units) and to the groups of small units operated privately devoting their work to documentary, educational and informational production.

The history and internal structure of the movement has been told elsewhere,[1] but to understand its present position we should remember that the British documentary makers were employed almost exclusively by the Ministry of Information and the Service departments during the war, thereby enjoying a certain degree of economic security which had been unknown before 1940. On the whole film-makers believed in the films they were asked to make as part of their national service. Considerable latitude was given as to treatment and technique by the official sponsors. From an economic point of view it meant that the documentary companies came inevitably to rely on Government sponsorship for their livelihood. Only a very few of the non-Governmental sponsors continued their financing of films during the war years, and such films tended to become less and less concerned with socially important subjects.

Although such films as *Desert Victory, Western Approaches* and the memorably magnificent *The True Glory* were successful at the box-office (by which I mean that they were booked well; not that they made a profit)[2] during the war years, this did not in any degree help to open up the commercial market to documentaries when the war was over. While I think it is true that documentary makers have found it difficult to dramatise effectively the subjects of peacetime post-war Britain so that such films evoke response in the cinemas, at the same time the rooted hostility of the Trade to allowing its screens to be used for any other purposes than entertainment in the Trade's meaning of the word did not encourage the speculative production of post-war documentaries. It did not matter what warm response documentary films received from the Press and, when they were shown, from the public audience, the Trade disliked the very idea of documentary in the cinemas for reasons given earlier. Thus, the producers found them-

[1] *The Arts Enquiry Report* on *The Factual Film* (Oxford University Press, 1947) has the most up-to-date record.

[2] It will probably never be possible to measure the British Treasury's receipts against the cost of these films because so much of the latter was incalculable owing to Service rates of pay, free facilities, etc.

selves mainly relying, just as in the war, on what films the new Labour Government through its newly-founded Central Office of Information required and what sponsors would continue production in an economy that held the nation in its grip.

The Central Office of Information which succeeded the Ministry of Information in May, 1946, has had some severe criticism made of it. On its side, excuses and alibis have been all too readily found. It is not a Ministry. It is subject to more rigid controls than its predecessor, and so on. The fact remains that the British Labour Government's film production programme, like its overall publicity, has not as yet been conceived on a national level or geared to the realities of Britain's position in world affairs. It has lacked imagination and confidence. The Central Office has to date pursued a policy that has brought a sense of frustration among even the toughest of documentary film-makers. Added to that, the interminable delays by committees and the financial disagreements apparently inescapable in the making of Government films have done much to bring British documentary into its present much-criticised position. With the cinemas virtually closed to any speculative production, with the economic uncertainty of post-war official sponsorship, with the reluctance of non-official sponsors to underwrite productions of a socially significant kind, is it any wonder that British documentary has lost something of its vitality and inventiveness since the war?

The documentary makers themselves are not wholly without blame. The obsession for regarding documentary film-making as a movement first and foremost has had the effect of suppressing the individual. Films are made by individuals, not by movements, a matter to which I shall return later. It is immensely important—and of considerable historic cinematic interest—that through the documentary method a whole school of film-making has been built up. That documentary makers the world over have common interests is expressed through the World Union of Documentary founded in Brussels, June 1947. That documentary needs have created methods of training and graduation unknown in other branches of the Film Industry is accepted. Equally important, a method of access to means of production by sponsorship as distinct from speculation has been established, and a substantial new audience has been gathered in the non-theatrical field. Documentary has achieved these things *through being a movement* with all the power and influence that this can mean.

At the same time, the needs of mass-production during the war years, when documentary producers were called upon to quadruple their output, has had the bad effect of standardising techniques and styles. The rapid growth of non-theatrical consumer needs, the policy to put out film after film into the cinemas often under a system of free-distribution, undoubtedly robbed documentary of some of its vitality. This is a criticism which can be made with fairness not only of British production but of the product of the National Film Board of Canada. The latter built up supremely well its highly-organised non-theatrical machinery and had excellent outlet in the cinemas of North America. But to meet this regular demand for its films it resorted to formula-produced pictures, in line with *March of Time* and the other screen magazines. Group production of this kind can be as cramping to the artist as the formula-conceived pictures from the studio assembly-line. If too much emphasis is put on uniform output, the creative and aesthetic urge is bound to suffer whatever the field. The individual contribution gets submerged in the group endeavour.

Moreover, I do not believe that we ever meant the term 'documentary' to cover such a multitude of sins as it is made to do to-day. What has in actuality occurred since those days twenty years ago is that there has been a need, greatly stimulated by the war, for many different types of factual and informational films calling for many divergent types of technique; but because most but not all of these films have used actual material and real people as distinct from sets and professional actors in the studio, the term documentary has been stretched to embrace them all.

The growth of non-theatrical distribution in the United Kingdom, and for factual British films overseas, the similar and even more impressive work in this field that has been done in Canada, Australia and the United States, is immensely encouraging and vital to documentary's future development in all its forms. Film distribution of this kind will one day enter into every sphere of civic activity and education. While I am the last person to deny this importance of the film for non-theatrical exhibition, with all its growing specific tasks of education, information and explanation, I nevertheless believe that it would be a thousand pities if the chapel-like atmosphere that has been allowed to enshroud the non-theatrical side of documentary were permitted to overshadow the virile, impulsive desires that give rise to the dramatic documentary which can inspire the millions in the ordinary cinemas.

The immediate post-war years of British documentary will not shine brightly when the overall story comes to be told. Its exponents have had inevitably to court official sponsorship because of the scarcity of other backing. More than ever dependent on Government support, British documentary has had to make concessions to bureaucracy which have temporarily damaged its quality.[1]

While discussing documentary, opportunity must be taken to make reference, if only briefly, to one or two events which have taken place overseas in this side of the Industry. Of outstanding importance was the founding of the National Film Board of Canada early in the war. The Board may well be held up as an example to other countries in the use of all visual media for education and information, provided that the dangers of standardised product are avoided. Although its technicians are still young and still learning, they have turned out a steady programme of short films of which they may well be proud. At the

---

[1] The recent appointment of John Grierson as Films Controller at the Central Office of Information may conceivably improve the position.

same time, the Board has taken films out to rural audiences and developed a worthwhile non-theatrical distribution and demand that is a model. Our own Central Office could learn much from it in this field. One day possibly we shall see the other Dominions with such Film Boards. Australia already has the beginnings of such a body but with progress to date not comparable with Canada.

Another development which must be included here was the sudden flowering of American documentary to meet the needs of war. Richard Griffith describes this at some length[1] but I must record my own respect for the fine work of those from Hollywood and elsewhere who were anonymously behind the making of such magnificent films as *The Fighting Lady, The Battle of San Pietro, Let There Be Light,* and of course, the famous *Why We Fight* series which provoked even the Soviet cinematographers to praise. It was as if the war suddenly gave to these men a release from Hollywood for which they had long been waiting. It is all the more sad that they have in most cases returned to the field of entertainment films where their work, interesting as it must always be, has not the same force as it had temporarily in their imaginative war documentaries.

If the difficulties of sponsorship, distribution and standardisation on which I have dwelt can be overcome, documentary has unlimited fields in which to develop into the future. But its films must be more human, warmer and full of understanding. As well as the vast programme of factual films required for national and international education, there must also be the individually-made film, the work of observation, impassioned in subject and theme. In the British Commonwealth of Nations, especially in the new Africa, there are themes to be filmed which open out our imaginations and our sense of drama. Documentary, particularly in Great Britain, has become too parochial. The work of the United Nations Film Board, so deeply inspiring in its original aims and manifestos, seems to have got bogged down in rather dull, flatly-made little pictures

[1] *Vide,* pages 460-464.

9. THE BIRTH OF A NATION, directed by D. W. GRIFFITH. [American, 1915]

10. INTOLERANCE, directed by D. W. GRIFFITH. [American, 1916]

11. HIS OWN HOME TOWN, directed by Thomas Ince. Charles Ray. [American, 1918]

12. BROKEN BLOSSOMS, directed by D. W. Griffith. Donald Crisp, Lillian Gish. [American, 1919]

lacking real international breadth, width and stature. Perhaps out of the new generation of documentary film-makers growing up to-day there will emerge new Flahertys, new Ivens's and new Basil Wrights who will go out to make films uninhibited by departments and committees and minor officials, to say nothing of internal intrigue.

*

The problem of the expression of the individual mind in film-making (except in the simplest of films such as *Nanook* or *Drifters*) has grown with the complex technological methods that are involved in production, and with the commercial needs of the Industry's promoters with their goal of world audiences. The more the film has become an Industry of magnitude and a powerful factor in world trade bargaining, the more carefully must we search for its creative impulses.

It is frequently held by screen-writers that they are the real creators of films in that they conceive the original characters and events which finally take shape in the finished film, and that the director and his team only carry out the writer's instructions. Although I respect highly the task of the screen-writer, especially when he or she writes originally and not merely adapts, and admit that he is frequently undervalued and underworked, I would suggest that only the director can be the main creative mind that really gives life and breath and emotion and meaning to the writer's ideas. The influence of the writer over the director can be extremely powerful, as for example the relationship between Prévert and Carné, Pressburger and Powell, Riskin and Capra, Nichols and Ford, and even Amidei or Fellini and Rossellini. Nevertheless, it is the director who remains in our mind when we think back over the films of these teams.

A good story can be ruined by a hack, rule-of-thumb director; a poor story can be made at least interesting technically by an imaginative director with his unlimited power over the instruments of the medium.[1] In practice, it

---

[1] *Naked City* is an example of the latter.

has been generally found that a small team of the key film-makers—the director, writer, cameraman, designer, with the producer as a sort of father-confessor—is the most desirable way of working with a good deal of generous give and take between them. The writer of an original story for a film is often without the technical experience (which certainly involves first-hand knowledge of editing shot to shot) to prepare a shooting-script. The writer engaged to adapt a novel or a play for the screen may be capable of taking it to treatment stage, but he needs technical experience to take it further into shot form. There are very few writers in motion pictures, as far as I know, who have actual physical experience of piecing shot against shot, of moulding form from fragments of film which is the final process that brings dead celluloid to life. In a careful survey of the outstanding films of the past forty years, I can think of only one writer whose influence spread far outside the actual words that he put on paper—the late Carl Mayer. But as Pommer and Freund remind us, Mayer did not end his work with the written script but kept in the closest touch all through with the shooting and editing of a film. In fact, he became a member of the production unit.[1] In the same way, Rossellini's main writer, Sergio Amidei, is constantly present during all the shooting, inventing dialogue and situations while the film is in progress acording to the possibilities of the locations. This improvisation and spontaneity is the secret of much of Rossellini's vital approach.

A recent tendency in feature production, especially in Britain, is for writers themselves to become directors. I applaud the move if the writer has first had a good sound training in the cutting-room. The writer-director who brings an editor on to the studio-floor to help him select his camera set-ups, and to tell him when to start and when to cut action seems to me to be avoiding his responsibilities (and his pleasures) as a director. It is phoney film-making.

I once wrote that the ultimate test of a film director is

[1] *Vide,* Appendix IV, pp. 711-713, 716.

to put him alone with a camera in a ploughed field and get him to make a film about it. To-day, many directors are so overpowered by the team with which they work that they become merely a skilled technician. The significant director is he whose personality, tastes and outlook on life as well as his store of knowledge emerge from the complex process of film-making. One knows that many skilled and gifted persons contributed to the making of a film like *Great Expectations* or *The Fallen Idol* or *The Miracle,* but through each of these films comes clearly and unmistakably the signature of Lean, Reed and Rossellini. I like a piece written about Rossellini by Hugh Barty-King: ' He "dreams up " a film in his mind's eye, and that's the eye that will orientate the whole production. There will be no other " eyes " earlier or later on in the long-drawn-out process of production to upset the balance, composition or meaning of the picture as first conceived. It will be his creation.' [1]

It would be impossible to imagine that *The Miracle* had been directed by, say, George Cukor; or that *Hamlet* had been made by, say, Fritz Lang; or that Alexander Korda had been responsible for *Crossfire;* or that Flaherty had made *Odd Man Out.* Yet in the group-movement of documentary mentioned earlier, it is often hard to tell these days who directed what. The standardised, almost inhuman product seems to have become the ideal of some of the younger documentary group in their desire to suppress personality. That is why the adult work of Flaherty, Ivens and Rossellini stands out with such strength.

Nevertheless, the technical processes of the medium are such that it appears that the skill of a film director must lie not only in his own gifts of filmic expression but in the capacity as well to organise and co-ordinate and inspire the skills of his fellow-workers. The more elaborate the picture in its technical requirements, the more essential becomes this capacity for co-ordination. The immense array of technical equipment, the double-figure staff of technicians and assistants each with their watertight Union-

[1] *Documentary '47* (Albyn Press, 1947).

defined jobs, the corps of electricians, carpenters, painters, plasterers, property-men and others, who although not answerable to the director are nevertheless contributors to what finally goes on the screen, the intricate processes of photography and recording, of developing and processing, and above all the fantastic cost of it all—can build up an iron curtain between the director and what eventually reaches the screen as his creation. The length of time in production also means that months possibly will elapse between the time when he visualises a sequence of shots in his working script and the time when he sees them assembled and projected. For months he must carry about in his mind a clear vision of what he expects it will all look like. He may well wish he were back in that ploughed field, camera in hand, and not a soul in sight. Small wonder that some directors flourish neuroses like mink-coats.

When Van Gogh walked along that sunny road near Arles, carrying canvas and paints and stool, he was free to set up his easel and paint as he felt inspired. Between him and his subject, and between his subject and his canvas there lay only his skill and his colours. But the film-maker, even pursuing the simple ways of a Flaherty or a Rossellini, is dependent on a myriad of materials and processes outside his control. The creator in films has an enormous task between the script and the screen.

*

The film is fundamentally an art based on observation. True observation is only obtained at first-hand. A film significant and affirmatory of life, can be called a micro-cosm of a microcosm. Thus it is imperative for film-makers (particularly producers, directors and writers) never to lose touch with the realities of living. Film-making can easily become such a one-track activity that its exponents tend to segregate themselves away from everyday activities. The very need to concentrate on their work limits their field of experience. I suggest that Wyler was only able to make

The Best Years of Our Lives with sincerity and understanding because he had in his Service capacity probably
mixed on equal terms with hundreds of Americans facing
demobilisation, and was in contact with the confused
emotions with which they faced reabsorption into civilian
life. Compare him with Wyler making *Mrs. Miniver,* who
knew and understood at first hand little of what he was
trying to express. Carol Reed's *The True Glory,* Rossellini's
Open City and *Paisan* were of people and events and
environments which had been experienced.

Here, perhaps, in this context is the right place to say
a word about the often-discussed fusion of the documentary
approach with the fiction entertainment film. The possible
merging of the two has given rise to some confused speculation. It is certainly true that a few British fiction films,
such as *Millions Like Us* and *The Way Ahead,* derived
something from documentary during the war. It should also
be remembered that the war itself demanded that some
subjects for entertainment films should be drawn from
reality. The Ministry of Information had as one of its
main aims the influencing of subjects for commercial studio
production. Technicians employed in the feature studios
were just as much working under terms of temporary
deferment from military service as were the documentary
people; and some of them felt, I believe, that their films,
although coming under the category of entertainment,
should none the less be a direct contribution to the war
effort.

In perspective, however, some of the British films so often
quoted as being examples of the fiction-documentary
marriage were ' documentary ' only in the sense that their
subjects were typical of something which had happened,
and that from time to time units left their studios and shot
in actual surroundings. I have in mind *In Which We Serve,
One of Our Aircraft is Missing* and *San Demetrio,* films
which in my opinion were much overpraised and, on
rescreening, reveal a crude and even amateur approach to
the observation of reality. The bulk in each was, in any

case, studio-shot. It should be made very clear that the mere use of real backgrounds in a film instead of studio reconstruction does not constitute ' documentary'. Recent British films like *Broken Journey, Holiday Camp, The Brothers* and *Daybreak* had genuine exteriors, but could not by any stretch of kindness be called documentary in approach, method or purpose. To transport actors, technicians, equipment and all the paraphernalia of the studio into a real street, or a real house, or to real countryside and to let the fictitious action take place there does not in itself induce a sense of realism. It just doesn't happen like that. Actors and their actions must have a sense of belonging to that place, must grow out of it, and implanting that essence is the art of the realist director. From his experience, from his power to observe, from his ability to merge players and action with environment will come the creative interpretation of reality, an understanding of the rightness of things, of things all of a piece, of things belonging.

That is the real essence of the art of Rossellini; the skill with which he blends actors with non-actors and lets the whole film emerge from actual surroundings. He does not worry his head about marrying ' documentary' with ' fiction'. He believes only that cinema is the art of representing reality and he goes as far as possible to reality with his camera and microphone in exactly the opposite manner to such a film as *London Belongs to Me*. He believes that cinema is only at the very beginning of discovering drama set in reality, and that the claustrophobic methods of the studio which have bedevilled film-making for so long are the reason why so many films have been theatrical, literary and artificial instead of cinematic.

In this Rossellini is not doing anything new. The use of reality dates back to the beginning of the cinema. Sennett in his early comedies worked just as the Italians do to-day. Renoir in *Toni* did the same. Rossellini is simply carrying out in practice what so many people have written and talked about for the past twenty years. It is what de Rochemont did in *Boomerang* and Dassin in *Naked City*. The documentary directors have been making films by these methods for years. Jill Craigie's *The Way We Live,* Watt's *Bill Blewitt,* Holmes's *Merchant Seamen* and *The Centre,* to name only a few from the British group, all attempted the method but were not able financially to extend to feature-length conceptions. What Rossellini has done is to blend into an indivisible unity the fictional incident and its realistic expression, and done it with immense effect because of his own dynamic and persuasive personality coupled with his inherent sense of cinema. His habits of working would not be practicable in America or England; Union rules alone would thwart his whole approach. His small unit, limited to essential people, is less like a team of film technicians than a circus troupe in which anyone does anything as need arises. The success of the picture comes before all else.

Carol Reed's *The Way Ahead* is fresh and purposeful after four years because it had real documentary meaning. It did not stem from a commercial studio but was inspired, conceived and executed mainly by technicians in uniform, given temporary release to produce the film through a commercial company, the whole idea deriving from an Army educational film called *The New Lot.* The major commercially-made British films attempting with some success to use documentary methods were *The Foreman Went to France* (one of the best of all war films), *The Gentle Sex* (a little theatrical and self-conscious), *Millions Like Us* and *Nine Men.* The often-quoted Launder-Gilliat film came to recognisable life in its factory sections only; the pre-war family life sequences, which occupied considerable footage, were gauche and embarrassing. *Nine Men,* like *The Way Ahead,* was a genuine work of film creation and, although partly studio-shot and reconstructed, lives remarkably freshly. Those who may have seen Zoltan Korda's Hollywood-made *Sahara* on the same subject would immediately have detected the fundamental differences between the two approaches. In my view, *Sahara* had all the phoney characteristics of a studio-made product.

Harry Watt is the only film-maker from the British documentary group so far to be strong enough to make an impact on the studio-mind. Wisely, perhaps, he has operated from distant Australia on his last two pictures, although his producer, Michael Balcon, obviously believes in what his director is trying to achieve. With a fine record of films—*Night Mail, Bill Blewitt, North Sea, Squadron 992, Target for Tonight, Nine Men* and *The Overlanders* —Watt has shown more understanding of the need for human qualities in documentary than any other British director. By the other documentary makers who have entered the commercial field, little influence has been exerted; if anything, the tendency has been the other way round. It is yet to be fully understood, I suggest, that the essential difference between fiction entertainment pictures and documentary is not only a difference in technical method (important though this is), but also a difference in approach to subject, indeed in the very reason why the director is making the film at all. Films such as *Boomerang* and *Open City* and *The Miracle,* documentary in technique, were nevertheless films produced on a commercial basis and made for money and entertainment, though entertainment was not the sole object in view. Yet the important purpose behind each, an expression of social outlook that is uncommon in the ordinary commercial picture, in no way detracted from their special appeal at the box-office.

It is to be deeply regretted that the British directors from the commercial studios who grasped and developed the realistic approach during the war should, like some of their American *confrères*, have turned back to purely fictional films, theatrically conceived and exhibiting no sign of their brush with reality, as soon as peace came. Contrast Reed in *The True Glory* and *Odd Man Out,* the Boultings in *Journey Together* (or *Burma Victory*) and *Fame is the Spur,* Asquith in *We Dive at Dawn* and *Fanny by Gaslight,* Launder and Gilliat in *Millions Like Us* and *London Belongs to Me.* Hopes of a significant British cinema began to fade when realism gave way to the romantic and theatrical.

To be technically brilliant in cinema to-day is not in itself enough. It is the use to which this skill is put which is the real test. Trite stories, geared to a 'teen-age level, will no longer hold for the technical mastery of our young directors or of those in other countries. Thus a fundamental question arises which can only be answered by their future films : Have they, talented with their skilful techniques, anything they want to express, or is their sole aim that of entertainment for its own sake? Are they seeking to perpetuate the ideology expressed by Mr. Terry Ramsaye quoted earlier, or have they any such aims in world cinema as Renoir, Rossellini, Wyler, Huston, Dmytryk, Chaplin, or Flaherty? That is something they must face. In all the booms and slumps of British films in thirty years, how very, very few have reflected anything of the mood and movement of their times.

*

This is the moment, especially in Britain, to emphasise and plead urgently for the need to experiment. Without new ideas and themes, new and vigorous personnel, new ways of using the camera and the microphone, new inspirations and incentives, the business of picture-making will decline. This is as true of documentaries, newsreels and cartoons as it is of feature production. We should always remember that when film-making in the past has become standardised and mass-manufactured, it has not taken long for the box-office to reflect the public's indifference. When stereotyped, rule-of-thumb methods dominate production, and films become the assembly-line output of departments or committees, audiences inevitably begin to dwindle, whether it be in the cinema or the village hall. That happened in entertainment films towards the end of the twenties as a result of Hollywood's standardised methods : it happened again some ten years later when the talking film tended to become mere illustrated gramophone records and only the war intervened; it is happening now.

The fine flowering of the French cinema in the middle

thirties came out of the experimental *avant-garde* period just previous; the renaissance of the British cinema during the war could never have happened if there had not been the experimental work of the documentary group before the war; the British documentary group in turn had learnt from the pioneer work of the Russians and of Flaherty. One hears of new *avant-garde* groups in America to-day, and the news is welcome. I wish we could say the same of Britain. I wish that the two millions which we are told have been lost on 'prestige' films, which added so little to our knowledge of cinema, had been spent on a few modestly-budgeted experimental films. I know that Mr. Rank has financed the Independent Frame method, films for children and a large new animation unit, but that is not what I mean. Experiment in stories and subjects, in styles and techniques, will always pay in the long run. But then, few producers look further ahead than this year's schedule. In feature, documentary, cartoon and newsreel, experiment is needed to-day more than ever before. Nothing will satisfy me until I hear that a proportion of each year's production budget at the major studios is set aside for experiment; not only to bring on new creative craftsmen, but to allow, just for once, some of the established film-makers to do what they feel passionately urged to do with the screen-medium. Such a policy would pay rich dividends in next year's normal product, and even richer twelve months later.

*

The year in which this book is being revised is without doubt the most critical of many critical years in the British Film Industry. Events have already taken place, and others are occurring as this is written, that will change and shape the whole future of British films for progress or decline. The placing on the Statute Book of the new Cinematograph Films Act has given a speck of hope to the independent producer by legislation that provides circuit bookings on fair terms to a set number of independent feature films a year. The Film Finance Corporation should eventually ease the economic difficulties of the independent producer. The forty-five per cent. quota should encourage producers both big and small. The four-year agreement between the American Motion Picture Association and the British Government should also provide more screen-space for British pictures, but may restrict the playing of our films in America; but we should strenuously resist here any attempt to influence our subjects and styles by Hollywood. The establishment of a Committee of Enquiry into Exhibition, if well set up and with full powers to investigate the facts, can be the first practical move towards the highly-desirable aim of separating production from exhibition interests.

In the non-theatrical field, the establishment with Government aid of an Educational Foundation for Visual Aids can either break the vicious circle of films in schools or set back the use of school films for ten years, according to what policy of sponsorship and distribution is adopted. The Report on the future of the British Film Institute (rather a mild document) can lead to a reorganisation, reconstitution and reassessment of that potentially important but inept body. The passing of the Local Government Act can open up a new era of municipally-owned cinemas if local authorities have the initiative to use fully the powers given them. Finally, the setting up of the British Film Academy can bring to the Industry some of that dignity and critical perspective which have been so notably absent all these years.

These are factors each of which will have direct bearing on the future of films in the many spheres of production, distribution and exhibition, both in the public cinemas and in the ever-growing field of non-theatrical performance. Their effects will presumably engage the close attention of all serious followers of the cinema, as well as of those actively involved.

*

With this book, as with the first edition eighteen years ago, we arrive at a turning-point in cinema. Hollywood has partially retained its hold over the British market, has temporarily (we hope) restricted native production in France, and has retained a very considerable control over what is shown throughout the Commonwealth, despite important inroads made there by Mr. Rank. But that is only part of the picture. The attention being paid to the cinema by the United Nations Organisation and its agencies, especially Unesco; the existence of National Film Boards in the two great countries of Canada and Australia; the fact that every day the film is being more widely discussed and understood—these things mean that eventually and inevitably an overpowering demand will arise that the screen be used for fuller purposes than it is used to-day. Across the world, from East to West, arise vast new audiences for films, the meeting of which has scarcely entered the calculations of any existing film industry. Old generations of film-makers will go their way, but all the time new young audiences are forming. They will not be content to let their mental inferiors dominate the screen.

*

I cannot end these notes without paying tribute to three men who, each in their own way when they were alive, made their contribution to cinema and influenced my thinking. Eric Knight, a Yorkshireman with the fire and faith of England in him, was the best critic of films ever to write in an American newspaper. His letters from Holly-wood in 1936 unforgettably document and indict that phantasmagoria of frustrated talent. Carl Mayer contribu-ted more than anyone to the whole Golden Period of the German Cinema. And Otto Neurath, who of all others I have met, understood most fully how the film could extend the consciousness of the international man-in-the-street.

These three men widened my experience and helped to open my eyes to the manifold ways in which the film, once its infinite techniques are mastered, can enrich and reward all human beings.

London   PAUL ROTHA
August, 1948

ACKNOWLEDGEMENTS

In addition to the acknowledgements made in the first edition of this book, which do not need to be reprinted, I am indebted in this revised edition to the many people who from time to time since 1930 have pointed out errors of fact in the original text. From many parts of the world, correspondents have sent valuable information and the new text has, as far as possible, been changed to meet their facts. My thanks are especially due to the directors and staffs of the Museum of Modern Art Film Library, New York, the Cinémathèque Française, Paris, the National Film Library, London, Dansk Kulturfilm, Copenhagen, the Czechoslovak Film Institute, Prague, and the National Board of Review of Motion Pictures, New York, for their unlimited help. These bodies, which are doing such fine work in the preservation of films, making them available for study, collecting data about film history and generally aiding in creating a wider appreciation of good films, have supplied me with much factual information and loaned still-photographs.

The book has been mainly re-illustrated and acknowledgements are due to the following companies, past and present, for permission to reproduce their stills : Albatross-Sequana, Arquis Film, British International Pictures, British National Pictures, Charles Chaplin Film Corporation, Ciné-Alliance, Cinégraphie Documentaire, Cineguild, Columbia Pictures, Contemporary Historians Incorporated, Coopérative Générale du Cinéma Français, Crown Film Unit, Dafu-film, Defu-film, Deutsche Film-Gemeinschaft, Ealing Studios, Elekta Film Slavia, Empire Marketing Board Film Unit, Films Marcel Pagnol, Films of Fact, First-National, Fox Film Corporation, Frontier Films, G.B. Instructional Ltd., G.P.O. Film Unit, Grafton Films, Hakim Brothers, Lenfilm, London Film Productions, Mejrabpom-Russ,

ACKNOWLEDGEMENTS

Metro-Goldwyn-Mayer, Minerva Films, Mosfilm, Néofilm, Nerofilm, Nordisk, Organizzazione Films Internazionali, Palladium-Film, Paramount Picture Corporation, Paul Rotha Productions, Photosonor, Prana-Film, Réalisations d'Art Cinématographic, R.K.O.-Radio Pictures, Robert Flaherty Productions, Selznick-International Pictures, Sigma-Frogerais, S.N. Pathé-Cinéma, Société Générale de Films, Sokal-film, Sovkino, Soyuzdetfilm, Svenska-Biograf, Tobis Regina, Transcontinental, Twentieth Century-Fox, Two Cities Films, Ufa, United Artists, Universal, U.S. Department of Agriculture, Vostok-kino, Vufku-kino, Warner Brothers.

PUBLISHER'S NOTE TO 1967 EDITION

For this new edition of *The Film Till Now*, Paul Rotha has added a Postscript, briefly mentioning important developments in international cinema during the 1960s. He re-states his beliefs and objectives as a film-maker and summarises the main changes which have taken place in the industry since he wrote his book almost forty years ago.

Apart from minor corrections, the text remains complete and unaltered, but the single comprehensive index is a new feature. There are also twenty-six new illustrations of outstanding post-war films, bringing the total to 200, and these have been rearranged to appear in chronological order.

1930

TO THOSE
AMONG CINEMA
AUDIENCES
WHO WONDER WHY
AND THINK HOW

1949

TO ALL THOSE WHO ARE READY TO RECEIVE
A BETTER KIND OF FILM IF ONLY PRODUCERS,
RENTERS AND EXHIBITORS WILL HAVE
THE COMMON SENSE TO PROVIDE THEM

1967

AND TO THE MEMORY OF
ERIC KNIGHT (1897–1943)
CARL MAYER (1894–1944)
RICHARD WINNINGTON (1903–53)
WHO OVER THE YEARS SHARED MY APPROACH
TO THE ART OF THE FILM. IT WAS BY WAY OF THE FIRST EDITION
OF THIS BOOK THAT I MET THEM

13. THE PHANTOM CARRIAGE, directed by Victor Seaström. [Swedish, 1919]

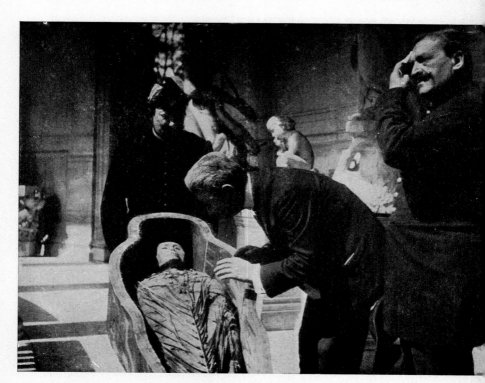

14. LA CIGARETTE, directed by Germaine Dulac. Signoret. [French, 1919]

15. THE CABINET OF DR. CALIGARI, directed by ROBERT WIENE.   WERNER KRAUSS.
[German, 1919]

16. THE GOLEM, directed by HENRIK GALEEN.   PAUL WEGENER, ALBERT STEINRÜCK.
[German, 1920]

PART ONE
THE ACTUAL

I

THE DEVELOPMENT OF THE FILM

The development of the film may be regarded from three different points of view : the Scientific, the Commercial, and the Aesthetic.

The first is concerned with the mechanical advance of the instrument and its technicalities, dealing with the workings of the projector, the intricate mechanism of the camera, the various methods of sound reproduction by discs or sound-strip[1] on film. These it is not proposed to consider, except where the actual machinery of the instrument has direct bearing on the expression of the theme which the film is unfolding.

The second covers the amazing growth of the film as an industry, which here will be briefly recorded.

And the third views the progress which the film has made since its birth as a medium of dramatic expression, including its limits and its delimits. It is with this aesthetic aspect of the cinema that this survey is primarily concerned.

Except historically and technically, the birth and early years of the cinema are neither interesting nor particularly brilliant in aesthetic achievement. Accounts of financial successes and failures in tawdry commercialism are depressing. It suffices to mention a few salient facts and dates in order to gain a perspective of the position to-day without undue tedium.

(a) *The Commercial Development of the Film*

It seems generally agreed that, for all practical purposes, Edison started the ball rolling in 1887. Having perfected the phonograph, he desired to supplement the sound images with another mechanical device which would present visual images alongside those of sound. It is extraordinary to

[1] For definitions of these and other technicalities, such as sound or visual image, etc., see the Glossary in Appendix II.

observe that this ambition of Edison, which brought the film into being, is precisely the opposite to the aim of the present-day producer, who attempts to supplement his visual images with their recorded sounds. This astonishing fact is worth serious consideration. The visual film was thought necessary to accompany the sound record. Fifty years later, sound is deemed necessary to accompany the visual film. Many dialogue films made since 1930 have been, in fact, glorified, illustrated, gramophone records.

Edison's first efforts apparently resulted in pictures of microscopic size in spirals upon a cylinder, somewhat similar to the early gramophone record. Some time later, strips of film were made out of collodion and experiments were also carried out with celluloid, but it was not until samples of the first Eastman-Kodak film, constructed on a nitro-cellulose base, were obtained by Edison in 1889 that the original cinema machine came into being. This was called the Kinetoscope. Experiments proceeded in Edison's laboratory at West Orange, until at length it was possible for one person at a time to look through the peephole of the machine and to see a series of pictures, some fifty feet in length, representing a person in movement—jerky and interrupted, perhaps, but nevertheless *movement*. It is said that the first actual cinematic record was that of a sneeze, performed by an assistant in the laboratory, one Fred Ott, whose name surely will go down to posterity on this account alone.

In 1894, the Edison kinetoscope was presented commercially to the New York public, and hundreds of these machines were sold in the open market. The subjects of Edison's films made at his laboratory were chiefly boxing-matches, dances, and variety turns, all of which were suitable to show off the capabilities of the new invention on account of their movement. But the limitation of these films being viewed by only one person at a time gave rise to a demand for a machine like a magic lantern, which would project the pictures on to a screen so that they could be seen by a whole roomful of people. Edison, however, disliked the proposal, believing that collective showings would rapidly exhaust the market, and he omitted even to patent his device in foreign countries.

Meanwhile, other experiments were in progress in Europe, all of them aiming at a combination of Edison's kinetoscope with the magic lantern, for the projection of the film on to a screen. A year later, in 1895, Woodville Latham gave public demonstrations in America of a projector using the kinetoscope film pictures, but the process was crude and unsuccessful. About the same time both Robert Paul in London and the Lumière brothers in Paris, inspired by the exhibition of Edison's device in their respective cities, brought out projectors; Paul exhibiting his at Olympia and the Alhambra in the following year.[1] The principle upon which the modern projector is based, however, is that of Thomas Armat's machine, which was shown publicly for the first time at the Cotton States' Exposition at Atlanta, Georgia, in September of 1895. Armat's Vitascope, which was illegitimately coupled with Edison's name for box-office reasons, was then shown on Broadway and was an immediate success. It was not long before several other projectors were put on the market, with the inevitable result that in a short time there was turbulent conflict and litigation over patents, which was to last for several years in America and thus to hinder progress. A disastrous damper on the young industry was experienced also in Europe, for at a charity bazaar in Paris, in 1897, one hundred and eighty members of Parisian society were burned to death in a marquee, the cause of the fire being a cinematograph machine. This calamity had a depressing effect on the whole of northern Europe, and it was years before many people would countenance the presence of the diabolical engine.

Gradually the fifty-feet lengths of film used in the kinetoscope lengthened until, in 1897, eleven thousand feet of film

[1] Several of these early instruments, of historic and scientific interest, are included in the Will Day Collection of cinematograph equipment, which is housed at present in the Science Museum, South Kensington, London.

were shown by Enoch Rector in America, being a cinematic record of the Corbett-Fitzsimmons fight at Carson City, Nevada. Exceptionally dull as this enormous length of film must have been, its novelty was probably astounding. During the same year a film version about three thousand feet long of the Oberammergau Passion Play was made by Richard Hollaman. This was not a genuine reproduction of the real spectacle, as was advertised, but was manufactured on the roof of the Grand Central Palace—a fact, however, which did not worry the public when they became aware of the deception.

About this time also, some wonderful trick effects of fade-outs, dissolves, and other photographic devices now familiar were attained by Georges Méliès at the *Théâtre Robert Houdin* in Paris. Méliès actually had his own studio, which was constructed in 1896, and amongst other films produced a version of Jules Verne's *Trip to the Moon*.[1]

Although these novelties were widely successful, it was not until 1903 that the first real attempt to tell a story by moving pictures was made. This event was achieved by Edwin S. Porter's sensational *The Great Train Robbery,* eight hundred feet in length, with Marie Murray as the leading lady in what must surely have been the first cabaret on the screen. This film was rapidly succeeded by many other ' story-pictures ', as they were called, of a similar type, such as *The Great Bank Robbery, Trapped by Bloodhounds,* and *A Lynching at Cripple Creek.* Thereafter, for some years, there set in an orgy of one-reel melodramas.

The arrival of the story-picture almost at once gave rise to the need for suitable places in which to project these efforts, which resulted in the famous nickelodeon or five-cent theatre. The first of these was opened by Harry Davis, of Pittsburgh, a real-estate operator and the proprietor of a stage theatre. This excellent showman opened his nickelodeon in 1905 with *The Great Train Robbery* as the first stupendous attraction, much in the same way as

[1] For a detailed study of Méliès, see the well-illustrated and documented book by Maurice Bessy and Lo Duca (Prisma, Paris, 1945).

exhibitors in 1929 specialised in opening with *The Singing Fool* as soon as their cinemas were wired for sound. The immediate success of Davis's house inspired speculators all over the States to start similar shows, and it was not long before these nickelodeons sprang up everywhere. They were particularly remunerative in the big labour centres, where the universal language of the film appealed equally to mixed nationalities. It is of interest to note that Zukor, Laemmle, Fox, and Marcus Loew, all men of influence in the industry at a later date, ran and made big profits out of nickelodeons.

In Europe, story-pictures continued for the most part to be shown in concert halls and variety houses, and at such places as the London Polytechnic Institute. During this time there had come into being the famous Hale's Tours, which were conducted with great success for some years between 1903 and 1909. These consisted of panoramic and travelling shots of scenes in various countries, projected on to a screen at the end of a room which was arranged like the interior of a railway carriage. The spectators were given the illusion of a tour through some distant land, the screen variously showing the railway track and spectacular views of well-known ' beauty spots '. Effect was added to the performance by the whole carriage being rocked to one side whenever the screen showed the train rounding a curve. This may perhaps be regarded as the first attempt to achieve atmosphere; certainly the carriages may be looked upon as the forerunners of the vast ' atmospheric ' cinemas of to-day. The outside of the place was made to resemble the end of a carriage, with two rails, and an attendant dressed as a railway-guard. The gilded whiskered walruses who guard the portals of London's Empire and New York's Roxy would scorn to recognise their predecessors in these pseudo railway-guards, attracting attention by a screaming phonograph.

Out of the nickelodeons, music-hall shows, and Hale's Tours there developed the first cinemas, which carried on the profitable business and caused an increased demand for story-pictures. This led to the erection of film studios and the forming of stock companies of actors and actresses by the picture-makers. From the one-reel melodramas and slapstick comedies there emerged the longer story-films; and there grew up around the latter many names which were to become world-famous. In 1908, David Wark Griffith, a stage actor, was engaged by the American Biograph Company of New York as a scenario-writer and actor, and his great influence on the film was to manifest itself during the next ten years. About this time also, numerous one-reeler Westerns, with their cowboys and Indians, were especially popular with the ever-increasing film public.

From 1911 to 1914 the industry developed with astounding rapidity. The film, hitherto a thousand feet, grew in length. But the most sensational pictures now began to come from Europe, and had considerable influence on the American producers. In England, the Hepworth, the British and Colonial Kinematograph, and the London Film Companies were all creating a demand by the good quality of their steady output. France, with her national leanings towards spectacular pageantry, produced historical films of considerable length, the most renowned being Louis Mercanton's *Queen Elizabeth,* with Sarah Bernhardt in the title rôle. This picture created a sensation wherever it was shown and was bought for America in 1912 by Adolf Zukor (then an exhibitor in New York) in conjunction with Edwin S. Porter, Daniel Frohman and others. From Italy came a series of big productions or ' feature films ', as they were known, including a version of Homer's *Odyssey, The Fall of Troy, Faust, The Three Musketeers,* and *The Sack of Rome;* but greatest of all, the forerunner of every spectacle film since, was *Quo Vadis?* a veritable mammoth production of 1912, eight thousand feet in length. This also was bought and shown by George Kleine in America, where to that date the most pretentious effort had been *The Life of Buffalo Bill.* Since the day when American producers first saw *Quo Vadis?,* cinema audiences of the world have been presented with super-spectacle after super-spectacle. From *The Birth of a Nation,* Griffith's reply to the Italian picture at the end of 1914, through the years of *Intolerance, The Ten Commandments, Robin Hood, Ben-Hur, Noah's Ark, Metropolis, Secrets of the East* and *Casanova,* super-films abounded, developing to-day into *Broadways, Hollywood Revues,* and *General Cracks* of the singing, dancing, and talking variety. In the few years just before the war the feature film sufficed to build up the industry (increased audiences meant bigger film studios and larger cinema theatres), and in 1914 the opening of the Strand Theatre on Broadway marked a new era in the history of the cinema. The way was open for the position as it is to-day.[1]

With the outbreak of war in 1914, film production virtually came to an end in Europe. The road was left clear for America to secure for herself the supreme commercial control which she still holds. It was simply a matter of circumstance, of which the Americans were quick to take full advantage. That they made the best of their opportunity is only to their credit. But all was not easy for their producers. Financiers were at first reluctant to put their war gains into the film business. Great sums of money were lost, serious risks taken, and wild speculations made in those early days before the monied men of America realised the vast financial profits waiting to be reaped from the movies.[2]

Once started, however, the American producing firms made astonishing progress. Throughout the whole war period their output increased yearly, until 1918 found them completely dominating the world market, with distribution interests in foreign producing companies and theatre controls that extended into Britain, France, Germany, and the Far East. In Britain, their acceptance was widespread simply because there were no other films available, and because their shallow, superficial nature appealed to the post-war state of mind of the public. British companies

[1] This account omits reference to the important growth of the Danish and German film industries prior to the 1914-18 War.

[2] The reader is referred to the enthralling accounts of early American struggles in Samuel Goldwyn's *Behind the Screen,* Terry Ramsaye's *A Million and One Nights,* and Mrs. Griffith's *When the Movies Were Young.*

found it more profitable, and far less of a responsibility, to rent American films than to make their own. Moreover, American companies soon opened their offices in Wardour Street and on the Continent for their own distribution, and remain there still. A few attempts to produce were made in Britain, but the lack of both experience and capital rendered the resulting pictures unworthy of presentation. America continued with characteristic facility and slickness to make picture after picture of a hard, scintillating type. By her astute business methods, she kept the standard up to a certain technical level, calculated to appeal to the lowest grade of intelligence. Britain and Europe were littered with these glittering, metallic movies, whose chief appeal lay in their sex and salaciousness, until the time came when marketing pictures by one's and two's began to be ridiculous, and Hollywood took to selling a whole year's output to foreign exhibitors and renters before the films themselves even were made. By this means she tightened her hold on the foreign market. The ' star-system ', catchpenny titles, scandalous publicity, and a hundred other tawdry schemes were devised to sell the goods to the European public. Business being business, without honour or morals, these movies were taken by British exhibitors, and the public flocked to them because of the cheapness and accessibility of the cinema. By degrees, the masses became saturated with pictures of the worst type. They did not know that others existed. They do not know now that many others exist, nor are they given the opportunity to know. Rarely is any foreign film (save an American) afforded a fair chance of success in this country. As then, the movie is rampant; the film is dormant.[1]

There is no denying the view that the Americans would have been foolish to loose their hold on the world market;

[1] This position changed but little in the thirties and even in 1947, eighty per cent. of films shown on British screens was of American origin. The situation may be changed, however, by the arrangement arrived at by the British Government and American Motion Picture Association, March 11th, 1948, and fewer Hollywood films may be imported.

and the method they adopted for retaining that hold was the disposing of their films *en masse* to British exhibitors. They devised a simple but clever system of selling their second and third-rate productions by means of their super-films. For example, if a British exhibitor wanted a big picture—a spectacle film—which would be a certain box-office draw, then he had also to accept a number of poor pictures to show during the off-season. This was all there was to it, except that, as the method spread, the exhibitor began to book pictures before he had seen them, and probably before they were made, either on the strength of promises that they would be good or else by sample. It will readily be seen how this system led to the abominable practice of making films to type, encouraged of course by the evils of the star-system. If, for instance, Raymond Hatton and Wallace Beery made one comedy, the exhibitor was then coaxed to book five similar films to show during the next two years. Many examples of this stranglehold on both stars and directors are apparent, *viz.* the polished drawing-room pieces of Adolphe Menjou; the Emil Jannings *Way of All Flesh* type of film; the Clara Bow comedies; and the backstage and adapted stage-plays of to-day. All of these are *per recipe*. Such a mechanical method of making films is bound eventually to kill individuality in director and star. Obviously there can be no creative effort in pictures produced in this manner.[1]

But it was not only by these means that the Americans assumed control of the industry. It became popular at an early stage to rent big theatres for the premiere run of a film in order to secure prestige. A 'premiere' at a large cinema in London, Berlin, Paris, or New York is all-important to a film. In Britain the provinces are unquestionably influenced by the London reception. It is the Press reports after the first night which count the highest. Thus it became customary to launch any big new picture at a prominent theatre, and it will be remembered that numerous

---

[1] The observant filmgoer of the past eighteen years can add for himself many examples of this method both British and American.

American films had their first run at London theatres. This idea developed into the acquisition of theatres for premiere runs, not only in capitals but in the key-cities throughout a country. Competition led to the taking over of whole chains of cinema houses, which meant, of course, that any film a company liked to produce could be shown at every one of the houses on its chain, the box-office profits being taken direct. Nearly every big producing concern now owns its chain of theatres, or is associated with a company owning theatres, while most of the smaller film companies distribute their pictures through the larger firms. In London alone, Metro-Goldwyn-Mayer own the Empire; Paramount (the distributing side of Famous-Players-Lasky) the Plaza and the Carlton; Fox are building a new cinema in the Haymarket,[1] Provincial Cinema Theatres own over one hundred and twenty houses, including the New Gallery, the Tivoli, the Capitol, and the Astoria, as well as being associated with the Gaumont-British chain who control the Marble Arch Pavilion, Shepherd's Bush Pavilion, Avenue Pavilion, and many others.[2] Universal own the Rialto in London,[3] and the Rialto in Leeds; and so on. Thus the control of a chain of cinema theatres with a ' shop-window ' in London, and the advantage of group advertising, is one of the most important assets for a producing company. There is little doubt that the larger concerns will concentrate more and more in the future on enlarging their existing circuits.[4]

The struggle in Europe to break down American domination has been hard and long fought; but although much of the European output (Germany and France) has been superior to the Hollywood film, the vast organisations so

[1] This announcement of 1929 did not materialise, but the cinema built was the Capitol, later renamed the Gaumont, and owned by the Rank Organisation.

[2] All these theatres are now part of the Rank Organisation.

[3] The Rialto is now controlled by Sir Alexander Korda's British Lion Film Corporation.

[4] The concentration of the most important cinemas into fewer and fewer hands has been the significant tendency in the industry in Britain during the past eighteen years, and in 1945 lead to the British Government's publication of the Board of Trade Report called *Tendencies to Monopoly in the British Cinematograph Industry*.

liberally equipped financially have presented an insuperable barrier. Possession, one recalls, is nine points of the law. In order to gain real profits, a film made in Britain, Germany, or France must secure a showing in America. This at present is almost impossible. A great deal has been said by smooth-tongued publicity men about the Americans wanting British films, but there is little doubt that the Americans are definitely hostile not only to the British but to the Continental industry. They do not want foreign films in America, except as occasional curiosities, and do not intend to have them. Why should they? [1]

After the war, the predominant country in Europe to attempt producing pictures on anything like a big scale was Germany. (For the moment it is as well to leave Soviet Russia out of the matter, for although she started to build up an industry at an early date, she was not concerned with the outside market. She made films with a purpose for her own people.) Superb as many of the early German productions were, they failed to appeal to a public accustomed to American flashiness. Scarcely any of the early German films were financially successful, and few made money outside their country of origin, where the box-office receipts were not sufficient to warrant production of fresh pictures. Added to which, Germany, like most other European countries at that time, was financially poor, and to build up a healthy film industry very considerable capital is needed. The German film trade turned to the Government for support, and the response was forthcoming. But even with State help, bank subsidies, and, later, loans from American companies, the German industry was in a constant state of fluctuation. Her films, although far better quality than the American output, failed to secure adequate returns, and Hollywood, quick to recognise the brains behind these productions, began to rob Germany of her directors, players, and technicians, and to turn them to her own commercial uses. Some years later many of these returned the worse

[1] No significant change in this position can be reported eighteen years later, except for the vastly improved quality of British and French films.

for wear. Recent German productions tend to be Americanised, although some attempt has been made by Erich Pommer to combine Hollywood commercialism with the remnants of the great German school of 1919-25.

In Sweden, Denmark and France much the same story can be told. For some time Sweden tried gallantly to make films of good quality, but again financial failure was the result. One by one her best directors and players drifted across to Hollywood, where their work steadily deteriorated. France, although spasmodically producing interesting but isolated films, has never succeeded in sustaining a continued output. In Britain also, much the same situation developed, the Americans acquiring the most promising players for their own productions, leaving British directors to do the best they could with the remainder.

Thus, although European countries made every effort to produce films in the face of the Hollywood machine, these pictures and their makers were doomed to eventual failure, with the inevitable result that the brains were imported into America. Instead of remaining persons of individual taste, they became cogs in the great movie machine. I cannot recall one example of a European director who, on going to Hollywood, made films better or even as good as he did in his own surroundings.[1] For example, Murnau's *Four Devils* and *Sunrise* were not comparable with *Tartuffe* and *The Last Laugh;* Lubitsch's *The Patriot* came nowhere near *Dubarry* in dramatic power; Leni's *The Man Who Laughs* was a travesty compared with *Waxworks;* Dupont's *Love Me and the World is Mine* is not generally associated with his name; Seaström's *Thy Soul Shall Bear Witness* is preferable to *Name the Man.* Among players, contrast Emil Jannings in *The Street of Sin* with Jannings in *Faust;* Conrad Veidt in *A Man's Past* with Veidt in *The Student of Prague;* Greta Garbo in *A Woman of Affairs* (better photographed, it is true) with Garbo in *The Joyless Street;* Pola Negri in *The Flame* with Negri in *The Crown of Lies;* Lya de Putti in *The Scarlet Lady* with Lya de Putti in

[1] In view of Lubitsch's career, this point is now debatable in his case.

Manon Lescaut, and so on. There are few conclusions to be drawn from these comparisons. Perhaps these directors, when given *carte blanche* and the wonderful technological resources of Hollywood, lost their sense of values. Perhaps the attempt to make good films with accepted Hollywood box-office ingredients was distasteful to European artists, who decided to bluff the Americans by including a few facile camera tricks which the magnates would consider high art. Or perhaps, and this is probably nearer the mark, it was impossible to produce, let alone conceive, any work of real aesthetic value when surrounded by the Hollywood atmosphere of dollars and opportunism, where culture and sincerity seem to be unknown qualities. The finest picture is not painted by an artist who has small boys to light his cigarettes, perfected mechanical appliances to mix his paints, canvases which have been specially primed at exorbitant cost, brushes made from the hairs of a strange and rare beast in the Himalayas at twenty pounds a hair. Nothing but hot-house virtuosity can come out of that environment. Sincerity of purpose and surroundings bring out good work. Transfer the painter from his disordered studio into a luxurious apartment with every new-fangled contrivance to hand and he is at a loss. Thus, for instance, Paul Leni producing *Waxworks* with little money, the goodwill of three fine actors, handicapped by lack of lights, studio space and time, bound down by limits, was forced to use his ingenuity and to extract the utmost value from a sheet of paper.[1] But Paul Leni directing *The Man Who Laughs,* with millions of dollars to spend, a cast of thousands, with the flattering knowledge that he had only to ask for a thing and get it, became slack, drivelling, slovenly, and lost all sense of taste, cinema, and artistry. This may be applied equally to a hundred other films made under the same circumstances, even by Americans, as was the case with Josef von Sternberg's *The Salvation Hunters,* a much over-praised film, which contained a few elementary ideas

---

[1] The last episode, of *Jack-the-Ripper,* was made with the barest essentials of scenery and lighting, owing to lack of finance.

of cinema, ideas that Sternberg has failed to develop since Paramount elevated him to be a director.

*

It is important to note that there had been little attempt at combination, or working in common interests, on the American side of the business, although various producing concerns were well advanced on the road to prosperity. Despite the fact that, in 1915, the Motion Picture Board of Trade was formed in New York, followed two years later by the National Association of the Motion Picture Industry, neither of these boards had much status with the trade or the public. In fact, it is said that not until there had been repeated abuses by the trade, salacious productions, and several disastrous scandals involving leading personalities on the screen and the executive staffs, did the Motion Picture Producers and Distributors of America Inc. come into being (1922).[1] This high-sounding organisation was distinguished by having for its figure-head Mr. Will Hays, who specially resigned from the Postmaster-Generalship of the United States to take the position. The powers exercised by the Hays Organisation extended over a wide area, embracing the selection of movie subjects, general trading in films, international dealings with companies, the relations of the general public to the film industry, censorship, and taxation. Mr. Hays himself looks after the general interests of the cinema with loving kindness, by taking a hand in almost every affair and a large salary. From time to time strongly-worded edicts are issued from the great man's office, which lend suitable dignity to the concern but have little real meaning or effect. It was Mr. Hays who so shrewdly decided that Somerset Maugham's play *Rain* should not be made into a film unless it were renamed *Sadie Thompson,* thereby displaying great moral sagacity.

In 1925, the international aspects of the cinema began to cause endless trouble, both politically and industrially, to

[1] Now the M.P.A. (Motion Picture Association) under the leadership of Mr. Eric Johnston. For examination of the Hays Office, see *The Freedom of the Movies*, Ruth Inglis (University of Chicago Press, 1946).

17. WAY DOWN EAST, directed by D. W. GRIFFITH. LILLIAN GISH. [American, 1920]

18. THE FOUR HORSEMEN OF THE APOCALYPSE, directed by REX INGRAM.
ALICE TERRY, RUDOLPH VALENTINO. [American, 1920–21]

19. DESTINY, directed by FRITZ LANG.   [German, 1921]

20. TOL'ABLE DAVID, directed by HENRY KING.   [American, 1921]

governments and the Press. Europe suddenly awoke to the fact that the American control of the screen, with its steady flow of propaganda for the American people, their life and work, was exerting an influence on world trade. Americanisation not only of Europe, but of Asia, Africa, and Australia was being furthered through the entertaining medium of the cinema. Agitations arose in all countries, and, after heated discussions between the trade and their respective Governments, quotas were fixed. America herself tried to disguise the whole matter by importing foreign stars and directors so as to give the film an international appeal, and by sending her own production units to work abroad. In this way she hoped partially to evade the quota regulations and to retain her hold on the world market. She has been successful.

Quota restrictions on American films encouraged European production, and determined attempts in Britain, Germany, and France were again made to build up an industry. Many companies both large and small, some with negligible financial backing, made their appearance, and after a few months a number of films were available for exhibition. Few were really satisfactory, however, partly because the public was still saturated with flashy American pictures of low standard, and partly because British films were inferior to even the American movies. This was due to the lack of organisation, the scarcity of intelligent directors, and the unsuitable type of people of which the executives in British studios were comprised. In 1924, a publicity campaign was launched to help the British film. This campaign was perhaps the worst thing that could have happened. By extravagant articles from eminent hands in the Press, by debates in both Houses, by libellous accounts of foreign methods, by reported scandals about American stars, by a tremendous stirring of agitation amongst the public, the latter was browbeaten into a state of receptivity for British films. For months the Press told the public how good the British films then in the making were going to be. After all this publicity, with the public hypnotised into readiness to applaud the worst picture in the world because it was British, the promised films came, one by one. Upon this shamefully false foundation the present industry in Britain is largely based.[1]

The British Government's Cinematograph Films Act of 1927 decided that every distributing firm and exhibitor should show a five per cent. quota of British films, no matter what the films were like. Similar but more severe restrictions were passed in Germany and in France where, however, the position was slightly different. The German and French publics would rather see a second-rate film made in their own country than an imported movie. Moreover, German and French films made to supply exhibitors with their quota were of much better standard than the British product. In Britain, the home-made film was often so inferior that an exhibitor lost money while showing it, and had to make up the loss on next week's American picture. Some exhibitors actually decided to ignore the quota and pay the resulting fine, which they could well afford to do out of the profits from American programmes.

After a time, most of the smaller British companies collapsed, and the remaining big firms concentrated on producing a considerable number of pictures, with both British and foreign directors and players, which would bring in returns sufficient to build up their business on a sound basis. Such was the position when Hollywood chose to exploit the talking film. Four out of the numerous British firms (British International Pictures, Gaumont-British, British Instructional Films, and Gainsborough Films) had gained a small footing in the home market mainly by imitating American movies and American methods. This was also taking place on the Continent, where players and directors, who some years previously had drifted to Hollywood, were reappearing in their home countries. Hollywood was being left in the lurch, and,

[1] In fact, *British* films never lived down this ill-advised campaign until the very late thirties, and it is only within the last three or four years that the definition has come to be an asset rather than a liability.

moreover, there was evidence that the public were at last tiring of the mass-produced movie. Something fresh had to be devised to whet their jaded appetites.

How the talking film struck the industry in every country like a bombshell is recent history. How Warner Brothers, not knowing which way to turn in order to continue with their production, decided to gamble on the talking film, and how they achieved an astounding success; how all Hollywood rapidly followed in their wake; how the talking film hit the nascent British industry; how law-suits and injunctions took place over infringed patents of reproducing and recording apparatus; how the coming of the ' talkies ' was Britain's great chance; how the unrepentant masses flocked to the novelty of *The Singing Fool;* how the Americans keep their control of the world market—all this and more is scattered in the daily Press and is on everyone's lips.

*

The first British dialogue film of any merit, *Blackmail* (produced by British International Pictures and directed by Alfred Hitchcock), was shown to the Press and the trade in America. The New York critics generally agreed that it was well up to Hollywood standards. But nobody *bought* the picture in New York; nobody wanted it; and in order to present the film publicly the British company had to rent a theatre. Now *Blackmail* may not have been a particularly good film, but it was infinitely better than any American dialogue picture of the same time. But the opposition it met with was a hard blow to British International Pictures. Even the Dominions cold-shouldered it. Censorship authorities in Australia at first prevented the picture from being shown, but later withdrew their ban. Such are the difficulties a British film had to meet.

Meanwhile, it is said, America is thinking beyond the dialogue film, beyond even the colour and stereoscopic film; that she is scheming quietly for complete control of the

entertainment industry of the world; and that she intends
to achieve this by means of television.

At the moment of writing (October 1929)[1] there are two
forces that count in America—the Radio Corporation of
America, and the American Telephone and Telegraph
Company. These two gigantic concerns own and control
everything that matters in the entertainment industry.
Their present power is due to an outcome of mergers,
tie-ups, and combinations that have been taking place for
some years. They are rivals in the war for complete
control, but it is likely that their rivalry will culminate in
amalgamation.

The Radio Corporation of America, who have the
immense financial backing of the General Electric Company,
are allied with the Pathé film producing concern, and have
recently organised their own film company on a big scale—
Radio Pictures. They own a large number of cinemas,
having purchased the vast Keith Albee circuit of theatres
and variety houses. They are associated with the Victor
Gramophone Company, the *alter ego* of His Master's Voice.
They own also an invention for stereoscopic films called
the Stereopticon, which, it is said, is ready for the general
market and will make television a certainty. Finally, they
are extremely efficient in the making of sound film
apparatus, the R.C.A. process being used both in British
studios and cinemas.

The American Telephone and Telegraph Company are
rich in their association with film producing concerns, being
allied to Warner Brothers, Paramount, United Artists, Fox,
Universal, First National and Metro-Goldwyn-Mayer. It is
reported that through these firms they can control half of
the total number of cinemas in the United States. They are
connected with the Columbia Gramophone Company, and
through it are constructing the second largest chain of
radio stations in the world. Warner Brothers have bought

[1] For much of this information I am indebted to the *Morning Post,* in
whose columns there is steady antagonism to American domination of the
film industry (1929).

up all the leading publishers of light music, including the best-known firm in London, Messrs. Chappell. The Fox Film Company are also financially interested in the Gaumont-British Company of England, which, as has been stated, owns a large chain of theatres in this country. Five representatives of the Paramount Film Company have joined the board of the Columbia Broadcasting Company. The Western Electric recording apparatus, which is being installed in many cinemas in Britain with great speed, is a subsidiary concern of the American Telegraph and Telephone Company.

These are the two firms whose united objective will be the entire control of the entertainment of the world. Through the means of the film, the gramophone, the radio, and television will America dominate the world market.

*

Wheels within wheels, tie-ups and mergers, quick and quiet shifting of financial interests, acquisition of small companies in foreign lands, chains of theatres and cinemas increasing by one's and two's, defiance of quota acts—these are the ways of the commercial film.

*

Yet another difficulty to be encountered by the progress of the cinema is the acute problem of film censorship. As is generally known, copies of films differ according to the demands of the censorship regulations in the country of presentation. Whereas a critic in Berlin may applaud the editing and cutting of a certain sequence of G. W. Pabst's new film, this sequence may have been re-edited or completely deleted in the copy of the same film seen by a critic in London. That the aesthetic value of the film suffers thereby as a whole is, of course, obvious to all but the Press and the censorship committee itself, but even this latter body must at times realise the havoc it causes to films by deletions for so-called political and moral motives. Those interested in this aspect of the subject are referred to Mr. Ivor Montagu's valuable pamphlet, *The Political Censorship of Films* (Gollancz, 1929), but it would seem that unless all forms of censorship are either abolished or subjected to drastic revision there is no solution to the problem. The fault, however, lies equally with the producers and the directors. If they make films in which there are certain sequences that wilfully infringe the censor's rules they must obviously expect them to be severely edited before leave for public exhibition is granted. The root of the trouble lies really in the different rulings laid down by each country. Nevertheless, the present censorship of films in Britain undoubtedly needs stringent reform, for its ban on many harmless pictures is detrimental to the progress of the British film industry.[1]

Apart from this, frequent exception can be taken to the official reasons given for the rejection of a film. A case in point arose in connection with Germaine Dulac's *La Coquille et le Clergyman*. According to the Film Society's programme for 16th March 1930, this was banned from public exhibition by the British Board of Film Censors because it ' is so cryptic as to be almost meaningless. If there is a meaning, it is doubtless objectionable.' First, to confess ignorance of the significance of a film, and then to suggest that it is ' doubtless objectionable ', reveals a standard of criticism that is truly Gilbertian!

Mr. Kenneth Macpherson, writing on the sore subject of the destruction of films by the censor authorities, cites the case of *The Joyless Street*. The film was made in thirty-four days working at sixteen hours a day and when completed it was ten thousand feet in length, about the same as *Ben-Hur* or *The Big Parade*. France accepted the film, deleting two thousand feet and every shot of the ' street '

---

[1] To readers anxious to pursue the devious paths of film censorship, I recommend the relevant chapter in *The Arts Enquiry Report* on *The Factual Film* (Oxford University Press, 1946), *The Freedom of the Movies,* by Ruth A. Inglis (University of Chicago Press, 1947) and *Censored* by Morris Ernst and Pare Lorentz (Jonathan Cape and Harrison Smith, 1930).

itself. Vienna extracted all sequences in which Werner Krauss appeared as the butcher. Russia turned the American lieutenant into a doctor and made the butcher the murderer instead of the girl. After having run a year in Germany, an attempt was made to censor it. In America it was shown as *The Street of Sorrow,* and in Britain once, at a private performance of the Film Society.[1] That is the history of a creative work which contained less harmful matter than *Our Dancing Daughters* or *Hot for Paris,* and it gives some idea of the censor's power to destroy the qualities of any film.

There is no reason at all why many of the forbidden Soviet films, for example, should not be shown to special audiences of persons connected with the film trade and the Press, who might perhaps realise the shortcomings of their own work in this manner. Economically, also, foreign methods of production might be studied with advantage from some of these suppressed films.

(b) *The Development of the Film as a Means of Expression*

When considering the commercialism which surrounds the producing and exhibiting of any one film, the unscrupulous dealings and double-crossing which occur when a production is launched, it is surprising to discover how far the cinema has really advanced as a medium of dramatic expression. It has been seen how the film began its career and how it became popular with the public, but it is well to remember that the child film was nursed by a company of ' fur-dealers, clothes-spongers, and grocers ' (to use the words of Mr. Messel [2]) in whose hands it could hardly have been expected to rise above the lowest form of entertainment. Moreover, and the fact must be stressed, the primary aim of film producers is to make the maximum of financial return in the shortest possible time, a method hardly congenial to so intricate an art as the cinema.

The later part of this survey will show some of the real

[1] It was re-issued in the thirties in London with a synchronised sound track.

[2] *Vide, This Film Business,* by Rudolph Messel (Benn, 1928).

functions, capabilities, and potentialities of the film as a medium of expression, considered apart from any commercial point of view save that of general appeal. It is the aim here to preface these theories by actualities, to reinforce the potentialities of the cinema by analysis of the progress of the film until now, examining influences and estimating their worth, selecting some tendencies and rejecting others.

It is essential, in the first place, to assert that the film is an independent form of expression, drawing inspiration with reservation from the other arts. Furthermore, it should be remarked that the attributes of the film are derived from the nature of the medium itself, and not from other matters of subject, story-interest, and propaganda. It should also be remembered that the film is essentially *visual* in its appeal; and that light and movement are the two elements employed in the creation of these visual images. As I shall demonstrate later, the abstraction of the ' absolute ' film is the nearest approach to the purest form of cinema, far removed from the commercial film, and descriptions will be given of their ' simplist ' methods of psychological appeal through the eye to the mind of the spectator. Following this, there will be determined the other forms of cinema, descending in aesthetic significance through the epic and art film to the ordinary narrative film and the singing and dancing picture.

The scientific and mechanical advance of the cinema has developed with marked rapidity as compared with aesthetic progress, which has been either backward, or, in all but a few studios, absent. I have yet to explain that perhaps the greatest handicap imposed on aesthetic progress was the camera's misleading faculty of being able to record the actual. At an early stage, it was found that the camera was capable of registering a credible record of real scenes and events, thereby becoming a valuable asset to education, a reliable means of historical reference, and a potential method of discovery in the sciences. When put to these uses, the realistic properties of the film were good. Even to-day, the news-reel and topical budget are always welcome events in the evening's programme, especially when heightened in effect by sound. It must be emphasised, however, that no narration of story, or expression of dramatic theme, has place in this form of cinematic record. The appeal is purely *interest*. The audience is not asked to participate in the emotional feelings of stout gentlemen in top hats launching liners, or His Majesty opening a new home for destitute orphans. The audience watches the incidents with interest and listens to the dialogue in much the same way as it reads the evening paper. But when the camera came to be employed for the telling of a fictional theme, its realistic photographic powers were used instead of the creative imagination of the director, who failed to express the story *through* the camera. The latter almost at once became an instrument of photographic realism rather than a medium for the expression of creative imagination. Its real powers of distortion by means of exaggerated camera angle, slow-motion, and masking,[1] and of transposition were completely neglected in the hasty striving after the obvious goal of realism. The power of the camera to record the actual on the screen fooled the audience into believing that its sole pleasure lay in the recognition of familiar things. Thus, at the outset of the story-picture, the film began its career on a false basis and it hardly need be stated, has continued along these wrong lines (with a few notable exceptions) until the present day, when the dialogue film is further extending the desire for realism, as are also the stereoscopic screen and the colour film. The exact replica of an object, accurate in every detail and measurement, cannot give the same emotions of pleasure as the real object. A photograph of a person is a very poor substitute for the actual being. It lies in the hands of the creator to utilise his imaginative powers in the creation of the replica, which is his impression, expression, or mental rendering of the subject. Because

[1] The reader is referred to the full analysis of camera properties in Part II, Chapter III.

a picture is 'lifelike', it is not necessarily an exact rendering of the original. It is rather the artist's interpretation of the original, in which he has emphasised the salient characteristics. The spectator at once seizes upon the latter and recognises them as being akin to his own thoughts about the subject, which perhaps have been subconscious in his mind until the picture has brought them into sudden understanding. Further, the artist's conception may suggest thoughts about the original of which the spectator had no previous knowledge. This is particularly applicable to the film with its power of emphasis by the close-up. The very presence of commonplace objects takes on a fresh meaning when shown enlarged on the screen, when emphasised as playing a part in the whole pattern of life. And, above all, it is essential to remember that a picture can be a non-representative, as well as a representative, record of an object.

But it will be understood that actual progress of the film along its proper path has been slow, and is only defined in a small percentage of the many thousands of productions realised up till now. Mr. Charles Marriott has suggested that 'art is a matter of the medium in which it is executed and a just balance between using that material in the imitation of nature and of abstraction, the degree of naturalism and the degree of abstraction being limited by the material.' This matter of 'the medium in which it is executed' cannot be stressed too much with regard to the cinema, for only on rare occasions is the film used rightly as its nature demands. The pleasure of film appreciation lies in the recognition of small developments, which do not often comprise the whole. It is rare to find a film that is in itself a step forward. Indeed, sometimes it is a reward to find one single sequence in a movie which suggests an advance in the film's capabilities. However discouraging the present position of the film may be, the worst director may unconsciously put forward a fresh idea of interest. Someone has got to go on making movies, even if they do not stop to ask themselves whether progress is being made.

With the production in 1903 of *The Great Train Robbery,* the story-film was launched on its long and prosperous career. The incident, or action, of the film became of first importance. An excellent example, which shows clearly how mistaken were the ideas of the pioneer directors, was seen in the *Comédie Française* films of 1908. Members of this celebrated theatre were persuaded to perform famous scenes from several of the French classic dramas, including episodes from *Tartuffe* and *Phèdre*, and to act them as they would on the stage, exaggerating their gestures into the lens of the camera. It was calculated by the promoters of the scheme that the appeal of the well-known scenes, coupled with the popularity of the celebrated actors and actresses, would achieve a wide success. The fallacy of the idea is obvious, of course, and the result was quite ineffectual. But it suggested to Adolf Zukor the great possibilities of famous plays and famous players, which, as is now well-known, developed into Famous-Players and later into the Famous-Players-Lasky Film Corporation, one of the biggest producing concerns in the world.[1] From the time of the *Comédie Française* effort onwards, it became a natural course of events to appropriate subjects and persons hallowed by public approval, with complete disregard of their suitability, and to adapt them to the screen. This process is as common, if not commoner, to-day as it ever was. Stage stars are filling the film studios because of the dialogue cinema; any best-seller novel is bought for the screen; any name that comes into the public eye is snapped up for the movies. What of Elinor Glyn, Aimée Macpherson, Philip Yale Drew, and in the past Jack Dempsey, Georges Carpentier, and Steve Donoghue?

Gradually the acted story became the *raison d'être* of the film. Stage technique was modified, the gesture still being used in relation to the spoken word, and 'acting' became one of the necessary talents of the movie star. Upon this type of stagey performance, good photographic looks and the power of suggesting sexual passion has the infamous

[1] Later to become the Paramount Pictures Corporation.

star-system of Hollywood grown up, a system that has been slavishly copied in this country.[1] Quite frankly, this sort of thing is not film at all but merely ' living photography '.

Despite all opposition, the inherent assets of a medium inevitably assert themselves, and, in the case of the film, some of its simpler resources began to show at an early stage. This was not due, however, to any deep thinking on the part of the ' fur dealers and clothes-men ', but to a natural course of development. They were to be found principally in the 'slapstick comedy, the melodramatic thriller, and the spectacle film.[2] Of the three young tendencies, slapstick is the most interesting, for it utilised the fantasy capabilities of the cinema. It brought to the screen things that were unreal and impossible, but verified them by actual vision. All the devices of the camera, such as slow-motion, ultra-rapid motion, abrupt cessation of movement by camera stopping, and distortion, have their direct use in slapstick for achieving comic effect. This has now been augmented by the introduction of sound, which is capable of adding largely to comedy effect. In particular, reference may be made to the *Mickey Mouse* cartoon films, perfect examples of the sound and visual cinema. In an exceptionally early fragment of film prior to 1900, which was included recently in a souvenir film, *Royal Remembrances,* a motor-car ran over a policeman who was smashed by the impact into small pieces which subsequently rejoined themselves. This may be seen as an early example of consciousness of the capabilities of the medium. Years later, the same cinematic trick of breaking an object into pieces and re-assembling the fragments into a whole, was used for dramatic purpose in Eisenstein's *Ten Days that Shook the World.* The gigantic symbolic statue of the Czar fell and crumbled only to come together again with the assembly of the Kerensky Provisional Government. In

[1] Expansion of this viewpoint will be found in *The Rise of the American Film,* by Lewis Jacobs (Harcourt Brace, 1939), and *America at the Movies,* by Margaret Farrand Thorp (Yale University Press, 1939).

[2] This account unfortunately neglects the development of film fantasy as seen in the works of Georges Méliès *vide,* pp. 70, 114, 115.

devices of this kind, the mind of the audience is held between the fact that they know the incident which they are seeing is in reality impossible, and the veritable fact that there it is in actuality before their eyes. A wonderful state of mind with which to conjure! The great asset of the melodramatic thriller was its movement, exemplified in the chase-and-escape element, which displaced dull literary story-interest. The emotions of the audience when witnessing these melodramas of speed were roused to excitement by the action, and not by the meaning of the story. It was this call for movement that developed the faculties of the scenario-writer, who learnt to employ the film's capacities for parallel action and ' last-minute-rescues '. The value of the high-spot climax was appreciated and was led up to by the chase. It was from these melodramas and Westerns, with their essential fast movement, that the Americans learnt their slick flashiness which is the hall-mark of their movies to-day. On the other hand, this feeling for movement has led to the false assumption that American films have tempo in comparison with the early German and Swedish productions. It must always be stressed that movement of actors and material is only one form of cinematic movement. The function of editing is equally as important, being the intrinsic essence of filmic creation.

In the middle of the striving for photographic realism, there came the first real aesthetic advance in the cinema. Just after the war, the first genuinely imaginative film made its appearance amongst the hundreds of formalised movies. This break in the monotony, this gleaming ray of light, deserves our closest attention.

*

Like a drop of wine in an ocean of salt water, *The Cabinet of Doctor Caligari* appeared in the profusion of films during the year 1920. Almost immediately it created a sensation by nature of its complete dissimilarity to any other film yet made. It was, once and for all, the first attempt at the expression of a creative mind in the new medium of cinematography. Griffith may have his place as the first employer of the close-up, the dissolve, and the fade, but Griffith's contribution to the advance of the film is negligible when compared with the possibilities laid bare by *The Cabinet of Doctor Caligari*. Griffith and his super-spectacles will disappear under the dust of time, if they have not already done so, but Wiene's picture will be revived again and again, until the copies wear out.[1] In ten years this film has risen to the greatest heights, as fresh now as when first produced, a masterpiece of dramatic form and content. It is destined to go down to posterity as one of the two most momentous advances achieved by any one film in the history of the development of the cinema till now. *The Cabinet of Doctor Caligari* and *Battleship Potemkin* are pre-eminent.

Made for the Decla producing firm by Robert Wiene, of the Sturm group in the Berlin theatre, during 1919 (a period, it will be remembered, when expressionism and cubism were the doctrines of the advanced schools of the drama, the novel, painting, and sculpture in Germany, France, and Russia), *The Cabinet of Doctor Caligari* was released in March of the following year. It was handled in Britain at a later date by the Philips Film Company, now extinct. Wiene was almost an amateur in film production. The architects or designers, Walther Röhrig, Herman Warm, and Walther Reimann, were three artists absorbed with ideas of cubist and abstract art. It is only natural to assume that their intelligence saw in the making of a film an adventure in a new medium, a form of expression which they must have realised was wider and more receptive than the static stage and canvas, but an expression which to them

---

[1] Subsequent years have seen both the work of Griffith, especially in *Intolerance*, and *Caligari* take their true perspective. The reader is referred to the programme published in connection with the memorial performance of Carl Mayer's work, Scala Theatre, London, April 13th, 1947, in particular to the note by Erich Pommer on the inception of *Caligari*. *Vide*, Appendix IV.

at that date bore a distinct relationship to the other arts.[1] It is not surprising, therefore, that *The Cabinet of Doctor Caligari* is in some places more theatre than film, and that there is a distinct tendency throughout to illustrate the sub-titles with pictures. These faults, apparent now with a heightened knowledge of the film's capabilities, must be allowed for in the appreciation of the meaning of this remarkable picture. In technical accomplishment of camerawork, the film made little real progress. The photography, by Willi Hameister, revealed no new suggestion of camera-angle, all the scenes apparently being taken from a normal eye-level. Dramatic mood was achieved by contrasted lighting effects and by the design of the settings. Long shots and medium shots predominated, masked close-ups occasionally being used, and the old iris-in and iris-out method of beginning and ending a sequence was adopted throughout. The latter camera device was notably used for emphasising important matter, by opening or closing on to a face or a light, or (in the example cited on pp. 368, 380), on to the revolving roundabouts. These openings were not always circular in shape; the view of Holstenwal was discovered to the audience by a diamond-shaped iris, suitable to the twisted and angular houses of the distorted town.

The progress lay, rather, in the tremendous problem of how the camera was to be used. The result of Wiene's thought was sufficient to stagger the film production of the

---

[1] The following information, if reliable, is of considerable interest: ' When the scenario for *Caligari* was first handed to Wiene, the manuscript specified none of the style that appeared in the production. In form, the original scenario was conventional. But Wiene saw an opportunity of getting away from the customary by giving the scenes in *Caligari* settings and forms which intensified the thought and emotions of the characters and established a very positive relation between them and mimetic action. The authors did not want expressionistic acting and decorations. To this day they do not understand why the picture had success. Mayer, one of its authors (who later wrote the scenario for *The Last Laugh*), has come round to Wiene's attitude; the other (Hans Janowitz) still insists that Wiene should never have handled the production of *Caligari* in the abstract style he gave it.' (Excerpts from several articles by Barnet Braverman in *The Billboard*, in November, reprinted in *The Film Year Book*, 1926, New York). *Vide*, Appendix IV.

two continents out of its comfortable peace and calm.

In 1919, *The Cabinet of Doctor Caligari* put forward these dominating facts, which have lain at the back of every intelligent director's mind to this day: that, for the first time in the history of the cinema, the director had worked *through* the camera and broken with realism on the screen; that a film, instead of being realistic, might be a possible reality, both imaginative and creative; that a film could be effective dramatically when not photographic; and finally, of the greatest possible importance, that the mind of the audience was brought into play psychologically.

As a film, *The Cabinet of Doctor Caligari* asked everything of its audience. They were to take part and believe in the wild imaginings of a madman. They were to share his distorted idea of the professor of the lunatic asylum in which he (the lunatic) and they (the audience) were confined. The theme and the conception were absolutely remarkable.

The scenario was written by Carl Mayer and Hans Janowitz, and even now contains brilliant and absorbing story-interest. The continuity, perhaps a little difficult to follow, was well constructed and flowed with adequate smoothness. It is curious to note that after seeing *The Cabinet of Doctor Caligari,* it is the story, and its remarkable unfolding, which principally holds the imagination.

The settings, which were almost entirely composed of flat canvas and hanging draperies, furnished with such simple objects as ladder-back chairs and stuffed horse-hair sofas, were painted with two intentions in mind: primarily to emphasise the distortion of the madman's mind through whose eyes they were seen, and secondly to provide interesting decorative values of tone varying from rich velvety blacks to the purest whites. Wherever possible, the design and layout of the set enhanced the dramatic content or meaning of the scene. In the linear design of the painted floors, for example, the prominent, usually straight lines of pattern led the eyes of the spectator direct to the figures or objects of significance. The walls of the prison cell were

21. ORPHANS OF THE STORM, directed by D. W. GRIFFITH. [American, 1922]

22. GRANDMA'S BOY directed by FRED NEWMAYER. HAROLD LLOYD. [American, 1922]

23. WARNING SHADOWS, directed by ARTHUR ROBISON. RUTH WEYHER. [German, 1922]

24. VANINA, directed by ARTHUR VON GERLACH. [German, 1922]

arranged and painted in tall perpendicular planes, emp-phasising dejection. The prisoner, seated cross-legged on the floor, was the point to which all lines of the painted floor-pattern converged. Again, the warped and angular branches of the trees in the landscape strengthened the dramatic escape of Cesare bearing away the body of the unconscious Jane. The stool upon which the official-bound Town Clerk was seated was at least six feet high, sym-bolising both bureaucracy and the difficulty that Caligari had in obtaining attention. These are but a few examples of the emphasis of dramatic content by means of pictorial composition and settings.[1]

The lighting, also, was arranged from this point of view, in complete co-operation with the designers. When the murder of the Town Clerk was discovered, a magnificent scene was shown of a darkened room, its walls sombre and angular, with the single source of light directed on to the beautifully grouped draperies of the white sheets. No corpse was visible, only the motionless figures of the police-men in the half-light, but there was no doubt as to the content of the scene. Although the *décor* was largely angular, at times contorted and twisted arabesques, Matisse-like, aggravated the scene, as when Cesare made his noc-turnal entry in Jane's bedroom.

Of the acting there is not a great deal to be said, for the parts did not call for any great emotional skill beyond melodrama. This type of acting, together with heavy make-up, was characteristic of the atmosphere of the film. The titles, in accordance with the feeling of the whole, were irregularly lettered and strangely set out.[2]

[1] The following extract is relevant : ' The studio had a very limited quota of power and light, and on the day when we were notified (several days before the end of the month) my three artists (Warm, Reimann and Herlth) brought in a proposition that seemed to me absurd, and even reactionary—" Why not paint lights and shadows on the sets for this *Caligari* film? " ' From Carl Mayer's Debut, by Erich Pommer, in the Carl Mayer programme, published in connection with the memorial performance, London, April 13th, 1947. *Vide,* Appendix IV.

[2] This is not the case in the copy now to be obtained from the National Film Library, London.

It may, perhaps, be asserted that this film has dated. Technically, as regards camerawork, stock, lighting, this is correct and naturally inevitable. But in meaning, content, suggestion, treatment, and above all entertainment, *The Cabinet of Doctor Caligari* is as convincing to-day as when seen years ago. It is true, also, that surrealism and neo-realism have superseded expressionism in the minds of the *avant-garde,* but this does not alter the fact that expressionism plays a large part in the film. Nevertheless, it is curious to remark that although *The Cabinet of Doctor Caligari* was a revolution in cinematic tendency, it has never been directly imitated or copied.[1] *Raskolnikov,* directed by Wiene in 1923, and based on Dostoievski's novel *Crime and Punishment,* was assisted in dramatic emotion by Andrei Andreiev's cubist architecture, but could hardly be called an imitation. Rather was it an essay by the same director in a similar vein to an earlier success.

Comparison has also been falsely drawn between *The Cabinet of Doctor Caligari* and *Aëlita,* a film made in Soviet Russia by Protazanov with cubist settings. This is a delusion, for the sets and costumes of *Aëlita,* on which it is assumed the comparison is founded, were designed fantastically in order to express an imaginary idea of the planet Mars, and *not,* as in *The Cabinet of Doctor Caligari,* to emphasise the thoughts of a distorted mind. The cubist setting for Wiene's film was used purely because the audience were asked to imagine themselves thinking a madman's thoughts through the medium of the camera.

As a document of cinematic progress, the value of *The Cabinet of Doctor Caligari* increases year by year. Since its first showing, over ten years ago, it has been mentioned and referred to, criticised and revived, times without number. It has become celebrated. Practically all those who were connected with its production have become famous. There is no need to trace their course and recent successes; they are too well known. Only one word need

---

[1] This is incorrect. Carl Mayer wrote a script specifically for expressionist treatment, *Genuine,* in 1920, also directed by Robert Wiene.

be added, Robert Wiene never repeated his achievement. It is his sole work of genuine merit.[1]

*

Although the appearance of *The Cabinet of Doctor Caligari* set working the brains of people both in and out of the film industry, and although it was a clear finger pointing one path for the cinema, one film, however great, cannot change the output of vast producing concerns. With its new ideas on the use of the camera as an instrument of expression, Wiene's film certainly influenced some of the more advanced American directors, but taken as a whole the productions of Hollywood remained on their former level. What *The Cabinet of Doctor Caligari* did, however, was to attract to the cinema audience many people who had hitherto regarded a film as the low watermark of intelligence.

Not until 1925, however, was a film to appear which wholly justified the position of the cinema. During the intervening period many remarkable films were realised, chiefly in Germany and in Sweden, which evidenced that brains were at work in Europe, but these were of less significance than would first appear.[2] They naturally have their place in the gradual development and will be found dealt with more fully at a later stage. In 1925 *The Last Laugh*, the joint product of Murnau, Mayer, Freund, and Jannings, definitely established the film as an independent medium of expression. Unlike *The Cabinet of Doctor Caligari*, it had nothing in common with the theatre, but made full use of the resources of the cinema as known at that date. It was a remarkable example of filmic unity, of centralisation of purpose and of perfect continuity. It was made without sub-titles, with the single exception of a director's note, which changed the natural sad ending into a happy one, a

[1] Wiene died in Paris in July, 1938.

[2] Here, as elsewhere, the importance of the immediate post-war films of Denmark is overlooked. The reader is referred to *The History of Motion Pictures*, by Bardèche and Brasillach, translated and edited by Iris Barry (W. W. Norton and the Museum of Modern Art, New York, 1938).

superbly handled concession to the public. Everything that had to be said in this thematic narrative of an old hall-porter was said entirely through the camera. Not a written or spoken word was necessary to the correct unfolding of the theme. By psychological understanding, every action suggested a thought to the audience, every angle a mood that was unmistakable in meaning. *The Last Laugh* was cine-fiction in its purest form; exemplary of the rhythmic composition proper to the film.

After this date, 1925, the German cinema, to which students of the film were looking for further progress, began to decline, largely on account of the general exodus of talent to Hollywood. The art film (decorative in treatment and enveloped in an architectural environment of studio structures), for which Germany had built herself a reputation, was a commercial failure. The superb efforts of German creative directors drained the coffers of the industry, an unfortunate but indisputable fact. An argument for the failure of these films is the knowledge that the cinema is essentially modern, and modernism is, above all things, anti-romantic and experimental, reflecting as it does the spirit of the age. The German decorative films were for the most part romantic and spectacular, with a natural tendency towards the German love of the theatrical and the splendour of pageantry. Their tone was on a grand scale, at once serious minded and splendid, far from the superficiality of the American movie to which audiences were accustomed.[1]

About this time, between the appearance of *The Cabinet of Doctor Caligari* and *The Last Laugh,* the wide-felt influence of psycho-analysis, which had swept over the post-war schools of painting and literature, was making its mark on filmic treatment. Many films, both from France and Germany, bore effects of psycho-analytical study, particularly those by directors who were striving after

[1] For a full analysis and sociological study of the German cinema at this time, the reader is recommended to *From Caligari to Hitler,* Dr. Siegfried Kracauer (Princeton University Press, 1947).

naturalistic methods, such as Lupu Pick, Karl Grune, and G. W. Pabst. There will be seen in the later section dealing, with film psychology the important part played by the ' ineptitudes ' of life in the revealing of inward phenomena. An early example of this groping idea was found ingenuously in *Doctor Mabuse,* but unfortunate as parts of this melodrama were, there is no doubt that Fritz Lang was feeling along the right lines. During this stage also, the machinery complex, which had occupied the Vorticists before the war, re-arose in a glut of composite shots of trains, trams, factories, and all types of machinery. At one time it was almost impossible to see a film without a double, triple, or quadruple exposure shot of wheels. For some years, expressionism also had its sway with the German film, despite an occasional breakaway into isolated individualism. The Expressionists were interested in Man in general and not in the Individual. Although they made use of the representation of characters, the result was not regarded as personal experience but as the essential experiences of humanity. Thus, it was usual to find themes woven around the Man and the Girl, as in Grune's *The Street,* Pick's *New Year's Eve,* Czinner's *Nju,* Lang's *Destiny,* with additions in the form of Death the Stranger and The Prostitute. It is of importance to note that nearly all these films were entirely studio-made, whole palaces and streets being built, providing a feeling completely different from the open-air films taken on a real location.

Some time later, the theme interest seemed to have been focussed on individuals again and their peculiar characteristics, as with Pommer's jewel thief and policeman in *Asphalt,* and the two men and the wife in *Homecoming.* This was a swing round to the partial admission of the star-system, a feature of the Americanisation of the German studios. Very different in texture, for example, was *The Hungarian Rhapsody* in comparison with the moral seriousness of *The Wild Duck.* There was a tendency towards individualism in the new German film and a feeling for a more materialistic spirit, which was progressive. The first may be said to have been due to America; the second to the influence exerted by the Soviet films in Germany.

In contrast with the heavy morbidness and slow technique of the Swedes and Germans, the French school was marked chiefly by its directors' nineteenth-century delight in classical compositions and its continuous leaning towards spectacle. French films were roughly divided into two classes : the *avant-garde* of the *jeunes cinéastes* and the commercial film on the lines of *Atlantide, Michael Strogoff* and *Casanova*. Whereas the Germans had sought to gain their effects by a theatrical, traditional form of acting in conjunction with an environment of studio structures, the French experimentalists attempted the creation of atmosphere by a series of succeeding exterior compositions, usually of great pictorial beauty but non-dynamic. Nevertheless, although many of the *jeunes cinéastes* toyed with the cinema as their fathers had dabbled in their *ateliers,* several developed into directors of remarkable talent, as for example, René Clair, Jean Epstein, and Jacques Feyder, whose work must be considered apart from the usual *avant-garde* kindergarten product.

Meanwhile, it must be remembered that America was producing films in vast quantities during the years that the cinema was discovering its aesthetic qualities in Europe. The American cinema as a whole naturally demands wide investigation, which will follow at a later stage, but at the moment it is important to mention two outstanding tendencies that had grown up in Hollywood. A school of light, domestic, drawing-room comedy, displaying a nicety of wit and intelligence, had developed, to be carried eventually to as high a degree of perfection as this lighter side of film allowed.[1] It had its origin in Chaplin's memorable satire *A Woman of Paris* (1923), as well as in Ernst Lubitsch's brilliantly handled *The Marriage Circle,* made in the following year. It was probably the result of a fusion

[1] The supreme example to date (1930) is Ernst Lubitsch's *The Love Parade,* a brilliant combination of sophisticated, witty direction and perfected technical accomplishment.

between the existing school of Hollywood bedroom farce and the imported European talent, the latter being exemplified primarily by Lubitsch. Along these lines the majority of Hollywood's clever young men worked with a superficial skill, to produce many effervescent comedies and farces, sparkling and metallic, which provided light entertainment for the audiences of many nations.

In contrast with this movement in the studios, there had appeared a small group of directors who showed a preference for constructing their films around natural incidents and with real material; a tendency that had possibly grown out of the early Western picture. Robert Flaherty, Ernest Schoedsack, Merian Cooper, Karl Brown, and William Howard formed the nucleus of this group, to whom there should be added James Cruze, John Ford, and Victor Fleming, by reason of their isolated pictures which fall into this category. To Flaherty, however, must be given the full credit for the first film using natural resources, the inspiring *Nanook of the North,* in 1922, followed later by the beautiful *Moana,* in 1926. Other remarkable pictures characteristic of the naturalistic movement to be noted were *Grass, Chang, Stark Love,* and *White Gold,* all films that stood out sharply from the common run of American movies.

Apart from these two tendencies, only the work of Erich von Stroheim, King Vidor and Henry King, and the individualistic films of Chaplin and Fairbanks, emerged with real seriousness from the mass of machine-made movies up till the time of the dialogue film. Investigation of these, together with less interesting work, will follow.

Acknowledging the theoretical excellence of Pabst, the importance of Carl Dreyer's *La Passion de Jeanne d'Arc,* Clair's delightful comedies, Feyder's impressive *Thérèse Raquin,* and the domestic comedies of the American school, the most momentous advances of the cinema during recent years have shown themselves in Soviet Russia. Although the value which the Soviets attached to the resources of the film, and which they have developed with such skill, is constantly stressed in these pages, it must not be forgotten that the intensity of purpose so predominant in the Soviet film has been brought about by changed social conditions and political events since the revolution in 1917. Early Soviet pictures, such as *The Postmaster* and *The Marriage of the Bear,* contained little of the filmic creation of the present productions. When analysing the contemporary Soviet film, it has firstly to be understood that a production is seldom launched unless the theme contains some definite sociological or political meaning; because the Soviets have realised more than any other nation how powerful an instrument of propaganda is the cinema. It is partly out of the desire to express these contained ideas with the utmost possible conviction, and partly out of the exceptionally brilliant skill of the foremost Soviet directors, that the modern state of technical perfection in the science of the film has been reached. There has been a tendency in Britain and elsewhere, however, due to the always hasty enthusiasm of the intelligentsia, to call any film coming from the U.S.S.R. a masterpiece. This is very far from being the case, for actually there are not more than about half-a-dozen really brilliant film directors in Soviet Russia. There are, of course, many second and third-rate directors, as there are in Germany or America, but it has become fashionable to raise their work to unusually high standards in London. The whole situation is rather reminiscent of that when the intelligentsia 'discovered' Russia in the first decade of this century; when it became the fashion to read Tchekov, Dostoievski, Gogol, Gorki, and Turgenev without discrimination as to their merits; when no studio was complete without its samovar, and ikons were all the rage for interior decoration.

Every Soviet film is, to put it crudely, a picture with a political purpose, and it is the duty of a Soviet director to express that purpose as clearly, powerfully, and vividly as possible. Added to which, it must be remembered that the cinema in Soviet Russia has been fortunate in having the whole-hearted support of the Government, whose leaders have at all times fully recognised the value of the film for spreading their principles. Lenin regarded the theatre as a potential microcosm of the whole theories of Bolshevism, and determined to build a new theatre in Russia which would serve as a practical model for the people to learn from and to copy. The cinema, by reason of its limitless range and commercial superiority over the theatre, lent itself to the same idea. It will be recalled, for example, that the Government commissioned several films to be made in order to commemorate the tenth anniversary of the Soviet *régime*. *Ten Days That Shook the World* (original Soviet title, *October*)[1] and *The End of St. Petersburg,* were two of the results. Out of their efforts to meet this demand, Eisenstein and Pudovkin built up a form of film technique that is now unequalled for dramatic intensity. The same applies to more recent directors, to Dovjenko, Ermler, Raizman, and Turin.

It is certain that the first Soviet experiments in film editing, employing strips of celluloid as the basic material, which is the foundation of almost all their film technique, were due to Lev Kuleshov, an instructor and film director in Moscow. From his original theories regarding the relation and inter-relation of pieces of film, which we may place about 1922, there have been developed the principles of constructive editing. Pudovkin, having studied for a while with Kuleshov, carried the idea further by devoting himself to using raw material as the foundation for his filmic working; whilst Eisenstein, having made his first mass film, *Strike*, in 1924, proceeded to enlarge on his ideas of ' intellectual cinematography '. To these directors must be given the credit for the most advanced forms of contemporary cinema and their theories are to be seen reflected in the work of almost all the lesser-known Soviet directors. From 1924 onward, therefore, the most interesting developments in the cinema have taken place in the U.S.S.R., and it is to this newly-constructed country that we must turn for modern tendencies towards progress.

Of the film to-day, I find it hard to write, let alone to

[1] *Vide* footnote page 230.

tell, for the unbalanced state of the whole industry, together with the sweeping tide of the noisy dialogue film, are movements which strangle at the outset any attempt at progress in the cinema. To find the proper film it is necessary, first, to brush aside the sweepings from America and Britain, dissect the films from France and Germany with an open eye for second-hand virtuosity, and regard the new Soviet pictures with reservation in case they may be resting on their past successes. Of the wedded synchronised sound and silent film, co-ordinated into a filmic whole, there is as yet no concrete example, though one waits in anticipation for Pudovkin's *Life Is Beautiful*.[1] It is possible only to watch the dialogue film and utilise one's imaginative power. Of the silent film but few examples come laggardly to Britain, often enough to be hidden away unseen. Occasionally a few of these may find their lonely way to the Film Society, or to the affectionate screen of what is, at the moment of writing, London's only loyalist, the Avenue Pavilion.[2]

Of the feeling prevalent on the Continent it is difficult to say, for news is rare of the silent film, and words and static photographs are inadequate to express the dynamic of film technique. The ever-moving theme, the relation and inter-relation of thought expressed in moving images, is too elusive to be captured in print. It is, perhaps, only possible to sum up by disconnected statements of ideas, reactions, and observations.

The predominant characteristic of the film to-day is the growing tendency to find filmic expression by means of climactic effect. This process of image construction is the basis of Soviet technique, and has spread with rapidity into the minds of the more advanced German and French

[1] Announced as a sound film, *Life Is Beautiful* eventually appeared as a silent film. Pudovkin's first sound film was *Deserter*, in which he made many interesting new experiments with sound.

[2] In retrospect, it is possible to see now how much one owed to the management of the Shaftesbury Avenue Pavilion by Stuart Davis. Articles surveying the specialist cinema movement in retrospect were published in *Documentary News Letter*, June and July, 1940. Cf. footnote on p. 293.

directors. There seems, moreover, to be a distinct striving after some form of arithmetic or geometric progression in the arrangement of visual images during editing, in the relation and inter-relation of film strips. There is also a tendency to shorten the approach to a scene by the elimination of the long shot and the increased use of the close-up. The psychological effects made possible by the introduction of varied cutting by the Soviets is in the process of being carried to an advanced stage. Cross-cutting and inter-cutting are being utilised more as a method of insistence on the main object, than as the old-fashioned even distribution of dramatic suspense of the 'last-minute-rescue' variety. Symbolic inter-cutting is being employed as an aid to the emphasis of the central theme, as with the statue of Peter the Great in *The End of St. Petersburg*. It is a dual theme of symbol and individual, connected mentally by association of ideas and visually by similarity of the shooting angle. It is being found that emotional effect is to be more easily reached by an intercut comparison to a like emotional effect.

There seems prevalent in the film to-day a more sensitive feeling for the association of ideas, which is finding filmic expression in terms of contrast and comparison, mental and visual. There are directors who in their work seek to establish by suggestion, contrast, and comparison, what may perhaps be called a continuity of human thought. One is emotionally conscious that the content of a theme is constantly ranging over more than one idea at the same time, a double purpose of meaning for the expression of which the natural resources of the film are admirably suitable. This affinity of ideas is marked by a connecting link, which may be said to be, in its terms of contrast and comparison, the essence of filmic treatment, both in the mental association of ideas by symbolism and by the actual visual likeness of one thing to another.

Contrasts appear to take on various aspects. The contrast of space between the interior and the exterior; between the close confinement of walls and the spreading horizon of a landscape; between the occupied and the unoccupied;

between the full and the empty. The contrast of size, between the thick and the thin, the long and the short. The contrast of shapes, between the square and the circle, between a top hat and a cloth cap. The contrast of like-nesses, so well exemplified by Vertov's gas mask and skull. The contrast of extremes, between the worker underground and the top of the factory chimney. There is an association of ideas between the mouth of a bugle and the muzzle of a gun. There is a comparison of likeness between the poise of an athlete and the balance of a horse. There is a similarity of motion between the stroking of one's hair and the stroking of a cat. There is the comparison of form, used so much for easy transference of thought in dissolves and mixes. All these factors make themselves apparent in the uses of cross-cutting for effect. They are filmic methods of strength, emphasis, enforcement of meaning by the association of ideas.

To be considered further but not necessarily to be accepted, there are the new theories of montage construc-tion that have been put forward by Eisenstein. These embrace an entirely fresh method for the determination of the relation that lies between the film strips in the assembling of a picture from its contributory lengths of frames. Eisenstein seems concerned with the disposal of the old, orthodox principles of editing (*i.e.* according to the time lengths of shots, the relationship of shapes, the association of ideas, etc., all of which produce sensations in the minds of the audience, ranging from sudden shock to smooth transfusion according to the will of the director) by the adoption of a new method which will be governed by the physiological sensations produced by over-tones of the visual and sound images. He is experimenting with the arrangement of shots, scenes, and sequences according to their degrees of emotional pathos by creative impulse, cal-culating to arouse the nervous reflexes of the spectator into responsiveness. He believes that, instead of an audience seeing and hearing a film, they should sense it; sense being the clue to the fourth dimension or over-tone, to be found in the beats of music and in the interval that exists between one visual image on the screen and another. On the assumption that both visual over-tones and sound over-tones are magnitudes of the same dimension (time) and that both are physiological sensations, he proceeds to new methods of filmic construction by a process of tonal and over-tonal montage. Naturally one awaits practical expression of his theories with interest before offering comment; other, that is, than those made manifest by certain portions of *The General Line,* which were not concerned with sound reproduction.

In actual production there is a welcome tendency towards the use of real material in place of studios and professional players. The cinema shows distinct signs of becoming film instead of theatre. Outside the U.S.S.R., Jean Epstein, John Grierson, and Hans Richter are seeking subjects in the commonplace instead of the artificially constructed, and there are also the few natural resources films in America. But these examples of the real film are but drops in the ocean of the movies of the world, overshadowed and dwarfed by the menace of the dialogue cinema.

*

Ridiculous as it may seem in the short span of life during which the film has existed, the process of misuse of the medium is repeating itself. General tendencies at the present moment show the misconception of the film to be greater and more difficult to unlearn than ever before. Directors as a whole are still only beginning to understand the potentialities of the film as a medium in itself. Its limits and delimits still present a broad field for investigation. It is just being realised that mime and gesture and the consciousness of the inanimate transmit an international idea; and that the pictorial meaning of the film is understandable to all according to their powers of sensitivity. But the main object to-day appears to be the synchronisation of the sound of the human voice with the photograph of the moving lips, and to reproduce the sound of visual objects in order to make them seem more real. That this is the desire of the American producers and directors is apparent from their advertisements. In brief, the introduction of the human voice merely relieves the director of his most serious obligation, to convey meaning to the mind by means of the resources of the visual cinema. The act of recording dialogue is *not* a further resource, as some theorists like to imagine. The dialogue film at its best can only be a poor substitute for the stage. From an aesthetic point of view, sound can only be used to strengthen symbolism and emphasise dramatic action, and experiments on these lines will be successful and justified.

On the heels of the usurping dialogue film comes the introduction of the stereoscopic screen and the colour film. Both of these inventions, wonderful though they may be in themselves, seek to achieve the realism so antagonistic to an imaginative medium. The cinema, with the addition of these new inventions, will degenerate into theatrical presentation on a large and economic scale. The true resources of the film will be swept aside in the desire for a straighter and more direct method of story presentation. The duration of time that a visual image is held on the screen is already becoming longer. As Mr. Eric Elliott has so truly written : ' given a large stage scene with three dimensional effect, combined with colour and oral dialogue, it is tempting authors and producers to " put across " the sustained dramatic situation of the theatre proper.' [1]

Thus, there are few films which stand alone as achievements of real cinema, whilst there are many that miss greatness because of the negligence of the director or the obstinacy of the producer. Rare indeed is it to meet with an intelligent and sympathetic film producer; frequent indeed is it to meet upstart producers who make illegitimate claim to a knowledge of the film, riding roughshod over the conceptions of the director. If a film is to be a unity, clear cut and single-minded, the director alone must preconceive it and communicate its content to the audience through

[1] *Vide, The Anatomy of Motion Picture Art,* by Eric Elliott (Pool, 1928).

groups of interpreters of his vision, under his supreme command. The construction of a film from the first conception to the final product must be under the absolute control of the director. This is unhappily far from being the case.

But good films have been produced and good films will be produced in the future, although the opportunities to-day are more remote. Was it not René Clair who said that the zenith of the film was passed a few years ago? Yet, in Bryher's *Film Problems of Soviet Russia* (Pool, 1929), Pabst is said to have observed that ' Russia has taken one road and America has taken the opposite, but in a hundred years both will meet. England has taken neither, but will work out her own salvation independently, and in the end she will arrive at the same result.' This may be so, but I find it hard to agree when considering the present circumstances. Again, Mr. Chaplin has written that ' . . . it has been from the film itself, a device offering constant provocation to the imagination and senses of rhythm and colour that the sheer strength and crude grandeur of the motion picture industry have come. A giant of limitless powers has been reared, so huge that no one quite knows what to do with it. I, for one, am hopeful that Mr. Wells shall settle the question for us in his next novel.' [1]

Mr. Wells has written that novel, but the question is no nearer being answered. *The King Who Was a King* was full of a thousand ideas, gleaned from a scrutiny of the output of Germany and America, but there was precious little in the book that had direct bearing on the position of the film itself. I believe that Mr. Wells saw and realised the greatness of the film medium, but did not know quite what to do about it. And in any case his outlook was literary and not filmic.[2]

For the most part the cinema still lies in the hands of those who desire to make it the means of the greatest

[1] In the foreword to *Films: Facts, and Forecasts*, L'Estrange Fawcett (Bles, 1927).

[2] Personally, I was disappointed by Mr. Wells's excursions into the film medium and was one who found *The Shape of Things to Come* a bore.

possible financial return in the shortest space of time. One looks, therefore, to those in whose power it is to keep steady the direction of the advance of the film. To Chaplin, Fairbanks, and Flaherty in America; to Soviet Russia; to Pabst, Richter, and Pommer in Germany; and to the young men of France. With their whole-hearted and enthusiastic support, the film can be diverted from the abyss towards which it is heading.

25. FOOLISH WIVES, directed by ERICH VON STROHEIM. [American, 1922]

26. SALOME, directed by CHARLES BRYANT. ALLA NAZIMOVA. [American, 1922]

27. DRACULA (NOSFERATU), directed by F. W. Murnau. Max Schreck.
[German, 1922]

28. THE ATONEMENT OF GOSTA BERLING, directed by Mauritz Stiller.
Greta Garbo, Lars Hanson. [Swedish, 1923]

II

THE VARIOUS FORMS OF CINEMA

Before proceeding to a detailed investigation of the product and personalities of separate film-producing countries it is important to try and define the various forms of cinema. In this way it will be found that such tendencies as choice of theme and employment of real or artificial material for the camera, existing in individual countries, can be more easily classified or contrasted with tendencies in other producing centres.[1] For this reason, therefore, the various forms of cinema may perhaps be grouped briefly as follows :—

(a) *The Abstract, or Absolute, Film*

The abstract film, like Ruttmann's *Operas,* Richter's *Rhythmus,* and the late Viking Eggeling's *Symphonie Diagonale,* is as far removed from the commercial fiction film as is surrealism from the Royal Academy. The abstract film is a primary example of unity of filmic purpose. Briefly, it seeks to produce simple psychological reactions in the mind through the eye by the variation in rapidity of groups of abstract forms in movement, and by the relations of geometric figures changing their proportions, dissolving and displacing each other, thereby making visual abstract patterns. The result on the mind produced by the abstract film may be compared with that produced by the word patterns of the post-war school of poets, to certain forms of literature such as the work of James Joyce, and to music without melodic interest. For example, a series of disconnected words may suggest an incident, and by the welding of these disconnected sentences a complete whole can be built up having a psychological value.

[1] In *Movie Parade* (Studio Publications, London 1936), a different method of classification under subject matter was tried.

113

The film, with its cinematic properties of rapid movement, contrast, comparison, rhythm, expansion and contraction of forms, is admirably suited to present a series of abstract visual images to the eye, capable of causing strong emotional reactions. A sequence of swift impressions, of little interest singly, but arranged in relation one to another, has powerful psychological meaning.

A more recent form of the abstract film is the pattern film, which often uses machinery in motion or at rest, or architectural motives, for its material basis. Most successful in this manner have been Eugène Deslav's *La Marche des Machines*, Richter's *Vormittagsspuk*, and Joris Ivens and Francen's *Pluie* and *Le Pont d'Acier*.

The late Viking Eggeling was one of the pioneers of the absolute film and an excellent description of his method is given by Mr. Ivor Montagu in *Close Up* (vol. 1, no. 6). ' The basis of his work is line, and his patterns are mainly the varying positions on a two-dimensional plane, the screen, of his one dimensional figures, in contradistinction to the patterns of Richter and Ruttmann which are usually two-dimensional forms moving in three dimensions. The screen is a blackboard to Eggeling and a window to Richter and Ruttmann.' In contrast to this, Deslav's abstractions are patterns of photographic reality pieced together to make rhythmic unity.

The definite similarity existing between the absolute film and the early melodrama is significant, for the psychological appeal to mind and eye is identical. As Mr. Eric Elliott has pointed out, everything the cinema has so far actually demonstrated, and all its possibilities as they are seen now, should theoretically have been obvious the moment it became practicable to project a series of animated images in scenes on a screen. It is curious to note how far the directors in those primitive days realised the resources of the new medium (such as the rapidity of the chase) in order to fulfil their ideas and it is interesting to watch, for instance, George Méliès' *Trip to the Moon*, made in 1902, in which were used double-exposure and ' magical ' effects equal, if not superior, to those employed in Fairbanks' *The Thief of Bagdad* in 1923. Any form of art, however, that may have developed out of these crudities was extinguished when the centre of film production shifted from Europe to America at the outbreak of war in 1914.

It is impossible to give here an exhaustive list of abstract films, but amongst those of more than usual interest, apart from already mentioned examples, were *Filmstudie* and other works by Hans Richter; *A quoi rêvent les jeunes films* (1924-25) by Henri Chomette; *Le Ballet Mécanique* (1925) by Fernand Léger and Dudley Murphy; Eugène Deslav's *Montparnasse* and *Les Nuits Électriques;* Sandy's *Light and Shade;* Francis Bruguière and Oswell Blakeston's *Light Rhythms;* and works by Marcel Duchamp and Maurice Sollen.

At the time of writing, no abstract film has been shown in Britain incorporating sound as well as visual images, but the possibilities of sound co-ordinated with visual patterns for abstract effect are limitless.[1]

(b) *The Cine-poem, or Ballad Film*

Of this type of cinema there is little to be written because experiments in this direction have been few. Occasionally a single sequence in a full-length film stands out alone as a cine-poem, as a pure creation of a simple mood or atmosphere, based possibly on literary inspiration, which can be lifted direct from its surrounding sequences and be shown complete in itself. Most notable is, of course, Walther Ruttmann's fascinating Dream of the Hawks in *Siegfried,* the first part of Fritz Lang's *Nibelungen Saga.* The sequence, which was extremely short, purported to show Kriemhild's dream in which she was forewarned of Siegfried's death and of her own fate. This was done by means

[1] The additional cost of sound has, without doubt, done much to restrict experimentalism. The colour films of Len Lye, mostly financed by the British G.P.O. Film Unit, in the thirties, carried on the experimental tradition in *Colourbox, Rainbow Dance* and others. The pattern of abstract visuals cut to fit synchronised music by Oskar Fischinger and the colour films of Norman McClaren for the National Film Board of Canada, also fall into this group. Cf. Appendix I (iii).

of the silhouettes of two black hawks and a white dove circling in beautiful rhythmic actions against a grey background, the whole maintaining a moving decorative pattern.[1] Man Ray's short film *L'Etoile de Mer* was a filmic expression of Robert Desnos' poem and was of merit by reason of its transient light forms and movement. Much of it was photographed through mica masks, producing a soft effect of mistiness. Of *Emak Bakia,* Man Ray's earlier picture, he says himself : ' . . . a series of fragments, a cine-poem with a certain optical sequence, make up a whole that still remains a fragment. Just as one can much better appreciate the abstract beauty in a fragment of a classic work than in its entirety, so this film tries to indicate the essentials in contemporary cinematography.'

In this section should be included such short films as Alberto Cavalcanti's *La P'tite Lili,* a delightful burlesque of a traditional song of *La Barrière,* in which an effect of an old sampler was obtained by the use of coarse gauzes in front of the lens of the camera. Kirsanov's *Brûmes d'Automne,* a simple representation of the mood of a girl after a tragic occurrence, was moving in a slow, sentimental way, much of the mental state being suggested by throwing the lens of the camera in and out of focus. Silka's fable film, *La Ballade du Canart,* although crude in technical execution, may be called a cine-poem in conception, and deserved better treatment.

(c) The Cine-surrealist Film

This type of film is as yet represented by a few isolated examples only, though there are traces of surrealism in some Soviet films that have been seen, such as the opening sequences of Barnet's comedy, *The House in Trubnaya Square,* and portions of Dovjenko's *Zvenigora.* The appeal of the surrealist film is necessarily limited and production is due entirely to private resources. I believe, however, that

[1] Other more recent examples were Lotte Reiniger's prologue to the Pabst film of *Don Quixote,* and from time to time a ' dream ' sequence is notable in a fiction film, for example, *Farewell My Lovely* and *Odd Man Out.*

there is something to be learnt from its manner of treatment which can be applied on a wider scale in fiction films. Although the essential character of Luis Buñuel's *Un Chien Andalou* prevented it from being shown except to a restricted audience, there was much astonishing matter to be gleaned from it. Realising the primary aim of the surrealist movement to be the expression of dreams and thought tangents of an imaginative person provoked by material surroundings and placed on paper or canvas, it is natural that the film lends itself to an expression which demands ' imaginative velocity and moral nonchalance, unlimited risibility, and a sensitivity to the fantasy of the commonplace.' Buñuel's film, whilst containing some unpleasant material, was one of the most dynamic I have seen. It had an intensity of expression unknown in most examples of cinema, an intensity gained from the material and not from technical assembling. There was a fluid continuity that was amazing in its swift transference of thought, and mention should be made of the extraordinary acting of Pierre Batcheff.

Germaine Dulac's brilliant *La Coquille et le Clergyman* was also surrealistic in tendency, being a series of expressions of states of mind strung together with a beautifully defined thread of continuity. At moments it rose to great heights of dramatic intensity, due to the cleverly chosen angles, whilst the photography throughout was of the best quality. It was to be taken as an extreme instance of the domination of ideas over the irrelevance of situations. Neither of these films has been generally shown in Britain; but that of Dulac was presented to the Film Society on 16th March 1930.[1]

(d) The Fantasy Film

The potentialities of the film in the realm of fantasy are unlimited and are to be found hidden away in practically every side of general production. The inherent fantastic

---

[1] Buñuel's *L'Age d'Or*, and Cocteau's *Sang d'un Poête* now fall into this group while surrealist influence was marked in the films of Jean Vigo, *Zéro de Conduite* and *L'Atalante*. The scenarios (in English translation) of *Un Chien Andalou* and *L'Age d'Or* are contained in the appendices to *The Secret Life of Salvador Dali* (Vision Press, 1948).

nature of the cinema at once suggests a hundred ideas which are impossible of being expounded in any other medium. Notable instances which immediately occur to the mind are the charming silhouette films by Lotte Reiniger, of which mention can be made of *The Adventures of Prince Achmed* and *Cinderella*. There have been several imitations of Lotte Reiniger's work, but they can be detected with ease by their inferior craftsmanship. Another fantastic type was to be seen in Stanislas Starevitch's model film *The Magic Clock*, in which good use was made of the ' magic ' qualities of the camera. Whilst this type of fantasy cannot be called strictly cinematic there is nevertheless room for much development.[1]

Coming to the full-length fantasy film one recalls, of course, Ludwig Berger's exquisite version of *Cinderella* in 1923, with its superb baroque architecture by Rudolph Bamberger. I find this chiefly memorable for the marvellous battle of the witches, perhaps the best example of film magic yet made. Flashes of fantasy appeared in nearly all the films of the German middle period, notably in *Siegfried, Destiny, Faust;* in the early Russian *Morosko;* in Dovjenko's *Zvenigora;* in the spectacular Ufa production, *Secrets of the East;* in Fairbanks' *The Thief of Bagdad;* in Renoir's *La Petite Marchande d'Allumettes;* and in Clair's *Le Voyage Imaginaire*. There remains much to be accomplished, however, in this vein, particularly in the manner of Hans Andersen and the Brothers Grimm. The consummate ease with which magic can be achieved by double exposure and trick effects on the screen suggests the wide range of material waiting to be utilised.

(e) The Cartoon Film

The cartoon element goes back to an early stage in the development of the cinema, arising probably in the first place out of the humorous strip in the American newspapers. Although the laborious draughtsmanship, neces-

---

[1] The charming puppet model films of Georg Pal, and the recent work of the Czechoslovak puppet film producers require mention here.

sarily entailed in the production of the thousands of small drawings needed as material for smooth movement, has naturally limited the output of these animated cartoons, nevertheless those artists who have specialised in this form of cinema have nearly always achieved success. In the past the appearance of *Felix the Cat, Mutt and Jeff,* and *Aesop's Fables* were always greeted with enthusiasm.

But it is not until the recent Walt Disney cartoons of *Mickey Mouse* that the full value of such work has been realised. In point of fact, the Disney cartoons are not only funnier and better drawn than their predecessors, but they are far more filmically conceived and have the added advantage of mechanically recorded sound accompaniment. The possibilities afforded by the incorporation of sound with the drawn cartoon film are unlimited and, without showing ingratitude to the creator of *Mickey Mouse,* one foresees a wealth of imaginative material lying at the hands of the creative draughtsman of the future, particularly with the employment of flat colour.

To many writers at the moment, the Disney cartoons are the most witty and satisfying productions of modern cinema. Their chief merit lies in their immediate appeal to any type of audience, simply because they are based on rhythm. They have been compared with the early one-reelers of Chaplin, and the way in which they appeared unheralded, gradually to achieve an international acceptance, is not unlike that of the great comedian's early work. The real importance of *Mickey Mouse,* however, lies not so much in the clever draughtsmanship and amusing wit of Walt Disney as in the full advantage that is taken of synchronised sound. Whilst film theorists in every country have been fruitlessly arguing over the merits and demerits of sound images and their employment in counterpoint, Disney has put into use all the properties to be gained from synchronisation. In the burlesque accompaniment of distorted sounds that is wedded to the ever-moving figures of *Mickey Mouse* and his associates, there are to be discovered all the intrinsic qualities of sound in combination with visual images. The essential characteristics of the Disney cartoon films, where distorted linear images are matched with equally distorted sound images, are those of the visual-sound film of the future. In his earlier cartoons it was noticeable that Disney divided the appeal equally between the screen and the sound, both matching but neither governing the other. In his later pictures (*Springtime* and *Jungle Rhythm*) there is a tendency to fit the linear images to a definite melody, which is detrimental, for it impedes the free flow of the draughtsmanship. It has been suggested, also, that there is a feeling of vulgarity in the more recent examples, but that is a matter outside the range of this survey. As the best of Disney's work I would choose, without hesitation, *Mickey's Choo-Choo* and *The Jazz Fool,* both masterpieces of combined wit and humour expressed in terms of patterned draughtsmanship and sound, revealing a sense of cutting and of angle.[1]

(f) *The Epic Film*

Like fantasy, the power of the epic film is still but partially exploited, and, again, where experiments have been made in this direction they have been remarkably successful. The film is capable of showing the movement of masses better than any other medium, but it is necessary to differentiate between the epic and the mere spectacle film. By the film's control of space and time, it is possible to portray by massed movement the feelings and psychological reactions of a nation. The epic film conceives collective life as an end in itself or with, perhaps, an individual of more than ordinary significance emerging from the crowded background.

[1] The subsequent development of Disney is, in my opinion, one of the greatest disappointments in the cinema. In the typical Hollywood manner, he has appeared to concentrate on the elaborate development of the mechanics of his technique and paid less and less attention to the fundamental creative ideas underlying his work. Of his recent full-length cartoon films, for all their trickery and combination of real persons with animated drawings, I am afraid I admire only parts of *The Reluctant Dragon* and *Dumbo.* His greatest mistake was perhaps to introduce human beings, either real or drawn, into his films.

The greatest examples of the epic mass film were the world-famous *Battleship Potemkin* and *Ten Days that Shook the World* by S. M. Eisenstein. It seems incredible that a person drawn from any class or any part of the civilised world could witness these films without obtaining a full realisation of the spirit of the Russian people. They were political in that they dealt with political events; they were propaganda in the same way that the *The King of Kings* (that essence of hypocritical nonsense) was propaganda for the Christian religion. On the score of their epic quality, as apart from their propagandist intention, they deserve to be shown freely throughout the world.

Contrasted with these mass productions, Pudovkin's *The End of St. Petersburg,* which dealt roughly with the same events as *Ten Days that Shook the World,* was an example of individuals moving against a crowded background, of an epic theme seen through individuals. By circumstance of the scenario narrative a peasant boy was made to project from the masses, but was suggestive only of their mental state.

It is necessary also to include such films as *Grass* in this category, and to a very much lesser extent *Martin Luther,* which was, or should have been, epic in conception, as well as Abel Gance's vast picture *Napoléon.*

(g) *The Documentary or Interest Film, including the Scientific, Cultural anl Sociological Film*

This type of cinema has been recently explored with great success on the Continent and especially in Soviet Russia, where the interest picture has been made in great numbers. Films on how this thing is made and how that functions are often to be found in the average programme in Britain. Moreover, the treatment of these films is rapidly improving, as for example in Edmond Greville's fascinating picture of the making of watches at Tavannes in Switzerland, *The Birth of the Hours.* Instances of the various forms may be taken as (a) Geographic : *Pamyr, With Cobham to the*

Cape, Turksib and *Pori;* (*b*) Scientific : *The Mechanics of the Brain,* and many short films of surgical operations, etc.; (*c*) Sociological : *The Expiation,* and, of course, most of the ordinary Soviet films.   In Britain, special mention should be made of numerous nature films produced by British Instructional Films, all admirably made, as well as John Grierson's recent epic of the herring fleet, *Drifters.*[1]

(*h*) The Combined Documentary and Story-Interest Film

The growing desire to photograph reality rather than structural studio representations has rendered this form of cinema exceptionally popular of recent years and many outstanding pictures have been made on these lines.   The aim of combining story-interest with real material is altogether good and opens up vast and hitherto untouched material as subject matter for scenarios.   Prominent examples in this vein have been : *Storm Over Asia, Finis Terrae, Nanook of the North, Moana,* and *Chang.*[2]

(*i*) The Cine-Eye and Cine-Radio Film

With the school of the cine-eye and the cine-radio one immediately couples the name of its founder, Dziga-Vertov, and of his brother and cameraman, Kauffmann.   The group is a branch of the Vufkukino organisation of the Soviet Ukraine and so far has worked alone in the development of its theories.   The Vertov theory, in brief, assumes that the camera lens has the power of the moving human eye to penetrate every detail of contemporary life and its sur-

[1] No attempt can be made here to describe the whole growth of the factual film in all its many forms since 1929. *Documentary Film* (Faber & Faber, London, 1939, revised edition), does this to some extent, but probably the best account of the documentary film movement is in the *Arts Enquiry Report* on *The Factual Film* (Oxford University Press, 1946).   Of great importance, also, is the collection of John Grierson's writings, *Grierson on Documentary,* edited by Forsyth Hardy (Collins, 1946).

[2] The combination of personal story with documentary approach and technique is a subject of much discussion and theory these past ten years.   Recent outstanding films attempting this synthesis were : *Nine Men, The Overlanders, Boomerang, Grapes of Wrath, Millions Like Us, The Way Ahead* and *In Which We Serve.*

roundings, to an accompaniment of sound. Particular use is made of the scientific resources of the cinema, and all such technical devices as slow and rapid motion, abrupt cessation of movement, double and triple exposure, together with all the orthodox principles of montage as understood by the Soviet cinema, are included in its work. It has been aptly termed *la cinématographie sans jeu;* its limitations are at once obvious.

(*j*) *The Cine-Record Film*

(*a*) The representation of modern fact, without the introduction of story-interest, is to be found chiefly in current newsreels, both sound and silent, as distinct from the Dziga-Vertov theories and Walther Ruttmann's *Berlin*. For this purpose, the advent of the sound film has increased the appeal beyond measure. British Movietone News, Paramount News, Fox Movietone News, etc., are all excellent uses of good camerawork and sound reproduction.[1] To be mentioned also in this group are the numerous reconstruction films of war events, a feature of British production some years ago (*Zeebrugge, Mons, The Somme, The Battles of Coronel and Falkland Islands, ' Q ' Ships,* etc.).

(*b*) The representation of past fact, without the introduction of fictional story-interest, is an attempt to put on record the actual happenings of some past event. Carl Dreyer's film *La Passion de Jeanne d'Arc* can well be cited as an example of this extremely difficult accomplishment, as well as Cserèpy's mammoth production of the life of Frederick the Great, *Fridericus Rex*.

[1] Of all branches of cinema, the newsreels have perhaps been the least progressive since 1929. During the recent war, however, official Service cameramen showed great skill and courage in their coverage of the battlefronts. Films edited from their material, such as *Desert Victory* and *The True Glory*, set a new standard for actuality film-making. In this section, also, should be included the monthly issues of the American *March of Time*, the recently started *This Modern Age* series from the J. Arthur Rank Organisation, the *Why We Fight series*, supervised by Frank Capra for the U.S. Army, and many other examples of edited material. *Vide: The Arts Enquiry Report* on *The Factual Film* (Oxford University Press, 1946).

(k) *The Decorative Film and Art Film, as distinct from the Cine-Fiction Film*

This form of cinema is now almost obsolete, for the cost of production is inevitably greater than the returns from such a picture, if it is to be well done. No firm which has to satisfy its shareholders can afford to produce an art film for the sheer prestige of having done so.[1] Nevertheless, some notable and splendid examples of purely decorative films exist, most of them having been made during the early and middle periods of the German cinema. Perhaps the greatest picture of this kind is the first part of *The Nibelungen Saga, Siegfried,* made by Fritz Lang in 1923. No expense was spared on this magnificent film, which stands practically alone as an example of simplified decoration.[2] On a smaller scale, Paul Leni's *Waxworks* deserves mention if only for the fine architecture, but it is to be understood that this type of cinema is more related to the theatre than to the film. A number of small, one- and two-reel art films have been made from time to time, but most of them, like Robert Florey's *Loves of Zero,* are insignificant. Fairbanks' *The Thief of Bagdad,* although negligible after the greatness of *Destiny,* may be ranked as a pseudo-art film.

(l) *The Cine-Fiction Film*

This form of cinema naturally constitutes the bulk of the world's film output and may be roughly subdivided into four sections:

(a) Modern comedies, farces, satires, and dramas, etc.

Typical examples of these may be taken at random as: *A Woman of Paris, Thérèse Raquin, The Crowd, The Love of Jeanne Ney, Piccadilly, The Spy, Les Nouveaux Messieurs, Vaudeville, Foolish Wives, The Virginian, The Kiss,* etc.

(b) Unrealistic costume and historical romances and dramas, etc., as: *Tartuffe, The Patriot, Le Capitaine*

---

[1] *Pace,* Mr. Rank.

[2] It would be fair, I think, to place Laurence Olivier's *Henry V* and *Hamlet* in this group.

Fracasse, Forbidden Paradise, New Babylon, The Student of Prague, Scaramouche, Schinderhannes, Le Collier de la Reine, The Golem, Rosenkavalier, etc.

(*c*) Spectacle films, without apparent decorative motive, instanced well by *Ben-Hur, The Viking, Noah's Ark, The Ten Commandments, La Marseillaise, General Crack.* These mammoth productions are usually of negligible aesthetic value, serving only as advertisements on a large scale for their producing firms, who scatter wholesale publicity as to the number of persons taking part, how much timber was used, the average weight of the cast, etc. They geneially originate from Hollywood, for no other producing centre has the immense amount of money needed nor the time to waste.

(*d*) Pure comedies, including slapstick, as distinct from the drawing-room comedies indicated above. All Chaplin films come into this group, as well as those of Lloyd, Keaton, and the lesser comedians; and such films as *Moscow that Laughs and Weeps, Hurrah! I'm Alive, Rookery Nook, Les Deux Timides.*[1]

(*m*) *Musical, Dancing, and Singing Films*

These, usually on a large scale, have only been made possible by the advent of sound and dialogue reproduction. Already there have been outstanding successes in *The Broadway Melody, Fox Movietone Follies, Rio Rita, Broadway, Sally, The Hollywood Revue of* 1929, etc. There is little doubt that this type of light entertainment will be produced widely in the future to meet the constant demand for musical comedy, and with it will come the all-colour film and wider screen.

[1] The reader is referred to the greater breakdown of these types adopted in *Movie Parade* (Studio Publications, 1936).

III

THE AMERICAN FILM

By sheer ubiquity, American movies compel attention. Although they are, together with their British and German counterparts, the lowest form of public entertainment, their very number prevents their being ignored. In every country of the world where cinemas persuade both the hardworking and the rich to part with their money at the box-office, there is to be found celluloid of Hollywood origin, except Soviet Russia. Indeed, so far has the influence of the movie spread that its presence is noted not only in the cinema but in the wireless, the theatre, the Press, and in all matters of advertising. The star-system alone has penetrated the inner regions of every working-girl's heart, influencing her likes and her dislikes, her ideals and her dreams. Movies are a part of drawing-room gossip and dinner-table repartee. They have superseded the novel and the play as a topic of fashionable conversation. The first night of some movies may almost be as important a social occasion as the first night of an opera.

Nine out of ten newspapers notice movies in their columns, and at least ninety per cent. of those mentioned are American. The cinematic terms of ' close-up ' and ' star ' are incorporated in the vocabulary of the English-speaking peoples, as well as being used all over Europe. One in ten poster hoardings displays cinema programme bills. A vast majority of the titles displayed are American. Except for a handful of home-made movies (demanded by the quota regulations) and a sparse sprinkling of foreign films, the programmes of British cinemas are composed of Hollywood movies.[1]

[1] Eighty per cent. of British screen-space is at present occupied by Hollywood footage (October, 1947).

After some consideration, I have ultimately decided (with a few notable exceptions) to regard Hollywood much as I would a factory, managed and owned by a number of astute business men, who seek only large financial returns from the goods that they manufacture. Among the employees of these big firms is undoubtedly a number of artists, sincere in their aims, who sacrifice their intentions for the sake of a living, for which they are hardly to be belittled. It follows that the bigger the profits made by the owners for themselves and their shareholders, the vaster the business expands and the more pictures are manufactured. It has already been seen that American producing concerns, beginning in a small way by making one- or two-reel story-pictures, gradually developed the trade until, taking advantage of the situation offered by the first World War, they eventually assumed control of the world market.

Now the vagaries of public taste are well known, and it has been the constant occupation of the film producer to gauge that taste and to keep abreast with its fluctuation. But, not content with pandering to the public taste, the film producer has also set out to create public likes and dislikes by clever advertising and world-wide distribution of certain classes of films. In a business-like way, the film men of Hollywood have experimented with the appetite of the public, and they are not to be blamed from a commercial point of view for having turned out stereotyped productions when the public has shown its acceptance of such forms. When any new type of film comes from Hollywood and is successful, there quickly follows a swarm of similar but inferior pictures, trading on the success of the first.

To the shrewd observer of the cinema, the difficulty lies in differentiation between films demanded by public taste, and movies deliberately foisted upon the masses. The public does not by any means choose its own players. If a big American firm wish to put over Miss —— as a leading star, they can and will do so, by systematically presenting movies at their own chain of cinemas with that particular young lady in them. In time, seduced by an exhaustive publicity campaign, by press photographs of the young lady in her underclothes, and by repeated appearances of the new star, the public will sit back in its tip-up plush seat and believe that it has discovered a fresh favourite; whilst the producing firm will sigh with temporary relief and set about keeping the young lady where they have put her. The whole matter resolves itself into the problem of gently persuading the public that it likes a certain player in a certain type of picture, without the public becoming aware of the fact that it is being persuaded. There is, perhaps, a touch of Dziga-Vertov about it. Actually, it is simply the basic principle of advertising. Several players could be named who are stars simply because they appear with monotonous regularity three times a year. Obviously, in order to retain the ' popularity ' of their stars all over the world, no efforts have been spared by American producers in devising new methods for keeping their public and for the furtherance of constructing, packing, and selling their goods. There are practically no lengths to which a Hollywood firm will not go to sell a film.[1]

At this point it is of interest to sketch briefly the relationship of the public to the American cinema. From the early period of the first story-pictures until a year or two after the first World War, the American movie progressed in quality. It found constant support in the public primarily because of the novelty of the cinema itself. During the whole of this period, producers were assured of the loyalty of the public, which was continually on the increase. To many people, the film was still an innovation. They went to the cinema because it *was* the cinema, and not for any other reason. Nearly every big production converted more people to the ranks of the cinema-going public. *The Birth of a Nation, Intolerance, The Four Horsemen of the Apocalypse, The Big Parade,* and *Ben-Hur* all created new

---

[1] Of the many attempts to analyse and describe the growth of the Hollywood factories and the reaction of the American public to the movie, I find the best are *The Rise of the American Film,* Lewis Jacobs (Harcourt Brace, 1939) and *America at the Movies* Margaret Farrand Thorp (Yale University Press, 1939).

29. CINDERELLA, directed by Ludwig Berger. [German, 1923]

30. THE STREET, directed by Karl Grune. Eugen Klöpfer, Lucie Höflich. [German, 1923]

31. THE COVERED WAGON, directed by JAMES CRUZE. [American, 1923]

32. ROBIN HOOD, directed by ALLAN DWAN. DOUGLAS FAIRBANKS. [American, 1923]

filmgoers. In the same way, one single showing of *Battleship Potemkin* and *The Cabinet of Doctor Caligari* gains believers in the film proper. During this period, therefore, from about 1912 until about 1920, the very marvelling of the general public, watching every new film with mouths agape, was sufficient for the studios to become established on a practical basis, capable of mass production. To this golden era belongs the best work of Griffith, Thomas Ince, and Mack Sennett, together with the sincere efforts of William S. Hart and Douglas Fairbanks. These pictures had a roughness about them, an intensity of feeling and an air of honesty that have long since vanished in the up-to-date slickness of the Hollywood movie. It may, perhaps, be said that the first indications of the star-system were making themselves shown, but although individual personalities were gradually being associated with individual pictures, there was no wide exploitation of the fact. *He Comes Up Smiling* and *Reaching for the Moon* were seen because they were good cinema. They were invigorating and they were stimulating. They had not yet begun to be Fairbanks.

But from this stage the American cinema began to succumb to the personality process, resulting in the tyrannical reign of the star-system, the super-film, and the publicity bluffing campaigns, all of which were to develop to such an extent that they defeated themselves. The producing companies made their great mistake when they decided to cater for the taste of the music-hall patron. The enthusiasm of the real public had already fallen off when directors tended to repeat themselves. The standard of films had reached a rut; a groove out of which it had to be jolted if big business was to be continued. Some new weapon was needed to stir the public out of its apathy.

The Americans decided to recapture the attention of the public by the wholesale exploitation of stars; a process, if such it may be called, which was in its embryo with the success of films in which Chaplin, Fairbanks, Mary Pickford, Gloria Swanson, etc., played. The film business of Hollywood was to become one big game of bluff. Obviously, those who bluffed hardest (and no nation in the world is so accomplished in the art of bluffing as the American) made the most money. The film men began to work (and some of them realise it now) to the detriment of the prestige of the film. The cinema lost a public who loved it for itself and what it meant to them. They had no liking for vaudeville, for star turns on a big scale. In the place of the old filmgoer there arose a new type of audience, a vacant-minded, empty-headed public, who flocked to sensations, who thrilled to sexual vulgarity, and who would go anywhere and pay anything to see indecent situations riskily handled on the screen.

America exploited the star-system for all the dishonest business was worth. Competitions were organised; beauty contests arranged; vast correspondence ' fan mails ' worked up; widespread campaigns of personal publicity launched; marriages and separations arranged; whilst a public of the lowest and worst type responded with eagerness. They began to write letters to their favourite stars; how old were they; how much were they worth; how much did they weigh; what sort of face cream did they use; why were they married; what were their children like (if any) and so on. This was encouraged and fanned by the publicity men. In contrast with the audiences of early days, people now went to the cinema to see films because of the stars who were in them. They cared nothing for the films themselves, so long as they were shown close-ups of their idols.[1] The star became a fetish, inasmuch that such a demand was created for movies that producing companies were unable to make them quickly enough. Naturally the stars themselves commanded tremendous salaries that grew larger year by year. They became bloated and puffed up by their world-wide publicity. They took to playing three, four, and even five parts in the same film, achieved by means of

[1] Incidentally, one shudders at the gross abuse of the technical resources of the medium, in particular the misuse of the close-up.

double exposure. Audiences exulting and thrilled, feasted their eyes and thoughts on the form of the star. Many famous names occur at this time, names that rose up and were forgotten. A few stayed, but they were exceptional. The Talmadge sisters, Wallace Reid, Rudolph Valentino, Pauline Frederick, the inimitable Mae Murray, Nita Naldi, Richard Dix, Thomas Meighan, Tom Moore, Dorothy and Lillian Gish, Viola Dana, and scores of others, all possessed manufactured screen personalities. The ideal type for the film star was the blank-minded, non-temperamental player, steeped in sex and sheathed in satin, who was admirably suited to movie 'acting', which called for no display of deep emotions, no subtlety, no sensitivity, no delicacy, no guile. All through her career Norma Talmadge achieved success by looking slightly perplexed and muzzy about the eyes. But audiences worshipped her; wrote to her for signed photographs; hung them over their beds and got a thrill out of them; and told their friends how great an actress she was. The Rudolph Valentino affair was worked with such success that, after his death, a guild was actually formed of people who had never set eyes on him to perpetuate his name. The publicity departments played the handsome Italian, with the cauliflower ear and the hundred per cent. sex, so well that anything became possible. It was even rumoured that Pola Negri's playing in *Hotel Imperial* was due to the emotions she was undergoing at the time because of the death of her beloved Valentino! Is it to be wondered that no sane-thinking person could see anything at all possible in the vaunted aesthetic value of the cinema?

The star-system achieved for Hollywood and the cinema in general an unenviable reputation. It called forth denunciations and castigations from conservative constitutions and religious bodies, which, of course, it thoroughly merited. Not, that is to say, from a moral, but from a film point of view, for the morals of a film star are entirely his or her own affair. It was the star-system that should have been attacked; not its victims, but its sponsors, the American producing concerns. The star-system was nothing more or less than a flagrant prostitution of creative intelligence and good film material.

As has been indicated, bound up with the task of public acceptance of the star-system, there arose vast publicity campaigns organised by producing concerns to ' get across ' their own particular stars and pictures. America fights half her film battles with publicity campaigns. At least two-thirds of the film writers in the United States and in Britain are mere gossip writers, who retail more or less scandalous news that is sent to them from the studios. There are not twenty critics in this country who know the first thing about films save what the publicity sheets issued from the studios tell them.[1] Every company floods critics and editors of newspapers and periodicals all over the world with ready-made press publicity, until the journalists lose all sense of values. During the height of the star-system every available detail, the more personal the better, was published about American film stars. Papers were deluged with highly-coloured matter from big firms, each exaggerating the talents of their individual stars. These descriptions were typical of the hypocrisy and dissimulation of Hollywood. But producing firms realised as well that the tone of their publicity must be given the appearance of purity. From the public's outlook, it was the halo round the star that mattered. It was imperative to keep it unbroken. Both publicity departments and the Hays Organisation took every care to hide up any scandal or misbehaviour that should occur in Hollywood. Quite obviously, if scandalous accounts were circulated about some hard-faced, smoothly-shingled young virgin who played sweet innocent heroines, the general public were apt to become dubious as to whether they were having their legs pulled or not. This, however, does not prevent temporary scandals and movements in the divorce market from receiving current publicity. To counteract this, some thousands of photographs are circulated yearly of well-

---

[1] In retrospect my estimate was optimistic.

known film stars in familiar and entirely creditable attitudes. The public are saturated with this sort of publicity, and believe it all. A typical story is cited by Walter Kron, who quotes from a criticism by an American woman journalist, Louella Parsons, as follows: '. . . his work as Lord Nelson in *The Divine Lady* proved what a really fine artist he is. With an arm missing and blind in one eye, he still managed to have sex appeal.' Another favourite method of retaining public esteem is the personal appearance. ' Miss —— travels specially to London for the opening performance of her new film ', and so on.

The continued forcing of the star-system inevitably called for new faces and fresh talent, and before long producers were raking the world for suitable aspirants to film fame. This, in due course, led to the distressing habit of ' discovering' likely persons in countries thousands of miles from California, transporting them, buoyed up by false promises, to Hollywood where, after a few months of exaggerated publicity, they were forsaken without so much as making one film appearance, being left to find their way home as best they might. Although less guilty in this respect, British studios have tried the same devices of beauty competitions and the like. The chances are remote that the winner of any film contest has any cinematic talent whatsoever beyond an insipid, pretty face. All these disreputable methods of finding film ' talent ' are of no use to the progress of the cinema.

As time went on, the haloes of existing stars in Hollywood began visibly to pale. Producers were continually forced to find new stars. Fresh names began to replace the old favourites, and stars of the calibre of Dolores del Rio, Sue Carol, Lupe Velez, and Joan Crawford appeared from remote corners of the stage or studio crowd work. Productions became more and more costly. The spectacle film, which for some years had lain low, developed into the super-film, and once more casts of thousands, costing millions of dollars, were employed to attract the public. At the same time, hundreds of feature-films were made to type; and one became accustomed to whole groups of movies of the same variety. There was a craze for war films, air films, underworld films, mother-love films, night-life films, backstage films, Spanish films, costume films, etc.

At this juncture, it is felt necessary to retrace the years, in order to appreciate the influence of talent imported from Europe to American studios. Shortly after the first World War, as has been seen, Germany, Denmark and Sweden gave plentiful evidence of the genius and technical brilliance that lay in their studios. The magnates, astute as ever in their business outlook, realised that these European intelligences had delved down much further into the cinema than had those of the superficial directors of Hollywood. They recognised, moreover, that Britain and France admired the aesthetic qualities of the German film, and they determined to flavour their own movies with some of this evidently 'artistic' talent. Not only this, but the increasing necessity for the *international* cinema to quiet the suspicions of commercial influence, made the installation of the foreign element in Hollywood desirable. American producers, therefore, sought to refresh their shop-soiled productions by the influence of German and Swedish film technique, followed later by importations of French, German, and Hungarian players and directors. From then onwards, American firms acquired talent from Europe as soon as it made itself apparent. The tale of British actors who have made good in Hollywood is too old a wound to be re-opened.

The German and Swedish element in the Hollywood studios marked a new era in American film output. It is significant that although the majority of German films failed outside their country of origin, two were successful in the United States. *Dubarry* (renamed *Passion*) and *Carmen* (renamed *Gypsy Blood*) both directed by Ernst Lubitsch, with Pola Negri, were well received. As a result, Miss Negri went to Hollywood, to be followed shortly by Lubitsch, and it was not long before most of the remainder of the Europeans deserted the sinking ship and settled down in California. The list is too long to be given in full, but pre-eminent among the exodus were Emil Jannings, Conrad Veidt, Lya de Putti, Greta Garbo, Camilla Horn, Lars Hanson, Nils Asther, Greta Nissen, Dimitri Buchowetski, Paul Leni, Fred Murnau, Ludwig Berger, Erich Pommer, E. A. Dupont, Victor Seaström, and the late Mauritz Stiller. Yet not one of these directors or players, having been bought by dollars, but fell into the Hollywood groove of living. The movie kings housed and fed these valued importations like prize cattle, and succeeded after some struggling in taming them for their needs. A few broke loose after a time and returned to the European fold, where they have for the most part failed to regain their former status. So strong is the dollar influence of Hollywood that it is necessary to consider the works of these directors in two phases, the pre-Hollywood and the Hollywood period. For example, on the score of appearances, I find it impossible to accept the Murnau who made *Faust* and *The Last Laugh* as the same man who later made *Sunrise* and *The Four Devils*. Some link between the two pairs of films is sought in vain. They seem the work of separate persons : the first of an artist, working with sincerity among harmonious surroundings; the second, of a pseudo artist muddling under extreme difficulties of super-abundance.

Of the individual influence of the Europeans on the American movie more will be said later, but it is to be remembered that their work was to set examples for the younger Hollywood school of directors to imitate. Lubitsch's *The Marriage Circle* and *Kiss Me Again* type of film served as a copy-book to a dozen of the young directors. Monta Bell, Mal St. Clair, Victor Heerman, Frank Tuttle, Harry Beaumont, Roy del Ruth, William Wellman, and all the rest of these clever young men modelled their work on a mixture of Lubitsch and Chaplin. It was the era of a new type of comedy, not the slapstick of Lloyd or the ludicrous style of Keaton, but a suave, polished, slick, slightly-satirical, sexual comedy. It was a fusion, perhaps, of the American flair for brilliance and the German tendency towards the psychological. It was to produce the

Man, Woman, and Sin, Sex in Fetters, Broadway After Midnight type of movie. It was a new quality in the American film, quite different from the natural Western element and the spectacle picture, and has been tremendously successful. It is found to-day (1930) in the plentiful adaptations of Lonsdale and Somerset Maugham plays to the dialogue film. *Charming Sinners, Interference,* and *The Last of Mrs. Cheyney* are cases in point.

It is not illogical that such an industry as the American movie, possessing an aim of the maximum amount of profit from the minimum *necessary* expenditure of time and labour, should be constructed on an extremely well-organised basis. Whatever may be said against American methods, it cannot be denied that they have developed their system of working to a highly perfected state. No man finds employment in a Hollywood film studio unless he knows his job. That job is his business and he manages it as such. That is where the Hollywood studio differs from the British studio. The American film man knows nothing whatsoever about the aesthetics of the film, its possibilities or its development, and he cares less. He is out for his pay-check, and the making of movies happens to be the way he is doing it. He might just as well be engaged in a chemical factory or coal-mine, except that the movie life is a pleasant one. Organisation of studio work, about which so much is written in the second part of this survey, has been carried to excess in Hollywood. Each studio works according to its own plan. No fresh production is started without careful pre-consideration as to its type, the selling methods to be employed with the completed picture, and the mentality of the public to whom it is to appeal. A schedule of production for a year's output is the result of much deliberation. No reasonable period of time or amount of money is spared on a movie. Every official in every studio has his allotted time and a definite amount of money for his particular job. In fact, he is simply a cog in a highly-efficient organisation, manufacturing pictures according to formula. Moreover, the Americans are perfectly serious-minded in their movie methods. They thought of them; they developed them; and they have profited by them.[1]

The American film man is amazingly hard-working. His heart is thoroughly in his job. He understands the business so long as it remains business; as soon as it becomes something more, entailing appreciation of beauty, subtlety of wit,

[1] Cf. the following excerpt from *Kinematograph Weekly*, April 24th, 1947, in an interview with the British writer-director Frank Launder, on his return from Hollywood :

'Launder met most of the people worth meeting in Hollywood, and particularly those engaged in the more creative departments of picture-making, such as writers and directors. He found among them what he felt to be a feeling of frustration because of the curbing of original ideas.

'A great deal of this frustration he attributes to the state of mind which appears to exist in the "front offices" of the major companies. Rising costs have made the executives more than ever anxious for solid box-office success. The tendency in story selection therefore is to play safe : and the big majority of "front offices" to-day play safe by consulting the Gallup Poll and its subsidiary, Audience Research.

'These reputedly scientific public opinion probes have very definitely sold themselves to Hollywood. Long before a film is ready for production, in fact, as soon as a property is acquired, Audience Research gets to work. It offers the producers a comprehensive service. Everything you want to know about your subject. Checks are made on title, story trends, popularity of the period in which it is set, story ending, star values—in fact, anything and everything which can provide information in advance about the probable public reaction to the mooted story.

'Hollywood executives, asserts Launder, have a touching faith in the value of these probes; and these days it is a courageous and independent man who disregards their findings. In a business badgered by rising costs and labour troubles, which arise all too frequently, the Hollywood executive to-day is almost feverish in the search for some kind of insurance on his company's story investments. Most of them seem to believe that Audience Research is the answer.

'The result, says Launder, is that most writers with fresh and original ideas are restricted and limited. In the case of the more modest films, the writers often do little more than put into screen formula the findings of the research sleuths. Most of them have to trim their treatments according to the astrology of the questionnaires.

'Launder's experience is that nearly all the rank and file writers, among whom are many who are potentially brilliant, are filled with a sense of frustration, and even the king-pins of script-makers are irked and handicapped in a similar way.

'Originality, faith in a central idea and the bold development of it by a team of artist-craftsmen, the formula for picture-making that has produced so many fine and commercially successful films, means less in Hollywood to-day, according to "front office" standards.'

psychology of emotions, then he is as good as finished.   He
takes refuge in calling it modern, artistic and what is even
worse, highbrow.   The only highbrow films are those made
by dilettantes and intelligentsia (e.g. the American *Fall of
the House of Usher;* Florey's *Loves of Zero;* Len Lye's
Tusylava).   No pure film is futurist, *avant-garde,* highbrow,
or precious.   No Soviet film is advanced, or 'artistic', or
even difficult to understand.   (It is, on the contrary, made
for the simple peasant mind.)   But the Hollywood film man
would call *Ten Days That Shook the World* or *Mother* an
art-film, for the reason that they are a more natural form
of cinema than the sophisticated movie to which he is accustomed.   *The Last Laugh* was an example of the fundamental use of cinematic technique, yet the film man of
Hollywood and Elstree will avoid discussing it.   He is
afraid of it.   So also is the average film critic.   If he sees
any new film which he does not immediately comprehend,
he will call it 'highbrow' and leave it severely alone instead
of analysing its properties.   When the famous Soviet film,
Battleship Potemkin was shown in London in November
1929, not one of the regular newspaper critics was able to
give a clear, intelligent, broad-minded criticism of it.   They
shirked it by weakly calling it Soviet propaganda.   They
were ashamed to admit that their knowledge of the functions of the cinema did not allow them to analyse this outstanding film.   The average American film man can speak
of nothing but movies.   In Hollywood they talk films, make
films, and live films, entirely from a business point of view.
The average British film man knows little about films.   He
knows all about golf and football, but he has seldom seen
a recent production.[1]

All the big, but not necessarily good, films have come
from Hollywood, simply because no other country has the
money to make them, and even if they had, they would not
know what to do with them.   In America, the more money

[1] It is indeed pleasant, some eighteen years later, to report the
opposite.   There is probably more sensible discussion of films in British
studios to-day than in any other country.

expended on the production of a film, the greater it is in the eyes of the producers and also the public. How often has not the eternal slogan of the cast of twenty thousand players and the film which cost two million dollars been seen on London poster hoardings? [1]

Moreover, Americans appreciate the value of perfected technical accomplishment, which British executives do not realise. Hollywood companies know well that the general public will be the first to spot bad lighting, inferior camera-work, shoddy settings, and badly-designed dresses. They recognise the importance of the *real thing,* and they appreciate the public's liking for appearances. If silk brocade is needed for a curtain, the Americans will not use cheap cotton, because they know that the fake will be noticeable. They will go to interminable lengths to get things right. If the scenario demands, they will build London in Hollywood or go to Italy to film *Ben-Hur.* They would buy the suit off the King's back if they could get it, or failing that, have an exact replica made of it. The American movie producer and director are immensely painstaking, and that is to their credit. On the other hand, they will make mistakes about the simplest and most ordinary things. *What Price Glory?* was notorious for its military discrepancies. Money for new mechanical equipment, up-to-date camera devices, newly invented lighting systems or intricate laboratory appliances is never wanting. The Americans know the value of these necessities. Two-thirds of American movies ' get across ' in Britain solely because of their good dressing. Technical accomplishment plays a large part in the polish of the Hollywood movie. The quality of the photography is usually faultless. Moving shots and camera operating are always beyond reproach, no matter whether aesthetically they are being used rightly or wrongly. It is rare to see an American ' extra ' badly made-up. An American movie star's clothes are always exquisite. Cheapness and shabbiness are unknown in the Hollywood studios. For this reason alone, the American movie is always successful. The

[1] And still is to-day.

general public, judging largely from outward appearances and knowing little of the cinema itself, welcomes its glitter.

And, as is to be expected, Hollywood movies are slick, facile, and well-finished. At the same time, they display an absence of good taste, of intelligence, and, if the term is allowable, of culture. These qualities, so essential to the cinema, are lacking in the American film director and producer. It is these which they have tried to buy with dollars from Europe, which they have gradually found to be unbuyable.

There is found, then, at the close of the pre-dialogue period of the American film, a mixed selection of productions mostly being made according to formula. They have been well named ' committee-made pictures '. In most cases, the director is not his own master, being under the control of the producing board, the sole desire of which is to turn out a certain number of standardised pictures during the year. Directorial talent has been subdued and shaped into a single quality, the *raison d'être* of every Hollywood director worthy of his name, PICTURE-SENSE. Picture-sense controls the choice of theme, the treatment, the players, and the presentation. Hollywood has rigidly schooled herself into looking at every film from a picture-sense angle. The ingredients of a successful film, conceived from a picture-sense point of view, may be said to be : a strong, powerful theme (preferably sexual); a highly polished, quick-moving technique, employing all the most recent discoveries (usually German); a story-interest that will carry the sex, at the same time allowing for spectacle and at least two high spots; and a cast of international players.[1] Of such a type were *Flesh and the Devil, The Last Command, The Patriot, Wild Orchids,* and *The Kiss.* Hundreds of pictures based on this formula were being produced just prior to the general adoption of the dialogue film. The same idea was being carried out in Britain with *Piccadilly,* and in Germany with *Volga Volga.*

[1] Cf. Footnote on p. 137. Ought we not, then, to be more than usually grateful for a *Grapes of Wrath,* a *Crossfire,* a *Story of G.I. Joe* and a *Strange Incident* ?

American pictures are filled with people, for prominent among the movie beliefs of Hollywood is the conception that the general public is more interested in people than in things. Seldom is a landscape, or a piece of architecture, used in an American film for its own beautiful sake. (The work of Henry King and Robert Flaherty may be taken as exceptional.) Only as a background to people does the American producer allow nature to interfere. Typical of this belief is the film *White Shadows,* in which even the hard hand of Hollywood, personified in the haggard Monte Blue and sex-charged Raquel Torres, could not subdue the waving palms and mountainous cumulus clouds of the south seas, which Van Dyke's cameramen succeeded in photographing so well. In all probability there are a few directors in Hollywood who would, if given the opportunity, make films of sincerity, but they are continually manacled by the one great obstacle, picture-sense or box-office. They cannot afford to break away and attempt to produce on their own. The combines are far too strong. Only the star-producers of the Chaplin, Fairbanks, Pickford and Swanson group work alone and pursue their own methods, but even they are afraid of the demands of the distributors. Perhaps Chaplin only is in the position to make films as he really wishes, but even he cannot afford to make another *Woman of Paris.* Fairbanks and Pickford are to be sincerely admired for their efforts to create better American films. They realise, at least, that they are lacking in some of the essentials of good cinema, and are not afraid to go to the source for the benefit of learning.

The mentality of the American film magnate is perplexing. His futile mistakes and brilliant successes are a continual source of wonderment. The Americanisation of Emil Jannings is typical of Hollywood methods. In reviewing the position, it may be recalled that Paramount secured the ' world's greatest actor ', the man who shook the audiences of the entire cinema by his powerful performances in tragedy and comedy. In early days, he became known in *Peter the Great, Danton, The Loves of*

Pharaoh, as Louis XV in *Dubarry,* as Henry VIII in *Anne Boleyn,* etc. This was Jannings, the repertory player, with the stage and Reinhardt uppermost in his mind. From this came Jannings the film actor, finding his bearings in the new medium, dropping the old theatrical ideas and finding fresh filmic ones. During this period he did his best work, in *Waxworks, Nju, The Last Laugh, Faust, Tartuffe, Vaudeville,* in both comedy and tragedy. And then Jannings in Hollywood, with the picture-sense men running round him in circles, crying ' what shall we do with him, now we have got him here? ' like so many pet dogs round a bull. They looked at all his past films, diagnosed the successes, noted the powerful bits, rehashed them for stock, and decided to construct individual masterpieces based on small incidents in his former triumphs. The public would never recognise old wine in new bottles; they would be too occupied in acclaiming the world's greatest actor now starring in Paramount productions. Thus *The Way of All Flesh* was a clever reassembling of *Vaudeville,* the white-haired old man and all. Compare, also, *The Last Command* with *The Last Laugh,* with bits of *Vaudeville* thrown in to make up weight. Look again at *The Sins of the Fathers, The Street of Sin, The Betrayal,* and they will all be found to be revampings of the European Jannings. The transposition was, of course, well done, and the public acclaimed Jannings to be ' greater ' than ever. The ovation accorded *The Patriot* was unprecedented, and yet it was a very banal performance, in nauseating bad taste. Publicity from the Paramount studios lent glamour to the position. At one time, a London film journal actually printed a statement that Jannings, having had two reels of *The Last Laugh* shown through to him in Hollywood, sat back and deplored the bad acting. This, it is to be admitted, is clever publicity. Later, they sent Jannings back to Berlin, ' on holiday ', for he was considered of little use in the dialogue film. In order to cover up the injustice of the act, they presented him with the highest honour, the annual award of merit bestowed by the Academy of Motion Picture Arts and Sciences for the most notable screen work during the year. They actually dared to present this to him as he left Hollywood, with his dismissal in his pocket! Universal's mishandling of Conrad Veidt was of a similar nature. It was almost unbearable to watch Veidt's painful striving with the impossible rôle of Gwynplaine in *The Man Who Laughs,* when comparatively fresh in the mind was his exquisite performance in *The Student of Prague.* Imagine Universal, with 'Uncle' Carl Laemmle and all, murmuring thus: 'Here is this great emotional actor, who plays with such intense force that his mind appears warped, portraying on his narrow face the inner conflict of self with terrible truth, under contract to us. What part shall we put him over in? How can we make him greater still? Let us take away the use of his mouth, and make him act with his eyes and hands. Let us give him a permanent smile and then make him play tragedy. Think of the sensation . . .'

Searching for the true characteristics of the American film, as distinct from European influence, it is found that youth, vitality, space, and movement are the chief attributes of the movie. American traditions, generally speaking, date back only to the time of the civil war, and, as in her literature, many of her movies, especially those of the early war-period, carry themes relative to that event. Both commercially and socially, America has been far too busy to devote any sincere attention to the arts, with the result that there is no contemporary school of American painting recognised in Europe, and her literature is marked only by isolated achievements. The average American citizen has more sympathy with a mechanic or an engineer than with an artist or a writer. Painting or composing is a dilettante profession. Rudolph Messel in his analysis of the American mentality has traced the development of the cowboy mind from the days of the great gold rush into the modern-day healthy American with money as his sole aim.[1] Much of the American mind is occupied with a primitive instinct for fight and possession, an instinct that is the basis for many

[1] *Vide, The Film Business,* by Rudolph Messel (Benn, 1928).

movies (*viz.*, the early Westerns, with their gunmen and hard-riding cowboys; the recent vogue for underworld crook stories, with gangsters, etc.). Out of this primitive mind comes also the strong physical feeling, particularly in the dynamic American girl. Nearly every movie is saturated in sex stimulant; a quality that is increasing with the dialogue film, and is uppermost in almost every director's and producer's mind, not only in Hollywood, but in Britain, France and Germany. The most popular stars in Paris are Joan Crawford and Victor McLaglen (1929). Every girl chosen for a part in a British film is judged by her amount of sex, according to *outward* appearances. Yet one of the most sexual pictures ever produced was Room's *Bed and Sofa,* which contained the theme of a man's selfish attitude towards women, a state of mind which Room tried to counteract. Bound up with this sexually primitive, fighting, self-possessive state of American mentality is a warped sense of religion and a false pride of patriotism, both of which find expression in the movie. *The King of Kings, The Godless Girl, What Price Glory?* and *The Big Parade* exemplify this point.

Youth is one of the essentials of the American film. In the studios there is ever a search for youth, for with it go the vitality and dynamicism that are inseparable from the true function of the movie. Youth and movement were the keynotes of *Our Dancing Daughters, The First Kiss, Wings, The Legion of the Condemned, Beau Geste,* and countless others of the same brand. Clara Bow, Fay Wray, Charles Rogers, Richard Arlen, Nancy Carroll, Anita Page, Sue Carol are all symbols of the American drama of youth.

Pace, together with the combined motives of sex, youth, and spaciousness, is the chief reason for the success of the American movie. It was the vitality of movement in such films as *The Broadway Melody, Hollywood Revue, Ben-Hur, Beau Geste, College Days, The General, The Black Pirate,* and *Wings* which made them popular, as well as the underlying factors of publicity and the star-system. One rarely observes a European film with such pace as was con-

33. A WOMAN OF PARIS, directed by CHARLES CHAPLIN. ADOLPHE MENJOU, EDNA PURVIANCE. [American, 1923]

34. PARIS QUI DORT, directed by RENÉ CLAIR. ALBERT PRÉJEAN. [French, 1923]

35. GREED, directed by Erich von Stroheim.   Zasu Pitts.   [American, 1923–24]

36. NIBELUNGEN SAGA: SIEGFRIED, directed by Fritz Lang.   [German, 1923–24]

tained in these movies; but this pace is only movement of *material,* a distinction which is explained on page 341. Pace of material reaches back through the years to the silk-legged Mack Sennett slapsticks, to the fast-moving Westerns, where it touches the feeling for spaciousness. Every audience delights in the vast spaciousness of the Western cinema. The cowboy films with their valueless stories, their lean riders and flaxen-haired rancher's daughters in gingham frocks, brought to the screen a sense of unlimited horizons, of far-reaching desert. But the real Western is gradually fading from the American cinema. Instead there is the spaciousness of rooms, great, tall, ceilingless rooms; and of cities, with buildings reaching into the sky. Only on rare occasions is a small set seen in an American movie. To the Hollywood director, a dining-room must stretch away into infinity, with doors running up out of sight, and polished, reflecting floors. . . .

But space, sex, vitality and youth are but material from which the film director constructs his work. The pace of the American movie is not necessarily the pace of *film.* It is in the construction, in the best use of the resources peculiar to the cinema, in the employment of the properties and the attributes of the screen, that the Americans fail. They have no knowledge of the *rendering* of their material. They are unable to contrive its assembling, its relationship, its meaning with any degree of sincerity. In the filmic treatment and composition of this rich material, the American allows business to overcome the proper functions of the cinema. For this sense of filmic representation, for this real use of the cinema, it is imperative to turn to other countries whose traditions and culture make possible a better understanding of the values of the film as an instrument of expression.[1]

The dialogue film became an actual commercial certainty

[1] In making any study of the sociological aspects of the American cinema, the reader is recommended for background to Frederick Lewis Allen's two informal social histories, *Only Yesterday* and *Since Yesterday,* which unhappily were not available when the above paragraphs were written in 1929.

when the Warner Brothers' producing concern, on the verge of financial collapse as a result of the failure of their silent programme, decided to exploit the Vitaphone, a talking film apparatus on the disc method, for which they held the rights. The whole affair was a matter of chance, a shot in the dark, with a well-known variety artist as the box-office appeal. The gamble succeeded. To the general surprise of Hollywood, who had little faith in the dialogue film, the public of America received the novelty of the speaking and singing entertainment with open arms. It offered an alternative to the machine-made movie. Immediately a stampede took place among the producing firms, for within a short time Warner Brothers were making tremendous profits out of their venture. There was a rush by the companies to secure equipment, to convert their silent studios into sound-proof ones, to build new stages, to find suitable subjects, to test the voices of their stars, and to buy from the theatre all the adjuncts of the voice. Hollywood turned yet another corner in her crazy career. She threw aside all the ideas and processes by which she had built up her vast industry; she risked the adaptability of her directors to this new device; she chanced the success of her established stars, now that their voices were to be heard. She discarded all her well-tried systems and staked her opportunities of further success on the novelty of a new invention.

The results were not in the least surprising. The reaction of the public, who were taken unawares, was inevitable. They were as eager to hear this new invention as they had been to see the kinetoscope. Up till the present moment, the general interest of the public remains held by the dialogue film, but there are tendencies to show that the first craze is subsiding. There is a feeling of uncertainty abroad.

Of the types of dialogue film as yet observed, there are roughly four varieties : the adapted stage play, an obvious source to which producers immediately turned for ready-made dialogue; the thriller, being an extension of the old crook melodrama, with slang, bangs, and every conceivable noise; the sentimental, individual-appeal picture, which relies on the personality of one star; and the musical comedy, the backstage type of movie with a slight story-interest serving as an excuse for colour and syncopation.

In the first category may be placed *The Last of Mrs. Cheyney, The Doctor's Secret, Madame X,* and *Charming Sinners,* all of which were adapted stage plays, notable for their slow theatrical development, their sparkling dialogue and their uncinematic quality. In the second are such pictures as *The Perfect Alibi, Bulldog Drummond,* and *Dr. Fu Manchu,* being entertainment along popular lines but without any value. In the third, the sobbing performance of Al Jolson in *The Singing Fool* and *The Jazz Singer,* and the charm of Maurice Chevalier in *The Innocents of Paris,* being remarkable only for their variety elements. While in the fourth is the descendant of the super-spectacle film, with dancing and singing and colour, such as *The Hollywood Revue, The Fox Movietone Follies, On With the Show,* and *The Broadway Melody,* all of which suffer from their lack of camera movement and other filmic properties, being successful because of their musical numbers and chorus work.

There have also been individual experiments along the lines of Gloria Swanson's *The Trespasser* and the Pickford-Fairbanks' version of *Taming of the Shrew.* Both these productions have obvious merits, but neither can be considered within the range of genuine cinema. I have only seen two American dialogue films that have had true quality, King Vidor's *Hallelujah!* and Victor Fleming's *The Virginian,* and these only because of the use of sound for dramatic emphasis.

Mention has already been made of the use of sound in the accompaniment of the animated cartoon film. The *Mickey Mouse* cartoons have definitely achieved the beginnings of the wedded sound-and-visual-image film, which will be developed in the course of time.

IV

THE AMERICAN FILM (*continued*)

Among the countless movies made in Hollywood are many which demand inclusion in this survey, and investigation of their qualities can best be made through an examination of their individual directors, placing the productions in their allotted groups as they occur. It must be stated that whatever good and harm American directors and producers have done to the cinema, there are certain developments originating in Hollywood for which she must be given credit. For example, the Americans were the first persons interested in the cinema to discover that the filmplay possessed functions peculiar to itself. Although the original use of the camera as an instrument of creative imagination is not found until Wiene's *The Cabinet of Doctor Caligari,* Griffith certainly determined that the capabilities of the film were not to make a simple record of the material placed in front of the lens of the camera, but that they consisted in the reproduction of that material on a screen by a process peculiar to the film alone. Griffith, at an early stage in the history of the cinema, was the first director with the intelligence to attempt to organise the scenario-manuscript; to make dramatic use of the close-up, the fade-in and the fade-out, being technical devices of the camera which, although discovered before Griffith used them, had not been utilised as a means of dramatic effect.

The films of Griffith[1] are to be regarded as well-constructed models of contrasted tension, achieved by the gradual narration of consecutive incidents, with the action planned in such a manner that the dramatic tension of the film rises to a powerful climax at the conclusion. This climactic ending to the Griffith pictures found outlet in what is popularly called ' the last-minute-rescue '. Actually, this was simply a working-up of excitement towards the

[1] Died in Hollywood, July, 1948.

final sequence of action, thereby making a satisfactory rounding-off to the film. The continuity process of parallel action will be mentioned later in this connection. Griffith, moreover, was not only content to construct his climax from the actions of his characters, but he contrived the story so as to intensify the final struggle of the theme by using the conflicting elements of nature, of rain, snow, storm, and ice. This use of atmospheric environment heightened the Griffith climax to an almost indescribable pitch of emotion, well seen in the snowstorm, the melting river of ice and the awe-inspiring waterfall in *Way Down East*. It will be remembered that the elements increased in intensity towards the final struggle. In this example from *Way Down East*, Griffith used not only the available natural resources, but heightened the thrill of the rescue from the waterfall by the capabilities of the camera itself by contrasting two streams of movement. In this sequence of events, the snowstorm, the ice-floes, and the waterfall, each increasing in strength, formed a comparative background to the increasing despair of the characters themselves in the narrative. Love followed in the footsteps of despair. As a contrast to this turbulence of natural resources may be taken the gradual atmospheric changes in *America*, of twilight and of morning. Griffith is a master of natural effect; and his influence is seen in many Soviet films.[1] It will be found, also, that in his earlier and better films, Griffith always chose his characters from the normal stream of life, and developed their fictitiously constructed lives in a world quite normal to them. (*Isn't Life Wonderful?*, *The Birth of a Nation*, *Way Down East*, *America*, etc.)

The ' last-minute-rescue ', such a prominent feature of the Griffith film, had been used at an early date in *The Life of an American Fireman* (1903), and has been in constant employment since then. The girl at the guillotine; the

---

[1] Recall the mist scenes at Odessa in *Battleship Potemkin* and the death of the ' Partisan' leader in *Storm Over Asia*, both instances of natural atmospheric effect in the Griffith manner.

knife about to fall; the approaching riders flourishing the pardon; the little details that hinder the fall of the knife; the arrival of the riders at the last moment; these are the factors, so well used in *Orphans of the Storm,* so familiar to audiences throughout the world. Griffith improved the tension created by parallel action by addition of the close-up. He interspaced the alternate motives with a close-up of the hooves of galloping horses; the keen edge of the blade; the girl's neck bared; the excitement on the faces in the crowd; tears in the eyes of Miss Gish—and so on. Perhaps Griffith's cleverest use of the close-up was in the trial scene of *Intolerance,* an instance of subordination of the general to emphasis of the particular. The woman was hearing the sentence of death passed on her husband, whom she knew was innocent of the crime. On her face a subdued, anxious smile was half-hidden by tears. This was shown in close-up. Suddenly, a flash was seen of her hands gripped together in anxiety. Not once was her whole figure shown to the audience, but her emotions were rendered doubly dramatic by individual close-ups of her face and hands.

Griffith was at one time an actor and play-writer. He apparently wrote a film manuscript of Sardou's *La Tosca,* had it rejected, but was engaged as an actor to play in a one-reeler, *Rescued from an Eagle's Nest.* Against his own will, he started directing, being induced to make *The Adventures of Dolly* in 1908, which was followed shortly by *The Lonely Villa, The Avenging Conscience, The Sheriff's Baby,* and many others. His real work, however, was not until 1914, when *The Birth of a Nation* was produced as an answer to Italy's 'super' film *Quo Vadis?* of 1912. It was decided that *The Birth of a Nation* was to be the world's greatest film, in twelve reels, with many thousands of extras. In the customary manner of Griffith, a theme on a large scale was selected, based on the result of the enfranchisement of the negro, with added high-spot interest in the war of the North and the South and the Ku Klux Klan vendettas. Financially, the picture was a success, although much was said at the time about it being anti-Negro propaganda. Nevertheless, propaganda or not, all America, and later the rest of the world, went to see it, and if it achieved nothing else, it certainly placed the cinema as an entertainment and as a provocator of argument on the same level as the theatre and the novel.

The Birth of a Nation relied entirely on the cinema for its success, for it carried no well-known names as a box-office attraction. It stood alone as a film : and as a film it was triumphant. The chief faults to be found with the construction were in the slow, meaningless opening; the realistic replicas of Abraham Lincoln's study and the theatre in which he was assassinated; and the badly-handled, insufferably dull battle scenes.[1] Nevertheless, the importance of the film lay in its achievement of attracting the notice of serious-minded people to the expressive power of the cinema.

For his next picture Griffith again chose an immense theme, so vast that the film became unwieldy and depressing, and thereby defeated its own purpose. He sought to convey the idea that intolerance pervades the minds of all peoples, from past to present, dragging with it despair, murder, and ruin. The immensity of the idea (which would be turned down with scorn by any scenario department of to-day) was Griffith's undoing, for he was forced by the limits of time alone to treat the theme generally. *Intolerance* did not set out to tell a narrative; instead, it utilised four separate historical incidents, divided by centuries of time, to express one central theme. It has been said that *Intolerance* was the first attempt to use the film in its correct manner. The four incidents chosen by Griffith to illustrate his theme were : the fall of Babylon; the intolerance of the world and the Pharisees towards Christ; the massacre of St. Bartholomew; and a modern story of capital and labour, set in an atmosphere of misunderstanding, vicious gambling dens and corrupt orphanages.

[1] I do not find this to-day (1947); the handling of the battle scenes is one of the major virtues of the film.

These four separate stories were connected by a link, supplied by Walt Whitman's lines ' out of the cradle endlessly rocking ', which manifested itself in the form of Lillian Gish aimlessly rocking a cradle, appearing at regular intervals throughout the course of the film. The four stories were developed slowly, gradually working up into a Griffith crescendo, with quadruple action in the climactic ending, rounded off by a touch of symbolism. The Persians approached Babylon; Christ was crucified; the Huguenots were butchered; but the young man in the modern story was saved by a miraculous ' last-minute-rescue '.

Intolerance was, and still is, the greatest spectacular film. Its ingredients, the sumptuous feast of Belshazzar, the wild attack on the massive walls of Babylon, the scene at Golgotha, the struggling hordes of extras and the vast sets, have been at the back of every American producer's mind ever since. They are the urge and comfort of Mr. De Mille. They are indirectly responsible for the many imitations— *The Ten Commandments, Noah's Ark,* and the Hungarian *Sodom and Gomorrah,* all of which failed because they lacked the fierce intensity of purpose and skill of Griffith. *Intolerance* had the makings of a great film, but failed because of its own immensity. A film, even in twelve reels, cannot embrace the width and depth of a theme such as *Intolerance* sought to carry, without the elimination of detail. Under these circumstances the theme at once becomes superficial. The theme carried no power because of its *general* treatment. At the time of production, *Intolerance* had the reputation of being the most expensive film ever produced; the high reputation of Griffith from *The Birth of a Nation;* an air of mystery, for it was made under a veil of secrecy; but it was a failure because of its own intolerance. The American people were puzzled by its name, by its meaning, and by its hugeness. They took a dislike to it.[1]

[1] In retrospect this is perhaps an underestimate of *Intolerance.* Seen again in recent years, the film stands up well, especially its fine editing.

Of Griffith's later films there is not a great deal to be written. It is well-known that he did not live up to the promise of his first two achievements, that he brooded in the darkness, and tried to repeat his successes in a different guise. *Broken Blossoms,* inspired by a short story by Thomas Burke, is of interest because it was the forerunner of the sordid, dilapidated slum theme that has been present in the cinema ever since Griffith suggested it. The film succeeded for only one reason; it had no other asset to carry its weight across to the audience save the direction. Lillian Gish, despite her earlier playing, was not yet considered in the ranks of stardom; Richard Barthelmess was unknown; and the story was simple, tragic, and sordid, with no call for the spectacle of Griffith's earlier work. Yet *Broken Blossoms,* with all its morbidness, was a success. As a film it achieved great emotional power, due entirely to the strong direction. It created many things, the most significant being the establishment of Lillian Gish as a tear-stained slum girl, which she has been on and off ever since; it founded the school of dirt and depression among dirty plates and unswept rooms; and it influenced Stroheim in the making of *Greed.* Moreover, it showed producers that a simple, human story, without the box-office attractions of silk legs and spectacle, could be made successful if handled by an intelligent director. *Broken Blossoms* relied on the cinema for its success.

Orphans of the Storm, with its setting in the popular French Revolution, was another new undertaking for Griffith. It was romantic costume film technique as distinct from the reconstruction of the ancient world of *Intolerance.* Financially, the orphans were peculiarly pleasing, especially when it is remembered that costume films are usually considered to be failures even before they are made. They secured over a hundred thousand pounds in this country alone, being advertised as based on Carlyle's *French Revolution.* Actually, it was Hollywood's French Revolution, with little of the real Griffith, save in the construction of the ' last-minute-rescue ' at the guillotine. But Griffith was beginning to repeat himself. He seemed forced to go back over his ground and it became tiring to watch the rescue of Miss Gish, however strong Griffith's sympathies for her may have been. *One Exciting Night,* a thriller that excelled in thrills but nothing else; *America, Isn't Life Wonderful?,* and *Sally of the Sawdust Ring* were all reiterations of early Griffith methods. *Isn't Life Wonderful?,* an essay on the food shortage problem in post-war Germany, was meant to express an idea. But when he made this film, Griffith appeared not to have appreciated the progressive movements in the whole cinema around him. Later, he was forced to climb down from his fence of independence, join the Famous-Players-Lasky Company, and under their supervision made *Sally of the Sawdust,* a crude, sentimental picture of circus life which was financially successful. Since then he has continued to make a series of uninteresting pictures of unequal merit, among them being *Drums of Love, The Sorrows of Satan, The Battle of the Sexes* (notable for the playing of the talented Phyllis Haver and Jean Hersholt), and *The Lady of the Pavements,* with the vivacious Lupe Velez. He is now engaged on a dialogue version of *Abraham Lincoln.*

In general, the work of Griffith is notable for the expression of one central idea, a single theme carrying the film through from start to finish. This unity of purpose has been lacking in his recent films. Round this idea he constructs his scenario action and his characters, placing them in their natural surroundings, and finds players suitable for their sincere characterisation. It will be observed that once Griffith has moulded an actor or an actress into the desired shape, he seldom continues to use that player. Having employed them with great success for the expression of one or two of his films, he gives them to the smaller directors, by whom they are made into stars. As far as possible, Griffith works with raw material, and in this respect he resembles the Soviets. Lillian Gish is admittedly an exception to this theory, but she is perhaps the prototype of the Griffith heroine. Griffith nearly always creates his parts on the same characteristics. In particular the tear-stained, sobbing young woman, with or without child, smiling behind the misery with a wistful smile is recalled. Griffith's important work may lie in the past, in the early days of the spectacle film when theories on continuity and rhythmic construction were young, but he is a power in the American cinema that must be stressed. There is much to be learnt to-day from his early ideas, and his influence on the more eminent of Hollywood directors is marked. Both King Vidor and Erich von Stroheim learnt their early cinema from Griffith. Although his ideas are sentimental, his technique elementary, and his construction of the old type, it is upon them that much of the best of modern film treatment is built.

On turning to the work of Erich von Stroheim, a barrier is at once found to the true appreciation of his artistry by the fact that he has gained for himself (chiefly on account of his masterly bluffing of the American producers and by his display of meaningless magnificence) the status of a genius. It will frequently be found that when argument is broached about a Stroheim film, this powerful word is solemnly pronounced and further analysis, if any has been made at all, is impossible. I suggest, however, that just as Stroheim has bluffed Hollywood with such admirable neatness, it is equally possible for him to have deceived the intelligence of his ardent admirers among the *jeunes cinéastes*. It is not denied that Stroheim has made one exceptionally interesting and powerful film, *Greed*, but on the other hand it is asserted that his filmic knowledge is inadequate. He seems incapable of recognising the limits and de-limits of the cinema. The fact that *Greed*, in its original form, was twenty reels in length, and that two hundred thousand feet of film were shot when making *The Wedding March*, indicates neither the mind of a genius nor a great film director, as so many of his admirers seem to believe. On the contrary, his obvious incapability to express his ideas adequately in ten thousand feet of film shows clearly his lack of understanding of the resources of the medium. Added to which, Stroheim has unfortunately earned for himself the reputation of gross extravagance, and so great is the faith of Hollywood in vastness on any scale that, if Stroheim ceased to squander money on his productions, he would no longer be called a genius.[1] Whilst fully appreciating the fact that a director must have freedom in order to express his ideas, it cannot but be admitted that if he has to take nearly twenty times the amount of film actually used in the final copy, he has no idea of what he wants or how he is going to achieve his desired result, the two elementary qualifications of a director. Stroheim's greatest faults are his love of excess and his failure to express his mind filmically. He labours his points and repeats his arguments to the limits of boredom, losing thereby any subtlety or meaning that they might convey. Typical of this was the painful gold colouring in *Greed,* which very nearly wrecked the film, and the superfluous cherry blossom in *The Wedding March.* Both these attempts at atmospheric emphasis lost their effect by their redundancy. Instead of becoming suggestive, they became irritating.

Stroheim's best work is to be seen in small pieces. There are many sequences in his films that stand out alone for their extreme beauty and sympathetic feeling. This in itself suggests the lack of unity and central purpose of the Stroheim film. Frequently it is declared that he is hampered in his realisation by lack of money, but in consideration of the extraordinary licence allowed him in the past, this argument for his failure is hardly convincing. If Stroheim is the filmic genius he is said to be, then he will express his purpose under the limited conditions of film-making.

Admittedly, this awkward predicament of having to spend money in order to keep up appearances is regrettable, but Stroheim has no one to blame save himself. If it were

[1] It has been said subsequently, on good authority, that much of the extravagance credited to Stroheim was pure publicity build-up by his producers. *Vide: World Film News.* Vol. 2, No. 6. September, 1937.

possible to see Stroheim in small, separate sequences, it would then be correct to call him a superbly talented experimentalist. One of the most beautiful sequences realised in the history of the cinema was the short hospital scene in *The Wedding March,* exquisite alike in feeling, acting, simplicity, and lighting. Photographically, it was magnificent, the range of tones shimmering from deep velvety blacks to dazzling gauzed whites with perfect gradation. But the fact remains that if Stroheim suddenly dropped his pose, became serious, ceased his expensive bluffing campaign, and made a film of normal length, with a normal amount of money and in a normal space of time, producers would believe that they had been cheated out of their money, and the film would be regarded as a joke, whilst probably it would be a masterpiece.

It is said that Erich von Stroheim has led a stormy life in Hollywood trying to combat commercialism with artistic temperament. Perhaps it would be more truthful to say that Stroheim has commercialised his artistic temperament. No producing centre in the world save Hollywood would have accepted Stroheim's whimsical fancies. His ideas are always made to look as if they are conceived on a great scale, calling for vast financial resources, and naturally, when he carries them out, strict executive eyes are watchful of his movements. But Stroheim, carried away by his ' genius ', enlarges and extends his ideas as he puts them into realisation, far beyond original specification. As is only to be expected, trouble ensues between the two parties. It is remarkable that, despite Stroheim's failings, producing companies still continue to place their faith and money in him. The case of *The Merry-Go-Round* is almost too well-known to be cited. Report has it that Stroheim spent so long in showing a squad of soldiers how to salute in the Stroheim manner that the producers finally grew tired of the game, ejected Stroheim and put in Rupert Julian to finish the picture.

Stroheim was at one time an officer in the army of Franz Josef of Austria. Later, he came to New York to live alternately as gardener, ostler, dish-washer, etc., all of which are excellent occupations for a potential film director, for they breed an understanding of reality. He arrived in Hollywood about the beginning of the war, found work as an extra, and played the Pharisee in Griffith's *Intolerance*. His first achievement, however, did not come until after the war, when he directed and acted in *Blind Husbands*. Stroheim's acting as the superior, smart, salacious Austrian officer on holiday, with just sufficient power to seduce any woman he happened to meet, was outstanding for its truth. The film had a good reception, and he proceeded to make *Foolish Wives* in the same way. Once more he acted and directed, adding touches to the lascivious Austrian officer, and proved himself capable of progress. *Foolish Wives* will always remain an extraordinary film. It was subtly sexual and provocative. Old-fashioned in technique when seen by modern eyes, it nevertheless still retains much of its force and dramatic power. Following this came the disastrous affair of *The Merry-Go-Round,* with Norman Kerry and Mary Philbin, which was left unfinished by him. Soon afterwards, Metro-Goldwyn gave him the production of *Greed,* adapted from Frank Norris's novel *McTeague,* and Stroheim made the film on which his reputation stands to-day. Why and how Metro-Goldwyn came to give Stroheim the opportunity to make this picture still remains a mystery, for the theme of *Greed* was the last possible form of box-office appeal for Metro-Goldwyn, always a firm of showmanship, to be interested in.

Stroheim set out to show the loathsome results of a human being's passion for money; how it affected the woman whose passion it was; and how it reacted on the persons with whom she came into contact. The action was woven around a wedding and a double murder, with death in a torrid desert by thirst and exposure. *Greed* was the essence of sordidness, the depth of depression and the horror of distorted human nature. But it was sheer, undiluted truth; the essence of reality expressed in the powerful terms of the cinema. Not one ray of light, of warmth, of cheer disturbed its meandering length. It was the concentrated dreariness of life. From its opening among the tree-clad hills which surrounded the gold mine, through the depths of the dark squalor of middle-class life, to the murder of the wife and the final sequence in the valley of death, it was disturbing. The public that saw it loathed it, yet were fascinated. Americans frankly disliked it; its moral that money is worthless either roused their consciences uncomfortably, or was passed over unseen. They could not believe that someone had made a film about a man who murdered his wife because she had hoarded money. It was too near to life, too damning in its truth, too frank in its rightness. Stroheim's days as a dish-washer had shown him too much.

In *Greed,* more than in any other film, Stroheim strengthened his theme by insistence on detail and by the consciousness of inanimate objects. Stroheim knew the value of the camera's faculty for the selection of the particular. He used it as it had never been used before in the establishment of psychological atmosphere. The dingy wallpaper, the automatic piano, the dirty dishes, the unmade bed, the unemptied wash-basin, the brass bedstead, the soiled handkerchief, all these details, insignificant in themselves, were used to build up an effect of squalor. It was from *Greed* that Sternberg acquired his talent for using sordid material. There is also an affinity in the use of detail between Stroheim and Pabst. Both directors are aware of the consciousness of the inanimate. Both use objects rather than persons to create atmosphere. It is possible to see *The Joyless Street* (1925) and *Greed* (1923) on the same level. The opening scene of *Jeanne Ney,* most of *The Salvation Hunters,* and portions of *The Docks of New York* have distinct relationship with the bedroom of McTeague in *Greed.* The final sequence in the desert, with the sense of space, the blazing sun, the cracked sand, the shot mule, stands alone as a superb rendering of environment. *Greed* was Victorian, but it was cinema. Despite its faults, the gold coloration, the too sudden development of the wife's character, the ridiculous make-up of Gibson

Gowland, this was Stroheim's greatest picture. It is interesting to note that Stroheim's explanation for the length of *Greed*, said variously to have been anything from twenty to a hundred reels in its original version, was that he used no more film than was absolutely necessary for the filmic expression of the theme. This is an evasive statement typical of Stroheim, to which there is no answer. Nevertheless, the copy generally shown, about ten thousand feet in length, left much to be desired in editing. The film fell evenly into two halves. It is assumed that the transition period after the wedding was eliminated, an unfortunate act that took weight from the otherwise brilliant performance of Zasu Pitts as the hoarding wife. Her acting, under the control of Stroheim, had seldom been equalled by any other American screen actress

The next Stroheim picture was a reaction from the reality of *Greed*. It was a movie version of a popular musical comedy in the Ruritanian manner, complete with princesses and monocled lieutenants, flashing sabres and pink roses. *The Merry Widow* was as much a story-movie as *Greed* was a thematic film. Occasionally, amid the welter of crown princes and chorus girls, a stagey duel and a coronation in the true Hollywood manner (colour), there came a flash of Stroheim technique, a sparkle of wit akin to the *Forbidden Paradise* of Ernst Lubitsch. To his credit, Stroheim at least made the synthetic Mae Murray do something else than mince, and he handled John Gilbert as he has not been handled since. But despite this, the picture was nothing more than a typical Metro-Goldwyn adaptation of a musical comedy, with tuneful music and Parisian humour. Because it had been successful in the theatre, the producers calculated that *The Merry Widow* would be a successful, money-making movie. But why give it to Erich von Stroheim, the maker of *Greed*, to produce?

Stroheim pursued his luxurious way, passed into the hands of Paramount and began *The Wedding March* in June 1926. He finished the picture in the late spring of 1927. He spent over twelve months in trying to edit his

37. THE LAST LAUGH, directed by F. W. Murnau.   Emil Jannings.   [German, 1924]

38. WAXWORKS, directed by Paul Leni.   [German, 1924]

39. THE IRON HORSE, directed by John Ford.   [American, 1924]

40. FORBIDDEN PARADISE, directed by Ernst Lubitsch.   Rod La Rocque, Pola Negri.
[American, 1924]

vast mass of footage into some unified whole, calmly suggesting to Paramount that he should make two films out of it, until finally they lost their temper, and gave the bins of celluloid to someone else to edit. The successor, however, did no better than Stroheim, and the assembling was turned over to yet another professional cutter, who succeeded in condensing the original matter into about ten reels. Eventually, it was shown in Britain early in 1929, three years after it had been begun, and, as was only to be expected, was disjointed, erratic, and uneven in quality. Von Stroheim, of course, wished it to be clearly known that he entirely disclaimed the version shown to the public and washed his hands of the whole matter. Without prejudice, he had mainly himself to blame. In the copy presented to the public, *The Wedding March* was lacking in unity, uncertain in treatment, and crudely interspaced with cheaply written titles, but, for the student of the cinema, it contained some beautiful passages. The setting was Vienna; with a background of falling cherry blossom; sentimental beer gardens that were out of joint with some topical-news shots of the city at the beginning; a scandal-mongering and poverty-stricken court; and a coloured procession with a lifelike replica of old Franz Josef. It was burdened with little story-interest, being concerned chiefly with the tragic love of a prince for a poor but charming girl, and the fatal circumstances that compelled the former to do the will of his parents and marry according to his status. It was pathetic, appealing, and wistful; sentimental, charming, and Victorian. One recalls it now by a few isolated sequences. Prince Nicki's first meeting with the girl, when he is on parade and is unable to speak to her; the hospital sequence which has been mentioned (see page 157); the delightful interplay between Stroheim and Maude George, as his mother; and Zasu Pitts's exquisite playing of the lame princess, the compulsory wife of the unwilling Prince Nicki. Notable, also, was the use of heavily-gauzed photography for the love scenes, in contrast with the sharp, clear-cut camerawork of the butcher's scenes. Although the public version stopped short with the unhappy marriage of the prince and princess, to the grief of the poor but charming girl, the original conception continued the theme to a hunting trip in the mountains and the death of the limping princess. From an examination of the still-photographs of the latter, unshown part of the picture, it seems of greater interest than the first. Although it is improbable that the second half of *The Wedding March* will ever be seen, there is perhaps a possibility of its being shown as a curiosity at some future private film society performance?

After his retirement from Paramount, Stroheim started the direction of Gloria Swanson in *Queen Kelly,* in which Miss Swanson played the part of a prostitute. The film was apparently finished and in the cutting stage when dialogue made its unseemly intrusion. It was deemed unwise to attempt the synchronisation of the picture owing to its unsuitability as a talking vehicle for Miss Swanson. Instead, she went under the direction of Edmund Goulding in *The Trespasser,* while Stroheim went into *The Great Gabbo,* under James Cruze. Of this latter film I find it hard to write, for so cluttered up was it with singing, dancing, talking, backstage, musical comedy stuff, that Stroheim was given no chance with his part. Added to which, he was obliged to wear bad uniforms and was overpowered by the worst coloured sequences I have ever seen.

Stroheim as a director has given much to the cinema in an indirect and obscure manner. Stroheim as an actor is always a source of interest. Stroheim as a 'cinematic genius' is not to be suffered.

Charles Chaplin's greatest asset is his deep understanding of human nature; an understanding that has not been reached without contact with the low, depressing, morbid side of life; a contact with the under-privileged, the poor and the hungry. Chaplin, like Stroheim, Pudovkin, Eisenstein and other good directors, bases his sense of reality on his years of poverty and insignificance. Without the circumstances of his days of struggle, Chaplin would never have reached the heights to which he has attained. The financial profits of his pictures have meant little to him, except that they were a proof of the success of his message to the world, and that they have prevented him recently from the necessity of working for a firm other than his own. No man has made Chaplin what he is to-day save Chaplin himself. He believes in two things : himself and the cinema.

For his own films, Chaplin claims nothing but that they have amused and lightened the hearts of millions. If he hears that they are badly shown, with harsh musical accompaniment, he is irritated because the carelessness of others is destroying his purpose. For this reason, he welcomes the mechanically-synchronised musical score. There are moralists who say that Chaplin should be happy because he gives happiness and joy to others. But Chaplin, I believe, is an unhappy, disconsolate, and lonely man. He is constantly overwhelmed and saddened by the immensity of life. As an artist, Chaplin lives apart from the rest of humanity. What artist, who ever fulfilled the expression of his thoughts, was ever happy? For to realise them he has had to suffer, to experience bitter loneliness, and to endure the aching pain of loveliness. He has, too, to live in unrest. With Chaplin, I suspect, it is all this, for it is to be seen in his films. An artist such as Chaplin can live only, and have interest alone, in the work upon which he is engaged at the moment. This work demands intense concentration, as indeed does that of any real film director. When Chaplin is conceiving and producing a film, it is disastrous for him to have any thoughts but those related to that film in his mind.

Chaplin conceives every gesture, every scene, and every sequence of his films from every possible point of view. He possesses a tremendous power of visualisation, and a valuable knowledge of the psychological effect of the visual image. He was one of the first directors to realise the camera's capability for recording detail and movement. The language of Chaplin, like that of acrobats and clowns, is international, for it is visual in gesture and universal in theme. The idea behind every Chaplin film is easily understood by every one, according to their powers of receptivity. Chaplin realises that the camera records physical movement far more closely than the eyes of a music-hall audience. Miming before a camera lens is very different from gesturing before an audience. The projected image on the screen enlarges and enhances the smallest of movements. Like other great directors, Chaplin makes supreme use of camera emphasis. Little movements mean big things in a Chaplin film, and, moreover, his invention of detail is amazing. Three memorable instances occur to the mind. The unforgettable dance of the rolls in *The Gold Rush;* the inimitable crooked finger suggestive of the maggot in the apple in *The Circus;* and the magnificent pantomime scene of the David and Goliath sermon in *The Pilgrim.* These three incidents show with immeasurable force the marvellous sense of filmic detail possessed by Chaplin. He is a genius in the art of suggestion and inference.

In any other medium but the film his genius would be negligible. There is nothing in a Chaplin film which has not been put there for a purpose, and the effect of which has not been calculated. He pre-conceives the psychological effect on an audience of every small strip of film. For this reason his work is never littered with lavish display. It is his faculty for discovering expressive detail, as distinct from his individual personality, which renders Chaplin the supreme artist. *The Circus* alone showed how, by his unique inventiveness of mind, he transmuted the traditional methods of fun into real uproarious humour under the eyes of the traditionalists themselves. This was in the rehearsal episode—the William Tell act and the Barber's Shop business. Chaplin has never excelled the brilliance of this scene.

Chaplin has reduced misfortune, trepidation, disillusion, and suffering to emotions of laughter. His adventures are against the hard-hearted, the oppressors and the selfish, for he knows the smug complacency, the hypocrisy, and the

injustice of this world. He is continually fleeing from the
angry arm of the law, which wants him for some misunderstood or unconscious offence. Blows, insults, and abuse are
heaped upon him, and yet the audience roars at his discomfort. Deprived of all that he holds dear, companion-
ship, food, happiness, Chaplin remains a figure of fun to
the masses. To others, perhaps more sensitive, he is
pathetic, for in some way he is themselves, their lives and
their emotions. *The Circus* was one of the greatest
tragedies in the history of the film and yet it was magnificently funny. With his alert, sensitive, illimitable resourcefulness, his well-meaning, misunderstood kindliness,
Chaplin stands unique in the cinema. It is the resolution of
the man which secures the affections of the public to him.
There is no comparable effect to the feelings roused by the
closing sequence of a Chaplin film; that final defiant
gesture of every picture when, buoyed up by eternal faith
and hope, Chaplin fades into the distance, into, as it were,
the opening of his next film. There is a definite link between
all of the Chaplin comedies. When he is seen afresh, after
a lapse of time, he appears to have just come round the
corner from his last film, to mingle with another crowd of
idlers. Although his productions are now separated by
years, there is still that link, a continuity of idea between
one film and the next. Despite this, Chaplin is not a type;
he is not an actor; he is an individual searching for a
satisfaction which he may never discover. For this reason
alone, if dialogue is introduced into a Chaplin film; if there
is the slightest concession to the public taste created by the
producers, by the Warners, the Laskys, the Zukors, the
Foxes; then the Chaplin film as it is known, universally
appreciated and adored, will cease to be.

Each of Chaplin's pictures is a theme woven around one
character. He is naturally aware of his remarkable
individuality, for it will have been noticed that as the years
have advanced, he has been gradually eliminating the
caricaturish element from his pictures. With his own
development, the characters with which he peoples his

stories have become more reasonable and more real, until, in *The Circus*, they were quite natural. It is interesting to compare the supporting cast in the latter film with that of *Shoulder Arms*. The flowing false moustaches, the big noses, the fat stomachs, the ridicule, the slapstick are gone. Actually, it will be remembered that Chaplin began as a ' funny man ', evolved through these knockabout comedies a distinct personality, and eventually epitomised not only the down-trodden under-dog, but the disappointment and discouragement of the whole world. It is of point, for a moment, to recall Chaplin of *The Kid's Auto Races, The Immigrant, Sunnyside, The Kid, The Gold Rush,* and finally, *The Circus,* tracing the development of the leading lady and cast as well as of Chaplin himself.

By way of example, the treatment of Merna Kennedy in the last-named film was evidence of Chaplin's interest in feminine personality; a facet of his character which was largely responsible for the subtlety of *A Woman of Paris*.

As is now well-known, Chaplin was originally engaged for film work by Adam Kessel, who happened to see the young comedian when he was touring far from his London home in a pantomine-revue affair called *A Night in a London Club*. Kessel signed Chaplin for a year's work at Los Angeles, beginning in November of 1913, the pictures being made under the direction of the inimitable Mack Sennett. These comedies are usually known as the Keystone period, that being the name of the producing firm. Their character was pure slapstick with the customary ingredients—throwing of custard pies, falling down, hitting of people on the head and being hit back. In nearly all these early one- or two-reelers, Chaplin was not the pre-eminent member of the cast, with the exception of the second, the already mentioned *Kid's Auto Races* (1914), wherein he merely became funny by continuous repetition of the same motive. The film was without story and scenario, and is of interest merely because it represents Chaplin's appearance in the sphere which he was to make so peculiarly his own. Of this period, also, is *The Fatal*

Mallet, in which Chaplin and Mack Sennett alternately hit one another on the head in their rivalry to embrace Mabel Normand, who disconcertedly sat aside until Chaplin struck her in the rear with the toe of his boot. A year later, Chaplin supported Marie Dressler, at that time a well-known stage actress, in *Tillie's Punctured Romance,* together with Mack Swain, Mabel Normand, and Chester Conklin. This comedy was made in six reels, a hitherto unprecedented length, and took fourteen weeks to prepare as compared with the customary one week for a single reeler. Preceding this was *The Face on the Bar Room Floor,* one of the two attempts at burlesque by Chaplin, with Edna Purviance and Chester Conklin. From these crudities, Chaplin continued into the Essanay period and a series of comedies in the true slapstick manner followed, such as *Champion Charlie, Charlie the Perfect Lady* (in which he played without a moustache, again with Edna Purviance and Chester Conklin), *Charlie at the Bank, Carmen, Shanghaied, Charlie at the Show,* etc.[1] Many of these contained the dream element, being his fond imaginings whilst dozing over his work, and in them all he was beginning to assert the individuality of the later pictures. So successful were these from a financial point of view that, in 1916, Chaplin signed a contract with the Mutual Film Corporation, for whom he made many films, including *Easy Street, The Floorwalker,* the one-man effort *One A.M., The Fireman, The Rink, The Pawnshop, The Cure,* and many others, in most of which he was supported by Edna Purviance. Later, he made the famous Million Dollar Chaplins for the First National Company, including *Sunnyside, A Dog's Life, Shoulder Arms, The Kid, A Day's Pleasure, Pay Day, The Idle Class,* and *The Pilgrim,* the last two of which prepared the way for the Chaplin of to-day. Though conceived in terms of travesty, they were all excellent in their construction and their unification of Chaplin's personality. Not, however, until the United

[1] In some cases, these are the British release titles.

Artists' productions of *The Gold Rush* and *The Circus,* of 1925 and 1927 respectively, was there to be found the true realisation of the artist. Both these films were superb examples of cinema; their composition and continuity was flawless; their exposition of the genius of Chaplin unrivalled. Recollection of them makes it necessary to restate Chaplin's rare faculty of exact timing. Like the Soviets, he is aware, to the nearness of a frame, of the precise length for which a shot should be held on the screen. Although his filmic knowledge may not express itself in the same technique as the Soviet school, nevertheless it is unique in American film production.

Quite apart from his contribution to the cinema as a self-directed actor, it is of importance to recall Chaplin's single essay in the serious direction of others. Just in the same way as *The Cabinet of Doctor Caligari, Greed,* and *Battleship Potemkin* are landmarks in the development of the film, so *A Woman of Paris* was the founder of a type of film-movie that has flourished in Hollywood since its production in 1923. Chaplin wrote the scenario and directed the picture himself, and, as with the later comedies, it was well-balanced in tension and actional sequence, the continuity flowing with an admirable smoothness. He chose a simple, natural theme of a boy's love for a girl; a misunderstanding; the development of their separate lives, the girl as an intelligent *demi-mondaine,* the boy as a temperamental creative artist; their re-meeting and the boy's resultant suicide at the discovery of his lover's way of living. The actual story-interest was of little value; it was the thoughts and mental reactions of the characters that gave rise to the action which were of interest. But what mattered most was Chaplin's treatment. He not only introduced the audience to a cultured prostitute and an exquisite *roué* in a drawing-room setting of flowers and gilt furniture, but he dug deep down into motives so that beneath their superficial actions could be discerned the quick workings of their minds. By subtle direction he laid bare the reasons of their petty quarrels, their jealousies and contrary complexes. He attacked both man and woman-hood in this unforgettable film. He showed an under-standing of the machinery of human mentality that hitherto had been merely suspected from his own comedies. He was reminiscent, if the comparison may be allowed, of the wit and skill of Wilde. The joy of watching *A Woman of Paris* unfold its length was only equalled by that of *Bed and Sofa*. With both films the spectator experienced an inward sense of irresistible delight due, I believe, largely to the design and balance of the continuity. This is not, of course, to suggest for a moment that Chaplin and Room have any similarity, save in an understanding of the principles of continuity.

A Woman of Paris marked the first appearance of Adolphe Menjou in the suave, cynical, elegant, slightly humorous man-about-town rôle which he has so often repeated under inferior direction. The original part, under the genius of Chaplin, was inimitable in its fascinating, attractive, inscrutable, gentlemanly behaviour. Only on two other occasions has the *svelte* Menjou been so clever—in a modification of the Chaplin part in Lubitsch's *The Marriage Circle* and *Forbidden Paradise*. With all respect to the artistry of Lubitsch, his handling of Menjou lacked the knowledge of human nature possessed by Chaplin. With an estimable sense of gratitude and recognition for her long support, Chaplin gave the leading rôle in this brilliant satire to Edna Purviance. He himself appeared anonymously for a brief moment in the guise of a French railway porter.

Significant in Chaplin's direction was the use of the close-up for emphasis of detail. He was able on several occasions to suggest the atmosphere of a scene by the visual image of a single character. No one will forget the im-movable face of the *masseuse* during the beauty treatment of Miss Purviance, her mechanical procedure with her job whilst the girl friends called in to chatter. Chaplin here was treading on the ground of Eisenstein, but, it will be recalled, was treading unconsciously. The brilliance of this film is remembered by its small incidents. The delightful episode of the rope of pearls; the miniature saxophone (an instance of Chaplin's inventiveness); the box of chocolates; the pocket handkerchief; a napkin full of holes; these were the memorable details of this amazing film. Mention is also to be made of the great scene of the *demimondaine* at the bed of the dead artist; the breaking to the mother of the news of her son's suicide; the boy seated alone on his bed, distraught, with a flood of white light on the bedclothes dazzling out of the blackness of the room. These are episodes unforgettable for their dramatic treatment.

A Woman of Paris inspired Lubitsch's *The Marriage Circle,* and, following in its wake, a hundred other movies from the hands of the young men of Hollywood. As is generally the case, the imitations lacked the sparkle, the wit, and the intelligence of the master film.

Both Douglas Fairbanks and Mary Pickford are to be regarded with the warmest admiration, for they are good forces in the cinema. In the first place, neither of them is an artist; nor, in the second place, can either of them be said to have any real idea of the values of acting. Yet they have both, in their own way, climbed from obscurity to the heights of universal popularity. Through years of hard work, they have become stars; but, paradoxically enough, it is not fitting to call either of them products of the star-system.[1] Neither Douglas Fairbanks nor his wife have become what they are now by aid of their respective producing companies. Like Chaplin, they have made themselves.

It is to the credit of Douglas Fairbanks and Mary Pickford that they are fully conscious of their limitations and capabilities in the expression afforded by the film. Fairbanks, one feels, realises only too well that he is neither an artist nor an actor in the accepted understanding of the terms. He is, on the contrary (and of this he is fully aware), a pure product of the medium of the cinema in

[1] Douglas Fairbanks died December, 1939.

which he seeks self-expression. But knowing his own limits and those of Hollywood, he will surround himself with persons who make claim to artistry. He will bring from France Maurice Leloir, a specialist in historical costume, to supervise in Hollywood the designs for *The Man in the Iron Mask*. He knew well, in this case, that no American designer had either the knowledge or taste to reconstruct with any faith the costumes of seventeenth-century France. In the same way, Fairbanks saw the German films *Destiny, Waxworks, Sumurun*, and *Siegfried*, and realised their value as examples of fantasy then unknown in America. He determined to learn from continental intelligence. *The Thief of Bagdad* was a poor film, badly designed and conceived with false artistry, but nevertheless it is impossible not to appreciate the motive that underlay its production. Fairbanks made a definite attempt in this film to do something better, to step out of the Hollywood groove. He is to be admired for his courage, for there were few others in California willing to try the chance. *The Thief of Bagdad* was not a financial success; it was not a good production; but its presence lies to the credit of Fairbanks. Curiously enough it is in this wish to encourage the ' art ' of the cinema that Fairbanks strikes the wrong note. His most recent films have not had the rough power, the intensity or the vigour which made his earlier pictures such good examples of cinema. Of late years there has been too much of the ulterior motive, too much lavishness and too little Fairbanks. Disregarding the obvious advance in technique due to mechanical progress, *The Mark of Zorro* was a very much better example of the filmic abilities of Fairbanks than either *The Gaucho* or *The Man in the Iron Mask*.

It may seem ridiculous to claim that Fairbanks, an acrobat who is unable to put drama into his gestures or emotion into his expressions, is one of the outstanding figures in the world of the cinema. Yet, by reason of his rhythm, his graceful motion and perpetual movement of acting material, Fairbanks is essentially filmic. He has, it is true, no other

talent than his rhythm and his ever-present sense of pantomime, except perhaps his superior idea of showmanship. It
is certain that he sees in every situation of the past and of
the present a foundation for rhythmical movement. Just
as Chaplin learned to walk a tight-rope for the making of
The Circus, so Fairbanks has learnt to fence, to crack a
whip, to throw a lariat.

At first glance these gestures may be explained by the
Fairbanks enthusiasm, but they are to be attributed to more
important reasons than the sheer love of doing things right.
He saw in those accomplishments some basis for filmic
movement other than mere acrobatics. He realised that the
actions were superbly graceful in their natural perfection,
as indeed are any gestures born out of utility. He delights
equally in the swing of a cloak, the fall of the ostrich
feather in his hat, the mounting of his horse, the hang of
his sword, the slender form of his doublet. One remembers
the prologue to that early film *A Modern Musketeer,* a
small gem that could be shown by itself. In all his costume
pictures Fairbanks took the utmost pleasure in the
romanticism that the clothes of the period offered to him.
In *The Black Pirate, The Three Musketeers,* and *Robin
Hood,* he made every possible play with the details of the
period. He delighted in D'Artagnan's duels, in the Earl of
Huntingdon's tournament, in the Spanish Main romanticism
of the pirates. The Petruchio of *The Taming of the Shrew,*
jackboot on head and apple-core in hand, was a symbol of
the romance of Fairbanks. It needed a great man to carry
off that costume with grandeur. I can think of no other
personality in the cinema who could have so displayed the
courage of his convictions. In the same way that Chaplin
is the centralised character of his work, so is Fairbanks the
sole *raison d'être* of his pictures. Despite Mary Pickford,
he dominated *The Taming of the Shrew.* Although none
of his films has been nominally directed by him, he is nevertheless the underlying mind behind every detail, however
small. The spirit of Fairbanks is at the base of every
factor in his productions; behind every movement, the

design of the sets, the choice of the cast, the lay-out of the continuity, the construction of escapes and situations, the making of the costumes, the technical perfection of the camerawork, the drama of the lighting. The mind of the man governs the architecture of the whole.

I have complained that this personality of Fairbanks, this love of complete supervision, has recently superseded his actual playing. This 'art' complex has ousted the Fairbanks of youth and energy. Not for one moment is the control of the man regretted, nor is his love of detail to be discouraged, but nevertheless, I believe that this feeling for magnificence has dwarfed the roughness of the original Fairbanks spirit. The bandit of *The Gaucho* was tame in comparison with the cowboy of *Heading South*. There is no question that, in his last three films, the production has been in advance of the actual screen work of Fairbanks. The individual motion, the defiant gesture and the swinging stride have been belittled by the splendour of the environment. There has been a tendency towards top-heaviness. There has been too much Fairbanks the producer and too little Fairbanks the acrobat. In the concentration upon his love of costume, of romantic sets, he has limited the actions of his own playing. He has failed to justify the heroism of his own existence. In order to appreciate the full meaning of Fairbanks, it is necessary to return to his earlier work, where his own movement and grace ran through every foot of the film. One recalls *The Mark of Zorro*, the latter part of *Robin Hood*, portions of *The Three Musketeers*, and particularly *The Lamb*, *The Matrimaniac*, *A Modern Musketeer*, *The Knickerbocker-Buckaroo*, *Arizona*, and *Heading South*. It is true that after *The Thief of Bagdad* he made an attempt to return to the real Fairbanks in *Don Q*, but the old spirit was absent.

In all the early Fairbanks films his overwhelming personality dominated the pretensions of a story and the elaboration of spectacle. The film sufficed in that it was always the exuberance of Fairbanks that held the audience. The stories were always composed around the same familiar structure, the inevitable hero, heroine and villain. They were located in different countries in order to retain the freshness of atmosphere, through which moved the ever-restless figure of Fairbanks; the essence of enthusiasm, good spirits, adventure, disreputableness, chivalry, and courtesy. The one aim used to be good-heartedness, to be attained by effortless energy. One recalls in this respect, the Artcraft series : *Reaching for the Moon, He Comes Up Smiling, Down to Earth,* and, later, *Mr. Fix It.* These moral uplift films were quite distinct from the adventure themes, the open-air romanticism of *The Lamb, The Man From Painted Post* and *Arizona,* which culminated, after the first World War, in *The Mark of Zorro.* Briefly, it is perceived that Fairbanks has come from the moral uplift, *Say, Young Fellow* type of film, through the cowboy and the bandit to the costume romanticism of *Robin Hood,* and the other personal productions on a large scale. With the exception of *Don Q* and parts of *Robin Hood,* he has now cloaked the full meaning of his vigour under the mantle of his own desire for magnificence.

It is obvious that the movements peculiar to Fairbanks could not possibly be conveyed by any other medium but the film. Fairbanks could not be theatre or literature. All the attributes of the cinema go to help the movement that envelops his productions. The properties of the camera, its device of slow-motion, add grace to his sweeping curves of action. I find it curious in this respect that Fairbanks, who is usually said to keep well abreast with current film production, has not shown more interest in the mobility of the camera. There was, it is true, a long travelling shot in the opening of *The Taming of the Shrew,* and another at the end, but these were purely atmospheric and not in any way attached to Fairbanks himself. It is possible, perhaps, to visualise the rhythm of Fairbanks being followed by the smoothly swinging path of Fritz Arno Wagner's camera, as one remembers the latter's work in *Jeanne Ney.* In such a way could the Fairbanks motive be most powerfully expressed.

Nevertheless, I earnestly hope that Fairbanks will make some return to his old outlook, when his movement stood for all that was good in the material cinema. The 'art' and 'moral' influence with which he has tried to imbue his big productions has not been acceptable, even though set in a background of William Cameron Menzies's structures. Not too easily can *The Thief of Bagdad,* with its chocolate box minarets and ludicrous winged monsters, be forgotten; the wasted situations of *The Gaucho* still rankle; and *The Man in the Iron Mask* was a false conception of romanticism, despite the Leloir designs, with a prologue and epilogue that were among the tritest things seen on the screen. *The Taming of the Shrew,* for all its splendid entertainment and its exposition of Fairbanks, lacked the fire of the earlier films. Alone, *The Black Pirate* stood out as a brilliant film. Taken for what it was, a glorious collection of impossible situations in delightful settings, it was as good as anything that Fairbanks has ever done. It was rapid in pace, strong in feeling, and, above all, it was stimulating. With *The Mark of Zorro,* it is his best work.

With the coming of the dialogue film, it became a commercial necessity for both Douglas Fairbanks and Mary Pickford to divert their talent along fresh channels. Miss Pickford went ahead of her husband and made *Coquette,* a film that raised much controversy, but Fairbanks hung back, contemplating presumably the needs of this new mechanical invention. For some time there had been suggestions that these two famous persons should appear in the same film, a dangerous and perhaps disastrous undertaking. But if ever a suitable occasion arose for their dual picture, then it was in this new species of cinema. Thus, the only way in which a proper appreciation of *The Taming of the Shrew* could be obtained was by regarding it from a business point of view. It was a superb piece of showmanship. The choice of a Shakespearean play was astute, for it meant that the dialogue was safe from criticism. True, people would complain at the prostitution of the play, but criticism could not be levelled at the lines themselves. That it was Shakespeare's play mattered not one jot. It was a commentary upon husbands and wives; it afforded a chance for spectacle; it was in all ways an admirable vehicle for the two personalities to be launched in a new manner. As a film, it was excellent entertainment, but it could not be considered as a proper cinematic exposition of the talent of either Douglas Fairbanks or his wife.

Of Mary Pickford I find difficulty in writing, for there is a consciousness of vagueness, an indefinable emotion as to her precise degree of accomplishment. In vain she has been described as the Cinderella of the screen, with an air of innocence that touches deeply the chords of the strongest heart. She is said to be ' the sweet young girl that every man desires some day to have for himself '. This may well be, but Mary Pickford as a business woman, acutely aware of the selling power of her sweetness, is the more interesting personality. The breakaway from the stereotyped part has been difficult for Mary Pickford. She tried, it will be remembered, once before with Lubitsch's *Rosita,* but the public apparently preferred the *Little Annie Roonies* to the Spanish singing girl. Nevertheless, it was clear that she could not continue to play the child of fifteen, and *Coquette* was a perfectly justified appearance. In *The Taming of the Shrew* she was swept off her feet by the tempestuosity of her husband, which was after all precisely what the story demanded. One hankers inevitably after the Pickford of *Human Sparrows* and *Daddy Long Legs,* but the commands of time are to be obeyed. The future for Miss Pickford will be difficult.

Both Mr. and Mrs. Douglas Fairbanks are extremely serious about this film business. They realise their responsibility. They are both of extreme importance to the cinema. With Chaplin, Stroheim, and, to a lesser extent, Griffith, they are the outstanding figures in the American cinema. It would be wise not to under-estimate the value of their work. They have separately and jointly given much that is good to the film. One feels also that they both have much left to give in the future, but it is

41. KEAN, directed by Nicholas Wolkoff. Nikolai Kolin, Ivan Mosjoukine. [French, 1924]

42. THE LATE MATTHEW PASCAL, directed by Marcel L'Herbier. Ivan Mosjoukine, Marcelle Pradot. [French, 1924]

43. THE BIG PARADE, directed by KING VIDOR. JOHN GILBERT, RENÉE ADORÉE.
[American, 1925]

44. TUMBLEWEEDS, directed by KING BAGGOTT. WILLIAM S. HART. [American, 1925]

dubious whether this will be by way of the dialogue film. Rather they will achieve even greater significance, perhaps, by a careful research of their past work and a study of the methods of the continental directors.

*

The importation of European talent into the studios of Hollywood has been already remarked upon, and it is important to observe the developments of the foreigners in their new surroundings and their indirect influence on the American film. The coming of Ernst Lubitsch[1] into the fold of Hollywood directors marked a definite era in the standard of the movie, and his artistry, together with that of his *confrères,* left a distinctive Germanic strain in the younger American school. It is to be remembered that despite apparent faults, the love of lavish display and the concession to salacious appeal, the American movies were at that time (1920 to 1923) popular throughout the world. They were being produced, moreover, with a high degree of technical accomplishment. Germany, on the other hand, had developed a type of film utterly different from the movie, a heavy, slow-moving, darkly-lit, studio film, bordering on the one side the psychological, and on the other, the fantastic. It has been seen that the Americans, instead of regarding this European child as a rival, took it as an ally, and the majority of the Germans, only too precariously placed in their own fluctuating industry, were not slow to accept the proffered contracts from Hollywood. The result of this fusion has been some extraordinary films, notable for their mixed tendencies.

In Europe, Lubitsch had directed many films, most notable being *Dubarry, Sumurun, The Flame,* with Pola Negri, and *Anne Boleyn* with Emil Jannings, when he followed Miss Negri across to California. He was an extremely efficient director with a leaning towards spectacle, a subtle sense of wit peculiar to himself, and a definite feeling for the dramatic in the manner of Reinhardt tradition. Lubitsch in America developed into a curious un-

[1] Died in Hollywood, December, 1947.

known quantity, who combined flashes of dexterous artistry, imbued with cunning, with much rather dull and boyish sentimentality. He started his American period in a bad vein, being given Mary Pickford and George Walsh to direct in a Spanish film, *Rosita,* in which his Germanic mind was in opposition to the star value of Miss Pickford. He had no idea of Hollywood production methods, and became confused in his outlook. Save for a few scenes of pictorial beauty, the film was best forgotten. His next picture, however, was much more the true Lubitsch, for following in the path of Chaplin's *A Woman of Paris,* with a hint of the James Cruze domestic comedies, he made *The Marriage Circle,* a witty, superficial, amusing, intimate commentary on modern life in Vienna and Paris, as Hollywood conceived them. Lubitsch contrived to continue where Chaplin had left off, leaving out the cynicism and inner meaning and concentrating on the lightness of the framework. With this frippery, Lubitsch set off all the young men in Hollywood in the same vein, making himself from time to time several other comedies of a similar nature, such as *Three Women, Kiss Me Again, Lady Windermere's Fan* (from the Wilde play) and *So This Is Paris,* all delightful, effervescent movies. In between these sweetmeats came Lubitsch's one really brilliant film, a satire on Hollywood so subtle and so crafty that to this day many Americans cannot perceive wherein lay its sting. In the first place, *Forbidden Paradise* was conceived by Famous-Players-Lasky as a rollicking Ruritanian melodrama, with good opportunities for spectacle and a reliable box-office appeal. Ernst Lubitsch, however, for once forgetting that he was being clever on an American salary, treated this farce, in a moment of inspiration, in such a manner that it satirised with a nicety of wit the entire American movie system. The scenario was adapted by that admirable scenarist, Hans Kraly, from a play called *The Czarina,* which dealt with the amorous intrigues of Catherine of Russia, but Lubitsch brought the thing up to date, putting it in a Ruritanian setting. The amorous moods of the queen, the fiery revolutionary disturbances suppressed by handy cheques, the delightful ins-and-outs of the court intrigues, were handled by Lubitsch with a perfection of satire. The continuity was pleasingly smooth, and he employed deft touches in the use of the particular to reinforce the general that have seldom since appeared in his work. The Lubitsch of *The Student Prince* was a dull dog when compared with the witticisms of *Forbidden Paradise*. He chose for his players, Pola Negri, whose talents he knew well, and whose playing of the impassioned queen, exquisitely regal when in the presence of the court, and sexually alluring when alone with her favourite lieutenant, has never been surpassed in its kind; Adolphe Menjou, of Chaplin's schooling, magnificently subtle—his wide-hearted acceptance of the decorations that emblazoned the breast of the young lieutenant and the French ambassador will not be forgotten; Rod la Rocque, the essence of dashing lieutenants, innocent, good-looking and slender; and Pauline Starke, angelic as the virginal lady-in-waiting.

He had built the vastest of palaces in which to house his regally passionate queen, with shining floors, massive columns, and great sweeps of drapery that seemed to hang from heaven. He had the roundest of full moons; the most luscious of roses; the blackest of velvet for the Negri's imperial dresses, with trains that swished across the mirrored floors; and an exquisite chorus of uniformed officers and bearded revolutionaries. Beyond being a commentary on the frailty of women (in particular of queens), on sly chancellors and gallant officers, *Forbidden Paradise* was a most satisfying exposure of the false glamour in which Hollywood lived.

Of Lubitsch's other and more recent Americo-German work, there should be mentioned that extremely popular and successful film *The Student Prince*, and *The Patriot*, a return to the historical spectacle, in co-operation with his early actor Jannings. The first-named picture was calculated by Metro-Goldwyn-Mayer to be a really grand film, lavish in spectacle, superb and smooth in direction, splen-

didly photographed, with Norma Shearer, Ramon Novarro,
and Jean Hersholt as the players. *The Student Prince* was
typical of the Americanisation of Lubitsch. It was a
meaningless, superficial exposition of sexual sentimentality,
rendered acceptable to the public by a perfection of technical
accomplishment that has rarely been equalled. (For this
reason it was voted by the general public as ' the film of the
year '.) It was an example of the keeping up of appearances.
In reality, tearing aside the veil of glamour, Lubitsch's
famous subtlety had degenerated into a lot of men all taking
off their hats at the same moment and the interplay of
opening and shutting doors. Of old Heidelburg, where the
action was set, the film told not a thing, for the atmosphere
was that of the second-rate property rooms. As an instance
of sheer undiluted picture-sense, *The Student Prince* was
to be appreciated. As a film, in the development of
Lubitsch's career, it was worthless.

Like *The Student Prince,* Lubitsch's *The Patriot* was
hailed as the world's greatest film, with the world's greatest
actor, made by the world's greatest director, with a cast of
twenty thousand. It was none of these things, which were
due to Paramount's highly imaginative publicity department. It was a ridiculous travesty of Russian history; a
mauled version of Alfred Neumann's play; an absurd,
melodramatic, bestial display of bad taste. It is, of course,
well known that Jannings is a great actor in the theatrical
manner, with much gesturing, mouthing, gibbering, and
eye-rolling as his assets. That much is apparent from his
early historical films, *Danton, Anne Boleyn,* and later, from
Tartuffe and *The Last Laugh.* But the Paramount-Lubitsch-
Jannings team was nothing if not ludicrous. Whereas, in
his earlier German work, Jannings put sincerity, force, and
meaning into his gestures, in his Hollywood period there
was nothing but a bare framework. Jannings as the mad
Paul the First succeeded in being ridiculous, unnecessarily
lascivious, and, to an admirer of his better work, merely
pitiful. It was sad to see good material put to such prostitution. Lewis Stone, on the other hand, always a quiet,

restrained actor, played the difficult part of the treacherous Count Pahlen with dignity, reserve, and self-control, due not to Lubitsch or Paramount, but to his own personality. In short, *The Patriot,* despite its natural leanings towards cinema, was a mishandled, highly theatrical, over-acted, rather pathetic instance of Americo-German tendencies. It lacked not only unity, but sincerity, purpose, style, and dignity. Some persons, judging by the reception accorded the picture (it was showing in London during the fortnight when the *Evening Standard* was running a public competition for postcard film criticism), mistook the capering of Jannings for these qualities. It was yet another example of the subordination of talent, possibly artistry, perhaps genius, to the demands of the box-office mind.

Lubitsch is a director of interest, if only because he is always an unknown quantity. He makes such films as *The Flame* and *Sumurun* in Germany, *Forbidden Paradise* and *The Marriage Circle* in America, and completes the enigma by *The Student Prince* and *The Patriot.* For appreciation of his cinematic knowledge, it is necessary to untie the Hollywood wrappings and peer inside to discover the intelligence he once possessed.[1]

The undoing of F. W. Murnau has been much the same as that of Ernst Lubitsch, save that the process has been quicker and is manifest in a lesser number of films. Murnau, of Germany, is associated with *The Last Laugh, Tartuffe, Dracula,* and *Faust,* films of value which showed their director to have a very sensitive knowledge of the resources of the cinema, summarised in particular in the much-discussed *Last Laugh.* Murnau went to Hollywood at the invitation of the Fox Film Corporation, who gave him *carte blanche* for his productions in their name. Mr. Fox was all out to buy 'art' for his second-rate productions. He tried also to persuade Carl Mayer, the brilliant scriptwriter of many German silent films, including *Caligari, The Last Laugh, Vanina* and *New Year's Eve,* to go to

---

[1] An excellent analysis is Theodore Huff's *Index to the Films of Ernst Lubitsch* (Sight and Sound, 1947).

Hollywood to adapt Sudermann's *Trip to Tilsit* for Murnau to direct. Mayer accepted the Fox contract, but insisted on remaining in Europe to do the writing. Rochus Gliese, a famous German set-designer, however, accompanied Murnau. Murnau, taking the bull by the horns, took full advantage of Mr. Fox's generous offer. He built a city. He employed Charles Roscher so that he could use his name, as a cameraman, and chose (or was it Mr. Fox's doing?) Janet Gaynor and George O'Brien as his players. Herr Murnau was all set to make Mr. Fox a big picture. Brer Rabbit!

I am at a loss to describe the groanings and rumblings of the machinery as the ' rhythm ' of *Sunrise* unfolded. First, it must be understood that *Sunrise* was ' a new conception of the function of the motion picture; a new outlook on the depth of human nature.' Secondly, ' When you see *Sunrise,* you will see what can be done with new, untried material, when controlled by the hands of an artist.' Thirdly, ' *Sunrise* has a new technique.' Although these announcements, issued with the severest gravity, were probably due to Mr. Fox's new ' art ' film publicity department, they are significant of the price that Murnau had to pay for his Hollywood engagement. The theme of *Sunrise* was meant for intelligent people; it was very successful with housemaids and their boy friends. The picture itself was well done. The city looked really well. The technique was clever. Mr. Fox was perfectly sincere when he said that the picture was a masterpiece. It was. A masterpiece of bluff, insincerity, unsubstantial nonsense. To those who had read the lesson in the American work of Lubitsch, *Sunrise* was not a disappointment. A little foresight showed that Hollywod would dismember Murnau, just as she had Lubitsch, Seaström, Buchowetski. *Sunrise* turned out to be exactly what had been expected. At the same time, many London film critics bleated restlessly over the ' rhythm ' of the great picture. . . .

Murnau's second picture for Fox was *The Four Devils,* a 'story of the circus ring', which was (save for some moving camerawork) an uninteresting film. *Sunrise* was at least meritorious if only in a small way; but this second film, with its puling sentiment, its little boys and girls, its wicked men and sensual vamps, was Mr. Fox in his post-war days of white-haired mothers carrying baskets over the hill. The German director has made another film for Mr. Fox, but as yet it is in the future. In the meantime, I wait to hear of Herr Murnau's return to Berlin, where perhaps it will be possible for him to pick up the threads of cinema where he laid them down after *The Last Laugh* and *Faust*.[1]

Erich Pommer, whilst not strictly a film director, is nevertheless a producer, and the productions which have resulted from his control are all of considerable note. He left Germany after the making of *Vaudeville*, which was directed by E. A. Dupont, and supervised by Pommer. Exactly what the supervision of Erich Pommer amounts to is hard to ascertain with any degree of certainty, but the fact remains that there are directors, who, whilst working under him make excellent pictures, but are disappointing when alone. Dupont is a case in point. *Vaudeville*, from all standards, was a brilliant film and, on the strength of it, Dupont went to Hollywood to the Universal Company. There he made an unmentionable picture, *Love Me and the World Is Mine*. His later work in Britain *Moulin Rouge, Piccadilly*, and *Atlantic*, although of more merit than the Hollywood picture, still lacks the vitality and strength of the film supervised by Pommer. When Pommer reached Hollywood, on the other hand, he sat alone and demanded this and that; supervised Mauritz Stiller making *Hotel Imperial*, and afterwards *Barbed Wire;* and returned to Berlin to control Hans Schwartz on *Nina Petrovna* and *The Hungarian Rhapsody*, and Joe May on *Asphalt* and *Homecoming*. It is evident, from a consideration of the above-mentioned films, that Erich Pommer's supervision accounts for a great deal.[2]

[1] Murnau died in California, March, 1931, after having collaborated with Robert Flaherty in making *Tabu* in the South Seas.

[2] Pommer is now (1947) working in Germany, in the American Zone, to re-establish film production.

Hotel Imperial, although not a great film, was nevertheless one of the best productions that have come from America. The story was of an Austro-Russian war type, set in a captured town on the Galician front in 1915, and Pola Negri and James Hall played spy parts with distinction. It was opened with skill by the entrance of the Austrian officer into the captured town, an opening of deserted streets in the cold dreariness of dawn. Miss Negri was a servant girl in the hotel where the officer took refuge, and her playing in this first sequence was her best individual work in America. The whole of the first reel was superbly done, the empty streets, the deserted hotel, the girl about to begin her day's work, her hiding of the officer, his raving delirium. This was Pommer and Stiller using great skill. The remainder of the picture, especially the orgy scenes with George Siegmann as a drunken Russian general, were in the true Hollywood debauchery style which they manage to do so convincingly.

Technically, the production was of interest, for it was one of the first to be made on the composite set method. An eye-witness description of the sets is given by Mr. L'Estrange Fawcett, and deserves repetition.[1] ' Some may remember the use made of travelling camera in *Hotel Imperial*. The stage accommodating the hotel was one of the largest in existence and eight rooms were built complete in every detail, four leading off each side of the lobby, which ran the length of the building. . . . Suspended above the set were rails along which the camera, mounted on a little carriage, moved at the director's will. Scenes (shots) could be taken of each room from above from every point of view. . . . There were two objects—first, to enable Erich Pommer to experiment with angle photography, representing impressions of scenes taken from the point of view of a character watching the others. . . . Secondly, the story could be filmed in proper sequence. In *Hotel Imperial* an attempt was made to build up a cumulative dramatic

[1] *Vide, Films: Facts and Forecasts*, by L'Estrange Fawcett (Bles, 1927).

effect by following the characters swiftly from one room to another, by means of several cameras and rolling shots.' Pommer succeeded in giving to the film an air of intimacy that is lacking in most pictures. On this method, many films are made in German studios to-day, and the same idea was adopted by Edmund Goulding when making the dialogue version of *The Trespasser,* no fewer than fifteen cameras being used to pick up Miss Swanson at every different angle. To return to *Hotel Imperial,* it was to be ranked along with *Forbidden Paradise* as one of the best productions from the Paramount Company. Not only was it the come-back of Miss Negri, but it was the triumph of a star in a rôle that asked no sympathy.

Mauritz Stiller continued, without the controlling hand of Erich Pommer, and made at a later date that most extraordinary of all movies, *The Street of Sin.* This was a picture from a scenario by von Sternberg, with Emil Jannings, Olga Baclanova, and Fay Wray. No expense was spared on its making. The script was well balanced; the continuity good; the setting natural. Yet, for some obscure reason, it was one of the dullest films yet made. Most curiously, it defied analysis. It was made just previous to Stiller's death in 1928.

Victor Seaström, a Swedish director who travelled to Hollywood soon after the war, has a series of uneven films to his name, but, with the sole exception of *The Scarlet Letter,* has made little of the material given to him by his producers. *Confessions of a Queen, Name the Man,* and *The Tower of Lies* were dull pictures, and not until the woodland sequence of *He Who Gets Slapped* did any of the old Seaström poetry of his early Swedish films come to the surface. This sequence of the two lovers in the sunlight, away from the circus ring in which most of the story took place, was the only redeeming incident in an otherwise uninteresting heartbreak affair of Lon Chaney. Seaström's *The Scarlet Letter,* from the Nathaniel Hawthorne story, was of greater power but was unfortunately rendered farcical by the false morality of the producers. It was remarkable, however, for the playing of Lillian Gish as Hester Prynne, a very different woman from Griffith's young lady, and for the appearance of Lars Hanson, at that time (1926) just come from Sweden. The theme of *The Scarlet Letter* was gloomy, but Seaström raised its gloom to moments of great beauty. It was a film made in one key, for even the humorous relief of the stocks and the ducking-stool were fitted into the pattern of sorrow. Seaström's sweeping sense of landscape, so evident in his early Swedish pictures, was expanded and gave an enchanting atmosphere to the first love scenes between Miss Gish and Lars Hanson. A later picture by the same director, *The Wind,* was of less interest, but there was again evidence of his lyricism and poetry. This feeling for depth and space was common to all the Scandinavian directors in their pre-American work. It was found in Stiller's *Arne's Treasure, The Atonement of Gösta Berling,* in Brunius's *Charles XII*, in Seaström's *Thy Soul Shall Bear Witness,* in *Love's Crucible,* and in the work of Benjamin Christensen. With Seaström, it manifests itself in his shots of landscape, his feeling for the presence of the elements, his love of wind, sky, and flowers. Perhaps it is in accord with the dusty desert of the American Westerns and the chimneys and smoke of the Soviet workers' films. Perhaps it is due to the natural Swedish tendencies towards the beauty of nature and the rhythm of poetry. Seaström took this reality of nature with him to the mechanised studios of Hollywood, and it blossomed even in that hot-house atmosphere. It was to be felt in *The Tower of Lies,* in *The Wind,* in *The Scarlet Letter,* and in the short gem-like scene in *He Who Gets Slapped.* Nearly all the themes of Seaström are connected with the struggle of human beings against the common mass of humanity. He is concerned with individual persons and their relationship to their environment. There was Hester Prynne set against the narrow-mindedness of the conventional people in *The Scarlet Letter,* and Miss Gish striving in *The Wind.* In the latter, the wind itself was an outer emphasis of the inner struggle; a sort of Griffith-like use of the elements. So also did the flowers and tree roots help the lovers in *The Scarlet Letter*. But Seaström has ceased to develop. He remains stationary in his outlook, thinking in terms of his early Swedish imagery. He has recently made little use of the progress of the cinema itself. *The Divine Woman*, although it had the Greta Garbo of *The Atonement of Gosta Berling*, had none of the lyricism, the poetic imagery of the earlier film. It is true, however, that he rendered the Scandinavian less of a star and more of a woman than in any other of her American films. The lyricism of Seaström, of the Swedish film itself, with its snow, its wind, its trees, and flowers, its depth and width of land-scape, cannot flourish in the American factory.

Of other European directors who have had their fling in Hollywood, Dimitri Buchowetski has not been successful. In Germany he made several dramas of the historical costume type, with plenty of blood and thunder, such as *Danton, Othello,* and *Peter the Great,* with Emil Jannings. In America his pictures have been of little value, and number among them *Men* and *The Crown of Lies,* with Pola Negri; *The Midnight Sun; The Swan; Graustark,* with Norma Talmadge; and *Valencia,* with Mae Murray. Among others, Ludwig Berger, who directed the exquisite *Cinderella* in Germany, has made *The Sins of the Fathers,* with Jannings; Benjamin Christensen, *The Devil's Circus* and *Sorcery;* Alexander Korda, a Hungarian, *A Modern Dubarry* and *The Private Life of Helen of Troy;* Lothar Mendes has strung together *The Four Feathers;* and Michaël Curtiz, having made the semi-spectacle picture *The Moon of Israel* in Europe, went to Hollywood and joined Warners to direct *Noah's Ark.*

Quite recently, Jacques Feyder, the Belgian, who in Europe is associated with the brilliant realisation of Zola's *Thérèse Raquin* and the political satire *Les Nouveaux Messieurs,* made his first picture for Metro-Goldwyn-Mayer, *The Kiss,* in which he skilfully combined intelligent direction with the necessary proportion of picture-sense.

His treatment of Greta Garbo was more subtle than that usually accorded to this actress by American directors, but it did not bear comparison with his handling of Gina Manés in the Zola picture. But there was a freshness about *The Kiss* that raised it above the level of the ordinary movie and a use of camera angle which was reminiscent of Feyder's earlier work. One queried, however, why the film should have been set in France, when the atmosphere and types were so obviously American? Why does a studio take the trouble to transport a French director to Hollywood and then give him a picture with a French locale to direct? It seems odd.

V

THE AMERICAN FILM (*concluded*)

There are certain American directors of lesser standing than Griffith, Erich von Stroheim, and Chaplin, whose work, if not altogether brilliant from a filmic point of view, is at least of more intelligence than that of the common run of movie directors. One assumes, also, from certain flashes of cinematic feeling in their films, that these directors would in all probability make fuller use of their abilities if they were not entangled in the structure of the studio system, and dominated by the drastic demands of the production committees for whom they work. The pictures of King Vidor, Josef von Sternberg, Rex Ingram, James Cruze, and Clarence Brown are, generally speaking, of more than passing interest. In much of their work there is an idea, an experiment, a sense of vision, a use of the camera, a striving after something that is cinema, which is worth detailed analysis for its aesthetic value. But we must remember that these men are employees of large manufacturing firms and have inevitably to incorporate in their films at least two-thirds of that picture-sense quality so dear to producers. In the remaining third, there may be found some expression of the director's real opinion of the film subject.

King Vidor is probably the outstanding director of the young American school, and he has already shown remarkable versatility in the satirical, the mock-epic and the psychological film. His best known and most commercially successful work was the notorious *Big Parade,* although preferable from a filmic point of view were *The Crowd, The Politic Flapper,* and *Hallelujah! The Crowd* has been hailed in intelligentsia film circles as a great film. In Paris it is considered the greatest, if not the most successful, film to have come from Hollywood, although recently this belief has been overshadowed by the novelty of *White Shadows.*

Nevertheless, whatever lavish praise may now be accorded
The Crowd, it was not by any means the film that it
was said to be. It failed for several significant reasons.
Primarily, it was a literary and not a cinematic expression
of a theme, although the original conception was cinematic.
Vidor's theme was vast in its breadth; a man's ineffectual
struggle against the hostile indifference of the masses; a
young man's hopeless striving against the convention, the
unsympathy and the brute selfishness of the everyday
people who surrounded him. The film should have been
the spirit and the humanity of the crowd. It was called
The Crowd. Instead, it concentrated attention on the
human interest of a single individual. As the film stood, it
should in all senses of self-justification have been called
The Man. The relation between the man and the crowd
was ill-defined and slurred over. There was, afterwards,
no clear-mindedness as to either the man or the crowd. At
times there was a tendency to become interested in the
individuals; the crowd became meaningless and uninteresting. All through the film there was a feeling of
detail and no sense of the breadth of the conception. It was
easily possible to pay attention to the small actions of James
Murray and Eleanor Boardman, and hence to lose contact
with the theme because of their mannerisms. *The Crowd*
was not a unity. The interests were divided and subdivided
instead of being bound together into a forceful, filmic
whole, such as *The Last Laugh.* I have suggested that *The
Crowd* was filmic in its original conception and literary in
its treatment. It demanded the complete elimination of all
sub-titles. It should have been treated from the same
approach as Murnau's film, but from a mass and not from
an individual outlook. Not one of the ironical titles
infused into the film were of cinematic value. The script
should have been conceived and written by King Vidor and
not by a scenarist. Added to this, the opening sequence of
the man's boyhood and the death of his father were painfully unnecessary; the film should have opened on a broad
scale with architecture. The psychology of the separate

characters became twisted and inconsistent as the theme developed. The ending, for which presumably Vidor was not responsible, was beneath contempt. The treatment when considered apart from the theme (which is absurd) was good. It was Vidor's misfortune and lack of direction that the players were the film and not the theme. *The Crowd* was a sincere attempt on the part of Vidor to do something well; it was a failure because of his misconception of the theme and the regrettable picture-sense of Metro-Goldwyn-Mayer.

The question raised by *The Big Parade* was a big one, and it successfully occupied the British Press whilst Metro-Goldwyn's picture was playing to record audiences at the London Tivoli. Somehow or other, during the premier presentation of this film, a rumour arose that it was a big American publicity stunt. It was propaganda to the effect that it showed how America won the war. Whether this was so or not is no concern of these pages, but in any case the propaganda (if any) can hardly have been effective with any informed Briton. Like all war films manufactured in Hollywood, *The Big Parade* carried little of the real meaning of war. The film story had been written by Laurence Stallings, and the picture was given by Metro-Goldwyn-Mayer to King Vidor for direction. Apparently Vidor was not attracted to the idea, regarding it in the first place as ' just another war story '. The picture was made, and it seemed as if it would be an ordinary programme feature until, after it had been run through for a pre-view, Irving Thalberg, one of Metro-Goldwyn-Mayer's production heads, suddenly decided that it could be made into a great, stupendous, super film. It would be America's patriotic part in the Great War. It would put America on the map of Europe. Vidor, fired with this new impulse, remade the complete film from start to finish from a new angle. The result was overwhelmingly successful. Despite the detail discrepancies and the weakness of the ending, there is no doubt that *The Big Parade* was a most remarkable picture. Its power lay in the opening sequences, where an immense feeling that hundreds of thousands of people were being howled into war, none of them knowing its meaning, the women regarding it as a thing of romance, the young men as a chance for gallant heroism, was dramatically spread across to the spectator. King Vidor handled these scenes with a nobility not usually associated with the American cinema. But perhaps the most memorable part of the film was the departure of the men from their billets in the French village for the front line. The long line of rattling lorries, the convoy of aeroplanes overhead, the cobblestones giving way to the straggling forest, this was magnificently handled. I shall not attempt to decide whether *The Big Parade* epitomised war as it really was, or war as Hollywood and Metro-Goldwyn-Mayer imagined it to be. It is like comparing the naturalism of *Journey's End* or *The Case of Sergeant Grischa* with the many novelettes written about brave officers and brutal Germans. From a purely personal point of view, however, the short sequence in Pudovkin's *The End of St. Petersburg* told far more vividly of the reality of the front line than all the eleven thousand feet of *The Big Parade*. The latter film, nevertheless, succeeded in showing with sincerity the folly of the thing, if limited by an American standpoint.

Vidor was seen in a happier, less problematical vein of mind in that brilliantly clever satire, *The Politic Flapper*, and later in another picture of the same type, *Show People*. In the former particularly, Marion Davies was given the opportunity to show her versatility and her vivacity, and for pure enjoyment both these slight pictures were high among the American output of recent years. Of Vidor's earlier efforts it is unnecessary to write at length, for they were merely the training ground for his later proficiency. Among his work there may be mentioned *The Sky Pilot* (1921); *Peg o' My Heart* (1922); *His Hour* (1924); *The Wife of the Centaur* (1925); *La Bohème* (1926); *Bardelys the Magnificent* and *Proud Flesh*. He has recently completed a dialogue and sound picture, *Hallelujah!* one of the many negro pictures to come from America. It

45. THE GOLD RUSH, directed by CHARLES CHAPLIN.   GEORGIA HALE, CHARLES CHAPLIN.
[American, 1925]

46. STELLA DALLAS, directed by HENRY KING.   BELLE BENNETT.   [American, 1925]

47. BATTLESHIP POTEMKIN, directed by S. M. EISENSTEIN.   [Soviet, 1925]

48. VAUDEVILLE, directed by E. A. DUPONT.   EMIL JANNINGS.   [German, 1925]

was a film of great lyrical beauty, filled with the spiritual feeling of the South, and may be ranked, with parts of *The Crowd,* as being Vidor's best work. Although from a cinematic point of view the film was too divided into separate sequences with little conjoining continuity, there was no question that it carried with it a sincerity of faith characteristic of the coloured peoples. Most of the picture was taken on the Southern cotton plantations near Memphis, and all the minor players were chosen from the cotton workers.

Josef von Sternberg rose rapidly to directorship by the making of *The Salvation Hunters,* a dreary film which Hollywood thought exceptionally intelligent. Sternberg succeeded in making this picture independently of the big producing concerns, no mean feat, and credit must be given on that account to his enterprise and courage. Chaplin is declared to have greeted *The Salvation Hunters* as a great film, a masterpiece of Human Realism; listened awhile at the following chorus of praise instigated by his grave announcement; and then given out that he was only pulling their legs. Nevertheless, whether this was true or not, the picture was bought by United Artists. Its drab monotony of dock-life, its symbolic dredger, its squalid doorways, and its sudden, ineffectual ending are going down to posterity as a masterpiece. It is rather like the dustbins and garbage of Alberto Cavalcanti. In fact, it seems that if one can make a picture so dreary, so dull, and so depressing that it defeats criticism, then one will be hailed as a genius. The pseudo-success of *The Salvation Hunters* left an uncomfortable mark on the work of Sternberg. His apparent desire to appear clever often hinders him from becoming so. Sternberg gives the unfortunate effect of always trying to be great. His films are always self-conscious. They are *Sternberg* films.

Paramount-Famous-Players secured the services of this director, and for them he wrote some scenarios (*The Street of Sin*) and made some pictures. Amongst his clever qualities, Sternberg has acquired the necessary faculty of picture-sense. Nearly all his pictures for Paramount have been successful. *The Last Command, The Docks of New York, Thunderbolt,* and *Underworld* were good films, but not one of them conveyed the filmic intelligence with which he is usually credited. *Underworld* was one of the best of the gangster pictures so popular a short time ago, before the same idea was adapted to the dialogue and sound film. It held the spectator by a slow development, gradually increasing to a tremendous climactic thrill, a sort of Sydney Street encounter with the police. Sternberg showed here a feeling for pictorial values, a definite interest in filmic suspense, but the continuity, especially the flash back sequence, was weak. *The Last Command* was probably the best of the Sternberg Paramount pictures, but, as has been written, was virtually a re-make of the earlier Jannings films of the late German period.[1] This film may be taken as another instance of the committee-made picture of the pre-dialogue era. It was a cleverly blended mixture of the elements of Hollywood picture-sense with a Germanic use of the camera. The story was dramatic and powerful, necessitating the use of crowds and the Paramount property rooms. It was handled in a direct, polished manner, with a tragic ending, for Jannings must be tragic. The camera was used with a pleasant freedom, notably in the opening scenes in the studios. The setting had a double interest, for at that time ' Imperialist Russia ' (*à la Hollywood*) was in the vogue and the general public always likes to see the inside of film studios. The whole picture was turned out with the efficiency of a fifty-shilling tailor, an efficiency that the astute film observer has come to associate with the Paramount studios.

Sternberg has some sense of the dramatic and he never fails to exploit this in a heavy way. He used Bancroft in the same way as Jannings, but with considerable more success. *The Docks of New York* was a distinguished film, although superficial in treatment and pseudo-filmic in character. Taking shots through hanging iron chains did not

[1] Cf. pp. 135, 141-143.

establish the atmosphere of a place, although it may have created pretty pictorial compositions. Sternberg seems lodged in this gully of pictorial values. He has no control over his dramatic feelings (*The Street of Sin*) and very little idea of the filmic psychology of any scene that he shoots (*The Docks of New York*). He has, however, some feeling for the use of women. His contrast of Betty Compson and Olga Baclanova in the latter film was good. Despite all his faults, Sternberg will perhaps one day make a really interesting film, if, that is, he forgets that it is a Sternberg picture.

Rex Ingram as an outstanding film director is a matter of opinion. His work displays a certain feeling for theatrical cinema, a leaning towards the drama of individuals, and a rather clever-minded flair for American showmanship. Just as Sternberg is too much the director of the Sternberg picture, Ingram saturates his films with 'artistic' pretensions. Occasionally, in isolated sequences, Ingram forgets his artistry and quite by chance directs a really moving scene. Of such a nature were the shooting of Alice Terry as the spy, and the drawing of the submarine commander's character in *Mare Nostrum*. These two scenes were handled with a sympathy, a value of suspense remote from the Ingramish direction of *The Three Passions* and *The Garden of Allah*. The picture with which Ingram established his name and a long-term contract with Metro-Goldwyn-Mayer was, of course, *The Four Horsemen of the Apocalypse*. From a technical point of view, in consideration of its date (1921), *The Four Horsemen* was extremely accomplished. Ingram set out in this epic picture to make Valentino a hero, and the Germans the vilest brutes who killed for the sheer love of killing. He spared no effort in doing this, and successfully painted black white and white black, with no neutral tones to break the jar. Ingram showed the popular conception of war. *The Four Horsemen* arrived at a most opportune moment. It was exactly what the public wanted to see about the war. It was precisely what the Press had been writing about with so much enthusiasm. Ingram was an opportunist; so also were Metro-Goldwyn; the result was unprecedented in *The Four Horsemen*. Ingram did everything to make the picture popular. He raked up spiritual references from the Bible, and made his horsemen flit about in an eerie manner in the sky. He caused Valentino to slink around with a cigarette dangling from his lips, and established him as an international hero by letting him dance a tango with his natural grace. Above all, by doing these things with an eye to public appreciation, he established himself as a great director in the opinion of the public, of Hollywood, and of himself. From that time onwards it was simply a question of Rex Ingram productions.

Some time after the world-wide reception of *The Four Horsemen*, he made *The Prisoner of Zenda*. He used Lewis Stone, Alice Terry, and Ramon Novarro for his acting material, and he creditably obtained the utmost out of them. The theme was sentimental, as are all Ruritanian themes, but sweetly so, with scope for gentle handling. To-day, perhaps, when held against modern achievements, *The Prisoner of Zenda* seems dull and old-fashioned. It was far from being so when first shown in this country. It is memorable now chiefly for the clever acting of young Ramon Novarro as the dashing Rupert. Novarro, before his days of stardom, was refreshing and stimulating. His playing in *Zenda,* against the reserved dignity of Lewis Stone, was beyond reproach. Rex Ingram's direction was capable, in a straightforward manner. His next outstanding success was an adaption of Sabatini's costume romance, *Scaramouche,* and this he also handled with competency. He remembered Griffith's *Orphans of the Storm* and outdid the French Revolution in its own bloodiness. This time he made Lewis Stone the villain, Novarro the smiling hero, and his wife again the heroine. As a costume melodrama, of no weight or pretensions to being anything but pleasant spectacle, *Scaramouche* was with the best of its kind. It was lavish, crowded, brutal, charming, and amusing in turn. To-day, it is almost forgotten. Of Ingram's other American productions, none was outstanding, but for reference may be mentioned *Hearts Are Trumps* (1921); *Trifling Women* (1922); *Where the Pavement Ends* (1923) and *The Arab*, after which he transported himself and his wife across to the shores of the Mediterranean. *Mare Nostrum*, a melodrama of espionage, with dastardly Germans and some good submarine shots, was uneven but of better technique than the Hollywood films. *The Magician*, with Paul Wegener, was a bad adaptation of Somerset Maugham's novel, and is memorable only for an operation scene which was handled in the best Ingram manner. *The Garden of Allah*, save for some beautiful panchromatic photography at the end of the picture, was drearily done in the true Ingram tradition of a story straightly told, with flashes of humour in the choice of crowd types. This curious mania for eccentric types is typical of Ingram. He seems to take delight in searching out the ugliest of mankind, making 'them useful in a close-up. One recalls the man with the bomb in *The Prisoner of Zenda;* the revolutionaries in *Scaramouche;* the crowd in the bazaar in *The Garden of Allah;* the hunchback in *The Magician*. Later, *The Three Passions* was an effortless picture, distinguished only for Shayle Gardner's character study of a ship-builder. The film as a whole was one of the worst of Ingram's artistic attempts. Perhaps it is possible that this director will regain his old skill, but he will have to jolt himself out of a deep rut. Perhaps he, like Griffith, does not keep abreast with the current films of the world? Perhaps he, like so many other directors, has exhausted his knowledge of the film?

Clarence Brown is another American director who has shown short flashes of cinema in between long stretches of picture-sense. Some time ago, in 1925, his clever handling of *The Goose Woman* and of Louise Dresser aroused some interest. During the first portion of this film, while Miss Dresser played the drink-sodden prima donna who had fallen beside the way, Clarence Brown's direction was remarkable. He made her live in the filthiest squalor with gin bottles and geese, and at night she would hunch up her back over her precious book of press-cuttings, to read over the reports of her glorious days. So far the film was excellent, handled with sympathy, but the latter half was quite ridiculous, Miss Dresser, the direction and the film going to pieces. Among the many films credited to Clarence Brown were *The Light in the Dark* (1922); *The Eagle,* with Valentino at his best; *Smouldering Fires,* with Pauline Frederick, in 1925; and *The Trail of '98,* a film that was meant to be an epic, but succeeded in being a first-class super film, without interest to the intelligent-minded. *Flesh and the Devil,* however, made in 1926, was a film of more than passing cleverness. It was, it is true, another example of the committee-produced picture, with John Gilbert, Lars Hanson and Greta Garbo as the star appeal, but it contained short sequences that strengthened Clarence Brown's claim as a director. The copy shown in this country was maltreated, either by the censor or by special British editing, but it sufficed to show that in its original version *Flesh and the Devil* had some pretensions to be called a good film. The theme was sheer, undiluted sex, and Brown used a series of close-ups to get this across with considerable effect. Notable also was his use of angles, different indeed from either the customary German or American method, and the happiness with which he settled the characters in their environment.

The work of John Ford has been uneven, but there are to his credit two good films, *The Iron Horse* and *Three Bad Men,* made in 1924 and 1926 respectively. The former purported to tell the story of the laying of the first railroad across America in the teeth of the opposition of nature and the Indians. It was the type of film that America can make well if she sets her mind to it. It ranked on the same level with the epic quality of *The Covered Wagon,* and combined the best elements of the Western school with the more sophisticated direction of the Hollywood feature film. *The Iron Horse* was vast in its conception, and John Ford, despite the hindrances of a story-interest, handled it with a high degree of talent. It was not popular in this country, where audiences have no enthusiasm for railways being thrown across trackless wastes, but as a film it was fit to rank with any in the class of reconstructed fact. I remember with feeling the long line of railwaymen's camps on the progressing track; the spirit and adventure of the pioneers; the clever rendering of the manœuvres of the encircling Indians; and above all, the far-stretching landscape across which the steel track was to run. Ford's other film, *Three Bad Men*, was conceived in the same open-air spirit, dealing with the dramatic episodes of the gold-rush in 1877. In many remarkable scenes the incidents of this extraordinary event were brought out with reality. The dance hall, its oddly assorted patrons, the would-be-rich settlers, the pastor and his ruined chapel, were pieces in a pattern that Ford blended together with clever direction. The great moment of the picture was the astounding stampede, the mad, on-rushing race of the donkeys, mules, race-horses, and oxen, jogged forward by their lashing drivers towards the hidden gold. Through the whole film moved irresistible camaraderie, the likeable badness of the three disreputable companions, each of whom met their death by holding the real bad men at bay. The playing of Frank Campeau, Tom Santschi, and Farrell MacDonald was excellent.

Henry King, I feel, is one of the most sincere of American directors, whose work seldom receives the attention it deserves. He is to be numbered among those directors in Hollywood who, if they were allowed the chance, would make a film to compare with the product of any of the better European directors. All his productions contain points of definite interest, demanding a detailed examination for which there is not the space in these pages. To his credit must first be placed what was at its date one of the finest films America had produced, *Tol'able David* (1922), which was followed later by *Stella Dallas, Romola, The White Sister, The Winning of Barbara Worth* (a sophisticated Western), *The Magic Flame,* and the better parts of *The Woman Disputed.* In *Tol'able David,* Henry King expounded his theme with a delicate use of detail and a sympathetic employment of landscape for the emphasis of atmosphere. The material was distributed with a nicety of feeling rare in the American film; the continuity was balanced to perfection and flowed with admirable smoothness; and the characterisation, notably in the case of Richard Barthelmess in the name part, revealed a depth of character that has not been noticed in any later film by the same director. King learnt from Griffith all that was good, combining the spoil with his own filmic knowledge. The real value of *Stella Dallas,* a brilliant and deeply emotional film, was superficially destroyed in this country by the cheap and contemptible publicity that it received. It was diversely said to be ' the greatest mother-love picture ever made ', and that ' Mr. King had focalised in it all the creative artistry of his great career ', all of which was an attempt to put over Samuel Goldwyn's appreciation of the 'art' of the cinema. It implied, on the contrary, not only the strangeness of Mr. Goldwyn's mind, but the negligible amount of appreciation he possessed for the work of his own directors. The story of *Stella Dallas* was not of unusual interest, but it gave scope for a consistent character development over a space of time, and lent itself to delicate touches of direction. Its lesson lay in the superb handling of acting material, notably in the cases of Belle Bennett and Lois Moran, and also in Jean Hersholt's masterly rendering of the coarse riding-master. It was one of those rare films that rested on its treatment alone, a type of film not usually connected with America. Sympathy and delicacy are the two salient characteristics of Henry King's work, exemplified strongly in *Tol'able David* and *Stella Dallas.* He is a misunderstood and mishandled director; a man of deep cinematic mindedness, who struggles in vain against the overpowering and crippling demands of picture-sense.

*

Notwithstanding the plethora of movies of the man, woman, and sin variety, with which one is generally accustomed to couple the label of Hollywood and which constitute the greater part of its output during film history, there are a few naturalistic films that should be considered apart from the fiction film. They are to be differentiated, also, from the work of the directors who have just been discussed, with the exception of John Ford and James Cruze, who happily combine a sense of this open-air school with their cine-fiction.

In the first place there was the Western film, a form of cinema in which America excelled; and secondly, the more recent arrival of the south-sea island picture. The Western was perhaps America's nearest approach to real cinema. It was perfectly natural. It was, practically speaking, the Americans being themselves. Distinct from the sexual interplay of the drawing-room movie, the Western had its birth in the early days of the one- and two-reelers, and rose to its zenith towards the end of the post-war period about 1922 or 1923. Since then, it has degenerated into a more sophisticated form, as with *The Winning of Barbara Worth* and *In Old Arizona*. It has almost been displaced by the steel-girder and the office eye-shade, the dance frock and the dumb-bell, together with the products of America's dancing youth. There is, it is true, some indication of the revival of the Western in the dialogue cinema. Its natural scope for the use of synchronised sound, of horses' hoof-beats and of gun-shots, was the basis of Paramount's *The Virginian*, directed by Victor Fleming.[1] The use of American natural landscape and types in this picture was highly creditable, and, despite the limitations imposed by dialogue, it was amongst the best (if not the best) pictures to come from Hollywood since the opening of the dialogue period. *The Virginian*, because of its wonderful open-air atmosphere, lifted Victor Fleming in my estimation out of the rut of second-rate directors, although credit must also be given to J. Roy Hunt for his superb exterior photography.

During their day the Westerns were widely successful, for the cowboy spirit and dust of the desert are inborn in the true American of the old school. In its middle period of

[1] Died January, 1949.

William S. Hart, the Farnum brothers, William and Dustin, William Russell, Tom Mix, and Hoot Gibson, the Western film had an air of sincerity in its open stretches of sand, its fleeting horses, its smell of sage and gunsmoke. Not that I suggest that Americans once behaved precisely as did these rustlers and gunmen, but there was nevertheless some element of fact in the idealised cowboy. The spirit of openness seemed to have come quite naturally to the Westerns, and was in itself eminently suited to the functions of the cinema. It will be recalled that the story-interest of these fast-moving pictures was usually negligible; all that mattered was the hard riding, the spreading horizon of the desert, the crumbled *cañon* walls, the dusty hooves of cattle and mustangs, the heat and the cold, the rain and the wind. It was something the Americans understood. It was captured by the cinema with remarkable faith, very different from the studio reconstructions of ' Imperialist Russia ' and ' Medieval England '.

From time to time the Western film was stripped of its fictional trappings and was raised to the standard of an epic. It lost its story and became a reconstructed record of some great past achievement. Two examples of this have been mentioned, John Ford's *The Iron Horse* and *Three Bad Men,* but the pinnacle was reached in Cruze's *The Covered Wagon.* This was a film that combined the essence of the Western with the cinematic knowledge of Hollywood; a film of the men and women who set their faces and their wagons to the west in the giant trek across the plains. The production of this film was all the more remarkable in that its makers were the Famous-Lasky Company. It was an odd link in their tradition. It was their first breakaway from the drawing-room movie, a step that has since been followed up by *Old Ironsides* (*Sons of the Sea*), also directed by Cruze, and the *Chang* and *Four Feathers* type of picture. It was a direct development from the crude Western, but approached in an epic spirit; a sincere attempt to reconstitute past fact.

James Cruze, up to that time a maker of domestic

comedies and since then of pseudo-dramatic movies, must be commended for having accomplished his task with distinction. It was known at the time that he had some cinematic skill in direction, but his handling of space in *The Covered Wagon* was unsuspected. In the dream sequence of *Jazz* and in *To the Ladies,* Cruze was interesting. In *The Covered Wagon* he demanded serious consideration. He first learned his knowledge of the cinema in the early serials, a fact which is probably responsible for the open-air direction of this epic. Of his other pictures, all of which are worth notice, will be recalled : *The City that Never Sleeps, The Pony Express, Hollywood, The Beggar on Horseback, Merton of the Movies,* and *The Goose Hangs High.* His recent attempt at straight drama in *The Great Gabbo* was inferior to this earlier work, but some allowance is to be made for the superfluity of song-and-dance stuff, which was obviously added to ensure box-office appeal. It is hoped that Cruze will return to the space and truth of *The Covered Wagon.* He is a director who needs fresh air. He is misusing his intelligence in the factory.[1]

Of recent years, there have sprung up in Hollywood occasional but admirable attempts to use the natural resources of the American cinema. The Western has been partially replaced by the travel film which, although to a large extent experimental and only financed by the big companies if well-known stars are allowed to share the natural beauties, has the most prominent claim for the attention of the American industry to-day. These outstanding examples of the naturalistic use of the cinema are to be regarded as distinct from the advances made by Lubitsch, Chaplin, and Stroheim in the pure cine-fiction school. If they are not the direct development of the Western, then they are at any rate in relationship to it. They can be associated also with similar movements in Soviet Russia, Germany, and France.

The first American step in this manner was made by Robert Flaherty, and was the result of a film financed by

[1] James Cruze died, Hollywood, August, 1942.

Révillon Frères, the Paris furriers, as an advertising venture. *Nanook of the North,* the Eskimo film, although not entirely honest in that it purported to be what it was not, marked the starting-point of the American documentary picture, without plot or story but simply the continuity of a theme. Actually *Nanook,* which set up to be a film of the Eskimaux in the far north, was made on a latitude level with Edinburgh. The same theory of thematic continuity was found in Flaherty's other film, the beautiful *Moana.* Each in their own way, *Nanook* and *Moana* were supreme examples of the pure visual cinema. In form they were alike, opening with a quiet sequence that established the characters in their normal environment, emphasising only the swing of the bough of a tree, or the slope of the snow. With an unwinding thread of continuity each progressed without a litter of titles; the one telling of the warm, dark-skied south with its rich foliage and crystal water; the other of the bitter cold and ice, with the wind sweeping across the snow fields. Both films ended on a note of rest. *Moana* with the betrothed pair swaying in their dance against the sinking sun; *Nanook* with the moaning wind and the howl of the sleigh dogs. Each film told of the immensity of living; the urge to live; the width and breadth of the world. Of the two *Moana* was perhaps the finer. It had a warmness, not physical but spiritual, in handling that was missing in the coldness of *Nanook.*

In order to continue producing pictures, Flaherty next accepted a contract from Metro-Goldwyn-Mayer. It is said that he was to have had the making of *White Shadows in the South Seas,* but reasonably enough rejected the offer on account of the inclusion of a story and two stars. Instead, it was made by W. S. Van Dyke. To Flaherty must go the credit then, of inspiring the new movement in the American cinema that later gave rise to such films as *Grass, Chang, Stark Love, White Gold, White Shadows,* and *Trader Horn.*

Van Dyke is of secondary importance to Robert Flaherty. *White Shadows,* good as it was in places, cannot be compared with the quality of *Moana.* If Flaherty had made the former, there is little doubt that he would have surpassed *Moana*. If it were possible to consider *White Shadows* apart from the nonsense of the acting interest, a badly faked model of a shipwreck and a moral of white men ruining the sanctity of the islands, there remained some very beautiful landscape scenes. It is interesting to recall, moreover, that Van Dyke at one time was making Westerns, being responsible for a series of Buck Jones's pictures, *The Desert's Price, Hearts and Spurs,* and *Ranger of the Big Pines*. There would seem some reason, therefore, to place the credit for the best parts of *White Shadows* to the cameramen, leaving the blame for the story-handling to Van Dyke. It was significant, on the other hand, that Flaherty was currently kicking his heels at Metro-Goldwyn-Mayer's expense in Culver City, that suburb of Los Angeles. *White Shadows,* despite its cheapness of story, will remain memorable for its liquid sunlight, its gently swaying palms, its white clouded skies, its far-reaching stretches of hot sand and beach. The chief cameraman was Clyde de Vinna. It ranks with *The General Line* and *Moana* as being a perfect example of the beautiful decorative values of panchromatic photography.

Following up the success of *White Shadows,* Van Dyke attempted to repeat himself with *The Pagan,* a film made ridiculous by the intrusion of a Metro-Goldwyn-Mayer contract star. Mr. Ramon Novarro may be popular with nursemaids when he is practically in the all-together, but he had definitely no place (singing on his back in the water) in this purely pictorial picture. Is it possible to imagine the *Moana* of Flaherty as played by Mr. Novarro? Van Dyke has recently been sent by his company to Africa, complete with studio equipment, including not only generators and lights, but sound-recording apparatus for obtaining the noises of the jungle. The film is based on the tales of Trader Aloysius Horn, and will again be made against natural settings.[1]

[1] *Vide, Celluloid: The Film To-day* (Longmans Green, 1931), pp. 196-211, for a full assessment of *Trader Horn.*

In this same group of natural resources directors must be included Schoedsack and Cooper, Howard and Karl Brown. Ernest B. Schoedsack and Merian C. Cooper first achieved recognition by their film *Grass,* which was made among the Baktyari tribe of North-West Persia, during 1925. The picture was a vivid record of the almost insurmountable difficulties that faced the tribe when they migrated twice yearly in their trek for grass. One watched with suspense the extraordinary manner in which this band of half a million men, women, and children surmounted the snow-covered mountain range, and forded the roaring torrent that barred their way. The film was a marvellous photographic record, spoilt in this country by the insertion of irritating and fatuous titles, written by a Paramount writer called Richard P. Carver. After the success of *Grass,* the same pair went to the jungle country of Northern Siam, where they spent two years in taking records with the camera. Eventually *Chang* was capably mounted into a story form, and credit was due to the editors who worked up the theme to a highly emotional climax, which, as has been mentioned at a later stage, was rendered even more dramatic by the use of the magnascope.[1] *Chang* told the story of the family of Kru, a Lao tribesman, who built beyond the village in a clearing in the jungle, and of his struggle not only against the encroaching jungle but the beasts that lived there. Not one sequence of this admirable film dragged. Moreover, the spirit of the jungle was captured in such a manner that the audience seemed to live in it themselves. When the jungle awoke at the close of Kru's hard-working day, a wonderful feeling of stirring, of undergrowth moved by unseen forms, of branches swinging by other forces than those of the wind, spread into the spectators. Thus the film continued, until suddenly, as if by magic, the magnascope flooded the whole of one end of the cinema with the massed stampede of elephants. The emotional power of this climax was so strong, so overwhelming in its size and movement, that I have little

[1] Cf. pp. 341, 384, 385.

hesitation in calling it one of the most brilliant ever devised. Akin to the case of *Grass,* the titles, written specially by Achmed Abdullah, the novelist, were inclined to be absurd.

Satisfied with the phenomenal success accorded to *Chang,* Paramount sent Schoedsack and Cooper to the Sudan for the purpose of taking further camera records. But at this point, unfortunately, the producers remembered their picture-sense. Wishing to add to the success of *Chang,* which to all intents and purposes was a film of pure natural resources, Paramount decided to blend Schoedsack and Cooper's records in the Sudan with an adaptation of A. E. W. Mason's novel, *The Four Feathers,* adding for the sake of entertainment several stars and a pro-British moral. The resulting picture, a hotch-potch devised by Lothar Mendes, was put out to the public as being by the makers of *Chang.* Those who remembered the natural quality of the latter film were dismayed to find in *The Four Feathers* a devastating attempt to cut in a few shots of hippopotami charging and baboons escaping from a bush fire with a Hollywood movie of the worst type. The animal shots, nice enough in themselves, were totally out of place, having no relation to the rest of the picture. In this way does picture-sense spoil the only good work done by American directors. Producers have the entirely fallacious idea at the back of their heads that they are catering for the public taste. The situation is rendered the more significant by the preceding success of *Chang,* which stood on its own merits without the aid of Hollywood. This deplorable habit, popular with big producers, of incorporating a few excellent but irrelevant shots in an otherwise cheap movie, is typical of the picture-sense mind. They calculate that the public would not go for a film entirely composed of animals; but they will see the animals if smoothed down by Messrs. Clive Brook, William Powell, Richard Arlen, Noah Beery, and misty-eyed Fay Wray. *Wings,* whilst dealing with the air, was good; but when it descended to earth, to Clara Bow and the boys, it was unbearable. On these occasions, the intelligent public must take the bad with the good. It is the way of Hollywood.

Of other films to be added to this group of open-air productions, mention must be made of William K. Howard's *White Gold,* which attempted to appeal to two types of audience, the intelligent and the rest; and Karl Brown's excellent picture, *Stark Love,* with Helen Munday, Forest James, and Silas Miracle. Howard's film was made in the so-called Continental technique, meaning that he paid more attention to atmosphere than to individuals. Instead of the crowded dance-hall, only the shadows were shown; in place of a shot of the corpse, the hero looked behind the door and drew back with horror plainly written in his face. Howard also tried the repetition of single word titles with with some success, but the film as a whole was inclined to be laboured. He was also the director of some early Westerns, *Light of the Western Stars* and *The Border Legion.* Karl Brown's film, which was financed by Famous-Players-Lasky, was taken during 1927, among the primitive descendants of pioneers in the Appalachian mountains of North Carolina. The director had been the cameraman on Paramount's *The Covered Wagon,* and *Stark Love* was a reminder of the grandness of the pictorial beauty of the earlier film. The acting material was raw nature; the story-interest simple and convincing; the direction straightforward with a sense of dramatic value. The film was to be ranged on a level with Flaherty's *Moana* and Jean Epstein's *Finis Terrae.*

*

Returning to the ranks of the ordinary movie directors, there are found a large number of second and third rate film men. Much of their work is of little save passing interest, and does not call for further comment than that usually accorded to it in the daily Press. Most of these secondary directors are like popular dance tunes—they only tell for a short time. Movies are easily made, and just as easily forgotten. On rare occasions, one of their films contains some little device, some twist of the camera that is interesting, some odd close-up which for the moment holds

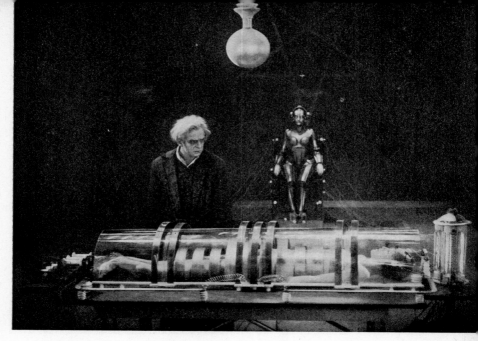

49. METROPOLIS, directed by Fritz Lang. Rudolf Klien-Rogge, Brigitte Helm.
[German, 1925–26]

50. THE STUDENT OF PRAGUE, directed by Henrik Galeen. Conrad Veidt.
[German, 1926]

51 THE BLACK PIRATE, directed by Albert Parker. Douglas Fairbanks, Billie Dove. [American, 1926]

52. THE TOWER OF LIES, directed by Victor Seaström. [American, 1926]

the spectator, but for the most part they are dull. Even as it is characteristic of big directors to convey a great deal in a few shots, so, on the contrary, these small directors tend to photograph much and say nothing. It is these film men who make a steady stream of pictures with which to fill the screens of the world. None of these movies is wholly good or wholly bad. Each is saturated with mental sob-stuff, high-spot thrills, alluring sexual positions, false patriotic motives, spectacular settings, and ravishing clothes. All are turned out with a polished, facile, slick technique. They are conceived, taken, and presented with one purpose in mind—picture-sense. Most of these directors have been in the business some length of time. They may be relied upon to turn out an average picture in a given length of production time, with any given star and any given story.

Herbert Brenon has been making pictures ever since he staggered America with the Annette Kellerman film, *The Daughter of the Gods,* in 1916, for which production he diverted a river from its course and altered the face of a landscape. Brenon, therefore, started his directorial career in the best tradition. Since that date he has produced a continuous flow of movies, mostly of the mock-sentimental kind, including versions of Barrie's *Peter Pan* and *A Kiss for Cinderella; The Side Show of Life; The Alaskan; The Little French Girl;* that very successful, popular film, *Beau Geste,* the forerunner of many similar pictures; and more recently, an adaption of Warwick Deeping's *Sorrell and Son,* a film of guaranteed appeal, but little filmic content. Brenon principally lacks imagination. His sense of pictorial values is sound, but his cinematic interpretation is negligible.

Raoul Walsh has made a curious assortment of films, showing at rare intervals a feeling for cinema and always a strong motive of picture-sense. Chief among his work ranks *Sadie Thompson,* an adaption of Somerset Maugham's brilliant short story and play, *Rain.* In this film, some three years ago, Gloria Swanson made her come-back to the screen and Lionel Barrymore acted with distinction.

Walsh did his best to tell the story of the fugitive from San Francisco, and the professional reformer who persecutes her until he himself is obsessed with sexual desire; but the contrived happy ending, which may have fitted in with United Artists' idea of picture-sense, was mediocre. Nevertheless, Gloria Swanson's performance was remarkable, and succeeded in placing her as an actress of talent far above the usual Hollywood standard. Walsh's second best picture was one of the war films so prevalent a few years ago, and as such was singularly unsuccessful. Despite its mock-heroic character, *What Price Glory?* was directed with some degree of vigour, and was, of course, satisfactory from a commercial point of view. Like the other American war films, it said nothing of the war itself except for a few sequences of blood and thunder. At an earlier date than this, Raoul Walsh had revelled in attempted fantasy, for he was responsible for the ice-cream mixture of *The Thief of Bagdad,* and others of an Eastern texture, such as *The Lady of the Harem.* To his credit, also, are to be placed the Negri film, *East of Suez, The Wanderer, The Loves of Carmen,* and *The Monkey Talks.*

Cecil B. De Mille is likewise to be reckoned among this group of directors, and although his work cannot be accepted with sincerity he is nevertheless a curiosity. Briefly one thinks of De Mille as a pseudo-artist with a flair for the spectacular and the tremendous; a shrewd sense of the bad taste of the lower type of the general public, to which he panders; and a fondness for the daring, vulgar, and pretentious. His productions number many, all of which by reason of their magnitude and publicity are well-known. In particular, he is responsible for *The Ten Commandments, The Volga Boatmen, The Road to Yesterday, The Golden Bed, The King of Kings,* and *The Godless Girl,* none of which demands further investigation.

Donald Crisp is a director of the good, honest type, with a simple go-ahead idea of telling a story. He has made, among others, one of the best of the post-war Fairbanks films, *Don Q,* and Buster Keaton's *The Navigato*r. In the same class are to be reckoned such men as Fred Niblo, who made the spectacle of spectacles, *Ben-Hur,* as well as *The Temptress,* and Fairbanks' *Mark of Zorro;* Victor Fleming, who ' handled ' Emil Jannings in *The Way of All Flesh,* made *Mantrap* with Clara Bow, a pseudo-epic in *The Trumpet Call, Lord Jim,* and *The Virginian,* for which last, however, he deserves warm praise; Rupert Julian, who directed *The Phantom of the Opera, Hell's. Highroad,* and completed *The Merry-Go-Round* when Stroheim left off; and Alan Crosland, maker of *Bobbed Hair, Three Weeks,* and that abominable costume picture with John Barrymore, *Don Juan,* followed by another as bad, *The Beloved Rogue.*

The leader of the sentimentalists and gauzed photography school is, of course, Frank Borzage, who makes pictures for Mr. Fox. He is principally known for that ' film of the year ', *Seventh Heaven,* which he followed later with similar eyewash, *The Street Angel.* Both of these pictures are generally considered as being beautiful, superb, artistic, and superlative in every way, but their titles are all that need be recorded of them.

George Fitzmaurice directs movies like *The Dark Angel* and *Love Lies,* about which there is nothing to say; Marshall Neilan takes the credit for the unfortunate *Tess of the d'Urbervilles, Diplomacy,* and *The Venus of Venice;* Sam Taylor has a knowledge of rough slapstick, and has made some of the Harold Lloyd comedies, Mary Pickford's *My Best Girl,* and lately, the dialogue version of *The Taming of the Shrew.* Tod Browning once made a film which was reputed to be of interest, *The Unholy Three,* and later *The Blackbird, Under Two Flags,* and *The Mystic;* Rowland V. Lee, directed *The Man Without a Country, Havoc,* said to be the best American war film, and *The Outsider;* whilst Allan Dwan made *Tin Gods* and *The Music Master.*

Among those whom I should class as better directors are to be recorded such men as Lewis Milestone, who made an excellent comedy in *Two Arabian Knights,* and has since directed a clever melodramatic film of the bootlegger type,

The Racket, with Louis Wolheim. Milestone is well aware of the right use of half-lighting, of well-chosen camera angles and of contrasted motives of tension with unexpected movement of material. Victor Schertzinger is another director who has done notable work, prominently in that excellent film, *Forgotten Faces,* where, although he was inclined to misuse his moving camera shots, he built up some dramatic situations. He has many pictures to his name, amongst which are *Man and Maid, The Wheel* and *Thunder Mountain.* E. H. Griffith was the maker of a sincere film, *Judgement,* a dramatic theme of a man's cowardice, and has also to his credit *Headlines* and *Bad Company.* Harry Hoyt will be remembered for his competent version of Conan Doyle's extraordinary story, *The Lost World,* a film in which Lewis Stone, Bessie Love, Wallace Beery, and Lloyd Hughes played with distinction.

Dorothy Arzner is a clever woman director who at one time wrote scenarios, took up editing (*The Covered Wagon*) and finally made a picture called *Fashions for Women.* Lois Weber is another woman director, who made that excessively dull movie, *The Sensation Seekers.*

To this long list are to be added the names of some of the older school, like Thomas H. Ince, Ralph Ince, King Baggott, Clarence Badger, Herbert Blache, Charles Brabin, Edwin Carewe, Jack Conway, Irving Cumings, William C. de Mille, Joseph Henaberry, Frank Lloyd, Sam Wood, and Edward Sedgwick.[1]

There are many younger men in Hollywood who, having had their schooling as scenario-writers and assistant-directors to already well-established film makers, are taken on and launched by the big studios. The majority of their work is best described as being modelled on the Lubitsch-Stroheim-Chaplin style : a well assorted medley of ideas gleaned from *The Marriage Circle, Foolish Wives,* and *A*

---

[1] The first three of these directors, at least, merit far more attention than they are given here (in 1929), and the reader is referred to Lewis Jacob's *Rise of the American Film* (1939), and to Miss Iris Barry's various publications and programme notes issued by the Museum of Modern Art Film Library, New York.

Woman of Paris. It is quite unnecessary to analyse such movies at length, for they nearly all conform to what has already been described as the formula of man, woman, and sin. They are slick, facile, flashy, well-photographed pictures, displaying here and there touches of Germanic influence in their camera angles. They are always rapid in pace, being briskly cut, with what are usually termed ' snappy ' titles. It will suffice to mention : Mal St. Clair (*Good And Naughty, The Show Off, Gentlemen Prefer Blondes,* etc.); Monta Bell, assistant to Chaplin on *A Woman of Paris* (*Broadway After Dark, Man, Woman, and Sin, Pretty Ladies,* etc.); William Wellman, who must be given praise for making *Wings,* although that film's merit lay with its fifteen cameramen, and *You Never Know Women,* from Ernst Vadja's story; Victor Heerman (*For Wives Only*); Sidney Franklin (*The Duchess of Buffalo,* with Constance Talmadge, and recently *Wild Orchids,* with Greta Garbo); Paul Bern, who wrote the script for *The Beloved Rogue* and made *Grounds for Divorce;* Frank Tuttle, scenarist for Allan Dwan's *Manhandled,* with Gloria Swanson, and director of *The American Venus* and *Blind Alleys;* James Flood, (*Three Hours*); Roy del Ruth, whose *Wolf's Clothing* was far above the average movie; and H. d'Abbadie d'Arrast, Chaplin's assistant on *The Gold Rush* (*A Gentleman of Paris, Serenade,* and *Service for Ladies,* all with Adolphe Menjou).

The titles of the above movies clearly indicate their subject and trend. They may be summed up, perhaps, in three titles, *The Popular Sin, The Waning Sex,* and *Blonde or Brunette.*

In the last eighteen months, there has arisen a number of new film directors who, owing to the dialogue film, have migrated from the stage. Many of the old silent film directors have also adapted their technique to the new demands of sound. In this group are to be found such men as Harry Beaumont, maker in the past of *Glass Houses, Gold Diggers,* and *Our Dancing Daughters,* and more recently of *The Broadway Melody;* Charles Reisner, who years ago directed Sydney Chaplin in *The Man on the Box,* and made *The Hollywood Revue* and *Chasing Rainbows;* and Marcel Silver, director of *Fox Movietone Follies.* With the dialogue period opened what may be called an era of new names as well as an era of new values. The introduction of this usurping mechanical achievement has rendered many of the old attributes of a film director no longer applicable.

*

Apart from the comedies of Chaplin, it is necessary only to mention the more recent work of Buster Keaton and the expensive knock-about contraptions of Harold Lloyd. Keaton at his best as in *The General, College,* and the first two reels of *Spite Marriage,* has real merit. His humour is dry, exceptionally well constructed and almost entirely mechanical in execution. He has set himself the task of an assumed personality, which succeeds in becoming comic by its very sameness. He relies, also, on the old method of repetition, which when enhanced by his own inscrutable individuality becomes incredibly funny. His comedies show an extensive knowledge of the contrast of shapes and sizes and an extremely pleasing sense of the ludicrous. Keaton has, above all, the great asset of being funny in himself. He looks odd, does extraordinary things and employs uproariously funny situations with considerable skill. The Keaton films are usually very well photographed, with a minimum of detail and a maximum of effect. It would be ungrateful, perhaps, to suggest that he tries to take from Chaplin that which is essentially Chaplin's, but nevertheless Keaton has learnt from the great actor and would probably be the first to admit it.

The Harold Lloyd comedies fall into a lower class, but are usually amusing. In my estimation, at least, Lloyd is not funny in himself and has none of the attributes of Chaplin, or even Keaton. His comedies are fast moving, vigorous in action of the material, being entirely contrived out of a series of comic situations. Lloyd movies are

excellent examples of the gag comedy. Many minds contribute to the nonsense of the escapes and chases and
ingenious escapades that go to make up *College Days,
Safety Last,* and *For Heaven's Sake.* There is no centralisation about a Lloyd comedy as there is in the Chaplin
film. There is no unity of character; no building up of
personality. The Harold Lloyd pictures are good fun.
They may always be relied upon for amusement of a harmless, light and thoughtless nature. They are essentially
physically stimulating. They serve their purpose in that
no audience is left dull or depressed after seeing a Lloyd
comedy.

*

From this brief survey of some of the more important
American films, it will have been seen that most of the output is ephemeral in value. Seldom will a Hollywood film
bear reiteration. It passes through the hands of the story-
writer, the selection committee, the scenario editor, the
treatment writer, the scenarist, the gag-man, the production
committee, the director, the cameraman, the art director,
the players, the title-writer, the professional cutter and the
film editor, until eventually the finished product is launched
on to the massed audiences, who are lured to see it by all
manner of persuasive advertising, exploitation stunts and
suggestive attractions. This life of a movie is precalculated
and preorganised from the beginning to the end.[1] Nevertheless, despite these conditions of manufacture, the mass
production, the obstinate committees, the uncreative
directors, the horrors of the star-system and the corrugated
iron environment, there are occasions when a single film,
the creative work of one man's mind, makes its appearance.
There are in Hollywood, fortunately, men of intelligence
whose very personality over-rides the machinery. With
wisdom and discretion they use to full advantage the organisation of Hollywood and its excellent technical resources.
From Chaplin, Stroheim, Griffith, at one time Fairbanks,

[1] Cf. p. 140.

Lubitsch, and Vidor, there have come films that are of the highest merit : *The Gold Rush, A Woman of Paris, Greed, Broken Blossoms, The Black Pirate, Forbidden Paradise*, and *Hallelujah!* In another category, produced under different conditions from those controlling the making of cine-fiction, there has been the individual work of Flaherty, Karl Brown, Schoedsack, and Cooper : *Moana, Chang, Grass, Stark Love*, and *Nanook*. These were films of great excellence that will endure and be studied in the future. On the whole, however, America's greatest achievements have been in her Westerns, her relatively few natural resources films, and her polished, satirical comedies. Due to the fusion of Chaplin and Lubitsch influence, the best of the cine-fiction films have been the domesticated comedies and the subtly-pointed bedroom pieces; films of the *Wolf's Clothing, So This Is Paris*, and *Serenade* variety. They comprise the lighter side of film production and have been developed to a state of perfection far beyond the dramatic tragedy of *The Way of All Flesh* school. In the dialogue film, the adaptation of stage plays from such writers as Somerset Maugham and Frederick Lonsdale indicates a tendency to continue along these lines.

Hollywood, before the coming of the dialogue film, was a factory of skilled workers, all of whom were able to produce films with a technique that had become polished by experience and efficient organisation. These men are adapting their practical knowledge to the new processes demanded by the visual and aural cinema along the line of least resistance. They are foolishly attempting to combine the widely divergent techniques of the stage and the film. But the public, many of them fresh to the cinema, support the new process in their love of novelty, sensation, and realism. Our filmic knowledge triumphs with ease over the past and the future evils of the cinema; but the present evils of dialogue and realism triumph over our knowledge to-day by reason of their commercial strength.

216

VI

THE SOVIET FILM

There is always a tendency to exaggerate the discovery of a new invention, a fresh philosophy, or an original theory of painting; similarly, the significance of the Soviet film has been largely over-rated by enthusiastic *cinéastes* in this country. Perhaps the primary reason why the discovery of the Soviet cinema has been more momentous in Britain than on the Continent is because, until comparatively recently, all productions from the U.S.S.R. have been withheld from public exhibition by the British Board of Film Censors. In consequence, fanned by eulogistic descriptions from abroad, there has risen a heated demand from the circle of film writers and experimentalists in Britain for the wholesale acceptance of Soviet films. Officially discountenanced, the forbidden productions have assumed gigantic importance as ' works of art ' in the minds of the British intelligentsia. All Soviet films are hailed as the supreme examples of modern cinema; all Soviet directors as filmic geniuses; with the result that the cult for Soviet films (still in great part forbidden) has become slightly hysterical and more than a little tedious in its parrot-like cry.[1]

Actually, the product of the Soviet film industry is to be surveyed with the strictest reservation. It is to be accorded the severest criticism, for it has been born of remarkable circumstances during a span of twelve eventful and restless years. Moreover, it should be remembered that the present state of the Soviet cinema has been made possible only by the social and political events that have taken place in Russia since the October revolution of 1917. But this is not to assume, as is often done, that a similar

[1] *Vide:* the contemporary issue of *Close Up,* Vols. 2-4 (1928-29).

progression of events would automatically produce a cinema such as that of the Soviets in Britain.

The Soviet cinema is immensely powerful. Its films carry social and political contents expressed so emotionally and with such a degree of technical perfection that the content may be accepted in the temporary admiration of the method. This has unfortunately been the case with the numerous over-young and over-enthusiastic *cinéastes,* which is suggestive of their lack of balanced critical faculties. Because of its full use of the resources of the cinema, the Soviet film to-day is in the position to influence an attitude of mind and an outlook on life. It is, in point of fact, produced for that very purpose. On this account, therefore, acceptance of a film produced in the U.S.S.R. as an example of filmic exposition must be guided by rigorous and careful deliberation. In hasty admiration of perfect technique, it is easy to accept content, theme, and meaning without thought as to their full intention.

It will be recalled that among the proposals of the Soviet Government when it assumed control in 1917, was the suggestion that all forms of expression to the public, such as the cinema, the theatre, the press, and literature, should be under the guidance of the State. The aim was, of course, that the new ideas and concepts of the Government should be widely circulated in the outlying areas as well as in the industrial centres. The theatre essentially was to become a unified form of drama, arising out of the social necessities of the masses. This aim has to some extent been successful, having evolved, during the process of rebuilding, a technique such as exists nowhere outside Soviet Russia. Incorporated in this constructive policy for the theatre was a similar but wider aim for the cinema. Originally, I believe, only a few of the Soviet leaders realised the capabilities of the film as an instrument of propaganda, considering the theatre the more powerful. But they have since become aware of the vast superiority of the cinema over the stage, both for economic reasons and for its greater breadth of representation, until now it is the principal medium of expression for the Government. The initial aim of the Soviet film was to reflect and interpret a new social civilisation in the making, as conceived by Marx and realised by Lenin, which resulted in a form of cinema demanding an entirely new scale of values. Lenin intended the theatre to be a microcosm of the complete theory of Bolshevism, to be admired and copied by the masses. But it was Lenin also who declared that ' of all the arts the most important for Russia is, to my mind, that of the cinema.'

The nationalisation of the Soviet film did not take place until 1919, but two years earlier, in December, a special Cinema Commission was held in Leningrad by the People's Commissariat of Education to lay down a future policy. The complete control of film production and distribution, however, soon passed into the hands of the Government and there began the development of the cinema along the lines of Lenin's policy. From that time onward, films were produced according to carefully laid plans, with certain types of films for certain audiences. The new cinema depicted the general policy of the Government and of the people; of construction and of creation. Further, all profit derived from the exhibition of films went to the realisation of better and more productions. Theoretically, it was an admirable state of affairs for the nurturing of a new form of dramatic expression.

Even as in literature themes are developed, ideas propounded, and problems solved beyond the mere exercise of writing and style, so the Soviet directors contrived to employ the visual images of the cinema to express, not, as in other countries, mere thrilling episodes and acrobatic sensations, but the spirit and heart of the people. Under the new policy a film was considered worthless unless it elucidated some new idea for the stimulation of mass thought. On principle, every film presented a problem or a theory which was definitely connected with the everyday life of the persons for whom it was made. A content of sociological importance was the basis of all productions; and

around this was woven a narrative story-interest. Added
to which, numerous pictures were made which depicted the
events of the Revolution and life under the Czarist *régime,*
both of which were, as was to be expected, treated to suit
the Government's purpose. (The exclusion of Trotsky, for
instance, in Eisenstein's *Ten Days that Shook the World,*
renders it inaccurate as an historical document. One
remembers, also, the distortion of historical events in the
French Commune film, Kozintzev and Trauberg's *New
Babylon.*) Commercially, aesthetically, and politically the
cinema was the ideal medium for the presentation of the
Soviet ideology.

We are to understand, then, that the Soviet film, such
as has been produced in increasing numbers as the years
have progressed, is designed to instruct, to develop, and
to connect up the thought and conditions of the outlying villages with that of the big towns; so that each man,
woman, and child in every district shall be made aware of
the social, scientific, industrial, and political progress of the
State. And in order to stimulate the interest of the masses
in the film industry, production is taken into their lives so
that they have opportunities to participate in realisations,
to write scenarios,[1] and to vote approval or disapproval of
a film's content before production takes place. There are
said to be organisations for the close co-operation between
producing companies and the people, so as to enable subjects of significance to all classes to be represented. But,
it must be remembered, Russia is a vast country with great
areas of thinly populated lands in the agricultural districts
where villages are separated by many miles. In order to
secure exhibition of films in these districts, therefore, there
are travelling cinemas, each of which takes a monthly route.
visiting about twenty villages. When it has completed its
round, it begins again with a new programme. Thus even
the most isolated villages are kept constantly in touch with

[1] Léon Moussinac in *Le Cinéma Soviétique* gives the following
information; that, in 1927, the Sovkino received no fewer than 2,000
scenarios from the public; whilst the Vufku-kino, in the same year,
had more than 1,300.

movements in the towns. Each of the latter has, of course, its cinemas, and statistics show a rapid increase in theatres during the last few years. The distribution of films takes place almost exclusively through Government channels; films carrying different contents being sent to various parts, according to the State's calculation of the needs of the populace in each district. In this way, the cinema reaches and influences the minds of the workers, the tradesmen, and the citizens in the towns, as well as the peasants in Siberia and the tribesmen in Turkestan.[1]

Hence, the content of every film is its *raison d'être*, whether of social, heroic, epic, historical, romantic, human, or national importance. Moreover, it is out of the desire to express this content with the greatest amount of emotional effect on the simple minds of the masses that the cinematic technique of Soviet directors has developed to a state of efficiency equalled by no other film-producing country in the world.

*

Soviet films fall into various classes, each made for a special purpose, and these are roughly as follow :

(*a*) General subjects dealing with life before, during, and after the Revolution, including satires, dramas, comedies, melodramas, etc. The usual aim of these pictures is to show the tyranny and oppression under the Czarist *régime* and the benefits derived from Soviet control. The subject is approached through various channels *viz.*, the *mass* or *epic film*, of comparatively contemporary interest, showing the masses challenging the old-established authority (*Ten Days that Shook the World, Battleship Potemkin, Strike*); the *individual film*, depicting the effect of the Revolution on a single person, or group of persons (*Mother, The End of St. Petersburg*); the *historical* or *monumental film*, dealing with the past historical events of massed revolt (*New Babylon, S.V.D., Revolt in*

[1] Cf. the development of non-theatrical distribution in the United Kingdom by the British Ministry of Information during 1940-45.

Kazan); the *reconstruction film,* portraying life under the advantages of the Soviet *régime,* the rebuilding of the New Russia and the formation of the Worker, the Citizen, and the Peasant, etc. (*The Fragment of an Empire, Life's Roads, The Peasant Women of Riazan, Pits, The Girl with the Band-Box*); and such films as Eisenstein's *The General Line,* which showed the State laying economic foundations for mechanised agriculture; Dziga-Vertov's *The Eleventh Year,* which reflected the economic and social development of the Ukraine under ten years of Soviet control; and *Turksib,* Turin's superb film of the construction of the Turkestan-Siberian railway.

(*b*) The educational, scientific, and cultural film, which is a form of cinema that the Government has developed to a wide degree. Instructional films are made about every conceivable subject: industrial, medical, geographical, ethnological, etc., and are shown widely with a view to improving education. Special films are made, for example, for the technical instruction of engineers and electricians, and for the officers and men of the Red Army, on field manœuvres, aerial defence and attack, etc.

(*c*) The news-reel, which, as in other countries, is a survey of the events of the week. It is, of course, largely used to popularise the leaders of the country.

(*d*) The children's film, both cine-fiction and educational.

For each of these groups there exists in every producing company separate scenario departments and information bureaux, which are capable of dealing with the various stages of scenario treatment. This highly developed organisation for the classification, cataloguing, and sorting of film scenarios is an important feature of the Soviet cinema. In no other film producing country is so much attention paid to the construction of scenario work. Under the control of the central bureau is the selection of themes for the year's output, so that the films may accord exactly with the aim of the Government, politically, socially, and financially. There exist also other departments which deal with the scenarios and manuscripts sent in by the people, and with the examination of literature, documents, etc., published in Russia and abroad that would make possible film material. The realisation of the films, once the subjects are chosen, is again a matter of close collaboration. The production units are allotted, according to their characteristics, to deal with such subjects as are deemed suitable to them. The workers in every studio (directors, cameramen, scenarists, architects, etc.) are all assessed, so to speak, with regard to their individual qualifications. In this way the achievement of perfect collectivism is attempted in film production.

The majority of the technicians and acting personnel go through special courses of training before assuming their positions in the studios. As is well-known, there exists the Moscow State School of Cinematography, which was founded in 1919 for the intensive training of workers in all branches of the industry. There are also several other schools throughout the country, in Leningrad and in the Ukraine. All producing firms have to give a certain number of positions in their studios to graduates from the State schools. In the latter, every section of film production is included, so that before entry into a studio a worker has some knowledge of film technique, acting, psychology, dramatic literature, make-up, acrobatics, dancing, etc., as well as his specialised skill in his particular job, be it scenario-work, assistant-direction, photography, lighting, set-construction, or in the laboratory. There exists also the Fex group, at Leningrad, for the sole purpose of experiment and *avant-garde* work. All the State schools are regularly visited by the better-known directors and technicians, who lecture and instruct on theory and on their practical experience of production work.

*

Briefly, then, the cinema is the main medium of the Commissariat of Education for the instruction of the people; and thus, we understand that the primary aim of the Soviet Government is to carry the principles of Communism by means of the cinema, not only throughout Russia, but to the farthest corners of the world. If the intellectual classes of foreign countries find their aesthetic ideal in these films (as is perhaps the case) then so much the better for the Soviet, since it will render it easier for their content to be absorbed.

*

It may be suggested that such an ideal state of conditions for film production cannot exist without some flaw in the pattern. The complete organisation, co-operation, and harmony of working conditions appear to be the dream-paradise of the *cinéaste*. There is, however, a serious drawback in the apparent happiness of the Soviet film industry; it lies at the root of the organisation, actually in the policy of the Government itself. There is a certain inward antagonism between the Government and the production units. The cinema is controlled by Communists whose sole aim is the spread of their faith; whilst the realisation of the best films is in the hands of the workers, who are also by way of being artists. As a result, a film director, who for some years past has been training his mind and has been contented with the policy dictated to him in his work, may now find himself in the position of being unable to realise his aesthetic principles if they do not conform to the wishes of the Government. He can only make a film of a subject approved by the controlling State bureau.

Although probably he has freedom of expression in actual technical representation, his aesthetic progress is limited by the demands of the production committee. Unless he is a Communist, his work may become stultified by the eternal theme of propaganda. It is ridiculous to suggest that the Soviet Government produces films for the sheer love of the medium. They do indeed make ' art ' films, but only for export in order to secure the appreciation of foreign intelligentsia. I have no hesitation in saying that the Soviet

53. HOTEL IMPERIAL, directed by MAURITZ STILLER. [American, 1926]

54. HUMAN SPARROWS, directed by WILLIAM BEAUDINE. MARY PICKFORD.
[American, 1926]

55. BED AND SOFA, directed by ABRAM ROOM. VLADIMIR FOGEL, NIKOLAI BATALOV. [Soviet, 1926]

56. MOTHER, directed by V. I. PUDOVKIN. [Soviet, 1926]

film director is as restricted in his self-development as his *confrère* in Hollywood is bound by the capitalistic methods of picture-sense and star-system. Neither is free to develop his knowledge of the cinema along an individual instinctive course. The Soviet director, it is true, has the benefit of being able to realise his own ideas of technical expression (*viz.* editing and cutting) which the German, American, and British director has not; but they are each equally prevented from progress in the realisation of their intellectual, spiritual, and creative conception of the film as a means of self-expression.[1]

The two Soviet directors, S. M. Eisenstein[2] and V. I. Pudovkin, have achieved during their evolutionary period the enviable position of being the most eminent directors in the world. They have been satisfied with State control over their themes and concepts whilst they have been otherwise interested in the perfection of their technique. But they are now in the extraordinary position of possessing a marvellous degree of technical accomplishment and of being unable to employ it freely to express their personal attitude towards life. Either they must continue to be good Communists, content to remain making films for the purpose of propaganda, or they must leave their native country and seek employment elsewhere. It is certain that if they are true artists, with the inevitable international outlook of an artist, they will never be allowed completely free expression of their minds in Soviet Russia under the present system of State control.

This remarkable condition of affairs can only be applied at the moment to the few eminent directors of the U.S.S.R. (Eisenstein, Pudovkin, and possibly Kozintzev, Trauberg, Turin, Dovjenko, and Ermler) for the majority of Soviet *régisseurs* are mechanical in their outlook and will be easily persuaded to manufacture a steady output of State-controlled films. The position will be rendered more acute,

---

[1] Cf. the subsequent development of Eisenstein, Pudovkin, Dovjenko, Turin, *et al.*

[2] Died in Moscow, February, 1948.

however, when the film schools produce further creative
mentalities. Even the iron rule of a Soviet *régime* cannot
suppress the birth and development of an instinctively
creative mind.

*

As might be expected from an industry organised under
a system of bureaucracy there is a network of producing
companies in Soviet Russia, each employing its individual
directors and units. The principal concerns are: the
Sovkino, with studios at Leningrad and Moscow; the
Mejrabpom-Russ, with studios at the same cities; the
Vufku-kino, at Kiev and Odessa, in the Ukraine; the
Goskinprom, at Tiflis in Georgia; the *Belgoskino,* at Minsk
in White Russia; the *Turkmenkino,* in Turkmenistan; the
Vostok-kino, at Baku; and the *Armenkino,* in Armenia.

The Sovkino, which came into being in 1925, employ
many directors, of whom the most important are S. M.
Eisenstein, Lev Kuleshov, Abram Room, Kozintzev and
Trauberg, Ermler, Olga Preobrashenskaia, Yuri-Tarich,
Popov, and Esther Schub. They are the sole distributors of
Soviet films abroad and the only importers of the foreign
product. To the Mejrabpom-Russ (a collective word
meaning the International Workers' Relief) are attached
V. I. Pudovkin, Y. A. Protazanov, Fiodor Otzep, Kon-
stantin Eggert, V. Obelenski, Zheliabuzhski, Boris Barnet,
V. R. Gardin, etc. The Vufku-kino, in the Ukraine, claim
Dovjenko, Dziga-Vertov, Kauffmann, Georgi Stabavoi,
Raizman, Kavaléridze, etc. Many other directors of
scientific and documentary films, as well as of cine-fiction,
attached to these and other companies, are far too numerous
for inclusion.

*

Until 1925, when the production of Eisenstein's *Battleship Potemkin* marked a new era in the technique of the

cinema, numerous films were realised by various producing concerns in Moscow and Leningrad—by the Sevsapkino, the Kino-Sever (Kino-North), the Goskino, and the Mejrabpom-Russ companies. Few of these pictures, however, have been shown outside Soviet Russia, and the possibility that they will now be seen is remote. In any case, I do not believe that they were of great value save as a training ground for the directors of to-day, nearly all of whom were engaged in some minor capacity during this early period. Pantelev, Doronin, Viskovski, Kuleshov, Gardin, Protazanov, Razumni, Zheliabuzhski, and Barski were some of the principal directors of that time; such men as Otzep, Nathan Zarkhi (later scenarist to the Pudovkin films) and Yuri-Tarich being employed as scenarists. Pictures of some interest to be connected with this era were *Palace and Fortress,* a large-scale historical production, by Ivanovski; *The Adventures of an Octoberite,* a political satire, by Kozintzev and Trauberg; *The Executioners,* a big production dealing with political events from 1905 to 1918, by Pantelev; *The Death Ray,* by Kuleshov, from a scenario by Pudovkin; *The Adventures of Mr. West Among the Bolsheviki,* a comedy of manners, also by Kuleshov; *The Cigarette Merchant of Mosselprom,* a comedy by Zheliabuzhski; and *The Tailor of Torjok,* by Protazanov. During this transition stage several art-films, theatrical in technique, were also produced, some being shown in Britain at a later date.[1] Of these may be mentioned *The Postmaster,* from the novel by Pushkin, scenario by Otzep and direction by Zheliabuzhski; *Morosko,* a folklore film by the same director; *Polikushka,* from the Tolstoi novel; and a macabre melodrama, *The Marriage of the Bear,* directed and played by Konstantin Eggert, from a script by Lunacharsky. These were produced by the Mejrabpom-Russ company and members of the first

[1] Mr. F. A. Enders, of Messrs. Film Booking Offices, London, was responsible for the handling of *The Postmaster* and *The Marriage of the Bear* in Britain. He also held several other films from the U.S.S.R. at that time, including the celebrated *Potemkin,* and *Aëlita,* but was unable to show them owing to censorship regulations.

Moscow Art Theatre took part in their realisation. To them is to be added the big decorative production of *Aëlita*, directed by Protazanov, from the play by Count Alexei Tolstoi. This was an extraordinary Martian fantasy, combining the events in Russia during 1917 and 1918 with a fictional story on the planet; it was notable for its wonderful massed grouping of crowds and for the cubist settings and costumes designed by Isaac Rabinovitch and Madame Alexandra Exter, of the Kamerny Theatre, Moscow. It has not been shown in Britain. The influence of the stage, in setting, lighting, and acting was strongly marked on these ' art ' films, there being no trace of the dynamic filmic properties that were later to become the main characteristics of the Soviet cinema.

The first experiments in film construction using strips of celluloid as the basic material, which are the foundation of Soviet film technique, appear to have been due to Lev Kuleshov. He was the director of several productions, including *On the Red Front, The Death Ray, Expiation*, and recently made *The Gay Canary* and *2 Buldi 2*, as well as being the founder of a school of cinematography. Kuleshov tried many experiments in the arrangement of pieces of film in different orders, finding that he could obtain remarkable effects by the relation, inter-relation, and juxtaposition of the various lengths. He logically maintained that in every art there was, first, a material and, secondly, a method of composing that material according to its nature; further, he determined that in the cinema, the material was the film strips of photographic record, and the composing was the act of editing, or piecing these strips together. His famous experiment with the actor Mosjoukine and the plate of soup, the coffin, and the little girl is probably too well-known to be repeated. Some time later, Pudovkin, who at that time was working on scenarios, became interested in the experiments of Kuleshov, and in 1923 they formed together a production unit and made *The Adventures of Mr. West Among the Bolsheviki*. This was followed later by Pudovkin's film, *Chess Fever*, in which José

Capablanca was made to appear to play a part merely by the cutting and composition of film strips. Thus it is from the original experiments of Kuleshov and Pudovkin that the modern school of constructive editing and cutting has developed. It is of interest to note Pudovkin suggests as a probable reason for the progress of editing among the Soviet technicians, that in the early days there was a shortage of film stock, and that whilst they were unable to find fresh film for their cameras, the Soviet technicians had ample time to evolve cinematic theories. Not only this, but they were forced to utilise what stock they had with the greatest care in order to get the best effects, which provided a contrast to the chaos and haste so characteristic of the studios of Hollywood and Britain at that time.[1]

*

The directors generally included in the left-wing, or most advanced school, of Soviet film production are S. M. Eisenstein, V. I. Pudovkin, G. Kozintzev and L. Trauberg, Lev Kuleshov, and to a lesser extent, Dovjenko, Turin, and Ermler. The work of Eisenstein, who was at one time trained as an engineer and an architect, is known by four productions. He has particular leanings towards the drama and comedy of the Japanese theatre and an immense interest in the work of Sigmund Freud. His early experiences were varied. He worked in the Russian army as a designer of field fortifications; he painted camouflage and propaganda on the sides of cattle-trucks and trains; he was employed as a designer in the workers' theatre in Moscow; he joined Meierhold, but was unable to agree with him; he studied Leonardo da Vinci and the reflexological school of Pavlov

[1] Almost all young technicians employed by John Grierson at the E.M.B. Film Unit in Britain in 1929-33 made their introduction to film technique by editing film already shot by other directors or cameramen for other purposes. In this way, they learnt to appreciate the value of celluloid before they were permitted to take a film shot themselves. Subsequent training at some British documentary units has followed this disciplinary method, which has done much to inspire respect for the materials of the medium.

at one and the same time; and he has a fondness for the melodramatic thrillers of Eugène Sue. In 1924 he made his first mass film, *Strike;* in 1925, *Battleship Potemkin,* which was originally planned as a section only of a larger film, *1905,* the latter idea being abandoned and the section being shown separately. In 1926, he began work on *The Old and the New,* known also as *The General Line,* but interrupted production in order to make *October,* later called *Ten Days that Shook the World,*[1] one of the several films commissioned by the Government in connection with the tenth anniversary celebrations of the Revolution. Upon completion of *Ten Days that Shook the World,* he returned to *The General Line,* finishing it in 1929. In all his films he has been assisted by G. V. Alexandrov, with Edward Tisse as his principal cameraman. I find it of significance that Tisse was originally employed in news-reel work, and thus is admirably suited to Eisenstein's impulsive method of working.

In his first three films, Eisenstein has been interested in the representation of the mass mind, in particular the mass challenging the established authorities. He has sought to express the mind of the people and not of the individual, and for this reason his work is to be placed on the epic scale. The theme of *Battleship Potemkin* is familiar. It concerned the revolt of the crew of a battleship against their officers on account of the bad food; the warm reception of the rebel ship by the townspeople of Odessa; the attack on the latter by the local military; and the final meeting of the battleship with the remainder of the Russian fleet. *Ten Days that Shook the World* was a representation of the events that followed the establishment of the Provisional Government in 1917; the flight of Kerensky; the attack on the Winter Palace; and the triumph of Lenin.

---

[1] As far as can be ascertained, it was the German distributors who sought to find more popular titles for Soviet films; hence *October* became *Ten Days that Shook the World* (presumably taken from John Reed's book of that name), *The Heir to Jenghiz Khan* became *Storm Over Asia,* and *The Old and the New* became *The General Line.* Subsequent film writers seem to prefer the German titles, and so I have changed to them in this revised edition.

Both of these films were supreme examples of advanced cinematography in that they were a synthetic combination of the emotional, the documentary and the absolute film.[1]

The intense dynamic vitality that is the keynote of Eisenstein's personality is the dominating feature of his cinematic expression. His films are unparalleled examples of ruthless, throbbing, vigorous direction. With absolute faith he remains true to the central aim of his theme. He does not seek help from outside sources, from irrelevant but symbolic references, as does Pudovkin, in the expression of his content. There are no isolated characters, no individual mannerisms or personal developments in his films. He works with broad vision, with the central theme of revolt as his one tremendous purpose. It was the collective spirit of the sailors in *Battleship Potemkin* and the feelings of the mass in *Ten Days that Shook the World* that gave those films their grand, sweeping, awe-inspiring quality. Throughout the former, it was the *line* of guards, the *twirling* parasols, the *breadth* of the lapping waves, the *sails* of the yachts, the *architectural rotation* of the steps, the *flapping* of the tent on the quay, the *wind under* the sheet that covered the captive sailors, the *mass-suspense* of the rebel crew as they waited for the fleet, that were significant. Similarly in *Ten Days that Shook the World,* it was the gigantic *statue* which guarded the streets, the *architecture* and *chandeliers* of the Winter Palace, the *floating pamphlets* in the river, the *banners* of the crowd, the *rifles* of the guard, that were the main factors of expression. Added to which, Eisenstein has a wonderful sense of pictorial composition and a unique feeling for the constant movement of his screen material. The lighting of his scenes is always so arranged and contrasted that the images never fail to convey their meaning at the first flash. He has, in company with Griffith and Abel Gance, an amazing sense of the pure visual image, apart from any interest in human character. It is

[1] The reader is referred to Eisenstein's Article, *The Fourth Dimension in the Kino,* published in *Close Up* (Vol. 6, Nos. 3, 4), in which is propounded his theory for the 'ideological film' and the evolution of intellectual cinematography'.

from his images, expressive only of collective spirit, that he constructs his main, vibrating theme.

Eisenstein is essentially impulsive, spontaneous and dramatic in his methods. He does not work from a detailed manuscript like Pudovkin, for he has not the deliberate, calculating mind of the latter. He prefers to wait until the actual moment of production and then immediately seize upon the right elements for the expression of his content. It is of note to recall that neither the famous steps sequence at Odessa, nor the misty shots of the harbour, were included in the original manuscript for *Battleship Potemkin;* but as soon as Eisenstein reached Odessa and found these features, he at once expanded his script to include them. He is thus a brilliant exception to the theory of complete preconception which is dealt with elsewhere in this volume.

He builds with a remarkable process of cutting, an overlapping of movement from one shot into the next that filmically gives double strength to his images. He seldom uses images without movement of material, unless it is to convey atmosphere (as in the shots of the gods and architecture in *Ten Days that Shook the World*), which he overlaps, thus emphasising the content. For example, the raising of the bridge in *Ten Days that Shook the World,* with the dead horse and the girl's hair as details, was so overlapped and shot from every available angle that the actual movement was synthesised into at least a dozen filmic movements. It is the *insistence* so produced that gives the work of Eisenstein such extraordinary strength. His films can only be described as producing the sensation of throbbing, pulsating, and prickling like that of a purring piece of machinery. The spectator is conscious solely of the insistence, the astonishing urge of expression. These are the characteristics of the Eisenstein film that Edmund Meisel incorporated in his musical scores for *Battleship Potemkin* and *Ten Days that Shook the World,* thereby rendering the presentation of these films doubly emotional. The key to the power of Eisenstein's direction is the relation that lies between the cutting and the material content, utterly different from the constructive editing of Pudovkin. The rhythmic cutting of Eisenstein is governed by the physiology of material content, whereas the editing of Pudovkin is controlled by the constructive representation of the elements of the scene, governed by the psychological expression of the content. In the words of Moussinac : ' *un film d'Eisenstein ressemble à un cri; un film de Poudovkine évoque un chant.'*

In his most recent work, Eisenstein seems to be divided in his outlook, his mass concept being split by the character of an individual. Throughout *The General Line* there was a division of interest between the character of Lapkina, the peasant girl, and the sociological content of the theme. It was, of course, a film definitely created for the purpose of instructing the agricultural community, to persuade them to adopt modern methods of machinery instead of their primitive ways, and from this point of view was probably successful. Cinematically, it was of interest in sequence construction and the rhythmic placing of titles, as well as in the superb beauty of the pictorial compositions. The individual types of the peasants, the great stretching shots of landscape, of wind, of storm, of clouds, were magnificent. The opening was conceived on a vast scale representing the immensity of the area of Soviet Russia and its millions of illiterate peasants. The whole conception was an enormous undertaking, and, taking into allowance the period of interruption for the production of *Ten Days that Shook the World,* Eisenstein may be said to have succeeded far beyond expectation in his task.[1]

As will have been gathered, Pudovkin is essentially the constructive director, perhaps more interested in the method of expressing his themes than in the themes themselves. His films contain more study, more deliberation, more calculation, more esoteric intellectuality than those of Eisenstein. Just as the themes of the latter are expressed through the collective spirit of people and things, so are Pudovkin's

[1] Cf. Eisenstein's new theories on tonal and overtonal montage, pp. 108, 109.

individual characters expressed through the themes. Pudovkin is scientific and analytical in his outlook; the builder of a film composition from small pieces, essentially psychologically dramatic. He is less spiritual and less physical than Eisenstein. He is more methodical and less visionary.

By profession originally a chemical engineer (a fact not without significance), he first became interested in cinematic representation through the experiments of Kuleshov, as we have seen. He has made five films to date, *viz.*, *The Mechanism of the Brain* (1926), in collaboration with the professors of Pavlov's laboratory at the Academy of Sciences, Leningrad; *Chess Fever* (1925); *Mother,* from the story by Maxim Gorki (1926); *The End of St. Petersburg,* one of the several films commissioned by the Soviet Government in connection with the tenth anniversary celebrations of the Revolution (1927); and *Storm over Asia.* He has also recently worked on a sound film, *Life is Beautiful.*[1]

The key to Pudovkin's direction lay plainly in *The Mechanism of the Brain,* for it gave an exposition of the methods which he employs for the selection of his visual images, based on an understanding of the working of the human mind. But most important of Pudovkin films to date was undoubtedly *Mother,* for in its brilliant realisation were found not only the elements of his constructive process, but a clue (in the opening scenes) to his future development in the phase of non-political cinema. It is to the treatment of the opening scenes in *Mother* that, I understand, Pudovkin has returned in the production of *Life is Beautiful.* In *Mother,* we discovered the scientific method of the decomposition of a scene into its ingredients, the choice of the most powerful and suggestive, and the rebuilding of the scene by filmic representation on the screen. In this respect, I recall the sequence of suspense at the gate of the factory; the gradual assembly of the workers; the feeling of uncertainty as to what was to happen. This was the result of an

[1] Cf. footnote, pp. 106, 564.

extraordinarily clever construction of shots and of camera set-ups in order to achieve one highly emotional effect. It may, perhaps, appear the simplest of methods, the basis of all filmic representation, but it needs the creative skill of a Pudovkin to extract such dramatic force from a scene. I recall, also, the scene with the falling of the clock; the discovery of the hidden fire-arms under the floorboards; the trial, with the judges drawing horses on their blotting pads; the coming of spring; the escape from the prison; and the final crescendo ending of the cavalry charge. It is impossible to describe the emotional effect of this film. Without hesitation, I place it amongst the finest works in the history of the cinema.

The primary weapon in the building of scenes is Pudovkin's use of reference by cross-cutting. In *Mother,* there was the constant inclusion of landscape, of nature, noticeable in every sequence. It was not symbolic, as with the porcelain figures in *The Living Corpse,* but the sheer use of imagery to reinforce drama. The shots of empty landscape in the opening; the trees and the lake cut in with the boy in prison; the breaking ice, rising by cross-cutting to a stupefying climax in reference to the cavalry charge. It is this breadth of reference that builds up the Pudovkin scene with such force.

The End of St. Petersburg, although a brilliant example of the methods of Pudovkin, had not the intense concentration of *Mother.* It had not the compelling force, the contact with reality that made the latter so great. The content sought to express the events of the war years, the overthrow of the Czarist *régime,* and the final establishment of the People's Government. It was, in other words, the transition of St. Petersburg to Leningrad. There were two subsidiary themes to the main purpose; the coming of the peasant boy to the city in search of work, and his experience in the war; and the story of the old Bolshevik and his wife. Above all was the overwhelming triumph of the Soviets. It was an astonishing film, composed with the full power of Pudovkin's filmic mind, at once overpowering and convincing. There were many memorable sequences : the peasant and his companion looking for work, coming to the Palace of Justice, the approach through a maze of columns to the base of one great column; the amazing scenes of hysteria at the outbreak of war, the fluttering banners and flowers; the shots of the war-front cross-cut with those of the stock exchange; the attack on the Winter Palace. Every sequence was a wonderful example of construction, of the values of cutting and of dramatic camera angles, but the film had neither the unity nor the universal understanding of *Mother*.

With *Storm Over Asia* Pudovkin rose to the height of his career in some sequences, whilst in others he lost the thread of his theme by interest in local environment. The whole effect was one of unevenness. In company with the two preceding films, it was a masterpiece of filmic construction, of referential cross-cutting, and of the representation of mixed mentalities. It opened with a series of landscape shots of distant hills, of small round huts, of great storm clouds; and from the distance the spectator was taken nearer by approaching shots. The whole of the first part up to the visit to the lamaserai was magnificent. Thereafter, the theme inclined to wander, to be interested in local detail rather than in the significance of that detail. There were moments of great power, however, as when the British soldier took Bair to be shot; the witty cross-cutting between the scenes of the general's wife dressing and the preparation of the lamas for the festival; and the terrific storm scenes at the close. These were Pudovkin at his best and most emotional, but the film as a whole was broken up and over-long.

As is well known, Pudovkin prefers, whenever possible, to work with raw material, building it in terms of filmic representation to achieve his desired result. Consequently he has filled his pictures with the most remarkable types of many nationalities. *Storm Over Asia,* for example, in its scenes of the fur market and the festival of the lamas brought material to the screen that had never before been

236

photographed. The types were as amazing as those of the peasants in Eisenstein's *The General Line*. Pudovkin has been very successful in his results with these naturalistic methods till now, and I believe that working on similar lines he will achieve even greater success. I am convinced that his principles of filmic construction, at once scientific, rhythmically structural, philosophic, and analytical, are those calculated to achieve the most powerful results.

To be included also among the advanced Soviet directors are two men of the younger school, G. Kozintzev and L. Trauberg, who have in collaboration realised several films, including *S.V.D.* (*The Union of a Great Cause*), *The Devil's Wheel*, *The Adventures of an Octoberite*, and *The Cloak*, from Gogol. They have, at the expense of their Government, studied film production in Paris and Berlin. Their principal interest, however, lies in their recent production, *New Babylon*, a film based on the events of the Paris Commune. Unlike other directors of the left-wing, who are chiefly concerned with the naturalism of their subject content, Kozintzev and Trauberg favour a form of costume melodrama, stylised and slightly romantic. For the expression of this heroic romanticism, they employ the recognised advanced forms of editing and cutting, as originated by the theories of Pudovkin and Kuleshov. *New Babylon*, although somewhat loosely composed and lacking the closely woven pattern of Pudovkin's early work, was conceived and realised with technical skill. The environment of the opening, cross-cut from the interior of the emporium to the café, was well established, as was the capture of the guns on the hill. The film suffered principally from over-length and a straggling continuity of narrative towards the end. It was, however, a progression from their earlier work, in particular from *S.V.D.*, which was a cloak and sword melodrama set in the Decembrist period, about the second decade of the nineteenth century. It was notable for its lovely scenes of the military in the snow-fields and an ice carnival. The chief merit of the direction of these directors lies in their brilliant handling of crowd work, of constant movement among turbulent pictorial compositions.

Of particular interest, also, among the younger school is the work of Alexander Dovjenko, one of the directors for the Vufkukino, of the Ukraine, who, although not technically of the left-wing group, is outstanding for his individuality of vision. In many peculiarities, Dovjenko is unique, not only in the cinema of Soviet Russia, but in that of the world. He has primarily an extraordinary faculty for adapting the characteristics of writers and poets as well as those of other directors, welding them with personal touches into his themes. He has no sense of completeness, little conception of a film as a unified whole, but he contrives nevertheless to charge his work with ideas that are universal. His two films, *Zvenigora* and *Arsenal,* were filled with poetic mysticism and magic, and were almost supernatural in their wild vagueness. He combines the mystical feeling of Dostoievski, Hoffmann and Gogol in his ever-wandering imagination. His ideas are disjointed and his filmic expression is as yet immature, for he has but limited knowledge of the exposition of his imagination in constructive cinematic terms. He has, however, a definite sense of the devices of the camera, instanced in the slow-motion opening to *Zvenigora,* and the abrupt cessation of material movement in *Arsenal.* His mysticism is fascinating. For example, in the latter film, a man lit a candle for his ikon; the features of Shevchenko, the national poet, grew disdainful; he leaned down from his picture and blew out the candle in the man's hand. Again, the soldiers were racing from the front with a sleigh on which was a coffin; in the village the widow waited beside a grave which was already mysteriously dug; the soldiers urged the horses to go faster; one of the animals turned its head and said: ' All right, we are going as fast as we can ! ' But, admirable as was the conception of this incident, it was not sufficiently effective in cinematic expression. It called for a dozen quick flashes of the horses and a title split among them.

Both *Zvenigora* and *Arsenal* were erratic but impulsively

created with a combined aesthetic and spiritual mysticism. Actually, even to the northern Soviets, much of Dovjenko's work is unintelligible, for he seeks to express legends and folk-lore peculiar to the Ukraine and illogical to a spectator unversed in the traditions of the locale. For this reason, *Zvenigora* was poorly received in Moscow and Leningrad, and I am informed that much of its curious incident, such as the placing of the bomb on the railway lines and the extraordinary dream sequence, was only understandable to a Ukrainian gifted in local politics. Memorable were the scenes of the old man on the grassy hillsides, wrapt in his magic visions; the digging for the imaginary treasure; the poetry of the trees and the slopes; the enchanting beginning of the Cossacks riding in slow-motion; and the passages in the woods with the brigands and the old man's evocations of hidden treasure.

It is my belief that in Dovjenko, Soviet Russia has a director of unprecedented vision, of wonderful imagination and of rare freedom of mind. If it is possible for him to learn through experience the right filmic exposition of his astonishing concepts (and he seems on the correct path in the use of camera devices), Dovjenko will develop into a cinematic artist of unique genius. With the exception of the work of Eisenstein and Pudovkin, and Turin's *Turksib,* Dovjenko's two films are the most stimulating and poetic yet realised in the U.S.S.R.[1]

*

In contradistinction to the work of the left-wing directors, whose principal interest lies in technical methods of construction and expression of content, the characteristic of the right-wing is the sociological purpose of their productions. Predominant in this group is Abram Room, who is a psychologist director interested in the exposition of the

[1] *Vide, Celluloid: The Film To-day* (Longmans Green, 1931), the chapter on Dovjenko's *Earth,* pp. 135-153.

interplay of emotions between an intimate group of persons. He is inclined to approach the narrative situations in his films through the reactions of the participants, bringing their inner thoughts to the attention of the spectator by a careful photographic selection of their small, possibly insignificant, outer actions. He suppresses the environment of the narrative, except where it can emphasise the human relationship, and employs external objects only when they are of direct consequence to his characters. It will be seen that in this detail, Room is in direct contrast with the methods of the left-wing. His direction is extremely simple and straightforward, relying almost entirely on the acting talents of his cast and narrative material for emotional effect. Each of his films has carried a strong sociological content, of personal, domestic, and contemporary importance. From a psychological point of view, Room seems primarily absorbed in the psychological and physical attitude of men towards women. This was the thematic basis of his best-known film, the notorious *Bed and Sofa,* which has met with approval in most countries, though it was refused public exhibition in Britain even after certain deletions had been effected. It was, however, shown privately to the Film Society, London, April 7th, 1929.

The sociological theme of *Bed and Sofa* was in sympathy with the general movement to raise the social level of women by the frank realisation of masculine selfishness. Room took the narrative of a husband, his wife, and another man, of universal consequence, and placed it in an environment of Moscow during the housing shortage problem. Out of the peculiar circumstances arising from the nature of the environment, he contrived situations that lent themselves to an expression of his motive. He carried the first two-thirds of his treatment of the eternal triangle with almost perfect direction, until at that point at which a decision had to be made in order to carry the moral content, he descended to a sentimental and banal motherhood feeling on the part of the wife, thereby destroying the intensity of the drama, but achieving his sociological motive. More-

57. MOANA, directed by ROBERT J. FLAHERTY.   [American, 1923–25]

58. THE GENERAL LINE, directed by S. M. EISENSTEIN.   MARFA LAPKINA.
[Soviet, 1926–29]

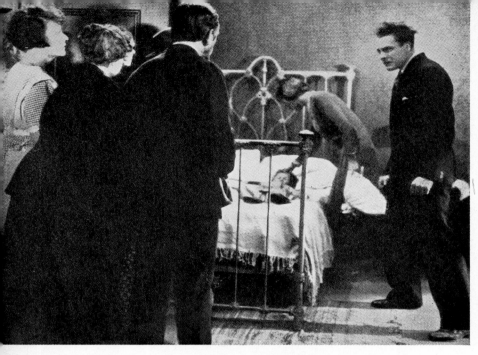

59. THE CROWD, directed by KING VIDOR. JAMES MURRAY, ELEANOR BOARDMAN. [American, 1927]

60. UNDERWORLD, directed by JOSEF VON STERNBERG. GEORGE BANCROFT. [American, 1927]

over, it was apparent that this sudden discrepancy, providing a weak conclusion to an otherwise brilliant film, was due to a concession to the policy of the producers, to wit the discouragement of abortion in the U.S.S.R. Aesthetically speaking, it was neither the logical nor natural ending for the first two-thirds of the film. Had *Bed and Sofa* been finished from the opposite point of view, I believe that it would have been one of the greatest films yet made. The mental understanding that controlled the direction of the earlier portions was amazing. The emphasis of contrasted moods, of space and compression, of sense of humour and depression, was conveyed to the spectator with tremendous psychological knowledge. There was no gesture, however small, on the part of the characters (admirably played by Nicolai Batalov, Ludmilla Semyonova, and Vladimir Fogel) which had not supreme significance in revealing the inner working of their minds. The construction of the situations was perfectly contrived, the continuity having a smooth fluidity that enveloped the spectator. The balance of the scenario and the arrangement of the alternating incidents were masterly. Technically, the cutting was so good as to be almost unnoticeable. I suggest that, despite the failure of the concluding sequences, *Bed and Sofa* was an unequalled instance of pure psychological, intimate, cinematic representation of human character.

Room's first film, *Death Bay,* was made a year previously, in 1925. It was of interest as the early work of a clever director, but was primitive in many respects, lacking the construction of *Bed and Sofa*. It is not worth detailed comment being notable chiefly for the sparkling quality of the landscape environment in the Black Sea district. He has since made *The Pits,* and *The Ghost that Never Returns* from a story by Henri Barbusse. The former was again uneven in texture, certain passages of intense emotional feeling between the girl and her lover in her squalid room being upset by the propaganda scenes in the workers' club and in the children's nurseries, as well as by the enforced ' glory of motherhood ' motive. From a pictorial point of view, some of the scenes in the glass factory where the men worked were of great beauty, but the melodramatic ending in the workers' theatre was poorly contrived. Once again, the spectator experienced the overthrow of what might have been a good film by the stressed introduction of propaganda, without which the film would never have been produced by the Government. It is impossible to ignore the purpose of such films, or not to appreciate their aim, but while it is understood it is also deplored.[1] From a sociological point of view, both *The Pits* and *Bed and Sofa* were probably admirable; but from the cinematic outlook, their emphasised moral motive was regrettable.

In the right-wing group is to be included also the work of Olga Preobrashenskaia, whose film *The Peasant Women of Riazan* has been much praised in intelligent film circles. Actually, however, when judged by the work of Room or the left-wing directors, Preobrashenskaia's direction lacks power and insight, although this picture was superior to the average American or European output. Olga Preobrashenskaia has three assets: a feeling for movement of material; a deep sense of natural beauty; and an idea of pictorial composition. But, as has been pointed out, these qualities are to be found in almost every Soviet production. She lacks conception and has a leaning towards the theatrical both in lighting and in acting, but the principal reason for the weakness of *The Peasant Women of Riazan* was once again the sociological propaganda. The concluding scenes with the children's welfare home and the ' new spirit ' were indifferent. There were certainly passages of great beauty, notably those of the waving ear-heads of corn, the scenes of the spring festival and the wedding of Ivan and Anna, but the film as a whole lacked dramatic value. Several other pictures have been made by the same woman director, including some for children which she should have done

[1] It is clear that at the time of writing, 1929, I failed to appreciate the problems of the Soviet directors in tackling themes of social education, so different from and so much more difficult than the revolutionary material of Eisenstein and Pudovkin. *Vide: Documentary Film* (Faber & Faber, 1939), pp. 125 ,126.

well, and she has recently completed *The Last Attraction,* a circus story, which is again said to be uneven and inferior to *The Peasant Women of Riazan.*

A further film of the same type was Yevgeni Cherviakov's *My Son,* which began in a maternity hospital and ended in an ambulance. It was yet another theme of child welfare work, and, according to accounts, the spectator was entertained by shots of babies eating, washing themselves, and sleeping, with a funeral and a ' last-minute-rescue ' as the high-spots.

*

The virtuosities of Dziga-Vertov and his group of the cine-eye have been called the *avant-garde* of the Soviet cinema. Actually, I suggest that, with the possible exception of Kauffmann, the group is going round in circles without being able to find a way out. Dziga-Vertov has instanced his theory of the cine-eye, a theory upon which he has based all his films and which the workers of the cine-eye group of the Vufku-kino organisation of the Ukraine attempt to develop year by year, as follows :

'. . . It is the evening performance at a cinema in a little village near Moscow. The local picture-theatre is filled with peasants and workmen from the neighbouring factory. A film is being shown without musical accompaniment. The only sound that breaks the stillness is the whirring machinery of the projector. An express train flashes across the screen. Then a little girl appears, walking slowly towards the audience. Suddenly, there is a startled scream in the house. A woman rushes forward towards the image of the little girl on the screen. She weeps and clasps a child in her arms. But the image on the screen has passed away. A train again flashes across the screen. The lights in the house go up. The woman is being carried out, for she has become unconscious. " What has happened ? " asks a visitor to the workman next to him. The latter turns slowly to look at him, and replies, " Ah, that, my friend, is the cine-eye. The girl whose image you saw on the screen fell ill some time ago, and recently she died. That woman who cried out and ran towards the screen, she was the girl's mother. . . ." '

The cine-eye group specialise in the progress of what they call in Soviet Russia the ' film without joy ', which can be associated in a mild way with the documentary picture. Briefly, the idea of the cine-eye is the cinematography of actual incidents and objects of everyday life. Vertov watches human expressions, mannerisms, and small incidents everywhere, photographing them at their most characteristic moments. He has no interest in films acted by professional players, which he considers theatrical. The method is a scientific, experimental study of the visible world. It seeks to collect and to catalogue for our pleasure and edification the actualities of contemporary life. It sorts out the pertinent from the irrelevant and places it on the cinema-screen.

The object of the cine-eye is to build an international language of the cinema. The ordinary cine-fiction film already achieves this to a certain extent, but in most cases it is a false rendering of fact. A record must be made and kept and shown of all that happens around us, apart from news matter which is adequately dealt with in the news reel. The roving lens of the camera has the power of the moving human eye. It can and does go everywhere and into everything. It climbs the side of a building and goes in through the window; it travels over factories, along steel girders, across the road, in and out of trains, up a chimney stack, through a park . . into the houses of the rich and poor; it stands in the street, whilst cars, trams, 'buses, carts flash by it on all sides . . . it follows this person down that alley and meets that one round the corner. . . .

The workers of the cine-eye made their first manifesto in 1923, published in a paper called *Lef*. But before this, from 1918 to 1922, Dziga-Vertov worked alone as the pioneer and experimenter of the cine-eye, until between 1923 and 1925 a small group was formed, numbering among them Kauffmann (Vertov's brother) and Kopaline. Since that date, the output of the group has increased, until now it may be said that the cine-eye group of the Vufku-kino is at the head of the documentary section of the Soviet cinema. The workers of the group rejoice in the name of the *kinoki,* and of their work may be mentioned *The Struggle under Czarism, The Truth of Lenin, The Sixth Part of the World, The Eleventh Year* (one of the several films commissioned by the Soviet Government in connection with the tenth anniversary celebrations of the Revolution), *The Man With the Movie Camera, Spring,* and *The Cradle.*

The cine-eye makes use of all the particular resources of the cinema, of slow-motion, ultra-rapid motion, reversed movement, composite and still photography, one turn—one picture, divided screen, microscopic lens, etc. It uses all the forms of montage in assembling and presenting its facts in a coherent order out of the chaos of modern life, and it seeks to establish a level of distinction among the thousands of phenomena that present themselves on all sides to the mind of the cine-director. All this was set down at length in a manifesto by Vertov in 1919.

The whole of the theories of Vertov were summed up in *The Man With the Movie Camera,* which, although a fascinating exposition of the resources of the cinema and a marvellous example of technical accomplishment, was totally devoid of dramatic value. Throughout the film the specta-tor was constantly being reminded of the camera, for it was continually being brought before the eye on the screen. The film was regularly punctuated by the interruption of a close-up of the lens of the camera, the camera itself, and the eye of the cameraman. We travel along watching a cameraman photographing a lady in a carriage. We see on the screen what the camera of the cameraman is taking. We see the cameraman as the lady in the carriage sees him. We are alternately the camera and we see what the camera sees; then we are seeing the camera seeing what we saw before. At that point, we cease seeing the camera and we see what we have just seen being developed and mounted in the studio-laboratory. ' Ah ', we say to ourselves, ' that is the cine-eye.'

Vertov was over-fond of cross-cutting for the purpose of comparison. From streets being washed to a girl washing herself; from motor-horns to a policeman holding up the traffic and back again; from the soft beds of the rich to the hard benches in the park; his cutting was generally short and staccato. He was over-inclined to flash a series of one-foot shots before the audience and blind them. Vertov in practice ran away from Vertov in theory.

The Eleventh Year was a record of the construction of the Ukraine during the ten years of Soviet *régime*. Its theme was man's attempted control over nature; of civilisation over the primitive. Where before there was waste ground, now there are towns. Water that was useless, now supplies the electricity for hundreds of homes. Thus the film went on with mines and pits and chimneys and smoke and workers. Kauffmann's picture *Spring* attempted to show the gradual transition from the Russian winter to the first signs of spring: the awakening of new life. It was admirably photographed and well composed into a beautiful pattern of shots.

With the coming of the sound film, the cine-eye theories expand to embrace the cine-radio. The camera becomes the ear as well as the eye. The *kinoki* become the *radioki*. They seek now to express their material in terms of cine-eye-sound, in the form of radio-vision. Eventually they will come to the simultaneous montage of visual and sound facts, sensitive to the touch and capable of being smelled.

The work of Dziga-Vertov and his *confrères* is necessarily limited. There are bounds to the amount of reality available even to his cine-eyes and cine-ears. He cannot, for example, record emotional scenes, except when taken out of doors and then they must be natural. By rejecting all forms of studio work, he sets inevitable barriers to his progress. Although from a technical standpoint I have full admiration for the pictures of Dziga-Vertov, I am convinced that he has been proceeding up a *cul-de-sac*, and that he is already at the end. His last film. *The Man With the Movie Camera*, was a wonderful piece of virtuosity, of montage, of material and of cutting, a perfect exposition of the cinematic values available to the director, but little else. Outside Russia his theories and films are only just becoming known, hence their enthusiastic reception by the intelligentsia and amateur film groups, but in his own country he is not considered to have achieved anything since the publication of his early manifestos. He is, in fact, rather out of date.

*

In Soviet Russia, as in other countries, there are many second and third-rate directors whose films, in comparison with those of the left and right wings, are not of unusual consequence. Their work, however, has met with considerable approval amongst the film literati, and it is usual to find their merits have been largely over-estimated. Typical amongst this group I should place such men as Georgi Stabavoi, Fiodor Otzep, Boris Barnet, Y. A. Protazanov, and Yuri-Tarich.

Stabavoi works for the Vufku-kino, having realised for them *The Man in the Forest, Calumny,* and *Two Days,* the last being his most important picture. He is a heavy-handed, deeply psychological director, capable of utilising dramatic situations to some effect, but is not considered of much importance by the Russian school. Otzep has made three films, *Miss Mend, The Yellow Pass,* and, in conjunction with Messrs. Prometheus, in Berlin, *The Living Corpse,* from the play by Tolstoi. He was originally well known as a scenario writer, being responsible for the manuscripts of *The Postmaster, Polikushka,* and *The Cigarette Merchant of Mosselprom.* He is not a director of any standing, his work being uneven and lacking in dramatic quality. *The Living Corpse,* which was one of the few films exemplifying Soviet technique to be generally shown in Britain, was of interest principally for the playing of

Pudovkin as Fedya Protasov, and for the editing, which was in the hands of the latter. It was obviously the product of a unit working in unaccustomed surroundings. Barnet is a director of comedies, usually of amusing incident and notable for an employment of trick effects. Two of his comedies have been seen, *The Girl with the Band-Box*, and *The House in Trubnaya Square*. Both were humorous as light entertainment, but not of cinematic importance. The latter contained all the elements of slapstick, being a burlesque on middle-class life in a block of flats in Moscow. There was a delightful Ford car that did tricks, an amusing election procession, and some comic theatre scenes. It was, moreover, a clever burlesque on many Soviet films. There was more than a gentle dig at Eisenstein's crowds and Dziga-Vertov's tramcars. Protazanov is a director of the old school, in company with Yuri-Tarich, Gardin, Dolinov, and Pantelev. He was the director of the big Martian fantasy, *Aëlita*, of *The Three Thieves*, *The Man from the Restaurant*, *The White Eagle*, and *The Forty-First*, none of which was of more than average merit. Yuri-Tarich has made two big spectacle films, *Ivan the Terrible* and *Revolt in Kazan*. Both were historical costume pictures, for the Russian loves his historical film, and were excellent pictorially. The list of directors in this class could be extended considerably, but their work, as a rule, is not worth detailed comment.

There are, however, three recent Soviet films that demand inclusion, *The Fragment of an Empire*, *Prison*, and *Turksib*, for their directors, Ermler, Raizman, and Turin, will be of future significance. The first is a member of a group of experimenters attached to the Leningrad Studio of the Sovkino, and *The Fragment of an Empire* was their fifth production. This film was the epitome of the Soviet sociological propaganda cinema, realised with an extraordinary skill of technical achievement. Its theme was the expression of the constructive work accomplished in Soviet Russia since the October Revolution, and its aim was to sum up the achievement of the workers and to reflect the ideals of the modern Government. It contained problems of cultural reform, of discipline among the workers, of friendship, and of the eternal universal question of love and marriage. The film was a complete document of the social and political life of contemporary Russia. The exterior scenes were taken in various towns, but were filmically composed into one great city, Ermler presumably desiring to express a universal concept of the newly constructed country. The narrative interest concerned an N.C.O., who was wounded and lost his memory in 1917, and regained it ten years later. He returned to St. Petersburg to discover Leningrad. In place of all that he knew in the past, he became involved in the new country of the Soviets. From a psychological point of view, the direction of Ermler was amazing. The subconscious process of the man's mind, particularly in the return of his memory through an association of latent ideas, was portrayed with extraordinary power. From death to emptiness; from emptiness to perplexity; from perplexity to understanding, the changing mental states were subtly revealed. As a representation of mental images, of reactions, of subconscious thought, the film was remarkable. The employment of technical resources was admirable; the cutting swift and slow in perfect modulation; the pattern closely woven. It is undoubtedly the outstanding film of the Soviet cinema after the two last productions of Eisenstein and Pudovkin.

Raizman's film of a mutiny in a prison, although less interesting than Ermler's compelling picture, was nevertheless a clever piece of cinematography. The opening was on a grand scale of clouds and architecture in slow dissolve shots, followed by the wind in a Siberian prison, and a dramatic escape. There succeeded the life in the prison under the new governor, the revolt that failed, the scene of prisoners at the church, the governor's party, and the release of the prisoners because of the Revolution. It was, in fact, the old theme, but directed with a high degree of skill, with contrasted lighting and clever cross-cutting.

Victor Turin's magnificent film of the building of the Turkestan-Siberian Railway was shown during March 1930, by the London Worker's Film Society. It was primarily a remarkable example of the organisation of material. The film was divided into parts, each dealing with a certain phase of the great undertaking. Thus the opening reels expressed the urgent need for the railway in order to link up the vast territories of the north and the south, showing the difficulties of the old, primitive methods of transport and irrigation. These were followed by scenes of the first surveyors, the assembly of the materials needed for the task, the gradual pushing out of the rail-road into the barren wastes, the first giant locomotive to make its appearance amongst the camels and horses, the triumph of man and machinery over nature, leading up to a final crescendo of the promise that the line would be open in 1930. The theme was handled with astonishingly skilful editing, the audience being worked up to an intense emotional crisis by the sheer brilliance of technique. Individual scenes of strong dramatic value abounded in every part, but especial mention may be made of the sand-storm in the desert, the coming of the water from the mountains to the land below, and the race between the first engine and the tribesmen mounted on their ponies and oxen.

*

A predominant feature of the Soviet cinema is the wide development of the interest picture and travel film for educational purposes. There is practically no subject, whether scientific, geographical, ethnological, industrial, military, naval, aeronautical, or medical which has not been approached by Soviet directors. It is quite impossible in a short space to give any idea of the vastness to which this side of the cinema has attained in the U.S.S.R. I can only mention a few films that were outstanding in each group, so as to indicate the range of the material covered. Firstly, there seems to be almost no essential part of the territories of Russia that remains photographically unrecorded. There has been a constant succession of production units leaving the various studios for the purpose of making film expeditions. In this section there was the wonderful *Pamyr*, the film of a joint expedition organised by the Leningrad Academy of Sciences and the German Notgemeinschaft; *The Heart of Asia*, taken in Afghanistan; *The Trail of a Meteorite*, made in the Siberian marshy forests; *The Way to India*; *Sea Warrens*, dealing with the migration of birds and the vegetation of the steppes, during spring and autumn, along the coast country of the Black Sea; *Comet*, a film of Tartar life; *The Men of the Woods*, an expedition into N.W. Siberia; *The Rails Go Ringing*, made by Leontiev in the engine sheds at Tiflis; and many others. Industrial and agricultural sections include such films as : *The Sunflower Industry, The Fight for the Harvest, Chaos and Order, Soviet Fordism, The Campaign for a Crop.* Medical and hygiene films have been plentifully made viz., *Ten Years of Soviet Medicine, The Morning of a Healthy Man, Mother and Child, Malaria*, etc.

*

It is difficult to write freely about the pre-eminent films of the Soviet cinema, for however much one may admire their technical excellence and acknowledge their unquestionable superiority over the product of any other film-producing country, it is impossible to ignore their primary social, political, and often anti-religious influence. The whole exstence of the Soviet cinema has come about through the urgent desire to express vividly and with the utmost effect the policy of the Soviet Government and the development of the principles of Marxism. Elsewhere in this survey I have written that the primary aim of the film at the present moment is entertainment. This statement must be qualified by the functions of the Soviet cinema, which have caused the film to be considered as a dominant factor in the social and political organisation of a country.

VII

THE GERMAN FILM

Not long ago,[1] it was general to look to the German cinema for the real uses of the film medium. A single German production meant a promised relief from the twenty American metallic movies which shouldered its London presentation. The simplicity of the German cinema then indicated that the intelligence and artistry, the creative imagination and craftsmanship, so essential to the production of a unified work of art, lay in the studios of Neubabelsberg and Staaken. It became customary to believe that a film coming from a German studio, made by a German director, cameraman, architect, and actors would be of a certain interest. During that period of the German cinema which culminated in *The Last Laugh* and *Tartuffe,* this was the truth. So far as was known at that time, the Germans were the only producers of imaginative films in the world, with the exception, perhaps, of a few isolated examples of the early French school and the beautiful pictures of the Swedes. Germany was wise in that she put her best talent into the creation of a film industry subsidised by the Government; but she reckoned without the influence of the American movie. The Germans were unable to realise that few people of intelligence and good taste ever went to the cinema. We know that the general public had become saturated with the artificiality of the Hollywood movie. It was quite unable to cope with the meaning that the serious-minded Germans contained in their films. The public had little, if any, experience of the cinema as a means of dramatic expression. They were shocked at and did not fully comprehend the sombre, darkly-lit, intensely powerful German film. They knew nothing of psychology,

[1] The middle twenties.

252

of decorative beauty, and of the intrinsic reality of the cinema. They continued to show interest in the Hollywood movie.

The German film flourished awhile, sparkled with individual efforts, developed technical resources to a pitch of perfection and brought new filmic conceptions to light on the support of her own audiences and those of France and Europe. But the German film languished for want of wider world support. The ideas of these films were conceived on a grand scale, demanding large finance for their realisation, but the returns were small. The real German film died quietly. Many of its creators went to Hollywood, while those who remained joined with fresh commercialised minds in the complete reorganisation of their industry on American principles. Hollywood took interest in her rival, nourished her, but stole her talent. The German cinema became American in its outlook and its characteristics became imitative of Hollywood.[1]

The films which the Germans produced in the years following the war were no more widely saleable outside their own country than those of the Swedes and the French. The position of the German film industry was founded upon an uneconomic basis. It must be recalled that film production in Europe was grievously hampered by the lack of sufficient financial resources; whereas America was preposterously wealthy. Whilst money was the last worry of Hollywood producers, in Germany (as later in Britain) it was the first. The German Government, realising that the showing of her films abroad would bring about advertisement after her ignominious war defeat, helped the industry with wholehearted support. It induced the Deutsche Bank to finance the biggest company, the Universum Film, A.G. (known to the world as Ufa), and then brought into play the *Kontingent* law, which drastically required every German distributor to buy one home production for every American

[1] The reader is referred throughout this chapter to Dr. Siegfried Kracauer's psychological history of the German film, *From Caligari to Hitler* (Princeton University Press, 1947).

film he handled. This ruling certainly encouraged the production in the studios, although it meant, on the other hand, that there was a chance of quality being flouted by quantity. But despite this subsidy, the German cinema continued to flounder, constantly becoming bankrupt, borrowing money from American firms, and taking twice the scheduled time to make a film. Interchange of studio personnel and players was adopted freely in order to keep the trend of production international. Many British and French stars were better known in Germany than in England. Recently, German directors have been working in British studios, failing to understand British temperament and trying to intermix German psychology with British bourgeois unintelligence. British firms produced in Germany but, even with the technical resources available, failed to justify their existence. All along there has been a slavish imitation of American methods. Germany finds it difficult now to produce a film that is characteristically German.

*

In surveying the German cinema from the end of the first World War until the coming of the American dialogue film, the output may roughly be divided into three groups. Firstly, the theatrical costume pictures; secondly, the big middle period of the studio art films; and thirdly, the decline of the German film in order to fall into line with the American ' picture-sense ' output. These three periods naturally overlap one another, and there have been isolated exceptions to the general trend. Such distinguished films as *The Cabinet of Doctor Caligari, The Student of Prague, Vanina, The Last Laugh,* and the films of G. W. Pabst, stand apart from the general run of production, in certain cases being advance examples of the type of film to come. The easily recognisable characteristics of the earlier German films were their feeling for studio representation, for simplicity of story and treatment, for a consciousness of camera fluidity, and for a dramatic, psychological understanding of events. The German film was born and bred in an atmosphere of studio structure, for seldom did the German director go outside for his exterior material. The outstanding feature of all the greater of the early German films was their decorative sense of architecture. At an elementary stage in their cinematic development, the Germans revealed a strong and not unwanted tendency towards filmic craftsmanship. An instance of this is the perfection to which German cameramen have taken the technical qualities of their photography. It was in Germany that the camera was first freed from its tripod, that it was first given the movement and life of a human being. But although they used their camera to its full capacity, the Germans still largely retained their studio-mind, approaching at times the artificiality of the theatre. They seemed unable to accept the possibility of the free spirit of the cinema, which is so important in later Soviet and French productions. Germany was unable to produce an *En Rade* or a *Battleship Potemkin*, but she did bring to the screen *The Student of Prague* and *The Last Laugh*. There is little doubt, however, that the studio-mind, with its love of craftsmanship and structural work, imposed limitations on the choice of theme and treatment, restrictions that have damaged the recent films of Erich Pommer: *Nina Petrovna, Homecoming,* and *Asphalt.* While it is admitted that studio architecture is absolutely necessary for certain exterior settings, which cannot be achieved on actual location (such as the creation of special streets and landscapes), nevertheless this artificiality is in opposition to the real aim of the cinema. Material that serves for filmic creation in the process of constructional editing has need to be the nearest approach to actuality, if not actuality itself.

The German film has contributed many valuable attributes to the cinema of the world. From the studio film there has been learnt the complete subordination of acting material, revealed so well in *The Student of Prague;* the pre-organisation of studio floor-work, including the composite set which allows for the taking of scenes in their correct sequence [1]; the unification of light, setting, and acting material (the central part of *Tartuffe,* and *The Last Laugh*); and the freedom of the camera as an instrument of expression, assuming the status of an *observer* and not of a spectator. The German cinema has taught discipline and organisation, without which no film can be produced as a unified whole.

The importance of the realisation of *The Cabinet of Doctor Caligari* has already been dwelt upon at some length. To reiterate, it was the first significant attempt at the expression of a creative mind in the new medium of cinematography. It broke with realism on the screen; it suggested that a film, instead of being a reality, might be a possible reality; and it brought into play the mental psychology of the audience. There has been a tendency of late to look back with disdain at the theatrical character of Wiene's film. It has been objected that *The Cabinet of Doctor Caligari,* in its structural co-ordination of light, design, and players, in its cubist-expressionist architecture, was pure stage presentation. It needs but little intelligence to utter this profound criticism, but it must be realised that *The Cabinet of Doctor Caligari* was produced under extraordinary circumstances. It is simple to look back now and diagnose the crudities of Wiene's work, with the most recent progress of the Soviet film and the American ' compound ' cinema fresh in mind, but in 1919 all theory of the cinema was extremely raw. It is only through such experiments as that of Wiene, *Warning Shadows, The Street,* and *The Last Laugh,* that advance has been at all possible. The narrow-minded film critics of to-day blind themselves to the traditional development of the cinema. They seize upon Dziga-Vertov and deny the existence of Carl Dreyer; they saturate their minds with the sound film and forget the intrinsic structure of visual images. It has been said that the admirers of *The Cabinet of Doctor Caligari* are usually painters, or people who think and remember graphically. This is a mistaken conception, for

[1] See description, pp. 184, 185, of composite set used in *Hotel Imperial.*

61. THE LOVES OF JEANNE NEY, directed by G. W. Pabst. Edith Jehanne. [German, 1927]

62. SUNRISE, directed by F. W. Murnau. George O'Brien, Janet Gaynor. [American, 1927]

63. THERESE RAQUIN, directed by JACQUES FEYDER.   GINA MANÉS,
    HANS VON SCHLETTOW.   [French, 1937]

64. THE ITALIAN STRAW HAT, directed by RENÉ CLAIR.   [French, 1927]

the true *cinéaste* must see and realise the importance of its realisation as well as that of *La Passion de Jeanne d'Arc*, *The Last Laugh*, *Tol'able David*, *Finis Terrae*, *Jeanne Ney*, and *Turksib*. Each of these films is related, each overlaps in its filmic exposition of thought. It is absurd to deny their existence on the grounds of theatricalism, expressionism, individualism, or naturalism. Without the creation of *The Cabinet of Doctor Caligari*, much that is admired in the cinema of to-day would be non-existent. It bore in it a suggestion of the fantasy that was to be the prominent characteristic of the art film. Some short time later, Kobe's *Torgus*, or *The Coffin Maker*, again with expressionist architecture, was another indication of the mystical fantasy which was to be the underlying motive of *Warning Shadows*, *The Student of Prague*, *Waxworks*, and others of a similar type.

The essence of the middle period German film was simplicity of story value and of actional interest that eventually led to a completeness of realisation fulfilled in *The Last Laugh*. Many of the themes were simple experiments in film psychology. Karl Grune's *The Street* was a reduction of facts to the main development of one character during a short period of time. It obtained its mood by the co-ordination of light and camera psychology rather than by the acting, which was crude and mannered. Arthur Robison's *Warning Shadows* was again a simplification of detail, a centralisation of incident into small units of space and time, decorated by a fantastic touch. *Waxworks* was yet another example. Nearly all these films contained the fantastic element. They were seldom wholly tragic or wholly comic. They were often melodramatic, as in the case of *Doctor Mabuse*.

Earlier than this middle period of simplicity and fantasy, there had been a wholesale production of theatrical costume films that made use of the German's natural love for spectacle and the property room. These served as a foundation for the stylised school of German film acting. At all periods of the German cinema, the actors have exerted a stabilising influence on the fluctuation of the various types of films. Their restraining presence helped towards the establishment of the film as a whole. One recalls, in this respect, the numerous films of Conrad Veidt, Emil Jannings, Alfred Abel, Werner Krauss, Bernard Goetzke, Julius Falkenstein, Albert Steinrück, Alexander Granach, Asta Nielsen, Henny Porten, Lydia Potechina, etc., in which the actors themselves steadied, and even in some cases dominated the direction.

With the German feeling for studio-craftsmanship came the decorative architecture and freedom of camerawork that were brought to a head in the big production of *Faust,* foreshadowed by Lang's *Destiny* and *Siegfried,* Robison's *Warning Shadows,* Murnau's *Tartuffe,* and Ludwig Berger's *Cinderella.* The decorative setting, based on traditional design with modern fantastic motives, played a large part in the German middle period. These fantastic productions began and ended with themselves. They carried no universal meaning, as did Karl Grune's *The Street* or *At the Edge of the World.* To this completeness, already partially achieved by the maturity of the traditional acting material, the splendid settings of Walther Röhrig, Robert Herlth, Otto Hunte, Erich Kettlehut, Karl Vollbrecht, Albin Grau, Rudolph Bamberger, Herman Warm, and others, added a final binding force. Their plastic columns, bulging mouldings, great flat expanses, simply decorated architecture formed an admirable background, never obtruding, for the acting material and simplicity of treatment of the period. It is of the utmost importance to grasp the significant part played by the architect and designer in the development of the German cinema. Indeed, it may be said without detriment to their directors, that two thirds of the aesthetic success of *Warning Shadows, Siegfried,* and *Cinderella* lay in their design. The first part of the *Nibelungen Saga* has never been equalled for sheer decorative beauty; the complete charm of *Cinderella* came from the decoration of Rudolph Bamberger. *Destiny, The Golem, Sumurun,* and *Waxworks* were equally superb in their creative architecture. This natural feeling for decoration, for simple but rich design, in the Düreresque and Baroque styles, was the real basis of the German studio-mind. Even in films of a popular type this wonderful sense for good design was prevalent. Unlike other countries, the experimentalists in the German cinema were able to embody their revolutionary ideas in films of general practicability. There was almost no German *avant-garde* school at that time, for the most advanced filmic intelligences were working in the commercial studios. This accounted to a large extent for the superior aesthetic value of the German film in relation to the rest of the world's output.

Towards the gradual decline of the decorative film, brought about by its own inbreeding, there arose a new type of cinema, less fantastic and more in touch with reality, but incorporating even more strongly the psychology of human emotions in the thematic narrative. This new form had been heralded to some extent by the appearance, in 1922, of von Gerlach's *Vanina,* adapted from Stendhal, with Asta Nielsen, Paul Wegener, and Paul Hartmann. In consideration of its date, *Vanina* was unique in its un-German feeling for fluidity of thematic conception. *Vanina* had breadth and space outside the customary studioisms of the period. Three years later there came *The Last Laugh,* which, as has been stated earlier, laid down the elementary principles of filmic continuity. It was, perhaps, an unequalled example of the co-ordination of production personnel. Murnau, Freund, Mayer, and Jannings worked collectively to produce a film that was a complete realisation in itself.[1] It expressed a simple, universal theme, unrelieved by incidental detail and cross purposes. It was a centralisation of environment, of setting, of atmosphere, of players, to one dominating purpose. It had a plastic fluidity that was made possible by a titleless continuity. It had a com-

[1] Carl Mayer actually wrote *The Last Laugh* for Lupu Pick to act and direct, and expressed himself to me as never wholly happy with Jannings' performance.

pleteness that for once was achieved by the architecture of the studio. It was the final outcome of the German craftsman's studio-mind. In the same year, as well as *The Last Laugh,* there was to come Dupont and Pommer's celebrated *Vaudeville,* Grune's *The Two Brothers,* Lupu Pick's *The Wild Duck* and *New Year's Eve,* and Pabst's *The Joyless Street.* With the exception of the last, these were all films with moral themes, close to the reality of modern life, treated with a new technique of moving camerawork and unusual angle of viewpoint. *Vaudeville* was, of course, the outstanding film that staggered the American producing companies when shown to them in the States. It was *Vaudeville* that took Pommer, Dupont, and Jannings to Hollywood.

Speaking broadly, for there are several notable exceptions, the German film entered into a decline after that date. The new productions, having lost the spirit and craftsmanship of the best German period (from 1921 to 1925) were constructed along the box-office lines of the American cinema. They were in the nature of a reaction from the work of the highest filmic intelligences in Europe at that time, because Soviet Russia was then but an unknown quantity, experimenting with theatrical pictures. There followed for some years a great number of second and third-rate German movies made to supply the *Kontingent* law, directed by such men as Richard Eichberg, Joe May, and Willi Wolff, with players like Harry Liedtke, Paul Richter, Mady Christians, Ellen Richter, Harry Halm, Liane Haid, Willy Fritsch, Lia Maria, Lilian Harvey, Jack Trevor, and Jenny Jugo. Many of these did not reach Britain, which only imported the best of the German output, but even from those which did it was obvious that they were lacking in the inventiveness of mind and originality of conception that had distinguished the earlier productions.

During recent years there has been an increased commercial co-operation between Germany and other European film-producing countries. The technical studio organisation of the German film industry was realised to be the most efficient in Europe, if not in the world, and both Britain and France interchanged production units with Germany. Many foreign firms were anxious to combine in joint productions realised by German technical resources. These pictures were an attempt to rival the constant flood of American picture-sense movies. Amid this heterogeneous mass of German films, however, there were still several individual works by pre-eminent directors who retained some intelligent interest in the cinema. Fritz Lang's *Metropolis* and *The Spy;* G. W. Pabst's *Secrets of the Soul* and *Jeanne Ney;* Fritz Wendhausen's *Out of the Mist;* the films of Elizabeth Bergner's Poetic Film Company, *Donna Juana* and *The Violinist of Florence;* and Walther Ruttmann's *Berlin,* were evidence that there still remained progressive *cinéastes* in Germany.

But generally speaking, German film production was rapidly becoming like that of Hollywood in external appearances. Many of the big pictures of 1928, for example, might have been the product of American studios. They were made for an international market, and little of the old German feeling for psychology and simplicity of treatment remained. Erich Pommer, on returning from Hollywood, attempted to combine the merits of the old German school with a new outlook of international picture-sense. Of his four pictures recently produced, *Nina Petrovna* and *Homecoming* were of better quality than the average American or German movie. They were not, I admit, good films in the sense that they were masterpieces of filmic expression, but they contained certain aspects of camerawork and architecture that were reminiscent of past achievements. There has been a tendency also towards the filming of melodramatic thrillers, light and artificial in story value, but constructed with a great deal of technical skill. Of such may be mentioned Fritz Lang's excellent *The Spy,* perhaps one of the best pictures of its kind; and Tourjanski's *Manolescu.* Pabst's *Jeanne Ney,* also, was melodramatic in action. There have also been a number of good, middle-class comedies made, of general entertainment value, such as *The Bold Sea Rover* (in Britain, *Hurrah! I'm Alive*), with that delightful comedian, Nikolai Kolin, and *Love's Sacrifice,* a light, polished picture of youthfulness, directed with admirable skill by Hans Schwartz. The old fondness for the spectacular historical film, which seems ever present on the Continent, has resulted in the large but quite unconvincing production of *Waterloo*, directed by Karl Grune, originally a simplist director; the same director's ill-conceived *Marquis d'Eon;* the sensational and theatrical film of *Martin Luther* (which revealed clearly the fallacy of the pageant picture); Ludwig Berger's version of *The Meistersingers,* a late example of the studio-mind; and *Schinderhannes,* made by the young director, Kurt Bernhardt.

The problem of the sound and dialogue film came to Germany in much the same disastrous way in which it stupefied France and Britain. For some time, German producing companies and directors stood aside to watch the procedure of events, until from month to month they issued announcements of forthcoming sound films. At the time of writing, no German film with mechanical reproduction of dialogue has reached this country, but several units are at work on productions. The situation of sound recording has been rendered difficult in Germany by reason of a patent war that exists between the Western Electric Company of America and the Klangfilm-Tobis-Siemens Co. of Germany, a conflict that alternates in victories and losses. The necessity of making bi-lingual dialogue films in German and English will assuredly place the production of intelligent films in a precarious position, for the Germans must needs meet the foreign market demands. So long as dialogue films are supplied by America, Germany must also adapt herself to their production, which is yet another step away from the German film of national characteristics.

*

I have not the space at command to analyse in full the work of Germany's many directors, but some notes may be written on the characteristics and techniques of her most significant *régisseurs*.

I complain elsewhere that Pabst is theoretically the great director, but that he has failed to justify fully his immense reputation since his second and sixth films, *The Joyless Street* and *Jeanne Ney*. Although this is adverse criticism of a director who has given many instances of his rare knowledge of the probing power of the camera, nevertheless, I feel that there is a general tendency to over-estimate any and every instance of Pabst's undoubted ability. But Pabst at his best, unhampered by limitations, uncut save by himself, is perhaps the one genius of the film outside Soviet Russia, approached, though in an entirely different manner, by Carl Dreyer, Chaplin, and René Clair. Both aesthetically and technically, his work is of the first importance in the European cinema. Investigation of his methods is difficult, complex, and hard to express in words. Pabst possesses a power of penetration into the deepest cells of human behaviour, and succeeds in psychologically representing the traits of his characters by filmic exposition. He is principally concerned with the development and understanding of the intricacies of the minds of his characters, and lays open their mentality by employing every resource available to the medium in which he works. It has been written in criticism that Pabst delights in the sheer use of technical accomplishment, as if he were simply a Monta Bell or a Mal St. Clair, but no more unwarranted statement has been made since the beginning of film journalism. It is impossible to witness the showing of a film by Pabst without marvelling at his unerring choice of camera angle for the expression of mood, or his employment of the moving camera to heighten tension. Pabst, probably far more than any other director (outside the Soviet cinema), understands the complete value of his instruments. *Jeanne Ney* has already been cited as a superb example of the uses of the camera as a means of dramatic expression; *Crisis,* although not revealing Pabst to full advantage (I have only seen the cut British version), was exceptionally interesting in its use of reverse shots and camera mobility.

Before he became interested in the cinema, G. W. Pabst was engaged in the theatre, and it was not until 1924 that he opened his film career with *The Treasure*. This was followed by the tempestuous and badly received *The Joyless Street* in 1925. Since that date he has made eight films, *Don't Play With Love, Secrets of the Soul, Jeanne Ney, Crisis, The Box of Pandora, The White Hell of Pitz Palü,* and *The Diary of a Lost Girl*. Of these, the two last named have not at the time of writing been shown in Britain, where the work of this remarkable director is not generally known.

The troubled history of *The Joyless Street* (see pp. 86, 87) has already been given, but the film which caused this extraordinary reception has not yet been described. It seems simple enough to write that *The Joyless Street* succeeded in showing the devastation that war conditions wreaked on the inhabitants of a small dark street in postwar Vienna, for there have been so many films which have dealt with similar circumstances. But with the genius of Pabst this film was different, for it tore away the American glamour, destroyed the romanticism, and exposed the stark reality of hunger and passion under distorted conditions. No film or novel has so truthfully recorded the despair of defeat, and the false values of social life that arise after war, as *The Joyless Street*. With unerring psychology by which he caused the smallest actions of his characters to convey meaning, Pabst brought to his picture moments of searing pain of mental anguish, of sheer unblemished beauty. His extreme powers of truthfulness, of the understanding of reality, of the vital meaning of hunger, love, lust, selfishness and greed, rendered this extraordinary film convincing. Like *Greed,* its significance went below the artificial surface of everyday life, turning up the deepest emotions. It was, perhaps, too true for the entertainment of the masses. Like *Greed,* it was too real, too devastating in its truth. It is recorded that Pabst himself once said,

'What need is there for romantic treatment? Real life is too romantic and too ghastly.' Mention has already been made of Greta Garbo in this film, for it is by this that one theorises on her beauty and ability. In Hollywood, this splendid woman has been wantonly distorted into a symbol of eroticism. But Greta Garbo, by reason of the sympathetic understanding of Pabst, brought a quality of loveliness into her playing as the professor's elder daughter. Her frail beauty, cold as an ice flower warmed by the sun, stood secure in the starving city of Vienna, untouched by the vice and lust that dwelt in the dark little street. Not only Greta Garbo, but the other players in this film were fascinating. I recall Asta Nielsen, superb as the woman who murdered for her lover, slowly realising the horror of her action, her eyes expressing the innermost feeling of her heart; Valeska Gert, the blatant, avaricious woman, who, under the thin guise of a milliner, kept the house patronised by the *nouveaux-riches;* Werner Krauss, the sleek-haired, wax-moustached butcher, secure in his pandering to the wealthy, with the great white dog at his side; Jaro Furth, the intellectual Councillor Rumfort, unable to understand the new conditions; Robert Garrison, the vulgar little speculator; and the others, Agnes Esterhazy, Henry Stuart, and Einar Hanson. When re-seen quite lately, the technique and technical qualities of *The Joyless Street* seemed faded (it was made in 1925), but the vital force of Pabst's direction was still present.

Of Pabst's psycho-analytical film, *Secrets of the Soul,* I can write but indifferently, for the copy reluctantly shown in Britain was badly mutilated in order to meet censor requirements; insomuch that its continuity straggled, gaps and interruptions that could not possibly have occurred in the original copy being painfully apparent. It had little story to relate, but was a simple demonstration of the theory of psycho-analysis. It was, for those sufficiently interested, a key to the working of Pabst himself. From the doctor's treatment of the patient with the knife-complex, and from the dream sequence, it was possible to discern the manner in which Pabst himself dissects his film characters. The picture was beautifully photographed, and was of interest for the scene when Werner Krauss recalled his thoughts and actions of the previous day, the incidents being isolated from their local surroundings and placed against a white background.

It took several years for the value of *The Joyless Street* to be appreciated, but when *Jeanne Ney* made its dramatic appearance in 1928, there were those who were eager to receive this new film by Pabst. It was, it is true, badly mutilated in Britain, and actually presented by the British renters, Wardour, under the fantastic title of *Lusts of the Flesh. Jeanne Ney,* which was based on the novel by Ilya Ehrenburg, was produced by Ufa, in Berlin, and apparently Pabst had difficulty in making the film in his own way. It was the time when the Americanisation of the German studios was in progress, and Pabst was told to make the picture ' in the American style '. Fortunately, Pabst had courage, and in *Jeanne Ney* he made a more subtle, a swifter, less tragic, and more dynamic film than *The Joyless Street.* At first glance, *Jeanne Ney* was a melodramatic spy story of communists, adventurers, a typist, a blind girl, with a murder and a diamond robbery. It is curious, at this point, to remark that all the stories chosen by Pabst are melodramatic, almost novelettish in incident. *The Joyless Street* was adapted from a serial story by Hugo Bettauer, in the Vienna *Neue Freie Presse,* and the narrative incident of *Crisis* was not much better. Instead, however, of this being detrimental, it proves only too conclusively how important is filmic treatment in relation to story value. The interest of *Jeanne Ney* was not in its actional incident, but in the individuals concerned, their thoughts, emotions and reasons for behaving as they did. From the superb opening sequence of the orgy, beginning with a close-up of the *émigré's* shabby boots, and the camera slipping away and tracking into every corner, *Jeanne Ney* developed from sequence to sequence with breath-taking power. Mood succeeded mood, each perfect in its tension and its understanding. The shooting of the consul, Jeanne's father, the restless curtains caused by the draught from the opening door, the quick-cut reverse shots; the inimitable, likable kindness of the smiling Communist *attaché,* with his kippers, and the wan smile of Jeanne; the parting in the drenching rain, the mud, the anguish of the farewell, the stark trees; the superbly conveyed atmosphere of the detective bureau, the types of the sleuth hounds, the dislike of Jeanne for her new work; the reunion of the boy and Jeanne, in the warm sunlight walking through the poor streets of Paris, the flowers, the sheer beauty of love and youth; the brilliant scene where little bald-headed Raymond Ney counts his imaginary money, the murder; the tremendous scene between the blind girl and the murderer; the hotel, its sordid shabbiness overcome by the love of Jeanne, the peace of their night, unsoiled by the contagious atmosphere of the house. . . .

The cutting of *Jeanne Ney* was executed with such skill that it seemed unnoticeable. Every cut was made on actual movement, so that at the end of one shot somebody was moving, and at the beginning of the next shot the action was continued. The eye was thus absorbed in the movement and the actual transposition from one shot to another became unnoticeable. Instinctively one recalled the overlapping cutting of *Battleship Potemkin,* and realised the similar aims of Eisenstein and Pabst in this respect. For this reason it will at once be seen how disastrous can be the effect of the censor's scissors. Pabst cut *Jeanne Ney* to a definite length; every shot had its place and meaning. The removal of only a few feet of such a film damages its balance, design, and *emotional* effect.

The photography of *Jeanne Ney,* by Fritz Arno Wagner, has been remarked on elsewhere, and it is sufficient to add that technically, for smoothness of panning and travelling shots, and for perfectly natural light values, it has never been surpassed. At Pabst's will, Wagner's camera nosed into the corners and ran with the players; photographed from below eye-level and down stairways; yet not once was the instrument misused. Every curve, every angle, every approach of the lens was controlled by the material that it photographed for the expression of mood. Sadness, joy, uplift, depression, exuberance, fear, morbidness, delight, were achieved by the position and mobility of the camera. Its viewpoints were regulated by the logic of the action. *Jeanne Ney* was a unified individual work. From start to finish it was conceived, controlled, and created by one sensitive but dominant mind—Pabst.

As a film, after the brilliance of *Jeanne Ney, Crisis* was a disappointment. As the expression of the character of a woman, a single individual, it was of passing interest. The story was a conventional plot of a misunderstood marriage; many of the same type have been manufactured in Hollywood. It is understood that once again the British version was considerably cut, whilst in Germany, Pabst refused to put his name to the production because of the editing. The film, as shown in this country, lacked stimulus. The direction again revealed Pabst's technical brilliancy for angles and pictorial composition, occasional moments rising to heights of intensity. The wife's hysterical collapse in the night club; the discovery of her brooding husband when she returned home; the vicious undercurrents of atmosphere that lay behind the cabaret scenes; these were handled with a technique that was equal to *The Joyless Street*. The centre of interest, however, was the compelling fascination of Brigitte Helm's Myra. Pabst was the first director to reveal the rare side to this actress, a quality that was not apparent in *A Daughter of Destiny, Metropolis, At the Edge of the World, L'Argent,* and her other pictures. In *Jeanne Ney,* Pabst was interested in the playing of Brigitte Helm as the blind girl. In *Crisis,* he came absorbed in the personality of Miss Helm herself. He succeeded in making her every movement exciting. Her strange latent power and underlying neurosis were here given their freedom. Her vibrant beauty, her mesh of gold hair, her slender, supple figure were caught and photographed from every angle. The intensity of her changing moods, her repression and resentment, her bitterness and cynicism, her final passionate breakdown in the Argentine club; these were constructed into a filmic representation of overwhelming psychological power. Pabst analysed and dissected the remarkable character of Miss Helm and built up out of the pieces a unified, plastic personality. Her curious, fascinating power has never been exploited with such skill. Gustav Diessl, as the husband, was beyond reproach, his whole outlook being enhanced by the low-level camera angles; while Hertha von Walther, as the dissipated girl friend, was strangely moving, her attractive smile at once understanding and scornful.

In each of his films, with the sole exception of the psychoanalytical essay, *The Secrets of the Soul,* Pabst has been concerned with some aspect of the character of women. His stories have been but a framework of incident on which to wind the theme of feminine character development. Every woman of Pabst's synthetic creation has had a curious, unnameable and hopelessly indefinable quality about her. He seems, in the building up of their filmic personalities, to be able to bring to the surface the vital forces of their being. Each actress employed in the films of Pabst assumes a new quality, not actually but filmically. He contrives by some unknown force to invest his characters with a quality of intense feeling, with strangely complex sexual or mental significance. In each of his succeeding films, he has sought more and more to express the motives that lie behind a woman's impulsive thoughts and actions. He appears to have the power of discovering a hidden quality in an actress, whatever her career may have been before she came under his direction. Like Greta Garbo—Asta Nielsen, Edith Jehanne, Brigitte Helm, Hertha von Walther, and Louise Brooks are almost ordinary when appearing in other films under other directors. But Pabst has an understanding, an appreciation of the intelligence, that builds the actual personality into a magnetic, filmic being.

It was, it seems, this hidden quality, this deeper, hitherto uninvestigated, side of feminine character that induced

Pabst to choose, after long searching, Louise Brooks to play Lulu in *Pandora's Box*. Lulu was the theme of Wedekind's two tragedies, *Erdgeist* and *Die Büchse der Pandora,* one being the sequel to the other, around which Pabst built his concept. Lulu was the final essence of the sexual impulse of woman; charged to the fullest extent with physical consciousness. The spring of her life was the attempted satisfaction of this insatiable impulse, and the power of man was the possible means of that satisfaction. She loved spasmodically, but with the strongest sensuality, until, sickening of her exhausted companion, he was indifferently destroyed. She was unable, moreover, to comprehend the ruthlessness of her devastation in her search for sexual satisfaction. She loved for the moment the man to whom she surrendered her body, but that love died like a flash when his exhaustion was complete. Her sentiment was hardened by the monotonous recurrence of the events which she had caused. She remained untouched by the death of her masculine stimulants. She had no interest in the vastness of life save sexuality and its accompaniments. She was childlike in her centralisation of material purpose. She was the essence of youth, with the eyes of a child, beautiful in appearance, and utterly attractive in manner. Her ultimate and only possible ending was her destruction by the passions which she aroused, killed by the lust-murderer, Jack-the-Ripper, in London.

In Louise Brooks, known to the public only by her American work (*The American Venus, Evening Clothes, The Canary Murder Case*), Pabst believed that he saw the hidden quality that could be filmically synthesised into Lulu. His judgement must undoubtedly, in view of his career, have been careful, but he failed to realise that in the transference of Lulu from the stage to the silent screen, he was to lose a link that vitally connected the external Lulu to her inner self. Wedekind caused Lulu to become a possible reality by the contrast of her outward appearance to the hard, naïve, passionate sentences that she spoke. By

reason of her unaffected utterances in combination with
her innocent appearance, Lulu became the essence of
woman, the despoiler. In brief, Lulu was an impossible
reality without the speech that Wedekind gave her. In the
medium of the film these words were absent; Lulu became
vacant and unconvincing, even under the direction of Pabst.
The audience was unable to connect the appearance of Lulu
with the magnetism that attracted men to her. The mistake
lay in the visual representation of a literary figure. It was
an attempt, basically at fault, to translate into a medium
of visual images a character that was originally expressed
by literature. It was an attempt that proved conclusively the
difference that lies between two entirely different forms of
expression. A character can be, and has been built many
times by visual images. So also has a character been formed
by the use of words and sentences. The latter may, perhaps, serve as the inspiration for the former, but never can
one be transcribed in terms of the other. Pabst conceived
Lulu as a literary concept, living possibly in his imagination, but failed to express that concept filmically. It will be
immediately suggested that the speech so vital to the exposition of Lulu might have well been supplied by the mechanical reproduction of dialogue. Such a consideration is
worthless, since by reason of its aesthetic impossibility it
would have only added a further load to the imperfections
of the cinema. Thus, having taken into consideration the
basic fault of *Pandora's Box,* we may be permitted once
more to admire the excellence of the cutting, of the use of
detail, of the chosen angles; of the introduction of the fog
at the end of the film to emphasise the increasing thematic
tension as the character of Lulu approached its fulfilment;
of the unfolding of the incident in seven essential scenes,
each built with clever montage.[1]

Neither of Pabst's last two pictures has been generally

---

[1] The 'specially arranged' British copy was a travesty, for the whole
meaning of the picture as well as its technical qualities were destroyed.
The significant part played by Alice Roberts in the German version
was omitted.

seen. The one, *The White Hell of Pitz Palü,* with its series of mountaineering catastrophes, is set in the Alps; the other, *The Diary of a Lost Girl,* concerns the revolt of a number of girls against the rigid rules of a reformatory. Both are stated to be notable for the camerawork of Sepp Allgeier, and they both have settings designed by Ernö Metzner, who made *Ueberfall.* The former film is co-directed by Arnold Fanck and Pabst; the first-named director being remembered for his beautifully photographed mountain film, *The Wrath of the Gods.*

There is a tendency, obscure but nevertheless real, to regard Fritz Lang as a more intelligent Rex Ingram. They are both expert showmen. But whereas Ingram's faculty seldom rises above a certain level of Hollywood picture-sense, Lang has definitely produced work that is of value. *Destiny, Siegfried,* and *Metropolis* were sufficient evidence of the fertility of his imagination and his sense of decorative design. Lang is further to be admired for his bigness of outlook and his power of broad visualisation. Both *Metropolis* and *The Woman in the Moon* were magnificently big cinematic conceptions, realised with every technical perfection of the cinema. It is impossible not to admire Fritz Lang in this respect. On the other hand, one regrets his entire lack of filmic detail, of the play of human emotions, of the intimacy which is so peculiar a property of the film. Only on rare occasions, notably in the tea-party scene between Gerda Maurus and Willy Fritsch in *The Spy,* has Lang revealed interest in human beings as such. As a rule, his characters are meaningless men and women, (heroes, heroines, and villains) swept hither and thither by the magnitude of his conception. And yet he has an instinctive feeling for types, for there is seldom an individual part in his films that is not distinctive.

Lang is accustomed to utilise the best film technicians in Germany for his vast studio conceptions. Karl Hoffman, Freund, Fritz Arno Wagner, Günther Rittau, the camera-men; and Otto Hunte, Erich Kettlehut, Oscar Werndorff, Karl Vollbrecht, the architects, have all worked in Lang's

65. STEAMBOAT BILL, JR., directed by CHARLES S. REISNER. BUSTER KEATON. [American, 1928]

66. SADIE THOMPSON, directed by RAOUL WALSH. GLORIA SWANSON, LIONEL BARRYMORE. [American, 1928]

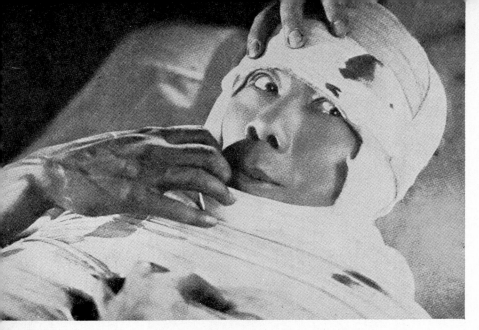

67. STORM OVER ASIA, directed by V. I. Pudovkin.   V. Inkishinov.   [Soviet, 1928]

68. TURKSIB, directed by Victor Turin.   [Soviet, 1928]

production unit. All Lang's scenarios have been conceived and written in collaboration with his wife, Thea von Harbou.

Both *Destiny* and *Siegfried* were supreme examples of the German art film. They were entirely studio-made, and in each the decorative value of the architecture was the binding force of the realisation. They were fantastic in that they were concepts of the imagination; they were decorative in that they employed a series of visual images, designed in black and white and intervening tones of grey, in a two-dimensional pattern. For sheer pictorial beauty of structural architecture, *Siegfried* has seldom been equalled because no company could afford to spend money as did Decla-Bioskop in 1922-23.[1] No expense can have been withheld on that extraordinary production, but in comparison with the cost, little money could have been made in return. *Siegfried* was far from being pure film, far from the naturalism of the Soviets or the individualism of Pabst, but it was restrained, simplified pageantry, rendered with a minimum of decoration to gain the maximum of massed effect. Who can ever forget the tall, dark forests; the birch glade, bespattered with flowers where Siegfried was slain; the procession of Günther's court, seen distantly through the mail-clad legs of the sentinels; the calm, silent atmosphere of the castle rooms, with their simple heraldic decoration; and above all, the dream of the hawks, a conception by Ruttmann, mentioned at an earlier stage? *Destiny,* also, was finely created, using every contemporary resource of trick photography and illusionary setting. Unlike *Siegfried,* which was a straightforward narration of story, *Destiny* was an interplaited theme of three stories, ' The Three Lights ', each connected symbolically with the main modern theme of the two lovers. The film was magnificently conceived and realised; played with unforgettable acting by Bernard Goetzke as Death the Stranger, Lil Dagover as the Girl, and Walther Janssen as the Boy. It

[1] Who, in 1929, could have foreseen the luxury allowed Pascal by J. Arthur Rank in *Caesar and Cleopatra?*

was a production that has been too soon forgotten and deserves revival.

Lang has made also two melodramatic thrillers of spies, gamblers, disguises, crooks, and police. *Doctor Mabuse, the Gambler,* was produced in 1922; *The Spy,* an improved version on the same lines, in 1927-28. In its original form, *Doctor Mabuse* was over seventeen thousand feet in length, and was issued both in Germany and in Britain in two parts. It was the first German film to reach this country (about the same time as Lubitsch's *Dubarry,* renamed *Passion*) and was regarded as remarkable in film technique by the American-influenced minds of British audiences. The story was of the usual *feuilleton* type, with murders, a Sidney Street defence of Mabuse's house against the police and the army, and fainting women, with a strong spell of hypnotism and psycho-analysis. The action, unlike Lang's other work, was rapid in pace and startling in incident, and was therefore preferred by some critics to his slow-moving pageant films. In certain respects it was interesting also as linking the pre-war long shot and chase elements with the tentative methods of the newer school. Six years later, Lang repeated his success twofold in *The Spy,* a story not unlike *Doctor Mabuse* of an international crook, with secret papers, a railway smash, complex disguises, and another final street battle. It was all splendid entertainment, superbly done. It was quick moving, thrilling, and melodramatic. Lang used again as his criminal genius the versatile Rudolf Klein-Rogge, who improved on his early Mabuse part. Technically, the production was brilliantly efficient, notably in Wagner's wonderful camerawork. In minor incidental effect, Lang had pilfered from far and wide. An excellent scene on diagonal steel-girder staircases looked as if it was taken from a Soviet film, but his 'plagiarism' was justified.

Of *Metropolis,* more wilful abuse has been written than praise, partly because the version shown in Britain was unhappily edited, many sequences being deliberately removed. The British copy was 'arranged' by Channing

Pollock, author of *The Fool*. The film, when it made its London appearance, was not enthusiastically received. H. G. Wells, amongst others, damned it as 'quite the silliest film . . .' As a matter of fact, *Metropolis* was very remarkable, based on a brilliant *filmic* conception. Had it been shown in its entirety, it might have afforded a wonderful exposition of cinematography. As with all of the German studio-films, the dominant keynote of the picture was its amazing architecture. It is not until we compare *Metropolis* with a British picture on the same lines, Maurice Elvey's *High Treason,* that it is possible to realise its value. There is not one member of the production units or executive committees, not one critic or film journalist in this country, who can afford to sneer at Fritz Lang's conception. *High Treason,* with its arts-and-crafts design by Andrew Mazzei, revealed only too clearly how poorly Britain produces a film of this kind. Though neither a great film, nor an example of pure filmic expression, *Metropolis* contained scenes that for their grandeur and strength have never been equalled either by Britain or America. Who, for example, could have handled the sequence when Rotwang transfers life and the likeness of human form into the steel figure with such brilliant feeling as Fritz Lang? *Metropolis,* with its rows of rectangular windows, its slow-treading workers, its great geometric buildings, its contrasted light and shade, its massed masses, its machinery, was a considerable achievement. Its actual story value was negligible; the architecture was the story in itself. Lang's recent production, *The Woman in the Moon,* a film purporting to show the journey of a rocket to the moon and the adventures of the crew there, has not yet been shown in London. From its still-photographs and conception, it appears to be quite as remarkable as Lang's other productions.

It is easy, perhaps, to call Fritz Lang a showman. but he is to be reckoned also as a director of decided film intelligence, of broad views, of rare imagination, of artistic feeling, who is not afraid to put his amazing conceptions into practical form, using every technical resource of the studio to do so. Lang is to be admired and studied for his courage and self-confidence. He has not, it is true, any knowledge of constructive editing in the Soviet sense, but he has initiative and a sense of bigness. His work is primarily architectural, essentially the product of the film studio.[1]

The names of Paul Czinner and Elizabeth Bergner are closely associated.[2] Until recently, when Czinner came to Elstree to direct Pola Negri, they have been interested in the productions of Elizabeth Bergner's Poetic Film Company. Czinner and Bergner's first film, however, was *Nju,* for the Rimax Film Company in 1924, in which the two other parts were played by Emil Jannings and Conrad Veidt. It has not been generally shown in this country. *Nju* was the essence of story simplification, of contrasted human emotions without irrelevant matter. Jannings was convincing as the humbly-married office-man, childishly innocent and delightfully in love with his wife. She was attracted by the smart young man. She was found out; a dramatic scene; she left the husband. The young man refused her and she threw herself into the river. The husband followed, not understanding. The young man stood alone in the room where the wife had been; the old charwoman swept round him with her broom. He went out.

There was something extraordinary about this film; an indescribable atmosphere of emptiness, of fatality. Elizabeth Bergner, Jannings, and Veidt simply stood about; Czinner caught the interplay of their thoughts. There was little attempt to tell a story; one felt that it just happened, and was recorded as it happened. It was marred only by the final child-interest. *Nju* left a feeling, rare in the usual completeness of a German film, that things would still go on. It was an incident that would be left behind by the lover and the husband in the

---

[1] Cf. *Celluloid: The Film To-day* (Longmans Green, 1931), The Films of Fritz Lang, pp. 227-238.

[2] They are, of course, married.

continuation of their lives. It had a feeling similar to that evoked by the last shot in *Vaudeville,* the wide open prison gates and the sky.

The second Paul Czinner-Elizabeth Bergner film was *The Violinist of Florence,* made for Ufa, (released in Britain under the ludicrous title of *Impetuous Youth*), and was outstanding for its lyrical beauty and poetic grace. It revealed an Elizabeth Bergner utterly unlike the Bergner of *Nju;* a small, elf-like child, with queer, wide-open eyes, watching and wondering; a child whose subtle emotions were revealed by Czinner's tenderness. Czinner began this film by presenting the reactions of the child to her father (superbly played by Conrad Veidt) and to her stepmother; a tangled mass of human emotions sorted out by the brilliant psychological direction. With the deepest interest one followed this child's thoughts; the scene of the flowers at the dinner-table; the mixing of the drinks; the scene at the boarding-school when she received the letter from her father; her joyous attempts to cross the frontier when she ran away from school; her wanderings in the hills, the cattle by the roadside—all this was most beautifully and sincerely done. Suddenly, about this point, the film achieved sheer Elizabethan cross-dressing comedy. Renée was mistaken for a boy and taken to Florence by an artist and his sister. Admittedly, in themselves, these latter sequences were delightful, but they were isolated from Czinner's opening and the main body of the film. It has even been suggested that they might have been a portion of another film, so different was their feeling. Nevertheless, despite this inconsistency, *The Violinist of Florence* deserved more appreciation than it was accorded. The third Czinner production, *Donna Juanna,* made for the newly-formed Elizabeth Bergner Poetic Film Company (in association with Ufa for distribution), was a light, romantic costume film, adapted from some old Spanish sketches by Tirso de Molina. Following the cross-dressing motive of the last portion of *The Violinist of Florence,* this film was typically Shakespearean, Elizabeth Bergner playing a ˉsort of Viola rôle, fighting a duel with her lover, and so forth. The poetic atmosphere of Spain, exquisitely photographed by Karl Freund, pervaded this new work of Czinner, which was wholly charming in both conception and realisation. Miss Bergner was again supported by Walter Rilla, who played in the former film, and by the delightful Erna Morena. Following *Donna Juana,* Czinner directed his own adaptation of Honoré Balzac's *Duchesse de Langeais,* for the Phœbus Film Company, renaming it *L'Histoire des Treize.* Bergner again played the lead, whilst Hans Rehman and Agnes Esterhazy supported her. Once more Czinner revealed his skill in direction, although as a whole the film was not of equal value to the earlier productions. Before coming to the Elstree studios to direct Pola Negri for the Whitaker production unit, Czinner made a version of Arthur Schnitzler's *Fräulein Else,* his last film with Elizabeth Bergner. This, like *Donna Juanna* and *L'Histoire des Treize,* has not been shown in Britain. Czinner may be reckoned as a director of considerable distinction, quite un-German in character, who, like Pabst, has an interest in natural individuals. His touch is light, fragile, and essentially poetic.

Much has already been written regarding the work of Murnau. Of his earlier films, *Phantom,* adapted from Hauptmann's story, and the pirated version of Bram Stoker's *Dracula* are known. The latter, produced in 1922, was possibly crude in its melodramatic acting, but nevertheless it contained much of considerable interest. There was a very definite feeling for camera angle in the establishment of a macabre mood, and effective use was made of projected negative and one-turn—one-picture camera devices for the suggestion of eeriness. Fritz Arno Wagner's camerawork was notably good, particularly a scene of frightened horses in the twilight and the close-ups of the architecture of the Count's castle. Murnau's *The Last Laugh* has been discussed earlier, and his *Tartuffe,* a production by the same team, is memorable for its superb simplicity. The scenario was again by Carl Mayer; the camerawork by Karl Freund; and the architecture by Walter Röhrig and Robert Herlth.

From the acting standpoint *Tartuffe* was a remarkable example of harmonious talent, typical of German completeness. The spectator felt that there was an underlying current of humour running throughout each sequence, a humour that was not without its vital dramatic moments. One recalls the crystal tear of Elmire that fell like a liquid pearl on the miniature of Orgon, the relationship of the figures one to another; the symbolic black figure of Tartuffe, with silhouetted thin ankles and clumsy square-toed shoes; the exquisite subtle beauty of Elmire, with curled wig, fragile dress, and gentle mien. Clever contrast was made between the closely held Bible of Tartuffe, its minute size symbolic of his hypocritical nature, and the open frankness of Orgon. *Tartuffe* constituted Jannings' third portrayal of comedy (former occasions being in *Waxworks,* in the final part of *The Last Laugh,* and later, of course, in *Faust*). It is difficult to forget Tartuffe descending the curved staircase—Tartuffe espying the image of Orgon's reflection in the teapot—Tartuffe listening, watching, suspicious, leaning on the handrail. The Elmire of Lil Dagover was fragrantly beautiful. I recollect her seduction of Tartuffe on the first occasion; her very gestures were fragile. Werner Krauss was as good as he can at times be bad. His portrayal of Orgon was all that was necessary, and was probably one of his best film parts.

The atmosphere that surrounded the characters enveloped the spectator. It was an atmosphere of simplification, of graceful curves, and wonderful detail of plaster and ironwork. There was no customary over-decoration. Unnecessary detail was eliminated to the better effect of the mass. I remember the beauty of the lace *négligé* in the final bedroom scene; the pattern of the bed covering; the porcelain clock on the fireplace; the reality of the square-toed shoes; the emphasis given to them in the scene of the hammock (a touch of genius); the design of Orgon's ring, and a hundred other points. All these were in perfect harmony, perfect taste, and of the highest tone. Every

detail and every mass was the result of creative forethought. It was this tone that was spread over the whole.
No matter where the characters moved or how they
gestured, the composition remained perfect. Molière,
Watteau, Boucher, and the French engravers of the
eighteenth century were embodied in the spirit of this film,
which was only marred by the unnecessary modern prologue and epilogue.

Murnau's last film in Germany, before he accepted the
Fox contract in Hollywood, was a realisation of *Faust*.
This film may again be taken as a consummate example of
German craftsmanship. Every detail, every mass, every
contrast of light and shade, emphasised the medieval
atmosphere. Mention will be made later of Murnau's use
of the art of Dürer and of Bruegel in his psychological
establishment of the period. Again, Karl Freund's photography was superb, and the production was a notable
instance not only of trick camerawork but of the Schuefftan
process of illusionary architecture. The Mephisto of
Jannings was completely delightful, the essence of refined,
subtle humour, of mischievous trickery and inimitable
devilry; the Marguerite of Camilla Horn, pure and flower-
like; the Faust of Gösta Ekman, a Swedish actor,
thoroughly competent; whilst Yvette Guilbert's playing as
Marguerite's aunt was an ever-memorable piece of sheer
artistry. The drinking scene between Jannings and Yvette
Guilbert stands as one of the finest sequences of humour
in the history of the screen. That such an artist as Murnau
should have gone to Hollywood to devote his filmic, philosophic mind to such banalities as *Sunrise* and *The Four
Devils* is infinitely regrettable.

In the two architectural productions of Murnau, *Tartuffe*
and *Faust*, his direction was closely bound up with the
design of Walter Röhrig and Robert Herlth, the acting of
Jannings and the camera craftsmanship of Karl Freund. In
the same way, the four outstanding films by Dr. Ludwig
Berger—*Cinderella, A Glass of Water, The Waltz Dream,*
and *The Burning Heart*—were the realisation of the

Ludwig Berger—Rudolph Bamberger team of workers. Bamberger was also the designer to Berger's version of the Meistersingers, *The Masters of Nürnberg*, a Phœbus production, with Rudolph Rittner, Max Gülstorff, Gustav Fröhlich, Julius Falkenstein and Elsa Wagner in the cast. It is by *Cinderella*, however, that Ludwig Berger is best known. Made in 1923, when the German cinema was at the height of its middle and best period, *Cinderella* was a film of the most beautiful fantasy, delicately conceived and realised with a perfection of decorative pictorialism. The touch of Ludwig Berger seemed magical, so completely entrancing was the subtle fabrication of this exquisite work. Bamberger, for his design, centred his theme around the charm of Southern Baroque art, making full use of the plastic moulding in which the German studio workers seem to excel. Technically, the ' magic ' in this film was brilliantly accomplished, for it was essentially cinematic. It was curious to note that Berger's design of pictorial composition was nearly always symmetrical throughout this picture— for he obviously centred his movement of acting material round a feature of the architectural composition. Thus it was observed that doorways, windows, gateways, alleyways, etc., were always set in the centre of the screen, the remainder of the composition moving around them. In the same year, Ludwig Berger made *A Glass of Water*, a film that nominally concerned Queen Anne of England, but actually there was no idea of historical accuracy for that would have been antagonistic to the decorative motive as well as to the environment of the picture. Once more Rudolph Bamberger's setting was in the spirit of South German baroque, whilst Helga Thomas, Mady Christians, and Lucie Höflich were again in the cast, with Rudolph Rittner and Hans Brausewetter. Although not realised with the charm of *Cinderella*, this film was nevertheless pleasing, tending perhaps to overlength. Berger's later picture *The Waltz Dream*, made in 1926, was one of the few German films to meet with success in America. It ran in New York for several weeks, appreciated by

American audiences as 'something different'. Actually, it was a charming comedy—as one would expect from Berger—sentimental and harmless, but not to be compared with the earlier *Cinderella*. Again, Mady Christians played with graceful comedy, supported by Willy Fritsch, who was at that time practically unknown, whilst the soft photography of Werner Brandes and the subdued richness of the Bamberger settings contributed to the atmosphere which Berger sought to realise. This director has made yet another German picture with Mady Christians and Bamberger, *The Burning Heart,* which has recently been synchronised, whilst in Hollywood he has directed *The Sins of the Fathers* with Emil Jannings, and a version of the operetta, *The Vagabond King.*

The name of Arthur Robison is at once associated with *Warning Shadows,* a film that by now is well known to all familiar with the development of the cinema. Actually, the credit for this unique work should be given equally to all the production unit, to Fritz Arno Wagner, the camera-man; to Albin Grau, the architect; and to Dr. Robison; as well as to the brilliant playing of Fritz Kortner, Gustav von Wangenheim, Ferdinand von Alten, Fritz Rasp, Max Gülstorff, Alexander Granach, and Ruth Weyher. The film was made without the use of titles, save at the opening for the introduction of the characters, but several quite ridiculous and totally discordant captions were inserted for its British presentation. At the time of production, in 1922, *Warning Shadows* was a remarkable achievement. Its purely psychological direction, its definite completeness of time and action, its intimate ensemble were new attri-butes of the cinema. It was a rare instance of complete filmic unity, with the possible exception of the unnecessary roof-garden scene. The continuity of theme, the smooth development from one sequence into another, the gradual realisation of the thoughts of the characters, were flaw-lessly presented. It carried an air of romance, of fantasy, of tragedy. Every filmic property for the expression of mood, for the creation of atmosphere, that was known at the time was used with imagination and intelligence. Its supreme value as an example of unity of purpose, of time, of place, of theme cannot be over-estimated. Of Dr. Robison's other pictures, mention need be made only of *Manon Lescaut* (1927), *Looping the Loop* (1928) and his recently completed work, *The Informer,* for British International Pictures of Elstree. For the production of *Manon Lescaut,* faithfully adapted from the immortal romance of the Abbé Prevost, Robison had the advantage of the design of Paul Leni, better known as a director. The acting material was well chosen, no easy task with a costume picture of this type, the Manon of Lya de Putti and the Chevalier des Grieux of Vladimir Gaiderov being admirable, whilst the supporting cast, particularly Siegfried Arno, Frieda Richard, and Lydia Potechina, were exceptionally competent. Robison succeeded in establishing an air of intimacy, of dramatic relationship between one character and another, of the deep passion that linked the two lovers, by a continual use of close-ups. The decorations of Leni gave to the film a reality that is lacking in the vast majority of costume pictures. His tendency to continue scenes through doorways and along passages lent a depth that prevented artificiality, a customary characteristic of such productions. The costumes, designed with a wealth of accurate detail that was fully revealed by the close penetration of the camera, were more faithful to their period, both in cut and wear, than any others that have been seen in historical film reconstruction. On the other hand, *Looping the Loop,* a curious contrast to Robison's earlier work, was a circus film—an environment which was popular at the time. It was not of especial interest, being a straightforward rendering of the usual circus story; a clown with a broken heart, a girl's flirtations, and an unscrupulous philanderer. The photography of Karl Hoffman was good; the settings of Walter Röhrig and Herlth consistent; and the acting of Werner Krauss as accomplished as usual. In brief, the production unit was worthy of better material. I have been given to understand, however, that the original negative was destroyed by fire and that the copy generally exhibited was made from an assembly of left-over ' takes '. Of Robison's British picture, *The Informer,* Liam O'Flaherty's story of gunmen and betrayal, it is hard to write, for although it obviously contained the elements of an excellent film, the silent version shown to the public was so badly edited that little of Robison's technique could be appreciated. In order to meet market requirements at the time, a version with added dialogue sequences was presented, but this does not enter into consideration.

Karl Grune has made one outstanding film, *The Street,* and a number of others that will be forgotten in the course of time. Made in 1923, Grune's *The Street* was again typical of the German studio-mind. Its chief value lay in its unity of theme, its creation of mood by contrasted intensities and movements of light, and its simplicity of treatment. Apart from these significant features, it was acted with deplorable melodrama, and its studio structure setting was hardly convincing. Nevertheless, for its few moments of filmic intensity, such as the celebrated moving shadow scene in the opening and the cleverly handled game of cards, it must rank as important. Grune's other films include *The Two Brothers,* with Conrad Veidt in a dual rôle; *Arabella,* with Fritz Rasp; *Jealousy,* with Werner Krauss and Lya de Putti; *At the Edge of the World,* an unconvincing pacifist theme, distinguished only for the settings by A. D. Neppach and the playing of Brigitte Helm; *Marquis d'Eon,* a depressing historical film, with Liane Haid badly miscast as the chevalier, notable only for the camera craftsmanship of Fritz Arno Wagner; *The Youth of Queen Louise,* a Terra production with Mady Christians; and *Waterloo,* the Emelka tenth anniversary spectacle film, badly staged at great expense, foolishly theatrical and lacking conviction. Karl Grune may have made *The Street,* but he has failed as yet to develop the cinematic tendencies displayed as long ago as 1923, becoming a director of the commercial type. The same may be said of Robert Wiene, who will, of course, long be remembered as the director of *The*

Cabinet of Doctor Caligari, but who, since that achievement, has done little to add to his laurels.[1] *Raskolnikov,* made in 1923 from Dostoievski's *Crime and Punishment* with a band of the Russian Moscow Art Players, was an essay in the same vein as *The Cabinet of Doctor Caligari,* but less successful. The following year, Wiene made *The Hands of Orlac,* with Conrad Veidt, for the Pan Film Company of Austria; a singularly dreary, melodramatic film, interesting only because of a few tense moments of Veidt's acting, and some cleverly contrasted lighting. Wiene has also made, in direct contrast to these heavy and slow productions, a light version of the opera *Rosenkavalier,* a delicate film of little lasting value.

Henrik Galeen is yet another director who has to his credit but one pre-eminent realisation, *The Student of Prague.* Galeen was first associated with the cinema as a scenarist, having been connected in this capacity with Paul Leni's *Waxworks,* Wegener's *The Golem,* and Murnau's *Dracula.* It will have been noticed by those interested in films of the past, that very frequently it is difficult to discern who exactly was responsible for the merits and demerits. Galeen, for example, probably had a great deal more to do with *The Golem* than the scenario, and similarly the complete production unit of *The Student of Prague,* including Herman Warm, Gunther Krampf, and Erich Nitzschmann, all well-known technicians, should receive credit. This remarkable film, almost un-German in its realisation, stands out during the transition period, when the decorative art film was being succeeded by the naturalistic film. Expressionist themes and cubist settings, so marked in the first German period, had developed into motives of mysticism and Baroque design, to give place again to the naturalness of the street, the town, and the individual. *The Student of Prague* combined both of these two latter periods. It had open spaciousness and dark psychology, wild poetic beauty and a deeply dramatic theme. Beyond this, it had Conrad Veidt at his best; a performance

[1] Died, Paris, July, 1938.

that he has never equalled either before or since. It was, possibly, theatrical—but it was, also, filmic in exposition. From the beginning of the students' drinking scene to the final death of Baldwin, this film was superbly handled. The conflict of inner realities; the sadness and joy of changing atmospheres; the storm emphasising the anguish of Baldwin; the rendering of the depths of human sorrow and weakness; the imagination and purity of treatment; the intensely dramatic unfolding of the theme; all these entitled this film to rank as great. The interior design was admirable, lit with some of the most beautiful lighting I have observed. As a film that relied for its emotional effect on the nature of the material, the lighting and pictorial composition, it was unparalleled. Two other productions go to the credit of Galeen, *Mandrake* (*A Daughter of Destiny*) and *After the Verdict,* a British production; but little can be said in praise of them, although it is only fair to add that the British version of the former film was completely mutilated in order to meet the censor's requirements.

Paul Leni's *Waxworks* was a typical example of the early decorative film, revealing, as would be expected from an artist of this character, a strong sense of painted, rather theatrical, architecture. As is probably known, the film purported to tell three episodic incidents of three wax figures in a showman's tent, developed by the imagination of a poet, the figures being Ivan the Terrible, Haroun-al-Raschid, and Jack-the-Ripper. The parts were played by Conrad Veidt, Emil Jannings, and Werner Krauss, respectively; the only occasion on which these three celebrated actors have appeared together in the same film. Their individual performances were magnificently acted in the theatrical manner. Leni's decorations were simply conceived, but *Waxworks,* whilst certainly being a film of exceptional interest, was not by any means great from a filmic point of view. Its significance lay in its exemplary methods of simplicity both in treatment and in design. Leni made also *Prince Cuckoo,* a film about which there is little on record and, as already mentioned, designed the settings for Robison's *Manon Lescaut*. His career in Hollywood, where he went in 1926, developed into two good melodramatic thrillers, *The Chinese Parrot* and *The Cat and the Canary,* which he followed with a travesty of cinematic methods, *The Man Who Laughs*. He died in 1929, having just completed an all-sound-and-dialogue picture for his American employers, Universal.

The work of Lupu Pick has tended to become over-praised and over-estimated. He played, it is true, a part of some importance in the gradual dawn of the German naturalistic school, with the production in 1923 of *New Year's Eve,* but this film itself was dreary. It was over-acted, in the worst German manner, by Eugen Klöpfer, a stage actor who knew little of the film, and it was made without titles. Pick's direction is principally characterised by a slow, deliberate development of plot and character, depending wholly on the acting value and narrative situations for dramatic effect. Apart from *New Year's Eve* (the English renaming of *Sylvester*) he is known chiefly by his dull version of Ibsen's *The Wild Duck; The Last Cab,* in which he played the lead; *The Rail;* and *La Casemate Blindée*. He came to Elstree in 1928, and made for the Louis Blattner Film Corporation, *A Knight in London,* a light comedy with camerawork by Karl Freund. His interest, therefore, really lies in the transitional nature of his earlier films. Dr. Arnold Fanck is associated principally with that superb mountain film, *The Wrath of the Gods,* a picture of great pictorial beauty. Recently he joined G. W. Pabst in the Alpine realisation, *The White Hell of Pitz Palü.*

*

Returning to the first period of the German film, that is the era of theatricalism and later the beginnings of the expressionist and art film, a brief note should be included on the Lubitsch productions, and others of a similar type. Apart from *Anne Boleyn* and similar historical pictures, Lubitsch directed a meritorious film, *The Flame,* with Pola

Negri, Alfred Abel, and Herman Thimig; as well as the Arabian Nights fantasy, *Sumurun*. To the Buchowetski historical pictures should also be added a version of Dostoievski's *Brothers Karamazov*, whilst mention must be made of Richard Oswald's *Lucretia Borgia* and *Lady Hamilton*, as well as the same director's *House in the Dragonerstrasse*, with Werner Krauss. More recently, Oswald has directed a spectacular French film based on the adventures of *Cagliostro*, with Hans Stüwe in the name part, and a war film, *The Fugitive Lover*, again with Hans Stüwe and Agnes Esterhazy.

In 1922 there was made the big Neuman production of the life of Frederick the Great, played with distinction by Otto Gebühr, with Erna Morena as Queen Christine. *Fridericus Rex* was of great length, so much so that a copy has long lain in London for lack of proper editing. By those who have seen the film in Germany, it is said to be a remarkably faithful representation of historical fact. The direction was by Arzèn von Cserèpy. Another big historical production was the Cob Film Company's *Martin Luther*, with Eugen Klöpfer in the name part, a film which recently caused some sensation in London by the British Board of Film Censors' ban upon its showing. The sensational ban was duly removed after some slight alterations had been made and the Board had perceived the foolishness of their action. Despite the publicity it received, however, the film proved to be not only dull but without any filmic justification. It was directed by Hans Kyser, a former scenarist to Murnau's film, *Faust*. Among other films of an early date, mention must be made of Carl Fröhlich's *Maternity* and *Tragedy*, both typical of their period; Leopold Jessner's *Hintertreppe*, made in 1921, from a scenario by Carl Mayer, with Henny Porten, Fritz Körtner, and Wilhelm Dieterle; and Frederick Zelnig's *Les Tiserands* and *The Blue Danube*.

With the later period of naturalism and reality there arose a number of directors, nearly all of whom are of significance, including Berthold Viertel, Fritz Wendhausen,

69. THE WIND, directed by Victor Seaström. Lillian Gish, Lars Hanson.
[American, 1928]

70. THE FALL OF THE HOUSE OF USHER, directed by Jean Epstein.
Jean Dubencourt, Charles Lamay. [French, 1928]

71. LA PASSION DE JEANNE D'ARC, directed by CARL TH. DREYER.   [French, 1928]

72. NEW BABYLON, directed by G. KOZINTSEV and L. TRAUBERG.   [Soviet, 1929]

the late Bruno Rahn, and Kurt Bernhardt. Viertel, who had at an earlier date made *The Wig* (with Otto Gebühr) and *Nora*, claims attention by reason of the *Adventures of a Ten-Mark Note*. This was a badly titled and poorly edited film, but the basic idea and some of the direction were noteworthy, despite unnecessary distortion of camera angles. Werner Fütterer was the outstanding member of the cast. Wendhausen, who has also to his credit *The Trial of Donald Westhof*, is chiefly notable for his brilliant film, *Out of the Mist*, with Mady Christians. This was a theme of German agricultural life, of a wayside hostelry, of a saw-mill, with a climactic ending of torrential floods. The direction was simple, going straight to the motive of every action that made up the narrative situations. The atmosphere of the woods, of the fairground, and of the sawmill was created with the greatest skill, Wendhausen realising the close relationship that lay between the people of the village and their land. The interior settings were exquisitely lit and the photography throughout was beautiful. As well as Mady Christians, Werner Fütterer was again in the cast, together with Lia Eibenschütz and Karl Klock.

Before his untimely death a short time ago, two pictures of the ' street ' type were associated with Bruno Rahn, the first being *Kleinstadtsünder* (*L'Auberge en Folie*) and the second, *The Tragedy of the Street*, which was shown in an abbreviated form in this country. Rahn followed on the lower-class reality that was started by Grune's *The Street*, and continued later by Pabst and Lupu Pick. *The Tragedy of the Street* was an intensely moving, deeply realised film of the Street; the feet that walk over its stones; and of the people to whom those feet, high heels and low heels, belonged. Asta Nielsen, that actress of erotic characterisation, played the elder of the two prostitutes; Hilda Jennings, the younger, who had dreams of escaping from the life she was forced to lead. To many, no doubt, the theme was sordid, possibly unpleasant, but Rahn infused its sordidness with a glimpse of happiness, a sudden appearance of all the sentiment of love and joyousness on which the woman had turned her back. Asta Nielson has never been greater than in this film; every moment of her slow acting was charged with meaning; the basin of black dye and the toothbrush; the buying of the confectionery shop with her savings; the final, overpowering tragedy. Throughout, all things led back to the street; its pavements with the hurrying, soliciting feet; its dark corners and angles; its light under the sentinel lamp-posts. Rahn's *Kleinstadt-sünder,* made just previous to *The Tragedy of the Street,* was a lighter theme than the latter, again with Asta Nielsen, Hans von Schlettow, Hans Wasmann, and Ferdinand von Alten. The pictures were produced by the Pantomin Film Company, both being superbly photographed by Guido Seeber. Kurt Bernhardt is a director of the young German school, who achieved rapid acclamation by his film, *Schinderhannes.* He has also to his credit, *Torments of the Night,* a modern theme with Alexander Granach and Wilhelm Dieterle. *Schinderhannes* contained a narrative placed in the year 1796 when the French army occupied the left bank of the Rhine—of a band of outlaws who opposed the *régime* of the French military. It was a difficult theme to treat with conviction, but Bernhardt, aided greatly by the camerawork of Günther Krampf, succeeded in making an extremely moving film out of its intricate incident. He attempted to develop the theme outside national feeling, to realise the characteristics and atmosphere of the period, and the sequence of events flowed smoothly to the finale of Schinderhannes' death as a national hero.

Among the more pretentious of the recent German productions, it is ·necessary to include the work of Hans Schwartz, Joe May, Tourjanski, and Volkoff. Schwartz was the director of an admirable domestic comedy, *Love's Sacrifice,* in which there played a new German actress of great charm, Kate von Nagy. He has a light touch, almost artificial at times, and a pleasing smoothness of handling. Under the supervision of Erich Pommer he made *The Hungarian Rhapsody,* a film obviously inspired by Soviet

influence (Preobrashenskaia's *Peasant Women of Riazan*)
that was hardly successful, but more recently directed
Brigitte Helm and Franz Lederer in *Nina Petrovna,* a
picture of considerable merit with elegant settings by
Röhrig and Herlth and some clever camerawork by Karl
Hoffman. Joe May, who is connected at an early date with
such films as *The Hindu Tomb* (with Bernard Goetzke) and
The Japanese Dagger, has also worked recently for the Ufa
Company under Pommer's control. *Asphalt,* a good con-
ception made unpractical by studio structure, and *Home-
coming,* a bad realisation of Leonhard Frank's fine novel,
Karl and Anna, distinguished only by Günther Rittau's
photography, were Joe May pictures. Tourjanski, a
Russian *émigré,* was responsible for the Anglo-German
spectacle, *Volga-Volga,* a film of interest solely for its
exterior photography, and *Michael Strogoff;* and Nicolas
Volkoff, who is associated with musical comedy spectacles
(*Casanova*), made for Ufa the well-staged but Americanised
Secrets of the East. Of the lesser-known German
directors, those whose names and work must be mentioned
are Jaap Speyer (*Conscience,* a powerful film with Bernard
Goetzke and Walter Rilla); Wilhelm Thiele (*Hurrah! I'm
Alive,* with the inimitable Nikolai Kolin); Erich Washneck
(*Jackals,* an excellent film with Olga Tschechowa and Hans
von Schlettow; *A Society Scandal,* with Brigitte Helm);
Willy Reiber (*Sturmflut,* a well-realised theme of the sea);
Max Glass (*Homesickness,* with Mady Christians and
Wilhelm Dieterle); Willi Wolff (*Kopf Hoch Charley,* with
Ellen Richter); Gerhard Lamprecht (*Under the Lantern,*
an underworld picture with Lissi Arna); and A. W.
Sandberg (*The Golden Clown,* with Gösta Ekman and
Mary Johnson), together with Max Mack, Rudolf Meinert,
and Manfred Noa.

*

The German has been a great cinema. It has produced
principles and processes that have been all-important contributions to the cinema of the world. From its individual

development there have come the freedom of the camera, the feeling of completeness, and the importance of architectural environment as part of the realisation. These have been brought about by the national aptitude for craftsmanship, for structure, for studioism. They have been a means to an end that in itself has not yet been discovered. It has been well said that the German film begins and ends in itself. This, with certain reservations, is true.

In recapitulation, it has been seen how the years immediately after the war gave rise to the historical costume melodrama, commercial products of the property room and Reinhardt (*Dubarry, Anne Boleyn, Othello, Merchant of Venice*). There was then *The Cabinet of Doctor Caligari*, with its decorative environment and its use of psychology, to be followed by other expressionist films, *Torgus, Raskolnikov, Genuine,* and later, *The Stone Rider.* From these there developed the decorative film, increasing in pictorial beauty to the culminating *Faust* (*Siegfried, Waxworks, Destiny*). Then began the feeling for reality, still by studio representation, with *Scherben* and *The Street,* followed in time by the work of Lupu Pick, Murnau, Czinner, Pabst, Dupont (*New Year's Eve, Last Laugh, Nju, Joyless Street, Vaudeville,* and *Baruch* [1924]); later by Rahn and Bernhardt; until there came the surrender to the American cinema—resulting in commercial melodrama, to be relieved only by the isolated films of Pabst, the large-scale studio-films of Lang, and the childlike psychology of Hans Behrendt's *Robber Band* and *Die Hose.* Finally, there is the crisis presented by the advent of the dialogue and sound film, the result of which has yet to be seen.

VIII

THE FRENCH FILM

French *cinéastes* have the disconcerting habit of denying the existence of the French film despite ever-constant proof to the contrary. But then the French *cinéaste* is a tiresome fellow, who is always dissatisfied with everything that takes place, and is burdened with a mind that chases itself in circles. Added to which, we are frequently given to understand by him that the failure of the French cinema is due entirely to its being French.

Apart from so discouraging a national outlook, few writers in this country appear to appreciate the significance of the French cinema, and even those who do have only reached that frame of mind with the recent importation of *avant-garde* productions into London. The reason for this lack of appreciation in Britain of the French product seems to be due to three causes; first, because much of the French cinema, save for the grand spectacular films, has been experimental in nature, and therefore a closed book to British film writers; secondly, because production in France has always been spasmodic; and thirdly, because there has been comparatively little opportunity for the close examination of the French film in Britain, except at the performances of the London Film Society.[1]

In short, then, the general ignorance as to the salient characteristics, influences, and tendencies of the French cinema is singularly profound, a fact that is all the more remarkable in that the French film is of extreme importance, not only to the cinema of Europe, but to a proper understanding of the cinema as a whole.

[1] Gratitude is to be accorded Mr. Stuart Davis for his enterprise in presenting at the Avenue Pavilion, London, a three-month's season of French productions during the autumn and winter 1929-30. This provided an excellent opportunity for the examination of some of the outstanding examples of the French school.

293

As stated above, the French *cinéaste* has strangely little regard for the capabilities of his self-created cinema. He appears to be always too interested in the films of other countries to take part in his own productions. In post-war days, he was the most appreciative critic of the German and the now extinct Swedish film; this, later, being displaced by a reaction to the constructive methods of the Soviets; whilst the whole time he has had a sneaking fondness for the American movie, first for its action, and now for its sex. The position is rendered the more curious in that several of the qualities which the *cinéaste* admires in the American cinema are indirectly derived from his own. Despite its increasing prevalence, the reason for this idolisation of Hollywood is hard to discover. The sole aim of the average French director seems to be to go to Hollywood, which surely is the last place in which to find a creative understanding of the cinema. But, notwithstanding all logic, the *cinéaste* has a constant craving after the metallic glitter of the movie, with its movement of acting material and mock-humanitarianism. The fully charged sex-appeal movie is the fetish of the French *cinéastes*. The natural acting material of France (Pierre Batcheff, Maurice de Féraudy, Philippe Hériat, Jim Gerald, Gina Manés) is suppressed in the fervent worship of Sue Carol, Florence Vidor, and Joan Crawford, and the physical toughness of George Bancroft and Victor McLaglen. They will deny the presence of the capricious Catherine Hessling in favour of Lupe Velez. They will ruthlessly condemn Epstein and Dreyer, but enthuse over von Sternberg and von Stroheim. *The Wedding March* is considered preferable to *En Rade; Our Dancing Daughters* to *Thérèse Raquin; White Shadows* to *Finis Terrae*. They will accept the *décor* of Cedric Gibbons and forget that it is almost wholly derived from the *Exposition des Arts Décoratifs*, held at Paris in 1925. It is this ridiculous state of artificiality that strangles the French cinema to-day, that prevents it from progressing along its natural course of development. There are fortunately, however, a few directors who have sufficient independence and are sane-headed enough to stand above this adolescent attitude of self-condemnation, such as René Clair and Jean Epstein, and it is to these men that we must look for the future of the French cinema in its purified form.

Meanwhile, the young *cinéaste* perpetually calls for youth in the film. The dynamic vitality of the American girl is his schoolboy downfall. He is incapable of achieving a true perspective of the cinema as a whole, of its widespread developments and traditions. He has, in fact, lost his sense of values when he calls *The Crowd* the greatest achievement of the American cinema.

*

In contrast to the cinema of the Soviets, collectivism in film production is practically unknown in France. This, it would seem, is partly due to the haphazard methods of the producing companies and to the natural disinclination of the French for co-operation. Nearly every film of interest which has originated from France has been the product of an individualistic artist mind. This characteristic is to be found equally in the experiments of the *avant-garde* and in the bigger realisations of Clair, Feyder, Epstein, and Dreyer. But perhaps the basic reason for this single-mindedness is that it is the logical outcome of the painter's studio so inherent in French tradition. One has but to recall the last two decades of the nineteenth century, when the marble-top café table bred the environment in which the *camaraderie* of Seurat, Lautrec, Van Gogh, Gauguin, and the rest had its origin. This group habit, so typical of Parisian intellectualism, has given rise to the cinematic artist and photogenic experimentalist, personified in Duchamp, Chomette, Deslav, Grémillon, Man Ray, etc., and which is so well instanced in their ' absolute ' cinematics, *L'Etoile de Mer, Montparnasse, Fait Divers, A quoi rêvent les jeunes films,* and others.

Much has been said to the detriment of the French *avant-garde* film, but, nevertheless, I believe that it constitutes an excellent grounding for the young film director. We know that it is the fashion for any young man of intelligence to borrow a few thousand francs and a camera and to make an abstract, 'absolute' film of Paris, selling it afterwards (if he is fortunate) to an advertising firm. But this is an admirable way for that young man to develop his filmic instinct, if by any chance he should possess any. In themselves, experimental films are of little significance, being mere object-lessons in cinematic values and the various uses of the resources of the cinema. They are a testing ground for the instruments of the film, and hence should be of the utmost interest to the big-scale director. In all experimental films there are to be found a dozen uses of camera devices and trick photography, which, with modifications, can be employed in the commercial film. René Clair's *Entr'acte,* made in 1923, may be cited as a typical example. It was realised from a scenario in the dadaist manner by Francis Picabia, and purported to be an exposition of the cult of the spontaneous dissociation of ideas. It exploited the theory, now discarded, of the irrelevance of material events and consequently was entirely antagonistic in conception to the essential organisation, selection, and construction of the cinema. Contained in its realisation, however, were various camera devices, now familiar, of slow-motion, the reversal of pictorial composition from left to right of the screen, and photographing a ballet dancer from below through a sheet of glass. Henri Chomette's *A quoi rêvent les jeunes films* (1924) was also in this category, the material content being entirely composed of light and speed, the human element being absent from the film save for the cine-portraits of Man Ray. It was an attempt at pure emotionalism. The environment of the *cinéastes* is completed by the cine-journalists, with their ephemeral outlook and easily impressed minds, who are ever busy in criticism and filmic theory. And behind them lies the group of little cinemas which specialise in the presentation of *avant-garde* work and intelligent films from other countries —the *Studio* 28, *Studio des Ursulines, Studio Diamant,* etc.

I hope the experimental contribution of the French cinema will ever be present in Paris, which is a fitting background for an *avant-garde* movement. The short capricious films of Germaine Dulac, Eugène Deslav, Georges Lacombe, Rouguier, Man Ray, Kirsanov, Grémillon are always mentally stimulating in that they seldom end with themselves. They are continually suggestive of new ideas, new shapes and angles, that may be of significance to the cinema proper. On the other hand, it is ridiculous to accept the *avant-garde* movement as the aesthetic zenith of the film, as so many of the intelligentsia seem to do. The experimentalists in the abstract and ' absolute ' film are interesting in their right place, which is the private cinema, but any attempt to thrust their work on to the public at large is merely absurd.[1]

Developed from the experimental groups there are a number of directors of some maturity, who have come to realise that a considerable amount of money is necessary for the production of any film of significance. Clair, Epstein, Cavalcanti, Renoir, have all had their training in the *avant-garde* before making larger pictures. Thus has come into being the principal characteristic of the French cinema, the single-minded production with the director or the cameraman, as the case may be, as the sole *metteur-en-scène*. Hence, Gance is the single creator of *Napoléon*, Clair of *Le Chapeau de Paille d'Italie*, and Feyder of *Thérèse Raquin;* whilst on a lower scale are Deslav's *La Marche des Machines*, Dulac's *La Coquille et le Clergyman*, and Kirsanov's *Brûmes d'automne*.

But this constant stream of experimental work does not mean that France's sole contribution to the cinema will remain in an empirical state, as so many like to assume. On the contrary, it suggests that France should possess a

[1] The coming of the sound film, the greatly all-round increased costs of production, the Trade Union requirements for minimum technical crews, all these have practically made experiment impossible. For a time in the thirties, the British documentary school offered opportunity for experiment, but even that has tended to disappear as documentary units became more and more dependent on sponsorship of a bureaucratic and unimaginative kind.

number of distinguished directors grown up through stages of experiment.[1] There is, however, a wide gulf between the French director and the French producer, well instanced by René Clair's relationship with Albatross-Sequana. With the exception of the Société Générale de Films, there exists no producing company in France which recognises the artist-mind of the French director. Producers seem unable to realise that, instead of organising their industry on an American basis, they must adapt their production schedule according to the directors whom they employ. This would result in a permanent policy of individually realised films, each with its controlling source in the artist-mind of the director. As mentioned above, this policy has been adopted by the Société Générale de Films and has resulted, to date, in two outstanding productions, *Finis Terrae* and *La Passion de Jeanne d'Arc*. The production plans of this enterprising company have, however, been temporarily suspended, owing to the problems raised by the dialogue film.

But it is useless to believe that this natural outcome of the French cinema, even if widely adopted, will ever flourish on a big commercial scale. The market for the French ' artist ' production must necessarily remain limited, for the French have not any idea of the entertainment of the masses. The appeal of such films as *La Passion de Jeanne d'Arc* is naturally restricted, but it is sufficient to ensure further production if unhampered by the side-issues of the dialogue film. The French cinema as a whole is incapable of competing with the vast commercial product of Hollywood, and no amount of ' quota ' regulations will make it possible. The opportunity of the French producing companies lies in the public which the American and British companies are creating by their steady stream of indifferent talking films. This public is definitely hostile to the product that is being thrust upon it from Elstree and Hollywood, and would· be receptive of good films from

[1] The subsequent development of the French feature film in the thirties and the distinguished work of such directors as Carné, Duvivier, Grémillon, Renoir, and Clément add further to this comment made before the full flowering of the French cinema.

any country. The French commercial development is gradual but sure, and if a better understanding could be reached between producer and director, and the companies would be content with small profits, there waits a public in this country which will receive their product.

*

Directly associated with the rise of the French film director from the environment of the artist's *atelier* and the marble-top table of the *boulevard* is his delight in the perfect composition of the visual image. The *cinéaste* has first and foremost a pictorial outlook, which is as discernible in the *avant-garde* films as in the large-scale spectacle productions of the French commercial cinema. In contradistinction to the slow morbid psychology and emphasis on dramatic acting values that mark the early German and Swedish films, the French cinema has always been characterised by its directors' love of classical compositions, almost in an early nineteenth-century manner. It is an outlook that bears comparison with the classicism of the painters Chavannes and David. The French director frequently sets out to create an environment solely by a series of succeeding visual images, often of great pictorial beauty in themselves but usually non-dynamic in material. There have been many attempts to establish thematic atmosphere with the barest framework of narrative content. Such was the intention of Cavalcanti's *En Rade* and Epstein's *Finis Terrae,* as well as numerous of the *avant-garde* films, *Menilmontant, La Zone, Tour au Large, Le Tour,* etc. Of recent years, with the interest shown by the *cinéaste* in the Soviet cinema, principles of cutting have been infused into the values of pictorial composition. But quite unlike the constructive policy of the Soviet director, the *avant-garde* seem to believe that material can be photographed anywhere and anyhow as long as the images themselves are of interest, and that by simply joining them together, according to their form and shape, a complete film will result. This fallacious idea is, of course, wholly antagonistic to the principles of constructive editing and cutting as understood in Russia. Instances of the chaos produced by this irrelevant method were to be seen in Silka's *La Ballade du Canart,* Man Ray's *Les Mystères du Château du Dé,* and Eugène Deslav's *Montparnasse.* Only one French example occurs where constructive editing has been rightly incorporated with beautiful visual images—in the often quoted *Finis Terrae.*

With the exception of the two recent comedies of René Clair, the French director has little real feeling for movement of acting material. It is on these grounds that the cine-journalist rightly attacks his own cinema, holding up for example the American action film, formerly in the Western and later in the underworld thriller. It is this failure to utilise movement of acting material that causes the French *grand* films, such as *Koenigsmark, Monte Cristo, Michael Strogoff, Casanova,* and *Le Joueur d'Echecs* to be unconvincing. Although pictorially these big productions seldom fail to please, their paucity of action often renders them depressing. The spectacle films, which are so typically French in their pageantry and pomp, are conceived in the latent spirit of eighteenth-century romanticism. Despite the fact that they are almost always extremely well done from a historical and visual point of view, the perfection of pictorialism does not prevent them from becoming frequently tedious and often exceptionally dull, as in *Le Miracle des Loups* and *La Merveilleuse Vie de Jeanne d'Arc.* For actual detail in reconstruction of settings and costumes the French are unparalleled for good taste and accuracy, but these *grand* films are negligible cinematically. On this account, therefore, despite their shallowness and entire absence of good faith, the American costume spectacles, such as *Ben-Hur, General Crack,* and *The Beloved Rogue* are preferable filmically to their French counterpart and certainly more commercially successful. This fact is all the more deplorable when one recalls the brilliant costumes and settings, so perfect in spirit and taste, of such a film as Gaston Ravel's *Le Collier de la Reine.*

The supreme example of the pictorial mind was instanced in that most remarkable of films, Carl Dreyer's *La Passion de Jeanne d'Arc,* where the very beauty of the individual visual images destroyed the *filmic* value of the production. Every shot in this extraordinary film was so beautifully composed, so balanced in linear design and distribution of masses, so simplified in detail that the spectator's primary desire was to tear down each shot as it appeared on the screen and to hang it on his bedroom wall. This was in direct opposition to the central aim of the cinema, in which each individual image is inconsequential in itself, being but a part of the whole vibrating pattern. In Dreyer's beautiful film the visual image was employed to its fullest possible extent, but employed graphically and not filmically. But more of *La Passion de Jeanne d'Arc* later. Alberto Cavalcanti (who, it will be recalled, was a set-designer before a *metteur-en-scène*) is another example of the pictorial but non-cinematic mind. *En Rade* was composed of numerous lovely compositions out of which was built an atmosphere of ships and the sea, but the film was definitely lacking in the dynamic vitality of the cinema. But in Epstein's *Finis Terrae* the visual image was constructively used. Every shot was of interest; first, psychologically in the filmic manner, and secondly, from a pictorial standpoint. Epstein worked with a cinematic, constructive mind, keeping the graphic visual design of secondary importance. The same cinematic relation between image and content was found also in Feyder's *Thérèse Raquin,* in which the influence of Germanic psychology was strongly marked in the arrangement of the images, Feyder also employing with subtle skill the contrast of light intensities to emphasise the expression of the dramatic mood.

Indirectly related to the French delight in the harmonious composition of images is a leaning towards the decorative, artificially created environment, which is again non-cinematic in its semi-theatrical artistry. This tendency towards sweetness of decoration I am almost inclined to describe as artistic embellishment, if I had not so great an admiration for French graphic art in its proper surroundings. The creation of the artificial environment, especially when inclined to become sentimental in the French film as compared with the expressionist and fauvist character of the early German pictures, is hostile to the proper aim of the cinema, which is primarily concerned with the representation of reality. In the French film, as in the German, this environment may at first sight be taken for a degree of fantasy. Actually, however, it is nothing of the sort. It is the syrup of sentimentality, destructive to the forcefulness of purpose of the cinema. It was seen at its worst and most decadent in the fairyland settings of Clair's *Le Voyage Imaginaire* and in Renoir's *La Petite Marchande d'Allumettes,* where it was strongly reminiscent of the Russian ballet and the decorations of the Chauve-Souris. Moreover, beyond setting, it spreads into spiritual themes until there is found the ' Spirit of France ' in *Napoléon,* with its fluttering eagle, the ' Rose of the Rail ' in *La Roue* and in Poirier's *vision d'histoire, Verdun.* It is a type of poetic symbolism, essentially nineteenth century in feeling, of spiritual sentimentality that is uncongenial to the architectural, contemporary essence of the cinema.

Of the present directors in France it has been said that the most significant are Jean Epstein, René Clair, Abel Gance, Carl Dreyer (a Dane who has recently worked in France with French material) and Jacques Feyder (a Belgian, who has directed in Germany and who is now in Hollywood).[1] The first two of these have developed from the *avant-garde* movement.

Epstein, who is of Polish origin, is characterised by his philosophy of outlook and his essentially cinematic mind, which has recently been influenced by the constructivism of the Soviet cinema. Amongst his early experimental work, usually conceived with a sense of mysticism and expressed by a variety of trick camerawork, mention may be made of *Mauprat, Le Cœur Fidèle, L'Affiche, La Glace à Trois Faces,* and *Six et Demi x Onze.* It was with his version of

[1] Died, Lausanne, 1948.

La chûte de la Maison Usher that he first claimed serious attention. He succeeded in this somewhat theatrical production in creating an atmosphere of macabre mysticism, rather after the manner of Murnau in the earlier *Dracula*. Chiefly notable were his uses of flying drapery, of low-lying mist, of gusts of wind and of the imagery of guttering candle flames, with which he emphasised the literary value of Poe's story. Regrettable were the poor model shots, clumsily contrived, which were destructive to the poetic atmosphere of the whole. Epstein was hampered by the interpretation of a literary theme in terms of the cinema. Utterly different, however, was his next work, the realisation of *Finis Terrae*. This was a film with practically no narrative content, taken from actual material on an island off the coast of Brittany. The theme concerned an injury to the hand of a fisherman, who was one of four gathering a harvest of kelp on the island of Bannec, and a quarrel that resulted from the accident. The value of the content rested on the interplay of the emotions and reactions of the characters to the incidental events. For the first two-thirds of his film, Epstein built the theme in preparation for a final climactic ending. In the last third he lost control, and by changing the location from the fishermen on the island to their mothers and the doctor, he failed to retain the unity of the earlier portion. Nevertheless, despite this mistake in scenario construction, Epstein made a film of great strength, of powerful psychological and pictorial value, that may be placed almost on the level of Flaherty's *Moana*. He has recently completed *Sa Tête*, which, although conceived on the same lines as the earlier film, is said to be more artificial in psychological construction.

The two best comedies realised in France have come from René Clair, who is perhaps the most delightfully witty and ingenious director in Europe. He has, moreover, that quality of employing movement of material which is absent from the work of most French directors. He has learnt freely from the American cinema, from Mack Sennett and from Lloyd, but his idol, of course, is Chaplin. Clair manipulates his adaptations with a degree of refinement that renders them peculiarly his own. His films, especially the two most recent examples, *Le Chapeau de Paille d'Italie* and *Les Deux Timides,* are more completely French in feeling than any other productions. He has an extraordinary skill in combining satire, comedy, sentiment, and fantasy. Originally a journalist on *L'Intransigeant,* he later took up acting, eventually becoming an assistant to Jacques de Baroncelli. His early films were all experimental in form, beginning in 1922 with *Paris qui Dort,* followed by the already-mentioned *Entr'acte, Le Fantôme du Moulin Rouge, Le Tour,* and *Le Voyage Imaginaire.* Few of these were of much consequence in themselves, but during their realisation Clair learned a thorough knowledge of the resources of the cinema, which was to be of great avail in his more ambitious later productions. In 1925, he accepted a contract wth the Albatross-Sequana producing firm, and for obvious commercial reasons his work became bridled and less wild. This limitation, however, brought out the best in Clair, for he was forced to extract the utmost out of the material provided for him by his firm. In *La Proie du Vent,* although hampered by an uninteresting scenario, he made a competent picture, with a few individual sequences of exceptional merit. Two years later he produced his best work, *Le Chapeau de Paille d'Italie,* a brilliant comedy deep in bitter satire of French middle-class life, and realised with a high degree of intelligence and cinematic skill. Around a simple dual theme of a man who was a little hard of hearing and the destruction of a lady's straw hat, Clair wove a film that was not only exceptionally witty, but a penetrating commentary on the pettiness and small-mindedness of the *bourgeoisie* who constitute such a large proportion of the French population. For this reason, the film was not a commercial success, the public being partially aware of its exposure and righteously indignant, with the result that Clair remained idle for a year, although still under contract to Albatross-Sequana. Finally, he was allowed to make another comedy, *Les Deux*

73. THE BLUE ANGEL, directed by JOSEF VON STERNBERG.   MARLENE DIETRICH, HANS ALBERS, EMIL JANNINGS.   [German, 1926]

74. APPLAUSE, directed by ROUBEN MAMOULIAN.   [American, 1929]

75. THE GHOST THAT NEVER RETURNS, directed by Abram Room. [Soviet, 1929]

76. ARSENAL, directed by Alexander Dovjenko. [Soviet, 1929]

Timides which, though less brilliant than its predecessor, was nevertheless of considerable note. His fire and wit were not given the freedom that had rendered *Le Chapeau de Paille d'Italie* so brilliant, but for use of technical trickwork in order to achieve funny effect it stands almost alone. Clair's fervent admiration of Chaplin is apparent throughout all his work, but that is not to say that he is in any way an imitator of the great comedian. Probably *A Woman of Paris* has had more influence on his outlook than the actual comedies of Chaplin. There is no question that Clair has very definitely his own individual sense of cinema and a mentality that I do not hesitate to place alongside that of the other big directors in the cinema for its refined wit and intelligence. I certainly suggest that *Le Chapeau de Paille d'Italie* is the most brilliant satirical comedy produced in Europe, to be grouped with Lubitsch's *The Marriage Circle* and Chaplin's *A Woman of Paris*.

Although Carl Dreyer's great contribution to the cinema lies in the production of *La Passion de Jeanne d'Arc,* his work at an earlier period was distinguished by a simplicity of handling and an understanding of psychological values in the development of character.[1] In 1924, he made *Heart's Desire* for Ufa, with a thematic narrative based on an artist's love for his adopted son and the latter's ingratitude. It was slow moving, unfolded with careful deliberation of detail, Benjamin Christensen playing Zoret, the artist, and Walther Slezak, the boy. Some time later he made *The Master of the House* (*Le Maître du Logis*), a Danish production telling the story of a lower middle-class flat occupied by a man, his wife, and three children, and the complications that ensued owing to the selfishness of the husband. The direction was quite straightforward, with scrupulous attention paid to detail and without any variety of angles or lighting. Yet it was powerfully done, intimate, and compelling. It had little success in any country save France, whither, on the strength of it, Dreyer went in

[1] There is an excellent study of Carl Dreyer's work to be found in *En Filminstruktons Arbejde,* by Ebbe Neergaard (Copenhagen, 1940).

1927 to make the immortal *La Passion de Jeanne d'Arc*.

It seems ungrateful to level adverse criticism at this beautiful film, for it was so moving and so intense that hostile opinion appears ridiculous. Nevertheless, despite the admiration evoked by the visual and spiritual meaning of this representaton of the last moments of the agony of Jeanne d'Arc, cinematically Dreyer's film was not great. Its overwhelming fault of the isolation of the visual images from the dynamic content has already been explained, and further comment on its lack of filmic texture is considered superfluous. But it remains to record that Dreyer deserved the highest praise for his marvellous representation of environment; his terrible and strong use of camera angle and camera movement for the close establishment of an intimacy between the characters and the audience that has rarely, if ever, been equalled; and for his splendid subordination of detail in settings and general atmosphere. He insisted that no make-up of any sort should be used by his acting material, with the result that the faces looked like burning copper with finely wrinkled textures against the stark white backgrounds. A strange power, an unprecedented insistence was given to the characters by this lack of artificial make-up. Across the screen spread great close-ups of eyes, a leer, the corner of a mouth, a smirk, a delicately marked hand, revealing with tremendous force the inward thoughts and emotions of the crowd, the judges, the monks, the soldiers, and above all, the expressions of Jeanne herself, hesitating, perplexed, enlightened, anguished, ever fascinating. For once there was no concession to public convention, no star, no high-spot, no box-office appeal, no 'last-minute rescue', nothing but the dominating direction of Dreyer. There is no question that *La Passion de Jeanne d'Arc* was extraordinarily powerful. From the opening to the closing shot it held, swayed, staggered, overwhelmed and tore at the spectator. It somehow contrived to get underneath and round the back of one's receptivity. It demanded the complete concentration of the audience from start to finish. I have no compunction in saying that it was one of the most remarkable productions ever realised in the history and development of the cinema, *but it was not a full exposition of real filmic properties.*

Dreyer's employment of the psychology of human emotions and reactions was profound. His sense of atmosphere was superbly expressed. The greater portion of the film was taken in close-ups from high and low level angles, the screen being constantly flooded with compositions so completely pleasing in themselves that they ceased to be contributions to the concatenation of shots. The greatest praise should be given to the whole production unit and the extraordinary playing of Mme. Falconetti as Jeanne. Eighteen months were spent on the film for the Société Générale de Films, and despite its demerit the film will ever be memorable.

The style of Jacques Feyder, who is a Belgian, appears to change with each of his interesting productions. It would seem he is naturally assimilative. He has adapted from the Germans and from the Swedes, but he has always adapted correctly and with sincerity. In his list of films are to be found, *L'Image* (from a scenario by Jules Romains); *Atlantide ; Gribiche ; Crainquebille*, from the Anatole France short story; *Visages d'Enfants; Carmen,* with Raquel Meller; *Thérèse Raquin,* from Zola, and a comedy, *Les Nouveaux Messieurs.* It is, however, in the two latter films that Feyder demands most attention. He is essentially a director of dramatic situations, of heavy conflict between disturbed emotions, and for such handling the material of Zola's *Thérèse Raquin* was admirable. It was made in German studios for the Défu firm, and its lighting and treatment were typically Germanic. But pre-eminent was Feyder's remarkable direction of Gina Manés, an actress who can be as good (as in *Thérèse Raquin*) or as bad (as in Molander's *Sin,* from the Strindberg play), according to the mind controlling her playing. Feyder's treatment of Thérèse, her inner mind, her unsatisfied sex, her viciousness and her sensuality was an amazing example of dramatic direction. By the smallest movement, by the flicker of an eyelash, by a sidelong glance at Laurent, by her partly opened mouth, by her calm composure at the Raquin home, and by her passion in the studio of her lover, the spectator was forced to share the mind of this remarkable woman. In the handling of Wolfgang Zeller, as Camille the husband, with his adjustable cuffs and cheerful bonhomie, Feyder was equally brilliant, bringing to the surface the pitiful desolation of the little man's life. Feyder built his film by the use of selected detail, by indirect suggestion, and by symbolism into a strong emotional realisation of a dramatic theme. He was inclined, it is true, to exaggerate the melodrama of the closing scenes by too heavy a contrast in lighting and by a sequence of double and triple exposure which disturbed the smooth continuity that was so well achieved in the first two-thirds of the picture. Nevertheless, *Thérèse Raquin* was a great achievement of dramatic direction, an example of the use of emphasis of detail to reinforce the content. The following Feyder picture was in direct contrast to the depression of Zola, for *Les Nouveaux Messieurs* was a comedy of politics adapted from a stage play, demanding satirical direction utterly different from the sombreness of *Thérèse Raquin*. It was not surprising that this film caused a flutter in the French political dovecote; that feeling at first ran so high that the censor intervened and prohibited it being shown in its country of inception, although later the ban was removed. The dominating feature of *Les Nouveaux Messieurs* was its biting humour. The foibles of the rival politicians were mercilessly exploited in a mute appeal to the intelligence of the spectator as a silent protest against the childishness of party political strife. Technically, it was interesting for some competent camerawork, with frequent use of low-level angles and clever composite photography, as in the confusion of thought in the telephone scene at the Trade Union Headquarters. The outstanding impression given by these two Feyder films, *Thérèse Raquin* and *Les Nouveaux Messieurs,* was the astonishing versatility of their director. Both, in their kind, could scarcely have been

more brilliant. Feyder's first film in Hollywood for Metro-
Goldwyn-Mayer was *The Kiss,* which has been mentioned
in the American chapter at an earlier stage as a clever
mixture of picture-sense and filmic intelligence.

Marcel l'Herbier is the supreme virtuoso of the French
cinema, his films at all times revealing a high degree of
technical accomplishment. His work suffers, if one may be
allowed the term, from over-intellectuality. He is essentially the cinematic aesthete rather than the film director.
His technique is too brilliant to be convincing, too clever to
be of purpose for dramatic expression. His recent film
L'Argent, from Zola, with its refinement of setting and
forced acting, was evidence of this sensitive intellectualism.
Of the many pictures to his credit, there may be mentioned
for reference *L'Homme du large,* in 1920, typical of the
first *avant-garde* movement; *Don Juan and Faust,* in 1921,
with Jacques Catelain and Marcelle Pradot, a curious mixture of Velazquez pictorial influence and the expressionism
of *The Cabinet of Doctor Caligari; El Dorado,* notable at its
time for distorted camerawork; *Le Marchand des Plaisirs,*
again with Catelain; *Le Vertige; L'Inhumaine; Le Diable
au Cœur,* with Betty Balfour and André Nox; *Le Feu
Mathias Pascal,* from Pirandello, with Ivan Mosjoukine
and settings by Alberto Cavalcanti; *L'Argent,* with
Brigitte Helm, Alfred Abel, and Marie Glory; and *Nuits
de Princes,* with Catelain and Gina Manés. L'Herbier is a
prolific director, always of interest, but seldom producing a
picture of complete merit.

Apart from his artist's appreciation of pictorial beauty,
Alberto Cavalcanti is not a director of cinematic films. His
selection of visual images and his delicate sense of environment are sincere, but his expression of theme and content
is not filmic in texture. He has but little idea of camera
position except for pictorialism and none at all of constructive editing for dramatic effect. These faults and virtues
are apparent in all his work, in the *décor* for l'Herbier's
L'Inhumaine and *Le Feu Mathias Pascal,* and the realisations of *Yvette, Rien que les Heures, En Rade,* and *Le*

Capitaine Fracasse. His most interesting work was in the burlesque cine-poem, *La P'tite Lili,* in which he touched a true note of poetic sentimentality. Although his films are littered with garbage and depression, they are always sweet natured. *Rien que les Heures,* made in 1926, was similar in aim to Ruttman's *Berlin,* but whereas the latter film was an impersonal selection of images taken during a day in a great city, Cavalcanti's handling was more human and intimate. Among a pattern of shots of Paris, interspaced at regular intervals by close-ups of a clock marking the hours, he followed the movements of an old woman and a young girl. Cavalcanti is not interested in the usual devices favoured by the *avant-garde,* being generally concerned with the slow unfolding of a human being's life. *En Rade,* set among the quays and ships of Marseilles, was a praise-worthy example of centralisation of environment, beautiful pictorially, but negligible cinematically. His last picture to be seen was a costume romance adapted from Gautier, *Le Capitaine Fracasse,* rich in seventeenth-century detail and atmosphere, but unfilmic in form. He has recently completed *Le Petit Chaperon Rouge,* with Catherine Hessling.

Jean Renoir, son of the famous painter, is recalled principally by three films, *Nana, La petite Marchande des Allumettes,* and *Le Tournoi.* The first was based on the Zola novel, with Werner Krauss and Catherine Hessling in a mixture of the *can-can,* Lautrec back-stage and Offenbach; the second was a charming, sentimental realisation of the Hans Andersen story, notable for the fascination of the irresistible Hessling and a wilfully artificial setting already commented upon; while the third was a costume romance, in the best French historical manner, scrupulously accurate but quite unconvincing.

Abel Gance is the *grand maître* of the French cinema, theoretically the apotheosis of great directors, but in practice always out-of-date with ideas. He spent five years on the production of *Napoléon,* a theme so vast that it defeated its own, Abel Gance's and everybody else's purpose. It was filled with imagination, technical devices, and ramifications of complicated scenario work, needing three screens on which to exhibit its lumbering bulk. It was tediously cumbersome and hopelessly overweighted with symbolic reference. Gance is essentially the employer of the symbolic image, with the 'Spirit of France' perpetually at the back of his mind. Solemnly we observe the eagles in *Napoléon;* the rails, wheels, and signals in *La Roue;* the parks and terraces in *La Zone de la Mort;* and the lily in *J'Accuse.* Mention should be made of his early films, *La Dixième Symphonie* and *Mater Dolorosa,* both outstanding at their time of realisation. He has now embarked on another stupendous theme, *The End of the World;* the year of presentation has not yet been calculated.

With the pre-war period of the French cinema I have little concern. It is mostly to be summed up in the characteristic productions of the Gaumont, Pathé, and Aubert companies, marked chiefly by their theatrical conception, stylised acting and the attention paid to story value. One of the most ambitious efforts was a several reel version in Pathécolor of Victor Hugo's *Les Misérables.* The domestic comedies of Max Linder, whom I am tempted to describe as a prototype of Adolphe Menjou, may also be recalled. Similarly, I do not intend to catalogue the many films produced during the early post-war years in France by various directors, but, if occasion arises, reference may be made to the work of the late Louis Delluc (*La Fête Espagnole,* in collaboration with Germaine Dulac, in 1920; *La Femme de Nulle Part* and *Fièvre,* both made in 1921); of Jacques de Baroncelli (*Le Carillon de Minuit, Le Père Goriot, Pêcheur d'Islande,* and *Réveil,* with Isobel Elsom); of Severin-Mars (*Le Cœur Magnifique*); and of Jules Duvivier (*La Tragédie de Lourdes*).

To these may be added Nicolas Volkoff's *Kean,* a film of considerable merit made in 1924; Léon Poirier's *Jocelyn, Verdun,* and *La Croisière Noire* (an admirable interest picture); Marc Allegret's travel film, in conjunction with André Gide, *Voyage au Congo;* the amusing work of

Germaine Dulac, *Arabesque, Mme. Beudet,* and *La Coquille et le Clergyman*; and the many short films of the *avant-garde,* too numerous for inclusion.[1]

*

From this, some slight estimate of the significance of the French cinema may be gained. That it is important is very clear, despite the efforts of the *cinéaste* and the cine-journalist to prove the contrary. Of the future of the French cinema it is impossible to write, for each step will depend on the precarious position of the dialogue film. Various experiments are being made with sound reproduction in France, but at the time of writing, no serious realisation has been seen, although several full-length dialogue films are said to have been completed.

[1] The French cinema is dealt with in some detail in *The History of Motion Pictures,* Bardèche and Brasillach, translated and edited by Iris Barry (W. W. Norton and the Museum of Modern Art, New York, 1938).

IX

THE BRITISH FILM

The British film is established upon a hollow foundation. Perhaps it would be more significant to write that it rests upon a structure of false prestige, supported by the flatulent flapdoodle of newspaper writers and by the indifferent goodwill of the British people; inasmuch that a film emanating from the studios of this country to-day is at once enshrouded in a blaze of patriotic glamour by the public, who actually feel that the product (with one or two notable exceptions) is unworthy of its esteem.

The whole morale of the modern British cinema is extravagantly artificial. It has been built up by favoured criticism and tolerance of attitude. If a few critics had consistently written the bitter truth about the British film, if they had criticised it ruthlessly and stringently according to its deserts, I am convinced that this country would have revealed at least half-a-dozen thoroughly capable, intelligent film directors and a group of perspicacious, courageous producers. Well-merited castigation would have laid bare, and therefore more easily remedied, the root of the evil. Instead, there have been British Film Weeks and National Film Campaigns which have nourished the cancer in the industry. As it is, the British film is spoon-fed by deceptive praise and quota regulations, with the unhappy result that it has not yet discovered its nationality.

The British film has never been self-sufficient, in that it has never achieved its independence. Léon Moussinac writes: ' *L'Angleterre n'a jamais produit un vrai film anglais* ',[1] a remark that is miserably true. The British film lacks honest conception. It has no other aim than that of the imitation of the cinema of other countries. For its obscure source it goes first to the American, and secondly, but

[1] *Panoramique du Cinéma,* Léon Moussinac, 1929.

313

more difficult to discern, to the German film. Of one thing I am confident, that the British film will never prosper, save as the child of the American cinema, until our producers bring themselves to recognise the value of experiment. Only on exceedingly rare occasions does a producing firm in this country countenance a new form of technique, a development of outlook, or anything that is alien to their conservative methods of working. British studios are filled with persons of third-rate intelligence who are inclined to condemn anything that is beyond their range. Producers, directors, scenarists, cameramen, art-directors, and their *confrères* are afraid of any new process, in case their feeble mentality is not sufficiently clever to grasp its significance. We are slow to learn from other film-producing countries, but we are always quick to imitate. But the danger lies in the disastrous fact that we generally imitate without under-standing, without probing to the base of the ideas that we adopt (as for example, the mixed technique of Asquith's *Cottage on Dartmoor* and the ill-designed *décor* of Elvey's *High Treason*). For this reason there has never been any school of *avant-garde* in Britain. I do not suggest that an advanced school of cinematic experimentalism is essen-tial, but I believe that it would stimulate the directors of the commercial cinema. There is, moreover, no school of thought for the furtherance of filmic theory, such as is found in other countries. There is none of the *enthusiasm* for the progress of the cinema which is so prevalent in France, Germany, Soviet Russia, and even America.[1]

On occasions, our studios burst into a flare of latent modernism that is usually deplorable. In such a vein was

[1] The first progressive movement distinguishable in British films was, in fact, just beginning as this book was written, with Grierson's *Drifter's* (1929) and the establishment of the small E.M.B. Film Unit. It was to take more than ten years for the influence of the British documentary film movement to make itself felt on feature production, and for the studio directors to discover a new realism. Cf. *The Fore-man Went to France, The Way Ahead, Nine Men, The Overlanders, The Stars Look Down, Millions Like Us, Waterloo Road*, etc. The Ministry of Information Films Division, under Mr. Jack Beddington, must be given great credit for intermixing the documentary and studio film techniques, as well as interchanging their respective exponents.

the already mentioned Gaumont-British film, *High Treason,* which was made by a director with over fifty productions to his credit. It is not, moreover, as if British studios were insufficiently equipped or inadequately staffed. On the contrary, the technical resources of Elstree, Welwyn, Islington, and Walthamstow are as good as, if not better than, those of almost any other country in Europe, a point upon which every foreign visitor will agree. The trouble lies in the way in which these excellent resources are employed. A good film and a bad film pass through the same technical process. The amount of good and the amount of bad in each depends upon the minds which control the instruments.

It need scarcely be reiterated that Britain is the most fertile country imaginable for pure filmic material. Our railways, our industries, our towns, and our countryside are waiting for incorporation into narrative films. The wealth of material is immense. When recently visiting this country, S. M. Eisenstein expressed his astonishment at the almost complete neglect by British film directors of the wonderful material that lay untouched. Why advantage had not been taken of these natural resources was exceptionally difficult to explain to a visitor. Oxford, Cambridge, Liverpool, Shrewsbury, Exeter, the mountains of Wales and the highlands of Scotland are all admirable for filmic environment. Nothing of any value has yet been made of London, probably the richest city in the world for cinematic treatment. Grierson alone has produced the fine documentary film of the herring fleet, the epic *Drifters.* This film, good as it was, is but a suggestion of that which waits to be accomplished. But what British company is willing to realise these things? British International Pictures, it is true, have made *The Flying Scotsman* under the direction of Castleton Knight, but what of it? Anthony Asquith made *Underground,* but became lost in the Victorian conception of a lift-boy, in place of the soul of London's greatest organisation. Instead, our studios give forth *Variety, Splinters, The Co-optimists,*

Elstree Calling, A Sister to Assist 'Er, and *The American Prisoner.*

What has been done with the Empire? It is well, first, to recall Epstein's *Finis Terrae,* Flaherty's *Moana,* Turin's *Turksib,* and Pudovkin's *Storm Over Asia.* The material lying unused in all parts of India, Kenya, Nigeria, Malta, Cyprus, is vast. There have been made *A Throw of the Dice, Stampede,* and *Palaver,* but what did they tell of those rich countries, save a superficial rendering? Without proper methods of film construction, without a knowledge of the capabilities of the cinema, it were best for this wonderful material to be left untouched.

*

The root of the trouble in this country lies in the conservative and narrow-minded outlook of the producing executives. There are not the men of broad vision, receptive to new theories and progressive ideas. (I do not here refer to the general adoption of the dialogue cinema, for that was a position forced upon British companies by American domination.) When the industry underwent a revival some years ago, after a decline period of inactivity, British producers seriously considered that it was more necessary to erect studio-cities than to train the young men who were to work in them. Every effort at that time was concentrated on making the public believe that Elstree was the new Hollywood; but the public shrewdly reserved its judgement until it should see the product of this studio-city.

Not only this, but producers lack the courage of their own convictions. When the dialogue film swept into Britain by way of the American-owned theatres in London, several directors in British studios were just beginning to grasp the rudimentary principles of film construction. They were groping and slowly developing for themselves some ideas on the theory of the cinema. But the whole studio organisation of this country was thrown into chaos by the American revolution of the dialogue film. If only one firm had remained level-headed when the tidal wave came, I am convinced that the best intelligences in British studios would have stood with it and would have acted independently of the dialogue innovation. If one company had been content with small profits and a gradual increase of its output, developing its knowledge of the silent film, there would have been some tendency, some initiative, some independence in the British cinema of whch to write. As it was, the studios tried to transform their inadequate knowledge of film-making into ' the new technique ', and continued with their slavish imitation of the American cinema.

The importation of foreign talent did not have the same influence in British studios as it did at an earlier date in Hollywood. It will be remembered that the work of Lubitsch, Murnau, Pommer, and Seaström had serious effect on the minds of the younger school of American directors. But in Britain, Arthur Robison, E. A. Dupont, and Henrik Galeen, three directors of talent, have had no effect on the Elstree school. On the contrary, their ideas were totally misunderstood and unappreciated in our studios. Foreign directors failed to discover in Britain the collectivism and team-work so vital to film production. They were unable to understand our idea of picture-sense and we were at a loss to interpret their filmic outlook. (*E.g.* Robison's *The Informer* and Galeen's *After the Verdict;* yet these directors had earlier been responsible for *Warning Shadows, Manon Lescaut* and *The Student of Prague.* The conclusion to be drawn is obvious.) Dupont alone attained to some measure of success in *Piccadily,* but only because he employed a German cameraman and architect.[1] The importation of foreign talent was due to the eternal craze for a picture of *international* appeal. Producers were convinced that the inclusion of a foreign star would give a film an instant attraction in other countries. For this reason, Lya de Putti, Lars Hanson, Hans von Schlettow, Anna May Wong, Olga Tschechowa,

---

[1] Werner Brandes and Alfred Junge; the latter subsequently made his home in England and created some of the best sets of the renaissance of British films. (E.g. *The Canterbury Tale, Colonel Blimp, A Matter of Life and Death,* etc.)

Gilda Gray, and others have played in this country, but the advantage is somewhat obscure, save that it has been successful in the suppression of natural British talent.

*

Analysis of the output of British studios since the war is impossible in the same way as has been done with that of other countries. Nor, on the other hand, is it proposed to give even a brief survey of the commercial development, for that has been lightly touched upon at an earlier stage. I am unable to discern a realistic, expressionistic, naturalistic, decorative, or any other phase in the development of the British cinema. Added to which, there are no tendencies to be traced, for British films do not have tendencies, unless allusion is made to the prevalence of cabaret scenes and war themes. I propose, therefore, to examine several isolated productions and the work of a few individual directors, who demand some notice.

Without hesitation, there is one production that is pre-eminent in the British cinema, Grierson's film of the herring fleet. As far as I am aware, *Drifters* is the only film produced in this country that reveals any real evidence of construction, montage of material, or sense of cinema as understood in these pages. Admittedly, Grierson was influenced in his work by the rhythmic construction of Eisenstein's *Battleship Potemkin*, but, as has been pointed out elsewhere, he gave to *Drifters* something that was lacking in the celebrated Soviet film. As is now well known, Grierson was connected with the preparation of the American version of the Soviet picture, and had, therefore, every opportunity to analyse the work of Eisenstein at close contact. Although Grierson failed to understand completely the construction of *Battleship Potemkin,* he nevertheless contrived to build a film of great strength and beauty in *Drifters*. Like Epstein's *Finis Terrae* and Ford's *Iron Horse,* the theme of *Drifters* was pure in filmic texture. The ships that sailed out at night, the casting of the drifting nets, and the climactic race home to give their haul to the markets of the nation was splendid film material. The film was filled with the beauty of labour and a sense of ships. It lacked, possibly, a universal idea of the sea by its concentration on detail, but it was so far in advance of normal British productions that to write unfavourably of it would be ungenerous.

There are several directors in and around British studios who, in my belief, would realise interesting films were they afforded the means. There are also, on the other hand, many directors who have failed to make use of ample opportunities when they have had them. And again, there is a large number of second and third-rate directors on whose spasmodic work it is impossible to comment in a book of this nature.

Although Miles Mander[1] has been connected principally with acting, he has made one film that provided evidence of his wit and intelligence in filmic expression. *The Firstborn*, made at Elstree two years ago, was almost entirely the product of Manders' creative mentality; the story, scenario, direction, and principal rôle being his individual work, supported by Madeleine Carroll. In the copy of *The Firstborn* shown to the public, however, the merits of the direction and the continuity were rendered almost negligible by the poor assembling of the material by the distributing firm. It is understood that the film was edited without the control of the director by a professional cutter, and hence much of Miles Mander's original conception was destroyed. As a light commentary on married life, flavoured with an environment of semi-political domestication, *The Firstborn* was conceived with a nice subtlety of wit. The treatment, especially of the eternal arguments and the dinner party, was sophisticated and clever. Mander has obviously a shrewd knowledge of feminine mentality and succeeded in transferring this into his handling of Madeleine Carroll. Had the film been well assembled, according to the original manuscript, I believe that *The Firstborn* would have been a unique instance of an English domestic tragi-comedy in the cinema.

[1] Died, Hollywood, 1946.

Probably Anthony Asquith is the most fortunately situated of British directors. He has certain ideas on cinematic representation, and he is happily able to put them into realisation. He has been concerned with four productions till now, *Shooting Stars, Underground, Princess Priscilla's Fortnight,* and *A Cottage on Dartmoor.* That he possesses a feeling for cinema was proved by all these films, but that he is still groping and undecided in his mind as to how to find expression for his ideas is equally plain. He has learnt varied forms of treatment from abroad, but has not as yet fully understood the logical reason for using them. He has studied the Soviet and German cinema, but has failed to search deep enough. His technique still remains, after four productions, primitively on the surface. In his last picture, for example, there were several instances of quick cutting and symbolic reference, but they were employed because of themselves and not as a contributory factor to the film composition. For this reason, Asquith's work appears that of a virtuoso, whilst in reality he is undecided in his mind as to what to do next. He is legitimate in borrowing from superior directors only if he comprehends that which he borrows and why he has borrowed it. His films seem principally to lack centralisation of purpose. This was exemplified in *Underground,* which, instead of being a direct exposition of the spirit of an inanimate organisation (and what superb material) degenerated into a movie of London 'types'. All his work has been unbalanced and erratic, and it is essential for him to lose his Victorian sense of humour before he can favourably progress. He has, on the other hand, some feeling for the use of dramatic camera angle, some ideas on dissolve shots, but an uneven sense of pictorial composition. He needs to receive a course in architectural construction in order to appreciate proportion; and to realise the relation that lies between the visual images and the expression of the theme.

The accredited pre-eminent director of the British school is, I suppose, Alfred Hitchcock, whose first dialogue film

77. BLACKMAIL, directed by ALFRED HITCHCOCK. JOHN LONGDEN, DONALD CALTHROP, ANNIE ONDRA. [British, 1929]

78. HALLELUJAH! directed by KING VIDOR. NINA MAE McKINNEY, DANIEL L. HAYNES. [American, 1929]

79. SOUS LES TOITS DE PARIS, directed by René Clair. [French, 1929–30]

80. ALL QUIET ON THE WESTERN FRONT, directed by Lewis Milestone.
Lew Ayres, Raymond Griffith. [American, 1929–30]

Blackmail has been generally accepted as the best of its kind. I believe, however, that Hitchcock's most sincere work was seen in *The Lodger,* produced in 1926 for Gainsborough. In this thriller melodrama, he displayed a flair for clever photographic angles and succeeded in creating an atmosphere of a London fog with some conviction. He continued with a series of unpretentious pictures, *Downhill, Easy Virtue, The Ring, The Farmer's Wife,* and *The Manxman,* but did not develop along the lines indicated by *The Lodger.* The production of *Blackmail,* although handicapped by poor narrative interest and the inevitable restrictions of dialogue, nevertheless showed Hitchcock in a progressive mood. His much commented upon use of sound as an emphasis to the drama of the visual image was well conceived, but inclined to be overobvious. Incidentally, the silent version was infinitely better than the dialogue, the action being allowed its proper freedom.

Although not strictly the work of British technicians, Dupont's *Piccadilly* was undoubtedly the best film of its type to be made in this country. It was moderately well constructed and expensively finished as such pictures should be, but was chiefly notable for the wonderful camerawork of Werner Brandes and the delightful settings of Alfred Junge. The action was slow where it should have been fast, and fast where it should have been slow, but taking it as a whole, *Piccadilly* was the best film to be made by British International Pictures. Dupont's first dialogue film, however, was an unprecedented example of wasted material. The theme was one of the most dramatic that it is possible to imagine—the sinking of a great liner. The film was based on a play called *The Berg,* which in turn was founded on the *Titanic* disaster of 1912. The facts available to the director were these : the maiden voyage of the largest liner in the world, supposed to be unsinkable; the striking of a low-lying iceberg; the sinking of the ship in less than three hours, with the loss of one thousand five hundred and thirteen persons. It was a tremendous situation, calling for an intense psychological representation of the reactions of the passengers and crew. It could have been one of the most powerful films ever made. It was one of the stupidest. First, the bathos of the dialogue was incredible; secondly, the acting was stage-like, stiff and unconvincing; thirdly, the actual shock of the collision was completely ineffectual. Technically, the photography was flat and uninteresting; the (unnecessary) model shots were crude and toy-like; and the mass of nautical errors was inexcusable; added to which there was a complete discrepancy of the water levels as the vessel sank. I can think of no other example where so fine a theme has received such inadequate treatment.

Comparison can be made with point between *Atlantic* and Pudovkin's *Storm Over Asia*. Both had great themes; each contained errors of detail. But whereas in the former, discrepancies were brought into prominence by the weak direction, in *Storm Over Asia*, the treatment of the film as a whole was so impressive that mistakes (in military detail, etc.) tended to be overlooked.

*

There are three groups of films that merit inclusion. The series of reconstructed war events made for New Era and British Instructional Films under the producership of Bruce Woolfe, by Messrs Geoffrey Barkas, Walter Summers, Michael Barringer, etc., including *Armageddon, Zeebrugge, Mons, The Somme, The Battles of Coronel and Falkland Islands* and '*Q*' *Ships*. All these were excellent examples of the documentary film. Three extremely amusing comedies directed by Ivor Montagu, *The Cure, Day Dreams,* and *Bluebottles,* from stories by H. G. Wells, with the ever-delightful Elsa Lanchester, were the best instances of comedy burlesque that I have seen. And the numerous *Secrets of Nature* films, made by British Instructional under Bruce Woolfe's producership, have always been admirable in conception and execution. They are, in fact, the sheet-anchor of the British Film Industry.

X

FILMS FROM OTHER COUNTRIES

There has been frequent mention in these pages of the Swedish cinema, which is now almost non-existent. During the years immediately following the war, Sweden produced a number of films that had great influence on the cinema of France and Germany. They were realised with exceptional visual beauty, being characterised by their lyrical quality of theme and by their slowness of development. For their environment, full use was made of the natural landscape value of Sweden, whilst their directors were marked by their poetic feeling. The themes were for the most part tragically conceived and treated from a heavy psychological point of view, two qualities that were chiefly responsible for the half-hearted acceptance of the Swedish cinema by foreign exhibitors and renters. In fact, it may be said truthfully that the Swedish film declined and died a natural death by reason of its national characteristics of poetic feeling and lyricism. Of the directors, most of whom have gone to Hollywood, mention must be made of Victor Seaström (*The Phantom Carriage, The Tragic Ship, The Exiles*), Mauritz Stiller (*The Atonement of Gösta Berling, Arne's Treasure*), and John Brunius (*Vox Populi, The History of Charles XII*).[1]

Both Italy and Spain are producing films, though, so far as I am aware, few of their recent productions have been shown outside their country of origin up till the time of writing. Before the war, however, Italian films were not infrequently presented in Britain, ranging from comedies to historical subjects. Of the latter, the most memorable is *Cabiria*, a classical theme from a scenario by Gabriele

[1] A notable omission from this chapter is the Danish Film, which before the first World War, was prolific. It was not only the Swedish but also the Danish cinema which strongly influenced the German directors in the post-war years, 1918-1924. (Cf. footnote, p. 99.)

d'Annunzio. With its extensive cast and elaborate sets—such, for instance, as the Temple of Moloch which anticipated the sequence of the Heart Machine in Lang's *Metropolis*—this super production was a remarkable feat for 1913, even though its cinematic properties were not pronounced. Hungary, Bulgaria, and Czechoslovakia have also entered the field of the film industry, but here there is as yet little to record.

By way of contrast, there is at the moment a flourishing film industry in Japan, where it is said that over five hundred productions are realised yearly by some ninety directors. This high rate of production, however, has only been reached of recent years, having come about through the national urge to overcome the American domination that took place during the war. Before the outbreak of war, Japan relied on France and Italy for supplying her programmes, but as was the case in all other countries, America took control of the market when the European industry was suspended. Directly after the war, Japanese production began to develop and it was not long before several companies were formed.

Until the present, the Japanese cinema has been too closely allied to the traditions of the theatre for there to have been any individual cinematic tendencies. For a long time the film was regarded as inferior to the stage, suitable only for the entertainment of the lower classes. For subject matter, also, the cinema relied largely on traditional costume plays, resulting in a large number of stylised, historical films adapted from conventional pieces of the past. These were notable for their beauty of setting and their excellent photography, being of particular interest as reconstructions of old Japanese customs and traditions. Moreover, another reason for the predominance of the historical film is the vigilance with which the censorship observes all pictures dealing with contemporary moral or social matters. Despite this, however, there are a certain number of modern themes produced, especially comedies, dealing with the peasantry and the lower middle classes.

The two prominent producing companies are the Nikkatsu and the Soetsiku, and although the latter was formerly the more important, it has now been superseded by the Nikkatsu. As in Soviet Russia, each concern has its own set of production units and players, there being little interchange of personnel. The Nikkatsu is said to employ the best acting material, having also at its command experts in Japanese antiquity and historical matters to supervise the traditional subjects. The Soetsiku, on the other hand, is more modern in its outlook and attempts to produce films of the naturalistic type with contemporary material, several of its technicians having learnt their trade in Hollywood studios. The chief studios are at Kamata, with a staff numbering about a thousand (including fifty directors), where only films on modern subjects are realised. The speed of production is astonishing, a full-length picture being completed in anything from a fortnight to a month, as compared to the usual six weeks or two months in Europe and America. This high rate of production is due to the Japanese desire to break down any attempt at American domination, a lesson which the British might well learn.

In India, also, there are a great number of films realised by purely native production units. Although the indigenous product is technically far inferior to the American and European films shown in India, nevertheless the former finds more favour with the vast Indian public. The majority of pictures are versions of well-known tales of Hindu mythology and religion, clumsily put together with many long-winded titles in several languages. The average length of a film seems to be about ten thousand feet, the audience being apparently willing to sit through any amount of film so long as it deals with a favourite subject. Moreover, owing to the differences of religion, the censor authorities have great difficulty in granting permission for exhibition in the various districts. There have also been a number of Indian pictures made by European producing companies, but most of these are singularly uninteresting (*Nuri the Elephant, Shiraz, A Throw of the Dice*).

PART TWO
THE THEORETICAL

I

THE AIM OF THE FILM IN GENERAL AND IN PARTICULAR

Analysis of the film is, perhaps, more difficult than that of any of the other arts. Since its beginning in the days of the Lumière brothers and Friese-Greene, the film has grown, retraced its steps, sprung in different directions at the same time, been hampered and impeded on all sides, in the most remarkable way, without any stock really being taken of its properties and possessions. Its very nature of light revealed by moving form defies systematic cataloguing of its capabilities. Its essentially mechanical basis is apt to lead the observer and the student up blind alleys. No medium of expression calls for such a wide variation of technical accomplishment as does the film. In literature, it is possible to check and to investigate new developments with comparative ease in contrast with the cinema; and as the late Arnold Bennett pointed out more than once, it is an insuperable task to keep abreast with modern literature. But even in literature, books in libraries or in one's own possession can be consulted, whereas when a film has had its limited run of a few weeks, access to it for examination or reference is a difficult matter. So few facts are actually put on record concerning current films that it is quite conceivable that a time may come when such important pictures as *Mother* and *Metropolis* will be but names at which future generations will wonder. Little record, even now, remains of some of the earlier German films made shortly after the war, whilst copies themselves become scarce as time goes on, either through wear or through accident.[1] Personal

[1] For example, there is, I believe, only one *complete* copy of *The Cabinet of Doctor Caligari* in existence, and certainly only one copy of *Dracula,* which is never likely to be shown unless privately. Of *The Peasant Women of Riazan* there is only a limited number of copies, the master negative being destroyed by fire. The same applies to *The Golem, The Mystic Mirror,* and *Destiny.* See footnote 1 on page 330.

experience, also, is necessarily restricted and seldom put on record. El Greco's *Agony in the Garden* may be consulted at almost any time with convenience, but in the case of a film it is only possible to rely on memory for reference, a precarious method of analysis.[1]

Furthermore, even to see a film is not necessarily to observe all its values, as Mr. Eric Elliott has remarked.[2] Scientific tests have shown that only sixty per cent. of a film is seen by an observer. What then of the remaining forty per cent.? The difficulty has, of course, been intensified by the introduction of the synchronised dialogue film and its accompanying sound. The loss to the visual image whilst the audience is trying to understand the dialogue must be great. It follows naturally, as in criticism of painting and music, that the better the dramatic construction of a film the more difficult it becomes to analyse that construction. The critic himself is inclined to fall under the power of the story, and another and more impartial viewing is necessary in order to appraise the numerous technical values.

A tremendous handicap is also experienced in illustrating filmic argument. It is possible only to suggest the different methods of film technique, of montage and of continuity, by giving examples that have been actually observed, taken from productions of all dates. In some cases the quoted instances may have been seen by others, but when the total

[1] Since the above was written, there have been set up several museums and film archives, most important of which are the Museum of Modern Art Film Library, New York, the Cinémathèque Francaise, Paris, the National Film Library, London, and the Czechoslovak Film Archive, Prague. In 1938, these bodies met and set up the International Federation of Film Archives. The Film Library in New York has done especially fine work, not only in preserving and making available for study important films of all countries, but in compiling programme notes, issuing pamphlets, holding special exhibitions and collecting probably the best library of books and other printed matter about the film in the world. Its Curator, Miss Iris Barry, is a distinguished film historian and critic of many years' experience, and the excellence of the Film Library is mainly a result of her devotion to the cinema.

[2] *Vide, The Anatomy of the Motion Picture,* by Eric Elliott (Pool, 1928).

film output for one year alone is considered, chances are against this. Furthermore, mere verbal descriptions are totally inadequate to convey the emotions excited by a film. It is, perhaps, to a certain extent possible to analyse the cause of these emotions, and from this point of view must examples be approached. For instance, it is beyond the power of my literary description to convey the mental and physical reactions to sequences of short-cutting and cross-cutting in Eisenstein's *Ten Days that Shook the World,* but one is able, I think, to explain the use of the method, how and why it was employed, and its place in the continuity and rhythmic structure of the film as a whole.

At a comparatively early stage, the cinema presented a range of values far beyond the complete understanding of any one human mind. For all intents and purposes a bad film passes through the same mechanical processes of studio, camera, and laboratory as a good one. The technical resources available to the film director when he is making his picture are without number. He can choose between tracking shots and direct cutting, between panning and flying cameras, between slow and ultra-rapid motion. He has available every conceivable means for the exposition on the screen of his selected theme. So wide are the resources in technical devices that theoretically there should be no reason for the making of bad films save the sheer incompetence of the director. He has crews of (in most cases) willing technicians to fulfil his orders, and in some studios almost unlimited money to spend in order to achieve the desired effect. Yet a survey of the film output since the first World War up till 1930 shows that the proportion of films in which full use has been made of technical resources is very small indeed. The reason probably is that before the child has learnt the power of his new toy, he is presented with another by the kind inventors. Moreover, there is no one to instruct him in the use of this fresh device. He can only experiment, and watch out of the corner of his eye to see how other people are using it. A director is given a camera 'dolly' with which to play, and

331

finding he can travel his camera all round the set, proceeds to do so in the film he is making at the moment, until he is interrupted by some more engineers who have brought along another device. Seldom does a director realise the absolute advantages to be derived from a new form of technical accomplishment and employ them with restraint in the right place and with the greatest effect. Instances of such virtuosity are innumerable. Travelling shots were employed for the first time in a German film, and almost immediately they became commonplace. They were used on every occasion, with total disregard to the nature of the action portrayed. Karl Freund once used a flying camera for a certain scene in *Metropolis*, because the upward flying movement of the instrument emphasised the struggle which Gustav Fröhlich and Brigitte Helm were experiencing in escaping *upwards* from the flood of water. A few months later, flying cameras swooped like locusts around Hollywood. Patient audiences were whirled across the room to look at a boot, because Lewis Stone looked at it in *The Patriot*. More recently, directors have been given the golden opportunity to let their players speak. The babel that ensues at the moment is appalling. It only remains for the stereoscopic screen and the all-colour film to come into general use for the director to have no excuse at all for producing a bad film. But there will be more bad films made than ever before, because all the technical resources of the cinema will form one great bundle of virtuosity, out of which only a few balanced minds will be able to pick the good from the bad. Chaos will be even greater than it is now, if such a state of affairs is conceivable.

*

During the last few years there has been much diversity of opinion as to what constitutes cinema in its purest form. Many believe that the presentations at the Avenue Pavilion in London used to represent true film art; others vaguely suggest Soviet films but call them Russian. Some talk loftily of the *avant-garde* of the French film and the numerous little Paris specialist cinemas; a few recall the great middle period of the German cinema. Whilst on all sides, from those who know, comes the mixed thunder of so many *Potemkins* and *Tartuffes, Bed and Sofas* and *Chien Andalous*. Nothing is very clear, which after all is quite understandable when we consider the almost hopeless tangle of ideas which strangles the arts as a whole at the present time. Conflicting opinions alternately cancel one another out; groups propound theories quite enigmatical to any save themselves; whilst advanced schools of thought are found in almost every country. That there is a new spirit moving in the theatre, in literature, in painting, in archtecture, and in the other arts is evident. It has scarcely touched Britain at all, and is at its strongest in Germany and Soviet Russia. But that it exists, and is to be found in some aspects of the cinema, is beyond doubt. The film is inclined to reflect the backwash of all these developments, holding up a mirror, as it were, to the current theories of art, sociology, and culture. Occasionally the spirit bursts forth into an outstanding and remarkable film, as in the case of Buñuel's *Un Chien Andalou* or Ernö Metzner's *Ueberfall,* but more often the cinema reflects the ideas of some two or three years earlier, such as the American and British pictures which have interior decoration taken direct from the *Exposition des Arts Décoratifs* of 1925 (*e.g.* the design by Cedric Gibbons in *Our Dancing Daughters* and that by Hugh Gee for *Tesha*). But it is perhaps possible to clarify the air by retrospection and to establish some sort of idea as to the present position of the film in relation to its surroundings.

It has been admitted that the silent film is essentially an independent form of expression, drawing inspiration from the other arts. With choreography it shares the power of movement; and with painting, mental communication through the eye. The recent dialogue film suggests comparison with the stage and its power of speech. Aesthetically, dialogue is in direct opposition to the medium, unless pure sound as distinct from the human voice is utilised from an impressionistic point of view.

But all art, whether painting, sculpture, music, poetry, drama, or film, has at base the same motive, which may be said to be the creation of a work in the presence of which an observer or listener will experience either pleasure or pain as the mood of the work demands. Moreover, it has been suggested that these reactionary emotions are aroused in the mind of the observer or listener by rhythm, either harmonic or discordant, which is determined by such manifestations of the various media as linear design, contrast in light and shade, metre, colour sensation, variations in light intensities, counterpoint, editing and cutting. Whether the spectator be highbrow, lowbrow, or mezzobrow, provided the creator of the work has expressed himself clearly in his medium, the appeal is the same though its power must vary in accordance with the mental receptivity of the spectator.

In the case of the film, it is this receptive power of the audience *en masse* which the Americans and the Soviets, the Germans and the French are trying to calculate, in order to render a work of art a popular success. That their methods should be different is naturally obvious when their respective national temperaments and the circumstances which govern production are considered. It has been seen that whilst Hollywood relies chiefly on the star-system and sex-appeal, Soviet Russia attempts to rouse the emotions of her own public by having in her films a definite applied purpose, preferably of contemporary social importance, and by the creation of rhythm—the basic motive of reactions— by means of a highly developed process of editing.

It has been written that ' in theorising about the cinema there are certain points which must be borne in mind and which should form the basis of all constructive criticism. In the first place, the cinema is dependent for its life on the good opinion of the public, and the average citizen is aesthetically indifferent.' (Vernon J. Clancey writing in *The Cinema*, 4th September 1929.) This may be true, but it should be remembered that the resources of the cinema, by which good directors seek to gain their effect on the minds of the audience, act unconsciously. An average citizen is naturally not expected to appreciate or even to become conscious of the montage of shots that appear before him on the screen, but he cannot help himself reacting to their content if they have been employed correctly. Soviet films, for instance, are made primarily to appeal to the mind of the working man, the labourer and the peasant, and are in most cases constructed with the essence of simplicity. We know that it is only because Soviet Russia has evolved her own theories of cinematography, that she has learnt how to use the properties of the film in their correct manner and to extract the utmost out of them. I find it hard to believe that any audience exists, taken at random in any cinema, which would not react immeasurably to the double-exposed, interrupted cutting of the machine-gun sequence in *Ten Days that Shook the World*. The reaction, however, would not be caused only by the dramatic value of the machine gun and the scattering crowd, but by the *cinematic treatment* of the incident. It would thrill and hold any audience with tremendous intensity. By way of contrast, it is only necessary to refer to similar scenes in such films as *What Price Glory?*, *The Big Parade*, and *Poppies in Flanders* to realise how Eisenstein relied on the subconscious mental qualities of the audience, qualities which he preconceived when cutting this incident. Only by such means as these, arising out of the attributes of the medium, can an audience be really stirred from its accustomed passiveness.

There has not been as yet, however, any scientific inquiry into the emotional effect produced by films on the public. It is well known that the simplest effects on the human mind connote the most subtle causes, being much more difficult to achieve than complex effects. Nursery rhymes and limericks, for instance, take as much, if not more trouble to compose than a lengthy piece of heroic verse. Chaplin alone is a superb example of the individual appeal to the public. He has taken the trouble to think how and why audiences throughout the world react to his individuality. All Chaplin films are brilliant instances of timing that have been effected only by analysis of the human mind, in the same manner as the Soviets' investigations and Pabst's absorption in psycho-analysis.

'Art', said the post-impressionists, 'is not truth, it is not nature; it is a pattern or rhythm of design imposed on nature.' The analogy to the film is at once apparent.

A film is primarily a dynamic pattern or rhythm (achieved by the editing and cutting) imposed on nature (the material taken, preferably the reality). It is governed pictorially by the use of light and movement in the creation of visual images, and mentally by psychology in the creation of mental images. Music and synchronised sound, used in counterpoint and contrapuntally, heighten the emotions of the spectator aurally and subconsciously. This dynamic mental pictorialism is, I claim, the most powerful form of expression available to-day to a creative artist.

In this theoretical section of the survey we shall be concerned primarily with two comparatively simple aspects of film creation, namely : the choice of a theme, which is to be a film's argument, its *raison d'être;* and the two steps in the expression of that theme, first, by scenario representation in literary form, and secondly, by the numerous orthodox technical methods peculiar to the cinema for the transference of the matter contained in the scenario on to the screen. This last step may be called the grammar of the film, arising out of its self-developed properties, and will be the subject of the two succeeding chapters. Investigation has already been made of a great number of films and their individual directors, but admittedly we have examined little more than the themes (or thematic narrative interest) of the films in question and the methods adopted for realisation by their directors. We have, as yet, to understand that there lies something beyond a theme and its technical expression, namely, the conception, attitude of mind, or *creative impulse* of the director himself.

336

81. LITTLE CAESAR, directed by MERVYN LE ROY. EDWARD G. ROBINSON, DOUGLAS FAIRBANKS, JR. [American, 1930]

82. MOBY DICK, directed by LLOYD BACON. JOHN BARRYMORE. [American, 1930]

83. MOROCCO, directed by JOSEF VON STERNBERG.   ADOLPHE MENJOU, MARLENE DIETRICH.
[American, 1930]

84. LE MILLION, directed by RENÉ CLAIR.   [French, 1920]

It is fairly apparent that a distinction can be made between the methods of expression employed by different directors. For example, it would not be difficult to distinguish between a film made by Lubitsch and a film made by Pabst, although the theme in both films was identical. It would simply be the matter of a distinction between methods of approach. Further, we know that Eisenstein constructs his films by a process of impulsive editing (based on complex forethought), according to his judgement of the material as being expressive of his principles of tonal and over-tonal montage. That is to say, we acknowledge that he selects his shots and determines their screen-length by the physiological-psychological sensations gained from their visual qualities and not (as does Dziga-Vertov) by a purely metric process of the number of frames to a shot. These are merely niceties of expression which are capable of being appreciated by every intelligent observer who is familiar with the principles of filmic representation.

But when we see and hear a film, or rather when we *accept* a film, we are conscious of something beyond its theme and technical expression. We become aware of the director. Our acceptance of the director's creative impulse, however, is governed by our degree of sensitivity, for we may or we may not be receptive to his inner urge of expression. We are possibly going to achieve contact with his creative impulse, whereby we shall appreciate his work to the fullest extent, or we are possibly only going to accept his theme by the simple technical methods adopted by him. In this way, we must distinguish between, on the one hand, a theme and its filmic expression and, on the other, the creative impulse of a director. It is one thing to accept *The End of St. Petersburg* and *Ten Days that Shook the World* as themes and examples of film technique, but quite another to accept *through* them the creative mentalities of Pudovkin and Eisenstein.

In this respect, therefore, it is clear that we are concerned not with the collective acceptance of a film by a number of persons, which is a matter of technical expression, but with the appreciation, according to degrees of sensitivity, that arises in the individual spectator. This is and must always be a matter of personal acceptance.

*

A film demands that a theme—either personal, impersonal or inanimate—shall be presented to the mind through the eye by the flowing relation and inter-relation of a succession of visual images projected on a screen. It further requires the theme to be emphasised by the full range of cinematic resources : by the use of the intimate to reinforce the general at a similar moment or in development; by the instantaneous pictorial vision of more than one idea at the same time; by symbolism and suggestion; by the association of ideas and shapes; by the varying high and low tensions caused by rhythmic cutting; by variation in the intensities of light; by the contrast and similarity of sounds; by all the intrinsic properties peculiar to the medium of the film. The film possesses the power of expanding and contracting the centre of interest, and of comparison by rapid change of the relationship of the trivial to the essential. By these means may the audience be compelled to accept the dramatic meaning of the theme and to realise its continually developing content.

Added to which, it is imperative that a film should be distinguished by a unity of purpose and should be single-minded in intention. According to the treatment of the theme, the dramatic incidents of the narrative may not be of primary interest to the audience, but rather the effect of these incidents on the characters who have provoked them by their behaviour. Again, the theme may be inanimate, recording the structure of some great organisation or industry, or expressive of some vast undertaking. And again, it may develop the intimate personality of a single being by plaiting together as a unified whole a continuity of selected incidents, which singly are of little significance.

In this manner, by utilising the means arising out of the nature of the medium itself, the film sets out to be a form of expression, presenting persons, objects, and incidents in a way entirely different from any other medium, and utilising resources unavailable in other means of artistic expression. It will be seen also that such values as ' acting ' and sets become but raw material for assembly in the final film construction. The complete insignificance of the star-system in this respect is obvious. In fact, I even suggest that there is no such thing as ' film acting '.

Provided that it is conceived in a filmic sense, the subject-matter of a film may be derived from anywhere. Every human thought, every incident of life or imagination can inspire a theme. The history of the world is a storehouse from which themes may be drawn at will. Choice can only be governed by sociological reasons; whether it be of interest or of no appeal to an audience. In the case of the fiction film, it is necessary for the plot to be well balanced and well constructed. Most good films are marked by the simplicity of their themes and their logical development of action. The theme may be found in a play, a novel, a magazine, a novelette, a newspaper, a history book, a memoir, an encyclopaedia, a dictionary or a fifteenth-century incunable. Better still, in the case of the semi-fiction picture, it can be found in the street, in the trains, in the factories or in the air.

There is a wealth of cinematic inspiration, for instance, in the paintings of the Flemish and early Dutch painters. For *La Passion de Jeanne d'Arc*, Dreyer went to the best possible source of inspiration in the medieval French miniatures, whilst in his crowd scenes there was the influence of Bruegel. The atmosphere of Murnau's *Faust* was gained through an intimate knowledge of the work and feeling of Dürer, of his grand pictorial value, whilst again there was a hint of Bruegel in the types of the townspeople in the plague-stricken city. Bosch, the Van Eycks, Lucas van Leyden, Hans Baldung Grein, and particularly the beasts of Lucas Cranach, have a definite filmic feeling that may be sensitively used for inspiration. El Greco, Goya, and more especially Honoré Daumier are rich in influential matter. The amazing types in Eisenstein's *The General Line* and Turin's *Turksib* recall the heads of Dürer and Holbein in their rich quality. In the film, it is possible to use such wonderful wrinkled features and twisted beards with great dramatic effect. Nearly all Soviet films are noted for their beautiful close-ups of striking heads, perhaps held only for a flash on the screen. But, as has been pointed out elsewhere, this influence of painting and engraving does not in any way signify the *transference* of a painting on to the screen. The illustrious Mr. De Mille showed his sublime ignorance of this in that travesty, *The King of Kings*.

It is obviously quite unnecessary to commission a celebrated author to write a story 'specially for the screen'. In all probability the celebrated author has not the least conception of the cinema, being chiefly concerned with the writing of novels, which he undoubtedly does very well. Again and again the lament of novelists is heard that their books have been ruined by adaptation to the screen. In many cases, they claim to fail to recognise their own characters and say that the plot has been distorted beyond redemption. This is due, first, to the absolute necessity to transpose the theme of any novel from literary into cinematic terms; and secondly, to the deplorable habits of wealthy producing firms, which frequently buy best-sellers at random without any consideration of their filmic value. Three outstanding instances of this pernicious habit may be found in: Universal purchasing the rights of *All Quiet on the Western Front;* Metro-Goldwyn-Mayer trying to make *The Bridge of San Luis Rey* into a film; and *The Case of Sergeant Grischa* being bought and given to Herbert Brenon, a *sentimentalist* director, to make. Yet another example, somewhat different, was Ufa's complete metamorphosis of the psychological situation in Leonhard Frank's *Karl and Anna,* a book that was already filmic, into a film called *Homecoming*. The greater number of film adaptations from literature are failures simply because scenarists attempt to embody a large amount of literary material in the relatively small space of a film.

When it is said that the visual images from which a film is built are light revealed by moving form, it is perhaps wise to qualify this statement. It is clear that there are at least four different movements present in the cinema, each of which has a definite bearing on the construction and pre-conception of a film. These may be said to be :

1. The actual *movements* of people, animals, and things (such as trains, motor-cars, trees, lifts, shadows, clouds, smoke, waves), being the *movements of the material* photographed in a single shot and which are the elements of the pictorial composition of the visual image on the screen.

2. The *movement* or mobility of the camera itself, being such movements as *panning, travelling,* and *crane* shots.

3. The *movement* existing through time and space between one visual image and the succeeding one in the progression of shots on the screen, by which may be understood the term *continuity* or fluidity of the development of the thematic narrative. This may alternatively be called the *theory of intervals* existing between one frame of film and another in direct cutting; giving rise to varying reactions from sudden shock to smooth transfusion in the spectator. By this means of *assembling* or *mounting* is the complete film composition constructed.

4. The *movement* of the screen itself, as has been publicly seen in the *magnascope,* or enlarged screen, and in the *triptych,* which is the ordinary central screen with a flanking screen on either side.

Each of these movements plays an important part in the expression of the dramatic content of the theme and in its construction.

Moreover, it should be understood that every visual image that appears on the flat screen on which a film is projected, is governed by contrasted intensities of light. The screen itself has no real interest, except in the final form of cinematic movement indicated above. Light on the cinematograph screen is rendered significant by means of form. It is form (*i.e.* the subject-material which is photographically recorded on strips of celluloid by the camera) that gives variations in intensity to the projected light. By means of such visually satisfying images their content or meaning is conveyed to the mind of the spectator through the eye. From a filmic point of view, the significance of form of the subject-material does not lie in its own properties but in its capability to reveal the variations of the intensity of the projected light.[1]

These principles of movement and intensity of light are the fundamental properties of the cinematic medium. Each will be found considered at length as it arises in the sections that follow on the medium as a means of expression of dramatic content. It is imperative, however, to establish such degrees of movement and principles of light before a general examination of the other properties of the film is possible.

---

[1] An admirable example of this was provided by Francis Bruguière and Oswell Blakeston's film *Light Rhythms,* in which the material consisted of static designs in cut paper over which various intensities of light were moved. The appeal of the film lay in the changing light values, which were revealed by the cut paper patterns.

II

THE PRECONCEPTION OF DRAMATIC CONTENT BY SCENARIO ORGANISATION

A film is essentially characterised by a unity of purpose which is present from the first to the last visual image projected on to the screen. This unity of idea, or central purpose, is unfolded shot by shot, sequence by sequence, and may be called the theme, or in the case of the fiction film, the thematic narrative.

It is strictly possible for an entire film to be preconceived in almost exact anticipation of every shot, except in such cases where sudden conditions (such as rain or mist) should occur during shooting, when some alteration in the scenario is justified. No single shot should be regarded as an isolated fragment, but must be reckoned as part of the moving pattern of shots and sequences out of which the film is constructed. Every shot of the many hundred that go to make up a full-length film is related to the preceding and succeeding shots, so that the complete film is related rhythmically.

A film is built, and the process of building has well been called *montage*.[1] The process of film construction is mathematical in its precision. It may be compared to building with a box of bricks. The unity of a film is achieved by the combination of the three acts of montage. Montage may be understood as the inclusive, creative, and constructive unity that is present from the birth of the first gleam of idea in the mind of the scenarist, to the final act of assembling the film strips by constructive editing and cutting. A film is brought into being by the development of the preconceived theme by

[1] Oxford Dictionary (1929) definition: ' Selection, cutting and piecing together as a consecutive whole of the separate *shots* taken in the making of a film. (F, f, *monter* to mount).'

343

cine-organisation of the three forms of montage thus:

(*a*) The *assembling* of the *thematic narrative*, first in the mind; secondly, in *treatment* form; and then in the shape of a *shooting-script;* including the reasoning employed in the choice of theme out of the countless available (as indicated in the previous chapter).

(*b*) The *assembling* of the *material* (as dictated by the shooting-script) that is to be photographed in the studio or on location, based on the power of observation and understanding of human nature possessed by the director, and its expression by the use of the full resources of the medium.

(*c*) The *assembling* of the *strips of film* bearing upon them the photographic images, in variations of length, light, movement of material, and intellectual values calculated to produce the greatest effect on an audience.

Cine-organisation is thus to be reckoned as the dominant factor of film production, for it controls the three acts of montage which create the film, make it a reality, and invest it with emotional power. A film is not significant as a dramatic expression unless the three acts of montage have been completely welded together in harmony.

The director is the sole *controlling* mind that organises the forms of montage. It is he who commands the fulfilment of cine-organisation. If a mistake should occur during any process of the three acts of montage, then the whole composition of the film may be thrown out of order. The director is to be considered as the central organiser of a number of workers (the scenarist, cameraman, designer, etc.), all of whose actions are in direct fulfilment of his wishes. The team work of a production unit is a natural outcome of the characteristics of the medium of the film. Although the construction of a film usually takes the following order of processes, *viz.*:

(*a*) The choice of theme, the treatment of theme, the shooting-script.

(*b*) The selection of acting material.

(*c*) The construction of studio settings and location of exteriors.

    (*d*) The filming of the material as indicated by the shooting-script.

    (*e*) The assembling of material (*i.e.* the strips of celluloid) by constructive editing and cutting, as indicated in the shooting-script,

it is not possible to divide this construction into independent stages, as is frequently done in large commercial studios. The work of each stage is directly contributory to the whole film composition, being controlled, as stated above, by the director. Thus absolute collectivism is an essential of efficient cine-organsaton.

*

Examination may now be made of the first act of montage, that is to say the assembling of the scenario. It has been seen in the preceding chapter that the variety of themes available to the director, scenarist or producer, is almost infinite, and that choice can only be governed by sociological or political reasons, or, in cases of the general commercial film, by whether a selected theme will be of interest to a large number of persons. For the simplification of argument, therefore, it may be assumed that a theme has been chosen. This theme is to be reckoned as the root-basis of the scenario. It is the motive for the realisation of the film and its entire justification as a means of expression, other, that is, than the creative impulse of the director. The theme indicates action, by which its meaning will be propounded. The action of the scenario is built up from a number of incidents and situations brought about by the characters and the relationship that exists between them. This, obviously, is determined by the imagination of the scenarist or director, being either a creative product or an adaptation from a literary work. The actional interest of the theme is set in an environment, which is either suggested by the nature of the theme, or is chosen as being suitable by the director. The general colour or atmosphere of the film is determined by the environment, and must be present in the film from beginning to end. Even a landscape, a piece of architecture, a natural condition of the weather, is to be absorbed into the developing action. The action and the environment are, in fact, inseparable.

At this stage, with the theme, the action and the setting decided, it is possible for the treatment to be written. This will consist of a descriptive narrative of the visual potentialities of the theme. Although written in purely narrative form, it will suggest clearly the filmic possibilities of the idea. It will not, however, be divided into terms of individual shots, which is strictly a matter of the organisation of the detailed shooting-manuscript, or plan. This latter is the final stage of the scenario-organisation and is the key from which the director will work.

In order that the completed film composition may be a unity, the entire expression of the theme as it will eventually appear on the screen is preconceived in the mind of the scenarist, and is set down by him shot by shot, scene by scene, sequence by sequence, in the form of a shooting-script. This preliminary literary expression of the concept contains the style, that is, the method of realisation, which the director will adopt during the taking and editing of the materal. The film manuscript is thus built out of at least a thousand separate shots, each dependent for effect on the other. By means of this composition of shots (eventually consummated by the editing, or final act of montage) the film is caused to vibrate as a whole, thus giving rise to various emotional reactions in the mind of the audience.

The qualities needed for this literary expression of the theme in filmic terms, the importance of which cannot be over-emphasised, are intense concentration and clarity of perception and visualisation. Preconception of the film shooting-manuscript makes exhaustive claims on the creative mentality of the director or scenarist. In a novel, a writer develops his theme by written descriptions; in a play, an author makes use of dialogue and stage directions; but a film scenarist thinks and works in terms of externally expressive visual images. A scenarist must always visualise his thoughts in terms of images on a screen in a cinema;

346

he must, moreover, be able to control, select, and organise the imaginary images as does a writer his words. He must be continually aware that each shot he describes and includes in his manuscript will eventually assume visual form on the screen. It is, therefore, not his words which are of importance, but the visual images that they define for the use of the director. The assembling of the film manuscript is, perhaps, the most exacting form of expressive writing. It demands without question even greater powers of concentration than the writing of a novel or the painting of a picture. Comparison may well be made with the composing of a symphony.

The director-scenarist[1] has, first, to create his theme in the form of mental imagery; then to express those images in literary terms in the form of a treatment; and finally to compose them in the shooting-script by employing every resource peculiar to the film for conveyance of dramatic content to the spectator. It is essential that the director-scenarist should have the fullest knowledge of filmic methods of expression, with which he can only acquaint himself by the study of other films and by experiment. Every property of pictorial composition, symbolism and suggestion, contrast and similarity in the association of ideas and shapes, the drama of camera angle, the rhythm achieved by various processes of editing and cutting, the technical accomplishment of camera mobility, trick devices, and the possibilities of studio settings, must be in the mind of the director, to be utilised in the right place, so that the dramatic content of the theme may be expressed with the greatest possible emotional effect. For the expression of every concept, there are a thousand and one shots at the

---

[1] Theoretically, the only possible writer of the film manuscript is the director, who alone is capable of transferring to paper the preconception of the film he is about to make. The theme, action, and environment may, however, be suggested to the director, who will translate them into his own terms of filmic expression. The special scenario departments for the mass production of films that are to be found in all big studios are ignored here. Their work can only consist of sorting and cataloguing possible material for themes, and the reader is referred, in this respect, to the scenario-bureaux of the Soviet cinema. (Cf. footnote, p. 220.)

disposal of the director, and it is assumed for the purposes of argument that there is no angle or position from which an object, person, or scene cannot be photographed, both terminals of the shot (the object and the camera) being either static or in motion. It is the task of the scenarist to select from the infinite number of shots in his imagination, those which are the most vividly expressive, in order that they may bring out the full significance of the scene, as required by the theme. The procedure of the shooting-script is the preliminary representation on paper of the eventual visual images on the screen. Both the director and the scenarist should think of all material, wherever they may happen to be, in terms of visual images, from which they can select according to their skill in filmic creation. It must be remembered that the camera, by means of visual images, digs deep into the inner reality of life; it penetrates the underlying currents of human emotions; it brings what I have called the consciousness of the inanimate to the spectator. The whole power of the film lies in the representation of themes and motives, presenting them filmically for the pleasure or sadness of the spectators, according to their degree of sensitivity.

In the preparation of the shooting-script, the director may be assisted by the cameraman and the designer, who are able to supplement his technical knowledge with their specialised experience of the capabilities of the camera as an instrument of expression and of the designing of sets calculated to emphasise dramatic content. I believe that the incorporation of draughtsmanship in the film manuscript is of the greatest importance in perfecting the representation of visual images. The scenario may not only be written, but may be drawn. In the first place, purely architectural diagrams of the lay-out of sets, travelling shots, panning shots, etc., should be included in order that a clear visualisation of the action of the characters in relation to the mobility of the camera may be possible. Added to this, the shooting angles and set-ups of the camera, as dictated by the imagination of the scenarist and the technical experience of the cameraman, may be indicated. Secondly, it is possible to emphasise the literary description of the selected visual images by means of drawings, which will be clues, as it were, to the actual shots on the studio floor or on location. At this point, a difficulty arises, for the literary descriptions in the scenario are usually concerned with movement of the acting material, which it is difficult, if not impossible, to convey by means of a drawing, the nature of which is essentially static. For this reason, therefore, the drawings should be in the form of footnotes, pictorial indications of the actual realisation, whilst the necessary movement of the players and the camera can be indicated by diagrammatic plans. The scenarist or director, as has already been stated, visualises the complete film in his imagination before it ever enters the studio to be fixed on strips of celluloid. It is only logical that there are many aspects of the visual images, such as pictorial composition and contrast of masses, that he cannot describe in his script by text. It is when the literary medium fails that the scenarist should be helped to a clear expression of his ideas by the draughtsmanship of the designer. When in the studio, the director should be able to work from drawings as well as from words in the realisation of the theme.

It will be understood, therefore, that three persons should have the organisation of the shooting-script in their control—the scenarist-director, the cameraman, and the designer. By means of their collective talent, there will result the nearest *absolute* approach to a complete film preconceived and set down on paper. Both visually and textually, the scenario will indicate the exact course of events in the studio, on exterior and in the cutting room. The textual description will still remain the prominent feature of the scenario, the draughtsmanship serving to augment the written description of visual images. It follows that with the aid of plans, diagrams, lay-outs, and descriptive text, the three composers of the film manuscript will be able to select more easily the best possible shots for the representation of the scenes which express the dramatic content of the theme. Moreover, the manuscript composers should be continually conscious of the varying relations of the visual image lengths (*i.e.* the length of time that each shot is held on the screen), for it is their rhythmic relationship which ensures the increasing or decreasing concentration of the audience. This detailed shooting-script will render more simple the two further acts of montage, already sufficiently complicated in themselves.

It is to be remembered that when shooting a film, a director is seldom able to take shots or scenes in their consecutive order of appearance. He cannot, for obvious practical reasons, begin by taking his first shot and proceed according to his scenario. For this reason alone, therefore, a well-organised shooting-script is absolutely vital for the final assembling of the film strips in the cutting room during the last stage of montage. If the shooting-script be vague, if every problem raised by the theme has not been filmically solved in terms of constructed shots, then the resulting film will be without composition and form. It must be clearly understood that a shooting-script is built up from sequences; the sequences from scenes; and the scenes from shots. Conversely, shots are edited into a scene; scenes into a sequence; and sequences into a unified filmic composition. The drawings included in the film manuscript are clues to the progressive movement of the film itself. They are a graphic commentary on the unfolding continuity of visual images. The basis of film construction is the plastic welding of visual images, or shots, into a complete interrelated whole. Each separate shot indicated in the shooting-script becomes a strip of celluloid; out of these strips, joined in varying orders and lengths according to story action and rhythm, is built the film as a whole.

In every way, efficient scenario planning eliminates surplus expenditure of time and money during the making of a film. With preconceived knowledge of exactly what material is desired, only a reasonable amount of footage of film stock need be taken. Furthermore, it is obvious that for a film to be produced with any commercial security, it must be constructed on a proper planned basis.[1]

*

A film, in developing its theme, attains dramatic effect by a series of visual images on the screen that succeed one another in a constant *forward* movement from the first shot to the last. This dynamic unfolding of the dramatic content of a theme by *continuity* may well be described as being the course of the narrative from incident to incident, from situation to situation, from mood to mood. Further, continuity may be said to be the psychological guidance of the mind of the audience to the different threads of the developing action of the thematic narrative. The continuity of a film is quite independent of the aesthetic value of any one scene. The development of the theme must be continuous. Not for one moment during the showing of a film can continuity possibly become exhausted. Although, as will be seen, ' actual ' time continuity may be suspended for the purpose of including shots of comparison, for parallel action or for reference to a scene that has gone before (so as to heighten the effect of the central theme), the continuity of the film continues to flow forward without cessation.

There exists no definite rule, or form of control, as to the order of appearance of visual images on the screen, save the principles of constructive editing and cutting. The importance of the last shot of a film may well depend upon the image seen in the three-hundred-and-forty-fifth shot. There is nothing but the mind of the director-scenarist to put the shots in their right place and in their most effective order of showing. This is preconceived in the shooting-script and takes material form in the final assembling work. It is a generally accepted fact that David Wark Griffith originally discovered that the development of incident need not necessarily be unfolded in the chronological order of

[1] In passing comment, there is little doubt that the weak spot in the British Film Industry is the inefficient organisation of scenarios (1929).

happening. Continuity may be compared with the unfolding of a plot of a novel. A close analogy is to be found, in particular, in the style of Conrad. Generally speaking, however, the change from one sequence to another is intended to indicate to the audience the progress of the plot of the narrative, though this can by no means be taken as a hard and fast rule. The arrangement of the order in which sequences are shown depends entirely on constructive editing.

The length of each individual shot (i.e. the duration of time that it will be held on the screen until cut, mixed or faded into the succeeding shot) may be taken approximately as varying from one second for twenty frames of film (fifteen inches) to twenty seconds for four hundred frames (twenty-five feet).[1] The time-length of shots should be roughly indicated in the scenario-plan, such estimates naturally being based on observation, since the time-length of every shot is controlled by the mood of the dramatic content of the scene in question. This variation in time-length of a shot is the basis of the rhythmic cutting, and such familiar processes as short, long, and medium cutting are governed entirely by the required mood. It may be well to add that this method assumes individual acting to be of secondary importance; primary consideration being given to achieving effect by image montage. Where acting is the only means of conveying the mood of a scene, a shot may be held on the screen for a considerable length of time, thus becoming akin to the stage. This, of course, is the predominant characteristic of the dialogue film, where image time-lengths are controlled by speech.

The continuity of time in the theme of all films is that of filmic and not actually recorded time. That is to say, the imagination of the spectator is very largely brought into play in the acceptance of the narrative from incident to incident.

The differentiation between 'filmic' time and 'actual'

---

[1] This reckoning is for silent film speed. Sound film speed, as almost universally used to-day, is 90 ft. per minute, or 1½ ft. per second.

85. WESTFRONT 1918, directed by G. W. PABST.   [German, 1930]

86. L'AGE D'OR, directed by LOUIS BUÑUEL.   [French, 1930]

87. DIE DREIGROSCHENOPER, directed by G. W. Pabst. [German, 1931]

88. KAMERADSCHAFT, directed by G. W. Pabst. [German, 1931]

time constitutes the whole basis of cinematic representation. When it is grasped that the formation of a scene, or situation, in a film is purely a matter of the constructive editing of visual images, then it will be seen that the film director creates his own ' time ', as well as his own ' space '. A scene is built up from a series of separate shots, taken from various angles, and, with the pieces of celluloid on which the shots are recorded, the director constructs the scene as it will appear on the screen. The very fact that the scene has been composed from various separate shots proves that it is not a direct record of the actual, and is therefore alien to the stage. The material with which the film director works is not ' real ' in the sense that it is actually recorded time or space, but is a number of pieces of celluloid on which real actions have been recorded. By altering the relations of these strips, filmic time is constructed. It will be remarked that between an actual event and the *filmic representation* of that event on the screen, there is a wide difference; the camera, at the director's or scenarist's bidding, picks out only such significant portions of the event as are necessary for its screen representation. This, in other words, refers back to the scenarist's selection of the best visual images for the expression of a scene. Suggested by the scenarist, recorded by the camera, created by the director in editing, there comes into being an element peculiar to the cinema—filmic time. This filmic time is controlled entirely by the three composers of the shooting-script. Further, it is clear that every situation in a narrative is characterised not only by its duration of time, but also by the space in which it takes place. It is perfectly possible for the action of a scene to be taken by the camera in several places remote from one another, but when the scene is filmically composed, the various places will appear to be one and the same.[1] By editing, preconceived

---

[1] Cf. Ermler's *Fragment of an Empire*, p. 249. More recent examples are the prologues of *World of Plenty* and *The World is Rich*, both edited from shots not only taken in different countries but taken from many different films, and the Capra series, *Why We Fight*.

in the shooting-script, there will have been created filmic space as well as filmic time.

Thus, the material from which a film is built consists of photographic images of persons, objects, and structures, either static or in motion, which can be assembled in whatever manner the scenarist likes, in order to express his theme. The element of real persons, objects, and structures, with their temporal and spatial conditions, are recorded photographically, to be altered according to the desire of the scenarist by the creative process of editing. Actual time becomes filmic time; actual space becomes filmic space; actual reality becomes, on the screen, filmic reality. To quote Pudovkin: 'The film assembles the elements of reality to build from them a new reality proper to itself; and the laws of space and time that, in the sets and footage of the stage are fixed and fast, are in the film entirely altered.' (*Pudovkin on Film Technique, Gollancz*, 1929.) Thus it will appear that filmic space and filmic time are the principles that primarily govern the continuity of the scenario beyond, that is, narrative interest.

In the construction of continuity, it is of interest to examine various methods of bridging a lapse of filmic time between the end of one sequence and the beginning of the next. There are several known methods of suggesting or representing this passing of time, the most usual being the fade-in and the fade-out.[1] The former represents a dark screen, upon which the visual image gradually assumes shape; the latter is the reverse process. It is common to end a sequence with a fade, indicating a slow, restful departure; the screen remaining dark until the first image of the succeeding scene is introduced. The speed of the fade is naturally controlled by the mood of the scene upon which it opens or closes. Another process is the dissolve or mix. This may be said to be the gradual fading of one image into another by a process of overlapping, so that the forms of the last shot of one sequence become lost

[1] See Glossary in Appendix II for definitions of some technical terms used in film production.

in the emerging forms of the first shot of the next. It would be possible, for example, to dissolve from a long shot of an object into a medium shot, and from the medium shot into a close-up. This method of approach (or retreat) can be very beautiful, and I would give as an instance the opening sequence of *Storm Over Asia*. It is not uncommon for the dissolve to be centred on the form of some object, or person, common to both sequences, so that the bridging is less harsh to the eye. This is a use of the association of like shapes. It is possible, for example, to dissolve from a person dressed in sports clothes sitting on a chair, to the same person wearing evening clothes sitting in an identical position in another chair in a fresh environment. A definite lapse of time and change of sequence is conveyed simply and restfully to the spectator in such a way. A dissolve is never harsh or exciting. Its mood is smooth and harmonious to the eye, involving a slow rhythm. It causes an instantaneous *mental* dissolve in the mind of the spectator. This has been very well described as the momentary condensation of a train of thought into another that has yet to serve its purpose. The aim of the dissolve is to associate the old with the new in the mind of the audience.

The customary method of dissolving has been explained as the gradual fading of one pictorial composition into another, but it has been rightly suggested that a process of rapid de-focus, cut, re-focus, from one sequence to another would be more harmonious both to the mind and to the eyes. This would be the association between the latent thought of the one sequence and the symbolism of the visual imagery of the sequence about to appear on the screen. (L. Saalschutz writing in *Close Up*, July 1929.) With this in mind, I would refer to a scene in a film edited by Pudovkin, *The Living Corpse,* where an experiment was made in using both dissolves and direct cutting as a means of expressing the content of a scene. A company of gipsy girls was dancing to the music of a band of guitars and mandolins. Pudovkin took a number of short flashes of the girls dancing, cutting direct from one flash to another.

He interspersed these with some double-exposure shots of hands plucking at the strings of the instruments, but dissolved from one shot into another instead of directly cutting. This meant that when flashes of human movement were being shown, it was permissible to *cut* from flash to flash, since the mood was that of dancing; but when flashes of the musical instruments being played were in question, the mood was melodic and hence the *dissolve* was more suitable than the cut, for the latter would be in conflict to such a mood. It would not have been aesthetically possible to cut visually from sound to sound, so the smoothness of the dissolve was required. A rhythmic combination of these two types of changing shots produced its own music in the imagination of the spectator.

Other technical methods for bridging the lapse of time are the employment of a written title, a direct cut from one scene to another, or by the rare method of drawing the visual image itself across the screen and following it with the next. This latter form was well seen in Cavalcanti's *Rien que les Heures.*[1] Titles employed for the purpose of connecting sequences are, as would be supposed, usually termed continuity titles. Their purpose is to give the audience an explanation, a connecting link between one situation and another, simply but effectively. There are also many familiar literary devices, usually symbolic, such as those of showing candles burning, calendar dates changing, full bottles dissolving into empty ones, cigarettes burning in an ashtray, etc., all of which are stock methods that appear again and again, indicating lack of resource on the part of the scenarist. As an example of almost perfect continuity and complete fluidity of development, *The Last Laugh,* from a scenario by Carl Mayer, was outstanding. Other films which can be mentioned in this respect were

---

[1] Since the above was written, this device, known as a 'wipe', has become widely used by its being made on the optical printer in the laboratory. Purist film technicians object to its use on the grounds that it is a two-dimensional device, as against the three-dimensional illusion of the 'mix' or 'dissolve'. It is true that 'wipes' of all types are used by editors to cover a multitude of continuity and editing sins.

Henry King's *Tol'able David,* Room's *Bed and Sofa,* and
the films of Eisenstein and Pudovkin.

The main continuity development of the theme set down
in the first place by the scenarist is, as has already been
explained, finally controlled by the constructive editing.
But it is clear that its course may be interrupted by certain
episodes and sequences which help to emphasise the whole
effect of the content. Certain incidents and scenes may be
re-introduced, suspending the actional progress of the main
theme in order to explain, perhaps, their appearance at an
earlier stage in the continuity. There are various principles
of relational development, such as contrast and simile in
the association of ideas, which are commonly employed to
heighten dramatic tension. The exact meaning of the
action taking place in the opening sequence of a film may
not be made clear to the audience until the film is half-way
through, when a comparison is made by a flash-back. A
familiar method also is to emphasise dramatic suspense by
means of parallel action. Shots from two different scenes
may be shown alternately, though they are both of the same
sequence and are developing to the same end. This is a
favourite method of drawing a film to an exciting climax.
The hero is on the point of being hanged. The riders
approach carrying his pardon. Alternate shots are shown
of each. The suspense as to whether the hero will be saved
or not is enhanced by quicker and quicker cutting, until at
the moment he is to be despatched, the pardon arrives. The
two sets of shots are mingled into one and all is well. It
is to be found in most Western films and in such old friends
as *The Orphans of the Storm* and *Don Q.*[1] The same effect
can be gained equally well by composite shots on the same
screen.

From this, it is but a step to the various other forms of
interrupted development of the theme by means of shots, or
even whole sequences, for the purposes of comparison,
either for direct contrast or for simile. It must, however,
be clearly understood that although these methods of com-

[1] Cf. page 148 *et seq.,* ' The last-minute-rescue '.

parison cause the suspense of filmic time continuity in order to heighten dramatic effect, the continuity of the development of the film itself still progresses.

Many examples of direct similes occur in the work of the Soviet directors and in the early films of Griffith.[1] Pudovkin is fond of building an effect by comparing the content of a scene with some object, or person, quite irrelevant to the narrative except symbolically. A scene of love and happiness, for instance, is interspersed with quick flashes of Sèvres porcelain groups of shepherds and shepherdesses, symbolic of the lightness and fragility of the love *mood* of the scene. In direct contrast, some shots of waving trees and sunlit country are cut in with a scene of combat and turmoil. Time continuity for the moment is interrupted, the dramatic effect of the combat is strengthened, and the actual continuity flows forward. Mention has been made on other pages of Pudovkin's skilful referential editing.[2] It is of point to remember that the drama of a thing lies not so much in the thing itself, as in the comparison of it with other things. An empty room is not so dramatic in itself as the thought of what that room was like before it was empty.

Similarity of content recurring at intervals throughout a film also appears as a form of comparison, but is strictly more connected with the actual plot of the narrative than with the continuity of the development. For instance, the recurrence of the same characters in a similar situation, so well handled in *Bed and Sofa,* was a matter of story construction. The exact balance of the recurring situations was a matter of continuity. The plot demanded that three people shared a room; a husband, his wife, and another man. The sleeping accommodation was confined to one bed and a sofa. In the first part of the film the other man had the sofa; in the middle of the film the situation was reversed; and in the end the problem was solved. There

[1] Elliott's *Anatomy of Motion Picture Art* (Pool, 1928) analyses the films of Griffith well in this respect.

[2] Cf. pages 235, 393.

was a nicety about the presentation of the changed situations that suggested careful balance and distribution in the continuity of development.

First, in his treatment and secondly, in his shooting-script, the scenarist has always to develop his action according to a design of varying degrees of tension. It is this variance in tension, ranging from high, exciting emotions to low, sad, and depressing emotions, that forces the mind of the audience to follow the unfolding of the film with interest. This attraction between the visual images on the screen and the mind of the audience is governed not only by the dramatic situations of the narrative (such as suspense, mystery, explanation) but also by the purely filmic methods of construction, *i.e.* editing and cutting. The use of crowds, of rapid physical movement, of dramatic situations, is in itself emotionally exciting, but this material is rendered doubly powerful by its filmic representation. Thus, the arrangement of high-spots at suitable intervals throughout a film is determined in the scenario construction. Sequences of high dramatic emotion (high-spots) must be balanced by sequences of low emotion (low-spots). Exciting incidents are to be modulated by sad incidents. Balance in the design of the film must be preserved in order to establish rhythmic structure. Incidents of varying dramatic intensity (or *mood*) must be distributed throughout the film in terms of contrast. High-spots are to be related to low-spots. Emotions are to be aroused in an up-and-down fluidity. Sequences are to be arranged according to their dominants or moods. It is possible to plot a graph of the dominants of a film, showing the inter-relation between the points of high and low emotion. The plotting of the graph of a film might be included as a further stage of scenario montage.

III

THE METHODS OF EXPRESSION OF DRAMATIC
CONTENT BY FILM CONSTRUCTION

It is proposed, for the purpose of simplification, to divide the processes by which the dramatic content of the theme of a film is conveyed to an audience into two separate sections. The first will deal with the construction of the silent film by means of visual images on the screen. The second will reason the uses of a combination of sound, dialogue, and visual images on the screen. Although these two processes may be considered as entirely different forms of cinema (believing, that is, the dialogue film to be spurious), certain properties are common to each, and in places will be found to overlap. For example, although visual images are employed in both cases, basically different ideas lie behind their conception. An intermediary stage has further been added, deliberating on the advantages to be gained from the use of recorded sound (as distinct from the recorded voice) as a resource of filmic exposition.

Although aesthetic principles render the silent film, reasonably reinforced by symbolic sound accompaniment, the only acceptable form of cinema, it is not to be denied that the dialogue film as seen and heard to-day is a form of cinema, its novelty and freakishness being commercially lucrative to American and British producers, and to those continental firms which take the same outlook. Beyond this, there must be visualised in the near future the stereoscopic and wider screen, the colour film, and the projection of coloured slides or secondary films on to the walls and ceiling of the theatre, all in combination with synchronised dialogue and sound, in an effort to establish what has been called the Compound Cinema. That these mechanical ' developments ' will come into general use there is little doubt, and in all probability they will be supported by a certain section of the community who applaud novelty entertainment. I am equally certain, however, that these new forms will never destroy the original and highest form of cinema, the silent, flat film with synchronised or orchestral accompaniment, which is indisputably the most effective medium for the conveyance of the dramatic content of a theme to the mind of an audience.

Examination may first be made, then, of the visual cinema.

(I) THE PROCESS OF THE VISUAL CINEMA

The silent film, in developing the continuity or progress of a theme, attains dramatic effect on an audience by a series of visual images on the screen. Long shots and close-ups, straight views and angular views, combine to demonstrate the character of the content of the theme. Only those images which have a definite bearing on this content are shown, and these are represented by means of carefully selected photographic angles, wholly or partially pre-conceived and indicated in the shooting-script. The greatest possible emotional effect can be achieved in the smallest amount of time by the arrangement of these visual images, the selection of which is governed by various principles of image montage. This arrangement is also included in the shooting-script, being carried out in the final act of assemblage. Complete freedom may be exercised in the choice of photographic angles and in the length of the shot (*i.e.* its number of frames). A film is not, by any stretch of imagination, a mere succession of shots taken at random, which can be described either singly or consecutively. Rather it is the relation, inter-relation and juxtaposition of these varying lengths of shot which, when combined into a whole, produce filmic effect.

Further analysis of these methods of expression of a theme may be divided into five sections, a sixth being added to consider the advantages, if any, to be derived from the stereoscopic screen and colour film. These sections can be described thus :

(*a*) *Film Psychology,* being the expression of inner reality by outward phenomena.

(*b*) *The Expressive Capabilities of the Camera.*

(*c*) *The Pictorial Composition of Visual Images.*

(*d*) *Constructive Editing and Cutting.*

(*e*) *Titles,* and the placing thereof.

(*f*) *The Visual Addition of Colour* and *The Stereoscopic Screen.*

*

(*a*) *Film Psychology*

The dramatic content of a fiction or semi-fiction film may be described as being the psychological reactions and emotions of the characters in a story, resulting from narrative situations which arise from the actions of the characters themselves or other material incidents.

The inner reality of the characters, their thoughts, desires, lusts, and emotions, is revealed by their outward actions. It is, furthermore, these outward phenomena which the camera photographs in order to recreate and transfer to the mind of the audience the inner reality of the characters in the story. It is by the subtle arrangement of the visual images (*i.e.* the editing) which photographically record these phenomena that the dramatic content is conveyed clearly to the audience. The camera itself is unable to penetrate the world before it, but the creative mind of the director can reveal in his *selection* of the visual images this intrinsic essence of life by using the basic resources of the cinema, *viz.,* editing, angle, pictorial composition, suggestion, symbolism, etc. And, in particular, it is the camera's remarkable faculty for the representation of detail that makes it possible to build up situations and events by putting their exact ingredients before the audience. Guided by the mind of the scenarist and the director, the camera eliminates from the screen everything

362

but material absolutely significant to the exposition of the dramatic content of the theme. Every visual image on the screen registers an impression on the minds of the audience, as also do the intervals that exist between the visual images, and out of a moving series of impressions is the whole effect composed. Hence, the complete attention of the audience lies at the director's will, and, therefore, in actuality the camera is the mind of the spectator. In this respect, there will be noticed the relevance of the Dziga-Vertov theory of the cine-eye.[1]

It is not unnatural, then, that the principles of psychoanalysis play a large part in the conveyance of dramatic content to the audience. It will be shown later, for example, in dealing with pictorial composition, that the smallest movement on the screen is immediately magnified in importance and becomes at once a source of interest to the spectator. From this it will be realised that the so-called symptomatic actions of Freud, the small, almost unnoticed and insignificant actions of behaviour on the part of a person, are highly indicative of the state of his mind, and are of the utmost value, when magnified on the screen, for establishing an understanding of that state of mind in the audience. For this reason alone, it will be seen how essential it is for a film player to be his natural self, and how detrimental ' theatrical ' acting is to film purposes. It is the duty of the director to reveal the natural characteristics of his players and to build these, by means of editing, into a filmic exposition of a personality, as required by the scenario. That is why, when approached from this point of view, the use of actual types is generally considered preferable to professional actors, a method of working adopted by the naturalistic directors. (Eisenstein, Pudovkin, Flaherty, Turin, and Epstein in his later period.)

Moreover, there is no limit to the depth of cinematic introspection. There is no state of mind which cannot be fully revealed by the resources of the film. The expression of such content may be said to be governed by the set-up

[1] Cf. pp. 243-247.

of the camera when the shot is taken; and the relation between the length of this shot (when shown on the screen) and that of the other shots which make up the whole sequence, and finally the film as a unity. It should be remembered also that both these two factors have been largely pre-conceived in the shooting-script.

Added to which, there is to be considered the very important part played by the presence of inanimate objects in the construction of a scene. An object in itself is an immensely expressive thing. It will possibly be symbolic. For instance, an aeroplane or a motor-car is immediately suggestive of speed; a rifle or gun of death; and so on. By reason of the camera's capacity for bringing detail to the attention of the audience, inanimate objects assume a dramatic significance in the establishment of mood. Their use is, of course, controlled by the editing. (Recall the Sèvres figures in *The Living Corpse;* the dirt and litter in *Greed;* the gallery of gods and the detail of architecture in *Ten Days that Shook the World.*) The film, more so than any other medium, forces the spectator to realise the consciousness of the inanimate.

It is, therefore, the mood or tension of a scene created by the characters which is to be transferred to the audience, or better still, in which the audience itself is going to participate. The existence and emphasis of this mood is established by the natural resources of the film.

Emphasis of mood is to be gained largely by contrast of light and of space, by angle, by symbolism, and by indirect suggestion. A memorable example of the contrast of space was to be found in *Bed and Sofa.* The story was placed in Moscow at the time when there was extreme shortage of housing accommodation. Out of this state of affairs, and rendered plausible by them, arose the story. It was necessary, therefore, to emphasise this shortage of space throughout the film, in order to substantiate the incidents of the story. Most of the action took place in a small room, too cramped for two, let alone three, persons. But the atmosphere of this confined space was not to be achieved only by shots of the litter and discomfort in the room itself. One of the three persons went out to work. He was seen working on the top of the roof of the Opera House, surrounded on all sides by sky. The width and breadth of the heavens provided a powerful contrast to the small room, where the three fell over each other in an effort to keep out of the way. The director in this film took advantage of natural circumstances to emphasise the content of his film, and to render it plausible to the audience.

As already indicated, a dramatic feeling of uncertainty, of perhaps slight fear, is to be obtained by emptiness. Long, deliberate shots of an empty room or corridor, after there has been a sustained sequence of vigorous, highly emotional action, produce a strong suggestion of tense atmosphere. Contrast of light and shade accentuates the mood of such a scene. In *The Joyless Street,* in a room lit only by the feeble rays of light filtering through the slats of a venetian blind, the presence of the murdered man was at once established although no corpse was to be seen. Atmosphere was conveyed by contrasted light; the mood of the dramatic content was achieved by indirect suggestion. Many similar scenes appeared in *The Cabinet of Doctor Caligari,* and, of course, in the often-quoted opening sequence in Karl Grune's *The Street.*

Throughout the course of Feyder's *Thérèse Raquin,* the audience was aware of the content of the narrative by subtle indirect suggestion. Thérèse went to see her lover Laurent in his studio. She leaned back on the couch; he sat brooding at her feet; the scene was charged with tension. On the wall behind them were pinned carelessly some of his drawings from the life, such sketches as are found lying about in so many artists' studios. There was nothing uncommon in their presence. But their meaning, although the direct effect on the spectator may have been unconscious, showed clearly the sexual reason for the meetings of these two. It was an example of the use of the incidental to reinforce the general, instigated by the intelligence of the director. In *Greed,* the central theme was the demonstration of the horror of a human being's intense passion for gold. This was emphasised by the presence of gold in every detail throughout the film. From the grinding mill in the opening sequence, to the bars of the canary cage, the teeth stoppings and the gilt picture frames, the keynote of the film was gold. Unfortunately, in this case, it was over-exaggerated by the use of part colorisation, causing the effect to be blatant.

It is then, by the flicker of an eyelash, the dropping of a cigarette end, the relation of one thing to another, the association of ideas and objects, that mood partially is suggested, emphasised and made apparent.

(b) *The Expressive Capabilities of the Camera*

The capabilities of the camera as an instrument of expression are almost unlimited. There exists practically no object or person that cannot be photographed. The appeal of the film lies in a transient series of visual images, presented to the eye on a screen flooded with light in a darkened place. The camera is the actual medium, the eye, through which all movement and all phenomena are captured. The camera swings here and there, catching unseen incidents and unnoticed aspects of life. This was well instanced by the Cine-Eye methods in *The Man with the Camera*. Flowers are observed to bloom; insects to crawl; birds to fly. Every movement, however fast or slow, in every direction, is recorded by the camera's eye. It noses into every corner, ferrets out information, returns to a normal position, and suddenly swings round on its own axis to observe the fresh movement of another person.

The camera as an instrument of expression in itself may be considered from four aspects : (*a*) the position of the camera and consequently the angle from which the shot is taken; (*b*) its power of distortion and of duplicating movement; (*c*) the movement of the camera in order to include other objects in its range, without change of scene by cutting and without movement of the actual position;

(*d*) the mobility of the camera in that it approaches, retreats or encircles the object that it is photographing.

In the early days of the cinema, all shots were taken from a standard distance away from the object, the influence of the stage still being uppermost in the mind of the director. It was deemed impossible to show a portion of a person on the screen. The actors were made to remain discreetly in the background, and gestured into the camera, adjusting themselves to it, as it were, and being extremely conscious of its presence. Griffith is claimed to have been the first director to have broken down this barrier, being rightly convinced in his own mind that facial expression was the all-powerful interpretation of the thoughts in the actor's mind for the purposes of film drama. This, as is well known, led to the introduction of the close-up, an element which altered the whole conception and outlook of the film. It was not until much later, however, that the real use of the close-up was appreciated, not so much for the dramatic expression on an actor's face as for the fact that it was a form of emphasis. Close-ups of objects and things became as important as the close-ups of a face. It was the idea of using the close-up to draw attention to a certain object that first threw a new light on film direction. An early instance of this was the shot of the galloping hooves of the horses cut in with shots of the riders themselves in the 'last-minute-rescue' of *The Birth of a Nation*.[1]

It was not until after the war, however, that the Germans realised that practically anything, when lit from the right source, was more dramatic if taken from a position different from the usual eye-level. From that day onwards the camera developed its independence, to be used rightly by a few directors for the strict emphasis of mood, and wrongly by many for the sake of sheer virtuosity. Even now, there are lamentably few directors who have any real knowledge of the use of camera angle, of when and how to employ it in order to achieve dramatic effect. Of those few, so that reference can be made to their work, mention

[1] *Vide, This Film Business,* R. P. Messel (Benn, 1929), p. 92.

may be made of Pabst, Pudovkin, Eisenstein, Feyder, Clair, and Dreyer.[1]

The first capability of the camera to be recognised, beyond the obvious fact of its taking the picture, is its power of distortion. Camera distortion is significant, for, by the very fact of throwing the pictorial composition of a scene out of perspective, it emphasises the mood of that scene. The angle from which a shot is taken must be controlled by the image that is being visualised and *not by the position of the camera.* The mood of the shot determines the position of the camera; not the artistic mind of a director who thinks the shot would look well if taken from the ceiling. The examples of misuse of camera angle, both for freakish and exotic reasons, are countless, and can only be compared with the abuse of the camera's own movements. They are present in nearly every American and British film. There is, moreover, little excuse for the use of freak camera angles. The choice of an angle should not be a disputed point, or even a matter of opinion. Provided the mood of a shot and its connection with the sequence is clearly indicated by the shooting-script, there is only *one* position in which the camera can be placed in order to render that shot most expressive of the mood required.

The camera, moreover, possesses the faculty of concentrating the eye of the spectator on some important detail on the screen, by narrowing down the field of vision on to the centre of interest. An old method was to mask over gradually the whole screen with the exception of one particular detail; or to begin a sequence by the iris-in method, starting on the most important object in the composition. This was freely used in *The Cabinet of Doctor Caligari* and *Birth of a Nation,* and other early films. Camera mobility and the recognition of the values of cutting have disposed of these methods, which were clumsy at their best.

---

[1] In recent years, several directors have made a serious study of camera set-up as a means of interpreting dramatic content. Their names deserve to be added to the above. Among them should be included Marcel Carné, David Lean, John Huston, Carol Reed and Edward Dmytryk.

89. MAEDCHEN IN UNIFORM, directed by Leontine Sagan. [German, 1931]

90. EMIL AND THE DETECTIVES, directed by Gerhard Lamprecht. Fritz Rasp.
[German, 1931]

91. CITY STREETS, directed by Rouben Mamoulian. Guy Kibbee, Sylvia Sidney.
[American, 1931]

92. QUICK MILLIONS, directed by Rowland Brown. Spencer Tracy.
[American, 1931]

It is common now to start a sequence on a close-up of some small object, the camera travelling away from it, round the set, finally picking up the chief source of interest. Hoffmann exploited this idea in *Nina Petrovna* until it became wearisome and smacked of virtuosity.

There are various properties of the camera, apart from the matter of its set-up, which are valuable for the emphasis of dramatic mood. The device of throwing a scene deliberately out of focus in order to denote the misty state of mind of a character (and, of course, the audience) is familiar.[1] In American films the employment of gauzes for softening the effect of lighting is not generally used so much with the desire to emphasise the mood of the scene as to make it look pretty. It is an offensive habit, and is to be found chiefly in sentimental films of the calibre of *Seventh Heaven*. It was an unfortunate feature, also, of *The Wedding March*, but there at least it was used to create atmosphere. The use of mirrors is also known, being seen at its best in Metzner's *Ueberfall*, for the brilliant representation of a man's subconscious thoughts.

Another form of pure cinematic resource is the projection of negative film on to the screen, which gives an effect of reversed values to the ordinary projection of positive. Instead of the screen image being in terms of black on white, the result is white on black. This was well used by Murnau in the rare version of *Dracula*, in order to convey the macabre atmosphere of the dark woods surrounding the Count's castle. A curious feeling of lifelessness is obtained by the use of negative in this way, due probably to the suggestion of the skeletons of the objects being photographed. Its effect in the case cited above was sinister; the gaunt, white branches of trees standing out in a ghostly manner against the black sky. It is a camera device frequently used by the French experimentalists, and in particular I recall it in *A quoi rêvent les jeunes films, La Marche des Machines,* and *Les Mystères du Château du Dé.* In

---

[1] A beautiful example of double-image distortion to simulate drunkenness was in Dmytryk's *Crossfire* (1947), cameraman, J. Roy Hunt.

Dracula also, was found the use of one-turn—one-picture, a device which produced an effect of erratic, jerky movement, giving the phantom coach a bizarre appearance as it moved through the woods.

Other devices of the camera connected with movement but expressive of mood are slow-motion, ultra-rapid motion, and the abrupt cessation of movement. Slow-motion is often to be seen employed in topical films to reveal the graceful actions of athletes and racehorses. Its place in dramatic themes is more interesting. Perhaps the best example was the opening sequence of Dovjenko's *Zvenigora,* a scene which showed a band of cossack brigands riding through some luxuriously foliaged countryside. Slow-motion was used during the scene, the effect being peculiarly beautiful as well as suggestive of the laziness, heat, and dust of the afternoon. It had also the asset of deliberately concentrating the attention of the spectator on the slowly moving horsemen, with their graceful, fascinating actions. Fairbanks has employed slow-motion in order to give his leaps and bounds added grace (in *Don Q*), but this can hardly be classed as emphasis of mood. Ultra-rapid motion and the abrupt cessation of movements, producing a petrified effect, have been well used in some Soviet comedies (*e.g.* Barnet's *House in Trubnaya Square*). For the extraordinary effects obtainable by cessation of movement, one remembers in particular Dovjenko's film, *Arsenal,* where its use was intensely emotional. It will be appreciated that the effects of these devices cannot well be described in words. They are wholly cinematic in texture.

Having considered the expressive properties of the camera at rest, it is permissible to examine the capabilities of the camera in movement. The mobility of the camera is an important factor in filmic representation that has only come to be used to its full capacity during recent years. But no sooner has the camera achieved its independence than it is again curbed by the advent of the dialogue film, which demands that the instrument be enclosed in a booth or box of some considerable dimensions, seriously limiting

its power of movement.[1] Some experiments are being made
to remedy this by enveloping the camera in a velvet cloak
to keep out sound, but there is no question that the dialogue
film has temporarily thrown the recently liberated camera
back once more into slavery. Karl Hoffmann's lament :
' Poor camera, alas; no more of your graceful movements,
no more of your happy-go-lucky shifts? Are you again
condemned to the same bondage and chains which you com-
menced breaking ten years ago?' is a stab at the dominant
commercialism of the American dialogue cinema.

At the time of the production of the first dialogue film,
the camera had just established its freedom. It must be put
on record, also, that the *principal* developments in the
capabilities of the camera took place in Germany, despite
claims to the contrary by smart American film writers.
Practically every photographic device which is used to
emphasise the dramatic power of a shot saw its origin in
German studios. It was Fritz Arno Wagner, Karl Freund,
Karl Hoffmann, Günther Rittau, Guido Seeber, Günther
Krampf, and their *confrères* who gave the camera its
independence from the hampering tripod. Assisted by her
unlimited finance and unparalleled capacity for annexing
any new development, Hollywood exploited this freedom
of the camera without any regard to its limits or correct
uses. It is seldom that camera mobility is used for any
purpose other than sheer virtuosity in American movies.

Camera mobility is completely justified in any direction
and at any speed so long as the reason for its movement
is expression and heightening of the dramatic content of
the shot. Its motion can be forward and backward, from
side to side, or up and down. It can move horizontally,
perpendicularly, diagonally, circularly and in combinations
of these actions in curved or straight movements. In
Jeanne Ney, Wagner's camera was in motion practically
throughout the film. So strongly was the dramatic content

[1] Even to-day, while the up-to-date ' blimp ' is a great improvement on
the old booth of the early talkies, camera mobility is more limited in
synch. shooting than in silent camerawork.

brought out, however, that the spectator was scarcely conscious of the movement. In Paramount's *Forgotten Faces,* a camera took flights round a room whilst a hold-up raid was in progress. A fine view of the wallpaper was obtained, but the drama of the scene was non-existent. The same applied to certain shots in Vidor's *The Crowd.* In such a way must sheer artistry be distinguished from shallow technical accomplishment.

Many instances of correctly used camera motion occurred in *Moana,* where the camera swung to follow the swaying movements of a tree; in *La Passion de Jeanne d'Arc,* where the quick, pulsating, backward and forward motion denoted the hesitant trepidation in Joan's mind; and in *Metropolis,* where a similar movement followed the hammer of the great gong calling the workers together.[1]

Obviously, the dimensions of the material forming the pictorial composition on the screen change in relation to the movement of the camera; but it must always be uppermost in the mind that the material governs the motion of the camera. Furthermore, there is a close relationship between the movement of the camera and camera angle, both being controlled by the mood of the material being photographed. All the properties of the camera itself, such as slow-motion and masks, as well as camera angle, which have been considered previously, have direct bearing on camera mobility. It should be remembered that the camera can approach an object from a low angle, gradually rising as it gets nearer, at the same time altering its course; arrive at the object and encircle it; and photograph the whole time in slow-motion. Each of these movements is justified, *if it is emphasising* the mood of the shot and its bearing on the dramatic content of the story.

As has been made clear, the expressive powers of the camera may be considered from four points of view; the

[1] John Huston's thriller, *The Maltese Falcon* (1941) photograped by Arthur Edeson, was an outstanding example of brilliantly used camera devices of all kinds especially movement related to cutting. The last two films of Rossellini, *Germany Year Zero* and *The Miracle,* also have remarkable camera movement.

first two with the camera at rest, the last two with the camera in movement. It is necessary, therefore, to differentiate between the two forms of movement. The first is that in which the camera position does not change, but the camera itself swivels either laterally or vertically, to include fresh objects in its range. The second is that in which the camera moves its position as a whole in order to approach or to retreat from the object being photographed.

The first of these actions, when the camera pivots on its own axis laterally, or tilts in an up-and-down motion, is generally termed *panning*, the obvious reason being that this action produces on the screen a panoramic view of the set or location in which the camera is placed. Its customary use is to connect two persons or things on the screen which are some distance apart, without entailing a separate shot. The movement must necessarily be fairly slow if it is not to offend the eyes of the audience, and hence it will be apparent that panning from a person standing at one side of a table to a person at the other, takes a greater length of time than would a direct cut from one visual image to another. A pan shot tends to slow down the action of a scene; cutting tends to quicken the pace. The only clue as to whether panning or cutting should be used in a certain continuity of shots lies in the mood of the scene. If the nature of the latter is to be quick and staccato, then panning will be useless to convey this tempo, cutting being the desirable method. If, on the other hand, the action is slow, dragging, and sad, panning slowly from one person or object to another will produce the required emphasis of mood. Like every other form of camera movement, panning is justified only by the mood of the scene being represented. These remarks apply equally to the perpendicular form of panning, which is more rarely used than the lateral. Both the merits and demerits of panning were apparent in Werner Brandes's camerawork, at Dupont's direction, in *Piccadilly*. Several highly dramatic moments in this film lost their effect on the audience because the camera dawdled in its panning, in the very place where direct, quick cutting should have been used. It may be added that the technical accomplishment of the camerawork in this film was of a high standard, and it was regrettable that it should have been misused.

The movement of the camera as a whole, in approach to or in retreat from the material being taken, is usually known as a *rolling* or *travelling* shot, or simply as *tracking*. Actually, the camera is mounted on a trolley or a camera tricycle, which enables it to be moved forward or backward or in an arc, as desired. The tripod head mounted on the tricycle permits the camera to pan at the same time as it is moving across the studio floor; thus almost any form of movement in any direction is attainable.

Great care should be exercised by the director in the use of a tracking shot, for the movement is apt to make the audience conscious of the camera's presence, *which is absolutely undesirable*. The shot should always be seen on the screen with the camera in motion the whole time, and not, as is usual, with the camera first at rest and then in movement. This beginning (or ending) of movement immediately makes the spectator conscious of the camera. There were many instances of both good and bad travelling camerawork in *The Patriot*, where the audience was never quite sure if it was intended to be the camera (which was also Emil Jannings) moving through the palatial corridors of Paramount Palace, or whether it was just an onlooker who trailed after Jannings as he wandered about in a half-witted absent-mindedness, in order to show the audience the artistic reconstruction of Imperialist Russia (Hollywood version).

This problem inevitably raises the complicated question of camera personification. Is the camera (as Chaplin insists) to be used as an unconscious observer, a hidden eye, or is the camera to take on the viewpoint of a character in the theme? When the camera moves across the room and ends in a close-up of a picture on the wall, is the audience to understand that it has itself moved across the room and is looking at the picture; or that the camera is personifying one of the characters going across the room; or yet again, that the camera may have followed an actor across the room, looking over his shoulder? This is a problem on which each director has (or should have) his own or somebody else's theory. Actually, it can only be settled by the dramatic content of the scene once more. Camera personification is to be used in certain shots where the dramatic content (according to the director) demands its use without the risk of the audience becoming camera-conscious. It is justified, for example, where the screen is showing the thoughts of a character in order to explain his actions. In most cases, however, it is preferable to adopt the unseen eye theory, and therefore assume that the camera is able to see anything anywhere without hindrance.[1]

(c) *The Pictorial Composition of Visual Images*

In considering the problem of the pictorial composition of visual images seen on the screen, it should be remembered that a scene is only photographic in its reproduction. That is to say, a certain arrangement and composition is necessary before an object or group of objects or persons, as the case may be, can be photographed. This arrangement (which is in the hands of the director and *not* in those of the ' art-director,' as is sometimes believed) can only take place in the studio or on location, when the material is capable of being actually composed. It can, however, and should be indicated by the draughtsmanship in the shooting-script. In cases where real material of landscapes is used, it is the task of the director to compose much in the same way as does a painter. (It is as well to recall, in this respect, the creation of filmic space made possible by constructive editing.) Although the principles of linear design that are generally accepted in regard to static composition in paintings and drawings do not strictly apply to the cinema (where the material is in almost constant motion),

[1] Robert Montgomery's much-publicised *Lady in the Lake* (1947) provided a valuable object lesson in how not to use camera personification.

they are nevertheless invaluable in filmic composition for presenting forms, not only in a pleasant manner to the eye, but for purposes of insinuation and suggestion in the expression of dramatic content.

When a film is projected in a cinema, the visual image on the screen represents a rectangular frame which the camera has isolated from all other possible points of view. Objects and persons within the limits of this picture frame (formed by the four sides of the screen) should be composed harmoniously so that balance and design are maintained. Irrelevant matter is to be discarded and the remaining important material is to be arranged with regard to its significance, as demanded by the dramatic content of the shot. As with a static composition, little things should be employed to lead the eye of the spectator to big things. Attention should be drawn to the significant object, or person, on the screen by the linear design of the composition, as well as by contrast in lighting. This is of particular importance in the conception and designing of studio settings, for the leading lines of a set should emphasise and support the dramatic content of the action taking place in it. *The Cabinet of Doctor Caligari* was an object-lesson of this co-operation between the film designer and the director.

Relation between the pictorial composition of visual images and the dramatic content that the scene carries must in all cases be insisted upon. There is a definite connection between the form of the composition and the dramatic content of the shot. Pictorial composition in the film connotes the maintenance of a balanced composition that is both in constant motion and in constant connection with the ever-changing dramatic content of the action. Just as continuity has to be sustained in the continuity of shots and sequences, so has the balance of pictorial composition to remain in constant harmony.

Paradoxically enough, although it should be the aim for the visual image to be beautiful in design, nevertheless that design should never be allowed to dominate the dramatic content of the image. It should always be remembered that a single visual image is but one of the great number which compose the whole filmic pattern; and that effect is not gained by *one* shot but by a *combination* of shots. A visual image is present on the screen primarily to express a meaning; the quality of that expression is aided by the design of the pictorial composition of the image. It will be recalled that the damning fault of *La Passion de Jeanne d'Arc* was, strangely enough, the beauty of the visual images, which were so pleasing in themselves that they were detrimental to the expression of the theme. In other words, I remember *La Passion de Jeanne d'Arc* as a series of very beautiful compositions, but not as a film.

When one separate visual image is seen on the screen there is usually movement present in some form, either of one or several objects or persons, taking place at the same time or in rotation. There are cases, however, when a series of wholly static compositions succeed one another in order to build up a solid atmospheric or psychological effect.[1] In these instances, the common rules of two-dimensional linear design govern the visual composition; whilst their order of appearance on the screen is a matter of assembling indicated by the desired mood.

The attention of the spectator is drawn to the meaning of the dramatic content of a shot principally by movement and contrast of light and shade. It is common knowledge that a moving object is apprehended by the eye very much quicker than a stationary one. In a shot of complete rest, a single small movement immediately attracts the attention of the spectator. Interest is at once aroused in the mind as to *why* the movement is taking place, *what* is its direction and speed, and what *bearing* has it, or will it have, on the other objects in sight or whose presence is known? When we realise that the spectators are focussing

[1] Refer to section of this chapter dealing with constructive editing and cutting, and note examples cited in *The Living Corpse, Camille, Ten Days that Shook the World, New Babylon*, etc. A series of static landscapes is also a favourite method of opening a film, *e.g. Storm over Asia, Turksib*, and *A Cottage on Dartmoor*.

their whole attention on a rectangular space, placed in the most advantageous position and the only conspicuous thing in a darkened house, it is obvious that the slightest movement on the part of an object, or person, on the screen at once compels the audience to watch it, fascinated by curiosity as to what is about to happen.

The movement of the acting material that makes up pictorial composition has been likened to the movement of the ballet. The ballet demands simplified physical movement, both in balance and in contrast. A dancer's first knowledge is that of rhythm. Rhythmic movement of gestures is essential in the maintenance of the harmonious pictorial composition demanded by the film. The ballet has been described as the ' art of flowing movements '. A close analogy is to be found in the cinema.

Perhaps the simplest, and incidentally the most impressive, form of movement in pictorial composition is a single repetitive motion. Its limited and monotonous repetition has immediate fascination. The knowledge that the movement can stray no further than its given path holds the mind of the spectator. A typical instance of this can be found in the motion of a crankshaft; a single allotted path which is followed again and again. Confined movement of machinery has been used with great power in many films (*Berlin, Drifters,* and, of course, *La Marche des Machines*). The constricted course and rhythm of a machine is not only compelling to watch but symbolical, also, of infinite though controlled power.

American movies have become especially notorious for their ' movement '. They certainly contain a great amount of action of material itself, but there the claim ceases. Fairbanks is the individual hero of the action school, and his amazing acrobatics charge his films with a sense of speed. Movement is prevalent, too, in all films of chase and pursuit, such as the Westerns and the touch-and-run comedies. Movement of this kind is stimulating and invigorating, which no doubt accounts for the wide audience success of such types of films.

In movement of pictorial composition, the eye of the spectator follows the direction of objects, or persons, in the space bounded by the margins of the screen. Pleasure is obtained by watching the moving objects, or persons, rhythmically changing their positions in relation one to another. Simple examples of this abound in the various abstract films of geometrical shapes, such as Sandy's *Light and Shade*.[1]

When there are two or more moving units in a composition, then the relative movements of these units, as well as their individual motion, have to be considered, either in terms of contrast or symmetrical balance. Two converging streams of movement naturally emphasise the point of convergence. Symmetrical balance may be obtained by circular movement, such as a ring of prisoners walking slowly round a sentry, who is perhaps the centre of the circle, a fact which is stressed by his being placed on the apex of a triangular shadow, which stretches across the prison yard. This example was observed in *Mother;* a similar instance was found, but with lesser effect, in *Vaudeville*. A more complicated form of circular movement was seen in Murnau's *Four Devils,* where the camera itself was moving in an elliptical path following a horse round a circus ring.

Direct lines of movement across the screen are affected by the same principles of two dimensional design. The co-ordinated movements of the crowds in that remarkable film, *The Golem,* have often been cited in this respect. Seen at times through a window, the crowds moved along narrow streets in straight lines and intersected straight lines across the screen. The fact that their direction was restricted and indicated by the walls of the streets added emphasis to their destination and intent. Probably the finest examples of streaming movement on various planes removed from the spectator were to be found in *Battleship*

[1] The value of movement, both simple and complex, is always well seen in absolute films, hence one of the reasons why they should be closely studied by directors, and not dismissed, as is usually the case, as mere ' highbrow ' fripperies.

Potemkin. Eisenstein's use of crowd movement is almost too well known to be quoted again. It is sufficient to recall the procession along the quay, balanced by the movement of the small boat; the townspeople of Odessa when they came in their hundreds to file past the dead body of the sergeant Waluckchuck; the scene of the three streams of movement, the crowd passing across the bridge in the distance at the top of the screen, the crowd on the right coming down the steps diagonally, and the crowd in the road in the foreground; and many shots of simple one-directional movement repeated again and again on the steps sequence. One recalls, also, how Eisenstein achieved co-ordination between pictorial composition and overlapping of movement by cutting.[1] It is of passing interest to compare the unforgettable scene on the steps of Odessa in *Potemkin* with the dreary procession in *Martin Luther*.

Repetitive movements on more than one plane were well used in *The Cabinet of Doctor Caligari* to establish the mood of the fair scene. The units of movement were the two whirling roundabouts placed at the same angle but at different distances from the audience, who were introduced to the scene by a small vignette, the screen gradually lightening in a circular movement to reveal the whole. The isolated vignette of the moving roundabout, however, definitely suggested the nature of the scene, preparing the audience for the more important action that was to follow.

The film is capable of representing movement of material in the most beautiful and stirring manner in order to establish and enhance atmospheric drama. Choosing at random, I remember the wind-swept clouds and the quivering branches of the solitary tree outside the cottage where Kean lay dying, in Volkoff's film of that name. The storm scene in *The Student of Prague,* when Veidt as Baldwin raved into the night to meet his second self at every turn, was filled with the tortured bending of trees, symbolical of the anguish raging in the student's mind. Again, the swaying earheads of corn, the hair of the

[1] Cf. pp. 232, 390.

reapers blowing in the wind, the rhythmic movement of the scythes, and the excited rush to the village at the sound of the bell, suggested the power and movement of nature in *The Peasant Women of Riazan.*

There are plentiful instances, also, of mood being emphasised by contrasted movement in light and shade, the most celebrated being in *The Street.* The bourgeois lay on the sofa in the darkened, motionless room, fascinated by the flickering shadows of the passers-by. The use of light and shade in *Warning Shadows* is too classic to be recapitulated.[1]

In the composition of large, heavy masses on the screen, it is more difficult to maintain balance than in the handling of direct lines of movement. The motion of a large mass may be considered both as an individual action, indicated by the dramatic content, and as a movement which alters the pattern of light and shade of the whole screen area. These two results of one action must be allowed for in the maintenance of the balance of the whole. The movement of a heavy mass in one portion of the screen immediately produces an unbalanced effect, which must be checked by a reciprocal movement of another mass or masses in other parts of the screen composition. Elementary examples of this are again to be found in experimental pattern films, such as those of the late Viking Eggeling. Movement of small masses, particularly when aggravated by light, produces emotions of excitement and action; whereas corresponding slow movements of large masses, notably when in shadow, produce emotions of depression, despair, and sinister dejection. The effect of these movements is heightened and lessened, as the mood of the scene demands, by the speed of the movement. With this in mind, it is significant to recall the effect of Emil Jannings's broad back and Pudovkin's use of sparkling points of sunlight on running water.

Certain properties of the camera, such as the distortion

[1] Other recent examples worth mention were in *Zoo in Budapest* (1933), *The Grapes of Wrath* (1940), *Great Expectations* (1946) and *Odd Man Out* (1947).

created by angle and concentration, have direct bearing on pictorial composition.[1] These peculiarities of the instrument should be reckoned with in the arrangement of the material being photographed. It has been understood that camera angle is used to emphasise and reveal dramatic content. There is, moreover, a relationship between the choice of angle and the arrangement of the pictorial composition, both of which are governed by the dramatic content of the shot. For example, the opening shot of the film *Blackmail* was a close-up, taken directly in elevation, of the hub of a revolving disc-wheel. Circular motion covered the whole screen area. There was little effect of movement. (People have complained since that they thought it was a gramophone disc.) Now this shot was intended to convey the feeling of speed, of the flying squad with which so much of the narrative of the picture was concerned, and the film was begun on this high note presumably to emphasise this. But the shot was ineffectual, for the reason that first, there was no contrast to the circular motion of the wheel; and secondly, there was no suspicion of dramatic angle. The shot was taken flat on. Had the director pre-visualised the meaning of that shot and its supreme importance as the highspot beginning, he would surely have taken it from an angle slightly above the wheel, showing the fast-moving tyre on the road as well as the fleeting edge of the curbstone. Thereby, he would have presented two contrasted movements in the one composition, emphasised by the dramatic position of the camera, which would have immediately suggested speed and its dramatic meaning to the audience. Compare, for instance, Fritz Lang's tremendously effective opening shot in *The Spy* with the example cited above. The case of the *Blackmail* opening shot was yet another instance of an enthusiastic director getting hold of a good idea but, in his enthusiasm failing to extract the utmost possible effect from it. It may be argued that a small shot such as this does not make much difference one way or the other. But these separate shots go to make up the whole, and in this

[1] *Vide, Citizen Kane's* photography by Gregg Toland (1941).

particular case, the shot in question was the keynote to the drama of the important opening sequence. It was imperative for it to have been as effective as possible. It is in these small matters that the work of the greater directors, such as Pabst or Pudovkin, is flawless. Instinctively, they select the most expressive and the most vividly dramatic angle. Once more, it is a question of the wide difference that lies between genuine artistry and slick virtuosity.

When considering the mobility of the camera, we have found that pictorial composition on the screen changed in relation to the movement of the instrument, and further that the camera's movement was governed by the material being photographed. Obviously, when the camera travels up to an object, the latter increases in size, altering thereby the pictorial composition. The reverse effect takes place when the camera is in retreat. An effect of growth and diminution in size is thus obtained, the whole screen composition altering in proportion.

Conclusion may be made, therefore, that as with other cinematic resources, pictorial composition is controlled by the dramatic content of the shot which it expresses. It will be evident, also, that dramatic effect during this second form of montage (*i.e.* the assemblage of the material to be photographed) is obtained by the use of movement in pictorial composition and camera position, as well as by camera angle and the consideration of film psychology.

A further point which may be raised in connection with the pictorial composition of succeeding visual images on the screen is the unity of light throughout the length of a film. Degrees of light values naturally differ with the nature of the scene but the quality of light should remain of equal intensity throughout a sequence, unless a change is dramatically indicated, such as by the switching off of an electric light or the fading rays of the sun. It is common to find that light values differ from shot to shot, which does much to impair the desired effect of emotional completeness. This is sometimes due to the practice of inserting lengths of news-reel for atmospheric effect or for crowd scenes, as well as for purposes of cross-reference by cutting (*vide, A Cottage on Dartmoor* and *High Treason*). This practice seriously interferes with the uniform intensity of light, which should be present equally in a long shot and a close-up during the same sequence. Powerful emotional effects, on the other hand, can be achieved by the subtle interplay of light values, by increasing and decreasing the intensity in accordance with the dramatic content. (*Thérèse Raquin, New Babylon, The General Line,* and *En Rade* were good examples of this nicety of light expression.)

*

Indirectly concerned with pictorial composition is the movement of the screen itself, a function that is as yet only in an experimental stage. From results already obtained, the *magnascope* may be reckoned of greater importance than a mere good advertising trick out of the bottomless box of the American showman. It has been called ' a form of close-up ', but although this is hardly correct, it is certainly a legitimate form of emphasis. To date, the magnascope has been used in London on four occasions : for the elephant stampede in *Chang* and for the sailing vessels in *Old Ironsides,* both at the Plaza Theatre during 1927; for the exciting aeroplane sequence in *Wings* and for the final desert fight in *The Four Feathers* at the Carlton Theatre in 1928 and 1929, respectively. It may be added that these were all Paramount films shown at Paramount theatres, and that the process exhibited was invented by Glen Allvine of the Famous-Players-Lasky Company. The idea consisted of a supplementary lens on the projector which magnified the scene from the ordinary screen area on to an additional enlarged screen, so that the images almost appeared to emerge from the screen on to the audience. Apart from its unquestioned aid to the dramatic high-spots of a film, the magnascope involves no fresh principles of pictorial composition, being merely an enlargement of the ordinary film frame. Its use, however, is severely limited, for the change from the ordinary to the larger screen necessitates a

93. THE ROAD TO LIFE, directed by NIKOLAI EKK. [Soviet, 1931]

94. CONGRESS DANCES, directed by ERIK CHARELL. CONRAD VEIDT. [German, 1931]

95. THE PUBLIC ENEMY, directed by William Wellman. EDDIE WOODS, JAMES CAGNEY. [American, 1931]

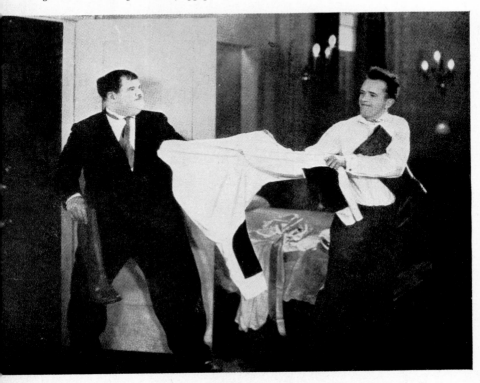

96. BE BIG, directed by HAL ROACH. LAUREL AND HARDY. [American, c. 1931]

complete re-adjustment of the eyes of the spectator; whilst the change back from the large screen to the small is a sharp anti-climax, requiring several minutes for the eyes to become accustomed to the different scale. From this it will be seen that the device becomes permissible only before an interval, or immediately before the ending of a film, in order to avoid the change. Another demerit of the magna-scope is that it causes the *frame* of the screen to become noticeable, which is undesirable, for it is the opening and closing movements of the screen margins which make the device possible. The fact of the screen altering its size during the progress of a film not only interrupts the con-centration of the audience, but makes them conscious of the screen itself, instead of the visual images upon it. The probable outcome of the magnascope will be the general adoption of larger screens in the majority of cinemas, for a larger screen area than that at present in use will un-doubtedly give an enhanced stereoscopic effect.

The triptych screen, which has been seen only at the London Tivoli for the presentation of Abel Gance's *Napoléon,* was not on that occasion particularly successful. The effect was too overwhelming for the receptive power of the audience and tended to confuse rather than to impress the mind. For this device, the film was projected in the normal way on to a central screen. When a high-spot was reached, two side screens flanking the centre one were brought into play, and two other films were projected in synchronisation with the main film. For example, one instance depicted Napoleon reviewing his armies. On the centre screen appeared a stream of soldiers on a large scale, whilst on the side screens were two further processions, the scene on the left being the same as that on the right, but reversed. The troops at first formed three separate scenes, but later they mingled, forming one great river of the *Grande Armée.* The effect was dramatic but confusing.

I understand that this multiple screen theory is being developed in New York, but I suggest that this ‘progress of the cinema’ is far from achieving the unity of purpose demanded by a film. For normal intents and purposes, the simple flat screen of customary proportions is all that is necessary. It would be more satisfactory if these enthusiasts spent their leisure in improving their knowledge of the film itself, rather than in evolving complicated methods of presentation. Mr. Harry Potamkin writes of a Compound Cinema, in which the rational centre screen is used for the projection of the main film, whilst slides or minor films are projected on to the walls and ceiling of the theatre to enhance the atmosphere of the main theme on the audience. The idea is admittedly novel, but it is doubtful if it tends to establish the film as a unity.

(d) Constructive Editing and Cutting

When analysing the final act of montage, which is the assembling of the various strips of film on which have been recorded photographically the incidents and material as indicated by the shooting-script, we can put aside all the resources of filmic representation that have so far been discussed. Camera angle, pictorial composition, movement of material and of camera, etc., have played their essential parts in the transference of the dramatic content on to strips of celluloid. It may be assumed that the content of the thematic narrative has been expressed to the fullest possible advantage by the resources of the film already utilised up to the time the picture leaves the studio floor, or the exterior location, as the case may be. There remains now the task of sorting out these strips of film and assembling them in an order of continuity of dramatic content. But it is essential to realise that a desired emotional effect cannot be gained by the mere indiscriminate assembling of bits of celluloid. The content that is photographically recorded on these strips must have been borne in mind by the director from the origin of the shooting-script. Thus far, this final act of assemblage has been kept in view throughout the whole procedure. Amongst the hundreds of lengths of film that wait to be assembled, there will be many meaningless bits that are useless in themselves, but each will play its part in the building of the whole. Frame by frame, shot by shot, sequence by sequence, the film as a unity will be constructed. This final relation, inter-relation, and juxtaposition of the varying lengths of film will produce cinematic effect on the audience, causing them to be roused in the most emotional degree.

It has been made clear that constructive editing is the process of arranging strips of film in an order that expresses the dramatic content of the story with the greatest responsiveness. The strength and mood of these reactions on the audience is affected by the methods of cutting, by variation in number of frames of each separate length of film and by the rhythm of material.

The elementary principles of editing are as follows. First, it should be the aim of the director never to use a shot on the screen more than once if it has been taken from the same angle of vision, unless he should desire to emphasise a particular viewpoint. The screen will thus be kept constantly fresh and interesting to the audience. To show a thing more than once from the same angle is to invite monotony. The means whereby this choice of angles is calculated are determined by the changing dramatic content of the action. (Reference may here be made to the earlier section of this chapter dealing with camera capabilities, in particular to the subject of camera angles.) Secondly, a shot should be held only long enough on the screen to be taken in by the audience during a medium tension of emotion. The spectator should only be allowed sufficient time to realise the significance of the image, which has been aided by the pictorial composition. Thirdly, short cutting (being the use of small lengths of film, usually close-ups, but not necessarily so) should be employed to create high and exciting emotions, by a succession of short flashes in rhythmic order on the screen. Fourthly, long cutting (being the antithesis of short cutting) should be used for obtaining sad and soothing effects, which can be deliberately intensified by the time-length of images on the screen. By varying combinations of these two extreme methods of cutting, together with the practice of cross-cutting by relation and contrast, almost any emotion of the human mind can be reached and made to react.

The power of editing in the hands of a capable director is unlimited. By a proper understanding of the method he can cause any audience to be sad, thrilled, pathetic, joyous, angry, sympathetic, etc., according to his will, and thus compel them to take interest in the content of the theme that he is expressing on the screen. It is the greatest resource of the cinema for stirring and holding an audience *en masse*. Its force is not, perhaps, generally appreciated. A notable instance was seen at the first presentation of Pudovkin's *The End of St. Petersburg* at the Film Society, London, on 3rd February, 1929. At one portion of the film, the action was worked to a crescendo by gradual short-cutting, with the title ' All power to the Soviets! ' at the peak of emotion. The audience was observed to start gradually stirring, then muttering, until eventually many persons rose to their feet, cheering and clapping. I do not believe that the word ' Soviets ' was of real importance, for had it been ' Royalists ' or ' Monarchists ' the effect would have been the same, due entirely to the emotions raised by the cutting. Much the same course of events took place among a working-class audience at the showing of Victor Turin's *Turksib,* at the Scala Theatre on 9th March 1930. The spectators in London were just as eager for the railway to be opened as were the peasants in Russia! This advanced process of editing and cutting, together with remarkable use of the other properties of the medium, renders Soviet films the most emotionally powerful in the world.

Pudovkin claims that every object, taken from a given viewpoint and reproduced on the screen in the form of a visual image, is a *dead* object, even though it may have movement, for this movement is that of material and not that of film. The object does not assume life until it is placed among other separate objects; until it is presented as being part of a synthesis of separate visual images. Every object brought upon the screen in the form of a visual image has not photographic but *cinematographic* essence given to it by editing. 'Editing is the creative force of filmic reality. Nature provides only the raw material.' (*Vide, Film Weekly,* 29th October 1928, translation by Ivor Montagu of the preface to Pudovkin's *Manual of Film Direction* and later published in *Pudovkin on Film Technique* [Gollancz, 1929].)

This, then, is the relation between the film and reality, An actor at his best is but raw material for his future composition in visual images when edited. He is only the clay with which the director works. A landscape is but a mere photograph until it assumes its place in the organisation of visual images. The extraordinary truth of this shatters at one blow the whole idea of the star-system. Where now is Clara Bow's 'It'? In brief, therefore, we are to understand that the film director works with actual material, creating out of it a filmic reality. He composes, it will be remembered, filmic time and filmic space out of real material. The true aim of the film director is not realism, as is generally but erroneously supposed, but a reality of his own construction.

Lev Kuleshov it will be recalled, logically maintained that in every art there must be, first, a material; and secondly, a method of composing that material arising out of the nature of the medium.[1] In the case of the film, we are now able to grasp fully the fact that the material is on the strips of film and the composing is the act of editing, which has been relegated in this present survey to the final act of montage.

In the assembling of the different strips of film, it has been seen that it is necessary to be able to manipulate the number of frames that make up each separate shot, for the combination of these varying lengths creates the vibrating rhythm by which the film as a unity achieves life and breath, slackening and tightening the attention of the audience.

In brief, editing resolves itself into the act of placing one

[1] *Vide,* pp. 105, 228, 229.

strip of film, bearing certain photographic images upon it, in front of or after another strip, recording either the same material seen from a different angle, or entirely fresh material. Two simple factors may be brought to bear on this relation between the two strips, each based upon the recognisable external characteristics of the pieces. First, film strips may be joined together according to a formulated scheme or metre, in harmony perhaps with the beats of synchronised music. Changing effects may be achieved by variations in the number of frames to a length, the balance of sequences (and consequently the whole film) being maintained by a repetition of the metre. The assembling may, therefore, be said to be a metric process of piece lengths, achieved by ' tape measurement '.

From this elementary metric method it is but a step to assembling according to the movement of the screen material (*i.e.* the movement of the players, objects, etc., recorded on the film strips). The assembling determined by the metric process may be strengthened by a rhythmic relation of material movement between the separate piece lengths. The movement contained in one shot may be continued into the next. Further, the predominant movement in a series of shots may be carried into the predominant movement in the succeeding series (*e.g.* the rhythmic movement of the soldiers descending the steps of Odessa in *Battleship Potemkin* merging into the rhythmic movement of the perambulator; the rhythm of the waving corn stalks in *The General Line* becoming submerged by the downward movement of the rain. Cf. also the bridge scene in *Ten Days that Shook the World*, page 232, and the cutting of *Jeanne Ney*, page 267).

Beyond such assembling of shots by rhythmic and metric relations, further factors may be applied to the juxtaposition of film strips. For example, in a given sequence of shots, as well as there being an increase (or decrease) in movement of screen material and a formulated scheme for assembling according to numbers of frames, there may also be increase (or decrease) in the intensity of light values (from light to dark, or *vice versa,* as the sequence unfolds), as well as increase (or decrease) in intellectual values (as in the gallery of gods in *Ten Days that Shook the World,* which were arranged in the order of a descending intellectual scale). Moreover, as Eisenstein has pointed out, there is no difference between the physical movement expressed by simple metric or rhythmic assembling in a sequence and the movement of the intellectual process within that sequence, save that one results in a physiological effect and the other a psychological effect on the audience.

Although each frame is one of a number, which in succession produce movement in a shot, it is possible also to use purely static shots to build up effects with cutting. A series of shots, each one static, achieves an emotional effect quite different in feeling from a succession of shots showing movement. For example, Eisenstein in *Ten Days that Shook the World* brought all the religions in the world to bear upon a certain point, simply by a succession of ' still ' shots of religious symbols, such as the Buddha, the Cross, and savage heathen fetishes. It was, so to speak, the director's comment on the action of the context, exemplary of ' intellectual cinematography '. Again, when establishing the environment of tradition and pompous imperial taste in art at the Winter Palace, in St. Petersburg, he used a series of static shots, taken from dramatic low-level angles, of cornices and capitals, column-shafts and chandeliers—a solemn comment on wasted magnificence. A sudden realisation of disgust was raised in the mind of the spectator at this luxury, so useless and so meaningless, by a simple, slow succession of silent, still, visual images. More recent examples of this method were seen in Kozintzev and Trauberg's *New Babylon.*

The effect of movement in cutting may be measured by contrast with a stationary object, just as dark is given value by light. This form of contrast may frequently be achieved by means of the process of cross-cutting from a moving object to a stationary one, and repeating the procedure. An admirable example may be found in a cavalry charge. In order to gain the greatest effect of this action on an audience, alternate close-ups are shown in rapid succession of the hooves of the horses in fast movement over the cobblestones, and of the static, bronze hooves of an equestrian statue. The alternate cross-cutting from swift action to static rigidity, when repeated, achieves remarkable dramatic intensity, far more powerful in every way than a conventional shot of the charge as usually employed, as for example in *Balaclava*. Many other examples of cross-cutting abound. In the night-club scene in *Crisis*, Pabst wished to arouse in the mind of the audience the emotions created by syncopation and jazz. He obtained this by taking a shot, with his camera travelling backwards, of a pair of exhibition dancers coming forward with typical rhythmic movements, cutting alternately from close-ups of their heads to close-ups of their feet. In this way he achieved a cinematic result impossible with a straight shot of the pair. During the opening sequence of *Berlin*, Ruttman wished to express the rhythm of an express train. He intercut short flashes of the wheels, of the telegraph wires and of the rails with one longer shot of the coupling between two of the coaches. Thereby he obtained an effect of 'three shorts and a long', as it were, causing the audience to visualise an emotion that they had experienced themselves in reality. Similar effects of cross-cutting to achieve rhythmic movement were found in the railway scenes of Room's *Bed and Sofa*, and in Dziga-Vertov's telegraph wire sequence in *The Eleventh Year*. Much of the secret of arousing these feelings in the audience lies in the subtlety with which emotions latent in their minds are awakened. Often it is not desired to stir fresh emotions but to create old ones by stressing the rhythm, which was probably unrecognised by the observer before it was seen on the screen.

By constructive editing it is possible to convey the dramatic content of an occurrence without even showing the actual happening. Pudovkin gives an instance of an explosion, which he used in *The End of St. Petersburg*. In order to render the *effect* of this explosion with absolute fidelity, he caused a charge of high explosive to be buried and had it detonated. The explosion was terrific, but filmically it was quite ineffective. So by means of editing, he built an explosion out of small bits of film, by taking separate shots of clouds of smoke and of a magnesium flare, welding them into a rhythmic pattern of light and dark. Into this series of images, he cut a shot of a river that he had taken some time before, which was appropriate owing to its tones of light and shade. The whole assembly when seen on the screen was vividly effective, but it had been achieved *without employing a shot of the real explosion*. In another instance, in *Mother,* he obtained effect by symbolic intercutting. The son was in prison. He received a note, passed to him surreptitiously, informing him that he was to be set free on the following day. The task was to show his joy filmically, and to make the audience participate in it. The mere photographing of the boy's face lighting up with joy would have been ineffectual and banal. Pudovkin showed, therefore, the nervous play of his hands and a big close-up of the lower half of his face, his lips faintly twisting into a smile. With these shots he cut in others of a brook, swollen with the rapid flow of spring, of the play of sunlight broken into points of light on the water, of birds splashing in the village pond, and finally, of a laughing child. By composing these into a whole, it was possible to give the emotions which the boy felt in prison when he knew that he was to escape. But it is, of course, to be realised that this constructive editing of material is primarily a matter of preconception in the film's script. The extension of the method is apparent and it will be appreciated how wide is the scope opened up by its potentialities.

An interesting point which arises in the rhythmic juxtaposition of film strips, is the overlapping of movement of the material from one shot into another. It is customary to find that when one visual image succeeds another on the screen, both showing an object moving in the same direction but each viewed from a different angle, the movement in the second shot begins where the movement in the first left off. But there may be an overlapping of movement, in that the *same* piece of action is in reality seen twice by the audience from different viewpoints. This is not by any means to be taken as an instance of careless cutting. On the contrary, it emphasises the movement of the pictorial composition and enhances the dramatic effect of that movement. Allusion has already been made to the fact that the line of soldiers in *Battleship Potemkin* descended over many steps more than once when seen on the screen. The same effect was experienced when the statue of the Czar fell to pieces and then came together again in *Ten Days that Shook the World,* and also in the famous scene of the raising of the bridge. It was seen again in the felling of the trees in Turin's *Turksib.* This practice of overlapping movement encourages and makes use of latent dramatic content in the mind of the spectator. It serves to weld the images into a firm whole by a process that can perhaps be described as dovetailing. Its neatness and precision are both comforting and stimulating. It adds, as it were, a sort of double-kick to the movement.[1]

In such pattern films as *La Marche des Machines* and *Skyscraper Symphony,* it is common to find an effect of balance built up by a series of succeeding shots, with the weight distributed diagonally on alternate sides of the screen in each image. For example, a shot is shown of a steam shovel on one side of the screen, followed by the same shot reversed so that the steam shovel is seen on the other side. This, in turn, is followed by a double exposure shot combining the two preceding shots, one on top of the other, so that the steam shovel appears on both sides of the screen simultaneously. The same has been done with shots taken of a building from below, the roof first cutting the screen diagonally from left to right and then from right to left. It is a matter of balanced design. The same method can equally well be applied to movement. A shot showing an

---

[1] There are numerous examples of this overlapped movement in the documentary film of *The Times* newspaper, *The Fourth Estate* (1939-40).

object moving across the screen from left to right may be succeeded by a shot showing the reverse action. This will reveal the close connection that exists between editing and the pictorial composition of the visual images. The use of dissolves and mixes in cutting in sympathy with the mood of the content has been considered earlier, and the reader is referred to the example taken from *The Living Corpse* cited on pages 355, 356.

It will have been observed from these brief remarks on the building of a unified film that every frame and every shot is of the utmost significance to the composition of the whole. It can be understood, therefore, how deep a resentment is felt by a director when many shots and even sequences are removed from his completed film in order, perhaps, to meet a censor's requirements, or to conform to an executive's conception of box-office. Theoretically the removal of one shot from a complete film throws out the unity of the balance, even as pieces of stamp-paper stuck over the nude parts of pictures in the National Gallery would destroy appreciation of them as whole compositions. The outcry in the Press at such an act of vandalism can well be imagined; but few realise to what an extent a film may be damaged by an official board or by a renter. It is not to be wondered that the only course left open to the director so affected is to disclaim his own work, a film on which he has perhaps spent months of care and toil.

(e) The Placing of Titles[1]

The literary value of *titles* or *sub-titles* (frequently mis-called ' captions ') is strictly a matter of scenario planning. It has been seen that a title is employed in a film to connect sequences in smooth continuity and also to introduce characters to the audience. When it is not mere super-fluity, the general use of titles is mostly due to an

---

[1] These remarks have been left in this revised version because in view of the developments in educational films, titling is still an important element in film technique.

insufficient employment of the resources of the medium Theoretically, the use of a title from a literary point of view is unwarranted if the full cinematic properties of the medium have been utilised by the director. That this is possible has been conclusively proved by such films as *The Last Laugh, Warning Shadows* and *New Year's Eve*. Titles are only really justified in the cultural and educational film for explanatory purposes.

A title should be visual as well as literary. Its place among the continuity of visual images must be decided by pictorial qualifications as well as by meaning. A well-titled film is one in which the titles harmonise with the visual images so perfectly that their presence *as titles* is not remarked. The length of a title must be considered in ratio to the speed of the scene in which it is inserted. Quick, exciting action needs short, succinct titles, at times simply a single word flashed at the audience. For this reason, the Soviet directors use split titles and repetitive wording. Slow, deliberate action, on the other hand demands slow, deliberate titles.

Titles may be used as a means of preparing the audience for a scene by suggesting in advance the dramatic content that is to be unfolded. A perfect example of this was quoted by Mr. Sergei Nalbandov (writing in *The Cinema,* 7th August 1929) from the film *Mother.* A title ' Waiting ' preceded a shot of a cavalry platoon, which was awaiting the coming of a procession towards a prison. The meaning of this title was bound up with the close-ups which succeeded it on the screen, of the hoof of a horse pawing the ground and a rider adjusting the buckle of his straps.

A title is often to be rendered more potent by splitting it into sections among a series of visual images. A title begins with a few words; it is cut to a series of visual images; the title continues; again it is cut to a series of relevant shots; the title finishes; it is succeeded by a further flow of images. Greater stress of meaning, of pictorial rather than of literary value, is gained by this division. A case in point was to be found in the introduction of the workers in the early part of *The End of St. Petersburg.*

Simple repetition of a title at spaced intervals is also found to be dramatically effective by its very rhythmic insistence. The same title may punctuate a film at given moments, driving home not the meaning of the title, but the meaning of the sequence and the whole meaning of the theme. This was used with much feeling with the title ' Mother ', in the film of that name, and was also a conspicuous part of the construction of *Ten Days that Shook the World, New Babylon,* and *Turksib.* This fact may be given support in that when I saw for the first time a copy of *Battleship Potemkin,* the titles were in Russian, a language incomprehensible to me, and yet their pictorial quality added greatly to the drama of the film.

An appreciation of the titling of Victor Turin's *Turksib* appeared in the Sunday *Observer,* for 23rd March 1930, and is worth citing : '. . . I have been waiting a great many years to see a film in which the titles would play a definite part in the visual and emotional progress of idea . . . In *Turksib* the titling is inseparable from the sweep of the film . . . I cannot describe the curious assault on the senses of those moving arrangements of letters, the cumulative effect of the final titles with their massive cadences. The words of *Turksib* are images; integral, triumphant, menacing. They are symbols of disaster and determination, fear and terrific jubilation. They have no longer sound or aural meaning—they are eye-images, mute, rapid, and wrought from the emotional fibre of the film itself.' This criticism is all the more interesting in that it comes from the pen of an advocate of the dialogue film.[1]

Other interesting experiments with the placing of titles have been attempted, notably by Pudovkin, who makes a practice of inserting spoken dialogue titles at the moment of

---

[1] The titles in the British version of *Turksib* were designed and inserted by John Grierson. This method of split-titling and the dynamic use of lettering was later explored at great length by the Empire Marketing Board Film Unit, in particular in its short ' poster ' films and 'trailers', and in *Contact* (1932).

utterance but not in conjunction with the visual image of their speaker.

It may be remarked that the design and word lay-out of a title should be as simple as possible. The quietest form of lettering should be used; the wording should be of the briefest and clearest nature; the ground should be dark, with the lettering a dull grey. The customary title is positively sparkling, with white scrawly lettering jumping about on an imitation leather background, which is the exact opposite to the requirements of a visual title. Various devices exist for the expansion of lettering, and may be used in accordance with the dramatic need of the title.

(f) *The Visual Addition of Colour and the Stereoscopic Screen*

The novelty of colour has always been a trick out of the showman's big box, and has been produced from time to time as an attractive selling addition to a super film. The advent of the dialogue and sound film is considered by some persons to make colour and stereoscopic effect a necessity. It depends entirely from what point of view we regard the cinema. The coloured stereoscopic film will give, when combined with sound and dialogue, a sense of realism. This, as has been explained earlier, is in the opposite direction to the proper aim of the film, which is reality. At the present moment, the marvellous decorative values that result from the use of panchromatic stock are more than sufficient for the needs of a director whose ambition is to convey dramatic content. It is necessary only to recall the beauty of *The General Line, Moana,* and *La Passion de Jeanne d'Arc* to realise this. But colour as an asset to showmanship is a different matter altogether.

In the history of colour films an episode in bright tones has often provided a novel attraction to jaded audiences, and its inclusion has generally been a concession to the taste of the masses. It will be remembered that Griffith used colour for certain of the sensational portions of *Way Down East* in 1920, but as Mr. Eric Elliott shrewdly observes, he had the discretion to restrict these coloured sensations to irrelevant pieces of action that were of little dramatic value, such as the dress parade (*vide, The Anatomy of Motion Picture Art*, Eric Elliott [Pool], 1928). In 1922, Stuart Blackton made *The Glorious Adventure* with the glorious Diana Cooper in colour, achieving, I believe, considerable commercial success. A year later, Metro-Goldwyn-Mayer's *Toll of the Sea* in Technicolor, with Anna May Wong and Kenneth Harlan, is said to have presented colour in almost acceptable tone values; and later still, Stuart Blackton repeated his success with *The Virgin Queen*. America produced *The Wanderer of the Wasteland* and France a gaudy *Cyrano de Bergerac*. After a time, it became fashionable to include a colour sequence, as often as not as the high-spot of the picture, and in this patchy vein are numbered parts of *Ben-Hur, Michael Strogoff, Casanova, The Fire Brigade, The Sea Beast, The Merry Widow*, and *The Wedding March*. Douglas Fairbanks's *The Black Pirate*, which was entirely in colour, was more successful, but it is understood that he will not repeat his experiment. Since that date, colour films have been produced plentifully, but I have seen none which has been satisfactory.

Although, up to the present, colours glow and pale at alternate moments (reds are revolutionary, yellows are dirty, greens are sickly, grass like that in fruiterers' shops, skies like aluminium, and flesh tints jaundiced), there is definite promise that the technical process will be soon perfected and generally on view. Assuming the possibility of perfect colour reproduction, however, it is hard to see where its use is of more value than the already existing beauties of panchromatic stock. It certainly holds out no advantages for the purpose of enhancing dramatic values. On the contrary, the most serious objection to be levelled against the colour film is its tendency to submerge the admirable photographic qualities of the visual image on the screen and hinder it from fulfilling its proper functions. The curious softness that will be produced by correct tone values all over the screen area will lack contrast and will immediately deaden dramatic effect, despite any resulting stereoscopy. Furthermore, it will be an intense strain to distinguish the presence and movement of separate objects in the coloured composition. Attempts will be made to imitate the drama contained in static paintings, which will fail miserably in the essentially dynamic medium of the film. There will be a sort of pre-Raphaelite dullness about the colour film which will deaden general appeal. The crispness of black and white, with intervening tones, is eminently desirable for the dramatic expression of filmic content. In the monochrome film of to-day, the natural tendency of the eyes of the spectator is to flow from the dark parts of the screen to the light. In the coloured screen composition, the eyes will wander aimlessly over the various forms without discrimination. Colour will tend to slacken the concentration of the mind of the audience. Spectators will easily be led away from the centre of interest by colour emotions, peculiar to each person. No two people see the same colour alike. The effect will be chaos instead of unity. Finally, it is impossible to believe that colour will improve, either dramatically or pictorially, films of the calibre of *The Cabinet of Doctor Caligari*, with its terms of contrast; *Siegfried*, with its wonderful striped and spotted decorations, its mists and black tree trunks; *La Passion de Jeanne d'Arc*, with its detailed textures and shimmering backgrounds; or *Thérèse Raquin*, with its subtle intensities of light values and sparkling points on the dress of Jean-Marie Laurent. Practically the whole dramatic and decorative effect of these works, perfect in their own class as they stand, would be lost by the use of colour, granting every possible perfection of the technical process.

The use of amber or blue-tinted stock, which produces a pale colour tint evenly over the whole screen area, is another matter for consideration. This method of tinting

97. "M", directed by Fritz Lang.   [German, 1932]

98. LA MATERNELLE, directed by Jean Benoit-Lévy and Marie Epstein.
Madeleine Renaud.   [French, 1932]

99. AMERICAN MADNESS, directed by FRANK CAPRA.   WALTER HUSTON.
[American, 1932]

100. SCARFACE, directed by HOWARD HAWKS.   GEORGE RAFT, PAUL MUNI.   [American, 1932]

the whole scene is justifield in that it enhances the dramatic effect, provided, that is, the tone is kept even with the volume of light throughout the whole sequence in which it is used. Both blue and amber tones are capable of helping the atmosphere of night and sunlight. All-over colour tints are also used to good advantage in certain silhouette films, where their inclusion has been a part of the decoration, in the same way that colour is part of a book decoration. The use here is not to attempt either realism or reality, but for the purpose of pure decoration.

In the past, apart from, say, the early Pathécolor films which were clumsily tinted all over with various hues, there have been some curious experiments with colouring certain portions of a visual image, such as a fiery cross or a blood-stained dagger. The idea seems crude in the extreme and wholly unnecessary.

With the general adoption of perfected colour films will also come the use of the stereoscopic screen, which purports to give visual images three, instead of two, dimensions. Beyond promising to present an illusion of solidity, without either advantage or disadvantage to the pictorial composition, it is difficult to see quite what asset, beyond novelty, the stereoscopic screen will possess. Its harm to the general conception of the film will, on the other hand, be great. Firstly, it must be realised that three dimensions will not enhance the pictorial value of the visual images except by suggesting an illusion of depth, which the screen already possesses in the movement of camera and players. Actual solidity of objects will tend to enhance realism. Secondly, the stereoscopic screen is of much larger dimensions than the customary screen,[1] and this will influence directors to adopt a more theatrical form of technique. There will be a tendency to hold the duration of a scene on the screen longer and longer, already the pre-eminent characteristic

[1] It is understood that the Spoor-Bergen process, which uses a film half an inch wider than the present standard one and three-quarter inch material, demands a screen forty feet wide, enabling a right illusion of depth to be given, and will eliminate the close-up. One more nail in the coffin of the real cinema!

of dialogue films. Gradually the powerful resources of cutting and editing will be forgotten and instead there will be long scenes lasting for minutes. There will be movement of players but there will be no movement of film, a characteristic that already marks the American film. The real functions of the resources of the film will no longer be possible with the colour-stereoscopic-and-dialogue film.

I fear that, year by year, realism will usurp reality in the cinema. Less and less imagination in the mind of the audience will be called for by this 'progress'. As Mr. Elliott observes, 'An imaginary depiction of a scene gives more reality in drama than does actual presentation.' The realistic effect aimed at by the colour-stereoscopic-and-dialogue film destroys the pictorial, symbolic, psychological, and imaginative properties of the film. Obviously, the stereoscopic screen is capable of presenting remarkable effects, but these will be catch-penny and sensational as distinct from the function of the film as a medium of dramatic expression. The new forms of the illegitimate cinema will, of course, be heavily financed by America, who includes these commercial opportunities in her vast scheme for capturing the entertainment market of the world. On these lines will the film retrace its steps, becoming a mechanical means for the theatrical presentation of spectacles superior commercially to the stage.

*

These, then, comprise the means of expression of the dramatic content of a theme by the visual form of the cinema. The natural properties of the film, arising out of its limits and delimits, have been considered at length. The projected addition of colour and stereoscopic effect have been investigated for any value they may bring to the cinema. It remains now to analyse the qualities of the dialogue and sound film, both as an integral part of the visual images on the screen and as an accompaniment in the form of the synchronisation of mechanically reproduced sound.

(II) THE VISUAL AND THE AUDIBLE CINEMA

In the preceding sections it has been seen that a film is built by the process of cine-organisation. This process has been divided simply into three forms of montage. To recapitulate briefly, the first act of montage is the assembling of the scenario by the preconception of the selected theme, as it would be expressed by the resources of the cinema. The second act of montage deals with these methods of expression during the actual process of taking the film photographically, as indicated by the shooting-script. The third and final act of montage consists in the assembling or mounting of the pieces of film bearing the photographic images, joining them in various lengths and positions in relation to one another in order to form a united whole. These three acts of montage are the means by which a story or theme is translated into a succession of visual images on the screen; which is capable of producing considerable emotional effect on any given audience of people in any part of the world.

Further, a supplementary section was added in order to consider the possible advantages that might be derived from two technical inventions, the colour film and the stereoscopic screen, with a view to adding them to the already existing forms of cinematic expression. For the purpose of argument, perfection was assumed in the mechanical process of these inventions, and it was found that neither contributed in any degree of value to the powers of expression already belonging to the film.

It is of urgent importance now to estimate the value, if any, of synchronised sound and dialogue reproduction as a means of expression of the dramatic content of a theme. Again, for all intents and purposes, perfection of the mechanical device is to be assumed.

General agreement has been reached by writers and

theorists on this exceptionally interesting new invention, that the sound-dialogue-visual film must be considered as a form of expression quite separate from the silent visual film with which these pages are principally concerned.[1]

It is necessary first to show, then, why this separation of the so-called two techniques is impossible; secondly, why the combination of the two techniques, when including direct-reproduced dialogue, is equally unfeasible; and thirdly, how, with the use of synchronised *sound* alone, it is possible to conceive a film as a unity, employing *sound* as a resource of the cinema, and incorporating it in the three forms of montage out of which a film is built.

(a) *The Sound-Dialogue-Visual Film*

It will be agreed that the aim of the sound-dialogue-visual film is the same as that of the silent visual film with musical accompaniment. To wit, to express cinematically the dramatic content of a theme or story so as to produce the greatest possible emotional effect on the mind of an audience.

The silent film seeks this effect by means of a succession of visual images on the screen. The sound-dialogue-visual film seeks the same end by means of a series of visual images on the screen *combined* with the reproduction of the voices and sounds of those images. In the first case, the appeal of the film lies absolutely in the vision of the images on the screen, soothed and emphasised by a musical accompaniment. In other words, the mind of the spectator is appealed to through the eye, the music being a subconscious supplement that by its apparent sympathy aids the smooth reception of the images. In the second, the appeal of the film is divided jointly between the sight of the images on the

---

[1] The number of articles, arguments, discussions, lectures, manifestos, conversaziones and debates on the merits and demerits of the talking and silent film has been positively amazing. The general public have had ballots; the Press have had columns; and the atmosphere in the studios themselves has been unprecedented. Probably no other invention for public entertainment has had so much free publicity as the 'talkie'

screen and the reproduction of the spoken dialogue and sound of those images. Screen and dialogue are seeking reception in the mind of the audience through the eye and ear.

Now it is an accepted and established fact that illumination of the mind by *visual* impression is practically instantaneous, whilst the *literary* meaning of speech requires an appreciable amount of time to produce its effect. The sensation caused in the mind by a visual image is not only sharper, but more apprehensible and more lasting than that caused by sound or speech. The eye is capable of associating ideas very much quicker and of creating a more definite impression in a given period of time than the ear. But when a visual image is seen on the screen and dialogue is synchronised to its action, although the visual image is received quicker than the dialogue, the latter commands more attention, for it is *literary* and non-imaginative. There results immediate confusion in the joint appeals of the *reality* of the visual image and the *realism* of the dialogue. Continual adjustment and readjustment of the senses occurs, which is an inconceivable state of mind for the sympathetic reception of the dramatic emotions of a film as a unity. Dialogue and the visual image cannot thus be divided in their appeals if dramatic effect is to be achieved. They can only be considered as a unity.

But it has been decided that the most dramatic possible method of telling a story is by a succession of pictures. No power of speech is comparable with the descriptive value of photographs. The attempted combination of speech and pictures is the direct opposition of two separate mediums, which appeal in two utterly different ways. If the two are wedded, one must be subordinated to the other, and at once division of appeal will occur. For this reason a silent visual film is capable of achieving a more dramatic, lasting, and powerful effect on an audience by its singleness of appeal than a dialogue film, in which the visual image is, at its best, a photograph of the voice. *Blackmail,* one of the so-called good dialogue films, will be completely forgotten

405

in a few months by those who have seen it. *Battleship Potemkin,* seen four years ago, is as vivid in the mind now as it was then. Immediately a voice begins to speak in a cinema, the sound apparatus takes precedence over the camera, thereby doing violence to natural instincts.

A theory, not without considerable interest, has been advanced that any compound which relies on the joint appeal of the two senses of sight and sound must utilise to the full the powers of its component methods. The balance between sound and sight will vary with the power of each to interpret the progressive development of the dramatic content of the theme. The synchronised film is to vary between sight accompanied by sound or silence, and sound accompanied by sight.[1] But this again is directly opposed to the interests of the film as a unity. If any sort of consistent dramatic effect is to be made on an audience, division of appeal between sound and sight is simply courting disaster. It has been evidenced over and over again that a film *must* be a single united whole in order to achieve strong emotional effect, and the moment that both eye and ear are brought into conflict the success is negatived.

Of the resources of the cinema that are used during the process of cine-organisation and out of which a film is built, it has been clearly seen that the final act of montage (the assembling or editing) is the dominant factor of the construction. For the further progress of the film, therefore, the only factors that need be taken into consideration are those capable of emphasising the cinematic result produced by the assembling. With the advent of the possibility of utilising synchronised dialogue and sound, it is necessary to consider how these new values affect the assembling.

It will have been understood that the final act of montage attains its desired effect by the conjoining of pieces of film into a whole. That is, no single piece of film is of value without its surrounding context. Now the addition of sound and dialogue to the visual image on the

[1] Mr. Vernon J. Clancey, writing in *The Cinema,* 4th September, 1929.

screen will tend to emphasise its isolated significance by reason of the fact that, as the sound and dialogue take longer to apprehend than the visual image, the duration of time that the shot is held on the screen will be determined by the sound and dialogue *instead of by the assembling*. Dialogue, by very reason of its realism, represents real time and *not the filmic time* of the visual image. Obviously this is in direct opposition once more to all the dominant factors that have been proved to achieve emotional effect by visual images.

At once it will be observed that synchronised sound and dialogue impose severe restrictions on the process of film construction, whereas before there was none. Moreover, it is quite impossible to entertain the prospect of a film in which visual images play a part without their being organised by creative montage. Added to this, dialogue imposes such restrictions on the director that all forms of cutting and cross-cutting become impossible. In fact, as has been realised by ' Mercurius ' in the *Architectural Review* (June 1929): ' The significance of symbolism and (visual) imagery, the stimulating and sedative effect of short and long cutting, the interplay of the personal and the inanimate, the contrast between the general and the particular; in short, practically all the attributions of the silent film which make the reality of cinematic art are forced into subjection by the illusion of synchronised speech.'

Again it is found that the reproduction of dialogue demands almost stationary action in its accompanying visual image, which prevents freedom in the development of the action during any sequence. Thus action has to progress step by step, destroying, as it jerks forward, both rhythmic continuity and harmony.[1] It is no longer a film. It has returned to the early photo-play of theatrical tradition. Moreover, it is to this state of retrogression that the stereoscopic screen and colour film are forcing the cinema.

There can only be one legitimate use for the dialogue

---

[1] Heart-rending evidence of this was clearly instanced in what must be one of the worst films ever produced, *The American Prisoner*.

film and that is the topical newsreel. Here the appeal to the mind is quite different, for there is no aim at dramatic effect in news-speeches. They are simply a record in which the interest lies more in the speech than in the visual image. They are not constructed films seeking to achieve the dramatic effect of a story. They are an elementary form of the cinema ' without joy ', and, considered as such, are only of casual and historic interest.

It may be concluded that a film in which the speech and sound effects are perfectly synchronised and coincide with their visual images on the screen is absolutely contrary to the aim of the cinema. It is a degenerate and misguided attempt to destroy the real use of the film and cannot be accepted as coming within the true boundaries of the cinema. Not only are dialogue films wasting the time of intelligent directors, but they are harmful and detrimental to the culture of the public. The sole aim of their producers is financial gain, and for this reason they are to be resented. Any individual criticism that may be made of them may be considered as having no connection with the natural course of the film. This, as will be seen, lies in the plastic moulding of sound and visual images.

*

(b) The Sound and Visual Cinema

The mechanical reproduction of sound, considered apart from the audible properties of speech, is an added resource to the already existing factors of filmic representation. Sound is to be included among these factors, having its place in all three acts of montage, and assuming final position as the basis of the musical score which accompanies the film.[1]

Generally speaking, a musical accompaniment to a film is considered desirable and has been customary through the years. It is essential, however, for the musical score to be

[1] Some indication of what will be possible is apparent from Arthur Honegger's musical composition, *Pacific 231*.

ıction of the film, and not simply an
lar pieces suited to the theme by the
ı in a cinema-house. Certain attempts
ng the last few years to meet this
_pecially composed score, notable instances
being Edmund Meisel's music for *Berlin, Ten Days that
Shook the World,* and *Potemkin,* and that by Darius Milhaud for l'Herbier's *L'Inhumaine.* Meisel has also written
a score for mechanical reproduction, *The Crimson Circle,*
which was a moderately successful experiment. The
obvious difficulties of circulating music for orchestras and
the varying quality of the latter have rendered these
attempts limited, except in the cases of the theme song,
which was considered a part of the popular appeal of a
movie and has been exploited widely by American firms.
The mechanical reproduction of the sound film, however,
admirably fulfils this desire for a specially composed score,
and on this count alone is to be welcomed as a definite step
forward in the advance of the film. Assuming the
perfection of mechanical reproduction, the synchronised
score is better suited in every way to the presentation of
a film than the orchestral accompaniment of the past.

Sound, then, has to be considered as a means of dramatic
expression of the content of the theme, in conjunction with
the succession of visual images on the screen. It must be
realised, however, that in the case of the sound film, the
combination lies between sound and sight, and not, as in
the dialogue film, between speech and sight. The differences
are apparent. Sound has not to be understood *literally*
as has dialogue and does not interfere with the visual
appeal of the screen. On the other hand, it inclines, if
used rightly, to emphasise and strengthen the meaning of
the visual image. It is essential to realise the importance
of this difference between the sound of objects and the
sound of speech, for therein lies the essence of the advance
or the retardment of the cinema. It is to be clearly understood, also, that the question of filmic time and actual time,
so damaging in the dialogue film, does not enter into the

matter of the sound film. Sound is the result of the action seen in the visual image, which is not lengthened or altered in any way to suit the sound, as must be the case with reproduced dialogue.

Thus, although built into the construction of the film, sound does not interfere with the visual reception of the images. There are now *sound images* as well as visual images, each of which will express the *same* dramatic content in harmony, or in contrast, one with another. Sound images that are recorded during the taking of the visual images will be an integral part of the composed musical score, if they have any significance as regards the visual image. Both sound and visual images build up the same effect. They are united in their appeal.

The wealth and richness of sound material available for dramatic emphasis is almost unlimited. The sounds of the world are to be combined with the sights of the world. Already Pudovkin has spoken of the whisper of a man, the cry of a child, the roar of an explosion. ' It will be possible to combine the fury of a man with the roar of a lion.' There is the sigh of a multitude to be heard in contrast to the dropping of a pin. The sound of the wind and the sound of the sea. The sound of rain, leaves, animals, and birds; of trains, cars, machines, and ships. These are to be woven into a unity in counter-point with their visual images, but never in direct conjunction with them. Even as the camera's power of distortion is used for dramatic emphasis, so will the distortion of sound be used. In the same way as an effect is built out of pieces of film by the act of montage, so will little portions of sound be built up into new and strange noises. The process of short cutting in visual images will be paralleled in the mixing of sounds. Even as visual images mix and dissolve one into another so will sound images mix and dissolve, according to the nature of the scene and as indicated by the scenario montage. Similarly, in the same manner that overlapping of movement is used in editing for strengthening and deepening effect, so will sound images be overlapped with both melodic and discordant effect, as the mood of the dramatic content of the scene demands.

Contrast of sound will be used in the form of the relationship of sound volumes. It will not be possible, except in rare cases, to cut direct from one sound to another as with the visual image, unless there is a background of music to soften the contrast. For instance, it will be possible to cut from the loud, angry sounds of a turbulent crowd to the sound of the crowd when hushed, and to strengthen that contrast not by the silence of the crowd, but by the shuffling of one man's foot.

In order that the powers of editing and cutting may be used with absolute freedom, the scenario-organisation must be arranged so that the sound images may be synchronised, if desired, after the taking of the incident. The sound images are to be fitted to the visual images in the final act of assembling. Both are controlled by the one aim. This indicates that it is essential for the sound images to be included with the visual images in the preconceived shooting-script.

Only in this way can synchronised sound images be wedded to the continuity of visual images on the screen in such a manner that both go to build a film as a unity with a singleness of mind and a centralisation of purpose. Thus will it be possible to construct a film as a plastic composition, capable of achieving unprecedented emotional effect on any given audience. By cine-organisation of the three forms of montage; by use of the true resources of the cinema which have arisen out of its nature; by preconception of the result and the power of being able to achieve that desired result by means of the film's capabilities of dramatic expression; by these means will a film be made.

*

In retrospect, it has taken roughly twenty-five years (1900-25) to discover the fundamental basis of film creation in the work of Kuleshov and the Soviet directors. During this time, the film has developed attributes and properties peculiar to itself; it has become completely alienated from the hampering traditions of the theatre; and it has succeeded in establishing itself as an independent form of expression utterly representative of the spirit of the twentieth century. From 1925, there have been realised practical examples based on the filmic theories of Kuleshov and his fellow-workers, resulting in the most momentous achievements of the cinema. And now in 1930, the film has returned to its original ideas; has become in still closer relation to theatre; and aims once more at realism and photographic representation. The advent of the sound and dialogue film marks the opening of the second cycle in the history of the cinema. Discoveries that have taken twenty-five years to evolve are being thrown aside in the interests of showmanship and commercialism; magnificently the film neglects its proper qualities and returns to the confines of the theatre. But just as in the primitive days the film developed despite the misconception of producers and directors, so am I confident that the offending dialogue will pass as soon as its showmanship possibilities become exhausted, and the way will be left open for the great sound and visual cinema of the future.

PART THREE
THE FILM SINCE THEN

by
Richard Griffith

INTRODUCTION

When *The Film Till Now* was being written in 1929, the motion picture was in crisis. In the short space of a year the silent film had disappeared, to be replaced in the theatres and in the hearts of most audiences by films featuring synchronised dialogue and music. It is hard to realise to-day the emotional impact of this revolution. Few people can remember more than dimly what it was like to see silent films at the time of their production[1] and majority opinion, now as then, assumes that since the invention of the talkies represented mechanical progress it automatically meant aesthetic improvement. But to the film enthusiasts who were the first passionate readers of this book, the sound upheaval came as very death.

Whatever improvements it might have developed if it had survived a few years longer, the silent film at its best had by 1928 attained singular completeness as a human experience. To walk into a darkened theatre, to focus upon a bright rectangle of moving light, to listen somewhat below the level of consciousness to music which was no longer good or bad in itself but merely in relation to what was on the screen, and above all to watch, in a kind of charmed, hypnotic trance a pattern of images which appeared and disappeared as capriciously as those pictures which involuntarily present themselves to the mind as it is dropping off to sleep—but which, also like those of the mind, gradually mount to a meaning of their own—this was an experience complete and unique, radically unlike that provided by the older arts or by the other new media of mass communication. It bade fair to become the characteristic art-experience of our time.

This new experience had by the end of the silent film era acquired an intense and devoted cult of intellectual

[1] And not, as is now possible, in revivals charged as they inevitably are with personal reminiscence and nostalgia.

adherents, bent on analysing and rationalising a pleasure which for the movie millions largely operated on the level of the subconscious. Vachel Lindsay in America, Guillaume Appollinaire in France, were pioneers in discovering aesthetic virtues in the primitive films of the early century, and after the first World War the intellectual cult of the cinema sprang up simultaneously in many countries. The aspirations of its adherents took many forms. In Germany and America, many of them took the direct route of finding what movie jobs they could, gradually learning their trade in the industries of their countries. Some, in France, insisted on making films as they felt they should be made; the *avant-garde* of the twenties. Others speedily discovered that film-making is the most expensive form of creation, and their activities were mostly confined to theoretical discussion and analysis of the isolated examples of film art which sporadically issued from the commercial studios.

These were the *cinéastes*. Like all enthusiasts, they gradually sought each other out, formed societies, engaged in international correspondence, and sought to influence majority opinion on behalf of their standards and ideals. Their leadership came mainly from Britain which, though it had produced few films and no good ones, seems to have been a fertile field for the ideal of cinema perfectionism. It crystallised partly around an institution, the London Film Society,[1] and partly around a highbrow magazine, *Close Up*.[2] 'The Film Society', as it was known throughout the world, made it possible for the *cinéastes* in Britain to see esoteric films which found no commercial market, or foreign films of a political tinge which British censorship found repugnant. In its choice of programmes it sought to confound the philistines by purifying the film of all borrowed elements and isolating what was unique to the new medium.

---

[1] Formed in 1925 and held its first performance on 25 October at the New Gallery Kinema, London. Many films imported into Britain by the Society were later given a commercial release. The last and 108th performance of the Society was given on 23 April, 1939.

[2] First published, July, 1927; last published, September, 1933.

101. I AM A FUGITIVE FROM A CHAIN GANG, directed by MERVYN LE ROY. PAUL MUNI. [American, 1932]

102. WILD BOYS OF THE ROAD, directed by WILLIAM WELLMAN. [American, 1933]

103. **THE PRIVATE LIFE OF HENRY VIII**, directed by ALEXANDER KORDA. CHARLES LAUGHTON. [British, 1933]

104. **SHE DONE HIM WRONG**, directed by LOWELL SHERMAN. MAE WEST, RAFAELA OTTIANO. [American, 1933]

Close Up was equally purist, but was concerned with the film in society as well as the film *per se*. As edited by Kenneth Macpherson and Winifred Bryher from Switzerland it represented the views of advanced young people throughout the world who were preoccupied with the possibilities of the machine-age as they conceived it. In this mutely vivid art, comprehensible in every language and to nearly every culture, even very primitive ones, the cinema enthusiasts believed they had found a form which could not only meet the highest aesthetic standards, but also, in its intimate appeal to all peoples, could become a universal language.

In retrospect, the *cinéastes* seem to have wanted at one and the same time to sophisticate the film and to exploit its mass-appeal. Yet there was much evidence at hand to support their hopes. Films of simple beauty and elemental emotion had enchanted the highbrows; films of considerable intellectual complexity had been comprehended by the masses and were not without influence on the course of public affairs. The more advanced *cinéastes* believed that the barriers to popular understanding of works of art were mostly verbal, that this art which dealt entirely in imagery, whose form corresponded so strikingly to the processes of the mind itself, could carry almost any intellectual burden. After the success of the great Russian films, ideologically complex but reaching illiterate peasants with enormous force and lucidity, it seemed that they must be right.

The advent of sound brought all these hopes and speculations to a dead stop. The film, which had ranged so far and spoken so eloquently to people everywhere, was suddenly battened down inside the sound stages and behind the language barrier. What Lillian Gish had called ' a species of emotional and . . . informational Esperanto ',[1] had given place to a new Babel. Worse, the very basis of film art had been destroyed. Substituted for it was the derived art of the stage. The first sound films were quite literally

[1] Lillian Gish. *A Universal Language*, Encyclopaedia Britannica, 1929 ed.

photographed theatre. And, as none other than Thomas Mann had pointed out, one of the most important discoveries that had been made about the film was that, in spite of superficial resemblances, it had less in common with the drama than with most of the other traditional arts. With affinities to the ballet and to formal music, films of the silent days most closely approached that kind of poetry which is epic in style and narrative in form. As Mann says, ' They are living shadows. They speak not, they are not, they merely *were*—and were precisely as you see them. And that is narrative.' The tense of the drama is always present.[1] Films, even at their most intimate and intensely experienced, have a quality of retrospect. Moreover, the techniques of the two media, however similar-seeming, are fundamentally incompatible because one is properly dominated by the ear, the other by the eye. Shaw's statement about stage acting, ' Gesture falls on the beat of the line ', summed up two thousand years of theatrical experience. When stage plays were first made into sound films, his dictum was applied to all the movements of the actors. Accordingly, all the editing and camera devices which comprise the instrumentality of the film were accommodated to the sense and rhythm of each line of dialogue. The resulting films were without form of their own, neither did they reproduce the feeling of the theatre. They seemed more like the mummies of plays, mounted for exhibition in a museum.

That this form of taxidermy should permanently be substituted for the art of the silent film was to the *cinéastes* unthinkable. They decided that this was merely a phase which would pass as soon as sound had exhaused its novelty, and blamed ' Hollywood ' for exploiting this perversion of the medium.[2] When at last it was clear that the silent film had been permanently replaced, the bewilderment

---

[1] Except where the theatre has been influenced by the film, e.g. *On Trial, Lady in the Dark*, etc.

[2] Ignoring the fact that the motion picture industry itself had accepted sound only with the greatest reluctance.

and consternation of the *cinéastes* was complete. Some bade farewell to the screen, considering the art of the film 'proper' to belong to history, like the secret of manufacturing Etruscan ware. Others sought to accommodate themselves in some way to sound without compromising their original stand on first principles. The conclusions arrived at by the majority are well represented in the closing pages of Part Two of *The Film Till Now*.

As early as 1928, Eisenstein and Pudovkin had actually provided a way out. Like a few other eminent directors revered of the intellectuals (Lubitsch, for example), they hailed the invention of sound at the very time that their disciples were bewailing it. In a manifesto published throughout the English-speaking world as well as in Russia, the deans of Soviet cinematography made clear that they considered sound an important and exciting extension of the medium, and that they regarded the early photographed plays as transient misuse of the new dimension. In view of the exhilarating possibilities their manifesto opened up and of the fact that that important film *Hallelujah!* (1929), by King Vidor, had in the first year of the talkies miraculously accommodated dialogue to the classic structure of the silent film,[1] it may seem difficult to understand now why *The Film Till Now* ends on so uncertain and negative a note. The pages (403-12) on the future of the audio-visual cinema have a perfunctory air; their confident prognostications barely conceal a sense of loss, a nostalgia for that which had been and never would be again. For Paul Rotha, and the devoted film disciples whose spokesman he often was, were beginning to perceive that something else had come to an end besides the silent film.

Like the French film *La Passion de Jeanne d'Arc* (1928) which, as Iris Barry points out, both characterised and marked the close of silent film experiments in Europe, *The*

---

[1] Rotha's indifferent estimate of *Hallelujah!* may derive from the fact that he was comparing it with the great silent films which immediately preceded it. When seen to-day in relation to current films, it seems a matchless achievement, cf. pp. 147, 192, 193.

Film Till Now epitomised and signalled the end of the first era of thinking about the motion picture. The *cinéastes* of the twenties had regarded the art of the film in the manner of classical criticism. They tried to analyse each great film as though it were entirely the product of individuals constructing their works on the basis of fundamental principles. Each work was judged for the most part on its conformity to those principles, and was treated as if it existed in a socio-economic vacuum without allegiance to anything but aesthetics. The audience for these films was regarded as a passive factor, accepting or rejecting the works put before it according to its degree of taste and education. The enormous popularity of the cinema was thought to depend not upon content or style, but purely upon the intrinsic powers of the medium itself; it was believed that given full use of those powers any theme, however esoteric, could be made exciting to the mass public.[1] The extent to which this argument from the powers of the medium is true is now obvious to any one who has thoughtfully seen a motion picture. What is equally true but not obvious to the intellectuals then (and to many of them not even now) is that the film's popularity derives principally from the fact that it is in a profound sense a *popular* creation. Not only commercial trivia but also great masterpieces are created of, by and for ' the people ' in much the same sense that medieval ballads were a creation of ' the people '.[2] This is as true of Eisenstein and Pudovkin as of Chaplin and Disney. Had it been otherwise, these great film creators might never have come into their greatness. They grew and prospered because they had the common touch. Other minds and other talents, equally keen in their instinct for the medium, fell out of the race or descended to hackwork

[1] In his second book *Celluloid*, which holds to the principles of *The Film Till Now*, Rotha continues this theme : he seems to urge a sort of conspiracy among intellectuals to exploit the physical reflexes which a certain kind of montage can produce to impose upon the public themes and attitudes remote from their values.

[2] *Vide*, Otis Ferguson, *Life Goes to The Movies*, *Films*, Vol. 1, No. 2, 1940.

because they could not or would not accommodate themselves to the time-spirit, or because they insisted upon pursuing themes remote from the sympathies, or alien to the experiences, of average audiences. This, as film history continues to demonstrate, is the basic condition of survival. An artist may use what virtuoso methods he likes in his films so long as his subjects are emotionally important to the majority; if they are not, he cannot work at all.

It is clear in retrospect that when the people embraced this new art they were bound to make it their own, and that therefore the most functional intellectual approach to cinema must be that of research into the economic, political, and cultural patterns which it was bound to reflect. But it is understandable that the *cinéastes* should have adopted the outlook with which they came to be associated. The motion picture was invented only fifty years ago; its development from a means of recording to a method of narration took place in less than half that time (1903-1922). The whole silent era was therefore essentially an experimental era. It *seemed* then that films were the work of individual artists because it was a pantheon of talented individuals who were discovering and perfecting the resources of the medium. And those creators were given a degree of freedom inconceivable to-day; M-G-M could permit Stroheim to make *Greed*, Goldwyn to distribute *Caligari*, Paramount to finance Flaherty, because the capacities of the film were still being explored. No one was yet certain what the public would accept. But by the latter half of the twenties the medium was highly developed and, what is even more important, the most profitable box-office formulas had become manifest. It had become practicable to standardise film production in anticipation of mass-standardised taste. Producers were no longer interested in experimenting with what they could now regard as a predictable product. This fact, and the influence of the world economic depression on public taste, were of final importance in determining the course of the medium. It was primarily they, and not sound, which gave its character to the contemporary film.

For as long as they could, however, the *cinéastes* clung to their belief that it was the unseemly intrusion of the dialogue film into the aesthetic paradise of the silent experimental films which had brought film art, as they understood it, to a standstill. Bryher and Macpherson washed their hands of the cinema and dismantled *Close Up* in 1933, while the Film Society and its increasing imitators had a thin time finding enough new material of the right degree of purity to present to their members. Others among the film aesthetes re-thought the whole problem of mass-communications and came to a new channel for their energies. They discovered that while the ' art ' film might be commercially impossible when served up as entertainment, its methods might powerfully serve the ends of propaganda. In radical contrast to their previous pursuit of the ' pure ' film as an end in itself, they now began to speak of ' films which serve a purpose beyond themselves.'

Serving a purpose beyond just film-making has been the main intellectual approach to the cinema ever since. In America, the energies of serious men have been principally devoted to the attempt to turn the Hollywood cameras on to the problems of modern existence. In Britain, a different course was undertaken. Under the guidance of John Grierson, a devoted group of educators, journalists, scientists—and former film aesthetes (among them Rotha)—created what has come to be known throughout the world as ' the British documentary film movement '. How documentary tried to make itself economically independent of the cinemas, how it absorbed the technical methods of all kinds of film-making in all countries, how it identified itself with the aims of government and industry and all those agencies which do the world's work, how it became an instrument and a force which was later to be used as a major weapon of war : all this is the story of Rotha's third book, *Documentary Film* (1936).[1] The fact that one of the principal exponents of film aesthetics in 1929 should have

[1] See also *The Arts Enquiry Report* on *The Factual Film* (Oxford University Press, 1947).

developed into a leading spokesman for the purposive use of film for social ends is conclusive testimony to the change that came over serious thinking about the rôle of the motion picture in contemporary life.

Because Rotha had written *The Film Till Now*, his entrance into the documentary film field in 1930 signalled the shape of things to come for many a group of film enthusiasts across the world way outside the United Kingdom. Perhaps the mainspring of his initial interest in the documentary method was the freedom of aesthetic experiment it allowed; but with each film he made from *Contact* (1932) onwards, he moved closer to the social implications of his subjects. *Documentary Film* first published in 1936 was a long, long way from *The Film Till Now* of 1930 in theory and philosophic base but by the time it was published Rotha had already realised its principles in action. His specific relation to Grierson and the documentary group is well-known in Britain. What is probably not so well-known is the extent of Rotha's personal influence by precept and example throughout the world. Quite precisely, he performed the strategic task of bringing into the international documentary camp the very considerable number of persons—some of them in key positions in relation to documentary's interests—who were in the first instance concerned with the film for its own sake, and who could only be led to a consideration of its social rôle by the exhortation and example of a film-maker and film-historian who, they knew, shared their own basic love for the medium. This, it should be realised, was one of the jobs to be done; I hope it is as recognised in Britain as it is overseas how well it was done.

Rotha's becoming a producer in 1935 was received with mixed feelings by the audience he had created as a director. The necessity in the interests of the whole documentary field for him to assume this responsibility was felt, but it was also felt that something had been lost. *Cover to Cover* (1936), *Today We Live* (1937) and *New Worlds for Old* (1938)—especially the latter—revealed flashes of the old drive to explore new territory, but it was a drive now diffused and partially expressed through others. The appearance some years later of *World of Plenty* (1943) confirmed the conviction of more than one observer that it is doubtful strategy to exploit talent in a supervisory capacity while actual creation is given over to routinists. It might, perhaps, be the other way round? Not only was *World of Plenty* a highly personal film; it was also the intimate product of the impact of two minds upon each other during the course of a long friendship. Between them, the late Eric Knight and Rotha developed a new form in this pioneering film. It reflected all the things they held in common; learned knowledge of the history of the medium, deep and instinctive feeling for its capacities and, where subject was concerned, a high anger against the folly and waste of heedless exploitation. It was the anger which gave a dimension to *World of Plenty* beyond that of Capra's *Why We Fight* series. It appealed to the people in their own interest at long last, not in the interest of the Nation or the Flag, not even in the interest of Education and Progress. It *spoke* directly *to the people,* over the heads of governments and agencies and institutions and causes, even the best, even the most disinterested, which was perhaps why the latter were shy of it. In doing so, it brought the people into the argument and almost for the first time in cinema made them their own advocates.

Most films hardly even try any more to speak to the audience in a voice it can believe. *World of Plenty* did it. Rotha's last film *The World is Rich* (1947) did more. It demonstrated that, as the semanticists would say, a question properly put dictates its own answer. The novelty, socially speaking, is that the audience is challenged to test the truth of what it sees and hears rather than be crushed by the authority of a Jovian commentator and scriptwriter. The measure of these Rotha films is not to be found in the striking distribution and profound effect which they have achieved throughout the world, nor in the audience allegiance they command. In a way that is still not altogether clear, they have flung down the gauntlet to all other lines of documentary development. They relegate lyricism and impressionism and mere factual statement to a very minor rôle. They make *The March of Time* think-film seem hoarily distant. They induce the reflection that while the *Why We Fight* technique created emotional unity around known values, it suggested and could suggest no way of solving the problems which threatened those values —except, perhaps, to fight some more. They raise the question : is it worth while for documentary, in a world crisis which has all the appearance of finality, to treat of subjects or to raise issues which cannot be brought to their outcome by the immediate and direct pressure of public opinion?

*

This addendum to *The Film Till Now* will concern itself principally with the relationship between a film and its world audience, and what was happening to that audience in the past eighteen years. The original edition of this book, written at the end of the experimental period, logically devoted itself to the developing grammar of the film. Now that the medium itself has matured, it is the uses to which this powerful instrument is put that require analysis.

The question may occur to some : how is it that, all through a period which has been focussed on ends rather than on means, *The Film Till Now* has survived as a classic film history? I am anxious to answer out of my own experience. ' Nowadays ', a prominent educator has said, ' thousands of young people seem to feel that the movies are their destiny.' And they search in their thousands for some way of uniting their destiny with that of the movies. In the babyhood and youth of the movies it was inevitable that Hollywood should seem the only locale, and bigness the only goal, of their efforts. But ever since 1930 this book has been lying in wait for them. They have happened upon it in their schools and colleges; it has loomed out at them from the shelves of small-town libraries; and it has

kept alive their enthusiasms in the long discouragement of
waiting for the chance to practise its precepts. Many, among
whom I am happy to number myself, found that even after
they had arrived at some form of motion picture activity,
what *The Film Till Now* had to say about the medium and
its principles and possibilities remained at the backs of their
minds as the goal to work toward. I do not think it possible
to exaggerate the importance of the consciousness of such a
goal in its effect upon actual movie work from day to day.
The endless stream of poverty-stricken or bankrupt films
which flows past us from week to week has its source in
large part in the fact that their makers literally do not know
that films ever have been (and therefore ever could be)
made in any other way. On the other hand, an increasing
number of craftsmen—Huston, Dmytryk, Kanin, Rossellini,
to name but a few—show a growing awareness of how
their own work can be enriched through a knowledge of
films of the past and what is to be learnt from them. They
know that Stroheim's cutting principle did not die with
Greed but is there for the taking; that the structure of the
Odessa steps sequence in *Potemkin* can be accommodated to
other themes and locales—and that only by this process of
absorption and refashioning of first principles and historic
examples can the medium continue to grow.

Beyond this teaching rôle, *The Film Till Now* has
another importance. It is the work of a man infatuated
with his subject. No one could read it, then or now, without being infected with some of its strict regard for the
essence of the medium itself. And that is basic. The
camera is a hard taskmaster. For whether it be in the
cinema of ideas, of information, or of amusement no film
can reach an audience where it lives unless it is first of all
a film. All hail, then, to the *cinéastes,* and to their one-time
spokesman who now practises what he then preached in a
world greatly changed! Whatever their mistakes about
dialogue, however baseless some of their optimism and
some of their pessimism, they loved the thing they sought
to protect. We need a matching love to-day. ' For the fire

cannot kindle nor the flame leap up, until there has been long intercourse with the thing in itself, and it has been lived with.'

RICHARD GRIFFITH

New York
June, 1948

THE AMERICAN FILM: 1929-48

(I) Subjects and Themes

If the talking film was repugnant to the aesthetes, it was no less so, at first, to the Motion Picture Industry. Synchronised sound and dialogue had been a theoretical possibility since the invention of the movies. All that was lacking was an adequate device for amplification of the projected sound. This was supplied by the development of the telephone repeater in 1914. Research could have solved the final difficulty of electrical recording in a very short time and the sound engineers early turned to the obvious source of finance to support the research, the Industry itself. But the corporation executives were not interested. Secure in the familiar pattern of movie-making which they had created and with which they felt at home, they saw no reason to disturb the profitable routine of silent film production. A few fanatic pioneers, like Lee De Forest, continued to experiment chiefly with the support of the telephone and phonograph interests; but they might have gone on fiddling on the fringes for years had not desperation caused one of the major Hollywood studios to break ranks and sponsor the sound film.

In 1924-25, Warner Brothers were facing bankruptcy. Lacking access to the theatre-chains controlled by their larger competitors, they could not obtain adequate distribution for their often excellent films. Within the existing industry set-up, there was no way out for them; they had to try something new. With what remained of their capital they equipped a sound studio and threw themselves into the gamble of making a synchronised film. The first result was John Barrymore's *Don Juan,* in which recorded music took the place of that customarily furnished by an orchestra in the theatre pit. Everybody agreed that this was a step forward in the presentation of movies but it did not seem a revolutionary one. Nor did the flat, middle-Western voice of Will H. Hays, slightly 'out of sync.' with his image on the screen, encourage anyone to believe that this form of speech-film had the bright future he predicted for it. But Warner's were committed to their gamble; they had no choice but to push on. They persuaded Al Jolson to accept shares in their nearly bankrupt company in lieu of salary for appearing in a screen version of a recent stage hit, *The Jazz Singer*. This film, finished at the end of 1926, was indifferently acted and directed, its story banal and heavily sentimental. Silent, or even with a synchronised musical score, it would have passed unnoticed in the stream of mediocre pictures. But at its end the voice of Jolson spoke to Eugenie Besserer : ' Hey, Mom, listen to this.' Then he sang two songs. To hear these two songs and the five words that introduced them, New York and then the world queued up for months.

Hollywood was still unimpressed. Only two or three theatres in the country were equipped to show sound films, and it seemed a waste of ' the stockholders' money ' to invest in expensive machinery to produce films whose novelty value was sure to be brief. But the novelty persisted. Through the last sunny years of the twenties when everybody was making money, at least on paper, the Industry was suffering from a mild slump. Movies were bigger, slicker, and showier than ever, but their profits were disconcertingly small in proportion to the huge amounts invested in them. Meanwhile, the renegade Warner's were making amazing sums from their sound pictures which, although they could only be shown in a few theatres, never seemed to stop running there. By the beginning of 1928, the executives of the other companies got around to deciding that perhaps they had better investigate sound. It could do no harm, and maybe a few of these novelty ' talkers ' might bolster the dwindling income from the ' regular ' product.

The results of their investigations were startling. They

learned that any sound film, no matter how bad, could fill any theatre, however ratty while across the street their most super silent picture played to empty seats in the most sumptuous of motion picture cathedrals. They learned that countless exhibitors were installing sound equipment, and that the Western Electric Company could not keep up with existing orders much less serve the vast theatre chains; that Warner's had a similar lead in building sound-stages for production; that it was not only possible but highly probable that their tardiness in adopting sound could destroy their dominant position both in production and in exhibition; and that it might already be too late.

The panic that followed, well described in William de Mille's *Hollywood Saga,* was immediate. Stars, directors, writers, producers, even the studios themselves, were locked in a struggle for survival, the single test being whether or not they could adapt themselves to sound. Many could not on the simple score of illiteracy. Many others lost their battle because the particular gifts which had made them acceptable in silent pictures seemingly had no place in the talkies. The players suffered most. Early sound recording was faulty in the extreme, and voices either recorded dissonantly, or revealed traits of character strikingly at variance with the screen personality built up by publicity and type-casting during the silent days. Worst handicap of all was the fact that no one quite knew to what he was required to adapt himself—the sound film as a method of story-telling was an unknown quantity. Most producers assumed that films from now on would be replicas of stage productions, and resorted to wholesale importation of Broadway playwrights, stage managers and actors, meanwhile relegating the old stars and directors to limbo along with all the principles of film construction which had been slowly developed through the silent years.

Like the producers, the Broadwayites in their triumph assumed that all they had to do was to transfer the New York stage bodily to Hollywood and photograph it. In the late twenties that meant drawing-room comedy, then the fashion. But the fashion was confined to New York. To rural movie audiences, these recorded plays came as a shock and a puzzle. Years before, the silent film had accustomed moviegoers to Lady Diana Delatour, Lord Kildare and the stately homes of England. Through literal transcription of Barrie, Lonsdale and Maugham, the screen now revived these characters but this time asked the movie-goer to take them seriously. In the photographed play of 1930, Lady Diana was evidently intended to be a real person. She was usually played, for one thing, by Ruth Chatterton, who didn't look like Pola or Gloria in the least, and whose manner was human not divine. But while the moviegoers had accepted Lady Diana when she was pre-sented in terms of sweet Elinor Glyn, her real self bored and nonplussed them. Miss Chatterton seemed to them much too sensible a woman to waste her time in the delicate Lonsdale effort to decide whether or not she really loved her husband. In greater America in the year 1930, a woman might dislike her husband or she might love him, but she was seldom in doubt about it. The fact that Lady Diana's indecision was expressed through dialogue made her more than ever irritating to the majority, to whom it seemed that 'tea-cup drama' got nowhere. It left its characters where it found them, and the interim of polite badinage had no more connection with fundamental emo-tions than a game of pingpong.

This attempt to use the subjects and methods of another art failed because the life represented in the photographed play, actual though it might be, was outside the experience of American audiences and alien to their values. Something more than a year of this 'tin-pot substitute for theatre' made clear that, contrary to the expectations of both aesthetes and businessmen, sound was to make no essential change in the American film as a popular entertainment because the values and outlook of the audience *remained fundamentally the same*. They still wanted youth, beauty and the common touch in their players, action in their nar-rative, and a familiar conscientiousness about the underlying moral values. Even the ability to recite dialogue, that literal shibboleth, turned out to be of secondary importance. Janet Gaynor, with the voice of a talking doll, made a triumphant talkie début in a film in which she also sang, and continued her successful career for nearly a decade. Many other silent favourites also survived the transition. It began to be seen that it was not the movie players and directors, but the imported talents from Broadway who had to adapt themselves to the sound film in order to survive. Few of them did, and of those few, only those intelligent enough to shed their proscenium manner for the restrained acting required by the intimacy of camera and microphone.

Meanwhile, the social forces which were really to shape the future of the American film were beginning to operate. The beginning of the sound era roughly coincided with the collapse of the stock market and the onset of the great economic depression of the early 1930's. But while the remainder of the American economy swiftly disintegrated, movie box-office grosses continued at an all-time peak. Wall Street pricked up its ears; here, apparently, was a depression-proof industry.

The continued popularity of the talkies was perhaps in part due to their continuing novelty, as the development of sound mechanics brought one new technique after another. More fundamentally, it was due to the fact that movies offered the cheapest amusement that was available to the newly-impoverished millions. But as the depression developed, as the economic pinch turned into actual penury for at least a fifth of the American nation, even the movies were not cheap enough. Box-office grosses dropped alarmingly. By cutting production costs, the studios might have weathered this storm, which lasted only through a few years of the New Deal. But the Industry had long been overcapitalised and, in distribution, overexpanded. Seeking monopoly, the most powerful major companies had invested heavily in theatre-chains which in those lean days turned out to be highly overcompetitive. By 1932, every Hollywood studio was in financial difficulties. Paramount and

105. EXTASE, directed by GUSTAV MACHATY. HEDY KIESSLER. [Czechoslovak, 1933]

106. FORTY-SECOND STREET, directed by LLOYD BACON. RUBY KEELER, WARNER BAXTER, GINGER ROGERS. [American, 1933]

107. LADY KILLER, directed by Roy del Ruth. Mae Clarke, James Cagney. [American, 1933]

108. IT HAPPENED ONE NIGHT, directed by Frank Capra. Clark Gable, Claudette Colbert. [American, 1934]

Fox went through successive receiverships and reorganisations. R.K.O., which had failed to make a profit since its foundation, changed administrations every year. By story-formula, by the star-system, by the control of distribution outlets, the producers had endeavoured throughout the twenties to create a standardised system for the mass production and mass consumption of films, more or less in indifference to public preferences. After 1930, this was no longer possible. Under the depression, the American public was undergoing new experiences, forming new attitudes, which had to be incorporated into films. The study of the 1930's was how to make film product approximate to the changed social outlook of the audience.

*

The way to the future was pointed by the *gangster* film cycle, which succeeded ' tea-cup drama ' late in 1930. Films dramatising the life and death of machine-age criminals had been familiar since Josef von Sternberg first dealt with the notorieties of Chicago in *Underworld* (1927). This sophisticated film, and Lewis Milestone's *The Racket* (1928), exemplified the subjective treatment of crime towards which silent technique naturally led directors of the period. The coming of sound shifted the emphasis from the criminal mind to criminal behaviour, enhancing the violent elements of the crime saga. The mere addition of recorded sound itself added immensely to the physical effect of the gangster film. The terrifying splutter of the machine-gun, the screaming of brakes and squealing of automobile tyres, were stimulants equal in effect to the headlong suspense developed by the introspective silent technique.

More important still, sound brought to the crime films those corroborative details which identified the underworld as a familiar segment of contemporary American life. The gangster talkies were written by newspapermen and playwrights, veteran observers who knew the metropolitan world and its cesspools at first hand. Maurine Watkins, Bartlett Cormack and Norman Krasna had all written gangster plays before going to Hollywood. John Bright and the late Kubec Glasmon had been news-reporters in Chicago. To the gangster himself, these knowing writers added the racketeering night-club proprietor, the gold-digging moll, the ' mouthpiece ', the strong-arm henchman, the moronic sycophant. Individual films began to explore the colourful details of the half-world and to depict unusual and ingenious criminal methods. Melodrama was the staple ingredient of the cycle, but as writers increasingly dominated the gangster films of 1930 and 1931 they formed a documentary mosaic, a panorama of crime and punishment in an unstable society. George Hill's *The Big House* (1930) showed prison as a breeding-ground for crime. *Little Caesar* (1930) traced the rise of a snarling hoodlum to the position of virtual overlord of a modern city, terrorising business and paralysing the police. *The Secret Six* (1931) was equally frank in depicting the vigilante methods used to combat organised crime when the law failed. The last big gangster films of this cycle made explicit the emergent fact that the gangster had become a popular hero because only an outlaw could achieve success in the economic chaos of depression America. Both *Smart Money* (1931) and *Quick Millions* (1931) made their heroes argue that a man was a fool to go into legitimate business when it was obvious that business methods applied to crime yielded much bigger returns.

Most extraordinary of all, *The Public Enemy* (1931) told the now-familiar story of the rise and fall of a gangster in terms of his social environment. The leading character (James Cagney) moved as though propelled by fate, by the inevitable doom of those born to the slums. This biography of a criminal dared the little-used and generally unsuccessful episodic form in order to detail every stage in the formation of the hero's psyche. As a boy, the futile mediocrity of his middle-class family is contrasted with the excitement of city streets where every saloon and poolroom is an invitation to excitement and, incidentally, to virile adulthood. A bar-room piano-player teaches adolescent boys dirty songs; in return, they pick pockets and he acts as their 'fence'. The petty crooks and ward heelers of the neighbourhood approvingly watch their progress from minor thievery to the organised robbery of fur warehouses and, finally, to the biggest bonanza of all, the liquor racket. It is as though they had gone to school and after rigorous training passed their examinations to general approbation. Their lives as adults are detailed with a realism new to the screen. In danger more from rival gangsters than from the police, they move uneasily from apartment to apartment, their surroundings at once luxurious and sordid, their women women and nothing more. Towards the end of the film, Cagney indicates his boredom with his current mistress by pushing a grapefruit in her face. A few minutes later, his befouled corpse is delivered to his mother's doorstep as though it were the day's supply of meat.

The intentions of Bright and Glasmon in this film were undoubtedly sociological; the reactions of audiences were frequently romantic. Young girls longed to have grapefruit pushed in *their* faces, and the tough, not to say sadistic heroes in the persons of Cagney and Clark Gable became the beau ideal of men and women alike. The gangster cycle, growing more harrowing with each picture, was box-office throughout the early years of the talkies. But though audiences in general did not recoil from the opened cesspool, its stench offended more delicate nostrils. The Daughters of the American Revolution, the American Legion, and that greater legion of women's clubs and business men's clubs which run the machinery of community life in the United States, disliked this focussing upon 'America's shame'. They pointed out, truly enough, that audiences sentimentalised the gangster and envied his life of unrestrained violence and excitement. Useless for the Hays Office to reply that the gangster films were grim object lessons against crime, and that their moralising was nearly always vocal and specific. To small-town civic leaders, the films seemed morbid, unpleasant, and somehow unpatriotic. The major portion of American film revenue comes from small towns. Hollywood gave in. In the spring of 1931 the gangster film was a staple product; before the beginning of the next year it had vanished from the screen.

Its disappearance marked the first instance of a paradox which has plagued the Motion Picture Industry ever since. A story 'theme' becomes popular enough with general audiences to warrant a cycle of films to be built round it. But the 'theme' itself is repugnant to the upper middle-class who, though they form only a small percentage of total motion picture patronage, are organised and articulate. Then, although the cycle's box-office warrants its continuance, it is abandoned in deference to the pressure groups. Yet these attempts to curb or guide public taste are seldom wholly successful if they are in opposition to the time-spirit. The gangster as stencil disappeared, but his influences remained. The crime films had brought the habit of a naturalistic approach to the screen. Their best-known contribution was a new swiftness of continuity which lifted the movies out of the dialogue doldrums of the photographed play. In pictures which revolved round the events of murder, pursuit and capture, speech became speedy and succinct. This brief dialogue blended with the staccato rhythm of films based on action to produce vivid impact. In 1931 Norbert Lusk said of *Smart Money*: 'Every word has the force of a newspaper headline.'

Once they learned that speech need not carry the story, directors and writers began to use it as an atmospheric adjunct. Edward G. Robinson's famous 'So you can dish it out but you can't take it', was one of the many phrases the gangster film brought into general circulation. Screen dialogue took on an idiomatic crispness in the mouths of Robinson, Cagney, Joan Blondell, Ruth Donnelly, Marjorie Rambeau, Chester Morris, Allen Jenkins, and Warren Hymer, very able players brought from Broadway.

The end of the gangster era found the screen equipped with a corps of efficient actors whose brilliant thumbnail characterisations gave audiences a sense of acquaintance with the background of events ordinarily remote from their lives. The cycle had given jobs to writers whose knowledge of the seamy side of American life was drawn from experience and was articulate and controlled. Above all, it had accustomed audiences to seeing contemporary life dealt with from a critical point of view. Except in *The Public Enemy*, the gangster films had avoided tracing the social backgrounds of crime. Yet the exhaustiveness of their naturalistic detail was in effect a tacit statement that the slum, and therefore society, was responsible for uncontrolled twentieth-century crime. It was this unpleasant implication, perhaps, more than the danger that the crime film itself might breed criminals, that lay at the bottom of the boycott of the gangster film by the small-town civic clubs.

But it was too late to turn back the clock. The new critical attitude, along with speedy continuity, idiomatic dialogue and naturalistic acting remained a characteristic of the sound film. It was the essential element in the *confession tale*, the next movie cycle, and one of the most symptomatic trends in popular entertainment since literacy and the ballot became universal.

*

The confession tale is the lineal descendant of those servant-girl stories which have been a constant factor in American and English popular literature since the days of Richardson, and to-day are a *genre* by themselves in the American magazine field (*True Story, True Confessions, True Romances, True Life, True Love*). These crude stories were originally intended as wish-fulfilment for shop-girls and servant-girls. On the screen, they gained a much wider audience acceptance. They were an answer to the frustration of the middle-class woman to whom industrial civilisation had given a taste for luxury and adventure, and who saw no way of achieving either in the economic depression of the thirties except by trading on her sex. But she wanted the sanction of morality too, and the movie formula neatly resolved her conflict. Watching Helen Twelvetrees in *Millie* (1931), she learned that you accepted money and a penthouse from a man because you ' trusted ' him to do right by you. Was it your fault if he turned out a cad, and if you were forced into a life of luxurious sin through the loss of your ' reputation ' ? Miss Twelvetrees said No, and proved her point by the tears she shed over her vanished purity. But her regret was *too* lachrymose— the game was hardly worth the candle if you had to cry that much to win. Constance Bennett's method of achieving the same end was far more reassuring. In each of five pictures (*Common Clay,* 1930; *Born to Love,* 1931; *The Common Law,* 1931; *Bought,* 1931, and *The Easiest Way,* 1931), Miss Bennett was seduced by a rich man and left to her fate. Far from weeping on the sidewalk, she fought for her man so intelligently that she eventually won a wedding ring from him. (In all cases he was, of course, physically desirable as well as wealthy.) Miss Bennett, articulate, shrewd and resourceful was unbelievable as a stenographer or an artist's model, but it was because of this very superiority to type that hers proved the popular variation of the confession formula.

The original confession tale in fiction paid at least lip service to the canons of bourgeois morality, as did silent film versions of similar stories. But as the business graph slid downward, rationalisations of the heroine's conduct grew more perfunctory and more fantastic. In the fall of 1932, darkest and most reckless hour of the depression, three films summed up the cycle in the round. In *Faithless,* Tallulah Bankhead went on the streets to get food and medicine for her sick husband. In *Call Her Savage,* Clara Bow went on the streets to get food and medicine for her sick baby. In *The Blonde Venus,* Marlene Dietrich became a rich man's mistress to get money to send her husband to Vienna to be cured of radium poisoning. When he finds out where the money comes from and casts her off, she too resorted to street-walking taking her six-year-old daughter with her. The attrition of conventional morality implied by these films is well indicated by Norbert Lusk, most astute of popular critics, in his review of *Faithless* :

' Another girl goes out on the street and, to use the old reliable phrase, sinks to the gutter, but what of it? Her husband takes her back when he hears about it, and with a gentle wisecrack brushes away any twinge of shame that may remain, proving again the current movie doctrine that it's not what you do that counts, but what you can get away with. In this case the young wife hustles to pay her husband's doctor's bills. When she confesses, her conduct is not only condoned but also wins a compliment from him on her nobility of character. What manner of hero are they offering us on the screen to-day? '

The hero of the confession tale did not matter, of course. He was at best the *deus ex machina* who arrived at the end of the picture to offer love and respectability to the heroine worn out by her sexual activities. Only one film, Garbo's *Susan Lennox* (1931) approached an honest treatment of the male response to the street-walker heroine. Miss Garbo's Helga is separated from her lover and in the usual manner loses her reputation before she meets him again. But lo, instead of receiving her with open arms, he is tortured by her lapse, when he can neither forget nor forgive. Their eventual reunion is a desperate measure, the last resort of a love that can never be satisfied. But *Susan Lennox* was an eddy. The main current flowed steadily in the direction of overt glorification of the philosophy of women-on-the-make. By the third year of the depression, the economic independence of women, so newly won, so precariously held, had collapsed almost completely and they were thrown back on the immemorial feminine position. In the harsh world of supply and demand, they had nothing to sell but sex.

In the high tradition of popular art, the screen became the confessional which gave them absolution. The shopgirl heroine herself was an incredible being both in concept and as embodied in glamour by Joan Crawford, Norma Shearer, and Barbara Stanwyck, but she was linked to the lives of her audiences by the idiomatic dialogue, the realistic minor characters, the setting of contemporary life, which sound had established as the background of the confession film. And the closer her screen adventures moved toward the experiences of her actual prototypes, the more difficult it became for her to adhere to the old ideals. She had not forsaken them in spirit; she still wanted wealth, virility, *and* respectability. But life under the depression had taught her that one might have to be sacrificed if any was to be obtained. The increasing frankness of the films centring round her was an echo of her cynical despair. At first it was only an overtone. But, by the end of 1932, it clamoured from every episode of the confession film.

*

In 1930, Darryl Zanuck, then the newly-appointed production head at Warner Brothers, had announced that films produced by his studio would henceforth be based so far as possible on spot news. This policy, inspired by the success of the gangster film in dramatising headlines to popular taste, produced the *topical film,* for many years Warner's speciality and imitated by the other major studios. Ostensibly these pictures ' based on news ' were meant to do nothing more than capitalise on topics of current interest, with perhaps a modicum of moral homily. But as the topical pattern emerged, as writers grew bolder and players more accurate in their reflection of character, the topical film, like the two cycles which preceded it, became a mirror of the subterranean discontent with the American social structure which slowly rose through the depression years.

Individual films were generally vague and evasive; they attacked the special case and absolved the system as a whole, but in effect their statement was direct. Frequently their critical tone was veiled by comedy. *The Dark Horse* (1932) rendered the mechanism of American electioneering in terms all too familiar to the citizen. The stupid candidate for governor, ' Hicks, The Man from the Sticks ', is a tool in the hands of his campaign manager, who has him photographed in fishing-togs, newsreeled awarding blue ribbons to prize bulls, and made an honorary chief by a tribe of Indians. The film was released during the 1932 campaign for the Presidency, as was a similar satire *The Phantom President*. Both films painted politics as a racket, public officials as hypocrites, and voters as venal fools to be bought with flattery and government jobs. In like serio-comic vein, *The Mouthpiece* (1932) argued that lawyers were to be had for a price and were the bulwark of organised crime, while *Night Court* (1932) chronicled the misdemeanours of a grafting judge. News-reporters will commit almost any crime for the sake of a story according to *Scandal Sheet* (1931), *The Front Page* (1931) and *Five Star Final* (1931). *Is My Face Red?* (1932), *Okay, America* (1932), and *Blessed Event* (1932) were films based on the exploits of Walter Winchell, depicting the rise of the newspaper columnist who grows rich by ruining reputations—and who is adored by the public. *All-American* (1932) and *Rackety Rax* (1933) reported the professionalism that had invaded football, implying that American sport, that cornerstone of our mores, was a racket like any other. *American Madness* (1932) informed disappointed speculators that banking was a confidence game in which the honest man was left holding the baby. Complementing this corrupt picture of the professional and business classes, the serious-minded Richard Barthelmess starred in three conscientious films which scrutinised the plight of the under-privileged, as expressed in such problems as share-cropping, *Cabin in the Cotton* (1932); the psychological deterioration caused by unemployment, *Heroes for Sale* (1933); and the exploitation of the American Indian, *Massacre* (1934).

The majority of topical films were mere snapshots of American life. *I am a Fugitive from a Chain Gang* (1932), the apotheosis of the cycle, dealt directly with social abuse, but no picture could afford to be thus uncompromising unless it limited itself to so narrow a field as prison brutality. The average film avoided the direct social attack. Its exposition of the disorders of the body politic was often brilliantly realistic, but it ended without concluding. The spectator was left to decide for himself whether the instance of social disintegration he had witnessed was typical or isolated. Nevertheless, the topical films succeeded in voicing a blanket indictment of depression America because their effect was cumulative. *It's Tough to be Famous, Love is a Racket, Beauty for Sale*—what wasn't a racket, what couldn't be bought, in the third year of the depression? Nothing, answered the topical films, which found a sordid story behind every newspaper headline. Their strength as a movie cycle lay in the fact that the story was really there, and that audiences knew it. ' Work and Save ', the ancient maxim of individualism, had been succeeded by ' Anything Goes '. Success in business and love was still the goal of the American wish, but nowadays you get it any way you can—no questions asked. Why not? Everybody's doing it.

For the coincident first four years of the depression and of sound, the American film had approached real life as closely as it dared. The technique of sound and the changed outlook of the audience had brought American idiom, real characters and contemporary situations into the film-story. But though the gangster film, the confession tale, and the topical film had tried American society and found it wanting, their attack was negative. They had no constructive programme. In reality, their critical attitude was a hankering for the old days back, when work produced wealth, when there was room to breathe and a chance for everyone. They were a reflective and unconscious response to the despondency of a nation.

*

In the delirious air of the first months of the Roosevelt administration, the slowly-formed critical attitude of the early talkies weakened. The President was beginning to work his magic with the minds of the people, and the country turned to him for miracles because it seemed that only miracles could save. ' Confidence ' was the watchword he spoke against despair, and a sort of febrile confidence spread throughout the country. The movies reflected it instantly. Hollywood, too, was weary of panic and strife. Enthusiastically producers ' co-operated ' with the new administration and did their best to restore confidence by producing films endorsing the National Recovery Act and other New Deal methods of rejuvenating the economy. *Looking Forward* (1933) used the title of a book by the President to offer co-ordinated business planning (of a rather homespun variety) as an economic panacea. The elements in which confidence was supposed to reside were significantly portrayed in *Stand Up and Cheer* (1934), in which a Department of Amusement was created to laugh the country out of the depression. It is also significant that this picture included songs and dances, since the dominant cycle of the New Deal ' honeymoon ' period became the musical film, an unregarded corpse since it was done to death in the early talkies by literal transcriptions of dated operettas and musical comedies.

In the new cycle, *Forty-Second Street* (1933) and its successors discarded the artificial conventions of stage musicals and frankly divorced music and plot, introducing songs and dances for sheer divertissement. Gradually the musical film jettisoned all semblance of realism, and its structure increasingly approximated that of the revue. These blithe films multiplied. Warner's first monopolised the field with their slangy, contemporaneous *Gold Diggers* series, which were so successful that Paramount and M-G-M followed suit with annual *Broadway Melodies* and *Big Broadcasts*. As might be expected, the cycle has developed into a permanent genre, filling the place left vacant by vaudeville and offering a vehicle for special skills and talents much as the silent film had done for athletes like Fairbanks. Its highest point so far has been achieved in the charming dance-comedies of Fred Astaire and Ginger Rogers.

At the time it was resuscitated in the early New Deal days, the appeal of the movie-musical lay in its scatter-brained indifference to logic, its provision of licit escape, and in its linkage with the spirit of 'confidence'. This sudden access of fantasy reflected the desperate wish of the majority for an easy way out of the economic impasse. But the habit of realism was strong upon Hollywood and, side by side with the musical film, the confession tale and the topical film continued their sordid analysis of changing customs. Basically they were little affected by 'confidence', though after the advent of the New Deal they became less tragically serious. The Jean Harlow-Clark Gable comedies (*Red Dust*, 1932; *Hold Your Man*, 1933; *China Seas*, 1935) continued the confession and gangster traditions but they laughed at amorality as much as they sentimentalised it. It was easy in the atmosphere of confidence to deride situations hitherto regarded as grave. It was easier, too, to regard them frankly, to dismiss the fog of rationalisation and sentimentality which so often negated the realism of the depression days, to paint with rueful amusement folly at full length.

It was her honesty that brought instantaneous, universal success to Mae West. The 'heroine' of *She Done Him Wrong* (1933) and *I'm No Angel* (1934) made a bid for no one's tears. Far from reforming in the last reel after the manner of the confession gals, the final fade-out found her wealthy, wicked, and beloved. As for her 'reputation', 'It's not the men in my life that worry me', says Miss West, 'it's the life in my men.' It was precisely this irreverence which brought about the downfall of Mae and her school. The middle-classes had borne with Hollywood's implied criticism of their institutions during the economic crisis, perhaps because they themselves felt critical of a society which seemed to be collapsing around them. But the New Deal had (mistakenly) given them the hope that the road forward was to be the road back, and they made haste to repair the breaches in the façade of the American tradition. What was coming out of Hollywood irritated and dismayed

444

them. Here was the realistic, the critical, the by-now merrily irreverent movie telling its audiences that romantic love was hypocrisy, a biological joke; that the government ordained by the founding fathers was run by hypocrites in the interests of big business; that the 'American way' in business itself was a cut-throat competition but little removed from racketeering. Just as in the case of the gangster film three years before, there slowly gathered during 1933 and 1934 a sentiment in the church, social and business organisations to use their power to muzzle and repress the screen—or better still, to direct its popular vitality toward more sanctioned goals. The result was the Legion of Decency.

The arguments advanced by the Legion in favour of screen reform had been heard before—they echo down the ages—but the methods of this remarkable polyglot organisation were uniquely successful. It hatched in the Roman Catholic Church, whose possession of the immemorial machinery of repression formed its nucleus and base. The Legion was created by the Council of Bishops to review films and classify them under the headings 'Passed', 'Objectionable in Part', and 'Condemned'. These findings were announced from pulpits. Communicants were urged to stay away from films deemed partly objectionable, and were told that attendance at those 'condemned' by the Legion would constitute a venial sin. At the same time, the Church invited other denominations to join in this campaign, the object being to force Hollywood by mass boycott to give over its exposures and sensationalisms and make what were vaguely described as 'good' films. Ordinarily, Protestant Americans are reluctant to ally themselves with Rome for any reason, but the respectable so urgently felt the need for screen reform that the holy alliance was consummated. In the great cities, especially those with a large Catholic population, the widely-publicised campaign actually caused a small drop in theatre attendance. But not much, and not for long.

The campaign was never felt disastrously at the box-office because the irreverence of the film towards established morality had sprung straight from an attitude of mind typical of the movie's audiences. The Legion's ban actually acted as a shot in the arm to many a film which might otherwise never have attained any publicity at all. Nevertheless, the pressure from civic leaders was so strong that Hollywood felt it prudent to bow. A 'Production Code' had been compiled by the Hays Organisation as early as 1927 from the rulings of the six State censor boards, but had chiefly been more honoured in the breach than in the observance. Now it was revivified and rewritten, reputedly with the aid of the Catholic hierarchy, and the studios agreed to be guided by it. A branch of the Hays Office, headed by the prominent Catholic layman, Joseph I. Breen, was established in Hollywood to pass judgement upon all scripts; none rejected by Breen could be produced until it was changed to meet the requirements of the Code. These were significant. Designed primarily to geld the sexual content of films, they also forbade criticism or humour aimed at the cloth, the bench, the armed services or ' the accepted canons of American morality '. The Code has straitjacketed Hollywood ever since. Resourceful writers and producers have wriggled out of it from time to time, but for the most part it has not been seriously challenged by any major studio. So, for the second time in the sound era, an articulate and energetic pressure group succeeded in imposing on the film an uneasy cast of respectability.[1]

*

Searching about for new subject matter to accord with Decency, Hollywood now beat a rapid retreat from the contemporaneousness which had been its stock-in-trade since sound. The end of 1934 brought a sudden revival of interest in history and legend, and a ransacking of the literary archives for simple tales of the wholesome virtues.

[1] *Vide, The Freedom of the Movies,* Ruth Inglis (University of Chicago Press, 1947).

American history and the legends clustered about it had already received treatment in the early sound film, but such a serious biography as D. W. Griffith's *Abraham Lincoln* (1930) exerted little influence, and *Alexander Hamilton* (1931) was simply George Arliss interfering with the course of history. Films with a more valid, because more instinctive, claim to popularity were *Billy the Kid* (1930) and *Moby Dick* (1930), legends dear to the American heart because they portrayed the old, free days when opportunity was as boundless as the unfenced prairie, when danger was the tangible menace of physical combat instead of the fear of losing a job—above all when behaviour was neither restrained by law nor inhibited by the binding force of convention. These occasional pictures, like the perennial Western, succeeded because they opened an avenue of escape toward less trammelled times. Edna Ferber's and Wesley Ruggles' *Cimarron* (1931) was at once the apotheosis of all the qualities that made the Western popular and a shrewd study of changing cultural patterns. Yancy Cravat, Miss Ferber's protagonist, was the ideal Western hero. The first half of the picture was the thrilling story of his exploits in subduing lawlessness and transforming the wilderness, until finally the town of Osage has become too tame and he is ready to move on. It was at this point that the picture divided in two. Yancy's wife, Sabra, stepped into the foreground and became the principal character. For Sabra refuses to leave Osage. While we have been watching her husband's picturesque adventures, she has been building security for herself and her children. Through her anti-liquor, anti-vice, beautify-the-city campaigns, Osage had become the modern American town, founded on feminine values.

Miss Ferber's picture of the transition from masculine to feminine America was exact, and its conclusions ineluctable. But the points made in its analysis were lost on both its audiences and Hollywood. As a popular picture, its power lay in the fact that it transported audiences back to the days of freedom, not in its exposition of why that freedom had vanished. *Cimarron,* the American cinema's one accurate study of social history, exerted little influence. Other pictures of the pioneer past made before the onslaught of Decency were merely nostalgic. *The World Changes* (1933) and *The World Moves On* (1934), (both titles were misnomers), set the sturdy past against the degenerate present, and argued that all will come right again if only we return to the old ways. The influence of depression psychology on these films was marked. Their glorification of the 'American way' was frenetic; they ended in doubt. Intended to be reassuring, they seemed instead a tinny whistling in the dark.

Indeed, American history raised too many problems to be acceptable to the spirit of Confidence. The escapist tendency which followed Decency found a more fertile field in the idealism of 'classic' nineteenth-century literature. The early depression years had witnessed the success of such simple tear-jerkers as *Daddy Long Legs* (1931), *East Lynne* (1931), *Rebecca of Sunnybrook Farm* (1932) and *Smilin' Through* (1932). Their success, and the triumphant popularity of Katharine Hepburn's *Little Women* (1933), enabled the Legion of Decency to point out that the public obviously did want 'good' films. Hollywood was impressed by the box-office backing for this argument, and producers began to ransack nineteenth-century writing for counterparts of Mrs. Alcott. They made a great discovery. They found Dickens.

Dickens, and after him Barrie, overran Hollywood. *David Copperfield* (1934), *The Mystery of Edwin Drood* (1934), *Great Expectations* (1935), *The Little Minister* (1934), *What Every Woman Knows* (1935), and *Quality Street* (1937) transported audiences out of harsh America into England—not the England of documentary films, but England as upper-class Americans wanted to believe it still existed, a right, tight land, a *cosy* land where all's warm and happy and Mother Britannia knows best. While British producers were fabricating *Chu Chin Chow* and *Jew Süss,* Hollywood was proving that England's all right, even in

109. CRIME WITHOUT PASSION, directed by Hecht and MacArthur. Claude Rains, Margo. [American, 1934]

110. CHAPAEV, directed by the Brothers Vassiliev. Boris Babotchkin. [Soviet, 1934]

111. L'ATALANTE, directed by Jean Vigo. Dita Parlo, Jean Dasté.
[French, 1934]

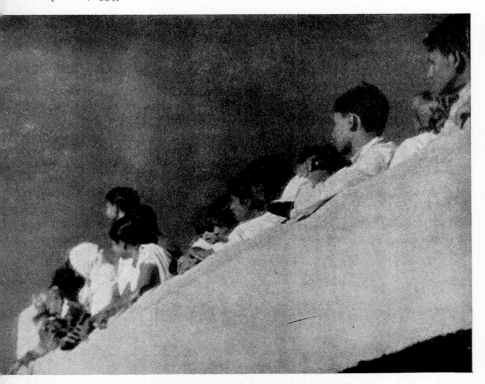

112. THE SONG OF CEYLON, directed by Basil Wright. [British, 1934–35]

her colonial policy, with *Clive of India* (1935) and *The Lives of a Bengal Lancer* (1935).

Censored history and the winnowed literature of capitalism's great period pacified the middle-class and brought it back into the theatres. The escapist trend made the screen respectable in the eyes of those who have always a little feared it, and it enabled the Hays Organisation to issue pronouncements on progress. But the escape it provided had no solid basis in either creative impulse or audience demand. The Decency fervour and its by-products were a transient interruption of the reflexive process by which the film-story approximates ever more closely the agitations of the popular mind.

*

The great majority of American intellectuals, already left-wing in spirit, saw in the Roosevelt administration a partial fulfilment of their hopes. At the other end of the scale, the enormously increased number of the under-privileged and the dispossessed instinctively followed the man who promised them escape from the economic trap. These two extremes formed, during the thirties, the major portion of the left-wing of American political thought, in which individual differences were to some degree submerged in united support of the New Deal. Over against them lay the middle-class, professionals, business men and that vast group of office workers whose sense of property had not been destroyed by the depression. Although this class must be termed conservative in contrast with the left-wing, its ideas were confused and uncertain. It had no love for the *status quo*, it was profoundly uneasy about the New Deal's programme, and it had no programme of its own. It stood for the preservation of values already lost.

Chiefly the spirit of the middle-class took the form of inchoate opposition to the experiments of the administration. But on the articulate levels it endeavoured to formulate a policy. Many of America's most popular writers have never merged with the nation's intellectual groups.

Coming to the city from farms and small towns, they have retained the values and viewpoint of the middle-class. Their ideal is discovered in what corresponds to the Edwardian period in England, the first tender years of the new century, when America was still a great small town. It was in their eyes an epoch of invention, of 'healthy competition', of progress, of humanitarian reform. Above all, it was thought of as an era of good feeling in which the 'classes' were hardly conscious of their identities. It was the individual who counted, who made his own way in the world and, feeling pity for those less strong and assertive than himself, helped his unfortunate fellows. It was this individual feeling of kindliness which popular writers— Clarence Budington Kelland, Struthers Burt, Damon Runyon, Isabel Paterson, Rose Wilder Lane—considered the element missing from contemporary life. By its revival, they thought, the world of the day-before-yesterday could be restored.

Such was the *fantasy of goodwill* created by middle-class writers and principally enunciated in *The Saturday Evening Post*, a magazine patently dedicated to the interests of big business. The principle found film embodiment through picturisation of stories by the *Post's* most popular authors, and, on the screen, found its natural exponent in Frank Capra, considered by many to be the most capable director developed by the talkies.

Capra won his spurs directing rough-and-ready melo-dramas in the days when his studio, Columbia, was still struggling toward size and importance. The economy and forcefulness of his cinematography bear the marks of this training, but his claim to significant popularity lies in a temperamental affinity to the middle-class outlook. Coming to America from Sicily as a boy, he seems to have absorbed its psychological atmosphere the more completely because he looks on it with an objective, therefore a visual, eye. This ability to express ideas in terms saturated with emotional associations has enabled him to give its appropriate form to the fantasy of goodwill.

Capra's first highly succesful film was *Lady for a Day* (1933), based on Damon Runyon, in which a hard-boiled gangster raises wretched Apple Annie to affluence so that she may appear respectable to her long-lost daughter. It was not made clear whether the old woman goes back to her street-corner after her daughter leaves, but no one asked questions because the picture was so obviously a fairy-tale. What gave it importance beyond customary fantasy was the *milieu,* which was that of contemporary life. And that was made logical by the implicit suggestion that public enemies are just little boys at heart, who will do any one a good turn when fate lets them.

This feeling achieved the status of an idea in Capra's most famous film *Mr. Deeds Goes to Town* (1936), adapted from Clarence Budington Kelland's *Saturday Evening Post* serial. Its setting was the Broadway of the topical films; its characters cynical, merciless, governed by gangster morality. They, too, were once young and ardent, but they have come too far, lost their virginity, sold their birthright for success. What they fear most is sincere emotion, for it reminds them of what they have lost. Perforce they laugh at Longfellow Deeds with his naïve greeting-card poetry, his honesty, his deep content. To them he is an incredible anachronism. He is, apparently, meat for their exploitation, just another hayseed to be given the time-honoured runaround, and they are only following the appropriate formula when they tempt him to use his wealth, to cut himself off from the kind of life to which he was born. But Mr. Deeds, unexpectedly, is not tempted. Wealth to him is something to share, and after his disillusionment with his slick advisers, he uses it to give homeless farmers and labourers a chance to set up for themselves. Through this consistency, he triumphs. For the Broadwayites are eventually moved by him. In his life they see what theirs might have been. And since they are really men of goodwill at heart, they end by applauding his rejection of the metropolis and all that it stands for.

The thesis of this sentimental comedy was welcomed by

huge sections of the American public. What need for the social reorganisation proposed by the New Deal if prosperity and peace could be recovered by the redemption of the individual? This idea, absolving the middle-classes from realistic thinking about the forces which governed their lives, has proved perennially popular. The stalemate implicit in it is indicated by Capra's subsequent work, all of which continues to exemplify the fantasy of goodwill. With the exception of the pretentious *Lost Horizon* (1938) and the farcical *Arsenic and Old Lace* (1944), each of his films has used an American social, political, or economic problem as its springboard. *You Can't Take It With You* (1938) inveighed against the influence of foreign 'isms'. The significantly titled *Mr. Smith Goes to Washington* (1939) probed the corruption of national politics. Most ambitious and daring, *Meet John Doe* (1941) examined the seedbeds of fascism in the United States. *It's a Wonderful Life* (1947) was a vivid portrayal of dog-eat-dog methods in small-town business.

Capra depicted each of these situations with striking naturalism. Characters, events, and atmosphere were recognisable to, and within the experience of, every American. The solutions provided were always fantastic. In each film, a messianic innocent, not unlike the classic simpletons of literature,[1] pits himself against the forces of entrenched greed. His inexperience defeats him strategically, but his gallant integrity in the face of temptation calls forth the goodwill of the 'little people', and through their combined protest, he triumphs. Nothing could be further removed from the actual experience of American audiences than that triumph, and nothing could have suited them better. Such a blend of realistic problem and imaginary solution epitomised the dilemma of the middle-class mind in the New Deal period. As I wrote in 1939 of *Mr. Smith Goes to Washington*: 'Its significance, it seems to me, lies not in its truth or falsity but in its persistence as an idea

[1] And closely akin to the silent film character created by Harry Langdon, whose pictures Capra directed at the beginning of his career.

and its popularity with audiences. Individual idealism is no solution for any practical problem, but it is the totem people worship when every other way out cuts across their thinking habits. A film which embodies this phenomenon enjoys, to my mind, an importance beyond itself. It is to be evaluated less as a mirror of life than as a document of human psychology, an index to the temper of the popular mind. *Mr. Smith Goes to Washington* is such a film, and the classic example of its type.'

Capra's panacea for mental strife was not available to everyone. Settled, middle-aged people might dream of a solution through Christian brotherhood, but the younger generations found it harder to believe in. The individualist tradition had been too profoundly shaken by the depression to offer them real hope. ' The loss of credibility in former values ', writes Lewis Jacobs, ' the breakdown of the smugness and self-confidence of the jazz era, the growing bewilderment and dissatisfaction in a " crazy " world that does not make sense, has been reflected in a revival of comedies of satire and self-ridicule . . . epitomised, perhaps, in the title of one of them : *Nothing Sacred.*' [1] This cycle, known as the *screwball comedy*, began with Capra's *It Happened One Night* (1934) and especially with the equally successful *The Thin Man* (1934). The flip insouciance of this picture seemed at first glance a part of pre-Decency cynicism. But the aimless lives of the protagonists are redeemed by gaiety and goodwill; they atone for all shortcomings by being kind and charming. Above all, they find in marriage an adventure which blots out the insufficiency of the world outside it. Subsequent films in the cycle—the best known were *My Man Godfrey* (1936), *The Awful Truth* (1937), and *My Favourite Wife* (1937) —continued to emphasise escape from a meaningless existence into an imaginary world dominated by personal relationships. ' Emblematic of this new regard for the " wacky " ', continues Mr. Jacobs, ' are new hero and

[1] *The Rise of the American Film*, Lewis Jacobs, (Harcourt Brace, 1939), p. 535.

heroine types. Among the women, Carole Lombard is the most outstanding in her " screw-ball " activity. Beautiful, frustrated, she asserts intense dissatisfaction with existing conventions and deep bewilderment in seeking justification of her desires. . . . Among the men, perhaps the most representative of the rebels are Fred MacMurray, Cary Grant, and Melvyn Douglas. These men are seekers of one sort or another; they point to maladjustments by pretending with childlike simplicity that they do not exist. They enter into conspiracies with themselves or comrades, telling long stories or building up long situations which are unconventional but which seem right . . .' Beginning with *The Thin Man*, the heroes and heroines of most of these films are married. Only in the private world of marriage can they construct the phantasies which substitute for a meaningful relation to the world.

*

Though the escapist film cycles which followed Decency have continued successfully through the pre-war and war years, they have not monopolised the screen. Side by side with the public which sought release in fantasy there existed, or grew up, an audience for the realistic dramatisation of social problems. The influence of the depression, the leadership of Roosevelt, the controversy over the New Deal, the rise of documentary journalism, all the forces of a period of tension had made this inevitable. Labour disputes, standards of living, abuse of power, were after all no longer outrageous topics for public discussion. They were phrases on everyone's lips, and because of their value as news the screen could treat them in the category of the topical film, with an assurance of public support that would have been lacking before the depression.

The topical films of the early depression days were, it will be remembered, entirely negative in their criticism of American life. The new cycle added idealism to criticism. These films were made in the reformist spirit of the New Deal itself. Warner Brothers, through their long experience with topical and gangster films, took an easy lead over other studios in developing this cycle, and they appear to have done so consciously; for many years the company slogan was 'Good films—good citizenship'.[1] These ambitious producers gathered round them a team of writers and directors who were both trained technicians and earnest intellectuals, eager to put their mastery of a mass-medium at the service of social enlightenment. Conscientiously they set themselves the problem of dramatising public issues within the limits of what the box-office said was popular entertainment. The result was an extremely remarkable series of films which came closer to the American scene as the majority experienced it than films had done since the early days, when their audience consisted exclusively of the poor and humble. *Black Fury* (1935) considered a strike in a coal-mining town, of all milieus, and showed it being broken by goons hired by the mine-owners. *Black Legion* (1937), taking its theme from contemporary headlines, showed the operations of a secret society, decked out with all the paraphernalia appropriate to the Ku Klux Klan, which had as its veiled purpose the intimidation of labour unions. *They Won't Forget* (1937) was an outspoken indictment of lynching in the South. *Angels with Dirty Faces* (1938), *High Sierra* (1939), *City for Conquest* (1940), and *The Roaring Twenties* (1939) revived the gangster cycle but focussed on the social sources of crime. When called upon to voice blame for the social evils they depicted, these films saved themselves from censorship and pressure groups by employing dummy scapegoats, and by treating a general problem as though it were an isolated case. In *Black Fury*, the well-meaning employers are ignorant of the fact that they have hired strike-breakers. What the films had to say nevertheless came through. Writing construction was their secret. Each began with a long, carefully-documented opening which set the stage so

---

[1] It is hard to reconcile this policy and its products with Mr. Jack Warner's evidence at the Committee on Un-American Activities, Washington, November, 1947. *Vide: Hollywood on Trial,* Gordon Kahn, (Boni and Gaer, 1948).

carefully that the spectator, if he knew anything of American life, could not avoid drawing the logical inferences, no matter the phoneyness of the ending. All that had been learned about the making of sound films was employed to force audiences to recognise this scene as *their* scene, and these problems as *their* problems. As intelligent as the novels and plays by which they were influenced, and far more vivid, these films were the real social literature of their period.

None of them was so sensationally successful, as box-office or as propaganda, as to cause a stampede in the direction of the social film, but they exerted deep influence on the content and technique of Hollywood production. Directors and writers at other studios, belatedly reaching intellectual maturity, wanted to show that they, too, like Warner's, could make good films in the service of good citizenship. Norman Krasna's and Fritz Lang's *Fury* (1936) attacked lynching even more savagely and successfully than did its successor, *They Won't Forget*. Lang's *You Only Live Once* (1937) and *You and Me* (1938) reminded the public, as did William K. Howard's *Mary Burns, Fugitive* (1935), that the constabulary of the United States, frustrated by the inadequacy of law in the face of organised racketeering, were now using extra-legal means to capture criminals, and that in doing so they frequently punished the innocent with the guilty. Samuel Goldwyn solemnly contemplated housing problems in *Dead End* (1937). The South, contemporaneously characterised by President Roosevelt as ' the nation's Number One economic problem ', came in for analysis in *The Toy Wife* (1938), *Jezebel* (1938—a Warner film), and Jean Renoir's recent *The Southerner* (1945), not forgetting those earlier studies in decay, *Coquette* (1929) and *The Story of Temple Drake* (1933). John Ford's *The Grapes of Wrath* (1940) and Lewis Milestone's *Of Mice and Men* (1940) capitalised on the popularity of Steinbeck's books to challenge the conscience of a nation that had allowed its human and material resources to be impoverished by greed and planlessness.

And while they were disinfecting these social sores, Hollywood's crusading craftsmen endeavoured to formulate a positive approach. Direct support of the New Deal on the screen was impossible, but tribute to the generalised spirit of modern democracy was impregnable to pressure-group attack.

In this approach, too, the Warner studio took the lead. A series of biographical films, usually starring Paul Muni or Edward G. Robinson, (*The Story of Louis Pasteur*, 1936; *The Life of Emile Zola*, 1937; *Juarez*, 1939; *Dr. Ehrlich's Magic Bullet*, 1940; *Reuter's*, 1941) dramatised the contributions to democratic life of healers, research scientists, newspapermen, and humble revolutionaries. Laid in the past, smelling a bit of the lamp, these films were none the less earnest and vigorous attempts to convince the electorate of the possibility of a rational society based on science and education. They held their own at the box-office with purely commercially-inspired films, and conferred sufficient prestige upon Warner's and the Industry at large to warrant their continuance. Their most important effect, like that of the films which criticised American life, was gradually to accustom both audiences and movie-makers to the idea that the screen could legitimately take its place beside the printing-press as a channel for the discussion of public issues.

Writing at the end of the first decade of the talkies, Lewis Jacobs concluded his *The Rise of the American Film* with these words : ' The graveness of the past ten years has seen the content of movies take on a more serious tone. A depression-hit America has focussed the movies' attention upon social corruption, economic discrepancies, political maladjustments, and has started a search for a code of personal and social values that will not rest entirely on sex and affluence.' [1] The trend toward realism in the narrative film was quickened after 1936 by two other factors, not unrelated; the rise of the documentary film and the increasing threat of war from the fascist powers.

[1] p. 538.

Although the documentary film as a movement began in Britain as early as 1929, and was firmly established by the early thirties, it did not take root in the United States until the middle of the decade. Isolated individuals and groups did attempt to make documentaries, but under Soviet rather than British influence, and the 'agit-prop' methods used struck little response in the large American public.

Then the *March of Time,* in 1934, with its 'new kind of pictorial journalism', blended newsreel material with staged scenes to interpret the background of news events. Two years later, in 1936, Pare Lorentz, a movie critic without previous technical experience, produced *The Plow that Broke the Plains* under New Deal sponsorship. Influenced in its methods by both British and Russian examples, the material of this film about the Dust Bowl was sufficiently 'American' to enlist the sympathies of audiences hitherto unfamiliar with the direct dramatisation of factual material. His second film, *The River* (1937), produced for the Farm Security Administration, attracted national attention with its Whitmanesque commentary and the timeliness of its appeal for flood control and soil conservation. The documentary film had arrived; Lorentz was suddenly a great man. But where were his films, and others like them, to achieve future sponsorship and distribution? Hollywood-conditioned in spite of themselves, the documentary film-makers at first sought to retrieve their production costs in the customary manner through theatre distribution. But the Industry was indifferent, if not hostile, to this new kind of film and potential competitor. The *March of Time* had had to fight its way into the theatres, and it is said that *The River* achieved national distribution only through polite pressure from the government agency for which it was produced. It was clear that the documentarians would have to follow the example of Britain and obtain finance from government, business, or educational institutions—and accept the limitations of purpose which such sponsorship imposed. Lorentz succeeded in persuading the Roosevelt administration to set up a U.S. Film Service which would produce films propagandising the policies of all departments of the Government. He gathered round him such major talents as Robert J. Flaherty, inventor of the documentary approach, and Joris Ivens, the Dutch documentarian at that time in the United States, and for the moment it looked as though he had established a base of operations for documentary comparable to that created by John Grierson and others in Britain.

The first films augured well: Lorentz's *The Fight for Life* (1939), and Ivens' *Power and the Land* (1940), achieved the theatres, and both advanced that blend of factual observation and dramatic construction which was becoming the characteristic form of the documentary. But before Flaherty could complete his epic of erosion, *The Land*, a Congress now alienated from the New Deal decided that government film propaganda was needless and, indeed, un-American. It abolished the U.S. Film Service. *The Land* was never shown in the theatres. After that, as before, it seemed that documentary in America had nowhere to go. Industry, which had helped support it in Britain, was cold to sponsorship proposals coming from film-makers tinged with New Deal radicalism. Education was interested but cautious, and its budgets not of a magnitude to enable concerted film production. A few films of excellence, such as *The City* (1939), a dissertation on municipal planning financed by the Carnegie Corporation, made their occasional appearance, but they were sporadic. The little group of enthusiasts who constituted the American documentary 'movement' lacked salesmanship. They lacked the organisational—and inspirational—ability of a Grierson. So American documentary floundered on into the war years.

The war saved it, gave it sudden purpose and direction. For several years before 1939, the documentary-makers had been trying to warn the country of the rising menace of fascism. In 1937 Joris Ivens had collaborated with Ernest Hemingway in filming *The Spanish Earth* behind the

Loyalist lines. The next year, he and John Ferno went to China for *The Four Hundred Million*. Herbert Kline filmed Munich (*Crisis,* 1938-9), and the fall of Poland (*Lights Out in Europe,* 1940). Although Hollywood craftsmen rather patronised the documentary people (the attitude was mutual), these early anti-fascist films were not without their influence in California. Walter Wanger ventured *Blockade* (1938), a timid fictionisation of the Spanish war, and the ubiquitous Warner's enabled Anatole Litvak to film the wholly admirable *Confessions of a Nazi Spy* (1939) which, borrowing from the *March of Time* as well as from dramatic documentaries, gave the electorate an account of Nazi operations in America as illuminating as it was exciting. Slowly the documentary people and the fiction film-makers began to hunt in couples : famous stars and writers provided commentaries for independently-produced documentaries, and a few of the fact-film men found jobs in the studio short-subject departments. All belonged to the same anti-fascist committees. Then Pearl Harbour drew both groups into the direct service of the war. The documentarians for the most part made films for the Office of War Information and related agencies, while Hollywood talent dominated the armed forces. John Ford was made a lieutenant-commander in the Navy, Frank Capra assumed command of the Army's orientation and education film programmes. The results were revolutionary.

In peacetime American documentary had been a luxury project, promoted and supported by ardent groups of intellectuals, tolerated or ignored by everybody else. In a competitive economy by no means dedicated to the progress of enlightenment, its function was unclear. In war, it met a need which everyone felt and everyone understood, the need to hearten and strengthen millions of people to meet, not hardship only, but the incessant strain of acting always in the common interest at the expense of their own. This need presented itself less urgently to the makers of civilian Office of War Information films than to those who made films for the armed forces, which was precisely why the record of the old-line documentarians was less impressive than that of the Hollywood technicians dealing for the first time with factual material. The O.W.I. men were first set to work to make ' morale ' films for domestic civilian consumption, couched in a hortatory mood psychologically appropriate only to the beginning period of the war. Later they addressed a task even less directly related to the immediate experiences of their audiences; they made films about peacetime American life designed to ' sell ' the rest of the world on the United States. Little wonder that the O.W.I. films seemed routine, a repetition of peacetime documentary methods rather than a fresh start. Only in films directly related to what was happening, such as Helen Van Dongen's war-history, *News Review Number Two*, did the O.W.I. advance the technique of factual exposition.

By the nature of their position, the Army film-makers had a greater, because a more demanding, opportunity. The needs they met were definite, vital, and urgent. They had to train men in complicated and unfamiliar tasks, mostly alien to their instincts and training. They had to try to explain why the Allies were at war, why war could not have been avoided, how it was to be fought, and what those soldiers who survived it might hope for in the world beyond war. And all this had to be done from scratch, for no adequate Army film-making service had existed before Pearl Harbour. Hastily gathering round him such men as Anatole Litvak, Leonard Spigelgass, John Huston, the late Eric Knight, Anthony Veiller, Frank Capra plunged into the production of the now-celebrated *Why We Fight* series of orientation films designed to explain to soldiers the causes and progress of the war up to America's entry into it. At first relying upon fictional techniques, the men from Hollywood soon learned a respect for the dramatic value of the human countenance and the unstaged scene. Deprived of star glamour and production value, drawing their material from newsreel archives and combat film photographed at random on the fighting fronts, they were forced back upon the basic resources of the film medium; the editing principle emerged as the definitive factor in the conception and execution of every film. Capra, with his instinctive command of editing, created the basic form of the *Why We Fight* series, a complex elaboration of the *March of Time* pattern of interpreted events. These emotionalised history lessons culminated as dramatic poems in the last films of the series and in the Anglo-American *The True Glory* (1945) by Carol Reed and Garson Kanin.

The *Why We Fight* series deserves close examination by students of film technique. The formidable power of the film medium can be seen at its source in these elementary examples of the effects to be gained by the composition of images in counterpoint with sound, music, and speech. In particular, their use of imagery commands attention. The hackneyed symbols of popular sovereignty come alive in these films; the words and voices of statesmen—incomparably, of course, of Roosevelt—take on new meanings through association with images. To give but one example : over a scarred Italian battlefield, littered with the corpses of soldiers, floats the sound of ' Go Tell Aunt Rhoady ', an old American folk song. The instantaneous response of this juxtaposition is both emotional and intellectual; it conveys an idea, but an idea saturated with emotion. Such devices existed in embryo before the war and were used intermittently, but it remained for the *Why We Fight* series to develop them fully and to use them to solve the problem of giving dramatic construction to factual material. Doubtless these films will shortly be surpassed (the earlier ones already look awkward and uncomplex compared with the later), but there is little doubt that they already constitute the major influence on post-war efforts to use the medium for persuasive purposes.[1]

While this orientation series was being completed, Capra sent out units headed by first-rate craftsmen to film the progress of the war at first hand. After a rather abortive

---

[1] It is of interest to record that the series was greatly admired and analysed in detail by the Soviet cinematographers, most of whom agree with the above remarks.—P.R.

first effort, *Tunisian Victory*, imitative of but far from comparable with the British *Desert Victory*, the units hit their stride with such films as William Wyler's *Memphis Belle*, *The Fighting Lady* (produced by Louis de Rochemont for the Navy), and John Huston's *Report from the Aleutians* and *The Battle of San Pietro*. These films—especially Huston's—forsook the epic scale of *Desert Victory* and the Russian battle friezes for a more intimate and personal approach—a soldier's view of battle. The best of them emerged as screen poems lyrically celebrating the courage of ordinary men and charged with an agonised hatred of war and killing. It was perhaps this latter quality which accounted for the comparative scarcity of films of this kind. After a few experiences, the U.S. War Department grew less than anxious to permit independent-minded directors to travel freely through the combat zones and film what they saw as they felt it. Military difficulties to this kind of film-making were perceived, or invented; what material actually was filmed was closely scrutinised in the Pentagon, and finished films were delayed in reaching audiences.[1] In short, the opportunity to bring to the screen the experiences of the enlisted soldier was by-passed as much as possible.

By-passing the by-passers was the job of the resourceful Col. Leonard Spigelgass, in charge of the *Army-Navy Screen Magazine*, a 'pictorial report from all fronts' (including the home-front). This soldiers' newsreel had to be compiled from stock material photographed by wandering Signal Corps cameramen without direction from headquarters; it was found too 'difficult' to send out specially instructed camera crews expressly charged with the duty of shooting specifically for the *Screen Magazine*. As such it might have become a meaningless and random series of observations of the war. But editorial policy

[1] Huston's *Let There Be Light*, a record of the rehabilitation of psychic casualties and surely one of the greatest films ever made, was entirely suppressed by the U.S. War Department on the ground that it was too harrowing for civilian audiences, although it was addressed to them.

insisted that no item be included which did not bear on the overall strategic and political objectives of the war. Soldier-writers were found who were qualified to interpret G.I. experience. The enlisted man's view was steadily held to. Editors and writers worked together as one, moulding nondescript material into a pattern recurrently recognisable with each issue. The purpose was to recreate the G.I. world on the screen as G.I's saw it and thereby gain their trust in this particular form of news-narration. The technical experiment involved was a refinement upon the ideas of Dziga-Vertov and the experiments of the *Volksfilmverband* in Berlin in the late twenties, but was developed much further; late issues of the *Screen Magazine* achieved poetic and dramatic as well as ideological power. Taken as a whole, it represented one of the furthest points to which the drive to ' emotionalise facts and rationalise emotions ' has been developed—a development which has abruptly ceased.

With the end of the war, Spigelgass and his gifted corps of writers and editors dispersed to other fields. And no one with comparable analytical powers in America is now working in the field of interpreted news, as recent issues of the *March of Time* attest.

*

Did the American public really want to see the war on the screen? Nothing to do but test the situation by adapting the first material to come to hand—the spectacle of Europe prostrate under the Nazis—to routine melodramatic patterns. Literally scores of films were cut to this measure, but conviction was not helped by familiar Hollywood figures in Nazi uniforms, or by writing that conveyed no flavour of Europe. Even Jean Renoir and Fritz Lang were unable to conjure up the anguish and heroism of the underground on the California sound-stages. The public tolerated these films, but no one was impressed by them. The newsreels and war documentaries had brought real war too close. Films of patriotic fervour of

113. LA KERMESSE HEROIQUE, directed by JACQUES FEYDER.   [French, 1935]

114. TONI, directed by JEAN RENOIR.   BLAVETTE, DELMONT, CELIA MONTALVAN.
[French, 1935]

115. A NIGHT AT THE OPERA. THE MARX BROTHERS. [American, 1935]

116. MODERN TIMES, directed by CHARLES CHAPLIN. PAULETTE GODDARD, CHARLES CHAPLIN. [American, 1936]

the old type (*The Eve of St. Mark*) and the lone picture which dared admonish the isolationists into silence and conformity (*The War against Mrs. Hadley*), were equally coolly received. The public was no more interested in these things than was Hollywood. The public, civilian and military, was interested in three things only—the experience of being in a war, the hope of winning it quickly, and the more desperate hope that there would emerge a world rational and humane enough to justify the horrible sacrifice. As this mood crystallised, Hollywood slowly mobilised to satisfy it.

There came first a batch of films designed to glorify America's allies, to instil confidence in their fighting ability, evoke sympathy for their sufferings, and celebrate the nobility of their national aims. M-G-M's *Mrs. Miniver*, starring Greer Garson and directed by William Wyler, took the country by storm—a country so recently isolationist, so nearly outright anti-British. Then Lillian Hellman prepared for Samuel Goldwyn *The North Star*, an original screen-play which must have been the first serious attempt to portray Soviet Russia on the American screen. It was followed by two other glorifications of the Russian war effort, *Song of Russia* and *Days of Glory*, and by the hollowly pretentious account of the experiences and conclusions of Ambassador Joseph E. Davis, as adapted from his book *Mission to Moscow*. The virtues of the minor allies were portrayed in minor films: *Bomber's Moon*, *Paris Underground* (France); *Hangmen Also Die* (Czechoslovakia); *Chetniks* (Jugoslavia); *The Moon is Down* (Norway), and so on. Though some of these films were successful, and all held their own with ordinary commercial productions, their favourable reception owed little to their execution, which was indifferent to the point of carelessness. The fact that Hollywood responded so perfunctorily to the popular hope that their allies were people with whom they could live in peace in the world beyond war, may have been a sign that the hope itself was perfunctory, or that it was based on nothing more substantial than a will for peace unsupported by knowledge of the obstacles lying in wait for it. The series summed itself up in *Wilson,* a biography at once superficial and heavy, which exhorted us to fulfil the late President's hopes by supporting the United Nations. It is hard, now, not to think that Hollywood's timidity in making such empty gestures was justified. In the changed political climate of the post-war period, even these tepidly internationalist films are being used as weapons against the Industry.[1]

The final phase of the war brought a cycle which satisfied what everybody in America most deeply wanted to know— what was happening to their sons and husbands, what were they thinking and feeling, in the midst of the vast and bloody campaigns which stretched round the world? The best of these, *Guadalcanal Diary, A Bell for Adano, They Were Expendable, A Walk in the Sun,* were surprisingly convincing inasmuch as they were made with the usual studio methods. Their veracity was not so much a matter of advice by technical experts as of the fact that World War II was the best reported event in world history. The radio and press made everyone who could read, and some who could not, aware at least in part of the sight, sound, smell, and feel of war. This widespread sense of the reality of combat penetrated even the studios' golden gates. It was one thing to glamorise the guerillas and the underground, quite another to risk popular scepticism by perpetrating phoney theatricals on a subject about which people knew something and felt deeply. It is significant that these films employed newsreel and documentary story-construction when they could, and that the best of them were based directly on the eye-witness accounts of brilliant reporters. As was almost inevitable, the most compelling of them was William Wellmann's *The Story of G.I. Joe* (1945), from the news stories of Ernie Pyle, who perhaps more than anyone made the American people see the war through soldiers'

[1] The reader is referred to the remarkable 'proceedings' at the Committee on Un-American Activities, Washington, November, 1947. Some part of the 'proceedings' is published in *Hollywood on Trial,* Gordon Kahn, (Boni and Gaer, 1948).

eyes. In spite of occasional artificialities, *G.I. Joe* is to my mind the greatest of war films. Possibly *Westfront 1918* was superior in technique, but there was about Pabst's approach a cold and generalised abstraction which is the antithesis of the intimacy and humanity of *G.I. Joe*. Final judgement must wait on time, but I feel that Wellmann's film deserves to stand beside *Three Soldiers,* Brady's Civil War photographs, and the pioneer work of Ambrose Bierce and Stephen Crane, as one of the great American documents of warfare.

*

The end of the war found Hollywood once again at a loss for themes. The Industry confronted a public weary of the conflict, but so steeped in violence that anything less seemed tame. The war was immediately tabued as story material, countless scripts featuring soldiers were either scrapped or re-written to strip the soldiers of their uniforms while leaving their guns in their hands. Where could armed civilians find a plausible setting? There was only one possible answer : the gangster film was revived with a bang, and with an accent on violence and sadism unprecedented in the depression days. Resort to such films was not merely a hasty commercial improvisation as their emerging pattern reveals. They are symptoms of universal fear and insecurity. In these films, brutality is nearly always linked with insanity. Either the individual, or the world in which he moves, or both, are as unrelated to reality as in the hag-ridden German films of the early twenties.

The proposed remedy for this sudden spread of madness throughout the world is, of course, psychiatry, a science belatedly endowed by Hollywood with godlike powers. The significance of the flood of *psychological* films, and of the fact that psychiatry is represented in them as a witch-doctor cure, needs no underlining. This popularity of the analyst's couch as a place of healing and absolution is rivalled to-day only by that more ancient confessional, the Church. Beginning with *The Song of Bernadette* and *Going My*

Way, the cycle of religious films has become staple. To the hope held out by the psychiatric films of making us whole men again, the church pictures add the promise of eternal life to a world seemingly bent on speedy suicide.

This myth-making activity is necessarily the dominant function of the screen in a post-war era fraught with greater social and personal dislocations than even the war had brought. Whatever the scene or theme, the American camera is mostly turned inwards these days—and the example of the post-war German film again inevitably comes to mind. But some in Hollywood are attempting to draw attention to the real problems from which the unreal arise. They are mostly returned soldiers, and mostly producer-directors with enough prestige to make their own films outside the mass-production studios. William Wyler's *The Best Years of Our Lives,* Capra's *It's a Wonderful Life,* Edward Dmytryk's *Crossfire* are calls to sanity and reason. They approach real issues. They use with skill and taste the techniques of popular entertainment. They are successful, if unconstructive. It is not too much to say that they represent the most intelligent way to use the mass-media in the public interest. With that bow to the courage and resource of their talented creators, it is necessary to add that whether their example will, or can be followed, is much in doubt. Under the pressure of outside events, the American Motion Picture Industry is in a transition much more crucial than the sound upheaval with which this survey began. The loss of income from impoverished Europe threatens radical change in the luxurious production methods of the past. The possibility of Government action under the anti-trust laws to divorce production and distribution would utterly revolutionise the structure of the Industry. The flood of crime and brutality on the screen will undoubtedly provoke repressive efforts from conservatives, who are already engaged in attempting to purge the Industry of ' Communist influence ', meaning apparently the influence of any one who has read a book. Between these winds of doctrine, the deciding factor has always been in the past what Kracauer calls 'Those psychological dispositions which stem from the slowly moving foundations of a people's life.' As all that has been recorded here has tried to show, the future of the film under the American system of economy and the American habit of mind is bound up with the future experiences of its audiences. In 1948, that future has never been less predictable.

(II) DIRECTORS, WRITERS, AND PRODUCERS

Though most of the leading directors of the silent period survived the coming of sound, their former commanding position was greatly altered. Because of the necessity of writing dialogue in advance, it was no longer possible for them to improvise whole sequences on the set or on location. They were chained to the script, which tended to become more exact and detailed in its editing and shooting instructions. This situation played into the hands of producers. By 1935, directors were complaining that they were asked to start shooting the day they were handed the screen-play, and were not permitted to take part in the editing at all. The power of the writer correspondingly increased—though only because it was through him that the producer was able to control the shooting of the film. The effects upon production were soon apparent. As King Vidor remarked : ' The supervisor, with his lack of visual imagination, is unable to fill in the gap between the scenario and the finished article. Consequently the order that each detail of the script be so obvious and over-written that . . . the ultimate whole is all too obvious and dull.'[1]

For a time writers rejoiced in their new eminence. Many of them denounced (they still do) the ' myth of the director', and claimed themselves the single creators of the films they wrote, as much so as if they had been plays or even novels. True it undoubtedly was that most directors had been

[1] Cited in *The Rise of the American Film,* Lewis Jacobs, (Harcourt Brace, 1939), p. 459.

reduced to the subordinate position they occupy in the theatre. But it was equally true, and came to be more and more obvious, that in the sound era as in the silent, every important film was in most essentials the creation of an individual director. And, as the writers themselves found their ideas altered beyond recognition when filtered through the producer, they began to aspire to work more closely with directors. During the latter half of the thirties, the craftsmen began to try to form writer-director ' teams '. At about the same time, the Screen Directors' Guild pressed the producers to permit directors to work on the script with writers, and to edit at least the first rough versions of their films. Success in this endeavour is still unachieved in full Complete freedom is obtained only by those teams, or individual directors, whose prestige enables them to get backing for their own production units. Even then, their intentions are frequently modified by the national distribution chains through which they are bound to release their films.

King Vidor's career illustrates the difficulties that have faced serious directors since the experimental period of the film ended. His first sound film, *Hallelujah!* (1929) was, as indicated, a remarkable achievement. Seen to-day (1948), it is revealed to have all the flexibility of the silent film at its best. No visible concession has been made to the mechanical difficulties which caused other distinguished directors to turn out mediocre pictures in the first years of the dialogue film. The imaginative use of sound and music at times realised the best theoretical hopes of Eisenstein and Pudovkin; the brief dialogue was almost startlingly documentary in a way seldom since encountered. This was the halting yet vivid speech of everyday life, and to hear it again to-day makes the talk in other films, even the best, seem laboured affectation. Add to this the fact that the entire film was shot on location in the South, at a time when sound cameras supposedly were immovable from their glass-enclosed booths in the studios, and Vidor's achievement seems nearly incredible.

This superb technique was applied to a theme as formidable and challenging as any the movies have approached. Vidor undertook to film the Southern Negro ' as he is ' ; to dramatise what the Swedish anthropologist, Gunnar Myrdal, calls the American dilemma. The cast was chosen mostly from among non-professional negroes, and no white men appeared in the film. Daring, yet the device itself defeated Vidor's intent. The negro was portrayed in a vacuum. Because his position in white society was never referred to, his behaviour appeared to arise from his own nature rather than from environmental pressures. For this reason, *Hallelujah!* has sometimes been denounced as a vicious ' attack ' on the race. It was hardly that. Negro crime was shown, but compassionately, and the dignity, wisdom, and emotion of the race furnished the true motif. There can be no doubt that King Vidor offered his tribute to the negro with utmost sincerity, but the contrast between his brilliant technique and an important but inadequately analysed theme was to continue to be characteristic of his career.

During the early thirties, Vidor made a series of undistinguished box-office successes. The material of some of them (*Billy the Kid, Street Scene*) must have challenged his imagination, but the unimaginative supervision of which he complains prevented any of them from becoming much more than well-made movies. In 1934, he struck out for himself. Financing production out of his own pocket, he made *Our Daily Bread* for United Artists release. This curious film tried to offer a solution to the most vital of the great depression's problems—unemployment. Two jobless city workers, husband and wife, are offered a deserted farm by their uncle. As they struggle to master husbandry, there passes by them on the highway the endless, tragic stream of the dispossessed, wandering the face of the nation in search of work. Some of them are offered shelter for the night and wistfully ask to stay on. Thus gradually there grows up a co-operative community : ex-farmers teach the young husband how to work his land, even the tailor and

471

the blacksmith who stop over find uses for their long-neglected trades. Up to this point the picture is both fascinating and credible—poignant, indeed, in its evocation of the revival of human fellowship in the midst of misery. Whereupon Mr. Vidor, as though he were still working for M-G-M, introduces a blonde vampire—the old-fashioned word is justified—whose attempt to take the owner away from his wife supersedes all problems of marketing farm produce, irrigating the land, or fending off the sheriff! For no better reason than that the picture demands an end, this ' problem ' is solved, and the young husband awakes from his tawdry dream of love to be reminded that impending drought threatens all the hopes of his little group. The final scenes, in which the men bring water to the fields while the women rejoice in their fertility, are as brilliant as the preceding sequence was inept. Frequently compared with Pudovkin, they seem to me more like what D. H. Lawrence might have wished to put on the screen, which is to suggest faults as well as virtues. *Our Daily Bread* was given a gold medal by the League of Nations for its humanitarian overtones. But it also won first prize at Mussolini's Venice Film Festival, and the Nazis hailed it as new justification for *Blut und Boden*. King Vidor, sincere in his approach and eloquent in cinematic detail, had nonetheless produced an equivocal film. To his credit be it said that he alone of all the Hollywood craftsmen had the courage to try to say anything at all. But his talent for the camera exceeded his intellectual understanding of the theme. Other defects aside, the basic premise that the way to face the problems of industrial civilisation is to retreat from industrial civilisation was no contribution to the thinking of the time.

Despite the blonde vampire, *Our Daily Bread* was a box-office failure. There followed a series of potboilers; *The Wedding Night, So Red the Rose, Stella Dallas*. In 1938 M-G-M sent King Vidor to England to film A. J. Cronin's best-selling *The Citadel*. This was the least flawed of Vidor's recent films. Solid rather than brilliant in technique, it gave him an impregnable theme of the sort which he could wholly understand and give life to. Here were social facts which could be expressed in immediate human values. The well-constructed story piles incident upon pregnant incident toward the conclusion that the practice of medicine in the modern world is either an act of dedication or of racketeering—with no middle ground. Perhaps the integrity of this picture is evidence of what many have long thought: that Vidor needs a first-class writer, a mind as analytical as his is instinctive, to realise the rôle of social analyst to which he obviously aspires. Be that as it may, he has been as much at a loss since *The Citadel* as he was before that film.

When America entered World War II, rumours were many of what the director of *The Big Parade* intended to do. What finally emerged was the film first grandiosely called *America,* finally *An American Romance.* Filmed in colour, it described the rise of an immigrant workman to industrial power, whereupon he turns against the labour unions formed by his one-time comrades. The resolution of this impasse resolved nothing, neither did it appeal particularly to the public. More than any previous film, it revealed the confusions in Vidor's mind, his inability to penetrate the surface phenomena of social and economic life to the basic determining issues. Since this abortive and damaging effort at a big social film, he has recouped his commercial position by directing Selznick's colourful *Duel in the Sun.* For many of his quondam admirers, this was the last straw. But in view of the record, it is still too soon to give Vidor the kiss of death so often bestowed upon him in the past. His command of the technique of the sound medium is rivalled by few Hollywood directors. Whatever his intellectual shortcomings, he has interested himself in the actualities of modern existence more consistently than any other American director since the twenties.

Josef von Sternberg, too, fought the battle of Hollywood, though for rather odd reasons of his own. He seems now to have lost out completely. At first supremely successful, he has pursued an empty pictorialism which eventually interested neither the public nor his admirers among the critics. His career in sound began in Germany. Imported by Erich Pommer to give Ufa's talkies a rousing send-off, he produced in Berlin his celebrated *The Blue Angel* (1929) starring Emil Jannings, whom he had directed in Hollywood. Perhaps the most skilful and vivid of all Sternberg's talkies, the film also made social history by introducing Marlene Dietrich as—in Dr. Kracauer's words—' Lola Lola a new incarnation of sex. This petty bourgeois Berlin tart, with her provocative legs and easy manner, showed an impassivity which incited one to grope for the secret behind her callous egoism and cool insolence. That such a secret existed was also intimated by her veiled voice which, when she sang about her interest in love-making and nothing else, vibrated with nostalgic reminiscences and smouldering hopes. Of course the impassivity never subsided and perhaps there was no secret at all.'[1]

Dietrich has often been called Sternberg's *femme fatale*, the implication being that the gradual attrition of his talent was due to the necessity to centre his films around her. It was, perhaps, the other way about. It would appear, actually, that he used her as box-office bait so that he might pursue his strange, compulsive preoccupation with pictorial composition. From the six pictures which he made with her in the ensuing five years, *Morocco, Dishonoured, Shanghai Express, Blonde Venus, The Scarlet Empress* and *The Devil is a Woman,* action and even continuity were progressively drained away in favour of an ordered flow of a pattern of images, often lovely in themselves, sometimes floridly vulgar, but always empty of real dramatic meaning. Even the presence of Dietrich could not attract the public to the last of these, and as for her famous impassivity, far from subsiding, it was deliberately preserved for the purpose of making her a mere figure in the formal design of Sternberg's pictorialism. That this was not the fault of Miss Dietrich, subsequent performances

---

[1] *From Caligari to Hitler,* Dr. Siegfried Kracauer. (Princeton University Press, 1947), p. 217.

amply demonstrate. In 1935 Paramount separated this Trilby and Svengali of the studios, and the star herself is said to have realised that her career would have concluded abruptly had she continued with the director who discovered her. Sternberg's future seemed blank, but at this moment Peter Lorre, newly arrived in Hollywood from Berlin after the success of *M*, induced Columbia to secure Sternberg to direct him in a version of *Crime and Punishment*. Although produced quickly, and unfavourably compared by critics to the then-current French version by Pierre Chenal, the picture was a creditable achievement for Sternberg. Handicapped by crude writing and the off-type casting of Lorre as Raskolnikov, Sternberg nevertheless evoked something of the nightmare atmosphere of Dostoievski with the camera alone. His characteristic ' dissolves ' removed the action to the subjective plane, as did the insistence on streets, stairways, doors, lamp-posts, and other inanimate objects which seemed to observe, and even participate in, Raskolnikov's duel with himself.

The rest of Sternberg's career to date has been a series of misadventures. He went to England to make Robert Graves' *I, Claudius* for Korda, and a grandiose production was launched only to be abandoned after a few weeks' shooting for reasons that have remained obscure. Then M-G-M hired him to ' build ' Hedy Lamarr to stardom after her success in *Algiers*. Apparently he merely attempted to Dietrichise her, for the studio dropped him. After two years of inactivity, he returned to direct Arnold Pressburger's gaudy version of the old stage melodrama, *The Shanghai Gesture* (1941). Though profitable, it was ridiculed by the critics and, except for an Office of War Information short, *The Town*, Sternberg has been idle in Hollywood since then.

It is said that Sternberg lacks knowledge of dramatic construction and of cutting values. This is more apparent than real. Both *Underworld* (1927), his first successful film, and *Sergeant Madden* (1938), his last but one, are models of continuity and structure. *Morocco* (1930), his first Marlene Dietrich film in America, has seldom been equalled as an example of the proper function of dialogue. The narrative is unfolded through images, sound and music, speech merely punctuating or accenting the progress of the story. *The Devil Is a Woman* (1935) employed the flashback device more brilliantly than any film I can recall.[1] In a story told by one man to another, Sternberg's characteristic 'dissolves' give the episodes the air of memories rather than of actual events. That ludicrous film *The Shanghai Gesture* contained the memorable crane shot, several times repeated, in which the camera hovers over the gambling casino, searching out its febrile and foolish viciousness—an image reminiscent in feeling of van Gogh's 'Night Café'. In view of these achievements, there can be no question of Sternberg's great talent for the medium, nor of the fact that he has a highly individual style entirely invented by himself (though owing something, perhaps, to the German example of the twenties). The Sternberg problem is a problem of taste, not of ability. He portrays endlessly vice, corruption, the helpless and fatal pursuit of pleasure—but he does not portray it as a realist, or as a moralist. Evil, to him, is romantic. He gloats lovingly over scenes and incidents repugnant to normal minds. This is the key to his celebrated pictorialism. Kracauer says of *Metropolis* that Lang denies the humanity of his enslaved workers by making them move in ornamental patterns, very much as the Nazi party did at its Nuremberg spectacles. Sternberg makes a formal pattern of degradation. He is seemingly unable to work otherwise, even under commercial compulsion. I do not think it too extreme to compare him with D. W. Griffith, as a man of sentimental outlook, unable to employ his great abilities within the frame of the time-spirit.

With the possible exception of Orson Welles, Rouben Mamoulian is Hollywood's only eclectic director. Imported from the New York theatre in the early days of sound, he impressed Hollywood by restoring camera mobility at a

[1] Even more brilliantly than in Carné's *Le Jour se lève*? (P.R.)

time when his Broadway *confrères* were chaining it to the studio floor. It was clear in his first film *Applause* (1930) that here was a man who had studied the resources of the film medium through systematic examination of its classic works. *City Streets* (1931) employed symbols reminiscent of Pudovkin. *Dr. Jekyll and Mr. Hyde* (1932) revived the subjective camera of *The Last Laugh* and utilised the very slow 'dissolves' associated with Sternberg. *Love Me Tonight* (1932) was patterned after Lubitsch's Maurice Chevalier musicals, and showed also the influence of René Clair's Paris films. Each of these pictures was arresting, accomplished, yet it was impossible wholeheartedly to admire them. They smelt of the lamp. Mamoulian seemed incapable of absorbing the principles behind the work of the screen's masters; he literally reproduced their actual achievements. Seeing a film of his was like watching an anthology of the styles of other craftsmen.

For the next three years he was set to directing 'glamorous' vehicles for feminine stars (Garbo, Dietrich, Anna Sten). His touch was unnoticeable in these films. In 1935 Pioneer Pictures, a concern formed by John Hay Whitney to experiment with the three-colour Technicolor process, engaged him to direct their first feature, *Becky Sharp*. In the ball before Waterloo, Mamoulian made the first attempt at using colour to emphasise mounting emotion. The ball scene is at first prettily pastel, but as the guns are heard and the men mount and ride off, the colour gradually changes to a threatening red. Designed by Robert Edmond Jones, this sequence smacked more of the experimental theatre than of truly cinematic methods. The film as a whole was abruptly episodic and prudently censor-proof.

The following year Mary Pickford engaged him to film *The Gay Desperado,* considered by his disciples to be his masterpiece. Carefully, knowingly directed, it again, as in *Love Me Tonight,* employed the methods of the Clair and Lubitsch musicals, but achieved freshness as a comic fantasy by satirising not only its material but its own

477

methods. Undoubtedly it contained some of Mamoulian's best work, but as a whole was no more effective than the sharp-edged comedies turned out every year by the big studios (*Sing and Like It, Professional Sweetheart, Pigskin Parade*).

Since 1936, Mamoulian has made fewer and fewer films. Such productions as *High Wide and Handsome* and *Blood and Sand* hardly displayed any recognisable personal touch. The studios seem indifferent to him. Perhaps he, too, has grown indifferent, or has become absorbed in his work in the theatre and the opera; he staged the admirable Broadway version of Gershwin's *Porgy and Bess*. At any rate, even his academic interest in the resources of the camera is no longer evident.

*

Outwardly, the position of Ernst Lubitsch during the thirties and forties was as commanding as in the silent era, but in actuality it was much less. Delighted by the inception of sound, his initial contributions to its technique were greater than those of any director working in America, with the exception of Vidor and Sternberg. His first talkies, *The Love Parade* (1929), *Monte Carlo* (1930), and *The Smiling Lieutenant* (1931) set the mould of the best Hollywood musicals, discarding stage conventions, and employing music, speech and action in a rhythmic counterpoint as sharply witty as his famous cinematic tropes of the silent days. He owed much, however, to the early European musicals of René Clair and Wilhelm Thiele. At the end of 1931, he directed his own dramatic talkie, the junior Rostand's *The Man I Killed*. In it, a youthful Frenchman is tormented by the memory of an enemy soldier he killed in the war. Although the German was killed in combat, to the Frenchman it is as though he had committed murder. Frantic, driven, he seeks out the boy's family in Germany to confess and atone. They take him for their dead son's friend; he must stay and assume the boy's place in their lives. Gradually, his sensitive friendli-

ness overcomes the German father's bitter hatred of France.
Redolent of the pacifist optimism of the early thirties, this
film is more than a little equivocal when seen to-day.
Lubitsch, the cynic, the ironist, was unable entirely to convince himself that humanity would be saved through disinterested love. Lewis Jacobs mentions ' the scene in the
church where the camera moves past the praying officers
and reveals their guns beside them.' [1]   Nevertheless,
Lubitsch's treatment of the somewhat artificial idea was
serious and adult. Grave, thoughtful, unrelieved, the film
bade fair to become a commercial white elephant, and
Paramount, frightened, changed the title to *Broken Lullaby*.

Was Lubitsch, too, frightened? In the subsequent fifteen years he attempted nothing that was not well within
the tried formulas. Increasingly he turned to supervising
the work of others. In 1935, Paramount made him executive head of their studio and shouldered him with the
particular task of salvaging the career of Marlene Dietrich
after the fiasco of her last films with Sternberg. The result
was the witty *Desire* (1936), and the outmoded *Angel*
(1937). Everything he made after that (*Bluebeard's
Eighth Wife, Heaven Can Wait, That Uncertain Feeling,
Cluny Brown*) has been standard Lubitsch, and rather tired
Lubitsch, with the single exception of the sharply amusing
Ninotchka (1939). Here, with the aid of Garbo's brilliant
performance and of Melchior Lengyel's mordant story, he
wittily satirised the foibles of both Capitalism and
Communism. But such cynical neutrality was more in
keeping with the spirit of the twenties than with the
agonised world of the past decade. Lubitsch had ceased
to lead. The change in his Hollywood status was indicated
by the fact that, though respected, he no longer had a school
of imitators, nor broke fresh paths toward technical innovation. It is significant that his most successful film of the
forties was *A Royal Scandal*, a refurbished version of
Forbidden Paradise, with Tallulah Bankhead replacing

[1] *The Rise of the American Film,* Lewis Jacobs (Harcourt Brace,
1939), p. 359.

Pola Negri. All his films were immutably based on the famous 'touch'. Lubitsch died at the end of 1947.

Fritz Lang's American career began brilliantly. His first Hollywood film, *Fury* (1936), written by Norman Krasna, was an impressive social document. This story of mob-hysteria and attempted lynching was set so solidly into the American scene that no spectator could deny the truth of what he saw, or entirely dissociate himself from the guilt implied. Like Capra, Lang seems to see life in the United States more vividly and visually than a native could. The sociological and dramatic strength of *Fury* lay in the detail with which Lang cross-sectioned the entire community in which the attempted lynching took place. What interested him was not so much the incident which provoked mob-hysteria, as the buried strata of small-town prejudices and hates which it brought into the open. His attack went deeper than condemnation of mob-violence. It indicted fully the society from which violence grew. An uncertain ending alone marred this impressive film, which otherwise was in craftsmanship and vigour almost the equal of *M*. A more complete verdict on *Fury* must wait upon its revival. More thoughtful, more human, essentially more in touch with the reality it treated than other ' social ' films of the period, it exerted little influence in spite of its fame. Its imaginative realisation of the daily lives, habits, and attitudes of its characters did not succeed in showing any of the contemporary craftsmen how to escape from their oratorical habit of writing into truly cinematic construction.

But Lang seemingly could not even learn from himself. His next two films, *You Only Live Once* (1937) and *You and Me* (1938) defended reformed criminals from social persecution. Their somewhat thin argument was rendered the more doubtful since both pictures veered toward melo-drama, after a perfunctory bow in the direction of their official themes. *You Only Live Once* was taut and effec-tive as entertainment; *You and Me* disjointed and wan-dering. The latter is historically the more interesting. Its attempt at poetic narration, while it fell oddly on the ears

117. WE FROM KRONSTADT, directed by EFIM DZIGAN. [Soviet, 1936]

118. LA BELLE EQUIPE, directed by JULIEN DUVIVIER. JEAN GABIN, VIVIANNE ROMANCE.
[French, 1936]

119. FURY, directed by FRITZ LANG.   [American, 1936]

120. MR. DEEDS GOES TO TOWN, directed by FRANK CAPRA.   GARY COOPER.
[American, 1936]

of 1938, was a forerunner of much else, and its prison scenes were Lang at his very best, compassionate and angry.

You and Me, a box-office failure, dismayed and puzzled Hollywood, and for a time Lang was idle. Twentieth Century-Fox cautiously entrusted him with the direction of routine Westerns (*The Return of Frank James, Western Union*) and eventually, at the urging of Kenneth Macgowan, allowed him to film *Man Hunt,* (1941), from Geoffrey Household's unique novel, *Rogue Male.* This polished melodrama somewhat restored his prestige. In 1943, the vogue of anti-Nazi films permitted him to make *Hangmen Also Die,* centring round the assassination of Heydrich, the Nazi 'Protector' of Czechoslovakia. Considering its elements—espionage and counter-espionage, the very stuff of Lang's best work—it was curiously uneven and unconvincing. Lang, working with American actors on an American theme, had produced *Fury.* Lang trying to re-create his own Central Europe on a Hollywood set, was completely at sea. This had been the experience of other imported directors before him, and is an apparently inescapable dilemma. Perfunctorily praised for its patriotic intent, *Hangmen Also Die* hardly advanced Lang's career, or cast much light on the European underground. At the end of the war, he joined forces with Walter Wanger and Joan Bennett to form Diana Productions, his own unit. Presumably his purpose was to escape as much as possible from commercial restrictions, but the results so far hardly bear out these good intentions. *The Woman in the Window, Scarlet Street,* and *The Secret Beyond the Door* are acceptable thrillers in the style currently popular, but they might have been made by any of the studios and show only occasional signs of their director's technical inventiveness.

It is said that Lang searches endlessly for suitable film material, and works tirelessly on his own scripts for months before production. His failure to find important stories, or to bring them to the screen importantly, may perhaps reflect a good deal more than his fear of the commercial market.

It is almost inescapable to suppose that his own outlook is involved. To attempt to express the dislocations of this age of anxiety in terms of melodrama is an interesting and thoughtful idea. But it needs a deeper approach than Lang has ever brought to it, even in *M*, even in *Doctor Mabuse*. His films, for all their painstaking craftsmanship, are apt to emerge as melodramas thinly tied to current events. Their topicality seems to have a commercial rather than a philosophic origin.

The work of Frank Capra has been considered in detail in the first part of this chapter. The most valued and the most powerful director in Hollywood, his work has not been fully appreciated by many critics. His sentimental outlook has put them off. But there can be little question that he is a first-rate film maker. As ingenious as Lubitsch in inventing action and business, his most salient talent is that of editing. He approaches his films as might Griffith, or Eisenstein; their issue to him is a matter of analytical construction. His editing skill was the basis for the excellence of the *Why We Fight* U.S. Army films, which have also been treated earlier.[1]

Capra's only Hollywood rival in terms of commercial and critical prestige is John Ford. He is actually more admired and more praised than Capra. There is a feeling outside America that Ford fights harder to use the screen for worthwhile purposes, that to him the box-office is a necessary evil. His career during the past fifteen years has alternated between pictures produced at studio instructions and productions which, for reasons of his own, he has fought to make. Ford adapted himself readily to sound technique and began at once to make intelligent use of it. *Men Without Women* (1930) carried on the virile tradition he established with *The Iron Horse* and *Three Bad Men*. *Arrowsmith* (1931) was a resourceful version of a novel difficult to adapt to the screen. *The Lost Patrol* (1934) was a *succès d'estime*, and its reception by the critics laid the foundation for what has since become the cult of Ford.

[1] *Vide,* pp. 461, 462.

His celebrated *The Informer* of the following year crystallised the cult and established widely his reputation.

It is a curious reputation, based on the fact that Ford had to coax his producers, R.K.O., to allow him to make *The Lost Patrol* and *The Informer,* that both were made on extremely low budgets, that at first they were weak at the box-office only to recoup their losses later on as a result of swelling critical acclaim. This is a fine-sounding success story, but one that will unfortunately not bear analysis. As great contributions to the screen, both films were doubtful. It is true that they contained subject matter of a maturity from which the screen usually shies, but the treatment was anything but mature. It was romantic and sentimental, right down to the very details of the camerawork. Margot Grahame introduced *The Informer* as a whore on a street corner; but camera and lighting transmogrified her into an image of the madonna. This pretentious, adolescent symbolism continued throughout the film. The power of Liam O'Flaherty's story was dissipated in a welter of camera pictorialism so studiously ' artistic ' as to betray Ford's—and his admirers'—ardent desire to have the screen acquire prestige through reduplication of the effects of more traditionally respectable media. Only in one sequence, the night in the brothel, did his direction bring out the Dostoievskian implications of the narrative and its characters. For the rest, this famous film's reputation, like that of other ' art ' films from the days of *Caligari* on, rests mainly on a self-conscious and basically false use of the camera.

Spurred by his prestige success, and still interested in Ireland, Ford persuaded R.K.O. next year to permit him to make *The Plough and the Stars* (1937), but at the cost of including Hollywood ' names ' in the cast. The resulting inadequate transcription of the celebrated play should not be blamed on Ford. For several years thereafter he directed commercial films of uneven merit, of which the best were Mr. Goldwyn's horrendous *Hurricane* (1937) and the Western *Stagecoach* (1938), which took its place beside

The Informer as a Ford cultist piece. Widely acclaimed as an intelligent use of the materials of the typical Western, it certainly achieved excitement and suspense, but I cannot see that its virtuosity equalled that of Ford's more recent *My Darling Clementine* (1946). This quite remarkable film also told a melodramatic tale, but one which depended for its force on the actualities of Western life seventy years ago. Melodrama or not, it was an eloquent and convincing account of the folkways of the cattle country in a period of growth, settlement, and economic transition. Ford has rarely surpassed his camerawork and his invention of action than in this recent film.

In 1939, Ford attempted a biography, *Young Mr. Lincoln,* with what was, to me, great success. His account of an incident in the early life of Lincoln succeeded in suggesting all that was latent in the character of the obscure young prairie lawyer. This film was, incidentally, the first signal of Hollywood's approaching emergence from the artificiality of the sound stages. Since the first talkies, nearly every scene of every film had been shot inside the studios, however difficult or costly it might be to reproduce landscapes and city streets on the lot. In *Young Mr. Lincoln,* Ford took his actors outdoors for many scenes, and for the first time in years audiences saw actual sunlight fall on the faces of favourite stars.

He attempted to extend this naturalism in his next film, *The Grapes of Wrath* (1940). This brilliant and courageous achievement, by which Ford is best known, while it made necessary changes in plot and prudent concessions to political prejudice, preserved the essence of Steinbeck's monumental epic of agricultural mass-migration. For the first time, millions of Americans saw their faces, and their fate, on the entertainment screen. The folkways, speech habits, idioms and emotions of a vast suppressed minority were dramatised to the life by Ford, with a power, humanity, and compassion wholly admirable. Difficult as it must always be to transform a work of art in one medium into an achievement of equal quality in another, Ford can be said to have succeeded in all essentials. In this film, more than in any of his ' arty ' ones, more than in *The Long Voyage Home* or in *The Informer,* he strove for the look and sound of actual life. If the actors occasionally looked like actors, even without make-up, if the carefully filtered skies and landscapes were reminiscent of the familiar skies and landscapes of the studios, this was perhaps inevitable. It was as though Ford and his technical staff, being out of practice so long, actually had forgotten how to photograph the stuff of life, even when given Darryl Zanuck's *carte blanche*. Such defects were incidental to this film, though significant of the effects of Hollywood's general practice. What mattered, what matters to-day, is that Ford succeeded in producing a noble picture of emotional and social significance to every American. It understates the case to say also that *The Grapes of Wrath* contributed vitally to the political education of American voters.

How Green Was My Valley (1941), a careful version of Richard Llewellyn's novel, was Ford's last important film before he entered the Services. A series of episodes linked by the newly-popular narration in the first person by the leading character, it could not match in the Twentieth Century-Fox studio the sincerity of the British *The Stars Look Down* (1939), on the same theme. But it was a moving film, and another example of Ford's increasing interest in the problems of modern existence. During the war he made a number of films for the U.S. Navy, including *The Battle of Midway,* and then returned to direct *They Were Expendable* (1945) for M-G-M. In a sense this document of the Japanese attack on the Philippines was his last Navy film; it is said to be one of the most vigorous and eloquent of all his films. *My Darling Clementine* (1946) has already been described; for sheer inventiveness of camera placement and camera angle, it has no match in recent years. It is a throwback to an almost-forgotten cinematic tradition.

Ford's latest film, *The Fugitive* (1947) produced independently in Mexico with Merian C. Cooper, is at the moment the centre of a bitter controversy, mostly of a political tinge. Graham Greene's novel, *The Power and the Glory*, told of a decadent priest, symbol of the decay of the church in general, who is restored to his faith and his duty to his people through his sufferings under an anti-clerical dictatorship. The film transforms this study of conscience and divided personality into a simple conflict between a humanitarian church and an authoritarian state. More : the methods of this state and its protagonists are ruthlessly totalitarian, but its slogans and speeches are those of liberal democracy. Arthur Knight has said of *The Fugitive,* ' it is a film that Franco will enjoy.' This is perhaps excessive, and certainly must have been far from Ford's intentions; yet he must take the responsibility for an inadequate and misleading approach to a complex theme of great importance. Perhaps the responsibility should also be shared by Dudley Nichols, who has written most of Ford's best films to the benefit of both. Certainly, the correct statement and resolution of this conflict was a script problem.

Wherever the blame for the implications and effects of this film lie, Ford must answer for them. For *The Fugitive* was made to his own taste, independent of the restrictions of Hollywood supervision. It is perhaps significant that the technique of *My Darling Clementine* here becomes, as it were, over-ripe. The camera dwells too lovingly on this desert land inhabited by peasants; its eye is pictorial, romantic rather than realistic. Here, as in preceding films, there can be no question of Ford's enormous talent for the medium, or of his drive to explore and disclose life as it is actually lived. It is equally clear that he needs the collaboration, and perhaps the guidance, of a temperament less sentimental than his own. Without it, his command of the film medium is apt to be put to the service of confused thinking.

Lewis Milestone's career in sound began auspiciously. *All Quiet on the Western Front* (1930) created a sensation by restoring camera mobility and cutting complexity in the days of static photographed plays. Seen to-day, it is still powerful. Its pacifism is fantastically out of the contemporary argument, its histrionism and dialogue theatrical, but its rendering of trench warfare intense and real. In *The Front Page* (1931), he attacked and solved the problem of photographing a stage play within the limits and resources of the screen. This film taught many other filmmakers the lessons Milestone himself had learned from the Russians concerning cutting and the functional use of sound. His leadership at this period in Hollywood was unquestioned and his promise unlimited, for his films were commercial as well as critical successes. But in the succeeding decade, his career has been uncertain and his talent fitful. *Rain* (1932), in Norbert Lusk's words, ' dwindled to a mere drizzle ', and it is difficult to remember anything about such films as *Paris in Spring* and *Anything Goes*. Here and there along the way he tried interesting things : *The Captain Hates the Sea* (1934), a mordant study of the foibles of pleasure-seekers, in which the late John Gilbert gave a memorable performance; *The General Died at Dawn* (1936), an odd attempt to treat a Clifford Odets script in the portentous manner of Sternberg. Milestone's come-back occurred in 1940 with his production of Steinbeck's *Of Mice and Men* for Hal Roach. Produced simultaneously with *The Grapes of Wrath,* it is every inch the equal of that remarkable film. Although the story is more intimate, less epic, than the saga of the Okies, Milestone succeeded in making it point from the particular to the general. Under the surface life of a Western wheat ranch, his camera discovered the menace and insecurity of industrialised existence, and the loneliness of men forced to adapt to it. Depending heavily on actors and dialogue, this was nonetheless an eloquent film.

Momentarily back in his stride, Milestone soon lost the pace again. His war films, *Edge of Darkness* (1943), *The North Star* (1944), and *The Purple Heart* (1944), were routine treatments of familiar material. *A Walk in the Sun* (1945), had the bite of reality in its soldier characterisations, pointing up Lewis Jacobs' summation : ' Like many directors, Milestone needs subject matter that is real and that he can believe in.' [1] Whether he strives for such material is something of a mystery. Milestone at his best is a director of top competence with a style of his own; but it would be difficult, even for a connoisseur, to tell who directed the majority of his films.

*

William Wyler has steadily progressed from his beginnings in the silent days and now has reached a high peak of ability. *Counsellor-at-Law* (1933), *Dodsworth* (1936), *These Three* (1936), *Come and Get It* (1937) and *Dead End* (1937), derived from novels or the stage, were truly *adapted* to the screen. With *Jezebel* (1938) Wyler achieved new complexity. This weak play was transformed into a telling recreation of the old South, its code, speech, manners, and its implicit doom. This was a vividly pointed and mature film. Before entering the U.S. Air Force, Wyler skilfully transcribed to the movies *Wuthering Heights* (1939), and *The Little Foxes* (1941), taking leave to make that bonanza of wartime sentiments, *Mrs. Miniver* (1943).

After his admirable Army documentary, *Memphis Belle*, Wyler returned to direct *The Best Years of Our Lives* (1946) for Samuel Goldwyn. This document of American psychology establishes Wyler as the equal of any director in Hollywood in his command of the medium. The story, with its profusion of characters and motives, might easily have become a static literary piece. But throughout its great length, it is the camera that speaks. Not only in such scenes as that in which the disabled sailor looks out of the nose of the plane at dawn over his native city, or that in which the ex-Air Force captain flies again in imagination; even sequences seemingly dominated by dialogue draw their life from camera placement and cutting construction.

[1] *The Rise of the American Film,* Lewis Jacobs (Harcourt Brace, 1939), p. 489.

Scenes such as those in Hoagy Carmichael's saloon challenge comparison with the analytical approach of Pabst and Stroheim. This film solves narrative problems which have troubled directors since the beginning of the sound era. It remains to be seen whether other directors, or Wyler himself, can match its preservation of thematic coherence in the face of such a wealth of material.

While William Wyler drew his themes mainly from the stage, William Wellman relied upon the topical material furnished by the journalists who came to Hollywood as writers in the first years of the talkies. *The Public Enemy* (1931), brilliantly as it was directed, drew its major strength from careful writing. On the other hand, *Wild Boys of the Road* (1933), derived from the Russian *Road to Life,* and *The President Vanishes* (1935), a heavy-handed anti-Fascist parable, were better directed than written. Wellman's vigorous style matured with *A Star Is Born* (1937), a devastatingly frank study of Hollywood, and two excellent comedies, *Nothing Sacred* (1937) referred to earlier, and *Roxie Hart* (1941). In 1943, Twentieth Century-Fox unaccountably permitted him to make *The Ox-Bow Incident* (*Strange Incident* in Britain), a sombre story of a lynching, in which deliberate sadism rather than mob-hysteria was emphasised. Somewhat over-artful, and so abrupt in construction as to suggest story difficulties caused by censorship, the film had a fundamental reality which evoked much critical admiration. Wellman's best work is in *The Story of G.I. Joe* (1945), which is also one of the masterpieces of the sound film. One of the many attempts at applying the documentary approach to semi-fictional material, the film is something of an object-lesson in the difficulties involved in such an attempt. Beginning awkwardly and artificially, it gathers strength as acting is gradually subordinated to spontaneous behaviour and as the story is told mutely, through indirection rather than statement. The final sequence of the death of the captain is beyond praise or criticism—an authentic piece of cinema.

Frank Borzage is usually dismissed as the sentimentalist

of the screen, but the integrity of his best work cannot be so easily by-passed. *A Farewell to Arms* (1932) contrived to make its Hemingway original look cheap. For the phoney (and essentially sentimental) realism of the novel, Borzage substituted a frankly romantic approach. This gain in honesty was a gain in power : the human consequences of war were typified in a story of two lovers. *Little Man, What Now?* (1934) and *Three Comrades* (1938) preceded the war-time anti-Nazi films by many years and were immeasurably superior to them. In these two pictures Borzage examined the German mind and exposed the seeds of Nazism; the affinity of his style with the German travelling camera of the ' golden ' period, and with the German flair for giving inanimate objects a life of their own, is not without significance. Borzage has ceased to do interesting work, but the three films mentioned above, together with his *Bad Girl* (1931), deserve to be remembered.

Of other directors who received their training during the silent period, Stroheim was finally permitted by Fox to direct a sound film, *Walking Down Broadway* (1932), later re-edited and re-shot by another director as *Hello Sister* (1933). The original version, reputed to be forty reels long, was described by an official of the company as suitable for showing to a psycho-analysts' convention, and to that only. Since that time, Stroheim has continuously acted in French and American films, but has never been given the direction of another picture by Hollywood. Cecil B. De Mille's position in the talkies is even more fantastic than his rôle in the silent era. From *The Squaw Man* (1914) to *Unconquered* (1947), nothing in his outlook or sense of values has altered in the slightest. During the past fifteen years, he has made no effort to keep up with fashions in technique or subject matter, and has long since ceased to exert the influence that was his in the early twenties. Yet the phenomenal grosses of his films demonstrate conclusively that there is a vast subliminal public for pseudo-religious and patriotic subjects, however

' dated ' these themes appear to other directors. Perhaps it is not so simple as that. Crude as his films may be, they are of the stuff of cinema. His recreation of the ancient world in *The Sign of the Cross* (1932) was an achievement not matched by anyone else, and *The Plainsman* (1936) was admirably constructed as well as vastly entertaining.

Henry King has continued at the top of the commercial heap throughout the talkies, but the painstaking craftsmanship of his silent films is less and less evident. *State Fair* (1933) and *Jesse James* (1939) were imaginative renderings of Americana, but *Lloyds of London* (1936) and *In Old Chicago* (1937) are more typical of his work in sound. The late W. S. Van Dyke achieved world fame with his adroit comedy, *The Thin Man* (1934); a year earlier he had made a last film in the style of his *White Shadows* and *Trader Horn*. *Eskimo* was a synthetic *Nanook*. He was also responsible for *San Francisco* (1936), *Marie Antoinette* (1938) and many other box-office successes. Victor Fleming's perennial career reached a climax with the colossal *Gone With The Wind* (1939), most publicised and most commercially successful of all movies to date. His direction of this telescoped encyclopaedia was creditable, as it generally is. Fleming's talkies include an excellent version of *Treasure Island* (1934) and the sharp-edged, Jean Harlow, Hollywood satire, *Blonde Bombshell* (1933). Edmund Goulding began his sound career promisingly with three pictures which he wrote and directed: *The Trespasser* (1929), *The Devil's Holiday* (1930), and *Night Angel* (1931): these were good examples of film construction, and evidenced intelligent use of sound. When Hollywood showed no interest in these experiments, he relapsed into photographing plays and novels which he has done ever since with monotonous success.

Frank Lloyd, who entered films in 1910, reached his peak with *Mutiny on the Bounty* (1935). Studded with stars and over-complex in story, this was none the less a remarkable piece of film composition. The feeling of the sea, of sailing ships, and the magic of the South Sea Islands, were imaginatively evoked through the camera alone. Literary at times, the main drive of the story was visual, and Lloyd's handling of his mass of material was capably selective. Since then, he has produced and directed big-time action pictures of no particular distinction, with the exception of his recent *Blood on the Sun* (1944), an effective war melo-drama somewhat marred by censorship.

Wesley Ruggles, who began as a Keystone cop, made the pioneering sound epic, *Cimarron* (1931), and has also directed *I'm No Angel* (1934), *I Met Him in Paris* (1937), and *Sing You Sinners* (1938). Gregory La Cava, who composes his films as he shoots, has made *The Half Naked Truth* (1933), *Gabriel Over the White House* (1933), *Private Worlds* (1935), *My Man Godfrey* (1936), and that close-textured study of the under-privileged, *The Primrose Path* (1940). Michael Curtiz, famed as Warners' most successful box-office director, has made *The Cabin in the Cotton* (1932), *Black Fury* (1935), *Angels with Dirty Faces* (1938), *Casablanca* (1943), and *Mission to Moscow* (1943). Mervyn Le Roy guided two pictures of great social interest, *I Am a Fugitive from a Chain Gang* (1932), and *They Won't Forget* (1937). Howard Hawks, a very good all-rounder, stays in the mind with *The Crowd Roars* (1931), *Scarface* (1932), *Ball of Fire* (1941), and Raymond Chandler's *The Big Sleep* (1947). Raoul Walsh, who will be remembered from silent days, deserves mention for *The Roaring Twenties* (1939), with its attempted documentary use of newsreel, and *High Sierra* (1941) from John Huston's script. Henry Hathaway staged the slick thriller, *Lives of a Bengal Lancer* (1935), and more recently adapted documentary technique to the fiction film, under the tutelage of Louis de Rochemont, in *The House on 92nd Street* (1945), and *13 Rue Madeleine* (1947). His *Kiss of Death* (1947) was one of the most convincing and realistic of the revived gangster cycle, utilising actual backgrounds as did its immediate predecessors.

Other directors who had begun film-making in the silent period and who have carried on competently, include

Clarence Brown, Sidney Franklin, Rowland V. Lee, Allan Dwan, E. H. Griffith, Jack Conway, Sam Wood, Frank Tuttle and Harry Beaumont. Tod Browning disappeared after making a sound film of considerable imagination, *Freaks* (1932), while Monta Bell and Mal St. Clair have descended to making minor comedies.

*

Among directors whose experience is confined to the sound film, George Cukor and William Dieterle were the first to assume importance. Cukor occasionally attempts to explore the medium as such—more or less after the manner of Hitchcock—as in *What Price Hollywood?* (1932) and *Gaslight* (1944), but for the most part is content with conventional adaptations of stage successes, old and new (*Our Betters*, 1933; *Camille*, 1937; *The Philadelphia Story*, 1940). He is, in a manner of speaking, a William De Mille or Maurice Tourneur of the talkies, tasteful, meticulous, but without interest in, or flair for, the film itself. William Dieterle, a Reinhardt actor who had played in early silent German films, emerged in the United States with an excellent satire, *Grand Slam* (1932), and gained prominence with *The Story of Louis Pasteur* (1936), *The Life of Emile Zola* (1937) and *Blockade* (1938). The virtues as well as the faults of these big films were mostly attributable to their writers, but Dieterle achieved great compliment because of their crusading spirit. Shortly he became the producer-director of ambitious films (*The Hunchback of Notre Dame, All That Money Can Buy*) which failed to support either his critical or commercial reputation. His unquestionable talent was submerged in a welter of dialogue and ' production values '. To-day, as in the early thirties, Dieterle is a director of routine films.

Rowland Brown, ' the hero who once socked a supervisor ', is the martyr of Hollywood in the eyes of fellow-craftsmen, but his status affords him few opportunities. His first film, *Quick Millions* (1931), demonstrated what seemed like complete mastery of the sound film : ' extraordinarily adult ', says Lewis Jacobs, ' in its conception, editing, and appeal.' [1] Thereafter he was announced for picture after picture, but in each case (with the exception of *Hell's Highway* and *Blood Money*) removed from control early in production. He is said to have completed *The Devil is a Sissy* (1936) from his own script, but the film was almost entirely re-made by another director—a companion piece, so to speak, of Stroheim's talkie which emerged as *Hello Sister*. Like Stroheim, he seems naïvely unable either to come to terms with the studios, or to cajole them into doing things his way. Brown rarely works to-day, except in an advisory or co-writer capacity.

Garson Kanin, a bright young man from Broadway, was brought to Hollywood by Goldwyn in 1936, and given a period of training in the cutting rooms and on the sound stages. Nothing materialised for Mr. Goldwyn from this sensible apprenticeship, but Kanin shortly induced R.K.O. to permit him to make *A Man to Remember* (1938), as a small-budget picture. It emerged as a ' sleeper ' to general critical acclaim. It was a remarkable first film, rich-textured, mature, and successfully emotional. Kanin followed it with an amusing and pathetic *genre* piece, *The Great Man Votes* (1939), and with the brilliant satire *Tom, Dick, and Harry* (1940). This penetratingly realistic version of a typical ' confession tale ' plot highlighted the dilemma of the contemporary working girl whose intelligence and imagination make her reach out for greater economic and emotional satisfactions than circumstances permit. One of the most original comments on American life made in the thirties, the film's only fault lay in the contrived dream sequences done in the dated manner of the experimental theatre of thirty years ago. Like many others, Kanin failed to realise that the art of movie magic lies not in making the impossible happen in an impossible world—but in making it happen in the demonstrably solid, real world of everyday. Sennett, Keaton, and Dovjenko have demonstrated this

[1] *The Rise of the American Film*, Lewis Jacobs (Harcourt, Brace 1938), p. 490.

over and over again, yet directors continue to conceive their dream-sequences in terms of soft-focus, bizarre furniture, and, latterly, of Dali (e.g. *Farewell, My Lovely*).

Entering the armed forces, Kanin directed one of the best documentaries of the war *Fellow-Americans* (1942). This extremely short film did no more than chronicle the emotional effects of Pearl Harbour, but so genuinely and with such sincerity that it deserves to be called the only mature film of patriotic feeling ever to be made in the United States. After doing restricted film work for the Office of Strategic Services, Kanin went to England to make, with Carol Reed, the great documentary, *The True Glory* (1945), which has been commented upon above. This film demonstrates conclusively how profound is Kanin's feeling for the medium, but he has made no subsequent films, devoting himself to playwriting since the end of the war. Incidentally, the screen version of his play *Over 21*, written and directed by Sidney Buchman, was the most thoughtful comment on the real issues of the war as they apply to American life that has yet emerged from Hollywood. Kanin's eventual return to film-making is a foregone conclusion, and is to be eagerly anticipated.

Orson Welles' *Citizen Kane* (1941) came to the screen with more advance speculation and fanfare than any film since *Intolerance*. Welles had done experimental work on Broadway in the middle and late thirties with the W.P.A. Theatre, and a modern-dress *Julius Caesar* and a negro *Macbeth,* but his fame derived from a series of striking radio broadcasts culminating in his sensational presentation of H. G. Wells' *The War of the Worlds*.[1] This broadcast was literally believed by thousands and caused panics in the eastern United States. The resulting notoriety brought Welles to Hollywood, where R.K.O. gave him *carte blanche* to produce, direct, write, and act in his own productions. The first of these was surrounded with portentous secrecy, but was rumoured to be an account of the life of William Randolph Hearst and was virulently attacked, after seeing it,

[1] October 30, 1938.

by Louella O. Parsons, Hearst gossip columnist. When *Citizen Kane* was finally unveiled it received an unprecedented *succès d'estime*. Its deforming lenses and foreshortened perspectives were hailed as revolutionary additions to Film Art. Cecelia Ager of *P.M.* said : ' It's as though you'd never seen a movie before.' All reservations were brushed aside as carping jealousy. Welles was almost universally hailed as an innovator whose horizons were unlimited.

In view of all this, and of the picture's renewed fame in Europe since the war, *Citizen Kane* deserves close examination. Its apparent aim, to appraise the life of a flamboyant newspaper publisher in terms of his actual contribution to society, was praiseworthy and, for the screen, daring. The method chosen to reveal him, that of refracting his personality through the memories of various people who had known him, shifts the emphasis from the public importance of his work to the dislocations of his personality, and the story rapidly becomes a sort of detective story in search of the key to his psyche. The solution eventually offered to that particular mystery is tinpot Freud, if not crackpot Freud. To say that Welles was distracted from his original aim by the temptations of his bravura material is part of the truth. It is more on the target, however, to point out that themes and ideas are of only perfunctory importance to Welles. Technical virtuosity is his true enjoyment. This is sometimes admitted by his admirers, who add that his virtuosity alone would make him a master. On the basis of the record so far, it is difficult to see why this should be agreed to. Most of his methods are crude and eclectic adaptations of devices invented by the film pioneers, and even those acclaimed as entirely new—the lenses and the perspectives—are chiefly devices which more experienced directors avoid because they call attention to the process of film-making. What is salient, however, is that all these florid innovations merely disguise a technique which is basically that of the stage. The camera flourishes serve as brilliant decorations for a story told through dialogue or

121. REMBRANDT, directed by ALEXANDER KORDA. [British, 1936]

122. NIGHT MAIL, directed by BASIL WRIGHT and HARRY WATT. [British, 1936]

123. THEODORA GOES WILD, directed by RICHARD BOLESLAWSKI. IRENE DUNNE.
[American, 1937]

124. DEAD END, directed by WILLIAM WYLER. MARJORIE MAIN, HUMPHREY BOGART.
[American, 1937]

through verbal narration. The key scene in *Citizen Kane* occurs when Joseph Cotten tells Welles why their friendship must end. In this scene we learn for the first, and last, time that Kane had once been a friend of the people and of labour, and had used his newspapers in their interests, but that self-absorption had transformed him into a power-hungry reactionary. Here alone is the theme clearly stated, and stated in a speech so long as to become a monologue. During this speech, the camera describes a complete circle around the figures of the two men, at last coming to rest at its starting point. The effect is not unlike those moments in early musical films when the camera wandered all over the set in order that the audience should not tire while a singer delivered a lengthy aria. Much the same comment could be made of the famous ' scene in three perspectives ' at the beginning of the film, the meat of which is also given through speech.

Welles was a very young man at the time of making *Citizen Kane,* and its initial success intoxicated him. Whereas he had the guidance of the veteran Joseph Mankiewicz during the making of *Citizen Kane,* he embarked alone on the writing and direction of *The Magnificent Ambersons* (1942). This film lacked the roots in community life which were the strength of the Booth Tarkington novel (Welles states that scenes indicating the growth of an industrial community were excised by the studio, but they do not seem to be organically missing) and, in spite of moments of skill and intensity, was essentially a literary film. Its great central set of the Amberson mansion would have been admirable on a Theatre Guild stage, but in film it limited and retarded the action. Before it was released, to renewed critical acclaim but to popular indifference, Welles had completed shooting on *Journey into Fear* (1943) and gone to Mexico to begin several films, including a bull-fighting story by Flaherty. In the midst of work, R.K.O. informed him that, due to his great costs and falling grosses, his contract had been cancelled; he was to cease production and *Journey into Fear* would be released as cut by the studio. It emerged as a confused fragment, for which Welles cannot be held responsible.

This curtailment of Welles' directorial career was regarded as little short of criminal on the part of Hollywood, but it is a little difficult to feel sympathetic. Immensely publicised, Welles had contributed little to the movies beyond a certain (indefinite) social outlook and a decidedly definite eclecticism. Nevertheless the garment of martyrdom was hung on him, and he was compared to Stroheim because Hollywood permitted him to act in the trivia of others, but denied him films of his own. In 1946, he was suddenly restored to favour and given a directorial assignment. *The Stranger* was better integrated than its predecessors, and its technique was more functional, but once again Welles raised all the issues without solving them, and the film expired in a welter of melodrama which approached the ludicrous. Welles may be, as his admirers claim, the potential Marlowe of the screen, but so far he has given us only prentice work, inflated by publicity and the admiration of the half-educated.

Preston Sturges was imported to Hollywood after the Broadway success of his play, *Strictly Dishonourable,* in the early thirties. After years of hackwork he emerged as a first-rate writer of screenplays (*Easy Living,* it is now clear, owed its brilliance to his screenplay rather than to direction) and became a director at the end of the decade with *The Great McGinty* (1940). This satire on crooked politicians was an echo of the comic realism of the depression days, but it impressed aesthetes and acquired a cult. *Christmas in July* (1940) was a clever little comedy which yet demonstrated that Sturges had more than flair; it evidenced definite talent for the medium. *The Lady Eve* (1941) continued what seemed to be the development of an excellent screen humorist and nothing more, when suddenly Sturges' career climaxed in the extraordinary *Sullivan's Travels* (1941).

This is a film of contradictions. No picture has ever more savagely satirised Hollywood. The distorted values, the essential inhumanity, of the film colony are glaringly highlighted, and the futility of inflated publicity punctured in a cross-country chase which out-Sennetts Sennett. Deflated also are the pretentious directors and writers who yearn to create Art on the movie assembly-line. But what is the issue? Chastened by the admonitions of producers, who tell him he doesn't know the life of the masses, nor their desires, an arty director goes forth to seek experience. He finds it, he drinks its bitterest dregs—and comes to the conclusion that the producers were right, that the masses don't want to solve their problems but to forget them in movie escapism. The cynicism of this vindication of the box-office is at the core of Sturges' outlook and has remained characteristic of him ever since. *The Miracle of Morgan's Creek* (1943) and *Hail the Conquering Hero* (1944) satirised the follies of wartime—military romance, hero worship, ' Mom ' idolatry, and small-town politics. In writing and direction these are brilliant films. But their essential statement—and they make a statement—is that human beings are dopes. Winning, lovable, amusing dopes, to be sure, but dopes none the less, and a man is a fool who says otherwise or tries to do anything about it. This is, of course, the essence of what passes for philosophy in Hollywood, but no one before has ever articulated it so boldly, perhaps because no one else had the talent to sugar-coat the pill and get away with it.

Sturges has the talent. He can make you laugh explosively for two hours together. He has a style and resourcefulness not seen in film comedies since the early days of Sennett, Chaplin, and Keaton. But his is an inverse kind of satire. He is not interested in crushing infamy, but in recording it and implying that nothing can be done about it. Somewhere he knows this. The defensiveness of *Sullivan's Travels* is implicit elsewhere in his films. He tried to escape from comedy in *The Great Moment,* a film about the discovery of anaesthesia which was taken away from him by Paramount and reached the screen as a comedy on a serious subject. Seeking independence, he made with

Howard Hughes and Harold Lloyd *The Sin of Harold Diddlebock* (1947), rechristened *Mad Wednesday*. This attempt to revive the style of the old Lloyd comedies began brilliantly with the last reel of *The Freshman*. But the original idea of showing what happens to a football hero once ejected into the cold, post-collegiate world, got lost in mechanical slapstick devices far below the level of the old Lloyd inventions. Sturges has now returned to the commercial studios. His future lies in his own hands because all his films are original creations, from script to screen. The question appears to be, what can he find to say that will not denigrate his self-assumed position as critic at large of things-as-they-are?

Of all the directors who have arisen since the sound film, John Huston shows the soundest talent, displays the most conspicuous feeling for the medium. Son of the actor, Walter Huston, he had led a vagabond life as actor, prize-fighter, and Mexican cavalryman before coming to Hollywood to write the screenplays for such of the Warner social dramas as *Juarez, Dr. Ehrlich's Magic Bullet,* and *High Sierra*. In 1941 he directed as well as wrote *The Maltese Falcon*. This Dashiell Hammett melodrama had been filmed twice before, and had nothing in particular to say, but it was immediately clear that Huston was a greatly gifted director. His success in evoking the semi-civilised Hammett world, so symptomatic of the actual world we live in, was largely a matter of camera placement and of the use of light and of inanimate objects. In 1942, he again used the enigmatic mask of Humphrey Bogart for melodramatic purposes in *Across the Pacific,* less successful than its predecessor, and struggled for social comment with a Bette Davis vehicle, *In This Our Life*. Like so many others, the war freed him from studio limitations and gave him fresh material and the opportunity to use fresh methods. His *Report from the Aleutians* (1943) was a strange, impressionist study of the war in the sub-polar waters of Alaska; his *Battle of San Pietro* (1944) was an outright attack on all wars, and the way in which this particular war was waged. The poetry of this film has already been remarked upon.[1] The extraordinary reality of its portrait of G.I. life has never been matched by any other director. Although I have characterised the picture as an attack, it did not editorialise. It disclosed the psychology of enlisted men by sheer observation. The character of this film was, of course, disliked by the U.S. War Department, which produced it. Colonels in the Pentagon fiddled with commentary and editing in an effort to modify its essential statement, but however it was changed around it managed to continue to say that war is an affront to the human spirit. Huston's last Army film was *Let There Be Light* (1945), a study of methods of mental therapy developed to rehabilitate victims of psychoneuroses resulting from combat. At once scientific and compassionate, the film achieved a documentary naturalism matched by no other. It has never been shown publicly. The War Department suppressed it on ' legal ' grounds.

Returning to Warner Brothers, Huston wrote and directed a version of *The Treasure of the Sierra Madre* (1947), from a novel by the mysterious B. Traven, of Mexico. This dissection of the disintegration of three men lured by gold inevitably recalls Stroheim's *Greed,* not only because of the central theme but also because of the backgrounds—squalor of cities and the threatening might of the desert—which play so powerful a rôle in the expression of the idea. The comparison is not unjustified, and the parallels are many and curious. Like *Greed,* the Huston film falters, the structure is uneven, the theme seems forgotten at times and the action wanders into irrelevancies. But it is many a year since a director in Hollywood has used action, the human countenance, and the brooding face of nature to take us into the minds, and the guts, of his characters. Forgotten devices once more come into their own in this film. The use of symbols is reminiscent not only of Stroheim but of Pabst, the creation of a climate of feeling which surrounds the action is the unmistakable

[1] Cf. page 463.

signet of the great film director, and the picture as a whole challenges, in its best moments, the best moments of any film made anywhere at any time. Huston's first-hand knowledge of life as most people live it, his ability to absorb the lessons of past film-making (without merely reproducing them, as in the case of Mamoulian and Welles) and the fact that he is able to construct and write his own films, suggest an unlimited future.

Vincente Minnelli came from Broadway to Hollywood to make musical films and, after some prentice work, directed *Meet Me in Saint Louis* (1944) and *The Clock* (1945). Both of these pieces of Americana were first-rate movies, racy, vigorous, and visual. They had a technical style and a human understanding which seemed to put Minnelli in a class with Huston and Kanin among the new directors. *The Clock* in particular was a true piece of cinematography. Since then, Minnelli has directed commercial films (*Yolanda and The Thief, Ziegfeld Follies, Undercurrent*) which give no indication of the film style which had been emerging in the previous productions. *The Clock* was attacked by screen writers, such as Stephen Longstreet, on the ground that its free use of the camera represented a reactionary step backward from the 'modern' screenplay in which the story is told through dialogue. Perhaps Minnelli took the hint.

Of other new directors, Stuart Heisler rose from the cutting room to direct such excellent films as *The Biscuit Eater* (1940) and *Along Came Jones* (1942), as well as the Army film, *The Negro Soldier in World War II*. Irving Pichel, once an actor, is one of Hollywood's most vigorous proponents of serious films, but his work (*A Medal for Benny, The Pied Piper*) has yet to show the intelligent grasp of film principles exemplified in his theoretical writings. Robert Siodmak, who directed in Germany and France in the thirties, employs Teutonic camerawork to enhance the effectiveness of shockers like *The Spiral Staircase, The Phantom Lady* and *The Killers*, all good of their kind. Another young director who has made his name during the war years and after is Edward Dmytryk. His thriller *Farewell, My Lovely* (1944) from Raymond Chandler's novel, excited almost as much interest as Huston's *The Maltese Falcon* had done in 1941. In 1945, Dmytryk went to England with Adrian Scott as producer on a joint Rank-Twentieth Century-Fox arrangement, and made *So Well Remembered,* a sincere well-made if too long film about the social struggles of a North Country newspaper editor. At the time, the film did not attract much comment, but I am told that Dmytryk caught the feeling and atmosphere of the industrial north in a way that many British directors fail to do. In 1947, again with Scott as producer, Dmytryk directed *Crossfire* for Dore Schary at R.K.O., which dealt with the dynamite theme of anti-Semitism with more honesty and fearlessness than any other Hollywood film. Extremely well-directed, with excellent dialogue from John Paxton, *Crossfire* is one of the very few outstanding progressive films to come from America in recent years, and it was successful box-office. It is ironic, to put it mildly, that Scott and Dmytryk were two of the personalities insulted and slandered at the Washington Un-American Activities travesty in November, 1947.

A producer-writer-director team which has also caused wide interest is Charles Brackett and Billy Wilder, with *Double Indemnity* and *The Lost Week-End.* Wilder, an Austrian who worked first as a writer in Berlin (*People on Sunday*) and then as a director in Paris, went to Hollywood in 1933 and collaborated with Charles Brackett on the scripts of *Ninotchka* and *Ball of Fire,* among others. His first direction assignments did not cause comment, *The Major and the Minor* (1942) and *Five Graves to Cairo* (1943), but the next year *Double Indemnity* showed Wilder as a first-rate craftsman with a fine sense of movie for melodrama. The film was in the same style as the other 'psychological' thrillers, *The Blue Dahlia* and *The Spiral Staircase,* with tough clipped dialogue by Chandler and fast-moving continuity reminiscent of Rowland Brown's

503

Quick Millions in 1931. Indeed, in technique these films rediscovered many of the technical virtues that made the early gangster cycle so well remembered. Wilder's next picture was from Charles Jackson's notorious *The Lost Week-End,* in many ways a disappointing adaptation which failed to transmit to the screen the subtleties of the original.

Much admired by the aesthetes, it caused a sensation because of its subject of a pernicious alcoholic, but it was no step forward for Brackett and Wilder. The last film of this team, *The Emperor Waltz,* is a semi-musical in the worst possible taste, conforming to all the well-worn Hollywood clichés. Wilder's most promising work to date is certainly the dynamic *Double Indemnity.*

Elia Kazan, noted for his stage direction in the theatre of experiment and ideas during the 1930's, finally came to Hollywood to direct the screen version of a popular novel, *A Tree Grows in Brooklyn* (1944). This was much more than a talented transcription *à la* Zanuck; it assumed the proportions of a piece of latter-day folklore, thanks largely to the director. Kazan's second assignment was one of Louis de Rochemont's semi-documentaries, *Boomerang* (1947). It actually was closer to documentary technique than any film to come from Hollywood since sound. Although the action was plotted script-fashion, it seemed to grow out of the life of the suburban community in which it was set down. Its story was based on an actual incident in the career of an American public figure (although its authenticity is hotly disputed in some quarters). Whatever the truth of this, the blending of staged scenes and actors with real people in their own milieus has rarely been accomplished with greater smoothness. Kazan's eye for the dramatic beauty of plain people, their faces, homes, daily tasks, and amusements evidenced a strict understanding of the camera's affinity for actuality. *Boomerang* stands out as one of Hollywood's more honest pictures, and much credit is due to de Rochemont for his producership. Kazan's third film, *Gentlemen's Agreement* (1947), was forced by virtue of the fact that it was adapted from a widely-read novel to use documentary material for background only, but its story was worth telling as literally as Kazan decided to set it forth. Laura Z. Hobson's exposition of the deep roots of prejudice, and the elaborately tangled rationalisations used by quite respectable and kindly people to justify it, inevitably had to be presented largely in terms of dialogue. There was no way round this difficulty, and Kazan should not be blamed for a picture which depended mostly on actors, their thoughts and speeches, for its impact. Films as intelligent and adult as this are rare. But even in this photographed novel, Kazan gives clear evidence of his knowledge of screen structure and flair for camera values.

*

Of writers who have become directors, Dudley Nichols is the best known. Highest paid, most respected, and most powerful of all writers of screen plays, his important scripts from 1930 include *Born Reckless, The Informer, Stagecoach, The Long Voyage Home, Swamp Water* and *For Whom the Bell Tolls*. Becoming a director, he has made *Government Girl* and the recent *Mourning Becomes Electra,* which he also produced. Nichols is a paradox. Like Pichel, his theoretical writings reveal a profound comprehension of the fact that film composition is an act having little in common with the theatre or the novel. But, as *Mourning Becomes Electra* suggests, his actual scripts and films stress literary quality and theatrical construction. His elaborate reproduction of the O'Neill play was a valiant attempt to accommodate a theme expressed almost entirely through dialogue to the demands of the camera. What emerged was probably the most intelligently photographed play we have ever been given. But it was not a film.

Clifford Odets, after his sensational Broadway success as a left-wing playwright, wrote numerous screenplays (including *The General Died At Dawn*) and in 1943 directed a film of great merit, *None but the Lonely Heart.* This picture, based on Richard Llewellyn's novel, showed a firmer grasp of film principles than has been shown by any other writer-director, with the exception of Sturges.

Writers, in order to exert significant influence on the films they make, must apparently enter production or direction, or at least add those skills to their attainments. Of all the hundreds who feed the studio mills, Lillian Hellman alone has achieved reputation and influence without moving into the more active phases of production. Even Miss Hellman is more noted for her skilful adaptations of her Broadway successes (*Little Foxes, These Three, Watch on the Rhine*) than for her original screen-play, *The North Star*. In spite of the pretensions of some ambitious authors, the writing of a screen-play in itself hardly approximates to creation. By its nature it is devoid of literary quality, or even readability, and the writer must constantly strain to indicate and suggest what later will be realised visually. Even if he is successful in doing so, his work is subject to change without notice by the producer or director, not to mention a platoon of other writers who may be hired later to inject comedy, pathos, spectacle, or whatever the box-office fashion of the moment may indicate. The writers who come closest to having some voice in the final shape of their original conceptions are, as indicated, those who gravitate toward direction, such as Charles Brackett and Billy Wilder, who become producers like Sidney Buchman, or achieve an anomalous position as advisers or consultants to producers (Claude Binyon, Anthony Veiller, Albert and Frances Hackett, Leonard Spigelgass). These latter have more influence than they are generally credited with. On the whole, however, writing for the screen is apt to be a matter of year-in, year-out hackwork, with no escape for the well-paid victim except in the direction of the studio set or the administrative office.[1]

Once ensconced in the front office, however, the sailing

---

[1] To those who have never met Sammy Glick, whose spectacular career epitomises the Hollywood of the thirties, I recommend an early introduction to *What Makes Sammy Run?* by Budd Schulberg (Jarrolds).

is not always smooth. An 'associate producer' is in the long run no more than an instrument of the executive producer, who is directly responsible to the directorate and the stockholders. These Titans, in order to pay dividends and at the same time pay themselves salaries commensurate with self-respect, keep both eyes firmly on the box-office, and that means stars, musicals, and melodramas. At least this is said to be the necessity. But the crusading Warners for many years made pictures of serious purpose to adequate financial reward, and Dore Schary, new executive head of R.K.O., proved with *Crossfire* that a low-budget picture with something to say could be immensely profitable.[1] Having dared to flout hoary box-office principles, the Warners and Schary have had political punishment meted out to them, not because they were wrong about what the public wanted, but about what their stockholders wanted. Between the myth of the box-office on the one side, and the very real prejudices of the owners of the Industry on the other, the enlightened and ambitious producer must steer a zigzag course, replete with backing, filling, and sailing before the wind. Sometimes results can be achieved by charm and cajolery, as in the case of the genial Kenneth Macgowan, who has been a power behind the scenes in many good Hollywood pictures (e.g. *Ox-Bow Incident*) and a yeasty leaven in American film and theatre for many years. Sometimes they must be sought by disguising the theme under melodrama or topical muck-raking, as Walter Wanger tried to do for years until he retreated to *A Night in Paradise*, *Smash-Up*, and *The Story of a Woman*.

Val Lewton, for example, is a producer of horror films which have achieved a vogue among the intellectuals, in particular *The Cat People* (1942) and *The Curse of the Cat People* (1943). His *Youth Runs Wild* (1944) about

---

[1] According to Adrian Scott, its producer, *Crossfire* cost under £150,000 and grossed over £750,000 in the United States alone. It took twenty-two days to shoot. (*The Cine-Technician*, Vol. 14, No. 70, January, 1948.)

juvenile delinquency in war-time, was said to be one of the best of the ' city streets ' school, and his *The Body Snatcher* (1945), with Boris Karloff, was almost certainly the superior of all horror films, at least in terms of literacy and mature approach. His last film, *Bedlam* (1946), also with Karloff, had a weak script, and since then he has been inactive because of illness. It is clear that Lewton's is the directing intelligence behind all films he has produced; they maintain approximately the same level of quality regardless of who writes or directs them. This quality has been achieved, moreover, on a small budget and to remarkable box-office response. Lewton's return to activity is eagerly anticipated, especially under the aegis of Dore Schary, who may be expected to permit him to handle more serious material than has fallen to his lot in the past.

Yes, the way of the producer is hard. But perhaps intestinal ulcers might be avoided with the aid of a little more intestinal fortitude. Disregarding all the shibboleths, Samuel Goldwyn has gone his successful way producing many excellent films to excellent public response, and it is clear from his public pronouncements that he fears no man. As for political punishment, which is just now Hollywood's fear Number One, the Congressional darts directed at *The Best Years of Our Lives* fell harmlessly because the public's liking for this courageous picture was too obvious to be ignored, and was spelled out in terms of the box-office. Mr. Goldwyn seems to know the secret of surviving the stigma of intelligence, taste, and integrity. But it is evidently a secret difficult to impart or to learn, because his example has been before Hollywood for thirty years and no one has yet followed it.

Technically, the future of the Hollywood film lies in a further working out of producer-writer-director relations.[1] But the shape of the future lies with what happens to the mass-psyche in a period of what Siegfried Kracauer calls ' ideological fatigue '. There are many signs that the movie

[1] Cf. *Creativeness Cannot Be Diffused*, Irving Pichel (*Hollywood Quarterly*, Vol. 1, No. 1.)

public would welcome courageous and challenging films, and just as many to indicate that the public will not ask for them of its own accord. Will it get them? The film-makers are singularly like their audiences. They too await the Messiah. In the meantime, they make musicals.

(III) THREE INDEPENDENTS:
CHAPLIN, DISNEY, FLAHERTY

Three of cinema's major craftsmen have contrived through the years to maintain a certain independence of the mass-production studios. Apart from the importance of their work, it is of the greatest interest to consider the means by which they have remained independent—and the cost. The first was able to go his own way because the fortune he earned at the peak of his world popularity gave him the capital power to produce his own films. The second, necessarily dependent on banks and cinema distribution chains, escaped studio dominance only by creating his own assembly-line film factory. The third has gone his own way by the simple expedient of refusing to make films any way but his own. If the price of such refusal to compromise was inactivity, he silently paid it. The result has perhaps been, as Iris Barry puts it, that 'Robert Flaherty has made fewer and better films than any other eminent director.'

*

Charles Chaplin's successful defiance of the universal adoption of the talking picture is now well-known, although his reasons for at first preserving silence were long misinterpreted. When *City Lights* appeared in 1931, it was widely believed that Chaplin was challenging both the aesthetic and commercial feasibility of the talkies, an impression confirmed by the fact that the film was in all its main respects a silent picture with conventional musical accompaniment. But *Modern Times* (1936) made it clear that Chaplin did not object to speech as such. What he was trying to do was to preserve the silence of Charlie. This central figure in the pantheon of modern mythology would cease to be universal once he spoke in any particular language, or gave himself a local habitation and a name. For twenty years Chaplin's great creation had projected mankind's futile rebellion against the oppressors' wrong and proud man's contumely. If he was now to find a tongue, he must at last be specified and individualised—but individualised in some figure which would still personify the free spirit of man and the wrongs it suffers. The course of history presented Chaplin with such a figure. In *The Great Dictator* (1940), Charlie the universal, Charlie the international vagabond, becomes a Jew, and the impersonal forces which crush and humiliate him are focussed in the person of Hitler. *And Chaplin plays both.* No greater culmination to the career of Charlie is conceivable. Years before it had been remarked that the common man of the twentieth century was epitomised in two individuals, Hitler and Chaplin. And it is Chaplin himself who makes the parallel explicit, in all its profundity and in all its portent. The Hitler he presents is nobody else's Hitler. He is foolish and brilliant and savage by turns because all his attributes spring from injury, from the fact that he is a damaged human being. And the Charlie of *The Great Dictator* is not quite Charlie. Not alone because he speaks. He is now dumb in another sense. Charlie's old insouciance, his smartness, his brilliance, his occasional indications of cruelty, have now been absorbed into the Hitler character. What remains is a more subdued figure, somewhat stupid, thoroughly bewildered, no longer indomitably bright and courageous—and this new Charlie is the very image of that *homme moyen sensuel* whom Lenin feared as the greatest danger to the future of rational society. These two creatures are halves of the same whole. Together they represent that obverse of the Golden Rule which civilisation has neglected down the centuries : those to whom evil is done, do evil in return. As if to make certain that he has driven home his point, Chaplin has

Charlie momentarily become Hitler. The human truth of
our time stands out supreme in these two figures and their
identification. Amongst all the banalities of anti-fascist
art there is nowhere a similar realisation of the nature of
fascism.

Few, even among Chaplin's admirers, are willing to
grant as much. It has been the fashion for almost twenty
years now to restrict praise to Charlie as an actor and a
' personality ', and to regard both his thinking and his film-
making as somewhat old-fashioned. There is no foundation for either belief, but such is the state of film criticism.
What misleads the commentators is their failure to regard
Chaplin's work as a whole, or to relate it to the overall
history of films.

The Charlie of the early and intermediate silent films
was a rebel against the suffocation of the individual by
society. Up to and including *City Lights,* this rebellion was
expressed in the form of a somewhat Victorian irony, and
it was this dated idiom which was mistaken for dated
thinking. (It is worth remarking that all of cinema's great
exponents suffer from the same handicap: the style of
Griffith, Stroheim, Pabst, even Eisenstein, betray all the
stigmata of bourgeois culture, even when they profess to
repudiate it.) This one-man rebellion of Charlie's was
tolerated by social optimists of all parties because it seemed
a last expiring effort of romantic individualism. But when,
in *Modern Times,* Chaplin specified the inimical society to
be an industrial one, all shades of opinion were disconcerted.
Chaplin had left Chaplinland and ventured into the real
world. His very presence was a criticism of that world,
but a criticism that led nowhere that anybody wanted to
go. He prescribed no remedy. He did not stigmatise one
faction in order to uphold another; he stigmatised them
all. He seemed an anarchist. He was as unready to save
the world for this as for that. Socio-economic prescrip-
tions for socio-economic ills were none of his. No one
could take comfort from him.

It is my contention that he does not now want, and never

has wanted anyone to take comfort from him. Comfort, despite the annealing power of laughter, is not his line of goods. He is a satirist, and satire has no allegiances. Momentarily *The Great Dictator* did comfort his admirers and reassure his critics. At last, they thought, Charlie has come over to our side. Their enthusiasm was short-lived (and, as I have tried to indicate, based on a misunderstanding of the film) for *Monsieur Verdoux* (1947) again revealed a Chaplin who stands with no party and is critical of them all.

The savage sub-title, 'a comedy of murders', indicates how passionately Chaplin intended *Verdoux* to shock his public. How well he succeeded is shown by the fact that the film has achieved almost no distribution, at least in the United States. This is in part due to the boycott propaganda campaign waged against the picture and its maker by such organisations as the Catholic War Veterans and such journalists as Westbrook Pegler, a campaign tinged with Red-baiting. But I do not think the film would have made its way in the cinemas even if it had not met organised opposition. Not that it is an unpopular picture in the usual sense of the term. People are not indifferent to it or bored by it. They hate it, as they hated Stroheim's *Greed,* and for much the same reasons.[1] No wonder. It faces its audience with the gap between what they say they believe and what they do. And it implicates everyone.

As is probably well-known, Verdoux is a business man whose business happens to be that of marrying women and murdering them after they have made their property over to him. He entered this business after a period of taking stock of himself. Employed by a bank for thirty years, he finds himself out on the pavements at the first sign of a depression. Pondering the reasons for this, he concludes that he has not adequately analysed and exploited his own assets. A man of his charm and resource does not belong behind a teller's window. He belongs in the big time—and the big time, to-day, is the business of murder.

[1] Cf. page 159.

125. THEY WON'T FORGET, directed by MERVYN LE ROY.   CLAUDE RAINS.
[American, 1937]

126. A STAR IS BORN, directed by WILLIAM WELLMAN.   FREDERIC MARCH.
[American, 1937]

127. LA GRANDE ILLUSION, directed by JEAN RENOIR.   PIERRE FRESNAY, JEAN GABIN.
[French, 1937]

128. SPANISH EARTH, directed by JORIS IVENS.   [American, 1937]

The episodes which succeed this premise are designed to substantiate it in a variety of ways, and to reveal more and more of its enigmatic central figure. As Mary Miller says of Chaplin,[1] ' He has presented us with a completely new and fascinating creation. Endowed with the inimitable rhythms and inflections of a voice hitherto kept up his sleeve, Monsieur Verdoux steps upon the screen. He has an indescribable hair-do. He wears a variety of the most excruciatingly funny costumes. All the old perfections of grace and timing accompany him. He has a whole bag full of new tricks and dexterities : in short, this debonair (and only, oh, so slightly sinister) murderer, who adores his wife and child and an occasional return to the peace and quiet of domestic bliss after the excitements and agitations incident on wooing and liquidating of his bigamous consorts, is absolutely irresistible. He is tender toward his invalid wife. He reproves his little boy for being cruel to his cat. It would be difficult to do justice to the felicities of his love-making. To the poetry of his diction and the choice of his words (" This Endymian hour ! " he exclaims, as he looks from a window at the moonlit night just prior to pulling off the most horrific of his murders) there is a touch of necromancy. Everybody in his cast succumbs to the peculiar spell of his demands upon them. Suffice it to say that in each of the murderous episodes, and in the scenes in which he manages to escape or to liquidate his pursuers, his skill and brilliancy is amazing. To this spectator at least he appears to have reached the very peak of his genius as an actor and a director.'

Verdoux himself is a great figure, perhaps the greatest yet created on the screen. Such is his fascination that it is difficult at first to see beyond him. But second viewing of the film reveals the fact that he is completely and throughout the film the vehicle of what Chaplin wanted to say. Even in such scenes of apparent pure frivolity as the wedding breakfast and the attempt to drown Martha Raye,

[1] *New Movies*, The National Board of Review Magazine, Summer, 1947.

there is an intention and a design behind the incidents—so much so that the spectator comes to watch each new sequence in suspense as to what Chaplin wants him to see this time. This is the classic method of satire, and the central figure its classic prototype. Verdoux represents a number of current beliefs carried to their logical conclusion : that business is business, devil take the hindmost, that a man's private and professional worlds are utterly divorced, that his first duty is to his wife and family, that society is indeed an anarchic collection of families at war. Considering the burden of abstractions which he had to bear, Verdoux is an amazingly, a triumphantly, human figure. Beneath his insouciance there is desperate strain and dreadful boredom. His success is as empty as any success we know. In this, too, he speaks for us and all too clearly.

To make explicit what he wants to tell, Chaplin divides the film in two and gives us an old and indifferent Verdoux, serene, ironic, and hideously composed in the face of his fate and of that of all the world. Only the greatest of masters could so flout cinematic construction, but the theme demands it, and here if ever is a film governed entirely by its theme. Against that theme there has been a terrific outcry, from the left as well as from the right. *Verdoux* is an offence to us, because we are an offence to ourselves. I do not think it my place to defend the theme, except to say that I believe the film will be very well understood a century from now, and that it is perhaps already understood in western Europe, if not elsewhere.

I can't leave *Monsieur Verdoux* without commenting on the criticisms that have been made of its technique and style. These have two sources. One is Hollywood, where technicians stare in bewilderment at a film which makes no effort to conjure up ' That light which brings a Garbo alive, but in which a Chaplin cannot survive.' The other is the group of eclectics to whom the signet of film art is fancy camerawork. To these, a film is badly directed unless the camera goes about its business ostentatiously, and this view carries great weight wherever the art of the cinema is still discussed. I would, however, urge anyone who is trying to think about the functions of the camera to look as hard at *Verdoux* as he has at any film produced since 1929. By the nature of its theme, *Verdoux* has to deliver a great deal of what it says through dialogue; it is nearly Shavian in this respect. The camerawork has been adapted to this necessity with an imaginative precision I find difficult to describe. The moving or panning camera, that salvation of George Cukor, is rarely employed, and then almost entirely in mute scenes. Camerawork in scenes of dialogue is used in short shots based on analysis of movement and action. I do not think it has ever been remarked how completely, how almost in the manner of Flaherty, Chaplin's camera is an observer, an attendant on action. All its uses are determined by the invention of ' Business '. Because Chaplin himself is most of the time the central figure on the screen, this has misled many into thinking that Chaplin's own pantomimic ability is the source of the sense of rhythm and ' timing ' which everyone feels on seeing a Chaplin film. But a brief survey of scenes in which Chaplin himself does not appear should suffice to establish the fact that this sense of rhythm flows throughout the whole film. Remark the first scene in *Verdoux*. All Chaplin's films bear witness to a fundamental *observational* use of the camera which is to be seen elsewhere at times in the early work of Griffith, Flaherty, Pabst, and Lubitsch and to-day of Rossellini, but which seems to have been forgotten— or never understood—by almost everyone else.

It remains to record that Chaplin now thinks of retiring from films and moving to England. It is a measure of the events of the past thirty years that the man who once was better known to more people than anyone who has ever lived, is no longer persona grata in the country whose Film Industry he helped to popularise throughout the world.

*

The universal success of Walt Disney's cartoons was one of the most puzzling phenomena of the thirties to movie magnates. One of them said, ' You spend a million dollars on a super-spectacle and they sit through it just to see Mickey Mouse.' Intellectuals and proletarians alike were passionately fond of this enchanting figure, and only less so of all the others of Disney's profuse creation. In a depression world, the Disney fancies provided the most eagerly-sought escape and release of all. In Disneyland, violence and repressed aggression might find outlet without harm, for everything ended in sweetness and humanity. There was no meanness in any of these anthropomorphic characters, not even in the villains who were comic rather than evil. It was pleasant to leave city streets and live with them awhile.

The secret of Disney's technical superiority over other screen cartoonists lay in two things : his understanding of the possibilities of distortion in draughtsmanship, and his feeling for film rhythm. Both are seen at their earliest and best in the first Silly Symphony, *The Skeleton Dance* (1929). The formal dance in this film, with its rhythmic accompaniment of expressive sounds and music, forecast the later work in which the whole animate and inanimate world seemed to dance to the measure of the arbitrary and mercurial sound track. In most of the Silly Symphony series, this dance was almost abstract and was performed for its own delightful sake. The forms of nature were continually metamorphosed in a pattern which began and ended with itself. These films, triumphs of imaginative draughtsmanship, were greatly enhanced by the addition of colour in 1932; to the wonderful changes of fluid outline were added a succession of colour transformations which also had a rhythm of their own. *Flowers and Trees* (1932) and *The Old Mill* (1937) represent the summit of Disney's technical achievement.

These films were widely admired and enjoyed, but they were second in popularity to the Mickey series and other Disneys which featured animal characters with well-defined human characteristics. The galaxy is too intimately known to require more than mention : Mickey and Minnie, Pluto,

Clara Cluck, and of course, the formidable Donald Duck, who soon took stage centre. Mickey had been becoming increasingly genteel since his early roughhouse days, and Donald emerged about 1933 as the heckler who disrupted his elegant conducting of band concerts and grand operas and magic shows. When Donald's popularity surpassed Mickey's, and he became a star himself, his violent rages took on a different motivation. No longer himself the disturbing element, he finds himself pitted against an environment which refuses to obey what are to him his quite simple wishes, and in an hysteria of exasperation he goes to extremes to force his surroundings to do his will. This type of exasperation has a long comic history and many relationships : it is akin to Buster Keaton's animation of the inanimate, and to Laurel and Hardy's attempt to be normal in an unreliable and treacherous world. Every film writer has pointed out how these characters figure forth the individual's contemporary dilemma, and Donald now served the same purpose. From providing escape for the world, Disney had now presented it with a symbol.

His success with short subjects reached its peak with the celebrated *Three Little Pigs* (1933) which, arriving just at the moment when its economy was recovering from the worst depths of the depression, struck the American nation in exactly the right mood. It had similar reverberations all over the world. This film made as much money for Disney as a feature might have done. But such extravagant hits were necessarily rare, and he began soon to face the same dilemma with which he had confronted others. The success of his Mickeys and Donalds had sounded the death knell of the two-reel comedies in the early thirties. The veteran Mack Sennett had been forced to retire from production because of Disney's competition; Laurel and Hardy had had to launch themselves in feature films. Now Disney faced the same necessity. His short films were more popular than any had been since the days of Chaplin, but shorts, by nature of the Industry's distribution system, do not make money. For all his popular success and prestige,

Disney's annual production scarcely did more than break even. He, too, must go into feature-length production.

His first full-length film, *Snow White and the Seven Dwarfs* (1937) more than fulfilled his financial expectations; it has earned many millions of dollars and is still in circulation. Adults as well as children enjoyed this resourceful and charming fairy tale on film. Some of his team's best draughtsmanship is in it, and it added many new creations to his pantheon of folk-characters. But there were signs that Disney was deserting the sources of his own strength. From *The Skeleton Dance* on, he had observed correctly that the camera is not to be used in conjunction with cartoon material as it is used to photograph the three-dimensional object. For camera movement and cutting, he substituted the dramatic irrationality of things and people which got larger or smaller, closer or further away by their own power, and not because the camera was moved toward or away from them. In *Snow White*, the drawing begins to imitate conventional camerawork and, alas, the directorial clichés of Hollywood story-telling. Disney had begun to try to imitate the real world instead of continuing to create a world of his own. His departures from reality now consequently showed up as glaring errors instead of fanciful tropes.

All this was brushed aside, or went unnoticed, in the first flush of *Snow White's* box-office triumph. Its financial success enabled Disney to build a large studio, hire an army of draughtsmen and set them turning out his Donalds and Mickeys on an assembly-line basis, while he himself plunged into the production of more and bigger features. Subsequent films confirmed the suspicion that Disney had turned aside from the free inspiration of his early days toward literalism. The moving camera in *Pinocchio, Bambi* and *Dumbo* observes the artist's characters against the illusion of a three-dimensional background. The style of the drawing more and more imitates romantic painting of the early century. That the motive for this switch was a yearning for culture and respectability was fairly conclusively demonstrated in *Fantasia* (1940). Disney's attempt to ' illustrate ' classical music. It was an attempt at academicism by a half-educated man. As such, it was highly praised by the half-educated, and heralded as ushering in an era of mass-appreciation of music—with the aid of drawings!

The intellectuals who had madly ' appreciated ' his early work now began to desert an artist out for the bourgeois accolade. Nor were audiences as appreciative as they had been. His later films no longer create the sensation once expected of them. They are merely the annual Disney contribution to the film programme. As though he realised that he could not sustain his fancy through two-hour pictures, Disney has for the last five years presented features which are actually collections of short cartoons strung together on a thin thematic thread. At the same time, he has sought to recapture interest by turning to new scenes and adding to its galaxy of stars. But Jose Carioca is a rather calculated figure as compared with the spontaneity of the early Donald, and seeing *Saludos Amigos, Song of the South,* or *Make Mine Music* is not the equivalent of watching an evening of his old shorts. What has happened, apparently, is that all his films, shorts as well as features, are now committee-produced, with all that that implies of formula and calculated effort. It is ironic that the picture which gave us an insight into the way his studio-factory now works, *The Reluctant Dragon* (1941), was one of the freshest and most original of his recent films.

His current production methods are usually justified on the ground that the distribution system makes them necessary. Certainly they have been financially successful. The films are regularly revived for children at holiday season (they take the place of Christmas pantomimes in the United States), and the merchandising tie-ups by which the Disney name is exploited by manufacturers represent a fortune in themselves. It would appear that Disney is the tragic prisoner of a success which he, like so many others, is only able to conceive of in terms of the big money. It is significant that the best work that has come from his studios, artistically and in every other way, is represented by the instructional and training films he has made for the War Department and the Office of Inter-American Affairs. They are intelligent, imaginative, educationally effective, and beautifully drawn. None of them was made for profit.

*

The adventures of Robert Flaherty in the thirties and forties much resemble his first battles with the film world in the pioneering days of *Nanook* and *Moana;* they were well sketched by Rotha.[1] But a new element in his personal struggle crept in when, after *Tabu* (1930), the sphere of his operations was removed to Europe. From that time on he had to contend not only with commercial stupidity and cupidity, but also with the criticism and, I am afraid, the envy, of some of his own disciples. Not even Stroheim's career contains a greater irony.

When Flaherty arrived in England in 1931, he was welcomed by the newly-developed British documentary movement. Led by Grierson, these enthusiasts hailed him as the inventor and master of the technique of camera observation which they meant to make their own. They looked to his presence to give new impetus and inspiration to the development of documentary in Britain. That all was perhaps not well was indicated by the fate of the first attempt at a Flaherty-Grierson collaboration, *Industrial Britain,* which finally reached the screen as a co-operative work of several hands. When Flaherty esconced himself on Aran for Gaumont-British, the islands became a Mecca; young men went there to watch and learn, to serve their apprenticeship. But *Man of Aran* (1934) took, as usual, three years to make, and they were years of momentous transition for British documentary. Its tyro directors had emerged from a period of absorption with technical problems, and were face to face with the problems of a world sunk in depression and moving toward war. In that

[1] *Documentary Film,* pp. 81-86, 116-120 (Faber & Faber, 1939).

mood, Flaherty's pre-occupation with the classic beauties and braveries of human existence seemed to them irrelevant if not actually evasive or dishonest.[1] Reacting against aestheticism, they insisted that documentary must deal with the actual problems of modern existence, or it was not documentary. Their point is, or was, at least arguable, if only because, at that period, too many *soi-disant* documentarians were really aesthetes in disguise, ready, willing, and able to fall permanently into the rut of lyrical impressionism. But no considerations of group unity, social realism, or propaganda for the greatest useful-ness of documentary could explain or justify the outburst of denigration which followed the appearance of *Man of Aran* in Britain. It had its echo among the even more politically-minded documentarians in the United States. The film made its way through the cinemas and as usual, gained enthusiastic admirers from among all kinds of people but, judging from their published comments, the documentarians were not among them. They denounced the film as a vehicle of reaction. They seized upon the honours it won from the Nazis and the Fascists as proof that Flaherty's aim was the glorification of the cult of the folk. They even minimised it as a work of art, though none comparable with it emerged from anyone's camera anywhere in the world in the years of its making.

I cite this not only to make the point that a film-maker who strives to maintain his independence has no friends, but also as a warning. Hindsight is easy, but it is necessary to suggest that the subterranean stubbing or ostracism of Flaherty's films was a major error for the documentary movement, the more so because it took place in public. Maybe Flaherty and his work have but little relation to the informational and propagandist aims of the documentary movement as they happen to be conceived by this or that exponent, at this or that time. Nevertheless, the world

[1] *Vide, Cinema Quarterly,* Vol. 2, No. 4, Summer, 1934, review of *Man of Aran* by Ralph Bond, Vol. 3, No. 1, Autumn, 1934, *Evasive Documentary,* by David Schrire and *Documentary Film* (Faber & Faber, 1939).

public responds to the humanism of his films as they have to the work of no other documentary director. More sensible strategists would have made use of that appeal as an advanced salesman for the whole documentary idea. Flaherty's prestige and relative popularity have had just that effect. But it is an effect he has had to get for himself, working for the most part against the grain.

Be that as it may, after *Man of Aran,* Flaherty once more stood alone, though in the midst of a flourishing movement based largely on the method he had founded. He is not one to show bitterness, nor to act on it if he felt it, but to put it mildly, he was chilled by the professional reception of his film. There followed two years of inactivity, after which Alexander Korda sent him to India to film a version of Kipling's *Toomai of the Elephants.* Doubtless Sir Alexander was thinking of the kudos which might accrue to him through Flaherty's reputation, but he was also thinking of the box-office. For the first time since the abortive *White Shadows,* Flaherty was accompanied on his journey by technicians from the studio. While Flaherty was scouting the ground, searching out the essential relation between the elephant and India, his colleagues were plotting a story. Eventually the two collided in stalemate, after which the battleground was transferred back to London. The final scenes of Flaherty's documentary of India were made at Denham, near London. Grierson sums up the result : ' *Elephant Boy* begins magnificently. Toomai is set on the back of the biggest elephant of all Mysore : in his youth and innocence giving a dignity to the Indian people one has never seen before on the screen. But the synthetic spectacle of studio camp scenes and West End voices brings the film at every turn to an artificial, different plane. . . . They say an elephant will go mad on the death of his master and that he will go more mysteriously mad *just before* the death of his master. Nothing of this. Synthesis steps in, and an actor, in a fake beard, lashes the elephant to give a more Occidental motive for madness. . . .'[1]

[1] *World Film News,* Vol. 1, No. 12, March 1937.

Flaherty sadly relinquished the film to Korda, and Sabu to Hollywood and the big money, and went back to his now-customary interim occupation of writing books and television plays. Shortly, Pare Lorentz, then at the head of the newly-created U.S. Film Service, invited him to return from England to the United States to make a film on the misuse of farm land and the resultant widespread agricultural unemployment. Disaster attended this project from the start. Without clear directives, Flaherty was sent out to film what he saw. Wandering (for the first time) the farms and fields of his own country, he brought back an epic poem of the land and its people which ranks with his finest camera achievements. To this an official commentary and story-line was added, a mishmash of the already sufficiently confused policies of the Department of Agriculture. It left *The Land* (1941) intellectually at sea, a state of affairs not helped by the fact that the United States was by now about to go to war. The problem was no longer agricultural unemployment but farm labour shortage. In view of this, Washington decided not to release the film, except non-theatrically, and it has never been shown to the large cinema public. But *The Land* will yet find its audience—not, let us hope, because of any cyclical recurrence of the economic situation it describes—but because, like every film of this master, it goes beneath the surface to the timeless essentials of the relation of man to the earth. Some of Flaherty's most felicitous moments are in this film, and some moments of horror which are new to his style, because he deals for the first time with the modern scene. His relentless camera, Helen Van Dongen's editing, make a machine cutting corn into a machine cutting lives. And we see those lives, cast off, broken down by the road-side, in the eyes which one starving woman turns into the camera. There is a dulled animal curiosity in those eyes, and some pain because she is squinting against the sun, but hardly anything human any more.

In the early months of America's participation in the war, Frank Capra engaged Flaherty to make a camera survey of the state of the nation for inclusion in war films. But picture-making under military supervision proved more irksome to him than even Hollywood's interference. The experiment was soon brought to an end. Nor were other wartime government agencies able to see what his talent could lend to their sometimes pedestrian propagandist activities. There were, however, those who could. The Standard Oil Company, casting about for a film man who could serve their public relations aims, happened upon the fact that Flaherty's first film, *Nanook,* sponsored by a commercial firm, was shown all over the world and hailed as a classic with no complaints that its finances might be tainted. The result was an extraordinary contract, providing complete finance by Standard Oil for Flaherty's next film, but leaving him its sole owner, with no obligation to repay the negative cost and with distribution rights entirely in his hands. *Louisiana Story* is now ready for release. On the surface it is a big, old-time Flaherty epic, the life of a small boy in the Louisiana swamps, complete with alligators, fishing, hunting, a pet raccoon, and an oil-well explosion.

But this small boy differs from his predecessors in Flaherty films. To his primitive swamps comes an oil-drilling outfit, which proceeds to discover and bring in a well from beneath the waters of the bayou. The complicated modern marvel of testing, sounding, and drilling for oil is seen through the wondering eyes of a boy. There must have been thousands of ' educational ' films produced during the last fifty years which tried to show ' the wonders of industry ' through the eyes of a child. The wonders of industry as they presented them remained more incomprehensible than wonderful, and the children were those familiar text-book ones known as John and Mary Smith. Here the boy is as palpably real as the swamps he lives in, and the process of oil-drilling is observed and described with a clarity and drama unmatched in my experience of seeing films. This is a *real* educational film; it is also a poem, and the two things work together.

They always have, in all Flaherty films, whatever their scope of reference. This particular scope of reference will satisfy his sociological critics at least to some extent. But that is not, and never has been, the point. Flaherty has been severely criticised for doing what every artist must do. He has worked within the limits of his talents. And I should like to suggest that those limits are not so very narrow after all, as his present film shows. They are certainly much broader than those of the vast majority of his surprisingly numerous detractors. The final fact is that his is a descriptive and dramatic eye which has no counterpart among film-makers. The result of that fact is that his films have outlived, and will outlive, all their contemporaries. They are as fresh to-day as the day they were made. In short, they were worth all the struggle to make them, a struggle that it is a pleasure to record has now become less bitter. Flaherty's experiences, films, contacts and influences have at last crystallised into a general goodwill which has outlived the bitterness of ephemeral partisan dispute. A mysterious, generalised expectancy surrounds the unveiling of his new film. In making its way through the cinemas, it may well make way for other documentaries besides his own, as indeed have all his films since *Nanook* in 1920.

II

THE EUROPEAN CINEMA: 1929-48

(I) THE FRENCH FILM

Nothing could have been more auspicious for the future of the French film than the production during the first two years of sound films of René Clair's *Sous les toits de Paris* (1929) and *Le Million* (1930). At a time when the language barrier had suddenly bereft every European film industry of its foreign market, Clair's marvellous comedies with music were achieving huge success in New York, London and in every capital of Europe. His development of a technique (closely akin to Wilhelm Thiele's and Lubitsch's) of creating a sound ' image ' in counterpoint to the visual is now well known; it has been fully described by Rotha.[1] It seemed at the time that Clair had solved the problem of sound film form, and that in doing so he had restored the international appeal of national films. For what could be more French than Clair, and what easier for anybody, anywhere, to understand than Clair's films?

It turned out to be not so simple. Clair's third sound film and his masterpiece, *A Nous la Liberté* (1931), did not travel far beyond the borders of *la patrie,* nor fare so well within them. Master of the medium, Clair could make it do any trick that pleased him so long as he was concerned with pointing up human folly for his own amusement and that of others. When he deepened his outlook, when his wit became satiric comment, he paid the price of restricting the appeal of his film.

A Nous la Liberté, the obvious and direct source of Chaplin's *Modern Times,* attempted to dissect modern industrial society. It seemed to ask the question : What's

[1] *Celluloid: The Film To-day* (Longmans Green, 1931), pp. 181-195.

in it for any of us? The answer given by the film was : Nothing, except the human vitality and capacity for enjoyment we can find within ourselves. This answer has been dismissed as romantic and mystical (though, Clair may well ask, what other film answer was available in 1931, or is to-day?), but there can be no doubt that he was this time depicting his characters in relation to the forces which drove them on. He gave us the same world to which we were introduced in *Sous les toits* and *Le Million,* the same gallery of infinitely human characters, but it was now a world of competitive strife and the characters in it were eagerly, though futilely, competing.

Because of the Chaplinesque note of futility, the film was viewed with some disfavour by the intellectuals of the time; perhaps justly, if we consider that it was a romantic futility and rooted in Clair's essential outlook. But hindsight suggests that a different view is possible. When seen to-day, *A Nous la Liberté* seems a prediction of the fall of France, and not a vaguely generalised one. The amazing sequence in which a dotard functionary makes a speech about *La Justice, La Liberté et La Patrie,* while his audience of magnates and aristocrats chase banknotes wildly round and round the courtyard, has an unanswerable finality. That was, flatly, all there was to say, as France was to learn before the decade was out. But France was not ready to listen in 1932. The film met a reception as cold as that accorded *The Italian Straw Hat* in 1927. Despite its extraordinary brilliance, despite the international audience Clair had created for his films, he found himself considered a sort of international traitor. Nor did he fare much better with his admirers elsewhere. They considered his social criticism too heterodox for the intellectual fashion of the moment.

What Clair thought he was saying in *A Nous la Liberté,* and what effect its reception had on him, is not known. But much as *Les Deux Timides* followed *The Italian Straw Hat,* the successor to *A Nous la Liberté* was a satire with the sting plucked out. *Le Quatorze Juillet* (1932) recreated

Clair's Paris and his Parisians, but purely for purposes of romance and sentiment. For all its skill and heart-warming charm, one might well call this film the creation of a French Frank Borzage. It was, naturally, highly popular in France. Clair's next film, and it is possible to say his last important one to date, was popular nowhere. *Le Dernier Milliardaire* (1934) was a return to satire, but for safety's sake its comment on industrial society and the people who live in it, was directed at a mythical kingdom. The result was disastrous. Deprived of the opportunity to satirise specific foibles of the French, the thinness of Clair's social outlook became uncomfortably apparent. James Shelley Hamilton's epitaph in the *National Board of Review Magazine* read : ' Casinario is perhaps a miniature of a topsy-turvy world, trying to maintain its place in the universe by desperate efforts to keep whirling faster. It is dizzying and hilarious. . . . The moral—if by any chance the young lovers who run away supply a moral—seems to be that if you can escape to a desert island you can be happy though naked—if you have a radio. *Le Dernier Milliardaire* comes nearest of all Clair's films to showing where he stands as a social commentator. Human stupidity and selfishness and folly, with their resulting woes to the race, do not stir him to reform or revolution or even bitterness—he remains amused and though deeply interested, detached. Perhaps he is convinced that there must be a different kind of human being before there can be a different world.'

This verdict would be inadequate if *A Nous la Liberté* stood alone to represent Clair's outlook, or if *Le Dernier Milliardaire* had been followed by stronger films. It has been followed by films hardly worth discussion at all. The hospitable Korda invited Clair to Britain in 1935, and there emerged a big production studded with Anglo-American stars and with an eye to the American market.[1] But *The Ghost Goes West's* spoofing of aristocracy and Babbittry was a poor echo of the old Clair. It was shallow comedy, totally unworthy of the creator of *Sous les toits*. In 1940

[1] Cf. pp. 546, 548.

129. QUAI DES BRUMES, directed by Mercel Carné. Jean Gabin. [French, 1938]

130. LA BETE HUMAINE, directed by Jean Renoir. Jean Gabin. [French, 1938]

131. NORTH SEA, directed by HARRY WATT. [British, 1938]

132. THE STARS LOOK DOWN, directed by CAROL REED. EMYLN WILLIAMS.
[British, 1939]

Clair went to Hollywood to direct Marlene Dietrich in *The Flame of New Orleans*. Except for a few minor touches, it was a dull routine comedy, as were its successors, *I Married a Witch*, *It Happened To-Morrow* and *Ten Little Indians*. Neither Hollywood nor Clair suited each other.

After the Liberation, Clair returned to France where, with American finance, he directed an elaborate starring vehicle for Maurice Chevalier, *Le Silence est d'Or* (*Man About Town*) (1947). To ensure United States release, it was given an English commentary over French dialogue, causing at least this spectator to reflect that *Sous les toits* needed neither commentary nor titles to reach an international audience. This, to me, is the measure of the decline of Clair's technical talent, just as the material and his handling of it indexes his retreat from satire. Once more he recreates Paris, for the sake of sentiment only, and to make sure that no one could be offended, it is the Paris of the remote 1900's. The subject matter provides further clues to Clair's mentality; it concerns the operation of an early film studio. Clair loved and drew much inspiration from primitive films, especially Méliès's and Chaplin's, and the impetus of *A Woman of Paris* nearly guided him into the seriously satiric path which Chaplin has since followed. *A Nous la Liberté* demonstrates that. Why he could not sustain his thinking is beyond my province to explain, but it is clear from the record that, like Lubitsch, he has had in the end to content himself with style for its own sake. And with the onset of that contentment, or discontent as the case may be, his style itself has begun to die.

The Italian Straw Hat and *A Nous la Liberté* were nearly as perfect as films contrive to be. Their qualities derived in part from an instinctive command of the medium and an intellectual assessment of its possibilities, in part from a satiric eye for the follies of the middle-class. But, and here is the point, their greatest vitality derived from their full-scale attack on the hypocrisy of a civilisation which refused to face up to its failures. It would seem that in time René Clair also began to refuse to face up to his, perhaps because he had no prescription for success.

*

Clair's masterpieces were created in a vacuum. The French film of the early thirties was dormant, if not altogether dead. Trivial comedies and starring vehicles were about the sum of its accomplishments, and it had almost entirely lost its foreign market. When French films are bad, they are very bad. About the middle of the decade, however, there began what has been called the French Revival. The period of the French *avant-garde*, which had started soon after World War I, was coming to an end and it is worth noting that its demise roughly coincided with the improvement in French commercial feature production. New directors such as Marcel Carné, Jean Vigo and Prévert appeared, and the talents of the older ones, Renoir, Grémillon, Duvivier, Feyder, matured. A series of ambitious feature films restored the prestige of French production and regained a specialist foothold in some of the metropolitan cinemas of Britain and the United States. It was from now that we date the cult of the French film. It has been the fashion for a decade among the American intelligentsia, and I suspect the British also, to admire French films above all others, just as in the twenties it was the Soviet films. French films were thought to have something to do with ' culture ', something to do with sophistication. The word most often used to describe them was ' mature '.

The prolific Julien Duvivier led the van of the French Revival. In 1932, his sensitive *Poil de Carotte* revealed an understanding of the sound medium. (He had previously made it as a silent film in 1925.) This film was composed in terms of film rhythm, without regard to the supposed requirements of literary narrative. As such, it succeeded in portraying abnormal psychological states by indirection, although its formal statement of the mental problem of the boy was somewhat abrupt and unscientific. It was an inferior picture to Jean Benoit-Lévy's masterpiece, *La Maternelle,* made about the same time and about which I have more to say later. *Poil de Carotte* was, I think, the first of a series of films which gave to the late Harry Baur something of the position in France which Emil Jannings had occupied in the early German silent films. *Marie Chapdelaine* (1934) laid in French Canada, revealed again Duvivier's understanding of the function of landscape and milieu in revealing his characters and telling his story. From this time on, however, Duvivier went the way of French cinema as a whole, which was the *theatrical* way. *The Golem* (1936), made in Prague, purported to be a sequel to the early German film of Wegener and Galeen. It had cinematic possibilities which were (with the exception of the apocalyptic last scene) ignored in favour of the exploitation of Harry Baur's theatrical acting as a mad Austrian emperor.

In 1937, Duvivier assembled the whole corps of French acting experts to appear in *Un Carnet de Bal,* a series of episodes strung on a sentimental theme of nostalgia for lost youth. This so impressed the intelligentsia that Duvivier repeated the formula in *Le Fin du Jour* (1938), a story about a home for old actors which emerged as a Thespian field-day. Another and perhaps more entertaining side of Duvivier was his 'gangster' film, intelligently made and exciting, *Pépé Le Moko* (1937). It was re-made feebly and stupidly in Hollywood as *Algiers.* The prestige of these films took Duvivier himself to Hollywood, where he directed *The Great Waltz, Tales of Manhattan, Flesh and Fantasy* and *Moontide,* none of them in any way distinguished. His first French film after the Liberation was *Panique* (1946), from Simenon, to which reference will be made later. His recent version of *Anna Karenina* (1947), a typical Korda cosmopolitan production in Britain with Vivien Leigh and Ralph Richardson, is a full-blown return to the theatrical style, singularly unimpressive and rather tragic from the maker of *Poil de Carotte* and *La Belle Equipe.*

There is no question but that Duvivier is an accomplished director. His best films are in the classic style, but the intermittent promise that he would develop a characteristic style of his own has never materialised. Perhaps this is because, while his work is expressive, he seems to have very little that he earnestly desires to express. This is confirmed by his easy yielding to the theatrical manner when it was in fashion, and his susceptibility to whatever subject-matter happens to be offered him at the moment. Every Duvivier film contains moments of craftsmanship so admirable that one wants to take him seriously, but how can one be serious about the body of his work as a whole?

In contrast, the films of Jean Renoir ask always to be taken seriously, thematically as well as technically. His first sound films, *La Chienne* (1931), *La Nuit du Carrefour* (1933) and *Madame Bovary* (1934) were theatrical or literary adaptations, distinguished only by that taste which always distinguishes Renoir. Then he suddenly made a film which challenged comparison with the most advanced work in all countries. Superficially a *genre* study of Provençal life *Toni* (1935) went beyond all its particular locale to evoke and define the passions endemic in a fixed and traditional way of life. Here the eternal conditions of nature ' acted ' in the film in the manner we associate with Flaherty; here the inner life of the characters externalised in behaviour patterns which recalled the sensitive camera observations of Murnau, Seaström, Pudovkin and Vidor at their best, comparable to-day with the work of Rossellini. *Toni* was a piece of cinematic composition in the most precise sense of that term. It is interesting to note that Renoir's producer on the film was Marcel Pagnol, later to make *La Femme du Boulanger*.

This complete and self-contained work was followed by Renoir's uncompleted *La Partie du Campagne* (1937) which, fragment though it was, had all the warmth and tenderness of Renoir at his best. Then came his ' official ' masterpiece, *La Grande Illusion* (1937). This is, with the exception of Dovjenko's *Arsenal*, the most telling shaft which the cinema has ever directed against the institution of war. It wished to consider that institution in all its aspects. It probed the necessity of war to any *élite* corps, which has no reason to exist without it. It demonstrated, to its own satisfaction, that ' little men ', even when they have the instincts of democracy, are inevitably led to the slaughter because they are too ignorant to realise that wars of all kinds are against their interests. It touched upon the possibility that there is some perversity in the nature of man which is drawn to the unreasonable and profitless destruction which is brought by war. It suggested that a war, once started, becomes something akin to an inundating force of nature beyond the control or direction of any individual group. It looked forward with doubt and irony toward a future which, not inevitably but in all probability, would repeat the past.

These sentiments were rife in the mind of the world in the year of Munich, and the film seemed to us a towering achievement. To-day its argument, besides being profuse and rambling, is wide of the mark. *La Grande Illusion*, though it was set in World War I, was actually an abstract discussion of war, and war, its causes and realities, is no longer abstract to any of us. It was the argument of the film that was everything to Renoir; the technical result was in complete contradiction to *Toni*. *La Grande Illusion* expressed itself entirely through dialogue and the actors who spoke it. Very accomplished actors they were, Stroheim, Gabin, and Fresnay, but their methods were of the theatre, all except Stroheim, whose vivid presence dominated and somewhat outbalanced the film. The last scenes were more truly cinematic, more emotionally effective because their situations were elementally human, but they too were fatally the projection of a literary argument. Nevertheless, the film was a determined attempt to comment upon events and if possible to influence them.

La Marseillaise (1938) was reputedly an attempt to combat reaction by reminding the French people of the beginnings of their liberty. The early scenes of the revolutionary army were marvellously fresh and living, in contrast with the usual stained-glass and dressing-gown rendition of history, but later Renoir bogged down in a detached and ironic contemplation of the follies of the Bourbons. Perhaps an analogy was intended with the *rentiers* and industrialists of contemporary France, but if so its terms and purport were not clear. For a revolutionary film about a revolution, the whole was scholarly, civilised, strangely remote from the passions of the people it was supposed to arouse. For all its humanistic excellence, it was markedly distant from the manner and method of films which really have aroused political passions, from *The Birth of a Nation* to *Potemkin*.

In the same year (no mean physical achievement), Renoir made a powerful and movingly human adaptation of Zola's *La Bête Humaine,* possibly the best thing that Jean Gabin did until *Le Jour se lève*. Its opening sequence of the railway locomotive, the atmosphere of the shunting yards, the superbly handled sex scenes, made it one of the more memorable films of the French pre-war period. After *La Règle du Jeu* (1939), which I have not seen, and the outbreak of war, Renoir became a colonel in the French Signal Corps. Through the efforts of Flaherty and others, he escaped to America from occupied France. His first Hollywood film, *Swamp Water* (1941), vigorously resumed the manner of *Toni*. Disagreement with Darryl Zanuck at Twentieth Century-Fox resulted in the film being given to another director, but for a greater part it was unmistakably Renoir. Its sinister evocation of the Okeechobee Swamp, its remarkable feeling for the folkways of backwoods America, pointed again the strange paradox of the European director who makes better American films than the Americans. The reverse of the paradox emerged when, in collaboration with Dudley Nichols, Renoir filmed a story of French resistance, *This Land Is Mine* (1943). It was as unsuccessful, unsatisfactory and unbelievable as Fritz Lang's similar *Hangmen Also Die*, though the milieu and the people were Renoir's own.

In 1945, he completed his best American film, *The Southerner,* a very notable achievement. Though marred by occasional artificiality and by a lyricism more in keeping with southern France than the southern States, it was a remarkable piece of naturalism. The conditions of existence and the psychology of the Southern sharecropper were delineated with grim truth yet with affection, and almost entirely in cinematic terms. Especially notable was the extremely short sequence of violence in a sleepy Southern town, as accurate a piece of reporting of the American scene as films have provided since the early gangster days. This work of social realism was followed, in violent contrast, by a remake of his earlier *La Chienne,* delightfully entitled *The Diary of a Chambermaid* (1945). Studded with stars, and wholly in the theatrical manner, it came off as a *tour-de-force* in a class by itself. The artificiality was deliberate. The stars were used not for their histrionic skill but as natural acting material, as though they were types from the street. Whether the players concerned were aware that they were being used for this purpose is problematical, but it was clear enough to the audience, especially the use made of Hurd Hatfield's empty good looks. Sold to the public on the implications of its title, the picture actually was a mordant story of the decomposition of French bourgeois society. Renoir's latest film, *The Woman on the Beach* (1947) is one of the unsolved mysteries of the cinema. Everyone who has seen it emerges from the experience feeling that the projectionist has muddled the reels, indeed that some are missing. Interesting, it is quite unintelligible.

Almost every Renoir film has been distinguished by taste, intelligence, and maturity of theme. Each is notable for its catholic, humane, and slightly ironic outlook on human experience. Such qualities are rare in films. So too are the inventiveness and the strict eye for compositional values that enrich his work. Why, then, do we feel a certain lack in nearly all his films? It would appear that, with one or possibly two exceptions, they are not quite composed in terms of the film medium. This is betrayed by their structure, which seems to be determined by literary and (in the theatrical sense) dramatic considerations, and in their marked absence of that rhythmic pace which is one of the distinguishing characteristics of the real film. It may be that Renoir's desire to express important themes makes him too dependent on literary script-writers, such as Charles Spaak and Nichols. It may be that he thinks of a film in terms of isolated scenes. Certain it is that, on the one occasion when he let an actual countryside and its people determine the form of his film about him, he achieved mastery. Only in *Toni* did he appear really to perceive, and to act on, the fundamental fact that the cinema is an art of observation.

Jacques Feyder[1] returned from Hollywood in the early thirties to make a series of films mostly centring around the personality of his wife, Françoise Rosay, a task which has rather formulised itself as Mme. Rosay grew older. Of his many films since sound, *La Kermesse Héroïque* (1935) was the only one to achieve a stature comparable with the silent *Thérèse Raquin*. This international success was a riotous farce concerning itself with the sixteenth-century occupation of a Netherlands town by Spanish troops. It delighted in contrasting the sedateness and pomposity of the burghers with the dashing virility of the military invaders, a fact in which some found fascist implications, though the majority of audiences were content to enjoy the sexual titillations so dexterously provided. In any case, *La Kermesse Héroïque* was one of the very few ' historical ' films in which people behaved like human beings rather than puppets. They wore their elaborate and beautiful costumes about their daily occasions with a convincing naturalness quite unique in this *genre*. The film has also been highly praised for its production of Dutch Renaissance architecture and for its lighting by Harry Stradling, which seemed directly borrowed from Flemish painting of the period. For the rest of Feyder's work, it is sufficient to

[1] Died Switzerland, May, 1948.

mention only *Pension Mimosas* and the recent *Portrait of a Woman,* filmed in Switzerland, in both of which Mme. Rosay was brilliant to little ultimate purpose. It may be too unkind to say that Feyder is Czinner to her Bergner, but his films in recent years have had little purpose beyond providing a showcase for her beauty and compelling talent.

The career of Abel Gance hovers so confoundingly between the ludicrous and the majestic that it is difficult to write of him without exasperation. His grotesque *Fin du Monde* (repudiated by its director in the manner of Stroheim because it had been cut by others), his revamped *Napoléon* with choppy sound sequences added, and his remake of *Mater Dolorosa* seemed to point to a fading career and a diminished talent. But *The Life and Loves of Beethoven* in 1935, abrupt and episodic though it was, was something of an achievement. Against all probability, it suggested the grandeur of its subject. Indeed, it might be said that Gance, in his two biographical films, is the only director who has actually recreated the aura of greatness on the screen, and given some key to what it essentially is in a gifted individual. His second *J'Accuse* (1939), called in America *That They May Live,* was as belated and irrelevant an anti-war preachment as *La Grande Illusion* of two years' before. Its Victorian manner and romantic outlook laid it open to the sneers of the determinedly fashionable. It was nevertheless a forceful and a fascinating film. Granted that its kind of individualistic pacifism had already been proved ineffective by countless plays and films, from *Miracle at Verdun* onwards, it none the less possessed a moral passion lacking in more up-to-date sermons, and its style was vigorously cinematic. In its first sequence, and in several others, one seemed taken back to the pioneer days when the camera excitingly expressed all a director had to say. No one has used Francen's tragic mask with greater intelligence. Gance appears now only to supervise the work of others, which is a pity. Pretensions, extravagance and dated outlook notwithstanding, he is more a director of films than almost any of them.

*

The directors discussed above had all won their spurs in the silent film and pursued their careers in sound on the basis of a style already created, though the fortunes of the world depression considerably affected them all. The new directors who arose during and after the French Revival of 1935 seemed not so much to create a new style as to work within one which was handed to them. With due allowance for technical advance, that style was the familiar one of the Film d'Art, the theatrical manner which the French cinema has never been able entirely to put behind it. The theoretical exponent and the most successful practitioner of this manner has been Marcel Pagnol, who contends that the motion picture is nothing more or less than a printing-press for the drama. His films *Harvest, La Femme du Boulanger* (1938), *The Well-Digger's Daughter,* and the *Marius* series were peasant dramas of the soil, and there were moments in all of them when the *paysage* came alive with great felicity. They were nevertheless all a variety of canned theatre, centring round the performance and personality of famous players, with Raimu usually taking stage centre. They were diverting and amiable; but they are not a part of purposeful cinema.

They were accompanied by another series of films, also theatrical in subject, concentrating on the French underworld, the half-world, the seaports and waterfronts, all strongly reminiscent of Simenon's novels. The most famous of these were Marcel Carné's *Le Quai des Brûmes* (1938) and *Le Jour se lève* (1939), and Duvivier's *Pépé le Moko* (1937), and they mostly exploited the tremendous personality of Jean Gabin. They all focussed on the individual against a background of poverty, violence, and crime.

Why did these French films of the late thirties ape the theatre, why did they concentrate on the lowest levels of French life? When I put the latter question to Dr. Siegfried Kracauer, he replied : ' Because, above that level, all was paralysed.' [1] Since there was no hope for even the most mildly reformist social action, the individual had to stand alone, seeking satisfaction in an anarchic world of instinct and propelled by something akin to the notion of fate which imbued German silent films of a decade and a half earlier. Occasionally, in the midst of these essentially theatrical films, the camera would give life to objects and environment, as in *Le Jour se lève,* just as Murnau's camera had done, or Stroheim's. These misty waterfronts and low dives were excellently rendered and photographed, but their ' life ' was a subjective one. They had meaning only in relation to the mental states of the characters who wandered so inconsequently and hopelessly through them. Beautifully made, sensitively acted, they were films of defeat in which the British and American intelligentsia discovered poetry. They possibly overlooked the one out-spoken film of all this period, Renoir's *La Vie est à Nous* (1936), which at least attempted to say something politically related to the France of the thirties.

Just as they had applauded the aesthetic qualities of the German silent films and ignored their implications, the American and the British intelligentsia were ravished by the French sound films of *Le Quai des Brûmes* type, and quite blind to the key they provided to what was actually going on in national life. The aesthetic admiration was less than justified in this case. The New York intellectuals were awed by the acting and dialogue in these films, and believed they represented the best that movies can do. It was the old story of reverence for the traditional. French films *reminded* them of values made venerable by long use in the ancient, hence respectable, arts. They were astonished if any one suggested that these were not real films at

[1] Author of *From Caligari to Hitler* (Princeton University Press, 1947).

all.[1] Even greater was their astonishment if the vaunted 'adult' quality of the French theatrical school was challenged. At the risk of confounding them again, I must suggest that I do not find so very 'mature' a romantic pessimism which clothed itself in pseudo-psychology but issued in fatalism. (Worse, perhaps, could be added if one delved into the *Blut und Boden* implications of the Pagnol films.) Taken together, all these pictures gave as clear an index to what was going to happen in France as did the above-described sequence from *A Nous la Liberté*. René Clair, however was aware of what he was saying, while succeeding films embraced the anarchic death which they described. They pointed forward, also, I suggest, to such post-war phenomena as existentialism.

*

Of films made under the Occupation, America has seen only Clouzot's much over-heralded *Le Corbeau* (1942), Marcel Carné's very much overpraised *Les Enfants du Paradis* (1944), and Jacques Becker's *Goupi-Mains-Rouges* (1943). As was to be expected, it would seem they were mainly films of frustration, exploring side-issues, searching escape from any social realism, dipping into the world of fantasy, films without hope of the future. Such was *Les Enfants du Paradis*, and I feel sure were also *Les Visiteurs du Soir* (1942), also by Carné, and Jean Delannoy's *L'Eternel Retour* (1943)[2] 'Tasteful commercial films', as Nicole Védrès calls them, inaugurated by the Vichy Government.[3] It seems that the French, when given a certain security of production, turned back to the Film

[1] The usual reply was: 'What about Sacha Guitry?' Guitry's films were widely thought to be cinematic because they used all the magical properties of the camera. In this respect, Guitry advanced exactly as far, and no further, than Méliès in 1900, whose films made excellent use of mechanical tricks but were essentially conceived in terms of the proscenium.

[2] I confirm Griffith's prejudgement, having seen the films in question and others.—P.R.

[3] *Penguin Film Review*, No. 1, August, 1946.

d'Art, but no doubt that was inevitable under the Occupation. They were possibly fortunate to have been able to make any films at all.

Post-war French films have been slow in arriving in New York, but display the same technical characteristics and subject-matter with which pictures of the late thirties familiarised us. Duvivier's *Panique* (1946), from Simenon, seems to be typical, still another reprise of that pessimism, supposedly realistic and cynical, which is really romantic. We have heard of a new outlook and a more vigorous style, as exemplified in René Clément's *La Bataille du Rail* (1946),[1] but these have not reached us. We await also Cocteau's *La Belle et la Bête*, and *L'Aigle à deux Têtes*, Carné's *Les Portes de la Nuit*, and Claude Autant-Lara's *Le Diable au Corps*, of which we have heard so much and which may reveal the new approach.

In the meantime, it remains to record that Pierre Chenal made a passable and much-praised *Crime et Châtiment* in 1935, and that Marcel l'Herbier continues to oscillate between empty intellectualism and still emptier commercialism, with the single exception of a stray film called *Le Bonheur* (1935), which told more of the truth about the relation between films and their audience than has ever been told before or since.

It is ironic that the films of the late Jean Vigo, made some fifteen years ago, have only just reached us, for they display that spirit of revolt and inquiry which subsequent French films so notably lack. *Zéro de Conduite* (1933) and *L'Atalante* (1934) were works of youthful genius, and it is futile to point out the occasional callowness of the former, or the unresolved problem of the latter. Both films reveal a humane intelligence and an instinctive mastery of the medium. The middle and concluding passages of *L'Atalante* challenge comparison with any study of character that has been attempted on the screen. They

[1] René Clément's film of the French railwaymen's resistance movement ranks only second to *Open City* as a genuine film of an occupied country. It has all the fire and vitality that Griffith misses from other French films.—P.R.

have something beyond Pabst and Stroheim. Their disenchantment is mature in the real meaning of the word. In Vigo, France lost one of her greatest exponents of the cinema.

All through the thirties Jean Benoit-Lévy continued to alternate between making educational films for the classrooms and an occasional fiction film on a sociological theme. The best of these was, of course, the wonderful *La Maternelle* (1932), made with Marie Epstein, a film of great distinction. This case-history was presented with a so deceptively school-teacherish sobriety that its warmth and vitality seemed to well up out of the incidents and the people themselves. Re-examination to-day reveals that it was built into the design of the film. Of all the many attempts to accommodate the documentary approach to a fictional story, this is one of the best because its technique, far from being adopted for its own sake, grows out of the sociological and psychological aims of the film-makers. Those aims are humble. They are the unpretending, ameliorative aims of the pedagogue, the social worker, the healer. But they, and the film they gave birth to, have more health in them than all the rootless metaphysics and pseudo-scientific psychology with which the French film has preoccupied itself ever since the sound films took over from the silent.

*

The French cinema, like France itself, faces a future of uncertainty, irrevocably bound up with the future of Europe. The film is reckoned the second most important industry in France, and state taxation on it is grievously heavy, absorbing some sixty per cent. of the total receipts of the Industry. Negative stock, good equipment and efficient studio-space are in short supply. The yoke of imported Hollywood films hangs heavy and French producers are said to have difficulty in getting their films distributed in their own country, let alone overseas,

France has, on the other hand, a wealth of gifted acting talent and very capable technicians. She has Grémillon, Autant-Lara, Clément, Carné, Renoir, Rouquier; and Clair is still there. Her great trouble is that production is, and always has been, spasmodic. Much of the time it seems that her best directors are not working. Observed Alexander Werth from Paris in the autumn of 1934: 'Renoir is not working. Feyder is not working. Jean Lods has had to find asylum in Russia. Jean Vigo is too ill to work. Epstein and Clair are tossing fanfares in the commercial circuit. Cavalcanti in England seems to have found freedom to experiment and carry on the tradition of the old days.'[1] Observed Nicole Védrès from Paris in the summer of 1946: 'During recent months the best directors, those who refused to make concessions and compromises, have scarcely done any work at all. Carné, Grémillon and Becker have completed nothing since 1944. Bresson has only made one film, and Autant-Lara is still **waiting** for a Paris release to show *Sylvie et la Fantôme*, while in the meantime we are bombarded with American films dating from 1935 to 1940.'[2]

This is a tragic state of affairs. What the French must solve, apart from the economic problem of continuous production and wide release, and what only two pictures so far have shown that they can solve—Malraux's *Espoir* (1939) and Clément's *Bataille du Rail*—is the adaptation of their natural instinct for cinema to themes and subjects, social and political, of the present. They will not do it by looking backwards. They will not do it at all unless the French Government reverses its policy towards the French Film Industry.

[1] *Cinema Quarterly*, Vol. 3, No. 1.
[2] *Penguin Film Review*, No. 1.

(II) THE BRITISH FILM

'England has never produced a truly English film.'[1] Moussinac's dictum in 1929 was no longer true when *The Stars Look Down* reached the screen ten years later on the eve of World War II. Carol Reed's film was essentially British; it was also nearly a very fine film. But that the dictum of the famous French critic is still even partly true, eighteen years after this book was first published, is cause for concern. Several films emerge in the past eight years which follow in the tradition set by Reed's picture, a tradition strongly influenced by the British documentary movement, but all too often during the past two decades the British cinema has either imitated Hollywood, or pursued a devious path of pseudo-internationalism. The honesty of purpose and contact with real life that distinguished a handful of British feature pictures during the years of war now seems unhappily to have got mislaid in the attempts to capture a world market for luxury films that are neither one thing nor the other.

In retrospect, three factors appear mainly to have hampered the development of any truly national expression in the British fiction film; the policies of American companies in their British activities; the odd cosmopolitan character of British studio personnel; and, ironically, the British documentary film itself, the mere fact of its existence. The importance of the first factor, again ironically, is underlined, and to some extent explained, by measures actually intended to combat it : the Cinematograph Films Acts of 1927 and 1938.[2]

[1] *Panoramique du Cinéma,* Léon Moussinac (Au Sans Pareil, Paris, 1929).

[2] There is not space here to elaborate the complex structural growth within the British Film Industry and its American relationships, but no full assessment of technical, aesthetic and social developments can be made without first understanding the economic background. The reader is referred to *The Arts Enquiry Report* on *The Factual Film,* Appendix A, (Oxford University Press, 1947), *Tendencies to Monopoly in the Cinematograph Film Industry* (H.M. Stationery Office, 1944), *Money Behind the Screen,* Klingender and Legg (Lawrence and Wishart, 1937), *Film Business is Big Business,* prepared by the Association of Cine-Technicians, (1939) and *Films: An Alternative to Rank,* Frederic Mullally (Socialist Book Centre, 1946).

133. THE GREAT BEGINNING, directed by ALEXANDER ZHARKI and JOSEF HEIFITZ.
[Soviet, 1939]

134. LE JOUR SE LEVE, directed by MARCEL CARNÉ. JACQUELINE LAURENT.
[French, 1939]

135. GONE WITH THE WIND, directed by VICTOR FLEMING. [American, 1939]

136. THE GRAPES OF WRATH, directed by JOHN FORD. JANE DARWELL.
[American, 1940]

For some years, in the early thirties, American audiences marvelled that the few British films they were permited to see were often directed and acted by people for whom there was no longer much demand in Hollywood. It seemed to us then, that British producers were wooing the American market by the extraordinary expedient of offering attractions which that market had already repudiated. Time has now altered the impeachment. It is clear, in retrospect, that many of those fading stars and technicians were sent from Hollywood to Britain by their American employers for a very good reason. In view of the Films Act of 1927, which was law for ten years, it was necessary for Hollywood companies to finance a certain number of films in Britain. How better to do this, and perhaps at the same time to discourage the appearance of native actors and craftsmen, than to use British studios as a burial ground for Hollywood has-beens? Such was the apparent policy for several years, and such indeed it could again become, now that it is once more politic for America to finance films made in Britain. Be that as it may, this example of American policy seems to have had great weight for British producers of the period. They, and American producers operating in Britain, produced vehicles for such players as Corinne Griffith, Bebe Daniels and Esther Ralston, whose very names were unknown to a new generation of American filmgoers which grew up with the talkies. Such a state of affairs could only have arisen from a business psychology such as is described earlier by Rotha. (*Vide* : pp. 140 *et seq.*)

The cosmopolitan influence grew partly out of this American policy, and partly out of the fact that British producers of the period obstinately believed that a Continental film-maker was inevitably more gifted than one of their own countrymen. Alexander Korda had made minor films in Europe before going to Hollywood in the mid-twenties to direct his wife, at that time Maria Corda, in a super-production *The Private Life of Helen of Troy* (1927) for First-National. Both the star and the film proved disappointing at the box-office and, after a few more uninteresting pictures (*Women Everywhere, Dance Fever, Her Private Life, A Modern Dubarry*), Korda was despatched by Paramount in 1931 to the Elstree studios. After one film for Paramount-British, *Reserved For Ladies,* which was incidentally better than anything he had done in America, Korda formed his own company, London Film Productions in 1932. With him was his old friend the late Lajos Biro, upon whom Korda has so often relied for guidance in his scripts. His first two pictures were *Wedding Rehearsal* and *The Girl from Maxim's,* both frothy, and then he invited Charles Laughton to appear in an inexpensive production which, with evident nostalgia for his more successful days in Hollywood, Korda titled *The Private Life of Henry VIII* (1933).

Everything about *Henry VIII* is so well-known that comment to-day may appear superfluous. It seems, however, to have been generally overlooked that this, the most famous and successful of British films overseas, had little British about it except its subject, its stars, and that it was made near London. Its story, direction, photography, settings and music were all by Continentals. In an interview with Stephen Watts at the time, Korda said : 'An outsider often makes the best job of a national film. He is not cumbered with excessively detailed knowledge and associations. He gets a fresh slant on things. For instance, I should hate to try to make a Hungarian film, while I would love to make one about the Highlands that would be a really national Scottish film—and indeed I plan to do so. The best Hungarian film I have ever seen was made by the Belgian, Jacques Feyder. I believe that Clair could make a better London picture than any of the English directors—a London film that would be international. I know there are people who think it odd that a Hungarian from Hollywood should direct an English historical film, but I can't see their argument. The greatest folly is to set out to try to suit everybody. It is the sure road to insincerity and artificiality. The result will be a mongrel film which belongs to no country.'[1]

The basic formula of the Private Life idea was probably derived from the Lubitsch films of the early twenties (among which, be it remembered, was Jannings' portrait of bluff King Hal in *Anne Boleyn*); the style and purpose were borrowed from John Erskine, whose novels, including *The Private Life of Helen of Troy*, were the American expression of the impulse to humanise, and to debunk, history which arose shortly after World War I. This barren sophistication seemed already to have exhausted itself before the economic depression, and the success of *Henry VIII* might, therefore, seem all the more surprising. The reason was not far to seek. It was the story of a man who had six wives.

This in itself was nothing to its discredit. The Italian film *Open City* earned a million dollars in America solely on the basis of pornographic advertising, not on its value as a great social document. But it was somewhat surprising that few in the British Film Industry took the trouble to analyse the sources of the film's appeal, apart from its scintillating technique. The box-office said that a film made in Britain *could* make money in the world market, if its production budget was not excessively high. It was now simply a question of more and bigger Private Lives, financed by the City and Insurance millions, with the magician Korda leading the van and the rest of the Continentals scrambling after him.[2]

Korda himself seems to have agreed with this diagnosis. The private lives of Catherine the Great, Rembrandt, Don Juan, and even the Gannets, were explored, but rather more expensively than Henry; the Fairbankses, the Czinners, Laughton when he could be lured away from California,

[1] *Cinema Quarterly*, Vol. 2, No. 1, Autumn, 1933.

[2] *Time and Tide* (29 September, 1934) stated that Count Toeplitz de Grand Ry, gave 'Korda the financial assistance Korda had failed everywhere else to get for *The Private Life of Henry VIII*', and *Catherine the Great*, as well as *Henry*, were presented as Korda-Toeplitz productions. Toeplitz later produced *The Love Affair of the Dictator* (cf. p. 551).

became his willing accomplices. He seems to have aspired to become a second Goldwyn, relying on quality alone. The studios which arose, it is said, with Prudential's money at Denham were intended to be an international Mecca, a rose-garden colony to which the gifted of all the earth would repair, and out of which were to come films which had to be great because so many admirable people from so many countries were connected with them. Among the flashing names that decorated the Korda diadem were: Jacques Feyder, René Clair, Josef von Sternberg, William K. Howard, Marlene Dietrich, H. G. Wells, Paul Robeson, Leslie Howard, Lothar Mendes, Laurence Olivier, Erich Pommer, William Cameron Menzies, Elizabeth Bergner, while even Winston Churchill, then in the political wilderness, wrote some scripts and Sir Robert Vansittart some lyrics. Such a galaxy of talent was expensive, and so were the super-productions which surrounded it. *Catherine the Great, Sanders of the River, The Scarlet Pimpernel, The Ghost Goes West, Fire Over England, Knight Without Armour, The Thief of Bagdad, The Four Feathers, The Drum,* and the abortive *I, Claudius,* were some of them, each far more costly than their prototype *Henry VIII.* Returns, on the other hand, were slow and meagre compared with the *Henry VIII* bonanza. Nevertheless, the financiers proved sympathetic for a while longer. The American market was believed to be the key to all, and Korda's purchase of shares in and election to the board of United Artists was presumably thought to be sure-fire insurance of ultimate commercial success.

From 1932 onwards, a steady stream of pictures had also been issuing from the newly-reorganised Gaumont-British Picture Corporation, under Michael Balcon's producership, of which we may remember the successful *Rome Express, Friday the Thirteenth, Jew Süss, Rhodes of Africa, Evergreen, Little Friend* and the thrillers of Alfred Hitchcock following on his early success in *The Lodger.* Only the latter films, such as *The Thirty-Nine Steps* and *The Man Who Knew Too Much,* forerunners of Hitchcock's later success in Hollywood, may have been said to have created an English style; most of the others are forgotten, including *Jew Süss*.[1]

In those boom years up till 1936, money was poured into production, much of it to *entrepreneurs* who had no knowledge or experience of film-making. ' In the boom period, £4,000,000 was invested in one period of ten months. Most of it disappeared and the great City geniuses are still wondering where it all went ', wrote the Association of Cine-Technicians.[2]

It would have amazed the financiers, and probably even Korda himself, to see what actually *did* happen in the United States to his films and those of the other producers. United Artists distribution amounted to no more than a mouse's share of the American market, and the particular share which British films got was a curious one. United Artists themselves owned no theatres in the United States; all the other major Hollywood producers did; consequently only small independent exhibitors (who usually could not get, or pay for, the best Hollywood product) booked the productions of Denham, Elstree and Shepherds Bush. The audiences which came to these small theatres were city slum-dwellers, small-town proletarians, farmers and cowboys. Even if they could understand the West End accents, which was more than doubtful, they could not understand the films. Some British pictures of the period certainly had ideas, taste and talent. There was only

[1] C. A. Lejeune's following remarks on that film are worth repeating : ' With all the sympathy in the world for the suppressed Jew, I fancy that there are other problems worthy of being tackled at some expense by our native film industry. At the cost of being repetitious, I suggest that there is still unemployment, there is still ship-building, and there is still farming. We have an industrial north that is bigger than Gracie Fields running round a Blackpool fun fair. We have a fishing fleet or two, and a railway system, and some fairly acute problems of education. Gaumont-British have made a thoughtful gesture in devoting the proceeds of the *Jew Süss* premiere to the fund for the distressed miners, but there is nothing, so far as I can see, to prevent them thinking still harder, and devoting to a film of British industry, British agriculture, or for that matter, British mining, the same care and money that they have spent so generously on a film about a little German municipality of two hundred years ago.' (*The Observer*, 1934).

[2] *Film Business is Big Business* (A.C.T., 1939).

one thing wrong with them. So many of them simply were not films in the sense that American audiences understood films. Most of them, commendably, centred round themes. But the theme was either 'implied' or stated in the dialogue, which was incomprehensible, or failed to materialise at all. Never by any chance was it built into the film as an essential part of the structure. Trade critics in the United States, puzzling to find the basic defect which we all sensed in British films at the time, characterised it as 'lack of continuity'. Climaxes, both of sequences and of a film as a whole, were elided. The major events always seemed to take place ' off screen '. That this technique, if such it could be called, was in direct opposition to all established cinematic method need not be emphasised. But its glaring inadequacy was pointed up in the United States by the fact that, for the distribution and exhibition reasons given above, British films were shown to the basic, the primitive cinema audience—children and very simple people, to whom the Western, the melodrama, and the slapstick comedy of Hollywood were the long accepted forms of entertainment. How could the products of the Denham rose-garden be expected to flourish?

I detail all this some twelve years later because it may have certain bearing on the present position of British films in the world market, an aim which seems to fascinate most British producers. As is well-known, the abrupt collapse of City-financed, mushroom-growthed British production took place in 1937, and for the remainder of the years of uneasy peace there was little film activity which added up to anything. Wrote the Association of Cine-Technicians : ' The collapse of the film production boom of 1937 has had far-reaching consequences. For thousands of technicians, electricians, carpenters, plasterers, make-up men, writers, actors and directors it was disastrous. The responsibility for the muddle, mismanagement and inefficiency was not theirs, but they were the first to suffer. Months of unemployment were to follow. Savings slowly disappeared, cars, houses and other personal possessions had to be sold up. A fortunate few succeeded in finding jobs outside the Industry altogether. But for the majority that was impossible. Their livelihoods depended on their specialised skill, and these men whose creative ability had gone into production of so many films now found that their services were unwanted.'[1] Korda himself, with controllers in the studio, managed to keep going by oscillating between Hollywood and London.

In 1937, possibly foreseeing the 1938 Films Act, Metro-Goldwyn-Mayer, who until that date had refrained from actual production in Britain, now started making films on a biggish scale, resulting in *The Yank at Oxford* (1938), *Good-bye Mr. Chips* (1939), and *The Citadel* (1939), all three using Hollywood stars and being directed by Americans, Jack Conway, Sam Wood and King Vidor respectively. These films ' made in Britain ' employed some local studio personnel and tied up two of Britain's best producers, Michael Balcon and Victor Saville, but they were presented abroad as American pictures and brought little credit to the British Film Industry as such. When the war came, M-G-M discontinued production.

For the most part, however, genuine British production was dormant until the advent of war, and of J. Arthur Rank into the film arena. Figures like Max Schach and Toeplitz de Grand Ry, who cut such glory a year or two before, faded as promoters of ' super-British ' pictures. Who now remembers *The Marriage of Corbal, The Love Affair of the Dictator*, and many like them? Only two films, apart from *The Stars Look Down*, merit mention at this time: Thorold Dickinson's very well-made, beautifully designed *Gaslight* (1940) which was subsequently suppressed when Hollywood bought the rights, and John Baxter's *Love on the Dole* (1941), a sincere attempt to picturise unemployment in the mid-thirties from Walter Greenwood's novel, held up from film adaptation by the Censor until the war had vanquished unemployment, but too studio-bound to be wholly authentic.

[1] *Film Business is Big Business* (A.C.T., 1939).

The great revival of British production since 1942, stimulated partly by wartime conditions and partly by Rank's manoeuvres (and capital power) are familiar. By comparison with any previous period, the British Film Industry to-day seems in an excellent position. But I want seriously to suggest that the position has, in reality, changed in no essential way since the first burgeoning days of Korda and his London Films; and that, for this reason, it is quite possible that the present boom could be followed by disastrous collapse once again within the foreseeable future, although one hopes the contrary.[1]

Rank's strategy seems to be based for the most part on, once again, capturing a substantial slice of the American market in order to recoup his high production costs. He is penetrating other overseas markets as well, but his main dependence is clearly on the United States. He has gone about this skilfully. Assuring distribution by complicated deals with American firms, he has reversed the former pre-doomed policy of Korda and Gaumont-British, and sought approval of metropolitan audiences. No longer are British films the last resort of hard-pressed exhibitors in the slums or the country towns of America. They are shown, with great *éclat*, on Park Avenue and even occasionally at Radio City Music Hall. Prestige is theirs. Every list of the ten best films of the year contains from three to six British productions vastly to the annoyance of Hollywood. They have replaced French films as the fad of the intelligentsia. But their vogue and prestige are hollow. They are liked by the upper income-level groups because they are literate, because they flirt with ideas, because they are invested with the traditions of the English theatre and of English acting. But how hollow this vogue and this prestige actually are can be demonstrated by the fact that

---

[1] Mr. Griffith is writing before the Anglo-American Film Agreement was signed and before Mr. Rank announced his £2 million loss on 'prestige' films destined for the U.S. market, and, even more important, before the fixing of the 45% quota of British feature films for British cinemas in the Cinematograph Films Act of 1948, which may result in even less playing-time for British pictures in the United States as a retaliatory measure for the high quota figure.—P.R.

Rank's distribution efforts in America are at a stalemate. He conquers the cities—a few of them—but he makes no progress with the small-town exhibitor or the independent theatre chains. Even *Great Expectations,* a huge success in New York, had its expectations disappointed nearly everywhere else. Until British films can move out from the cities into that hinterland which is really America, the Rank policy and its analogues cannot hope for real commercial success.

The reason is simple and familiar. British films of the war period and after are infinitely superior to their predecessors, technically speaking. Most of the earlier faults of continuity and structure have been corrected. But they seldom have roots. Delightful as it may be to watch such excellent transcriptions to the screen as *Henry V* (1944) and *Caesar and Cleopatra* (1945), it is difficult to think of them as anything but an antiquarian's version of a national art. *Colonel Blimp* (1943), *This Happy Breed* (1944), *Blithe Spirit* (1945), *A Matter of Life and Death* (1946), *London Town* (1946), *Black Narcissus* (1947) and *Vice Versa* (1947) are as much in the spirit of pre-war cosmopolitanism as though nothing vital had happened in Britain since 1935.

These are pictures for the chi-chi few. On the surface of the record, and to an American, it would seem that making films for the select few is the ideal of young British directors. Carol Reed started with the desperate, and desperately important, realities of *The Stars Look Down* in 1939 and arrives at the pseudo-metaphysics of *Odd Man Out* in 1947. Technically, he improves enormously; in subject matter and approach to life, he retrogresses. Michael Powell, another gifted technician, emerged from comparative obscurity with *The Edge of the World* in 1937 and apparently finds apotheosis as the co-director of pyrotechnical exercises sometimes quite brilliant but which have no real purpose related to life. Launder and Gilliat presented a moving little original piece of wartime Britain in *Millons Like Us* in 1943, and now are due to present

The Blue Lagoon, a faded ' naughty ' romance much sought by schoolboys thirty years ago.

The war years and after have seen the British studios produce some really brilliant technicians, among them David Lean and Carol Reed. Settings, dressing, lighting, editing, sound, trickwork, music especially—all these have made the grade since the dim days when Rotha first wrote this book. A lot of technicians and other studio personnel in Britain must have worked very hard, and in very grim circumstances in those war years. Mr. Rank is said to have given comparative creative and technical freedom to some of the directors working in his many companies, perhaps especially to the group who were gathered round Filippo del Giudice when he was in charge at Two Cities Films, and to the various teams working under Independent Producers Ltd.[1] The results, frankly, are disappointing. Not only have many of the films not justified their costs but they have not added anything notable to the real British cinema. If this is the full flowering result of creative freedom and unlimited money, perhaps there is something to be said for the discipline of strict producership? Technical virtuosity is just not enough.

Only Sir Michael Balcon, head of production at Ealing Studios since 1938, appears to have followed a wise policy of making pictures within a budget which is recoverable

---

[1] David Lean writes : ' J. Arthur Rank is often spoken of as an all-embracing monopolist who must be watched lest he crush the creative talents of the British Film Industry. Let the facts speak for themselves, and I doubt if any other group of film-makers anywhere in the world can claim as much freedom. We of Independent Producers can make any subject we wish, with as much money as we think that subject should have spent on it. We can cast whatever actors we choose, and we have no interference at all in the way the film is made. No one sees the films until they are finished, and no cuts are made without the consent of the Director or Producer, and what's more, not one of us is bound by any form of contract. We are there because we want to be there. Such is the enviable position of British film-makers to-day, and such are the conditions which have at last given our films a style and nationality of their own.' (*Penguin Film Review,* No. 4, October, 1947.) In view of this agreeable position, it is rather difficult to understand why several of Mr. Rank's most accomplished writers and directors— Carol Reed, Michael Powell, Emeric Pressburger, Frank Launder and Sydney Gilliat—have recently decided to emigrate to Sir Alexander Korda's stable.

from the British home-market. Not all his films are worth noting; some should perhaps be forgotten; but from his producership have come: *The Foreman Went to France* (Charles Frend, 1942), *Next of Kin* (Thorold Dickinson, 1942), *Nine Men* (Harry Watt, 1943), *Dead of Night* (1945), *The Overlanders* (Harry Watt, 1946) and *Hue and Cry* (Charles Crighton, 1947). These unpretentious films at least represented a style, a freshness of approach. They were British in character, although they had many faults of self-consciousness and adolescence. They were fundamentally sincere pictures and had a purpose.

Mention also should be made of Sydney Box as a producer, since *The Seventh Veil* (Compton Bennett, 1945) established him as a maker of reasonably budgeted pictures. Nothing as yet produced by him for Rank has reached high level, but films such as *Holiday Camp, Easy Money,* and *The Brothers,* suggest that he is interested in subjects set among the ordinary British scene. He lacks, possibly, good directors; but his pictures are perhaps preferable to the pseudo-art prestige films.

It seems clear in an overall estimate that Britain has still much to do to put her film house in order. Costs of production have got to come down, speed of making has got to be increased without sacrifice of technical quality, labour has to be less restrictive where creative processes are involved, and above all, film-makers—writers, directors, producers—must find stories from out of the living experience of the British people and not rely on the romantic past.

Which brings us to documentary. Its thesis, its growth, and its purpose are too well-known through the writings of Grierson and Rotha to require comment from me.[1] Its products are by now part of the intimate experience of all British and many American readers of this book. But it is necessary to point out that documentary was the most important, and almost the only, British contribution to

[1] *Documentary Film* (Faber & Faber, 1939); *Grierson on Documentary,* edited by Forsyth Hardy (Collins, 1946).

world cinema until the war years. All that has since appeared and which has had any substance, has been guided by its example and nourished by its experience. From *The Stars Look Down* and *Edge of the World* through *Next of Kin*, *Desert Victory*, *Target for Tonight*, *Western Approaches*, *Journey Together* and *The Way Ahead* to *World of Plenty*, *The World is Rich* and *Children on Trial*, the record of British film achievement is a documentary record. I risk repetition when I emphasise that this is because these films have had something to do with life in Britain *as it is lived*, and that British fiction films by and large seldom have anything to do with significant life anywhere.

This has everything to do with the future of the British film in the world market. Britain has neither the resources nor the flair for the mass-manufacture of popular entertainment movies *à la* Hollywood. Thank God she hasn't! But she has got the intellectual and emotional resources, and she is undergoing the experiences, which could make her the leader of the film of reality. I have no doubt that if the British Film Industry keeps that fact in mind first, last, and always, there will be plenty of foreign markets for British films, even if a new distribution method and a new system of profit and loss, has to be developed to accommodate them.

＊

Under the system as it has so far prevailed, it is not surprising that Alfred Hitchcock should be the only British film craftsman to achieve an international reputation and commensurate popularity, and then only since he has been in Hollywood.[1] This specialist in mystery stories needed no roots in national life for the kind of entertainment he purveyed. The escapist appeal of the mystery is international; it need give no more than the barest simulacrum of reality to achieve suspension of disbelief. To my mind, Hitchcock's success derives

[1] I think Griffith underestimates the international reputation gained by Carol Reed and David Lean, at least in Europe.—P.R.

principally from a calculated use of the resources of the medium, and particularly of cutting, which is related to Russian theories of montage as of the late twenties. Montage is used for its physical shock effect and, deliberately, to cause the sensation of surprise and fear. Like Lubitsch and Chaplin, the structure of his films is centred around the invention of incident, of business. His description of the opening sequence of *Secret Agent* (1936)[1] can be regarded as a classic exposition of the way purely literary or theatrical material can be re-worked into film form.

All of Hitchcock's successes—*The Man Who Knew Too Much* (1935), *The Thirty-Nine Steps* (1935), *The Woman Alone* (1937) and *The Lady Vanishes* (1939)—were based upon the invention of business and the deliberate alternation of chronology towards the end of suspense. Preposterous often, these pictures were visually and rhythmically gripping to an extent that often seemed more humanly convincing than more serious films. Oddly, it was Hitchcock's one serious effort, *Rich and Strange* (1931), in which his visual imagination failed him. Here he ignored the material implicit in his theme to concentrate on a talkfest between individuals.

Hitchcock's increasing reputation led him inevitably to Hollywood, where his pictures have continued the style of his British thrillers, but it is recently a style somewhat blurred by production supervision and star values. *Foreign Correspondent* (1940), *Rebecca* (1940), and *Shadow of a Doubt* (1943) were more or less up to his British standard, but more lately it has been increasingly a matter of *Spellbounds* (1946) and *Paradine Cases* (1947) in which cinematic construction has had to be subordinated to pseudo-romantic conflicts involving the highlighting of principal players. *Lifeboat* (1944), his one war-related film, was intended as an allegory of conflict between democratic and totalitarian ways of doing things. It was at sea in more ways than one, since the majority of critics agreed

[1] *Footnotes to the Film,* edited by Charles Davy (Lovat Dickson, 1938).

that the Nazi who was its villain came off far better than the exponents of democracy. The action of the latter in tearing the Nazi to pieces was hardly the finest example of democracy in action. Hitchcock is now set up in independent production in the hope of regaining some of his former freedom, but it is safe to say that he will remain a master entertainer in a limited field.

Carol Reed's first film to reach America, *Night Train to Munich* (1939), a melodrama in the Hitchcock manner, signalled the arrival of a first-rate British film craftsman. He had, I understand, previously made *Laburnum Grove* (1936) and *Bank Holiday* (1938), unpretentious films that at least were related to everyday things although too studio-bound to be convincing. *The Stars Look Down,* reaching America almost simultaneously with *Night Train to Munich* but withheld from release until John Ford's *How Green Was My Valley* had played the circuits in 1942, was in my opinion a major work. To compare it with Pabst's *Kameradschaft,* or with certain Russian films, does not altogether do it justice. It was richer, less symbolic, and more deeply rooted in human living than any film dealing with the working-class that I can recall. Stripped of all paraphernalia of ' agit-prop ', it cross-sectioned and chronicled one grim episode in Labour's struggle, displaying all the forces momentarily involved, and implying always that this is but a segment of a historic process. To appreciate this film as a step forward in the picturisation of social reality, one must compare it with the numerous films, some of them by important film-makers, which lost the actual lives of the people in a maze of argumentation and symbolism. But this, one felt, one *knew,* was actually what it meant to be chained to a coal mine for life. Moreover, the protagonist (played by Michael Redgrave) was not a ' class character ' but a living person. His behaviour-chart was the outcome of influences which presented themselves on the screen as parts of his environmental reality rather than as abstract dialectical forces. I would not be surprised if future historians decided that

The Stars Look Down was the first film which realised any substantial part of the goals of the advocates of proletarian art. I should be very surprised if any one disagreed that it was the first film which had a chance to touch the conscience of the middle-class.[1]

No subsequent film of Reed's, except *The Way Ahead* (1944), has lived up to the achievement of *The Stars Look Down;* many have been indistinguishable from the work of routine directors—*Gestapo* (1940), *Kipps* (1941), *Young Mr. Pitt* (1942). His last film, *Odd Man Out* (1947), was hailed by critics for much the same reasons for which they applauded John Ford's *The Informer,*[2] and it is to me nearly as hollow a film, abstract and orchidaceous, a postured illustration of a *passé* metaphysical thesis. It is skilful, yes, but its skill lacks relation to the monumental reality which was the stuff of *The Stars Look Down.* Only in the fine documentary compilation, *The True Glory* (1945), which he edited with Garson Kanin, and in the war-time army film, *The Way Ahead,* written by Eric Ambler, has Reed moved forward. This latter film was as intimately human, and at bottom as socially conscious, as the earlier film. It revealed again how masterly and dignified Reed can be when he deals with men in their own environment and in relation to the jobs they do. He is now with Korda making an adaptation of Graham Greene's short story, *The Basement Room,* to be called *The Lost Illusion.*[3]

Of other British directors, Anthony Asquith has seemingly become a routinist; his outstanding achievement in the talkie period was the pretty thing that was made out of Shaw's *Pygmalion* (1938), and I do not share the critical acclaim of *Way to the Stars* (known in America as *Johnny in the Clouds*). Asquith now seems obliged to

---

[1] This is one of the rare cases in which I find myself in disagreement with Mr. Griffith; the interested reader is referred to my review of Reed's film in *Documentary News Letter,* Vol. 1, No, 3, March, 1940.—P.R.

[2] Cf. page 483.

[3] Retitled *The Fallen Idol.*

adapt stage-plays of West End successes to the screen. With the possible exception of the submarine film, *We Dive at Dawn* (1943), he has not fulfilled the hopes one had of him after *Tell England* in 1930. Korda, when he directs a film personally, is a livelier director than most of those he hires, though his taste is inclined to a genteel refinement (*An Ideal Husband*, 1947). *Rembrandt* (1936) was a thoughtful picture, however, and one which it is still a pleasure to look at in Korda's favour, thanks also to Périnal's photography and Vincent Korda's settings.

Gabriel Pascal's versions of Shaw need no comment here. They are on the British conscience. Laurence Olivier's *Henry V* (1944) was probably the first instance of a legitimately photographed play, inasmuch as its structure was designed constantly to remind the spectator of the fact that it was a play and not a film. When the action moved out of the Globe Theatre, it moved into fairy-land, not actuality, and thus avoided that conflict between poetic speech and three-dimensional reality that has set all previous versions of Shakespeare at nought. Michael Powell's *Edge of the World* (1937) was an interesting, if slightly arty, semi-documentary, but his subsequent collaboration with Emeric Pressburger has resulted for me in second-hand Hollywood, plus a dubious social outlook of the ' Churchillian renaissance '. Undoubtedly a very gifted technician, Powell still seems unable to make up his mind as to what he wants to say. David Lean and Noel Coward's *In Which We Serve* (1942) was a condescending instance of class-consciousness, and Messrs. Coward and Lean continued this approach in *This Happy Breed* (1944) and *Brief Encounter* (1945).[1] Lean's *Great Expectations* (1946) was a handsome version of Dickens, except that it blurred and minimised the most meaningful protagonist, Magwitch. It revealed Lean, however, as a brilliant technician, sensitive and serious about cinema, probably the most skilful of all the young British directors, obviously waiting for real material of contemporary

[1] Again, I think, an underestimate of the latter film.—P.R.

137. THE UNIVERSITY OF LIFE, directed by MARK DONSKOI. [Soviet, 1940]

138. GASLIGHT, directed by THOROLD DICKINSON. [British, 1940]

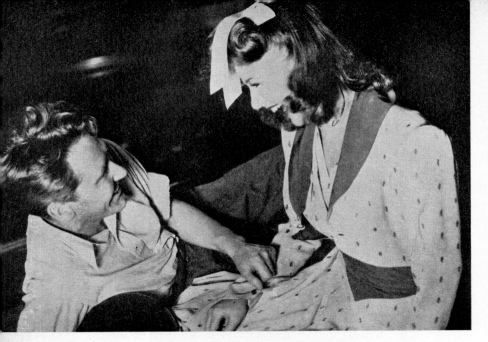

139. TOM, DICK AND HARRY, directed by GARSON KANIN. BURGESS MEREDITH, GINGER ROGERS. [American, 1940]

140. THE LITTLE FOXES, directed by WILLIAM WYLER. BETTE DAVIS. [American, 1941]

importance to come into his hands. It is disappointing that his next picture is again from Dickens, *Oliver Twist*.

It is no accident that Hitchcock's were the first British films to be really popular in the United States. The most popular of contemporary British pictures in this country, Mr. Rank's and Sir Alexander's super-productions included, are the murder mysteries like *Dead of Night* (1945) and *Green for Danger* (Launder and Gilliat, 1946). If Britain is to send us pictures distinguished only by skill and good taste, and not by vitality of subject-matter, they had better be murder mysteries. That seems to be a general verdict. When they star James Mason, that helps. But Britain no longer has Mr. Mason. She had better look first to filling her own home screens with genuine product.

(III) The Soviet Film

When the sound-film era was ushered in, Sergei Eisenstein was on his way to the West. The great exponent of the dialectical cinema had signed a contract with Paramount during a triumphal visit to western Europe, whither he had come to be deservedly welcomed by the intelligentsia. Behind him lay his sweeping revolutionary epics; ahead lay a unique attempt to adapt himself to, or ask concessions from, the capitalist film industry. It was to be a fruitless attempt and a long one in terms of the swift-moving events of the early thirties. Thus it came about that the first of Russian directors was absent from the scene during the crucial period when Soviet sound-film style was being evolved.

If the heads of Paramount reckoned that in signing Eisenstein they had merely acquired another tame European director for their stables, they were more than usually egocentric. Eisenstein regarded himself, and was regarded, as being on leave of absence from the Soviet Union. His adventure in California was in the nature of a Soviet experiment. Accompanied by Alexandrov and Tisse, and with Ivor Montagu as liaison officer with the alien West,

Eisenstein arrived in Hollywood and forthwith set about drafting scripts. For all the ministrations of Montagu, it was clear from the start that neither side spoke the same language. Eisenstein's address to the Academy of Motion Picture Arts and Sciences on the proper size and shape of the screen[1] fell on puzzled ears, and his draft scripts for *An American Tragedy* and *Sutter's Gold* seemed to have frightened the studio. It is difficult to understand why, since these were the ablest visualisations of literary material known to U.S. connoisseurs, and though both were penetrating examples of social analysis they did not call on the workers to arise. Perhaps it was their very completeness and detail that left the masters of Paramount at sea. At any rate, both films were re-written and filmed by others, and Eisenstein's contract was terminated.[2]

He had already made arrangements to produce a film in Mexico for the resourceful Upton Sinclair, who had secured sufficient independent financial backing to give the great Soviet artist his head. Eisenstein did more; he took the bit between his teeth and consumed more than two years in shooting hundreds of thousands of feet of film south of the Rio Grande.[3] Beyond being ' an epic of Mexican history ', no one, and this includes those closest to Eisenstein, seems to be quite sure what *Que Viva Mexico* was exactly intended to be. It was known that the film was to touch upon all the periods of Mexican history from the Aztecs till to-day, and anyone familiar with Eisenstein's work could safely assume that this epic panorama would not be allowed to sprawl out in episodes but would have a design and shape of its own, however grandiose. Speculation on the outcome was cut short when Sinclair announced that his financial resources were exhausted, that

[1] September 17th, 1930; reprinted in *Close Up*, Vol. 8, No. 1, March 1931, *The Dinamic Square*.

[2] Cf. contributions to the programme issued in connection with the Memorial Performance of Eisenstein's Work, May 2nd, 1948, published by the Film Section of the Society for Cultural Relations with U.S.S.R., London, in association with the British Film Academy and the National Film Library.

[3] *Op. cit.*, pp. 17-23. Marie Seton puts the total footage at 150,000.

Eisenstein and he could not agree on how to bring it to a conclusion, and that, as he held the rights, he proposed to make an arrangement with a commercial Hollywood producer, Sol Lesser, to edit the film and through whom it would be released. The resulting controversy was tumultous. Eisenstein's embattled partisans in the United States organised pressure groups, raised money, and threatened to seek legal means by which to take the footage away from its backers and send it to Eisenstein, who had already returned to the Soviet Union. Sinclair defended his actions on the grounds of economic commercial necessity. Shortly the controversy was embittered by the introduction of political issues. Meanwhile, Sol Lesser's version of the material, called *Thunder Over Mexico,* appeared at the end of 1933. This, one sequence of the original film, was praised or damned according to one's bias. It fell to Grierson to sum up what has become the final verdict : ' The clouds and the cactus will pass for great photography among the hicks, but they are, of course, easy meat for anyone with a decent set of filters . . . . The significance that Eisenstein might have added to the tale is not there; and types, acting and glycerined clouds cannot turn a simple tale of village rape into the passion of a people. There were other things up Eisenstein's sleeve. or he is not the dialectician I have always taken him for.'[1]

The absurdity of calling Eisenstein's a film which he did not edit is now sufficiently obvious, and it was only confirmed by the subsequent release of *Death Day,* edited from the original material by Sinclair, and of *Time in the Sun,* edited by Eisenstein's disciple Marie Seton from instructions and scenario notes which were, one gathered, more or less posthumous to the project. Apparently there was at no time a complete original script, and it is useless even to speculate upon what the film would have been like if completed by Eisenstein.[2] Perhaps another *Birth*

[1] *Grierson on Documentary,* edited by H. Forsyth Hardy (Collins. 1946), p. 54.

[2] Eisenstein's synopsis for *Que Viva Mexico* appeared in *Experimental Cinema,* No. 5. Reprinted with 36 illustrations (Vision Press, 1951).

of a Nation, or *Intolerance,* both of which were filmed
out of Griffith's head? Or *Que Viva Mexico* might have
joined the original versions of *Greed* and *Napoléon* as
projects inherently impossible of fulfilment. Eisenstein,
in the fragments which we saw of the Mexican footage,
came closer to the life of the common people than in any
of his masterpieces. But whether that life could have been
shaped into film form will forever remain an unanswered
question.

When Eisenstein returned to Moscow after this sadly
abortive experiment, he found a film world greatly changed.
He and Pudovkin had solved the problem of sound-film
technique on paper before he left,[1] but it fell to those he
left behind to discover how much of the theories expressed
in 1928 could actually be realised. The basic principle put
forward was that montage must apply to the sound track
as well as to the mute, and from this it followed that the
married film must be contrapuntal. Sound and visual images
would complement, not duplicate, one another. The
' compound cinema ' would be based on ' non-coincidence '.
The result, it was maintained, would be an even greater
intensification of the shock-effect of silent montage.

The first Soviet sound film avoided testing the theory.
The Road to Life (1931) by Nikolai Ekk included one
instance of disjunct sound, the famous scene in which
steam escaping from a locomotive expressed the grief of
hundreds of onlookers. For the rest, it was largely a
theatrical dialogue film, a form which it could hardly have
avoided since its content was reformist and Victorian (the
late Otis Ferguson described it as ' Louisa May Alcott on
a collective farm '). Pudovkin's first effort in the medium,
Life is Beautiful (*A Simple Case*), 1931, was a botch which
nobody has ever satisfactorily explained.[2] In view of its

[1] Cf. page 419. *Vide, Close Up,* Vol. 3, No. 4, October, 1928.
The Sound Film, by S. M. Eisenstein, V. I. Pudovkin, and G. V.
Alexandrov.

[2] *Life is Beautiful* was shown in Britain as a silent film by the Film
Society, May 21st, 1933. *Vide, Soviet Cinema,* Thorold Dickinson and
Catherine de la Roche (Falcon Press, 1948), p. 37.

emptiness and confusion, the fact that its use of disjunct
sound was unsuccessful seemed unimportant, but here, at
the beginning of things, was a warning for all to see that the
process of association on which the theory depended could
not be strained too far. Pudovkin did strain it too far,
and the result was either incomprehension or a completely
intellectual effect. It was literally true that Pudovkin's
intentions could not be understood by ordinary audiences
unless programme notes explained them, and many of his
supposedly most brilliant effects impressed the foreign
intelligentsia only because they had read about them in
advance. The trap into which both Eisenstein and Pudovkin seem to have fallen in their elaboration of the theory
of sound is the trap of symbolism—the ' formal-aesthetic '
fault of which their colleagues were soon to accuse them.
Actually, Ekk's brief use of disjunct sound in *Road to Life*
was nearer the mark, for he had sought in the scene for
some object of occurrence which would express the feeling
of the whole, much as Pabst in the silent days summed up a
passage by isolating a unit with his camera which would
mutely speak his meaning.

The sound-film medium seems to demand such treatment.
However defensible in theory, the association of sound and
image, or of image and image, cannot become too remote
or sophisticated without resulting in a fatal abstraction.
The medium does not consist only of composition of
material; the material makes demands of its own and
refuses wholly to follow the commands of the godlike
editor. But all this was not yet apparent.

The case of Pudovkin's flawed masterpiece *Deserter*
(1933) is now well-known. Here, too, his pursuit of
sound theories had unequal results, and his choice of
subject revealed a conflict and a quandary which was to
plague him and his colleagues more and more. *Deserter*
achieved greatness at isolated moments, when the ideas and
the material did not bear directly on the problematic nature
of the theme. Grierson sums up: ' When you come to
consider the continuing theme of the film you will be wise

to look for none, but content yourself with the vast description it gives of the world to-day : of high-powered industry, of unemployment, of poverty, of the accumulating fire of public effort, of the stresses and storms between men and men which economic disaster has brought in its train. The net effect is of great tragedy, in which the beauties of blue sky and morning, ships and machinery, young faces and hopeful faces, are strangely stifled in the common disaster . . . . For my part, I shall only record that no film or novel or poem or drama has sketched so largely the essential story or the essential unhappiness of our time, or brought them so deeply to the mind.'[1]

Meanwhile, less celebrated directors were attempting to cope with the struggles, problems, and achievements of the five-year plans. The efforts of Dovjenko (*Ivan* 1933), Vertov (*Enthusiasm* 1931, *Three Songs of Lenin* 1934), Macharet (*Men and Jobs* 1932), Ermler and Yutkevich (*Counterplan* 1932, *Peasants* 1934), have been described in *Documentary Film*, which also surveys the controversy that abruptly shifted the course of the Soviet cinema with the appearance of *Chapaev* in 1935.[2] It is suggested that the reader refers to Rotha's account of this period, for the controversy and its aftermath have been determinants in the subsequent course of the Soviet cinema. Briefly, Eisenstein and Pudovkin on the one hand, and Vertov and Dovjenko on the other, were denounced by the official leaders of the Central Committee for the pursuit of a barren intellectualism. The ' Soviet man ' had disappeared from, or had never appeared in, these mass-films and song-films. The way to bring him to life involved a return to acting and to stories centring around individuals. (*Chapaev*, with its developing ' class character ', represented the synthesis which was to be the way of the future.)

This triumph of the right over the left-wing of Soviet cinematography signalled a dilemma which was simultane-

---

[1] *Grierson on Documentary*, edited by H. Forsyth Hardy (Collins, 1946), p. 55.

[2] *Documentary Film* (Faber & Faber, 1936 & 1939), pp. 174-179.

ously plaguing the documentary-makers in Britain, as expressed in the following passage from Rotha : ' If significant propagandist motives are to be served, it is clearly not the slightest use making films which will appeal only to a limited section of the public . . . . If documentary is going to be significant, we must make films which will move the people and not just amuse our fellow-directors. If cinema is a branch of art at all, then it is the most vulgar branch because the most popular. And if the masses are interested in seeing individuals on the screen, then documentary must embrace individuals.'[1] This statement provides the real motivation for the Soviet revolt against typage and montage which, though expressed in theoretical terms, seems actually to have been motivated by the natural propagandist desire to reach larger audiences more intimately and more cogently.

To a certain extent Dinamov's criticisms of the left-wing were justified. Eisenstein, Pudovkin, and others were not only lost in intellectualism but in *aesthetic* intellectualism. The faults of *The General Line, A Simple Case, Ivan* and *Three Songs of Lenin* derived from an absorption in the medium for its own sake underlined by an implicit disinterest in the material treated and, possibly, an implicit distaste for the propagandist ends to be served. But it is to be questioned if the alternative method of the right-wing answered the dilemma any better. From *Chapaev* onward, the Titans of the twenties took something like a backseat; they appear to have functioned chiefly as ' artistic supervisors ', overseeing the product of entire studios but rarely directing individual films. That opportunity fell to the Vassilievs, Kozintzev and Trauberg, and a host of newcomers whose names were then unknown to Western *cinéastes*. Devotees of acting and narrative, they set to work to duplicate *Chapaev*—and did exactly that.

It had been expected that Dinamov's dictum would result in films which would centre around ' class characters ' drawn from the mass of Soviet humanity industriously

[1] *Op. cit.,* pp. 180, 181.

struggling with the problems of the second and third Five-Year plans. Instead, the return to the theatrical method brought with it a retreat to themes and scenes of the past. Not only the past of the 1917 revolution (*Baltic Deputy* 1935, *Lenin in October* 1938, *We from Kronstadt* 1936), and the 1905 revolution (the Gorki films), but all the way back to Suvorov and Peter the Great, even to Alexander Nevsky and Ivan the Terrible. Each of these films, and film series, had a specific propagandist aim. Most were well done within the limits of their deliberately adopted style. There is, of course, always room for experiment in the handling of historical material, even though some master-theorists and historians of the film have suggested, with a good deal of force, that it is not in the nature of the medium to deal with material so remote from contemporary life. But to find, as indeed we do in summing up, that costume drama as a *genre* for an entire decade largely dominated a State-supported and State-directed art, dedicated to assist in the transformation of an agricultural society into an industrial society, is to ponder deeply on the ways of leaders. The nature of the Soviet situation in the thirties demanded above all else that mass-propaganda serve two main purposes: to cushion the shock to the individual of necessitous collective regimentation, and to enlist the sentiments and loyalties of the complete population in the collective effort. It is difficult to see how any of the big films of the late thirties performed either function, except in the most indirect and remote way.

The return to the Actor, then, would seem as much an evasion of Soviet film problems as the earlier absorption with abstract film theory. The origins of this impulse to evade are given in part in Grierson's criticism: ' It is a commonplace of modern teaching that even with revolution, revolution has only begun. The Russian film directors do not seem to have appreciated this, for it would lead them to subject matter which, for the moment, they appear to avoid: to the common problems of everyday life and to

the common—even instructional—solutions of them. But
Russian directors are too bound up—too aesthetically vain
—in what they call their "play films" to contribute to
Russia's instructional cinema.[1] They have, indeed, suffered
greatly from the freedom given to artists in the first un-
critical moment of revolutionary enthusiasm, for they have
tended to isolate themselves more and more in private
impression and private performance. As much as
any bourgeois counterpart, they had given themselves the airs and ribbons of art. This has been
possible because the first Five-Year plan and the Second
have been too busy with essential services to get
round to the cinema. For the future, one may safely leave
them to the consideration of the Central Committee. One's
impression is that when some of the art and all of the
Bohemian self-indulgence have been knocked out of them,
the Russian cinema will fulfil its high promise of the late
twenties. It is bound to, for only its present romantic
perspective prevents it coming to grips with the swift and
deeply detailed issues around it. The revolutionary will
most certainly liquidate, as they put it, this romantic
perspective.'[2]

In terms of results, Grierson was optimistic, for ' the
romantic perspective' has persisted unaltered since these
words were written in 1935, as for example in such a
romantic picture as Gendelstein's *Lermontov* (1943). If
it has continued to be the perspective of theatre as against
intrinsic cinema, perhaps the choice meant nothing to the
Central Committee. Perhaps it was a Hobson's choice?
As between intellectualism and easy appeal to the masses,
there could be no choice but the second, in a period when
increasing external pressures made it essential to seize upon
any device which made for unity, even patriotism, even
nationalism. Yet there was a third alternative. The films
of Ermler, Yutkevich, and Macharet in the early thirties
(e.g. *Counterplan, Men and Jobs*) at least essayed that

[1] This is not true factually of Pudovkin and Dovjenko.—P.R.
[2] *Op. cit.*, p. 117.

'accurate industrial observation', that coming to grips with actual problems here and now, which seemed to Western sympathisers the first duty of the Soviet cinema in the immediate circumstances of the polity. Perhaps Central Committees are not always the best judges of their interest in areas remote from their immediate field of action? However that may be, the concept of documentary observation of contemporary Russia and its problems has never taken deep root in the Soviet film. Instructional films, in the classroom sense, are made in their hundreds. But the 'dramatisation of actuality' proceeds in terms of the traditions of fiction and the theatre. Who can say whether this represents conscious choice, or whether it indicates an aesthetic-propagandist immaturity reflecting a more portentous political immaturity?

Who, indeed, can make any final judgement upon the matter? The above account of the fluctuating fortunes of this faction and that is made in full knowledge of the fact that all factions, and all individuals, concerned are whole-heartedly devoted to the Soviet ideology. So great is this devotion that even a considerable perusal of Soviet film 'self-criticism' is scarcely enlightening. Everyone acknowledges his errors but always in terms of the greater understanding of an opponent's correctness. The general impression is not so much that of a directed verdict as of a continuing flux of ideas in which all are bewildered, commissars and craftsmen alike. The final blame, if that is the word, must nevertheless fall upon the craftsmen, for they are in a special position to which they have never before attained in the history of civilisation. They have, for the first time, the opportunity consciously to serve the highest interests of the community. The opportunity consists in clothing policy in flesh and bone. Merely to take orders is not enough.

*

Eisenstein's course during the remainder of his life is significant of the changed situation. He buried himself in the library, emerging from time to time to announce and even start a profusion of projects (*Moscow, La Condition Humaine, Bezhin Meadow*). Scenarios were prepared and footage shot for some of these, but none reached completion until the appearance of *Alexander Nevsky* at the end of 1938. What was happening in these years is difficult to assess. In 1935, he was severely reprimanded by the Central Committee as a formalist, and 'banished' for a long holiday. But between times he was by no means idle. He taught at the Higher State Institute of Cinema in Moscow, acted as artistic supervisor for Mosfilm, wrote innumerable theoretical articles, but none of this activity had issue in a personal film. So much of his writing at this period is speculation on the essential nature of the film, and of all art,[1] that our first conclusion might be that he had entirely retired from the controversy over propagandist ends and means which the 1935 conference had highlighted. But Rotha significantly points out: 'From the text of his G.I.K. lectures I should say that he understood the problem only too well, but was experiencing the greatest difficulty in doing anything about it but theorise.'[2] At any rate, the events of 1936 relieved him of the problem by providing a new channel for action which was completely non-controversial. It is generally conceded that, after the Moscow trials and the succeeding purge, all the energies of the Soviet Union were poured into preparation for the war that was now seen to be inevitable. Consequently Eisenstein, and with him the entire Soviet cinema, could by-pass with a clear conscience the basic and still unanswered problem of creating Soviet dramatic documentary and concentrate on films designed to rouse the fatherland spirit. *Alexander Nevsky* was exactly that. Acted and directed in the heroic manner, if not, indeed, operatically (two years later Eisenstein returned to the stage to direct *Die Walküre*), it was in style and approach as far removed from the Eisenstein of *Potemkin* and *Ten*

[1] It has been collected and translated by Jay Leyda as *The Film Sense* (Faber & Faber, 1943).

[2] *Op. cit.,* p. 178.

Days that Shook the World as is conceivable. Crammed with tremendous images, focussed on physical action, couched in black-and-white morality, *Nevsky* was nearly indistinguishable from a spectacle by De Mille or Curtiz, except for Eisenstein's discriminating taste and his supreme mastery of crowd scenes, and the absence of Errol Flynn. The arrival of the Mongol dignitary; the death agonies of Pskov; the Battle on the Ice—these gave opportunity for filigree imagery of a kind which had never appeared to interest him in the days of his revolutionary films. He seemed absorbed in recreating the face of the legendary past at the expense of any but the most elementary political theme.

After another abortive effort, *Ferghana Canal* (the scenario of which is of the greatest interest as an example of film writing), Eisenstein began preparations for *Ivan the Terrible*. These were interrupted by Hitler's invasion of Russia, the removal of the studios to Alma-Ata in Central Asia, and by other duties. Throughout the war period Eisenstein was working under tremendous strain, supervising many films, both fiction and documentary, while continuing intermittently with the shooting of Parts I and II of *Ivan*, which was projected as a trilogy.

Part I of *Ivan the Terrible* was released on the last day of 1944. This extraordinary and baffling film may never be completely understood, since the third part cannot now be finished. Like *Nevsky*, *Ivan* purported to be a reconstruction of a crucial period of Russian history for the instruction and edification of the masses. Far more than its predecessor, it elided theme, plot, character development, or exhortation, for the sake of concentrating upon what I can only call 'periodicity'. With terrifying vividness Eisenstein evoked from halls, costumes, processions, and from enormous close-ups of the faces of human beings, the atmosphere of medieval Russia—the immanence of chaos and blood and death. Through the holocaust moved its embodiment, the figure of Ivan, bearing within him the seeds of growth and death. The character was so much larger than life that comparison with the historical Ivan is futile, just as this version makes the old Paul Leni rendering of Ivan in *Waxworks* seem juvenile. The film and its central figure teemed with portent of what is to come, and perhaps all mysteries would have been resolved through the completion and release of the second and third films, though the reception of the second part throws doubt on this. Jay Leyda writes : ' Most of this Part II of the projected trilogy was shot during the production of Part I, but its cutting (including sequences in colour) was not completed until the beginning of 1946. Immediately upon the completion of the cutting, Eisenstein suffered an almost fatal heart attack, confining him to hospital for the remainder of the year. During this time screenings of his work-print aroused considerable critical controversy, of which he was unaware until his release from the hospital. At present he is completing Part II for release in 1948.' According to Ivor Montagu, the finishing of Part II coincided with a stroke. On his recovery, he found that his film had been categorised as ' giving a false impression of history ', and after a meeting with Stalin, he was working on remaking Part II and preparing Part III, when he died suddenly on February 10, 1948.[1]

James Agee and others have seen in Part I of *Ivan* a veiled allegory of the callousness of Stalinism to all human obstacles, and a protest against the rigidity with which it constricts artistic creation. To me, the case seems otherwise. I cannot conceive that anyone should seriously question Eisenstein's *intellectual* adherence to the philosophy of Communism or to the methods of the Politburo. To me, the keys to his latter career are two : the evasions of *The General Line,* and the statement, often attributed to Eisenstein himself, that he was ' a bourgeois at heart '. This great master remained interested only in the medium which he had so finely helped to create. His speculative mind, forever roaming through the ages of

[1] Memorial Programme of Eisenstein's Work, London, May 2nd, 1948, pp. 5-14.

human thought, could not easily come to rest in the problems of this year and next. *Ivan*, essentially, was a speculation on the nature of power—not Ivan's power, or Stalin's, but Power. As such, it was created *outside* the Soviet scheme of things, an involuntary heretic to its own cause.

Pudovkin's course has been much the same, so far as is known to us. His only film to reach America since *Deserter* was *General Suvorov* (1941), an historical pageant containing little to suggest Pudovkin's style or methods, much less his power and humanity. Nor did it exactly adhere to the line of history, the relationship between the General and the dynasty being prudently glossed over. Except for the great name attached to it, this might have been a routine historical film made almost anywhere in the world. It is a matter of much regret that his last film, *Admiral Nakhimov*, has not been made available to us.

There were elements in the early career of Alexander Dovjenko which might have suggested that he, alone of the old-line directors, would successfully adapt himself to the new dispensation. But apparently it was not to be. After *Earth* and *Ivan*,[1] Dovjenko made but one film of first importance. *Frontier* (1936) known also as *Aerograd*, was perhaps the first of the Soviet nationalist films and certainly was one of the most legitimate. The imagery of his characteristic style, sometimes employed for its own sake, here took on significance in relation to the theme. In linking the semi-barbaric ritual of the old believers with the equally barbaric punctilio of the Samurai, Dovjenko used unmistakably cinematic terms to express the sources of the political alliance between the enemies of the Soviet inside and outside the territory of the Union. Set over against this image of the primitive and the retrograde was his striking portrait of the Communist youth of the new generation, a portrait rather more lyrical than functional, perhaps, but suffused with the poetry and drama of which

[1] Discussed by Rotha in *Celluloid*, pp. 135-153, and *Documentary Film*, p. 175.

he is master. Moments in this film achieved again the summits of *Arsenal* and *Earth;* intellectually it went deeper than either. *Frontier's* nationalism stemmed from environment, character and political clash. As much cannot be said for his next film, *Shors* (1939), a biography of a young revolutionary hero of 1919 cut something to the pattern of *Chapaev.* Doubtless this resurrection of recent deeds had a powerful suggestive effect on the Soviet public, as has been proposed. Doubtless any film dealing with this material would have a comparable effect. But as an example of Dovjenko's style, or any film style at all, *Shors* was non-existent. It had very beautiful photography, by Ekelchik; a memorable opening sequence of battle among the sunflower fields; and a few moments reminiscent of the old Dovjenko, especially in the scenes of horses; but all this was overweighted by the ' policy ' line. As in *Chapaev,* as in them all, the ' development of class character ', the nature of friend and enemy, and even the strategy of the battles, was lost in a maelstrom of words. In this pseudo-epic there was little trace of the passionate poetic creator of *Arsenal* and *Earth.*

Lesser directors during this nationalist period concentrated principally on the revolutionary period and the twenty years preceding it. The *Gorki* trilogy (*Childhood of Maxim Gorki* 1938, *My Universities* 1940, *Out in the World* 1939), beautifully directed by Mark Donskoi, dramatised the coming of political and humanitarian consciousness to the first great writer to be adopted by the Soviets as their own. The *Maxim* trilogy of Kozintzev and Trauberg traced the development of still another ' class character ', an artisan youth who participates in the pre-revolutionary struggles and achieves full stature in October.[1] Alexandrov, one-time collaborator with Eisenstein, seems to have devoted himself to a kind of musical comedy career, with *Jazz Comedy* (1935), *The Circus* (1936) and *The Bright Path* (1940), none of which was

---

[1] *The Youth of Maxim* (1934), *The Return of Maxim* (1937), and *Vyborg Side* (1938).

in any way important. The career of the canonised leader of the Bolsheviks was elaborately acted out in Romm's *Lenin in October* (1937), and *Lenin in 1918* (1939) largely in terms of party politics and personalities somewhat obscure to the uninitiated. *Baltic Deputy* (1937) by Zharki and Heifitz, signalised the conversion of the intellectual to the new *régime* in the time of trouble; the rapturous reception accorded this film both within and without the Soviet Union, incidentally, was indicative of the extent to which the new method had taken root: it was principally applauded for the acting of a young man, Nikolai Cherkassov in the rôle of the septuagenarian protagonist.

So continued, and continue, these films of politicians, interspersed with rationalised interpretations of past Russian statesmen as the fathers of their people (Petrov's two films of *Peter the First,* 1937-38 and *Kutuzov,* 1944) From what reached America in the late thirties, the Russian studios at that date were almost wholly occupied with grandiose historical reconstructions ' humanised ' by theatrical acting, plentiful humour, and a political simplification of the facts. As costume films go, the Soviet renderings of history were among the best.[1] They were skilful, they were seldom absurd—and that is an achievement in this *genre.* But, except for an occasional introductory sequence devoted to conjuring up the atmosphere of a period, they seldom attempted any deeper understanding of the human chronicle than could be found in a child's schoolbook. It was not so much that they were ' official ' interpretations of events, nor that they were directed at a semi-educated audience; they seemed to lack any real concern for what they said.

Comparatively few major films dealt with contemporary life. Of these quite the most interesting was Sergei Gerasimov's *The New Teacher* (1939), a thoughtful and at times passionate consideration of the problems involved

[1] Strongly reminiscent of the German *Fridericus Rex* series of the twenties.

141. TARGET FOR TONIGHT, directed by HARRY WATT. [British, 1941]

142. THE LAND, directed by ROBERT J. FLAHERTY. [American, 1939–42]

143. CITIZEN KANE, directed by ORSON WELLES. DOROTHY COMINGORE,
ORSON WELLES. [American, 1941]

144. THE MALTESE FALCON, directed by JOHN HUSTON. HUMPHREY BOGART,
ELISHA COOK, JR. [American, 1941]

in the changeover from old to new which was still going on throughout Russia. Unlike most other Soviet films of the period, it was full of warmth and life, with beautifully observed details. Scores of small films celebrated Stakhanovism and the improvement in living-conditions announced by Stalin in his 'Now, comrades, life is better, life is brighter' policy after the conclusion of the second Five-Year Plan re-introduced mass production of consumer goods. Typical of these was Alexandrov's *Tanya*, which described the prize trip to Moscow awarded a girl worker for exceeding her quota. The brassy glitter of the Moscow jollification was repugnant to those Western critics who shrunk from the vulgarity of the new collective life (while finding picturesque the primitive peasant life as shown in the old revolutionary films). But to anyone interested in what was happening to the peoples of the Soviet Union, this film and its humble fellows were more revelatory—and more enjoyable—than a score of historical epics enacted by Honored Artists of the Republic. Here was a changing Russia, a Russia changing itself, and going about it with a gusto and vitality that signalled enjoyment of living. Such films as these provoked the comment that the Russian cinema was 'Americanising' itself. I should put it differently. The Soviet film at its beginnings shared with the American film that 'common touch' which endeared both to the masses. The return of this sense of the doings and concerns of ordinary people was to be welcomed in the rearguard of the Soviet cinema.

A memorable film just prior to the war was Vladimir Legoshin's *Lone White Sail* (1937), a film about children ostensibly made for children, but with an understanding and warmth that made it almost isolated among Soviet films of the late thirties. Sensitively handled, superbly photographed and produced, it came nearer to telling us how the new generation lived and felt and thought than any other picture, except perhaps *The New Teacher*, of the decade. We should not forget, also, the Soviet fondness for fantasy and fairy-tale storying, which they express so well in film with their mastery over the mechanics of trick-photography and model-work. We record, for their importance, Obratsov's *Land of Toys* (1940), and Alexander Rou's *The Magic Fish* (1938) and *The Little Humpbacked Horse* (1941), charming and fanciful pieces of film-magic.

*

Hitler's sudden blow in June, 1941, temporarily disrupted Soviet film-making. Before 1939 one anti-Nazi film, Adolf Minkin's and Herbert Rappaport's much-admired *Professor Mamlock* (1938) had expressed the official Communist view of the German *régime* with considerable insight and compassion.[1] But the Pact had put an end to such expressions, and it was with suddenness indeed that the studios were confronted with the necessity to make actual war films. The technical crudity of films for the first two years of the war was explained by the fact that the studios had been hastily transferred to Central Asia, with much resultant loss of technical facilities, just as the flat, black-and-white villain and hero character of the films themselves resulted from the experiences which the Russian people themselves were undergoing at the time. With large numbers of them under the Nazi heel, there was no room in their hearts for anything but hate of the ' Hitlerites ', and no demand for anything on the screen except portrayals of Nazis as devils incarnate and their Russian guerrilla and soldier opponents as knights in shining armour. If the Nazi portraits were absurd, the Russian heroisms were real enough, and both were entirely acceptable to their embattled audiences if hardly for export purposes. Probably none of these violent reactions to invasion (Donskoi's *Rainbow* 1944, from the prize novel by Wanda Wassilevska, was at once the most typical and the most elaborate) will be remembered. But the war evoked from Russia films which will not only be remembered but will also be closely studied by historians many generations from now. The vast Russian campaign

[1] Rappaport was Pabst's assistant on *Kameradschaft* (1931).

which, according to General MacArthur, stands unequalled in military history for its scale and grandeur, was spread across the screen in a frieze of edited documentaries which, in some of their qualities, take their place with the finest achievements of film art. *Moscow Strikes Back*, *The Siege of Leningrad*, *Stalingrad*, and *The Battle for the Ukraine* were monuments to Soviet achievement which will in all probability outlast all the admired fiction films. They also differed markedly from their Western counterparts, *Desert Victory*, *The True Glory*, and the Capra *Why We Fight* series. No attempt was made to describe military strategy : instead, all aspects of the war effort were simultaneously presented in a form not unlike the structure of *Intolerance*. No other films brought out the vastness of the war so forcefully, and none, except *The True Glory*, approached so intimately the human atoms in the enormous totality.[1]

Post-war Soviet films have been slow in reaching the United States. Alexander Ptushko, whose *The New Gulliver* (1935) brilliantly used puppets to reconstruct Swift's satire with a class-angle, directed *The Stone Flower* (1946), a rather weighty fantasy in Agfacolor made in the Barrandov studios at Prague. The veteran Yakov Protazanov produced that delightful legend, *Adventures in Bukhara* (1943), a Moslem folk-tale redolent of its period and setting. This simple and childlike film makes all other Oriental fantasies, from *The Thief of Bagdad* on, look ponderous. There has also been the *Festival of Youth*, a colour kaleidoscope of the great gathering of athletes from all the constituent republics of the Soviet Union in the Leningrad Stadium in 1946. An amazing spectacle of mass-movement well shot by some thirty-five cameramen (including some remarkable zoom lens shots), the film dazed by its repetitions yet at the same time remained an astonishing technical achievement. The much-heralded *réportage* film of the Nuremberg Trials was

---

[1] Many well-known directors worked on these films, including Dovjenko, Yutkevich, Dziga-Vertov, Gerasimov, Raizman, Belyaev, Varlamov, Zharki and Heifitz.

disappointing. Its ' English ' narration was naïve to the
extent of embarrassment, attempting to infuse melodrama
into visuals which were already dramatic in their
authenticity.

*

I have said that the Soviet historical films were among
the best of their kind. Yet there is a strong affinity between them and such Western commercial counterparts as
Juarez and *Zola*. The Hollywood liberals set the stage for
their triumphs of progressivism in the past because they
dared not set it in the present. The Soviet artists seem
to have clung to history because it enabled them to preserve
theatrical reconstruction as against that organisation of
observed reality which we have come to call documentary.
Historical reconstruction was, it is true, one of the policy
tasks handed down to them from on high, but unless all
signs fail, it was they who made it a major task. If this
be true, Grierson's criticism of Soviet sound cinema quoted
above still holds in 1948.

(IV) THE GERMAN FILM

' Irretrievably sunk into retrogression, the bulk of the
German people could not help submitting to Hitler. *Since
Germany thus carried out what had been anticipated by her
cinema from its ·very beginning,*[1] conspicuous screen
characters now came true in life itself. Personified day-
dreams of minds to whom freedom meant a fatal shock,
and adolescence a perpetual temptation, these figures filled
the arena of Nazi Germany. Homunculus walked about in
the flesh. Self-appointed Caligaris hypnotised innumerable
Cesares into murder. Raving Mabuses committed fantastic crimes with impunity, and mad Ivans devised
unheard-of tortures. Along with this unholy procession,
many motifs known from the screen turned into actual
events. In Nuremberg, the ornamental pattern of

[1] My italics.—R.G.

Nibelungen appeared on a gigantic scale : an ocean of flags and people artistically arranged. Souls were thoroughly manipulated so as to create the impression that the heart mediated between brain and hand. By day and night, millions of feet were marching over city streets and along highways. The blare of military bugles sounded unremittingly, and the philistines from the plush parlours felt very elated. Battles roared and victory followed victory. It was all as it had been on the screen. The dark premonitions of a final doom were also fulfilled.'

These are the final words of Dr. Siegfried Kracauer's *From Caligari to Hitler : A Psychological History of the German Film,*[1] which Paul Rotha has praised in his preface. I share his admiration for this remarkable book, and it is therefore with no apology that I shall refrain from retracing again the course of the German film from 1919 to 1933 because Dr. Kracauer has already done it so well.[2] What follows here is some account of the use made by the Nazis of the immensely efficient film plant and personnel which they inherited from the Weimar Film Industry. This report is, for obvious reasons, fragmentary. I venture to present it only because Dr. Kracauer does not deal with the Hitler period since 1933, and because while serving in the U.S. armed forces I had an opportunity to see many captured films not possibly available to film connoisseurs in the Allied countries.

In thus by-passing the films of the last years of the Weimar Republic and referring the reader to Dr. Kracauer, I do not intend to imply that either the films or the period are unimportant to a survey of *The Film Since Then.* Quite the contrary. The films themselves, the inspirations which brought them into being, and far from least their reception within and without Germany, are of the utmost consequence to the student of the rôle of film in contemporary life. They cannot be dealt with briefly

[1] Princeton University Press, 1947.

[2] *Vide* also, *Fifty Years of German Film,* H. H. Wollenberg (The **Falcon** Press, 1948).

without incurring a fatal superficiality. And Dr. Kracauer not only discusses them fully : in doing so he, perhaps quite consciously, brings to light one of the gravest weaknesses of film criticism, of all film cerebration, to date.

The Blue Angel, Westfront 1918, Kameradschaft, M, Die Dreigroschenoper, The Testament of Dr. Mabuse, and *Kuhle Wampe* stand with the finest and bravest films. Each made its creative contribution to the development of sound technique. All were conceived in a spirit of liberal-minded realism, and most had direct liberal propagandist aims. That was enough for all contemporary and most succeeding commentators. What Kracauer alone of all film writers perceived is that while the intentions of these films were good, the thinking behind them was wholly inadequate to the task their directors set for themselves. Addressing an immature audience, they employed intellectual terms which could not possibly exert any emotional spell over that audience. In so doing, their directors revealed not only political ignorance but also— one might almost say—an anthropological ignorance which is a fatal weakness in a film-maker whose purpose is to change minds and prepare the way for action. Combating immaturity, their films showed unmistakable symptoms of immaturity. When the liberalism for which they stood met its downfall, it was possible to perceive that that external defeat was preceded by, perhaps caused by, an internal defeat.

There was devastating evidence of this throughout the dismal last years of the thirties, the most conspicuous being the speed and ease with which certain German film-makers, who only a few years before were identified with social progress, accommodated themselves to the Goebbels' scheme of things. (In writing this, it is, of course, far from my intention to denigrate those brave German film-makers who left their homes rather than serve fascism, and many of whom lost their lives in the struggle against it.) The most extraordinary and baffling case of the ' accommodators ' is that of G. W. Pabst, one of the three or four greatest masters of the film medium, and for whom we all had the highest respect in the years before the war. From *The Joyless Street* (1925) to *Kameradschaft* (1931), most of his films seemed to American and British observers to be strenuous pleas for social and economic justice. When he left Germany after *Atlantide* (1932), after the accession of Hitler, we applauded his courage and integrity. We shared his frustration when he made the cumbersome three-language version of *Don Quixote* (1933) in the south of France, a film with which from start he had little sympathy despite its ultimate beautiful photography and settings. When he refused to work in Hollywood after one abortive film (*A Modern Hero*, 1934, with Richard Barthelmess), we said that here was a man to whom compromise was impossible.[1] When he seemed condemned to the direction of low grade melodramas in France in the late thirties (*Drame du Shanghai*), we raged against the System. And when, after the outbreak of war, he received Hitler's amnesty and returned hurriedly to Germany, some of us accepted the explanation that he was ill and feared French internment as an enemy alien; that he would retire to his castle in Austria and have no part of the war. When internal evidence suggested that Pabst had had a hand in the editing of *Feldzug im Polen* (*Baptism of Fire*), we

[1] The following excerpt from an interview with Pabst by Ludo Patris in Belgium, printed in *Cinema Quarterly*, Vol. 1, No. 4, Summer, 1933, is of interest :

' I am the most-attacked director in Europe and I pay dearly for my independence. After *L'Atlantide* I waited months and months for a proposition which I could accept without caving in. That's where candour leads you. . . . I don't reproach business men for gaining money, or for the desire to earn it. I dream of an understanding between the audience and the director, apart from the production. To appreciate each other they must understand one another. . . .'

' Do you foresee a reorganisation of production? '

' Rather the creation of another production better adapted to the needs of those for whom it will be intended.'

' Perhaps in collaboration with the State? '

' No! Hitler to-day and Stalin to-morrow! Under an obligation to direct oneself according to the wish of each Government. Never! There must be freedom to follow a determined line once and for all. . . . The cinema is the mirror of our epoch in which everything must be reflected and imprinted forever.'

refused to believe it for was he not the apotheosis of self-sacrificing democrats? As for the rumour that all during those years in Paris when he was supervising *kitsch* he had actually been an agent of Otto Abetz, we dismissed it as crude and unfounded slander. For my part, it took the evidence of the senses to convince me. Sitting in an Army projection-theatre in 1944, I saw before me the credit: *Paracelsus*: Regie: G. W. Pabst. After that, even I saw the light, and not from the credit-title alone. *Paracelsus* itself was proof positive. Vast, pretentious, impressive, shot in the Barrandov studios near Prague, it presented Werner Krauss, of all actors, as the apostle of Hitlerian enlightenment, and opposed to him none other than Fritz Rasp, the very Rasp of *Jeanne Ney* and *Warning Shadows,* no longer a symbol of decaying capitalism but a surrogate-figure for democratic science. This strange conglomeration was stage-managed and edited with all of Pabst's old-time brilliance, with superb camerawork and settings, but the result was a re-echoing emptiness, the shell of a film. Perhaps its director was, by then, the shell of a man?

Pabst's case is a subtle, knotty and perhaps an insoluble one.[1] I give its history in some detail because, though extreme, it is an all too significant commentary on film commentators, including the present writer. Our record has been for too long one of absorption in technique for its own sake, or alternatively of accepting sociological intentions

[1] Pabst is now known to be de-Nazified by the Austrian Government and has just completed a film in Austria called *The Trial.* (P.R.) Louise Brooks, whom Pabst brought to Germany from Hollywood in 1928 to play in *Pandora's Box* (*vide* pp. 270, 271) and whose whole life and career were altered thereby, told me (R.G.) in conversation that: ' None of us who knew Pabst well felt that we ever knew him at all. He was all things to all men, and nothing consistently. He would argue any side of any question with apparent complete conviction and sincerity, but to see this happen over and over was to suspect that he had no convictions at all. He worked like a scientist, presenting stimuli to his actors and watching their reactions with cold-blooded detachment. He never made any comment, never explained himself. I always felt he lived his life completely alone.' In contrast, the reader is referred to an interview with Pabst and Louise Brooks in Berlin at Christmas, 1928, by H.D. (*Close Up,* Vol. 4, No. 3, March, 1929).

at their face value. Unless such intentions are realistically oriented to the specific culture involved, they end in pathetic irony, or worse. The history of German films has demonstrated this finally. Kracauer's dicta on the liberal German films of the early sound era will seem over-harsh to some. They were so brave, so interesting! Yet it needs not *Caligari to Hitler* to tell us that they were neither brave enough nor interesting enough. Films of the future, of what future may be left to us in which to say a word for peace and freedom, must be intelligent as well as courageous and well-meaning. That is why I recommend Kracauer's approach as a model for critics, for all of us who have been so eager for excellence in films that we have been content with excellences irrelevant to the nature and mission of a mass-medium. Our part is now Polonius's : ' Pray you, be round with him '.

*

What was to be the course of the Nazi cinema? After the purgation of the German Film Industry of most of its non-Aryan elements, and the famous meeting at the Propaganda Ministry at which Goebbels held up *Potemkin* as the model which was to be overtaken and surpassed, it was natural to assume that German films would be as violently and monotonously propagandist as Hitler's radio rantings. The assumption proved false. Goebbels knew better than his master.

Munich, appropriately enough, produced the first all-Nazi film. After the events of March, 1933, the Bavaria Film Company rushed *Hans Westmar* into production and proudly presented it to Germany's new masters early in the following summer. But, far from welcoming it as proof of loyalty, Goebbels coolly informed the Bavaria company that it could not be released until all reference to Horst Wessel, the Nazi ' martyr ' whose story it purported to tell, had been deleted or concealed. The mangled film which resulted fulfilled the worst expectations of Western observers so far as violence and crudity were concerned.

Paul Wegener as a caricatured Communist leader ruled all Germany in the terroristic manner of Dr. Mabuse, with the *Deutsche volk* piteously impaled on his spear. The Nazis were saints. Their triumph occurred in a vacuum. This absurdity, far from being supported by the party, was hustled through the theatres under wraps. It made way the following autumn for *Hitlerjunge Quex,* written under the direct supervision of Goebbels and produced at Ufa, now completely State-controlled. To paraphrase Kracauer, this careful film gave the precipitate provincial producers at Munich to understand how such matters should be handled. Its first object was not to glorify Nazidom, except by indirection, but to destroy existing institutions and to use the energies thus released for party purposes. In particular it sought to drive deep wedges into an already disintegrating family life, and to exploit the sexual immaturity and general psychic infantilism of large sections of German youth. This exploitation was implicit as well as explicit : Gregory Bateson has suggested that, in the use of such motifs as the boy's desire for a knife and a key, the film may well have been unconscious of its own methods. In any case, it derived its major strength as propaganda from these buried appeals, rather than from such overt and childish scenes as that in which a Nazi leader weans a Communist from Moscow by telling him that the Germany in which they stand is ' *unser* Deutschland '. On the surface those two words alone reconvert the heretic, but the informed observer realises that his sudden conversion actually stems from antecedent events—events which have destroyed in his mind all basis for any political belief save a mystical one. So it was to be in all further Nazi political films. Their verbal arguments seemed childish to non-Nazi audiences, and the films were therefore dismissed at that valuation. But to the Germans the emotional conflicts implicit in their situations were real and urgent, and it was these, and not the sloganising, which had effective propagandist impact.

Direct political arguments, however, were rare after

1933. To the German cinemagoing public (increasingly cut off from foreign films as the years went on) things might have seemed to change very little, for the old cycles and motifs were resumed and carried on, or seemed to be carried on, in the familiar manner. Veidt, Pabst, Kortner, and Fritz Lang might be missing but Wegener, Krauss, and Jannings continued familiar rôles in familiar vehicles, and story content differed surprisingly little. World War I dramas and military musical comedies, full of barracks humour, held first place in popular favour, but so they had under the Weimar Republic. Outmoded theatrical pieces provided starring rôles for the eternal Lil Dagover, the returned Pola Negri, the new star of the Third Reich, Zarah Leander, and for occasional importations. Multilingual films with international casts such as had found favour in the first years of sound were occasionally produced, and French and other European production units continued to employ the matchless technical facilities of the Nazi sound studios. No new styles or story fashions were introduced, although there were occasional revivals or flashes of *Caligarisme,* as exemplified in the 1936 remake of *The Student of Prague.* Nationalist semi-historical films, such as those of Luis Trenker and Arnold Fanck continued, but were no more virulent than before. The expected wholesale onslaught of all-out Nazi film propaganda never materialised. It all must have seemed very much the same as before.

This impression can hardly have been accidentally conveyed. By 1938 Bavaria, the last of the independent production companies, had been absorbed into the State trust, and since considerably before that time the content and execution of all German films had been wholly under the control of Goebbels. In part, the policy of producing routine entertainment films derived from the fact that motion pictures had become a factor in the export aspect of Nazi economy; they were used as a means of peaceful penetration, as well as of obtaining foreign credits, particularly in France and South America, and therefore could not afford to offend too openly the national sentiments of other countries. More basically, one concludes, the policy had its origin in Goebbels' calculated decision never to allow Nazi principles to be discussed by the Germans (and thereby called into question). Nazi propaganda did not seek to convince but to impress. Consequently, such films as had direct propagandist inspiration generally concealed their aims or revealed them only briefly. They resembled Freudian dreams in that the principal 'wish', deeply embedded in irrelevant material, would appear in disguise and only for a moment. Creative and technical skill were customarily spent on the surrounding structure rather than on the central idea, embellishing the course of events with all sorts of corroborative details so as to induce a receptive and credulous frame of mind. A typical example of this occurs in a film the title of which I regret I cannot recall. It begins during World War I, and for many reels we follow the comic and dramatic war experiences of four infantry comrades so closely that we feel an intimate party to their friendship. Abruptly the war ends, the soldiers part, and it is ten years before we see them again. They are as distant now as once they were close : one an industrial magnate, another a Tyrolean farmer, the third a ruined speculator, and the last a schoolmaster. The magnate conceives the quaint idea of inviting them all— with wives and children—to a reunion at his mansion, and, even more quaintly, constructs the replica of a dugout in his drawing room, the better to conjure up the atmosphere of their former comradeship. Needless to say, this bit of *legerdemain* fails in its effect; the intervening years and experiences have divided them utterly, and the dugout rendezvous results in a violent altercation which centres around political differences. Up to this point the film has been shrewdly managed. One is involved with the feelings of the characters, and their political views are seen to grow very believably out of the lot in which they have individually been cast in the post-war world. The outlines of reality are present here. But suddenly in the middle of the quarrel, which is seen to be a hopeless one, a torchlight parade of the *Stahlhelm* passes the magnate's house. The protagonists, overcome by emotion, rush to the balcony and stand in reverent silence, partisans united by the knowledge of their German-ness.

Preposterous as is this ending, it does not rob the picture of effect, even for non-Nazi minds, because what has gone before has been presented with skill and insight. And this became the characteristic method of the comparatively few Nazi films which dealt directly with political events. It is significant that the majority of these centred around World War I, that festering focus of nationalist consciousness. In this milieu the Nazis could say what they liked, and still remain confident of ready belief on the part of the vast majority of Germans. Stemming from this taproot of popular emotion and actual experience, some of these 1914-18 films achieved considerable cinematic eloquence and maturity, notably the ambitious trilogy *Um Das Menschen Recht* (of which the first part only has been seen in the United States). Another popular—and safe— theme was that of Germany's irredentist populations. Typical of these was *Friesennot*, about a colony of Frisian Germans buried in the forests of Russia to which come representatives of the Bolsheviki bent on taking over. Here a bastard version of the technique of the old 'instinct' films was used to combine the irridentist theme with that of *Blut und Boden*: the climax is a folk-dance by male dancers which is the farthest the Nazi screen ever went in the direction of dramatizing primitive Teutonism.

For the most part, however, fiction films were far less direct. They contented themselves with routine stories, merely heightening those aspects of German life which fitted into the Nazi scheme.[1] All-out propaganda was

[1] When I asked Gottfried Reinhardt why an innocuous romance included a long and totally irrelevant scene showing the entrance of a cavalry unit into a Prussian town, he replied: 'For the same reason that American films feature unmotivated scenes of jazz bands and tap dancing. Germans are ready to watch any amount of marching, whether or not it relates to the plot.'

almost entirely confined to the documentary medium, in which the Goebbels ministry from the first took the greatest interest. The reasons for this policy decision and its ultimate consequences are brilliantly sketched in Kracauer's pamphlets *Propaganda and the Nazi War Film* and *The Conquest of Europe on the Screen.*[1] Everyone interested in propagandist methods and effects should read these keen analyses : they display not only what can be accomplished by means of a unified plan rigidly adhered to, but also lay bare the extent to which the characteristics of particular media resist the intentions of the master propagandist. This brief survey can do no more than refer to Kracauer's conclusions : that Goebbels was under powerful compulsion to annex all life to the Nazi system; no sphere of intellectual emotion or physical activity but must be swallowed up in the swastika world, for to leave out any would permit the free play of individual judgement in the by-passed area. Hence the urge to employ authentic documentary material which would testify to the ' reality ' of the particular film, but which could be manipulated by the editor into an image of reality suited to immediate propagandist needs. When documentary or newsreel shots resisted such manipulation, or were not available, the Nazi film-makers ' staged ' reality for their cameras in a manner never before attempted. The apotheosis of their efforts was the celebrated *Triumph of The Will* (1937) in which a Nazi convention, purportedly held for its own sake, was ' actually staged for the camera like some colossal Hollywood production' (Iris Barry). ' The deep feeling of uneasiness', says Kracauer, ' which *Triumph of The Will* arouses in unbiased minds originates in the fact that before our eyes palpable life becomes an apparition . . . .This film represents an inextricable mixture of a show simulating German reality and of a German reality manœuvred into a show.'[2] The triumph here was due to the fact that the

[1] Both published by the Museum of Modern Art Film Library, New York. The first of the pamphlets is also appended to *From Caligari to Hitler.*

[2] *Op cit.,* page 303.

mixture really was inextricable, except to the eye of the experienced analyst, and that it had been cast into the melting pot by a talent which we must, however reluctantly, recognise as one of the most brilliant ever to be concerned with films, that of Leni Riefenstahl. Let it suffice to say that this woman's knowledge of the power of editing images was profound, nearly as profound as Pabst's or Eisenstein's. The scene she surveyed so powerfully was obliterated with the destruction of the swastika atop the stadium at Nuremberg by American artillery. But the ideological artillery of America has yet to demonstrate that it can destroy, by matching, the psychic world which she created out of nothing with camera and shears. Nazi Germany is no more, but the challenge stands. It has not been met.[1]

Other characteristic pre-war ' documentaries ' may be represented by the extremely interesting *Wir Erobern Land* (1937) and *Für Uns* (1936); the first of these was a mystical dramatisation of the ' joys ' of labour camps, while the second gravely commemorated the martyrdom of Nazis who fell in the 1923 *putsch*.[2] The Goering-sponsored *Flieger! Funker! Kanoniere!* (1936) typified numerous films designed to glorify Germany's future in the air, and to hint that warfare, if it should come, would be no more than a spectacular parade stepped by modern mechanisation. The justly celebrated Ufa *kulturfilms* were left undisturbed by the Nazis, and continued to be produced without any apparent taint of Hitlerian scientific notions.

After September 1939, the Propaganda Ministry began to make the fullest and most energetic use of the film medium, but again the course of development was unexpected. With the single exception (so far as is known) of the violently anti-British *Oom Paul* (1939) there appeared

[1] Instructive comparisons can be made between the German *Triumph of the Will* and *Olympiad,* the Soviet *Festival of Youth* (*vide* p. 579) and the British *Olympic Games* film of 1948.

[2] It was fortunate indeed that the Museum of Modern Art Film Library had the foresight—and the courage—to provoke and endure unthinking criticism by importing these films from Germany before the war. They were of great importance in guiding U.S. psychological warfare, and remain among the few extant examples of Nazi thinking.

no examples of cinematic *Schrecklichkeit.* German fiction films seemed to continue as innocuous entertainment, lacking any direct reference to the war, any glorification of German arms and aims, any denunciation of the enemy. Certain films of this necessarily obscure period did contain heightened suggestions of the infallibility and eternity of Nazi philosophical principles. Toward the end of the war I saw three captured films, purporting to be biographies of Schiller, Diesel, and Paracelsus. In each case the protagonist was a thinly disguised Hitler: the obscure, untaught, self-educated man who confounds the professors with his brilliance, founds science and invention on his intuitions, and—in the instance of Schiller—fostered proletarian revolution on a purely nationalist basis.

Even more thoroughly than before 1939, Goebbels and his skilled craftsmen concentrated on the documentary, and particularly upon the manipulated newsreel, for their principal effects. Foremost among their weapons were the campaign films, *Feldzug im Polen* (*Baptism of Fire*) and *Sieg im Westen* (*Victory in the West*). The use made of the first of these is probably the best-known of Nazi successes in the strategic use of film. Specially edited versions of the Polish campaign films were shown to high officials in Denmark, Norway, Holland, and Belgium (and later, under similar circumstances, in Rumania and Yugoslavia) the night before these countries were invaded, and are credited with having greatly contributed to the paralysis which overcame the bureaucracies of these nations as the panzers rolled in.[1] These and subsequent news-compilations were a staple for Goebbels, but many other individual films and kinds of film were steadily employed or—increasingly, as Nazi troubles gathered—improvised to meet a particular situation. A French film made under the occupation, Clouzot's *Le Corbeau,* was retitled *Eine Kleine Stadt* and released in Germany as an example of the degeneracy of French provincial life.

---

[1] For subsidiary purposes of these films, and their effect on the German public, the reader is again referred to Dr. Kraçauer.

145. NATIVE LAND, directed by Leo Hurwitz and Paul Strand. [American, 1942]

146. WORLD OF PLENTY, directed by Paul Rotha. [British, 1942-43]

147. THE WAY AHEAD, directed by CAROL REED. STANLEY HOLLOWAY,
LESLIE DWYER, JIMMY HANLEY. [British, 1943]

148. THE OX-BOW INCIDENT, directed by WILLIAM WELLMAN. [American, 1943]

Captured American newsreels were cleverly strung together under the ironic title of *La Libre Amérique* and released in conquered France as an example of the degeneracy of American life. After the invasion of Normandy in 1944, a weekly 'youth newsreel', brilliantly photographed and edited, called on the youth of all Europe to repel the American and Asiatic barbarians with their bare hands. But above all, for ordinary civilian and army purposes the conventional newsreel was heavily relied upon. After 1940, it was expanded to forty minutes in length and consequently became a sort of second feature on every domestic entertainment programme.

This inflated newsreel, says Kracauer, was 'one of many devices which served to transform German audiences into a chain-gang of souls'. All these devices, as has been indicated earlier, teach the film student, the propagandist, the educator, many lessons. They teach what can be accomplished by a vast propaganda machine with absolute control at the top. They show that, thanks to the basic device of film editing, both fictional and factual material can be manipulated to any ends, even ends which contradict the real meaning of the material and which are contradictory to one another. For almost fifteen years they were thrown at German audiences with a steadily increasing intensity. We may well wonder if the chain-gang of souls, after such a psychological experience, can ever be released from their chains. But we may also consider whether that 'conflict with reality', which Kracauer also repeatedly emphasises, may in the end have rendered nugatory much of Goebbels' work. Nazi propaganda grew more efficient and more glittering with each passing year, reaching its apex of skill and effectiveness just before the collapse of the *régime*. But there were also, every year, increasing signs of resistance. The most striking instance is that of *La Libre Amérique* : its scenes of Broadway and Harlem night clubs and *le jazz hot,* supposed to be horrific examples of barbarism, actually delighted the French audiences for which they were designed. There may have been many similar reactions of which we do not know. As Grierson says: 'Where the Germans failed was in the fact that their cold-blooded cynicism spilled over and was spotted. You can impress other countries with your might and your will. You may even impress them with your new world order. But you can't start blatantly talking of conscience as a chimera; morals as an old wives' tale; the Christian religion as a dream of weaklings; and the pursuit of truth as bourgeois fiddle-faddle, without raising a few doubts in the hearts of mankind.' [1]

❊

At the moment of writing, no film made in Germany under post-war Occupation has been shown in the United States. One learns that production under licence has been started in the Russian, American and British zones. Activity seems to have been largest in the Russian zone in Berlin, where Defa, who have leased eighty per cent. of the technical facilities of the old Ufa, Aafa and Joffa studios, have already completed a number of feature films including *Die Mörder sind unter Uns* (*The Murderers are Among Us*), by Wolfgang Staudte, *Ehe im Schatten,* by Kurt Maetzig, *Somewhere in Berlin,* by Gerhard Lamprecht, a pre-Nazi director who made *Emil and the Detectives* in 1931, *Mein Fräulein Frau* (*No Place for Love*) by Hans Deppe, *Kolonne Stosstrupp* written by Friederich Wolff who scripted *Professor Mamlock,* to be directed by Slatàn Dudow who made *Kuhle Wampe,* and Büchner's famous *Wozzeck.* A promising schedule of new films is forecast. In the American zone, the veteran and much-respected Erich Pommer is slowly getting under production and has completed *Palace Hotel.* He has with him the old-time director Geza von Bovary and Erich Kästner, the author of so many brilliant light novels including *Emil and the Detectives* and *Fabian.* In the

---

[1] *Grierson on Documentary,* edited by H. Forsyth Hardy (Collins, 1946), page 174.

British zone, Helmut Käutner, would appear the most promising of the young directors, with his well-spoken of *In Jenen Tagen* (*In Former Days*), the adventures of an automobile with its owners in pre-war and wartime Germany. Those who have seen the above films all speak of their technical excellence reminiscent of early German days, but point out the tendency towards self-pity in their handling of most themes.[1]

That was not uncharacteristic of German production after World War I. Let us remember that the films of those years, suffused as they were with a general sickness of the soul, were hailed by America and the rest of Europe as supreme examples of artistic health—of that cultural superiority, indeed, which the Nazis later claimed as their exclusive possession.

(V) THE ITALIAN FILM

That the film is both response to and agent of a predominating social system was never more clearly demonstrated than in the case of Italy. For nearly a quarter of a century of fascism, nothing emerged from the studios of a country which had contributed importantly to the early motion picture that could possibly be taken seriously. Mussolini's men tried everything: the cultivation of exclusively native talent and themes, the importation of celebrated directors and stars, the imitation of the German, American, French, and even Swedish styles. Nothing availed. The monumental *Scipio Africanuses* and the musical *La Bohèmes* reflected nothing but the frozen values of a paralysed society. Even the fascists were bored by them.

This static picture was shattered into fragments by the Liberation. All the forces which had existed in suspension

[1] For this information I am indebted to *Penguin Film Review*, Nos. 2, 3, 4, and 5; Heinrich Fraenkel in *The Film Today* (Saturn Press, 1947) and *Documentary Film News*, Vol. 7, No. 61, (article by Arthur Elton).

behind the fascist façade burst forth violently and gave rise
to films exemplifying the nature of each and plotting the
course of each. Italian films of the past three years have
been more vital and vigorous than films anywhere else in
the world. In their concern for reality, for immediate
problems, for basic human concerns, they reveal themselves
as by-products of social revolution. Or they have up until
recently.

They are almost exclusively the product of young and
unknown men. Mussolini's industry and its personnel
seem to have disappeared as completely as the film industry
of pre-revolutionary Russia did in 1918. Roberto
Rossellini, pre-eminent among the new talents, had done
little with film before the partisan movement during the
last months of the Italian campaign. Immediately after
the Liberation of Rome, he and his friends gathered
captured cameras, slender finance, and actors from nowhere
and, against the background of Rome itself, produced the
extraordinary document of the German Occupation, *Open
City* (1945). This vast cross-section of the lives of the
insulted and degraded Italians contained also some remarkable sequences revealing how completely the Gestapo had
penetrated into every segment of the fascist state. No film
has ever equalled it in vituperation of the Nazis and their
even more despicable Italian allies. But the most impressive
sections of *Open City* were those which showed how all
kinds of ordinary Italians, from Catholic parish priest to
Communist partisan had, without help or leadership,
realised their common interest and found a way to action.
Such a thesis might have seemed mere apologia except for
the extraordinary reality of this production—a reality which
arose not only from the fact that it was filmed in the actual
streets and houses of Rome (some of the shots were taken
while the Germans were still there), but even more because
its characterisation of the Italian proletariat, from the
children to the very old, was honest, unsentimental, and
devoid of self-pity. It was not a justification of a people
who had succumbed earliest to fascism, and resisted it

least, but a description of their own shame and agony at their national disgrace.

Expressed in terms which everyone could understand, *Open City* created a sensation wherever it was shown.[1] It had been a long time since a film of such stark honesty had reached the screens of the world. Rossellini's second production achieved greatness. *Paisan* (1946) ranks with *Potemkin* in marking an epoch in the advance of the screen. It consists of six episodes, united in sequence by the progress of the American and British Armies up the Italian peninsula, from the first landings in Sicily until the day before victory. Filled with tumultuous life, they separately and together tell the story of two peoples, two cultures, formally united in aim and locked in a struggle with a common enemy, but too separate culturally and historically, too beleaguered by circumstance, to discover together their common humanity. The film's theses are as significant of contemporary dilemmas as was Pudovkin's *Deserter,* but unlike that film, *Paisan* is not cabinned and confined by a pre-ordained dialectic. It takes facts as they are. As fresh and unprecedented as are the methods of *Paisan,* it does not give the feeling of an ' experimental ' film. It seems the mature expression of minds deeply at grips with the problems of modern existence.

' Paisan ' was the American G.I.'s term of good-natured contempt for the ordinary Italian. The contempt is that of the world's best educated (but still hardly educated at all) and highest-paid proletariat for one of the most ignorant and miserable. The film is a weighing of that contempt for its origins and for its portent in a world now theoretically one. The soldiers landing in Italy find a village populace so fantastically ignorant that they cannot distinguish between their liberators and their oppressors. The soldiers puzzle over that fantastic ignorance, try to figure for themselves what it can mean, but at the first unfavourable sign they take the easy conclusion—' Why, that dirty Eyetie '. By the time the campaign has reached Naples and Rome,

[1] Cf. page 547. It created, however, little attention in Italy.—P.R.

the relation between people and soldiers seems to have crystallised around that misunderstanding. The G.I.'s expect to be exploited for their money and their good nature—and they are. The drunken Negro is sold for his boots, the besotted Lothario is picked up by the girl. The harbingers of democracy look wonderingly at these by-products of fascism. But when, in the person of the Negro, they get a glimpse of the hell of misery from whence rises all this ignorance and crime, the sight is too much for them, they turn and run. And they have learned nothing. Their hearts have been touched but not their minds. Civilised emotionally, they are nearly as intellectually at sea as the lowly peasants they despise.

Further up the peninsula, the pattern changes. In Florence and beyond it in the Po marshes, the liberators encounter Italians more politically advanced than they are themselves. The partisans know what they are fighting for, the nature of the enemy, and what was probably most surprising to the Americans, how to fight. The collision of the two cultures takes on more historic meaning in the isolated sequence in which the worldly American chaplains stand helpless before the humility—and the arrogance—of the monks who give up their food to bring about the salvation of a Jew and a Protestant. Altogether the position of the citizen-soldiers of the conquering army grows more equivocal as the film advances. In terms of their own experience of democracy, their contempt for the 'paisan' has basis. But Rossellini is not really defending him. The image put forward to replace both paisan and democrat is that of a third kind of man, the partisan.

Thus to set down the far reaches of thought which *Paisan* provokes is not to take the real measure of the film. Primarily it is a film about war and the effect of war; the overtones are there for the seeking. But more than any film we know, it is first and foremost drawn from the life. Ideas arise from the material, they do not control it, they hardly shape it. The line between documentary and fiction disappears as we watch ordinary men and women

enact experiences closer to them even than the revolution
was to Eisenstein's workers and peasants. Sometimes this
direct observation of life falters, or moves along a plotted
line. The Roman episode, with its Maupassant irony, seems
a rather too polished vignette—but its opening scene in the
café is a slice of actual life. When the Negro says to the
little paisano, ' I don' wanna go home ', we are perilously
close to a planted moral—but all humanity is in the actual
relationship of the two. In short the more Rossellini trusts
his genius for evoking their own humanity from his
' actors ', the more this film moves forward, away from
' art ' toward an emotional factuality that seems beyond
question. The concluding episode is one of the greatest
passages in cinema, triumphant vindication of the promise
of the work of all first-rate directors, from Griffith till to-
day. This is indeed ' the story of an action ', the very core
of film itself. But one hardly knew before how great the
medium could be, how deeply it could reveal the springs of
action from action alone, and make a comment from the
event itself.

It is hard to say how much of this comes from learned
skill. Rossellini and his team were men mainly without film
experience a few years ago, with the exception of the
writer Sergio Amidei. The men and women who people
their films are innocent for the most part of any
facility beyond doing things they know from their own
lives. It all comes out of experience, out of war and death
and the release of passionate emotions. Such an art seems
bound to follow the chain of events which brought it into
being, just as has happened in Russia in the last thirty
years. And there are signs to show that this is about to
come to pass, if it has not already done so.[1]

Rossellini, in both his films, holds up the image of the
partisan as the new man who can shape events toward some
more human scale of things. Other films reflect other
forces in the chaos of post-fascist Italy. Vittorio de Sica's
Shoe-Shine was an eloquent account of the degradation of

[1] Cf. p. 42.

homeless boys by stupid and corrupt officials, but its spirit was romantic and reformist in a now-discredited manner. Luigi Zampa's *To Live In Peace* is equivocal indeed. It describes and idealises that peasant inertia in the face of tyrannical force against which Silone struggled and which Carlo Levi records with some complacency in *Christ Stopped at Eboli*. The indifference to causes which it represents is precisely that ' force of habit of millions and tens of millions' which Lenin describes as a 'most terrible force'. And it is, also precisely, the deepest disease of Italian culture. Here it is rendered with affection.

Zampa's second film, *Angelina*, written and played by Anna Magnani, the brilliant and dynamic actress of *Open City*, starts in quite a different key, the key of Rossellini. Angelina and her sister proletarians act effectively against the corruption with which they are surrounded. As intelligently as the partisans they seize food from the black market and occupy decent homes built by their owners for more profitable purposes. Angelina's gift of leadership whirlpools her into the arena of national politics, and we seem about to witness the education of a working-class woman in the realities of the functioning of the State. The form of that education is curious to say the least. Flattered and duped by the profiteers, she is discredited with her supporters and jailed until she is powerless. What is the lesson she has learned? That the place of a wife and mother is at the side of her husband and children, not in politics. Anyhow, everything turns out all right. So moved is the capitalist by her plight that he turns over his housing project to the proletariat, and gives his son in marriage to Angelina's daughter—along with, presumably, half his industrial kingdom! Such a resolution of economic struggle has not been presented seriously on the screen since *Metropolis*.

Is this compromise a crude reflection of what has actually happened in Italy during the past year? Or does it represent the exhaustion of the revolutionary impetus which was the sole source of the emotional power, and the filmic force, of the Italian renaissance? Further films alone will provide the answer. It is important to note that Rossellini went to Berlin to make his third film, *Germany Year Zero*.[1] All current Italian films, including the inevitable operatic adaptations, are skilful and knowing, every inch the technical equal of their foreign competitors. But only those which have attacked with passion the problems of remoulding society have reached the world audience which, nowadays, every national film industry must seem to have to survive.

(VI) FILMS FROM OTHER COUNTRIES

Apart from the film production of those countries already surveyed, the record of the smaller nations in Europe has continued to be one of brave artistic attempt and all too often economic failure. In most cases lacking sufficient domestic market to ensure adequate cost of production, the smaller countries could only in rare instances secure enough outside distribution to keep their budding film industries going on anything but a spasmodic basis. Paradoxically, the coming of spoken dialogue both improved and worsened the position. It meant, in the first place, that some indigenous films had to be produced in a nation's own language because audiences would not tolerate imported pictures in a foreign language all the time, despite over-printed titles. Secondly, the use of dialogue still further restricted a picture's chances of being exported outside its country of production. With these factors in mind, it is remarkable how much production was undertaken in the thirties by the smaller countries. Occasional striking films, imbued with the unfamiliar values of cultures somewhat remote from those most frequently reflected on the screen, only served to emphasise their rarity

---

[1] Rossellini's last film, *Amore*, is in two parts; the first based on Cocteau's *The Human Voice* (English translation, Vision Press, 1951); the second, *The Miracle*, is an original story. Both are centred round Anna Magnani; neither is relevant to post-war Italy. *The Miracle* is frankly mystical.

and the standardisation of the product which flows through most of the world's projectors.

*

With their long and fine tradition in film-making in the early silent days, the Scandinavian countries have experienced the utmost difficulties in trying to regain their place in world cinema. Severely limited by the dictates of dialogue, comparatively little of their work has been seen overseas. In Sweden, the films produced since 1930 have been strongly marked by national characteristics, but from Gustav Molander's *En Natt* (1931) through *The Heavenly Play* (1944) and *Torment* (1946), (called *Frenzy* in Britain), none of its productions that we have seen has broken really fresh ground. Victor Seaström returned from Hollywood to Sweden to function primarily as an actor, and until recently Gustav Molander and some of the other veterans from silent days have carried on. Neither they nor their younger colleagues, however, seem ambitious to do more than film plays and novels with emphasis on dialogue. It is strange that these smaller nations, with the limitations put upon them by dialogue, do not attempt more experiment with international language techniques, as we saw in *Kameradschaft,* the Swiss *The Last Chance* and the Italian *Paisan*. Actually, Sweden's bucolic comedies, crude and good-humoured, have more freshness than the occasional big productions, which smack of the methods and ideological preoccupations of a declining realist theatre. *Torment* (*Frenzy*), directed by Alf Sjöberg, was highly praised for its ' daring ' theme, as well as for its direction and photography, by both American and European intelligentsia, but it is difficult to understand why. Its theme exactly reproduced the content of innumerable minor German films of the late silent period and early talkies, (mostly featuring Albert Lieven) and its camera technique stems from the same source.

One of Sweden's principal contributions since sound was Gösta Werner's *Midvinter Blott* (1945), a brilliant reconstruction of the winter solstice human sacrifice among the primitive Swedes, a beautiful piece of imaginative anthropology. There are also some documentary makers growing up in Sweden, among whom the most important and talented is Arne Sucksdorff. His two short films, *Sunshine Over Snow* and *Rhythm of a City,* were very lovely little compositions, full of poetry and human touches, international in their use of practically no speech but with excellent music. Sucksdorff's work is to be watched.

The main contribution of the Danes in recent years has also taken place in the documentary field where they have built up a considerable reputation for themselves. In view of the language problem, and the constant competition of Hollywood imported pictures, it is remarkable that this little country with only four million inhabitants still contrives to produce about ten feature films a year.[1] Denmark, we should recall, was making ambitious story-films as far back as 1906, and the famous studio of Nordisk just outside Copenhagen has many films to its credit in a long history. After the extinction of his Hollywood career, the Hungarian Paul Fejos found sponsorship in Denmark and the result was a series of anthropological studies, of which two, *The Bilo* (1937) and *Dance Contest in Esira* (1937) were the most notable. The work of George Schneevoigt, sometimes overlooked in the praise of Carl Dreyer and Sandberg, is also important. Apart from two early sound films, *Praestev : Vejlby* and *Hotel Paradis,* his films of Lapland and Finland, *Laila* and *Fredlos,* are said to be remarkable for their fine observation and for their use of natural sound on location. Apparently, he has not produced in recent years.

The work of Carl Th. Dreyer is probably the best known overseas of Danish directors, and then only to a limited audience, but his films are not in any way representative of Danish cinema, as were the films of Sandberg. His early work, such as *Leaves from Satan's Book* (1921) and

---

[1] *Vide, Motion Pictures in Denmark,* Ebbe Neergaard (Central Film Library, Danish Government, 1948) and *Documentary in Denmark,* by the same author and publisher, 1948.

Master of the House (*Maitre du Logis*) (1925), revealed an intelligent film mind and an interest in human detail. His sense of comedy, strangely enough, was said to be admirable in *Once Upon a Time*, (1922) but it was with *La Passion de Jeanne d'Arc* (1928), made in France toward the end of the silent era, that he attracted attention among film aesthetes. The film has been discussed at length earlier in this book, (*vide* pp. 301, 306). In France also, using a deserted *château* as a location, he made *Vampyr* (1931), its English version being called *The Strange Adventure of David Gray*. A film much applauded by the intelligentsia, its obscure mysticism, its diffused and meretricious photography (by Maté, who also photographed *Jeanne d'Arc*), its vague hints of the supernatural, have let the film become very much of a museum piece.

In between making films and while waiting for sponsorship, Dreyer turned to journalism, writing moving little stories sometimes based on first-hand observation of minor court cases, quite unlike his approach to film subjects. His last film, *Day of Wrath* (1944), made during the Occupation in Denmark, has created considerable discussion. 'Like *Jeanne d'Arc*, much of it deals with trial, torture and death by fire, but unlike the earlier film, it has an underlying quality of evil, (writes Rotha). A story of witchcraft and superstition set in the early seventeenth century, with very few characters and a limited locale, the film is one of unrelieved gloom and cruelty, despite the one or two love scenes between the devout Bishop's second and lovely wife and his son by his first wife. The story is not worth detailing. Technically, Dreyer's direction is slow and of the silent period, totally lacking any of the dynamic camera qualities that made *Jeanne d'Arc* such a graphic achievement. The acting is stilted and frozen, and one cannot help feeling that there existed no sympathy and understanding between Dreyer and his players. There was not a vestige of warmth or hope in the film, only the dominant theme that evil will ultimately triumph. The film lacks the pictorial beauty, the simplicity of *Jeanne d'Arc.* Without question, Carl Dreyer is a film artist of immense skill and, compared with much that runs through the projectors, *Day of Wrath* has qualities of honesty of effort and a certain dignity, but I cannot find myself alongside the many international critics who claim the film as a masterpiece of cinema; in fact, I can find little justification as to why the film was made at all. Why was it necessary to select such a cruel and evil theme? Possibly Dreyer was depressed and without faith of liberation from the Occupation.'

More typical of Danish artistic and technical standards are the films of Benjamin Christensen, one of the veterans of silent days, with their serious and always adult approach to social and psychological problems : *Children of Divorce* (1939) and *The Child* (1940), both for Nordisk. *The Burning Question,* directed by Alice O'Fredericks, dealing with abortion, was a further sociological subject which the Danes were not afraid to tackle on the screen. Among the young directors are Bjärne Henning-Jensen and his wife Astrid, who started as documentary makers but who made in 1946 their first full-length story picture, *Ditte Menneskebarn* (*Ditte—Child of the People*). This sensitive and beautiful study of an illegitimate country girl, set almost wholly in natural surroundings on Jutland, is one of the most successful attempts yet to blend documentary with fictional ideas. Its subtle psychological handling of the characters, its quite brilliant direction of children, its authentic acting of peasant life, made this film most memorable. These two young directors have just completed *De Pokkers Under* (*Those Confounded Children*), a film about the need for proper recreation facilities for children, again beautifully handled.

The Danish documentary group, for a while under the admirable producership of Mogens Skot-Hansen (himself no mean director and script-writer), has created quite a name for itself. Its many films, if sometimes a little over-impressionistic and unsure, at least show a variety of styles and techniques, and are always lively and imaginative. Of those made about the war, *Your Freedom is at Stake* (1946) was a remarkable compilation of the events leading up to the war, Denmark under the Nazis, and the Liberation. Some of the material was newsreel, but much of it was freshly-shot actually under German eyes by ten courageous cameramen in obviously the most dangerous conditions. Although its editor, Theodor Christensen (son of Benjamin, the old director), lacked the skill of a Helen Van Dongen or the editors who worked for Capra's *Why We Fight* series, the film had moments of tension and its sheer authenticity compelled attention. Its editor seemed to have difficulty in knowing what to discard from his great mass of footage, and the film consequently lacked dramatic cohesion. An excellent, fast-moving little film about the Resistance was Henning-Jensen's *The Brigade* (1945), actually made in Sweden in secrecy in anticipation of the Liberation of Denmark by the Allies. It had a brilliant musical score and a minimum of dialogue.

There is not space here to detail the many documentaries made about agriculture, road safety, blood transfusion and many other subjects under the auspices of either the Dansk-Kulturfilm or the Ministeriernes Filmudvalg, with their general excellence of photography and music. Shortly after the war, Arthur Elton, a senior British documentary producer, was invited to act as an adviser to the Danish documentary movement. A series of films on social services—typical titles were *The Seventh Age, People's Holiday, Good Mothers*—were made under his producership, directed by Torben Svendsen, Hagen Hasselbach, Astrid Henning-Jensen, Soren Melson, and others, revealing much good direction and human observation. The Danish documentary directors, like so many of their European *confrères,* cannot forget their love for impressionist effects and this can sometimes give a seeming superficiality to their films which is misleading. On the other hand, their films have a natural wit and an instinctive humour that is refreshing, often lacking in British documentary. Danish production as a whole is worth watching in the future; if economic obstacles can be overcome, it has an optimistic future ahead. The tenacity of its old company Nordisk to keep in production despite all setbacks and difficulties is something quite remarkable in the erratic history of European cinema.

*

Another country to take film production very seriously since the war has been Czechoslovakia, where the industry, both production and exhibition, was the first to be nationalised after the Liberation. The traditions of Czech cinema, however, stretch back to before the first World War but production in the twenties was very spasmodic. After the coming of the sound-film, more strenuous efforts were made to produce in dialogue in order to meet the home-market, but production still remained haphazard. Perhaps the only Czech film of the period to achieve a reputation (or should one say a notoriety?) outside its country of origin was Gustav Machaty's extraordinary *Extase* (1933), which unhappily became known more for its shots of Hedy Kiessler (now Hedy Lamarr) in the nude than for its very real qualities of good film-making. ' Reseen recently ' (writes Rotha), ' it reveals a powerful yet deeply sensitive approach to the psychological study of a sex-frustrated young wife. With much of its action shot in natural surroundings, Machaty's direction was as good as anything being made in Europe in the thirties. His use of editing to build up moments of high tension, such as the automobile drive to the level-crossing, his sense of movement and symbolism, and his very delicate handling of situations that could easily have become laughable, put him with the best directors of the period. It is peculiar that he has done nothing outstanding since, but is believed to be in the United States. *Extase* is a film which deserves restudy and re-evaluation, now that its appeal to the lascivious has had time to wear off, but it should be seen in its original full version. Its attempt to create a sound track which would be easily translatable for international markets by having only one sequence in direct synchronous speech is worth analysis, as indeed was its ingenious use of off-screen sound. The photography was superb.'

Also to be remembered from that period was an earlier film by Machaty, *From Saturday to Sunday* (1931), *Reka* (1933) by Rovensky, and *Pred Maturitou* (1932) by Innemann, each of which made considerable use of natural backgrounds, but did not achieve the quality of *Extase*. In 1937 Julien Duvivier, the French director, visited Prague to make another version of *The Golem*, but this film has been referred to earlier.[1] Also worth the record were some satirical comedies, quite crazy in conception, featuring that inimitable pair of actors Voskovec and Werich, directed by Jindrich Honzl, of which *Money or Life* (1932) and *Hey-Rup!* (1934) were the best.

With their fondness for beautiful photography and for their natural landscapes, it is not surprising that the Czechoslovaks made quite a number of documentary films in the thirties, some especially devoted to recording peasant life, such as Karl Plicka's *On the Mountains and in the Valleys* and Professor Ulehla's *Disappearing World*. Plicka himself is a very fine photographer and has had considerable influence in developing the pictorial sense of the Czechoslovak cameramen. Alexander Hackenschmied, that able cinematographer, made an experimental short film *Prague Castle* (1934), and with Hans Burger collaborated with Herbert Kline when the latter went to Czechoslovakia to make *Crisis* in 1938. Later he photographed Kline's *Lights Out in Europe* (1939) and then accompanied Kline to America where he worked on John Steinbeck and Kline's *The Forgotten Village* (1941), to me (Griffith) an arty and unreal account of Mexican superstition and education. Hackenschmied then turned director on his own account, made for the Office of War Information the humanist study *Valley of the Tennessee* (1945), and has recently directed the amusing and informative *Private Life of a Cat* (1946).

During the Occupation, Czechoslovak film production

[1] *Vide* page 531.

149. FIRES WERE STARTED, directed by HUMPHREY JENNINGS. [British, 1943]

150. NINE MEN, directed by HARRY WATT. [British, 1943]

151. THE DAY OF WRATH, directed by CARL TH. DREYER. [Danish, 1944]

152. DOUBLE INDEMNITY, directed by BILLY WILDER. BARBARA STANWYCK, FRED MacMURRAY. [American, 1944]

was almost wholly taken over by the Nazis and the huge studios at Barrandov, begun before the war, were completed by them. Equipment and technicians were imported from Germany, and Nazi film production was for a while centred in Prague. (Pabst made his *Paracelsus* film at Barrandov.) When the Liberation came, the Czechs were left with probably the best-equipped studio in Europe and an immense national enthusiasm for film-making. A few of their technicians had worked in Britain during the war, which had possibly some small influence on the technical development of their work on their return. With more studio-space than they could use themselves, the Czechs leased space in 1945 and 1946 to the Russians, and among the films made there was *The Stone Flower* (1946), a fairy-tale legend of heavy beauty shot in Agfacolor, with astonishingly clever trickwork. Of Czechoslovak post-war production, the most successful films have been those dealing with roughly contemporary themes, which only naturally for a while meant stories of the Resistance and Czech-German relationships at the time of Munich. *Men Without Wings*, by Frantisek Cap, *The Warning* by Martin Fric, *The Strike* by Stekly and *Stolen Frontier* by Jiri Weiss were all well-made technically and showed a remarkable advance on anything made in Czechoslovakia before the war. In their large-scale historical reconstruction films, such as *Warriors of Faith*, by Vladimir Borsky, they are less successful and tend towards a theatricalism which seems imitative of outside influences.

Since the war, great activity has taken place among the Czech documentary makers, now grouped together under Kratky Film which is the branch of the State Film Industry looking after short films. Like the Danes and the Poles, the Czech documentary makers tend sometimes to overmuch impressionism, but they have a poetic quality in their approach that is impressive. Kratky Film, under the producership of Eugen Klos, have ambitious production plans which, if carried out, will make Czechoslovak documentary important in Europe. Their distribution in their own cinemas is guaranteed, and they are building up a substantial non-theatrical circulation. Special reference here is needed to the development of the animated cartoon and trick, puppet and model films in Czechoslovakia, especially the group of technicians gathered round Trnka. These short films, mostly made in Agfacolor, have a freshness of ideas and a degree of imagination long-wanted in this highly-specialised branch of film-making, where Disney and George Pal have too long held their own. Working in Prague and at Zlin, the Czechs have certainly discovered a new standard of beauty and inventiveness, sometimes undershot with satire, in their drawn cartoons and their model films. Their delicacy and good taste make the American product look pretty gaudy and second-hand. In all, the Czechoslovak Film Industry has made a remarkable recovery since the Occupation; it has the facilities and the personnel to become a major production centre in the new Europe.

Among other countries to restart production, Poland is so far in an early stage with its Film Industry under the direction of a State controlled company, Film Polski. Lacking experienced technicians and equipment (there was little production of importance before the war), two or three feature films have already been made, of which Leonard Buczkovski's *Forbidden Songs,* a story of Warsaw under Nazi occupation, is said to be the most interesting. Polish documentary, as yet finding its feet, has produced several very uneven films, slow in tempo, among which the best have been *Locomotive, Poland's West* and *The Salt Mines of Wielieczka.* In Yugoslavia, ambitious plans are beginning to mature for a State Film Industry, which means starting from scratch for there was no pre-war production. The only film shown outside Yugoslavia so far was *Youth Railway,* which, despite all its crudities and technical immaturity, had an exuberance that reminded one of the early Soviet films. As with all these young nationalised industries, it is too early as yet to see how they will shape. They have enthusiasm and skill; some have and some have not adequate technical equipment. They may create a new European cinema, distinct from the French and the Scandinavians, which can mean much. A great deal will obviously depend on the creative freedom offered the individual, as distinct from expressing party policy through group production.

*

Holland has contributed much to world cinema, if not in terms of home-produced films then certainly in the production of artists. In the thirties, apart from the early films of Ivens, one recalls the over-long but very sincere *Dood Wasser* (1934) directed by Gerard Rutten, a story-documentary of the impact of new methods on the farming community resulting from the reclamation of the Zuider Zee; and the disappointing Jubilee film of Queen Wilhelmina, by Edmond Greville, the Anglo-French director. But Joris Ivens, John Ferno and Helen Van Dongen are the three lustrous additions to cinema's roster from Holland.

Ivens's masterpiece *New Earth* (1931-34) is one of the milestones of documentary. Begun as a *réportage* of the draining of the Zuider Zee and its conversion into farmland, a theme similar to that of *Dood Wasser,* it emerged as a passionate attack on the economic methods which permitted dumping the products of the new-won ground into the sea, thereby anticipating the messages of the Rotha films *World of Plenty* and *The World is Rich.* Brilliantly observed, and even more brilliantly edited for propagandist purposes, it summed up as the record of a tragedy typical of modern life, that of a project begun on an epic scale and ending in anticlimax. Ivens had previously made *Philips-Radio* (1930), an exploration of sound-film possibilities which was one of the first industrially sponsored documentaries, and later, in the Soviet Union, *Komsomol* (1932). Following an exposure of mining conditions in Belgium, *The Borinage* (1933) with Henri

Storck, which had to be made secretly, Ivens went to the United States. With American sponsorship, he made with Ernest Hemingway the brave anti-fascist films *The Spanish Earth* (1937) and *The Four Hundred Million* (1939), the latter being probably the most authentic film to be made about China, both of which have been mentioned earlier.[1]

In 1940, Pare Lorentz commissioned Ivens to make *Power and the Land,* the record of a day in the life of an American farm centring round the coming of electricity to rural districts and the human advantages it brings to farmers and their families. The film is an argument for rural co-operatives, but it is also, and deeply, an emotional impression of farm life, of planting and of harvest, of family relationships, of love for the land. During the war, Ivens worked for the U.S. Army Unit with Capra and for the National Film Board of Canada, and later became Film Commissioner for the Dutch East Indies, setting up head-quarters in Australia against the day when the Japanese should be driven out and peace and democracy be brought to the Indonesians. When neither peace nor democracy materialised, Ivens publicly broke with the Dutch Government, tore up his valuable contract, and determinedly added injury to insult by producing in Australia *Indonesia Calling!* (1946), a short *réportage* of the revolt of the Sydney waterfront workers who refused to load arms for the Dutch to be used against the embattled Indonesians. Made with practically no money and with every obstacle from the authorities, this film is typical of Ivens's whole career, and explains why his waits for sponsorship have often been long. But his fine attitude, uncompromising and strong-principled, has won him more than it cost, including the respect and admiration of sincere film-makers everywhere. Almost all of his films are uncompromisingly political and propagandist, but they differ from other political propaganda in being directly related to the people, and revealing a serene and sunny belief in people whatever the darkness of the age. Ivens has now returned to Europe

[1] *Vide* pp. 459, 460.

and is making a film about the Slav peoples, shooting in Poland, Yugoslavia, Bulgaria and Czechoslovakia. He is without question the most-travelled and internationally-minded of all documentary film-makers.

As is well-known, Helen Van Dongen has edited all of Ivens's films, except the most recent; they worked on equal terms as joint creators, a collaboration which has been one of the most fruitful in film history but which has tended to obscure Helen Van Dongen's own quite distinct talent. That talent came into its own with the two war-record films, *Russians at War* (1943) and *News Review No. 2* (produced for the Office of War Information) of which she was producer as well as editor. These two films can be set against the Capra *Why We Fight* newsreel compilations on the one hand, and the Rotha argument films on the other, to indicate a third possible use of compiled material. *Russians at War* was a description of behind-the-lines activities in the vast Russian arena; *News Review No. 2* was an even vaster account of fighting on all fronts round the world during two years of war. Both had the function of expressing the unity of the struggle for all participants however distant from one another. This binding together of human beings in a common enterprise was achieved almost without the aid of commentary, which was in both cases negligible and important only for identification of places and events. The factor governing the editing was the *content of the shot;* Helen Van Dongen sought through her material for examples of human behaviour which expressed similar feelings and derived from the same springs of action. This was not thematic illustration in the manner of Ruttmann's *Melody of the World.* The theme arose wordlessly out of the material as edited. Helen Van Dongen's subsequent association with Robert Flaherty, as editor of *The Land* (1941) and associate-producer and editor on his new film *Louisiana Story,* has been a happy and fortunate one for them both. But it is to be hoped that she will find opportunity to resume the production of compiled films. No one at work to-day observes more subtly the implications and possibilities of isolated shots, nor has a surer instinct for the links between them.

John Ferno (formerly Fernhout) photographed *New Earth, The Spanish Earth* and *The Four Hundred Million* for Joris Ivens, and accompanied him to the United States where he struck out on his own as a director. Previously, in 1934, he had been a member of a Franco-Belgian expedition to the Pacific and brought back what is still the most extraordinary of his films, *Easter Island*. Beautifully observed, beautifully constructed, this impressionist study of relapse and decay had both aesthetic and scientific authority. Its editing, in which Henri Storck assisted, made functional use of the ' wipe ' which is unique in the history of this dubious but popular editing device. Again and again in shots of the monolithic statues on the island the screen seemed to break open to reveal behind them the disease and poverty of the miserable descendents of the anonymous sculptors. Maurice Jaubert's superb music also aided in contributing to the unity of what is perhaps the finest example of film anthropology outside the work of Flaherty. In the United States, Ferno directed *And So They Live* (1940) and *Puerto Rico* (1941) both of which were also first-rate studies of broken cultures though limitations of sponsorship and purpose prevented them from achieving the wholeness and the maturity of *Easter Island*. For the British Ministry of Information, he directed and photographed at the end of the war in Europe two moving and brilliantly shot records of Holland's Liberation, *Broken Dykes* and *The Last Shot*, the latter being forbidden an American release by the Ministry lest it distract the American public from Britain's need for dollars to the Dutch need for food.

Since the Liberation, Dutch film activity has been limited to a group of documentaries and some interesting educational films for children. It is obvious that in Holland there is great enthusiasm for good cinema, but there is a lack of production experience to crystallise the technical skill that is available. Dutch film-makers have achieved their reputation almost wholly working outside their own country.

Henri Storck is the outstanding figure in Belgian film production, which is chiefly confined to documentary and interest films centring for the most part about Belgian art, architecture and history with occasional excursions into the Congo. Storck produced the feature story-documentary *Les Maisons de la Misère* (1938), photographed by Ferno, a striking indictment of the living conditions of the slum proletariat of the Belgian mining district. He has recently made an interesting study of the Belgian painter Delvaux, and is now engaged on a documentary-biography of Peter Paul Rubens.

One film from pre-war Hungary needs mention here, Georg Hoellering's pictorially superb *Hortobagy* (1936), a film of horse farming made in the silent style. Paul Fejos's *Marie*, from the same country, scarcely needs record. Among other European countries, there is reported to be considerable production in Spain since Franco, and some in Portugal, but none has been seen by us. Switzerland during the thirties, proved a haven for anti-Nazi refugees from the German Film Industry and, it is asserted, for some who were not so anti-Nazi either in their opinions or in the capital they brought to finance their work. The outstanding Swiss film before the war was *The Eternal Mask* (1937), directed by Werner Hochbaum and featuring Olga Tschechowa. This psychoanalytic case history began carefully and intelligently, but degenerated into over-simplification of both neurosis and therapy. Altogether too reminiscent of *Dr. Caligari* (for which it was indiscriminately praised) it achieved subjective conviction only in the long sequence in which the protagonist loses control over himself. Since the war, Switzerland has been a happy hunting ground for French, British and American producers in search of striking locations and cheap facilities. Lazar Wechsler's two skilful productions, *Marie-Louise* and *The Last Chance* (the latter an unequal but generally meritorious drama of refugees and allied soldiers) achieved international honours, and their American success was sufficient to induce Loew's International to finance the Wechsler production *The Search,* directed by Fred Zinnemann, from M-G-M in Hollywood, and featuring Alice McMahon, Jarmila Novotna and Montgomery Clift. This product of an international team of film-makers is one of the important events of 1948. Absorbing, tragic, hopeful, it vindicates belief in the possibilities of the enacted film using documentary background and theme and removes many of the objections to actors in documentary. Its technical success derives from the fact that its story grows direct from its theme (hence documentary setting is always appropriate) and that its actors' effectiveness comes from their being cast to national type more than from their skill or training. Most significant of all, its approach to material was dictated by a mature understanding of the requirements of propaganda in the United States. Its direct emotional appeal to the American matriarchy has greater potentialities for success than any political or economic argument for the reconstruction of Europe. Its fate at the box-office will be carefully watched and may do much to determine the possibility of future politico-commercial experiments of the same kind in the United States.

*

Outside Europe, Palestine is a small nation with an ambition to native production but is faced with the ubiquitous problem of not having a home-market large enough to repay costs of production. Films made in Egypt, poor in quality, have been supplying the whole Middle East Arabic-speaking countries but this leaves the matter of the Jewish community unsolved. Spasmodic attempts at production have been made from time to time but have resulted in little of real importance. In 1933, a Polish unit visited Palestine under the direction of Aleksander Ford and made a story-documentary *Sabra,* with a cast drawn from the Habima Theatre, the National Theatre of Palestine. It was an uneven film, a story of a pioneer group of settlers, their struggle for water and their fight against the Arabs. Years later Herbert Kline, the American documentary film-maker, took a unit there including Meyer Levine, the film critic, and Floyd Crosbie, the photographer of many American documentaries. Their film *My Father's House,* a documentary with a human story, is not yet released having been edited and synchronised in New York. The equipment left by this unit was taken over by Norman Lourie, of Palestine Film Productions, who has made a moving and quite good short film on one of the Dead Sea settlements, *The House in the Desert* (1947). Another film reported completed, *The Soil,* on the Ben Shemen's Children's Village, has been made by a mixed team of technicians some from European production in the old days. *The Great Promise,* directed by Josef Leytes, shown widely in Great Britain, was not more than a glorified travel picture.

There is not much of real importance to record of indigenous film-making in Asia and Africa. *Shakuntala* (1947) and *Sable Cicada* (1938) revealed little change in Hindu and Chinese methods of producing films based on mythology and religion, and the addition of sound seems to have confirmed both national cinemas, as well as the Japanese, in their adherence to stage traditions. The Indian films, produced in great numbers and still at great length, seem bound to historical and religious subjects and usually overloaded with songs. For a time during the war some quite good documentaries were made in India under the supervision of, first, Alexander Shaw and later, J. B. Holmes, both loaned from the British documentary group, but production now seems almost to have lapsed. There is talk of re-establishing the Information Films of India unit but to date it has not materialised. The Indian People's Theatre Association has launched into film production and its first work *Children of the Earth* (*Dharti ke Lal*), a theme of hunger and famine in a Bengal village, is said to strike a new and progressive note in Indian production but it has not, at the time of writing, been exported. One hears of the production of contemporary Chinese films on sociological themes but again no examples have come to hand. Egypt has a flourishing industry according to accounts, but its work is confined to the Arabic-speaking world. In Morocco, at Casablanca, there is also film activity, as yet unseen in Europe or America.

Film-making in Argentina and Mexico has lately been on the increase. A few Mexican productions, such as *Maria Candelaria* (1945), starring Dolores del Rio, have achieved American and British distribution in English versions, but they are not in any way outstanding except for occasional good camerawork. The Argentine films, such as have been shown, do not call for comment.

In the British Dominions, far and away the most outstanding development was the setting-up, at John Grierson's initiative, of the National Film Board of Canada in 1941. The complete transformation of Canada from a country which produced almost no films at all into a major factor is now well-known through *The World in Action* series, edited by Stuart Legg, and many other war-related films produced under the general supervision of Grierson. Using a nucleus of British technicians, or Canadians with British documentary training, the National Film Board concentrated on producing a large output of *réportage* and compilation documentaries, at the same time building up distribution both in the theatres and non-theatrically at home. It developed direct production on substandard colour and it encouraged animation experiment, being fortunate enough to have the services of the young Scotsman Norman McClaren. The latter's *Chants Populaires* series have reached a new level in synchronised animation, with much skilled draughtsmanship and design. Grierson resigned from the Board in 1946, and it is now carried on by Ross McLean, who has a team of young men and women whose talents, developed during the war, are making such excellent contributions as the recent psychiatric films *The Feeling of Rejection* (1947) and *The Feeling of Hostility* (1948). The National Film Board is a unique venture in national publicity and education through visual media; it is indeed a model to other nations. Its future will depend not only on its obviously fine teamwork but on whether it can develop personalities whose creative contribution can rise above the general need for continual output.

Australia during the past decade has made some efforts to create a national cinema of its own. *Forty Thousand Horsemen,* which reached the United States in 1941, was a lively account of the Australian Expeditionary Force in Egypt and Palestine during the first World War; its lack of star-names did not much militate against it at the American box-office, for the native personalities disclosed had a charm of their own. Harry Watt's *The Overlanders* (1946), already mentioned in the British chapter, was a remarkable effort of what really amounted to a British unit on location. Such use of native themes and material promises much for what could be done in Australia and gives hope for the future of the Australian National Film Board, set up along much the same lines as that of Canada but lacking, one understands, both full authority over subject-matter and adequate funds. Under the producership of Stanley Hawes, ex-British and Canadian documentary movements, several short documentaries have been completed, of which *School in a Mail-Box* (1946) was the most outstanding. During the war, Australian cameramen-directors covered much ground, and a notable short film to emerge from them was *Kokoda Trail,* by Damien Parer, which made his death in action in 1944 a great loss to Australian cinema.

To conclude this chapter, it is fitting to mention again the work of units sent overseas from documentary producing countries, because not only are the films themselves valuable in widening the screen's horizons but the impact of a visiting unit may sometimes do much to inspire and help local production. From the days when Basil Wright made the memorable West Indian films *Windmill in Barbados* and *Cargo in Jamaica* (1932), and Rotha made *Contact* (1932) half across the Asias and the Africas,

British documentary makers have been going overseas more and more for themes and material. Shaw's *The Future's in the Air* (1937) for Imperial Airways of the England-Australia air-route, John Taylor's *Dawn of Iran* (1938), Hawes's *Wings over Africa* (1938), Ralph Keene's *Cyprus is an Island* (1946) and *A String of Beads* (1947) in Assam, John Page's series of West African films, Jennings's *Voices of Malaya* (1937), Eldridge's *Three Dawns to Sydney* (1948), Chambers's *The Bridge* (1946) in Yugoslavia, and many more all mark the spread overseas of film ideas and film techniques. Ivens, Kline, and others from other nations have done the same, while the war gave many technicians the opportunity to shoot and make films in countries far from their normal bases of activity. All this, if it continues, can widen our perspectives and cement relationships. The more film units can travel and operate overseas, the more likely are we to see broken down the standardised product so beloved of the studios.

APPENDIX I

THE PRODUCTION UNITS OF SOME
OUTSTANDING FILMS

The years between which this selection has been made are 1914-48, and thus omits the primitives of Méliès, Porter and Griffith. The choice represents purely the personal point of view of the author, and the reader will almost certainly discover for himself various omissions.

Although every attempt has been made to check the accuracy of the following data, no guarantee can be given that some errors, or mispellings, may not have occurred. The date given to each film is the year in which the film was made, and not the year of its release.

Acknowledgement is made to the Museum of Modern Art Film Library, New York; the Cinémathèque Française, Paris; the National Board of Review, New York; and the National Film Library,. London, for their generous help in supplying and checking data.

I. FICTION FILMS

ADVENTURES OF BARON MÜNCHHAUSEN, The

1942 *(sound)*   GERMAN

Production	Ufa. Farbfilm-Verfahren
Direction	Josef von Baky
Scenario	Berthold Burger
Design	Werner Krien
Music	Georg Haentzschel
Set Construction . . .	Emil Hasler Otto Gülstorff
Trick Work . . .	Konstantin Irmen-Tschet

With : Hans Albers, Hans Brausewetter, Herman Speelmans, Werner Scharf, Ilse Werner, Leo Slezak, Käthe Haack, Brigitte Horney.

AEROGRAD (FRONTIER)

1935 *(sound)* SOVIET

Production	Ukrainfilm
Direction and Scenario	Alexander Dovjenko
Photography . . .	Edward Tisse, M. Gindin
Design	A. Utkin, V. Panteleyev
Music	D. Kabalevsky

With: S. Stolyarov, N. Tabunosov, I. Kahn, S. Shkurat, E. Mozhimov, V. Dobronravov.

ALL QUIET ON THE WESTERN FRONT

1929-1930 *(sound)* AMERICAN

Production	Universal
Associate Producer . .	George Cukor
Direction	Lewis Milestone
Scenario . . .	Maxwell Anderson, Del Andrews, Lewis Milestone, George Abbott
Photography . . .	Arthur Edeson
Design	Charles D. Hall, W. R. Schmidt
Music	David Broekman
Editing	Edgar Adams
From a novel by . .	Erich Maria Remarque

With: Louis Wolheim, Slim Summerville, Lew Ayres, Raymond Griffith, John Wray.

AMERICAN MADNESS

1932 *(sound)* AMERICAN

Production	Columbia Pictures
Direction	Frank Capra
Scenario and Dialogue	Robert Riskin
Photography . . .	Joseph Walker

With: Walter Huston, Pat O'Brien, Kay Johnson, Constance Cummings, Gavin Gordon, Robert Ellis, Burton Churchill, Arthur Hoyt, Edward Martindel, Edwin Maxwell, Robert Emmet O'Connor.

APPENDIX I

A NOUS LA LIBERTE

1931 *(sound)* FRENCH

Production . . . . Films-Sonores-Tobis
Direction and Scenario . René Clair
Photography . . . Georges Périnal
Design . . . . Lazare Meerson
Costumes . . . . Renée Hubert
Music . . . . . Georges Auric

With : Henri Marchand, Raymond Cordy, Rollo France, Paul Ollivier, Jacques Shelly, André Michaud, Germaine Aussey, Leon Lorin, William Burke, Vincent Hyspa.

ANNE BOLEYN

1920 *(silent)* GERMAN

Production . . . . Messter-Union-Film
Direction . . . . Ernst Lubitsch
Scenario . . . . Fred Orbing, Hans Kraly,
                    Norbert Falk
Photography . . . Theodore Sparkuhl
Design . . . . Kurt Richter
Costumes . . . . Ali Hubert

With : Emil Jannings, Henny Porten, Aud Egede Nissen, Paul Hartmann.

ARSENAL

1929 *(silent)* SOVIET

Production . . . . Vufku-Kino (Ukraine)
Direction . . . . Alexander Dovjenko
Scenario . . . . Spinel, Müller
Assistant Direction . . Lazar Bodik
Photography . . . Daniel Demutski

With : Semyon Svashenko.

ATALANTE, L'

1934 *(sound)* FRENCH

Production . . . . J. L. Nounez-Gaumont
Direction . . . . Jean Vigo
Scenario . . . . Jean Guinée
Adaptation and Dialogue . Jean Vigo, Albert Rière

Photography	.	.	.	Boris Kaufman
Assistants	.	.	.	Albert Rière, Pierre Merle
Design	.	.	.	Francis Jourdan
Music	.	.	.	Maurice Jaubert

With : Dita Parlo, Jean Dasté, Michel Simon, Louis Lefèvre, Gilles Margaritis, Rafa Diligent.

ATONEMENT OF GOSTA BERLING, THE

1923-1924 *(silent)* SWEDISH

Production	.	.	.	Svenska-Biograf
Direction	.	.	.	Mauritz Stiller
Scenario	.	.	.	Ragnor, Hylten-Cavallius
Photography	.	.	.	J. Julius
Design	.	.	.	Vilhelm Bryde
From a novel by	.	.	.	Selma Lagerlöff

With : Lars Hanson, Greta Garbo, Jenny Hasselquist, Mona Martenson.

BALTIC DEPUTY

1937 *(sound)* SOVIET

Production	.	.	.	Komsomol
Direction	.	.	.	Alexander Zharki, Josef Heifitz
Scenario	.	.	.	L. Rachmanov
Photography	.	.	.	M. Kaplan
Design	.	.	.	N. Suvorov, V. Kalyagin
Music	.	.	.	N. Timofeyev

With : Nikolai Cherkassov, M. Domasheva, B. Livanou, O. Zhakov, A. Melnikov.

BAS-FONDS, LES

1936 *(sound)* FRENCH

Production	.	.	.	Albatross
Direction	.	.	.	Jean Renoir
Scenario	.	.	.	Charles Spaak
Photography	.	.	.	Jean Bachelet, Jacques Mercanton
Design	.	.	.	E. Lourié, H. Laurent
Music	.	.	.	Roger Désormières

With : Jean Gabin. Louis Jouvet, Vladimir Sokolov, Suzy Prim, Junie Astor, Le Vigan, Genin.

153. HENRY V, directed by LAURENCE OLIVIER. [British, 1944]

154. WESTERN APPROACHES, directed by PAT JACKSON. [British, 1944]

155. LES ENFANTS DU PARADIS, directed by MARCEL CARNÉ.   ARLETTY, LOUIS SALON.
[French, 1944]

156. LA BATAILLE DU RAIL, directed by RENÉ CLEMENT.   [French, 1944–45]

APPENDIX I

BATTLESHIP POTEMKIN, The

1925 *(silent)*   SOVIET

Production . . . . 1st. Studio, Goskino
Producer . . . . Jacob Bliokh
Direction . . . . S. M. Eisenstein
Associate Director . . G. V. Alexandrov
Assistants . . . . A. Antonov, M. Gomarov, A.
                        Levshin, M. Shtraukh
Photography . . . Edward Tisse
Musical Score . . . Edmund Meisel

BEAU GESTE

1926 *(silent)*   AMERICAN

Production . . . . Paramount
Direction . . . . Herbert Brenon
Scenario . . . . Paul Schofield, John Russell
Photography . . . J. Roy Hunt
Design . . . . Julian Boone-Fleming
Music . . . . . Hugo Riesenfeld

With : Ronald Colman, Ralph Forbes, Neil Hamilton, Alice
Joyce, Noah Beery, William Powell, Victor McLaglen, Mary
Brian, N. Trevor.

BED AND SOFA

1926 *(silent)*   SOVIET

Production . . . . Sovkino
Direction . . . . Abram Room
Source . . . . F. Komanov
Scenario . . . . Victor Shklovsky
Photography . . . Grigori Giber
Design . . . . Sergei Yutkevich

With : Nikolai Batalov, Ludmila Semenova, Vladimir Fogel.

BEGGAR ON HORSEBACK, The

1925 *(silent)*   AMERICAN

Production . . . . Paramount
Direction . . . . James Cruze
Scenario . . . . Walter Woods
Photography . . . Karl Brown
From a play by . . . George Kaufman, Marc Connelly

With : Edward Everett Horton, Esther Ralston, James Mason.

BEN-HUR

1926 *(silent)*   AMERICAN

Production	Metro-Goldwyn-Mayer
Direction	Fred Niblo
Scenario	June Mathis, Carey Wilson
Photography . . .	Karl Struss, René Guissart

With : Ramon Novarro, May McAvoy, Betty Bronson, Francis X. Bushman, Carmel Myers.

BEST YEARS OF OUR LIVES, THE

1946 *(sound)*   AMERICAN

Production	RKO-Radio Pictures (Sam Goldwyn)
Direction	William Wyler
Scenario	Robert E. Sherwood
Photography . . .	Gregg Toland
Music	Hugo Friedhofer
From a novel by . . .	Mackinlay Kamtor

With : Myrna Loy, Frederic March, Teresa Wright, Virginia Mayo, Dana Andrews, Cathy O'Donnell, Hoagy Carmichael, Roman Bohnen, Harold Russell.

BETE HUMAINE, LA

1938 *(sound)*   FRENCH

Production	Hakim Brothers
Direction	Jean Renoir
Photography . . .	Curt Courant
Design	E. Lourié
Music	Joseph Kosma
From the novel by . .	Emile Zola

With : Jean Gabin, Simone Simon, Ledoux, Carette, Blanchette Burnoy, Gerard Landry, Jenny Helia, Germaine Clasis, Berloiz, Jean Renoir.

BIG PARADE, THE

1925 *(silent)*   AMERICAN

Production	Metro-Goldwyn
Direction	King Vidor
Scenario	Harry Behn
Photography . . .	John Arnold
From a play by . . .	Laurence Stallings

With : John Gilbert, Renée Adorée, Karl Dane.

BIRTH OF A NATION, The

1915 *(silent)*   AMERICAN

Production	Epoch Film Corpn.
Direction and Scenario .	D. W. Griffith
Assistant Direction .	George A. Beranger, Thomas E. O'Brien
Photography . . .	G. W. Bitzer, Karl Brown
Editing	James E. Smith

With : Lillian Gish, Wallace Reid, Robert Harron, Spottiswoode Aiken, Henry B. Walthall, Mae Marsh, Donald Crisp, Raoul Walsh.

BLACK LEGION

1937 *(sound)*   AMERICAN

Production	Warner Brothers
Direction	Archie Mayo
Scenario	Abem Finkel, William Wister Haines
Photography . . .	George Barnes
From a story by .	Robert Lord

With : Humphrey Bogart, Erin O'Brien-Moore, Dick Foran, Ann Sheridan, Helen Flint, Robert Barrat.

BLACK PIRATE, The

1926 *(silent)*   AMERICAN

Production	United Artists
Direction	Albert Parker
Scenario	Lotta Woods, Jack Cunningham.
Photography . . .	Henry Sharp
Design	Karl Oscar Borg

With : Douglas Fairbanks, Billie Dove, Donald Crisp, Sam de Grasse, Anders Randolph.

BLIND HUSBANDS

1919 *(silent)*   AMERICAN

Production	Universal
Direction and Scenario	Erich von Stroheim
Assistant Direction .	K. C. Stewart
Photography . .	Ben Reynolds
Editing	Frank Laurence, Eleanor Fried

With : Erich von Stroheim, Sam de Grasse, Gibson Gowland.

BLUE ANGEL, The

1929 *(sound)*   GERMAN

Production	Ufa
Supervision . . .	Erich Pommer
Direction	Jósef von Sternberg
Scenario	Karl Zuckmayer, Karl Vollmöller, Robert Liebmann
Photography . . .	Gunther Rittau, Hans Schneeberger
Design	Otto Hunte, Emil Hasler
Music	Friedrich Holländer
From a novel by . . .	Heinrich Mann

With : Marlene Dietrich, Emil Jannings, Kurt Gerron, Rosa Valletti, Hans Albers.

BOOMERANG

1947 *(sound)*   AMERICAN

Production	Twentieth Century-Fox
Producer	Louis de Rochemont
Direction	Elia Kazan
Scenario	Richard Murphy
Photography . . .	Norbert Brodine
Music	David Buttolph
Based on an article by .	Anthony Abbot

With : Dana Andrews, Jane Wyatt, Lee J. Cobb, Sam Levene, Taylor Holmes, Leona Roberts, Philip Coolidge, Ben Lackland.

BRIEF ENCOUNTER

1945 *(sound)*   BRITISH

Production	Cineguild
Producers . . .	Anthony Havelock-Allan, Ronald Neame
Direction	David Lean
Scenario	Noel Coward
Photography . . .	Robert Krasker
Design	L. P. Williams

With : Celia Johnson, Trevor Howard, Stanley Holloway, Joyce Carey.

BROKEN BLOSSOMS
1919 *(silent)*   AMERICAN

Production . . . . Famous-Players-Lasky
Direction and Scenario . D. W. Griffith
Assistant Direction . . Harry Carr
Photography . . . Hendrik Sartov, G. W. Bitzer
From a novel by . . . Thomas Burke

With : Lillian Gish, Richard Barthelmess, Donald Crisp.

CABINET OF DR. CALIGARI, THE
1919-1920 *(silent)*   GERMAN

Production . . . . Decla-Bioskop
Direction . . . . Robert Wiene
Scenario . . . . Carl Mayer, Hans Janowitz
Photography . . . Willi Hameister
Design . . . . Walther Reimann, Hermann Warm, Walther Röhrig

With: Lil Dagover, Conrad Veidt, Werner Krauss, Hans Heinrich von Twardowski, Friedrich Feher, Rudolph Lettinger.

CHAPAEV
1934 *(sound)*   SOVIET

Production . . . . Lenfilm
Direction and Scenario . The Brothers Vassiliev
Photography . . Alexander Segaev, A. Xenophontov
Design . . . . Isaac Makhlis
Music . . . . . Gavril Popov

With : Boris Babotchkin, Boris Blinov, Varvara Miasnikova, Leonid Kmit, I. N. Pevtsov.

CHILDHOOD OF MAXIM GORKI, THE
1938 *(sound)*   SOVIET

Production . . . Soyuzdetfilm, Moscow
Direction . . . . Mark Donskoi
Scenario . . . . I. Gruzdev

Photography . . .	P. Yermolov, I. Malov
Music	Lev Schwartz
Based on . . .	Maxim Gorki's autobiography

With: Alyosha Lyarsky, V. O. Massalitinova, M. G. Troyanovksy, E. Alexeyevna, V. Novikov, A Zhukov, K. Ziubko, S. Tikhonravov, Igor Smirnov.

CHRONICLE OF THE GRIESHUUS, The

1923 *(silent)*   GERMAN

Production . . .	Union-Ufa
Direction . . .	Arthur von Gerlach
Scenario . . .	Thea von Harbou
Photography . .	Karl Drews, Fritz Arno Wagner, Erich Nitzschmann
Design . . .	Professor Pölzig, Robert Herlth, Walther Röhrig
From a story by . .	Theodore Storm

With: Paul Hartmann, Lil Dagover, Arthur Kraussneck, Rudolph Rittner, Gertrud Welcker, Gertrud Arnold, Rudolph Forster, Josef Peterhans.

CIMARRON

1931 *(sound)*   AMERICAN

Production . . .	RKO-Radio Pictures
Direction . . .	Wesley Ruggles
Scenario . . .	Howard Estabrook
Photography . .	Edward Cronjager
Design . . .	Max Ree
From a novel by .	Edna Ferber

With: Richard Dix, Irene Dunne, Estelle Taylor, William Collier, Jnr.

CINDERELLA

1923 *(silent)*   GERMAN

Production . . .	Decla-Bioskop-Ufa
Direction and Scenario	Ludwig Berger
Photography . .	Gunther Krampf, Karl Becker
Design . . .	Rudolph Bamberger

With: Helga Thomas, Frieda Richard, Paul Hartmann, Herman Thimig, Mady Christians, Olga Tschechowa, Georg John, Lucie Höflich, Leonhard Haskel, Max Gülstorff.

APPENDIX I

CIRCUS, THE

1925-1927 *(silent)* AMERICAN

Production . . . . United Artists
Direction and Scenario . Charles Chaplin
Photography . . . Jack Wilson, Mark Mariatt,
     Roland Totheroh
Design . . . . Charles D. Hall

With : Charles Chaplin, Merna Kennedy.

CITIZEN KANE

1941 *(sound)* AMERICAN

Production . . . . RKO-Radio Pictures
Direction . . . . Orson Welles
Scenario . . . . Herman J. Mankiewicz, Orson
     Welles
Photography . . . Gregg Toland
Design . . . . Van Nest Polglase
Music . . . . . Bernard Herrman

With : Orson Welles, Agnes Moorehead, Harry Shannon,
George Coulouris, Joseph Cotten, Everett Sloan, Ruth
Warwick, Ray Collins, Dorothy Comingore.

CITY LIGHTS

1928-1930 *(sound)* AMERICAN

Production . . . . United Artists
Direction and Scenario . Charles Chaplin
Photography . . . Henry Cronjager, Roland
     Totheroh, Mark Mariatt
Design . . . . Charles D. Hall

With : Charles Chaplin, Virginia Cherrill, Harry Myers.

CITY STREETS

1931 *(sound)* AMERICAN

Production . . . . Paramount
Direction . . . . Rouben Mamoulian
Scenario . . . . Max Marcin, Oliver P. Garrett
Photography . . . Lee Garmes

With : Sylvia Sidney, Gary Cooper, Guy Kibbee, Paul Lukas,
William Boyd.

CONGRESS DANCES

1931 *(sound)* GERMAN

Production	Ufa
Producer	Erich Pommer
Supervision . . .	Karl Winston
Direction	Erik Charell
Scenario	Robert Liebmann, Norbert Falk
Photography . . .	Karl Hoffmann
Design	Walther Röhrig, Robert Herlth
Music	Werner R. Heymann
Costumes	Ernst Stern

With : (English Cast) Lilian Harvey, Henri Garat, Conrad Veidt, Lil Dagover, Reginald Purdell, Helen Haye, Gibb McLaughlin, Spencer Trevor.

COUNTERPLAN

1932 *(sound)* SOVIET

Production	Lenfilm
Direction	Frederic Ermler, Sergei Yutkevich
Photography . . .	Z. Martov, A. Ginzburg V. Rappoport
Design	B. Dubrovsky-Eshke
Music	Dmitri Shostakovich

With : V. Gardin, B. Tenin, B. Poslavsky, A. Abrikosov, T. Guretskaya.

COVERED WAGON, THE

1923 *(silent)* AMERICAN

Production	Famous-Players-Lasky
Direction	James Cruze
Scenario	Jack Cunningham
Photography . . .	Karl Brown
Editing	Dorothy Arzner
From a novel by . . .	Emerson Hough

With : Lois Wilson, J. Warren Kerrigan, Ernest Torrence, Alan Hale, Tully Marshall.

APPENDIX I
CRIME ET CHATIMENT

1935 *(sound)*   FRENCH

Production	Générale Production
Direction	Pierre Chenal
Scenario	Pierre Chenal, Marcel Aymé
Dialogue	Marcel Aymé
Photography . . .	Mundviller, Colas
Music	Arthur Honegger
Design	A. Bazin
From a novel by . . .	Dostoievsky

With : Pierre Blanchar, M. Ozeray, Harry Baur, Aimé Clariond, A. Rignault, Lucienne LeMarchand, Marcelle Geniat, Bergeron, Marcel Delaitre, Douking, Paulette Flambert, Sylvie.

CRIME WITHOUT PASSION

1934 *(sound)*   AMERICAN

Production	Paramount
Direction and Scenario	Ben Hecht, Charles MacArthur
Photography . . .	Lee Garmes
Design	Albert Johnson

With : Claude Rains, Margo, Whitney Bourne, Stanley Ridges, Paula Trueman, Leslie Adams, Greta Granstedt, Esther Dale.

CROSSFIRE

1947 *(sound)*   AMERICAN

Production	RKO-Radio Pictures (Dore Schary)
Producer	Adrian Scott
Direction	Edward Dmytryk
Scenario	John Paxton
Photography . . .	J. Roy Hunt
Design	Albert D'Agostino, Alfred Herman
From a novel by . . .	Richard Brooks

With : Robert Young, Robert Mitchum, Robert Ryan, Gloria Grahame, Sam Levene.

CROWD, The

1927-1928 *(silent)*   AMERICAN

Production	Metro-Goldwyn-Mayer
Direction	King Vidor
Scenario	King Vidor, John V. A. Weaver
Photography . . .	Henry Sharp
Design	Cedric Gibbons, Arnold Gillespie
Editing	Hugh Wynn

With : James Murray, Eleanor Boardman, Bert Roach, Estelle Clark.

DANTON

1921 *(silent)*   GERMAN

Production	Wörner-Film
Direction and Scenario	Dimitri Buchowetski
Photography . . .	Arpad Viragh
Design	Hans Dreier

With: Emil Jannings, Werner Krauss, Conrad Veidt, Maly Delschaft, Robert Scholz, Ferdinand von Alten, Eduard Winterstein, Hilde Wörner, Charlotte Ander.

DAY OF WRATH, The

1944 *(sound)*   DANISH

Production	Film-Centralen-Palladium
Producer and Director	Carl Th. Dreyer
Scenario	Carl Th. Dreyer, Poul Knudsen, Mogens Skot-Hansen
Photography . . .	Carl Andersson
Music	Poul Schierbeck
Design	Lis Fribert
From a novel by . .	Wiers Jenssens

With : Thorkild Roose, Lisbeth Movin, Sigrid Neiiendam, Preben Lerdoff, Olaf Ussing, Anna Svierkier.

DEAD END

1937 *(sound)*   AMERICAN

Production	United Artists (Sam Goldwyn)
Direction	William Wyler
Scenario	Lillian Hellman
Photography . . .	Gregg Toland
Design	Richard Day
Music	Alfred Newman

With : Sylvia Sidney, Joel McCrea, Humphrey Bogart, Wendy Barrie, Claire Trevor, Allen Jenkins, Marjorie Main, Billy Halop.

DESERTER

1933 (*sound*)   SOVIET

Production	Mejrabpomfilm
Direction and Scenario .	V. I. Pudovkin
Scenario	N. Agadjanova-Shutko, M. Krasnostavski, A. Lezebnikov
Photography . . .	A. N. Golovnia
Design	A. Kozlovski
Music	I. Shaporin

With : Boris Livanov, M. Aleshehenko, A. Besperotov, S. Gerasimov, E. Gliser, K. Gurniak, A. Konsovski, A. V. Kovrigin, T. Makarova, Tchistiakov.

DESTINY

1921 *(silent)*   GERMAN

Production	Decla-Bioskop
Direction	Fritz Lang
Scenario	Thea von Harbou
Photography . . .	Erich Nitzschmann, Fritz Arno Wagner, Herm. Salfrank
Design	Walther Röhrig, Robert Herlth, Hermann Warm

With : Bernard Goetzke, Lil Dagover, Walther Janssen, Rudolph Klein-Rogge, Georg John.

DIABLE AU CORPS, LE

1947 *(sound)*   FRENCH

Production . . .	Transcontinental Films
Direction	Claude Autant-Lara
Scenario	Jean Aurenche, Pierre Bost
Photography . . .	Michel Kelber
Design	Max Douy
Music	René Cloerec
From a novel by . .	Raymond Radiguet

With: Micheline Presle, Gérard Philipe, Denise Gray, Palau, Jean Debucourt.

DITTE—MENNESKEBARN

1946 *(sound)*   DANISH

Production . . .	Nordisk
Direction and Script .	Bjärne Henning-Jensen
Assistant	Astrid Henning-Jensen
Photography . . .	Verner Jensen

Music . . . . Herm D. Kuppel
From a novel by . . Martin Anderson Nexo

With: Tove Mäes, Maria Garland, Ebbe Rode, Edwin Tienroth.

DOCKS OF NEW YORK, THE

1928 *(silent)* AMERICAN

Production . . . . Paramount
Direction . . . . Josef von Sternberg
Scenario . . . . Jules Furthman
Photography . . . Harold Rosson

With: George Bancroft, Betty Compson, Olga Baclanova.

DOUBLE INDEMNITY

1944 *(sound)* AMERICAN

Production . . . . Paramount (Joseph Sistrom)
Direction . . . . Billy Wilder
Scenario . . . . Billy Wilder, Raymond Chandler
Photography . . . John Seitz
Music . . . . Miklos Rozsa
Design . . . . Hans Dreier, H. Pereira
From a novel by . . James M. Cain

With: Fred MacMurray, Edward G. Robinson, Barbara Stanwyck, Tom Powers.

DRACULA (NOSFERATU)

1922 *(silent)* GERMAN

Production . . . . Prana-Film
Direction . . . . F. W. Murnau
Scenario . . . . Henrik Galeen
Photography . . . Fritz Arno Wagner, Gunther Krampf
Design . . . . Albin Grau
From a novel by . . Bram Stoker

With: Max Schreck, Alexander Granach, Gustav von Wangenheim, Greta Schroeder, G. H. Schnell, Ruth Landshaft, John Gottowt, Gustav Botz, Max Nemetz, Wolfgang Heinz, Albert Denohr.

DREIGROSCHENOPER, DIE

1931 *(sound)* GERMAN

Production . . . . Deutsche-First National
Direction . . . . G. W. Pabst

Scenario	Leo Lania, Ernst Vajda, Béla Balázs
Photography . . .	Fritz Arno Wagner
Design	André Andreiev
Music	Kurt Weill

With : Rudolf Forster, Carola Neher, Fritz Rasp, Valeska Gert, Lotte Lenja, Vladimir Sokolov, Reinhold Schunzell, Herman Thimig.

EARTH

1930 *(silent)*   SOVIET

Production	Vufku-Kino (Ukraine)
Direction and Scenario	Alexander Dovjenko
Photography . .	Daniel Demutski

With : S. Shkurat, S. Svashenko, P. Masokha, N. Nademski, V. Mikhailov, E. Maximova.

EMIL AND THE DETECTIVES

1931 *(sound)*   GERMAN

Production	Ufa
Direction . . .	Gerhard Lamprecht
Scenario . . .	Billy Wilder
Photography . .	Werner Brandes
Design . . .	Werner Schlichting
Music	Allan Gray
From a novel by .	Erich Kästner

With : Fritz Rasp, Kathe Haack, Rolf Wenkhaus, Olga Engl, Inge Landgut, Rudolph Biebrach.

END OF ST. PETERSBURG, The

1927 *(silent)*   SOVIET

Production	Mejrabpom-Russ
Direction . . .	V. I. Pudovkin
Assistant Direction .	Mikhail Doller
Scenario . . .	N. A. Zarkhi
Photography . .	A. N. Golovnia
Design . . .	S. V. Koslovski

With : Vera Baranovskaia, A. Chistiakov, I. Chiuvelev, V. Obolenski.

ENFANTS DU PARADIS, Les

1944 *(sound)*   FRENCH

Production	S.N. Pathé-Cinema
Direction	Marcel Carné
Scenario and Dialogue .	Jacques Prévert
Photography . . .	Roger Hubert, Marc Fossard
Design	A. Barsacq, R. Cabutti, A. Trauner
Music	Maurice Thiret, Joseph Kosma

With: Arletty, Jean-Louis Barrault, Pierre Brasseur, Maria Casares, M. Herrand, L. Salou, P. Renoir.

EN RADE

1927 *(silent)*   FRENCH

Production	Néofilm
Direction and Scenario .	Alberto Cavalcanti
Assistant Direction . .	Claude Heymann
Photography . . .	Jimmy Rogers
Design	Erik Aës

With : Catherine Hessling, Nathalie Lissenko, Georges Charlia, Philippe Hériat, Thomy Bourdelle.

EXTASE

1933 *(sound)*   CZECHOSLOVAK

Production	Elekta Film Slavia
Direction and Scenario .	Gustav Machaty, Robert Horky
Photography . . .	Jan Stallich
Music	Dr. Breece

With: Hedy Kiessler, Albert Mog, Jaromir Rogoz, Leopold Kramer.

FALL OF THE HOUSE OF USHER, The

1928 *(silent)*   FRENCH

Direction	Jean Epstein
Photography . . .	Lucas
Adapted from the story by	Edgar Allan Poe

With : Margaret Gance, Jean Dubencourt, Charles Lamay.

FOOLISH WIVES

1922 *(silent)*   AMERICAN

Production	Universal
Direction and Scenario .	Erich von Stroheim
Photography . . .	William Daniels, Ben Reynolds
Design	Richard Day

With : Erich von Stroheim, Miss Du Pont, Maude George, Mae Busch.

FORBIDDEN PARADISE

1924 *(silent)*   AMERICAN

Production	Famous-Players-Lasky
Direction	Ernst Lubitsch
Scenario	Agnes Christine Johnston, Hans Kraly
Photography . . .	Charles van Enger
Design	Hans Dreier
From a play by . . .	Lajos Biro, Melchior Lengyel

With : Pola Negri, Adolphe Menjou, Rod la Rocque, Pauline Starke.

FORTY-SECOND STREET

1933 *(sound)*   AMERICAN

Production	Warner Brothers
Direction	Lloyd Bacon
Scenario	Rian James, James Seymour
Photography . . .	Sol Polito
Music	Al Dubin, Harry Warren

With : Warner Baxter, Bebe Daniels, George Brent, Una Merkel, Ruby Keeler, Guy Kibbee, Dick Powell, Ginger Rogers.

FOUR HORSEMEN OF THE APOCALYPSE, The

1920-1921 *(silent)*   AMERICAN

Production	Metro
Direction	Rex Ingram
Assistant Direction . .	Walter Mayo
Scenario	June Mathis
Photography . . .	John F. Seitz
From a novel by . .	Blasco Vincent Ibanez

With : Alice Terry, Jean Hersholt, Rudolph Valentino, Wallace Beery, Alan Hale.

FRONT PAGE, THE

1931 *(sound)* AMERICAN

Production	Howard Hughes
Direction . . .	Lewis Milestone
Photography . .	Glen MacWilliams, Bert Camm
Design . . .	Richard Day
From a play by . .	Ben Hecht, Charles MacArthur

With : Adolphe Menjou, Pat O'Brien, Mary Brian, Edward Everett Horton.

FURY

1936 *(sound)* AMERICAN

Production . . .	Metro-Goldwyn-Mayer
Producer . . .	Joseph L. Mankiewicz
Direction . . .	Fritz Lang
Scenario . . .	Bartlett Cormack, Fritz Lang
Photography . .	Joseph Ruttenburg
Design . . .	Cedric Gibbons
Editing . . .	Frank Sullivan
Music	Franz Waxman
From a story by . .	Norman Krasna

With : Spencer Tracy, Sylvia Sidney, Walter Abel, Bruce Cabot, Edward Ellis, Walter Brennan.

GENERAL, THE

1927 *(silent)* AMERICAN

Production . . .	United Artists
Direction . . .	Buster Keaton, Clyde Bruckman
Photography . .	Clyde Bruckman, J .D. Jennings

With : Buster Keaton, Marion Mack.

GENUINE

1920 *(silent)* GERMAN

Production . . .	Decla-Bioskop
Direction . . .	Robert Wiene
Scenario . . .	Carl Mayer
Photography . . .	Willi Hameister
Design . . .	Caesar Klein, Walther Reimann

With: Fern Andra, Hans Heinrich von Twardowski, Harald Paulsen.

157. THE LAST CHANCE, directed by LEOPOLD LINDTBERG. [Swiss, 1945]

158. THE STORY OF G.I. JOE, directed by WILLIAM WELLMAN. BURGESS MEREDITH.
[American, 1945]

159. OPEN CITY, directed by ROBERTO ROSSELLINI.   ANNA MAGNANI.   [Italian, 1945]

160. BRIEF ENCOUNTER, directed by DAVID LEAN.   CELIA JOHNSON, TREVOR HOWARD.
[British, 1945]

APPENDIX I

GHOST THAT NEVER RETURNS, The
1929 *(silent)*   SOVIET

Production	Sovkino
Direction	Abram Room
Scenario	Valentin Turkin
Photography . . .	Feldmann
From a novel by . .	Henri Barbusse

With : O. Jisneva, M. Shtraukh.

GOLEM, The
1920 *(silent)*   GERMAN

Production	Union-Ufa
Direction and Scenario	Henrik Galeen, Paul Wegener
Photography . . .	Karl Freund
Design	Professor Hans Pölzig, Rochus Gliese

With : Paul Wegener, Albert Steinrück, Ernst Deutsch, Lyda Salmonova, Hanns Sturm, Otto Gebühr, Lothar Müthel.

GOLD RUSH, The
1925 *(silent)*   AMERICAN

Production	United Artists
Direction and Scenario	Charles Chaplin
Assistant Direction .	Harry D'Abbadie d'Arrast, Charles Reisner
Technical Direction .	Charles D. Hall
Photography . . .	Jack Wilson, Roland Totheroh

With : Charles Chaplin, Georgia Hale, Mack Swain.

GONE WITH THE WIND
1939 *(sound)*   AMERICAN

Production	Selznick-International
Producer	David O. Selznick
Direction	Victor Fleming
Scenario	Sidney Howard
Photography . . .	Ernest Heller
Design	William Cameron Menzies
Music	Max Steiner
From a novel by . .	Margaret Mitchell

With : Vivien Leigh, Leslie Howard, Clark Gable, Hattie McDaniel, Thomas Mitchell, Barbara O'Neill, Victor Jory, Olivia de Havilland, Laura Hope Crews, Harry Davenport, Jane Darwell, Cliff Edwards, Ona Munson, J. M. Kerrigan.

GRANDE ILLUSION, La

1937 *(sound)* FRENCH

Production	Les Réalisations d'Art Cinématographic
Producer	Raymond Blondy
Direction	Jean Renoir
Scenario	Jean Renoir, Charles Spaak
Photography . . .	Christian Matras, Claude Renoir
Design	E. Lourié
Music	Joseph Kosma

With : Jean Gabin, Dita Parlo, Pierre Fresnay, Erich von Stroheim, Carette, Péclet, Dalio.

GRAPES OF WRATH, The

1940 *(sound)* AMERICAN

Production	Twentieth Century-Fox
Direction	John Ford
Scenario	Nunnally Johnson
Photography . . .	Gregg Toland
Music	Alfred Newman
From a novel by . .	John Steinbeck

With : Henry Fonda, Jane Darwell, Russell Simpson, Charles Grapewin, Zeffie Tilbury, Doris Bowden.

GREAT EXPECTATIONS

1946 *(sound)* BRITISH

Production	Cineguild
Producer	Ronald Neame, Anthony Havelock-Allan
Direction	David Lean
Scenario	Ronald Neame, David Lean, Kay Walsh
Photography . . .	Guy Green
Design	John Bryan, Wilfred Shingleton
Music	Walter Goehr
Costumes	Sophia Harris, Margaret Furse
From the novel by . .	Charles Dickens

With : John Mills, Valerie Hobson, Bernard Miles, Martita Hunt, Francis L. Sullivan.

GREED

1923-1924 *(silent)* AMERICAN

Production . . .	. Metro-Goldwyn
Direction and Scenario	. Erich von Stroheim
Assistant Direction .	. Eddie Malone
Photography . .	. Ben Reynolds, William Daniels, Ernest Schoedsack
Editing . . .	. June Mathis
From a novel by .	. Frank Norris

With : Gibson Gowland, Zasu Pitts, Chester Conklin, Jean Hersholt.

HALLELUJAH !

1929 *(sound)* AMERICAN

Production . . .	. Metro-Goldwyn-Mayer
Direction . . .	. King Vidor
Scenario . . .	. Wanda Tuchock
Photography . . .	. Gordon Avil
Design . . .	. Cedric Gibbons

With : Daniel L. Haynes, Nina Mae McKinney, William Fountaine, Harry Gray, Fanny Belle DeKnight, Everett McGarrity, Victoria Spivey, and the Dixie Jubilee Singers.

HAMLET

1948 *(sound)* BRITISH

Production . . .	. Two Cities Films
Producer and Director	. Laurence Olivier
Photography . .	. Desmond Dickinson
Sets and Costumes .	. Roger Furse, Carmen Dillon
Editor . . .	. Helga Cranston
Music	. William Walton
Adaptation . . .	. Alan Dent

With : Laurence Olivier, Jean Simmons, Felix Aylmer, Basil Sydney, Norman Wooland, Eileen Herlie, Stanley Holloway.

HENRY V

1944 *(sound)* BRITISH

Production . . .	. Two Cities Films
Associate Producer .	. Dallas Bower
Direction . . .	. Laurence Olivier
Adaptation . . .	. Laurence Olivier, Alan Dent

Photography	. . .	Robert Krasker, Jack Hildyard
Music .	. . .	William Walton
Design	. . .	Paul Sheriff
Costumes	. . .	Roger Furse
Editing	. . .	Reginald Beck

With : Laurence Olivier, Robert Newton, Leslie Banks, Renee Asherson, Esmond Knight.

HORSE FEATHERS

1932 *(sound)*   AMERICAN

Production .	. . .	Paramount
Direction	. . .	Norman Taurog
Scenario	. . .	Bert Kalmar, Harry Ruby, S. J. Perelman
Photography	. . .	Ray June

With : Groucho Marx, Harpo Marx, Chico Marx, Zeppo Marx, Thelma Todd, David Landau, Florine McKinney, James Pierce, Nat Pendleton, Reginald Barlow, Robert Grieg.

HOTEL IMPERIAL

1926 *(silent)*   AMERICAN

Production .	. . .	Paramount
Supervision	. . .	Erich Pommer
Direction	. . .	Mauritz Stiller
Scenario	. . .	Jules Furthman
Photography	. . .	Bert Glennon
From a story by	. .	Lajos Biro

With : Pola Negri, James Hall, George Siegman.

I AM A FUGITIVE FROM A CHAIN GANG

1932 *(sound)*   AMERICAN

Production .	. . .	Warner Brothers
Direction	. . .	Mervyn Le Roy
Scenario	. . .	Sheridan Gibney, Brown Holmes
Photography	. . .	Sol Polito
Editing	. . .	Wiliam Holmes
From a novel by	. .	Robert E. Burns

With : Paul Muni, Glenda Farrell, Helen Vinson, David Landau.

APPENDIX I

INFORMER, The

1935 *(sound)* AMERICAN

Production	RKO-Radio Pictures
Direction	John Ford
Scenario	Dudley Nichols
Photography . . .	Joseph H. August
Music	Max Steiner
From a novel by . .	Liam O'Flaherty

With : Victor McLaglen, Wallace Ford, Margot Grahame, Preston Foster, Una O'Connor, Heather Angel, J. M. Kerrigan, Donald Meek, May Boley.

INHUMAINE, L'

1923-1924 *(silent)* FRENCH

Production	Cinégraphic
Direction	Marcel l'Herbier
Scenario	Georgette Leblanc, Marcel l'Herbier
Photography . . .	Specht, Roche
Design	Mallet-Stevens, Alberto Cavalcanti, Claude Autant-Lara, Fernand Léger

With : Georgette Leblanc, Jacque Catelain, Philippe Hériat.

INTOLERANCE

1916 *(silent)* AMERICAN

Production	Wark Producing Co.
Direction and Scenario	D. W. Griffith
Assistants . . .	George Siegmann, W. S. van Dyke, Joseph Henaberry
Photography . . .	G. W. Bitzer
Assistant Photography	Karl Brown
Design	R. Ellis Wales
Editing	James E. Smith

With : Lillian Gish, Robert Harron, Mae Marsh, Sam de Grasse, Monte Blue, Erich von Stroheim, Bessie Love, Colleen Moore, Eugene Pallette, Constance Talmadge, Tully Marshall, Elmo Lincoln, Alma Rubens, Carmel Myers, Pauline Starke, Mildred Harris.

IRON HORSE, The

1924 *(silent)*   AMERICAN

Production   .   .   .   .   Fox Film Corporation
Direction   .   .   .   .   John Ford
Scenario   .   .   .   .   Charles Kenyon, John Russell
Photography   .   .   .   George Schneidermann

With: George O'Brien, Madge Bellamy, J. Farrell MacDonald, Gladys Hulette.

ITALIAN STRAW HAT, The

1927 *(silent)*   FRENCH

Production   .   .   .   .   Albatross-Sequana
Direction and Scenario   .   René Clair
Photography   .   .   .   Maurice Désfassiaux, Nicolas Rondakoff
From a play by   .   .   .   Eugène Labiche, Marc Michel

With: Olga Tschechowa, Albert Préjean, Jim Gerald, Paul Ollivier.

IT HAPPENED ONE NIGHT

1934 *(sound)*   AMERICAN

Production   .   .   .   .   Columbia Pictures
Direction   .   .   .   .   Frank Capra
Scenario   .   .   .   .   Robert Riskin
Photography   .   .   .   Joe Walker
Editing   .   .   .   .   Gene Havlick
From a story by   .   .   Samuel Hopkins Adams

With: Clark Gable, Claudette Colbert, Walter Connolly, Alan Hale, Roscoe Karns.

JOUR SE LEVE, Le

1939 *(sound)*   FRENCH

Production   .   .   .   .   Sigma Frogerais
Direction   .   .   .   .   Marcel Carné
Scenario   .   .   .   .   Jacques Viot, Jacques Prévert
Dialogue   .   .   .   .   Jacques Prévert
Photography   .   .   .   Curt Courant
Design   .   .   .   .   A. Trauner
Music .   .   .   .   .   Maurice Jaubert

With: Jean Gabin, Arletty, Jules Berry, Jacqueline Laurent, Bernard Blier, R. Genin, R. Legris, Jacques Baumer.

JOYLESS STREET, The

1925 *(silent)* GERMAN

Production . . . . Hirschel-Sofar
Direction . . . . G. W. Pabst
Scenario . . . . Willi Haas
Photography . . . Seeber, Oertel, Lach
Design . . . . Söhnle, Erdmann
From a novel by . . Hugo Bettauer

With : Jaro Fürth, Greta Garbo, Robert Garrison, Henry Stuart, Agnes Esterhazy, Tamara, Asta Nielsen, Einar Hanson, Werner Krauss, Valeska Gert, Grigor Chmara.

KAMERADSCHAFT

1931 *(sound)* GERMAN

Production . . . . Nerofilm
Direction . . . . G. W. Pabst
Assistant Direction . . Herbert Rappaport
Scenario . . . . Otten, Ernst Vajda, Lampel
Photography . . . Fritz Arno Wagner, R. Baberski
Design . . . . Ernö Metzner, Karl Vollbrecht
Editing . . . . Hans Oser

With : (German Cast) Alexander Granach, Fritz Kampers, E. Busch, Elizabeth Wendt, G. Püttjer, O. Höcker. (French Cast) : D. Mendaille, G. Charlia, A. Ducret, A. Bernard, P. Louis, Helna Manson.

KEAN

1924 *(silent)* FRENCH

Production . . . . Albatross-Sequana
Direction and Scenario . Nicholas Wolkoff,
                         Ivan Mosjoukine, Kenelm Foss
Photography . . . J. Mundviller, F. Bourgassoff
Design . . . . Lochakov

With : Ivan Mosjoukine, Kenelm Foss, Mary Odette, Nikolai Kolin.

APPENDIX I

KERMESSE HEROIQUE, La
1935 *(sound)*   French

Production	Tobis Régina
Direction	Jacques Feyder
Scenario	Charles Spaak, Jacques Feyder
Dialogue	Charles Spaak
Photography . . .	Harry Stradling
Design	Lazare Meerson

With : Françoise Rosay, Jean Murat, Alermé, Louis Jouvet, M. Carmentier, Pierre Labry, Micheline Cheirel, Bernard Lancret, Alfred Adam, Delphin.

KUHLE WAMPE
1932 *(sound)*   German

Direction	S. Th. Dudow
Scenario	Brecht, Ottwalt
Photography . . .	Gunther Krampf
Design	Scharfenberg, Höllering
Music	Hanns Eisler

With : Hertha Thiele, Ernst Busch, Martha Wolter, Adolf Fischer, Lili Schönborn.

LAST CHANCE, The
1945 *(sound)*   Swiss

Production	Praesens-Film
Producer	L. Wechsler
Direction	Leopold Lindtberg
Scenario	Richard Schweizer
Photography . . .	Emil Berna
Music	Robert Blum

With : E. G. Morrison, John Hoy, Ray Reagan, Lina Rossi, Tino Erler, Romano Calo, Maurice Sakhnowski, Therese Gihseova.

LAST COMMAND, The
1927-1928 *(silent)*   American

Production	Paramount
Direction	Josef von Sternberg
Scenario	John F. Goodrich
Photography . . .	Bert Glennon
From a story by . .	Lajos Biro

With : Emil Jannings, Evelyn Brent, William Powell.

LAST LAUGH, The

1924 *(silent)*   GERMAN

Production	Ufa
Supervision . . .	Erich Pommer
Direction	F. W. Murnau
Scenario	Carl Mayer
Photography . . .	Karl Freund
Design	Walther Röhrig, Robert Herlth

With: Emil Jannings, Georg John, Mady Delschaft, Emilie Kurz.

LATE MATTHEW PASCAL, The

1924-1925 *(silent)*   FRENCH

Production	Albatross-Cinégraphic
Direction and Scenario .	Marcel l'Herbier
Photography . . .	Guichard, Letort, Berliet, Bourgassoff
Design	Alberto Cavalcanti
From a novel by . .	Luigi Pirandello

With: Ivan Mosjoukine, Marthe Belot, Pauline Carton, Michel Simon, Marcelle Pradot, Barsac, Ioaure Douvane, Térov, Lois Moran, Philippe Hériat, Irma Perrot, Jean Hervé, Pierre Batcheff.

LITTLE CAESAR

1930 *(sound)*   AMERICAN

Production	Warner Brothers
Producer	Darryl Zanuck
Direction	Mervyn Le Roy
Scenario	Francis Faragoh
Photography . . .	Tony Gaudio
From a novel by . .	W. R. Burnett

With: Edward G. Robinson, Douglas Fairbanks, Jnr., William Collier, Jnr., Ralph Ince, Glenda Farrell, George E. Stone.

LONE WHITE SAIL

1938 (*sound*)   SOVIET

Production	Soyuzdetfilm
Direction	Vladimir Legoshin
Scenario	Valentin Kataev
Photography . . .	B. Monastirsky
Design	V. Kaplunovsky, S. Kuznetsov
Music	M. Rauchverger

With : Boris Runge, Ira Bolshakova, F. Nikitin, I. Peltser, M. Lyarov, N. Plotnikov, Svetiana Pryadilova.

LOVE PARADE, The

1929 (*sound*)   AMERICAN

Production	Paramount
Direction	Ernst Lubitsch
Scenario	Ernst Vadja, Guy Bolton
Photography . . .	Victor Milner
Music	Victor Schertzinger
Design	Hans Dreier
From a play by . . .	Leon Xanrof, Jules Chancel

With : Maurice Chevalier, Jeanette MacDonald, Lupino Lane, Lillian Roth, Eugene Pallette.

LOVES OF JEANNE NEY, The

1927 (*silent*)   GERMAN

Production	Ufa
Direction	G. W. Pabst
Scenario	Leonhardt
Photography . . .	Fritz Arno Wagner
Design	Otto Hunte, Victor Trivas
From a novel by . .	Ilya Ehrenburg

With : Edith Jehanne, Uno Henning, Fritz Rasp, Vladimir Sokolov, Brigitte Helm, Siegfried Arno, Jack Trevor, Hertha von Walther, E. A. Licho.

'M'

1932 *(sound)*   GERMAN

Production	Nerofilm
Direction	Fritz Lang
Scenario	Thea von Harbou, Fritz Lang
Photography . . .	Fritz Arno Wagner, Gustav Rabhje, Karl Vash
Design	Karl Vollbrecht, Emil Hasler

With: Peter Lorre, Ellen Widmann, Inge Landgut, Gustaf Grundgens, Fritz Gnass, Fritz Odemar, Paul Kemp, Theo Lingen, Georg John, Rudolf Blumner.

MADAME DUBARRY

1919 *(silent)*   GERMAN

Production . . .	Union-Ufa
Direction	Ernst Lubitsch
Scenario	Hans Kraly, Fred Orbing
Photography . . .	Theodore Sparkuhl
Design	Karl Machus
Costumes	Ali Hubert

With: Pola Negri, Emil Jannings, Harry Liedtke, Edward von Winterstein, Reinhold Schünzel, Elsa Berna, Frederich Immler.

MAEDCHEN IN UNIFORM

1931 *(sound)*   GERMAN

Production . . .	Deutsche Film-Gemeinschaft
Supervision . . .	Carl Froelich
Direction . . .	Leontine Sagan
Scenario	Christa Winsloe, F. D. Andam
Photography . . .	Reimar Kuntze, Franz Weihmayr
Music	Hansom Milde-Meissner

With: Emilia Unda, Gertrude de Lalsky, Marte Hein, Dorothea Wieck, Lene Berdolt, Erika Mann, Elsa Ehser, Hertha Thiele, Ilse Winter, Ellen Schwanneke, Hedwig Schlichter.

MALTESE FALCON, The

1941 *(sound)*   AMERICAN

Production	Warner Brothers
Direction and Scenario .	John Huston
Photography . . .	Arthur Edeson
From a novel by . .	Dashiell Hammett

With : Humphrey Bogart, Mary Astor, Gladys George, Peter Lorre, Sydney Greenstreet, Elisha Cook Jnr., Jerome Cowan, Ward Bond, Barton MacLane.

MANON LESCAUT

1926 *(silent)*   GERMAN

Production	Ufa
Direction	Arthur Robison
Scenario	Hans Kyser, Arthur Robison
Photography . . .	Theodore Sparkuhl
Design	Paul Leni
From a novel by . .	L'Abbé Prévost

With: Lya de Putti, Vladimir Gaiderov, Lydia Potechina, Siegfried Arno, Theodor Loos, Frieda Richard.

MARRIAGE CIRCLE, The

1924 *(silent)*   AMERICAN

Production	Warner Brothers
Direction	Ernst Lubitsch
Scenario	Paul Bern
Photography . . .	Charles van Enger
From a play by . .	Lothar Schmidt

With : Monte Blue, Adolphe Menjou, Marie Prevost, Florence Vidor, Harry Myers, Creighton Hale.

MATERNELLE, La

1932 *(sound)*   FRENCH

Production . . .	Photosonor
Direction	Jean Benoit-Lévy, Marie Epstein
Photography . . .	G. Asselin
Design	Max Rossi
Music	Edouard Flament

With : Madeleine Renaud, Mady Berry, Paulette Flambert.

APPENDIX I
MEN AND JOBS
1932 *(sound)* SOVIET
Production . . . . . Soyuzkino
Direction and Scenario . Alexander Macharet
Photography . . . A. Galperin
Music . . . . . S. Gerasimov, N. Krukov,
E. Bezalin

With : V. Stanitzyn, N. Okhlopov.

METROPOLIS
1925-1926 *(silent)* GERMAN
Production . . . . Ufa
Direction . . . . Fritz Lang
Scenario . . . . Thea von Harbou
Photography . . . Karl Freund, Gunther Rittau
Design . . . . Otto Hunte, Erich Kettlehut,
Karl Vollbrecht

With: Alfred Abel, Brigitte Helm, Gustav Fröhlich, Rudolf
Klein-Rogge, Fritz Rasp, Theodor Loos, Heinrich George.

MILLION, LE
1930 *(sound)* FRENCH
Production . . . . . Film-Sonores-Tobis
Direction and Scenario . René Clair
Assistant Direction . . Georges Lacombe
Photography . . . Georges Périnal, C. Raullet
Design . . . . Lazare Meerson
Music . . . . . Armand Bernard, Phillippe
Parés, Georges Van Parys
From a play by . . . G. Berr, M. Guillemaud

With : Annabella, René Lefèbre, Louis Allibert, Vanda
Greville.

MILLIONS LIKE US
1943 *(sound)* BRITISH
Production . . . . Gainsborough
Producer . . . . Ted Black
Direction and Scenario . Frank Launder, Sidney Gilliat
Photography . . . Jack Cox, Roy Fogwell
Design . . . . John Bryan
Editing . . . . R. E. Dearing

With : Eric Portman, Lili Palmer, Patricia Roc, Gordon
Jackson, Anne Crawford, Joy Shelton.

MOERDER DIMITRI KARAMAZOV, Der

1931 *(sound)*   German

Production	Terra
Direction	Fedor Ozep
Scenario	Fedor Ozep, Victor Trivas
	Leonhard Frank
Photography . . .	Fridl Behn-Grund
Design	Heinrich Richter, Victor Trivas
Music	Dr. Karl Rathaus
From a novel by . .	Dostoevsky

With : Fritz Körtner, Anna Sten, Fritz Rasp, Bernard Minetti, Max Pohl, Hanna Waag, Fritz Alberti, W. Hollman, Liese Neumann.

MONSIEUR VERDOUX

1946-47 *(sound)*   American

Production	Charles Chaplin Film Corpn.
Direction and Scenario	Charles Chaplin
Assistant Direction .	Robert Florey, Wheeler Dryden
Photography . . .	Roland Totheroh
Design	John Beckman

With : Charles Chaplin, Martha Raye, Isobel Elsom, Marilyn Nash, Robert Lewis.

MOTHER

1926 *(silent)*   Soviet

Production	Mejrabpom-Russ
Direction	V. I. Pudovkin
Scenario	N. A. Zarkhi
Photography . . .	A. N. Golovnia
Design	S. V. Koslovski
From a novel by . .	Maxim Gorki

With : A. Chistiakov, Vera Baranovskaia, Nickolai Batalov.

MR. DEEDS GOES TO TOWN

1936 *(sound)*   American

Production	Columbia Pictures
Direction	Frank Capra
Scenario	Robert Riskin
Photography . . .	Joseph Walker
From a novel by . .	Clarence Budington Kelland

With : Gary Cooper, Jean Arthur, George Bancroft, Lionel Stander, Douglas Dumbrille, Raymond Walburn, H. B. Warner.

MURDER

1930 *(sound)* BRITISH

Production	British International Pictures
Direction	Alfred Hitchcock
Scenario	Alma Reville
Photography . . .	J. J. Cox
Design	J. F. Mead

With : Herbert Marshall, Norah Baring, Phyllis Konstam, Edward Chapman, Donald Calthrop, Miles Mander.

NANA

1926 *(silent)* FRENCH

Production	Renoir Films
Direction	Jean Renoir
Scenario	Lestringuez
Design	Claude Autant-Lara
Photography . . .	C. E. Corwin, Asselin, Raleigh, Perie
From a novel by . .	Emile Zola

With : Catherine Hessling, Valeska Gert, Werner Krauss, Jean Angelo, Pierre Philippe, Claude Moore, Jacqueline Forzane.

NAVIGATOR, THE

1924 *(silent)* AMERICAN

Production	Metro-Goldwyn
Direction	Buster Keaton, Donald Crisp
Scenario	Clyde Bruckman, Joseph A. Mitchell, Jean Havez
Photography . . .	Elgin Lessley, Bryon Houck

With : Buster Keaton, Kathryn MacGuire, Frederick Vroom, Noble Johnson.

NEW BABYLON

1929 *(silent)* SOVIET

Production	Sovkino (Leningrad Studios)
Direction and Scenario .	G. Kozintzev, L. Trauberg
Photography . . .	A. Moskvin
Design	Y. Yenei

With : E. Kuzmina, D. Gutman, P. Sololenski, A. Arnold, A. Kostrichki.

APPENDIX I

NIBELUNGEN SAGA, The (Part I: SIEGFRIED)
1923-1924 *(silent)*   GERMAN

Production	Decla-Bioskop
Direction	Fritz Lang
Scenario	Thea von Harbou
Photography . . .	Karl Hoffmann, Gunther Rittau
Design	Otto Hunte, Erich Kettlehut, Karl Vollbrecht
Music	Gottfried Huppertz

With: Gertrud Arnold, Margarete Schön, Hanna Ralph, Frieda Richard, Rudolf Klein-Rogge, Paul Richter, Theodor Loos, Bernard Goetzke, Hans von Schlettow, Georg John, Rudolf Rittner.

NINOTCHKA
1939 *(sound)*   AMERICAN

Production	Metro-Goldwyn-Mayer
Direction	Ernst Lubitsch
Scenario	Charles Brackett, Billy Wilder, Walter Reisch
Photography . . .	William Daniels
Design	Cedric Gibbons
Music	Werner R. Heymann
From a story by . .	Melchior Lengyel

With: Greta Garbo, Melvyn Douglas, Ina Claire, Sig Rumann, Felix Bressart, Alexander Granach, Bela Lugosi, Edwin Maxwell, Gregory Gaye, Rolfe Sedan.

NOTHING SACRED
1937 *(sound)*   AMERICAN

Production . . .	Selznick-International
Producer	David O. Selznick
Direction	William Wellman
Scenario	Ben Hecht
Photography . . .	W. Howard Greene
Design	Lyle Wheeler
Editing	James Newcom

With: Frederic March, Carole Lombard, Charles Winninger, Walter Connolly, Frank Fay, Sig Rumann.

161. PAISAN, directed by ROBERT ROSSELLINI. MARIA MICHI, GAR MOORE. [Italian, 1946]

162. DITTE MENNESKEBARN, directed by BJÄRNE HENNING-JENSEN. TOVE MAES. [Danish, 1946]

163. THE OVERLANDERS, directed by HARRY WATT. [British, 1946]

164. GREAT EXPECTATIONS, directed by DAVID LEAN. MARTITA HUNT. [British, 1946]

ODD MAN OUT

1947 *(sound)*   BRITISH

Production	Two Cities
Direction	Carol Reed
Scenario	R. C. Sherrif, J. L. Green
Photography . . .	Robert Krasker
Design	Roger Furse, Ralph Brinton
Music	William Alwyn
From a novel by . .	J. L. Green

With: James Mason, Kathleen Ryan, F. J. McCormick, Robert Newton, W. G. Fay, Robert Beatty, Cyril Cusack, Denis O'Dea, Fay Compton, Beryl Measor.

OF MICE AND MEN

1940 *(sound)*   AMERICAN

Production	United Artists (Hal Roach)
Direction	Lewis Milestone
Scenario	Eugene Solow
Photography . . .	Norbert Brodine
Music	Aaron Copland
From a novel by . .	John Steinbeck

With: Burgess Meredith, Lon Chaney Jnr., Betty Field, Charles Bickford, Roman Bohnen.

OLIVER TWIST

1947-48 *(sound)*   BRITISH

Production	Cineguild
Producer	Ronald Neame
Direction	David Lean
Scenario	David Lean, Stanley Haynes
Photography . . .	Guy Green
Design	John Bryan
Editor	Jack Harris
Costumes	Margaret Furse
Music	Sir Arnold Bax
From a novel by . .	Charles Dickens

With: Robert Newton, Francis L. Sullivan, Alec Guinness, Kay Walsh, John Howard Davies, Mary Clare, Henry Stephenson.

APPENDIX I

OVERLANDERS, The

1946 *(sound)*   BRITISH

Production	Ealing Studios
Producer	Michael Balcon
Direction and Scenario	Harry Watt
Photography . .	Osmond Borrowdaile
Music	John Ireland

With : Chips Rafferty, John Nugent Hayward, Daphne Campbell, Jeanne Blue.

OX-BOW INCIDENT, The (STRANGE INCIDENT)

1943 *(sound)*   AMERICAN

Production	Twentieth Century-Fox
Direction	William Wellman
Scenario	Lamar Trotti,
Photography . .	Arthur Miller
Music	Cyril J. Mockridge
From a novel by . .	Walter Van Tilburg Clark

With : Henry Fonda, Dana Andrews, Henry Morgan, Victor Kilian, Harry Davenport, Matt Briggs.

PAISAN

1946 *(sound)*   ITALIAN

Production	Organizzazione Films Internazionali
Direction	Roberto Rossellini
Scenario	Roberto Rossellini, Federico Fellini, S. Amidei, M. Pagliero
Photography . .	Otello Martelli
Music	Renzo Rossellini
Editing . . .	Eraldo da Roma

With : Carmela Sazio, Robert Van Loon, Dots Johnson, Alfonsino, Gar Moore, Maria Michi, Harriet White, Renzo Avanzo, Bill Tubbs, Dale Edmonds, Cigolani.

PANIQUE

1946 *(sound)*   FRENCH

Production	Regina
Direction	Julien Duvivier
Scenario and Dialogue	Charles Spaak
Photography . . .	Nicholas Hayer
Design	Pimenoff
Music	Jacques Ibert
From a novel by . .	Simenon

With : Viviane Romance, Michel Simon, Paul Bernard.

PASSION DE JEANNE D'ARC, La

1928 *(silent)*   FRENCH

Production	Société Générale de Films
Direction	Carl Th. Dreyer
Scenario	Carl Th. Dreyer, Joseph Delteil
Photography . . .	Rudolph Maté, Kotula
Design	Hermann Warm
Costumes	Jean and Valentine Hugo
Historical Adviser . .	Pierre Champion
Music	Léo Poufet, Victor Allix

With : Falconetti, Silvain, Maurice Schutz, Ravet, André Berley, Antonin Artaud.

PEASANTS

1935 *(sound)*   SOVIET

Production	Lenfilm Studios
Direction	Frederic Ermler
Scenario	M. Bolshintsov, V. Portnov, Frederic Ermler
Photography . . .	A. Gintsberg
Music	V. Pushkov

With : E. Younger, B. Poslavsky, A. Petrov, E. Korchagina-Alexandroskaia, Nikolai Bogolyubov.

PHANTOM CARRIAGE, The

1919 *(silent)*   SWEDISH

Production	Svensk Filmindustri
Direction and Scenario	Victor Seaström
Photography . . .	Julius Jaenzon
Design	Alexander Bako
From a novel by . .	Selma Lagerlöf

With : Victor Seaström, Astrid Holm, Tora Svennberg, Hilda Borgstrom.

POIL DE CAROTTE

1932 *(sound)* FRENCH

Production	Vandal and Delluc
Direction and Scenario .	Julien Duvivier
Photography . . .	Thirard, Monniot
Music	Alexander Tansman
From a novel by . .	Jules Renard

With : Harry Baur, Catherine Fontenoy, Robert Lynen, Simon Aubry, Maxime Fromiot, Christiane Dor, Louis Gouthier, Mme. Marthy, Colette Segal.

PRIVATE LIFE OF HENRY VIII, THE

1933 *(sound)* BRITISH

Production	London Films
Direction	Alexander Korda
Scenario	Arthur Wimperis, Lajos Biro
Photography . . .	Georges Périnal
Design	Vincent Korda
Music	Kurt Schroeder
Costumes	John Armstrong

With : Charles Laughton, Merle Oberon, Elsa Lanchester, James Mason, Robert Donat, Lady Tree, Binnie Barnes, Franklin Dyall, Wendy Barrie, Miles Mander, John Loder, Sam Livesey, Judy Kelly.

PROFESSOR MAMLOCK

1938 *(sound)* SOVIET

Production	Lenfilm
Direction	Adolf Minkin, Herbert Rappaport.
Scenario	Frederich Wolf, Adolf Minkin, Herbert Rappaport
Photography . . .	G. Filatov
Design	P. Betani
Music	Y. Kochurov, N. Timofeyev

With : S. Mezhinski, E. Nikitina, O. Zhakov, V. Chesnokov, B. Svetlov, N. Shaternikova, I. Zonne, M. Tagianossova, V. Kisselev, T. Guretskaya, V. Merkuriev, V. Taskin, Y. Maliutin, Boris Shikhting.

APPENDIX I

PUBLIC ENEMY, The

1931 *(sound)* AMERICAN

Production	Warner Brothers
Direction . . .	William Wellman
Scenario and Dialogue .	Harvey Thew
Photography . . .	Dev Jennings
Editing	Ed. McCormick
From a story by .	Kubec Glasmon, John Bright

With: James Cagney, Eddie Woods, Jean Harlow, Beryl Mercer, Donald Cook, Joan Blondell, Leslie Fenton, Rita Flynn, Louise Brooks, Mae Clark.

PYGMALION

1938 *(sound)* BRITISH

Production	Gabriel Pascal Productions
Direction . . .	Anthony Asquith, Leslie Howard
Adaptation . . .	W. P. Lipscomb, Cecil Lewis
Photography . . .	Harry Stradling
Music	Arthur Honegger
From a play by . .	George Bernard Shaw

With: Leslie Howard, Wendy Hiller, Wilfred Lawson, Marie Lohr, Jean Cadell, Scott Sunderland.

QUAI DES BRUMES, Le

1938 *(sound)* FRENCH

Production	Ciné-Alliance
Direction . . .	Marcel Carné
Scenario and Dialogue .	Jacques Prévert
Photography . . .	Schuftan
Design	A. Trauner
Music	Maurice Jaubert
From a novel by . .	Pierre MacOrlan

With: Jean Gabin, Michele Morgan, Michèl Simon, Pierre Brasseur, Delmont, Le Vigan.

QUICK MILLIONS

1931 *(sound)* AMERICAN

Production	Fox Film Corporation
Direction . . .	Rowland Brown
Scenario . . .	Courtney Tenett, R o w l a n d Brown
Photography . . .	Joseph August
Editing	Duncan Cramer

With: Spencer Tracy, Marguerite Churchill, Sally Eilers, John Wray, George Raft.

APPENDIX 1

RACKET, The

1928 *(silent)*

Production	Caddo Company (Howard Hughes)
Direction	Lewis Milestone
Assistant Direction . .	Nate Watt
Scenario	Del Andrews
Photography . . .	Tony Gaudio, Dewy Wriggley
Design	Julian Fleming
Editing	Eddie Adams

With: Thomas Meighan, Marie Prevost, Louis Wolheim, Henry Sedley, Sam de Grasse, Lee Moran, Lucien Prival, George Stone, Skeets Gallagher.

REMBRANDT

1936 *(sound)* BRITISH

Production	London Films
Direction	Alexander Korda
Scenario	Carl Zuckmayer
Photography . . .	Georges Périnal
Design	Vincent Korda

With: Charles Laughton, Elsa Lanchester, Gertrude Lawrence, John Bryning, Richard Gofe, Meinhard Maur.

ROAD TO LIFE, The

1931 *(sound)* SOVIET

Production	Mejrabpomfilm
Direction	Nikolai Ekk
Scenario	Nikolai Ekk, A. Stolper, R. Yanushkevich
Photography . . .	B. Pronin
Music	Jacob Stoliar
Design	Ivan Stepanov

With: Nikolai Batalov, V. Vesnovsky, R. Yanushkevich, M. Dzharofarov, Ivan Kyrla, A. Novikov, Mikhail Zharov, A. Scriabina.

APPENDIX I

ROBIN HOOD

1923 *(silent)* AMERICAN

Production	United Artists
Direction	Allan Dwan
Scenario	Lotta Woods
Photography . . .	Arthur Edeson
Design	Wilfred Buckland
From a story by . .	Elton Thomas

With : Douglas Fairbanks, Wallace Beery, Enid Bennett, Sam de Grasse, Paul Dickey.

SADIE THOMPSON

1928 *(silent)* AMERICAN

Production	United Artists
Direction	Raoul Walsh
Photography . . .	Oliver Marsh, George Barnes, Robert Kurrle
From a story by . .	W. Somerset Maugham

With : Gloria Swanson, Lionel Barrymore, Raoul Walsh, Blanche Fridirici, Charles Lane, Florence Midgley, James A. Marcus.

SAFETY LAST

1923 *(silent)* AMERICAN

Production	Pathé (Hal Roach)
Direction	Fred Newmeyer, Sam Taylor
Scenario	Hal Roach, Sam Taylor, Tim Whelan
Photography . . .	Walter Lundin

With : Harold Lloyd, Mildred Davis, Noah Young, Bill Strother, Westcott B. Clarke.

SALOME

1922 *(silent)* AMERICAN

Production	Alla Nazimova
Direction	Charles Bryant
Photography . . .	Charles Van Enger
Design and Costumes .	Natacha Rambova
Based on Drawings by .	Aubrey Beardsley

With : Alla Nazimova, Mitchell Lewis, Nigel De Brulier, Rose Dione, Earl Schenck, Arthur Jasmina, Frederick Peters, Luis Dumar.

SCARFACE
1932 *(sound)* AMERICAN

Production . . .	Howard Hughes
Direction . . .	Howard Hawks
Scenario . . .	Seton I. Miller, John Lee Mahin, W. R. Burnett
Screenplay . .	Ben Hecht
Photography . .	Lee Garmes, L. W. O'Connell
From a novel by .	Armitage Trail

With : Paul Muni, George Raft, Ann Dvorak, Karen Morley, Osgood Perkins, Boris Karloff, C. Henry Gordon, Purnell Pratt, Vince Barnett, Ines Palange, Harry J. Vejar, Edwin Maxwell, Tully Marshall, Henry Armetta, Bert Starkey.

SHE DONE HIM WRONG
1933 *(sound)* AMERICAN

Production . . .	Paramount
Direction . . .	Lowell Sherman
Scenario . .	Harvey Thew, John Bright
Photography . .	Charles Lang
Music and Lyrics .	Ralph Rainger

With : Mae West, Cary Grant, Owen Moore, Gilbert Roland, Noah Beery, David Landau, Rafaela Ottiano.

SHORS
1939 *(sound)* SOVIET

Production . . .	Ukrainfilm
Direction and Scenario	Alexander Dovjenko
Photography . .	Y. Ekelchik
Design . . .	Maurice Umansky
Music . . .	D. Kabalevskv

With : E. Samoilov, I. Skuratov, L. Lyaschenko, Y. Titov, V. Dukler, S. Komarov, G. Polezhayev.

SIR ARNE'S TREASURE
1919 *(silent)* SWEDISH

Production . . .	Svenska-Biograf
Direction . . .	Mauritz Stiller
Scenario . . .	Mauritz Stiller, Gustav Molander
Photography . .	J. Julius
Design . . .	Harry Dahlstrom, Alexander Bako
From a novel by .	Selma Lagerlöf

With : Eric Stocklassa, Bror Berger, Richard Lund, Axel Nilsson, Hjalmer Selander, Concordia Selander, Mary Johnson, Gustaf Aronsson.

SMALL TOWN IDOL, A

1921 *(silent)* AMERICAN

Direction	Erle Kenton
Scenario	Mack Sennett

With: Ben Turpin, Bert Roach, Phyllis Haver, Charles Murray, Marie Prevost, Dot Farley, Eddie Gribbon, Kalla Pascha, Billy Bevan.

SOUS LES TOITS DE PARIS

1929-1930 *(sound)* FRENCH

Production . . .	Films-Sonores-Tobis
Direction and Scenario .	René Clair
Photography . . .	Georges Périnal, C. Raullet
Design	Lazare Meerson
Music	Armand Bernard
Songs	R. Moretti, R. Razelles

With: Pola Illéry, Albert Préjean, Edmond Greville.

SOUTHERNER, THE

1945 *(sound)* AMERICAN

Production . . .	Loew-Hakim
Direction	Jean Renoir
Scenario	Dudley Nichols
Photography . . .	Lucien Andriot
Music	Warner Janssen
Editing	Gregg Tallas

With: Zachary Scott, Betty Field, Beulah Bondi, Bunny Sunshine, J. Carrol Naish, Jay Gilpin, Percy Kilbride.

SPY, THE

1928 *(silent)* GERMAN

Production	Ufa
Direction	Fritz Lang
Scenario	Thea von Harbou
Photography . . .	Fritz Arno Wagner
Design	Otto Hunte, Karl Vollbrecht

With: Gerda Maurus, Rudolf Klein-Rogge, Willy Fritsch, Lupu Pick, Lien Deyers, Fritz Rasp, Craighall Sherry, Hertha von Walther.

STAR IS BORN, A

1937 *(sound)* AMERICAN

Production	. . .	Selznick International
Producer	. . .	David O. Selznick
Direction	. . .	William Wellman
Scenario	. . .	Dorothy Parker, Alan Campbell, Robert Carson
Photography	. .	W. Howard Greene
Music .	. . .	Max Steiner

With : Janet Gaynor, Frederic March, Adolphe Menjou, May Robson, Andy Devine.

STARK LOVE

1926-1927 *(silent)* AMERICAN

Production .	. .	Famous-Players-Lasky
Direction, Scenario and Photography	. .	Karl Brown

With : Helen Mundy, Forrest James, Silas Miracle.

STARS LOOK DOWN, THE

1939 *(sound)* BRITISH

Production	. .	Grafton Films
Direction	. . .	Carol Reed
Scenario	. . .	J. B. Williams
Photography	. .	Mutz Greenbaum
Design	. . .	James Carter
Editing	. . .	Reginald Beck
From a novel by .	. .	A. J. Cronin

With : Michael Redgrave, Margaret Lockwood, Emlyn Williams, Nancy Price, Edward Rigby, Allan Jeayes, Cecil Parker.

STATE FAIR

1932 *(sound)* AMERICAN

Production .	. .	Fox Film Corporation
Direction	. .	Henry King
Scenario	. . .	Sonya Levien, Paul Green
Photography	. .	Hal Mohr
Design	. . .	Duncan Cramer
From a story by	. .	Phil Strong

With : Will Rogers, Janet Gaynor, Lew Ayres, Sally Eilers, Norman Foster, Louise Dresser, Frank Craven.

STONE RIDER, The

1923 *(silent)*   GERMAN

Production   .   .   .   .   Decla-Bioskop
Direction   .   .   .   .   Fritz Wendhausen
Scenario   .   .   .   .   Thea von Harbou
Photography   .   .   .   Karl Hoffman
Design   .   .   .   .   Heinrich Heuser

With: Rudolf Klein-Rogge, Georg John, Lucie Mannheim,
Fritz Kampers, Otto Framer, Gustav von Wangenheim, Paul
Biensfeld.

STORM OVER ASIA

1928 *(silent)*   SOVIET

Production   .   .   .   .   Mejrabpom-Russ
Direction   .   .   .   .   V. I. Pudovkin
Assistant Direction   .   .   A. Ledashchov, L. Bronstein
Scenario   .   .   .   .   O. Brik
Photography   .   .   .   A. N. Golovnia
Design   .   .   .   .   S. V. Koslovski, Aronson
From a story by   .   .   Novokshenov

With: V. Inkishinov, A. Chistiakov, L. Dedinstev, Anna
Sujakevitch, L. Billinskaia.

STORY OF G.I. JOE, The

1945 *(sound)*   AMERICAN

Production   .   .   .   .   United Artists (Lester Cowan)
Direction   .   .   .   .   William Wellman
Scenario   .   .   .   .   Leopold Atlas, Guy Endore,
                                      Philip Stevenson
Photography   .   .   .   Russell Metty
Music .   .   .   .   .   Ann Ronell, Louis Applebaum,
                                      Louis Forbes
Based on news-articles by .   Ernie Pyle

With: Burgess Meredith, Robert Mitchum, Freddie Steele,
Wally Cassell, Jimmy Lloyd, Jack Reilly, Bill Murphy.

APPENDIX I

STORY OF LOUIS PASTEUR, The

1936 (sound)   AMERICAN

Production	Warner Brothers
Direction	William Dieterle
Scenario	Sheridan Gibney, Pierre Collings
Photography . . .	Tony Gaudio
Music	Eric Wolfgang von Korngold

With: Paul Muni, Josephine Hutchinson, Donald Woods, Anita Louise, Fritz Leiber, Henry O'Neill, Dickie Moore, Walter Kingsford, Iphigenie Castiglioni, Herbert Corthell.

STREET, The

1923 (silent)   GERMAN

Production	Stern Film
Direction	Karl Grune
Photography . . .	Karl Hasselmann
Design	Karl George, Ludwig Meidner

With: Eugen Klöpfer, Aud Edege Nissen, Leonard Haskel, Lucie Höflich.

STUDENT OF PRAGUE, The

1926 (silent)   GERMAN

Production	Sokal Film
Direction and Scenario	Henrik Galeen
Photography . . .	Gunther Krampf, Erich Nitzschmann
Design	Hermann Warm
From a novel by . .	H. H. Ewers

With: Conrad Veidt, Werner Krauss, Agnes Esterhazy, Elizza La Porte, Ferdinand von Alten.

SUMURUN

1920 (silent)   GERMAN

Production	Union-Ufa
Direction	Ernst Lubitsch
Scenario	Hans Kraly
Photography . . .	Theodore Sparkuhl, Kurt Waschnek
Design	Kurt Richter, Ernö Metzner
Costumes	Ali Hubert

With: Pola Negri, Jenny Hasselquist, Aud Egede Nissen, Harry Liedtke, Paul Wegener, Ernst Lubitsch, Karl Clewing.

APPENDIX I

SUNRISE

1921 *(silent)* AMERICAN

1927 (silent) AMERICAN

Production	Fox Film Corporation
Direction	F. W. Murnau
Scenario	Carl Mayer
Photography . . .	Charles Roscher, Karl Struss
Design	Rochus Gliese
From a story by . .	Sudermann

With : Janet Gaynor, Margaret Livingstone, George O'Brien.

THERESE RAQUIN

1927 (silent) FRENCH

Production	Défu Film
Direction	Jacques Feyder .
Scenario	F. Carlsen, Willi Haas
Design	André Andreiev
From a novel by . .	Emile Zola

With : Gina Manés, Wolgang Zeller, Hans von Schlettow, Jeanne Marie-Laurent, Paul Henkels.

THEY WON'T FORGET

1937 (sound) AMERICAN

Production	Warner Brothers
Direction	Mervyn LeRoy
Scenario	Robert Rossen, Abem Kandel
Photography . . .	Arthur Edeson
Design	Robert Haas
Music	Adolph Deutsch
From a novel by . .	Ward Greene

With : Claude Rains, Edward Norris, Otto Kruger, Lana Turner, Elisha Cook, Jnr.

TOL'ABLE DAVID

1921 (silent) AMERICAN

Production	First-National
Direction	Henry King
Scenario	Edmund Goulding
Photography . . .	Henry Cronjager
From a novel by . .	Joseph Hergesheimer

With : Richard Barthelmess, Ernest Torrence.

TOM, DICK AND HARRY
1940 *(sound)*   AMERICAN

Production . . .	RKO-Radio Pictures
Producer	Robert Sisk
Direction	Garson Kanin
Scenario and Story .	Paul Jarrico
Photography . . .	Merritt Gerstad
Design	Van Nest Polglase, Mark-Lee Kirk
Music	Roy Webb
Editing	John Sturges

With: Ginger Rogers, George Murphy, Alan Marshall, Burgess Meredith.

TONI
1935 *(sound)*   FRENCH

Production . . .	Films Marcel Pagnol
Direction	Jean Renoir
Scenario	Jean Renoir, Carl Einstein
Photography . . .	Claude Renoir
Design	Marius Brouquier
Music	Bozzi

With : Célia Montalvan, Blavette, Edouard Delmont, Dalbau, Andrex, Kovatchevitch.

TREASURE OF THE SIERRA MADRE, THE
1947 *(sound)*   AMERICAN

Production . . .	Warner Brothers
Producer	Henry Blanke
Direction and Scenario .	John Huston
Photography . . .	Ted McCord
Music	Max Steiner
From a novel by . .	B. Traven

With : Humphrey Bogart, Walter Huston, Tim Holt, Bruce Bennett, Barton McLane, Alfonso Bedoya.

UNDERWORLD
1927 *(silent)*   AMERICAN

Production	Paramount
Direction	Josef von Sternberg
Scenario	Robert N. Lee, Jules Furthman
Photography . . .	Bert Glennon
From a story by . . .	Ben Hecht

With : George Bancroft, Evelyn Brent, Clive Brook, Fred Kohler, Helen Lynch, Larry Semon, Jerry Mandy.

APPENDIX I

UNIVERSITY OF LIFE, The

1940 (*sound*)   SOVIET

Production . . .	Soyuzdetfilm, Moscow
Direction	Mark Donskoi
Co-direction . . .	R. Perelshtein
Scenario	I. Gruzdev
Music	Lev Schwartz
Based on	Maxim Gorki's autobiography

With : N. Valbert, S. Kayukov, N. Doroskin, N. Plotnikov, D. Segal, I. Fyedotova, L. Sverdlin, V. Maruta, Pavlik Dojdev.

VANINA

1922 (*silent*)   GERMAN

Production	Union-Ufa
Direction	Arthur von Gerlach
Scenario	Carl Mayer
Photography . . .	Frederik Fuglsang
Design	Walther Reimann
From a story by . .	Stendhal

With: Paul Hartmann, Paul Wegener, Asta Nielsen.

VAUDEVILLE (VARIETY)

1925 (*silent*)   GERMAN

Production	Ufa
Supervision . . .	Erich Pommer
Direction and Scenario	E. A. Dupont
Photography . . .	Karl Freund
Design	Oscar Werndorff
From a novel by . .	Felix Holländer

With : Emil Jannings, Lya de Putti, Warwick Ward, Georg John, Mady Delschaft.

VIRGINIAN, The

1929 (*sound*)   AMERICAN

Production	Paramount
Direction	Victor Fleming
Scenario	Howard Estabrook
Photography . . .	J. Roy Hunt
From a novel by . .	Owen Wister

With : Gary Cooper, Walter Huston, Richard Arlen, Mary Brian, Chester Conklin, Eugene Pallette.

WARNING SHADOWS

1922 *(silent)*   GERMAN

Production	Defu
Direction	Arthur Robison
Scenario	Albin Grau
Photography . . .	Fritz Arno Wagner
Design	Albin Grau

With : Fritz Körtner, Ruth Weyher, Gustav von Wangenheim, Alexander Granach, Fritz Rasp, Ferdinand von Alten, Max Gülstorff.

WAXWORKS

1924 *(silent)*   GERMAN

Production	Neptun-Film
Direction	Paul Leni
Scenario	Henrik Galeen
Photography . . .	Halmar Lerski
Design	Paul Leni

With : William Dieterle, John Gottowt, Olga Belejeff, Emil Jannings, Conrad Veidt, Werner Krauss.

WAY AHEAD, THE

1943 *(sound)*   BRITISH

Production	Two Cities
Direction	Carol Reed
Scenario	Eric Ambler, Peter Ustinov
Photography . . .	Guy Green
Design	David Rawnsley
Music	William Alwyn

With : David Niven, Stanley Holloway, Raymond Huntley, Bill Hartnell.

WAY DOWN EAST

1920 *(silent)*   AMERICAN

Production	D. W. Griffith Productions
Direction	D. W. Griffith
Photography . . .	Hendrik Sartov, G. W. Bitzer
Editing	James E. Smith
From a Play by . . .	Lottie Blair Parker

With : Lillian Gish, Richard Barthelmess.

165. THE BEST YEARS OF OUR LIVES, directed by WILLIAM WYLER. DANA ANDREWS. [American, 1946]

166. MONSIEUR VERDOUX, directed by CHARLES CHAPLIN. [American, 1946–47]

167. THE WORLD IS RICH, directed by PAUL ROTHA. [British, 1946–47]

168. LOUISIANA STORY, directed by ROBERT J. FLAHERTY. [American, 1946–48]

APPENDIX I

WE FROM KRONSTADT

1936 *(sound)*   SOVIET

Production	Mosfilm Studio (Moscow)
Producer . . .	I. Weissfeldt
Direction . . .	Efim Dzigan
Co-Direction . . .	G. Berezko
Scenario . . .	Vzevolod Vishnevsky
Photography . . .	N. Naumov-Straj
Design . . .	V. Egorov
Music	N. Krukov

With : V. Zaichikov, G. Bushuev, N. Ivakin, O. Jakov, Misha Gurienko, P. Sobolevsky.

WESTFRONT 1918

1930 *(sound)*   GERMAN

Production	Nerofilm
Direction . . .	G. W. Pabst
Scenario . . .	Vajda
Photography . .	Fritz Arno Wagner, Charles Métain
Design . . .	Ernö Metzner
From a novel by . .	Ernst Johannsen

With : Fritz Kampers, Gustav Diessl, Claus Clausen, H. Mobis.

WIND, THE

1928 *(silent)*   AMERICAN

Production	Metro-Goldwyn-Mayer
Direction . . .	Victor Seaström
Scenario . . .	Frances Marion
Photography . .	John Arnold
Design . . .	Cedric Gibbons, Edward Withers
From a novel by . .	Dorothy Scarborough

With : Lillian Gish, Lars Hanson, Montagu Love, Dorothy Cumming, William Orlamond.

WOMAN OF PARIS, A

1923 *(silent)*   AMERICAN

Production	United Artists
Direction and Scenario	Charles Chaplin
Assistant Direction .	Monta Bell, Harry D'Abbadie d'Arrast, Edward Sutherland
Photography . .	Jack Wilson, Roy Totheroh
Design . . .	Daniel Hall

With : Edna Purviance, Adolphe Menjou.

ZERO DE CONDUITE

1933 (*sound*)   FRENCH

Production	Arquis Film
Direction and Scenario .	Jean Vigo
Photography . . .	Boris Kaufmann
Assistants . . .	Albert Rière, Henri Storck, Pierre Merle
Music	Maurice Jaubert
Lyrics	Charles Goldblatt

With : Jean Dasté, Robert Le Flon, Du Veron, Delphin, Mme. Emile, Larive.

II. DOCUMENTARY FILMS

BATAILLE DU RAIL, LA

1944-1945 (*sound*)   FRENCH

Production	Coopérative Générale du Cinéma Français
Direction and Scenario .	René Clément
Dialogue	Colette Audry
Photography . . .	Alekan
Music	Yves Baudrier

BATTLE OF RUSSIA, THE

1943 (*sound*)   AMERICAN

Production	Orientation Branch of the U.S. War Department
Direction	Lt.-Col. Anatole Litvak
Scenario	Lt.-Col. Anatole Litvak, Capt. Anthony Veiller, Cpl. Robert Heller
Narration	Walter Huston, Capt. Anthony Veiller
Music	Dmitri Tiomkin
Editing	Major William Hornbeck

(One of the *Why We Fight* series.)

B.B.C.: THE VOICE OF BRITAIN

1934-1935 *(sound)*   BRITISH

Production	G.P.O. Film Unit for the British Broadcasting Corporation
Producers . . .	John Grierson, Cavalcanti
Direction and Scenario .	Stuart Legg
Photography . . .	George Noble, J. D. Davidson, W. Shenton

BERLIN
(SYMPHONY OF A CITY)

1927 *(silent)*   GERMAN

Production	Fox-Europa
Supervision . . .	Karl Freund
Direction	Walther Ruttmann
Source	Carl Mayer
Photography . . .	Reimar Kuntze, Robert Baberski, Laszlo Schäffer
Musical Score . . .	Edmund Meisel

BORINAGE, THE

1933 *(sound)*   BELGIAN

Production	E.P.I.
Direction, Scenario and Photography . . .	Joris Ivens, Henri Storck
Music	Hans Hauska
Editing	Helen Van Dongen

BURMA VICTORY

1945 *(sound)*   BRITISH

Production	Army Film Unit
Producer	Col. David Macdonald
Direction and Supervising Editor . . .	Capt. Roy Boulting
Commentary . . .	Frank Harvey
Photography . . .	Battle Cameramen of Army Film Unit attached to the 14th Army
Music	Alan Rawsthorne
Editing	Sgt. Richard Best, Sgt. Frank Clarke

CHANG
1926-1927 *(silent)* AMERICAN

Production	Paramount
Direction and Photography	Merian C. Cooper, Ernest B. Schoedsack

CHILDREN ON TRIAL
1946 *(sound)* BRITISH

Production	Crown Film Unit
Producer	Basil Wright
Director	Jack Lee
Scenario	Jack Lee, Norah Dawson
Photography . . .	H. E. Fowle
Design	Edward Carrick
Editing	Alan Osbiston, Humphrey Swingler
Music	Clifton Parker

CITY, THE
1939 *(sound)* AMERICAN

Production	American Documentary Films Inc.
Direction and Photography	Ralph Steiner, Willard Van Dyke
Outline Scenario . .	Pare Lorentz
Music	Aaron Copland
Editing	Theodor Lawrence
Based on	Lewis Mumford's *The Culture of Cities*

CLOSE QUARTERS
1943 *(sound)* BRITISH

Production	Crown Film Unit
Producer	Ian Dalrymple
Direction and Scenario .	Jack Lee
Photography . . .	Jonah Jones
Design	Edward Carrick
Editing	Sidney Stone, Russell Lloyd
Music . , , .	Gordon Jacob

COASTAL COMMAND

1942 *(sound)*   BRITISH

Production	Crown Film Unit
Producer	Ian Dalrymple
Direction and Scenario .	J. B. Holmes
Second Unit Directors .	Ralph Elton, Jack Lee, R. Q. McNaughton
Photography . . .	Jonah Jones, F. Gamage
Design	Edward Carrick
Editing	Michael Gordon
Music	Vaughan Williams

CRISIS

1939 *(sound)*   AMERICAN

Production	Arthur L. Mayer
Direction	Herbert Kline, Hans Burger, Alexander Hackenschmied
Photography . . .	Alexander Hackenschmied
Commentary . . .	Vincent Sheean
Spoken by	Leif Erickson
Music	H. W. Susskind, Jaroslav Harvan

DESERT VICTORY

1943 *(sound)*   BRITISH

Production	Army Film and Photographic Unit and the Royal Air Force Film Production Unit
Producer	Major David MacDonald
Direction and Supervising Editor	Capt. Roy Boulting
Assistant Direction . .	Lt. Patrick M. Jenkins
Photography . . .	Battle cameramen of the Army Film Unit attached to the 8th Army
Music	William Alwyn
Commentary . . .	J. L. Hodson
Editors	Sgt. Richard Best, Sgt. Frank Clarke

677

DIVIDE AND CONQUER

1943 *(sound)*   AMERICAN

Production .	.	.	. Orientation Branch of the U.S. War Department
Direction .	.	.	. Lt.-Col. Frank Capra, Major Anatole Litvak
Scenario .	.	.	. Capt. Anthony Veiller, Cpl. Robert Heller
Narration .	.	.	. Walter Huston, Capt. Anthony Veiller
Music .	.	.	. Dmitri Tiomkin
Editing .	.	.	. Capt. William Hornbeck

(One of the *Why We Fight* series.)

DRIFTERS

1929 *(silent)*   BRITISH

Production .	.	.	. Empire Marketing Board
Direction, Scenario and			
Editing .	.	.	. John Grierson
Photography .	.	. Basil Emmott

FARREBIQUE

1945-1946 *(sound)*   FRENCH

Production .	.	.	. Ecran Francais and Film Etienne Lallier
Direction, Dialogue and			
Scenario .	.	.	. Georges Rouquier
Photography .	.	. A. Dantan
Music .	.	.	. Sauguet
From a story by	.	. Claude Blanchard

FIGHT FOR LIFE, The

1939 *(sound)*   AMERICAN

Production .	.	.
Direction and Scenario	.	Pare Lorentz
Photography .	.	Floyd Crosby
Music .	.	. Louis Gruenberg
Based on a book by .	.	Paul de Kruif

FIGHTING LADY, The
1944 *(sound)* AMERICAN

Production	U.S. Navy
Supervision and Editing .	Louis de Rochement
Photography . . .	U.S. Navy cameramen

FINIS TERRAE
1928 *(silent)* FRENCH

Production	Société Générale de Films
Direction and Scenario .	Jean Epstein
Photography . . .	J. Barthe

FIRES WERE STARTED
1943 *(sound)* BRITISH

Production	Crown Film Unit
Producer	Ian Dalrymple
Direction and Scenario .	Humphrey Jennings
Photography . . .	Pennington Richards
Design	Edward Carrick
Music	William Alwyn
Editing	Stewart McAllister

FORGOTTEN VILLAGE
1941 *(sound)* AMERICAN

Production and Direction .	Herbert Kline
Scenario . . .	John Steinbeck
Photography . . .	Alexander Hackenschmied
Music	Hanns Eisler
Narration . . .	Burgess Meredith

FOUR HUNDRED MILLION, The
1938-1939 *(sound)* AMERICAN

Production	Contemporary Historians, Inc.
Direction and Scenario .	Joris Ivens
Photography . . .	John Ferno
Music	Hanns Eisler
Editing	Helen Van Dongen
Commentary . . .	Dudley Nichols

GENERAL LINE, The (THE OLD AND THE NEW)
1926-1929 *(silent)*   SOVIET

Production . . .	Sovkino
Direction and Scenario .	S. M. Eisenstein, G. Alexandrov
Assistant Direction .	M. Shtraukh, M. Gomorov
Photography . .	Edouard Tissé
Design . .	A. Burov, V. Kovrigin

With : Marfa Lapkina.

GRASS
1924-1925 *(silent)*   AMERICAN

Production . . .	Famous-Players-Lasky
Direction, Scenario and Photography . .	Meriam C. Cooper, Ernest B. Schoedsack

HARVEST SHALL COME, The
1941-1942 *(sound)*   BRITISH

Production . . .	Realist Film Unit
Producer . . .	Basil Wright
Direction . . .	Max Anderson
Assistant Direction .	Bert Pearl
Scenario and Dialogue .	H. W. Freeman
Photography . .	A. E. Jeakins
Music	William Alwyn
Commentators . .	Edmund Willard, Bruce Belfrage

With : John Slater, Eileen Beldon, Richard George, Victor Woolf, Ernest Borrow.

JOURNEY TOGETHER
1945 *(sound)*   BRITISH

Production . . .	R.A.F. Film Unit
Direction . . .	Fl.-Lt. John Boulting
Scenario . . .	Fl.-Sgt. Terence Rattigan
Photography . .	Fl.-Sgt. Harry Waxman
Music	Gordon Jacob
Editing . . .	Reginald Beck, Sgt. Cliff Boote

LAND, THE

1941 *(sound)*   AMERICAN

Production . . . . U.S. Dept of Agriculture
Direction and Scenario . Robert J. Flaherty
Music . . . . . Richard Arnell
Editing . . . . Helen Van Dongen

LISTEN TO BRITAIN

1942 *(sound)*   BRITISH

Production . . . . Crown Film Unit
Producer . . . . Ian Dalrymple
Scenario, Direction and   Humphrey Jennings, Stewart
Editing . . . . McAllister
Photography . . . H. E. Fowle

LOUISIANA STORY

1946-48 *(sound)*   AMERICAN

Production . . . Robert J. Flaherty Productions Inc.
Direction . . . Robert J. Flaherty
Scenario . . . . Robert J. Flaherty, Frances Flaherty
Photography . . . Richard Leacock
Music . . . . Virgil Thomson
Editing . . . . Helen van Dongen

MAN OF ARAN

1933-1934 *(sound)*   BRITISH

Production . . . . Gaumont-British
Direction, Scenario and
Photography . . . Robert J. Flaherty
Assistant . . . . John Taylor
Editing . . . . John Goldman
Music . . . . . John Greenwood

MAN WITH THE MOVIE CAMERA, THE

1928-1929 *(silent)*   SOVIET

Production . . . . Vufku (Ukraine)
Direction . . . . Dziga-Vertov
Photography . . . M. Kauffmann
Assistant Editing . . E. Svilova

APPENDIX I

MERCHANT SEAMEN

1941 *(sound)* BRITISH

Production	Crown Film Unit
Producer	Cavalcanti
Direction	J. B. Holmes
Assistant Direction . .	Ralph Elton
Photography . . .	H. E. Fowle
Design	Edward Carrick
Music	Constant Lambert
Editing	R. Q. McNaughton

MOANA

1926 *(silent)* AMERICAN

Production	Famous-Players-Lasky
Direction, Scenario and	
Photography . . .	Robert J. Flaherty

NANOOK OF THE NORTH

1920 *(silent)* AMERICAN

Production	Révillon Frères
Direction, Scenario and	
Photography . . .	Robert J. Flaherty

NATIVE LAND

1942 *(sound)* AMERICAN

Production	Frontier Films
Direction and Scenario .	Leo Hurwitz, Paul Strand
Photography . . .	Paul Strand
Commentary . . .	David Wolff
Music	Marc Blitzstein

With: Paul Robeson, Fred Johnson, Mary George, Housely Stevens, Louis Grant, James Hanney, Howard da Silva, Tom Connors.

NAZIS STRIKE, THE

1942 *(sound)* AMERICAN

Production	Orientation Branch of the U.S. War Department
Direction	Lt.-Col. Frank Capra, Major Anatole Litvak

Scenario	. . .	.	Major Eric Knight, Capt. Anthony Veiller
Narration	. . .	.	Walter Huston, Capt Anthony Veiller
Music	. . .	.	Dmitri Tiomkin
Editing	. . .	.	Capt. William Hornbeck

(One of the *Why We Fight* series.)

NEW EARTH

1931-34 (*sound*)   DUTCH

Production	. . .	.	Capi
Direction	. . .	.	Joris Ivens
Photography	. .	.	Joris Ivens, John Ferno, Piet Huisken, Helen Van Dongen
Music	. . .	.	Hanns Eisler
Editing	. . .	.	Helen Van Dongen

NEXT OF KIN

1942 (*sound*)   BRITISH

Production	. . .	.	Ealing Studios for War Office
Direction	. . .	.	Thorold Dickinson
Scenario	. . .	.	Thorold Dickinson, Basil Bartlett, Angus MacPhail, John Dighton
Photography	. .	.	Ernest Palmer
Music	. . .	.	William Walton

NIGHT MAIL

1936 (*sound*)   BRITISH

Production	. .	.	G.P.O. Film Unit
Producer	. . .	.	John Grierson
Direction and Scenario		.	Basil Wright, Harry Watt
Photography	. .	.	H. E. Fowle, Jonah Jones
Music	. . .	.	Benjamin Britten
Verse	. . .	.	W. H. Auden
Editing	. . .	.	R. Q. MacNaughton

NINE MEN

1943 (*sound*)   BRITISH

Production	. .	.	Ealing Studios
Producer	. . .	.	Michael Balcon
Direction and Scenario		.	Harry Watt
Photography	. .	.	Roy Kellino
Music	. . .	.	John Greenwood

NORTH SEA

1938 *(sound)* BRITISH

Production	G.P.O. Film Unit
Producer	Cavalcanti
Direction and Scenario .	Harry Watt
Photography . . .	H. E. Fowle, Jonah Jones
Design	Edward Carrick
Music	Ernst Meyer
Editing	R. Q. McNaughton

OPEN CITY

1945 *(sound)* ITALIAN

Production	Minerva Film by Excelsa
Direction	Roberto Rossellini
Scenario and Dialogue .	S. Amidei, F. Fellini
Photography . . .	Ubaido Arata
Music	Renzo Rossellini

With : Aldo Fabrizi, Anna Magnani, Marcello Pagliero, Vito Annicchiarico, Nando Bruno, Harry Feist, Giovanna Galletti, Maria Michi, C. Sindici, Van Hulzen.

PRELUDE TO WAR

1942 *(sound)* AMERICAN

Production	Orientation Branch of the U.S. War Department
Direction	Major Frank Capra
Scenario	Major Eric Knight, Capt. Anthony Veiller
Narration	Walter Huston
Music	Dimitri Tiomkin
Editing	Capt. William Hornbeck

(One of the *Why We Fight* series.)

RIEN QUE LES HEURES

1926-1927 *(silent)* FRENCH

Production . . .	Néofilm
Direction	Cavalcanti
Assistant Direction .	André Cerf
Photography . . .	James E. Rogers
Design	M. Mirovitch
Musical Accomp. . .	Yves de la Casinière

With : Philippe Hériat, Nina Chouvalowa, Clifford Maclaglen.

APPENDIX I
RIVER, The
1937 *(sound)*   AMERICAN

Production	Resettlement Administration, U.S. Government
Direction and Scenario	Pare Lorentz
Photography . . .	Willard van Dyke, Stacy Woodard, Floyd Crosbie
Music	Virgil Thomson
Narration	Thomas Chalmers

SIEGE OF LENINGRAD, The
1942 *(sound)*   SOVIET

Produced	Lenfilm Newsreel Studios
Photographed by .	22 Soviet cameramen

SONG OF CEYLON, The
1934-1935 *(sound)*   BRITISH

Production	Ceylon Tea Propaganda Board
Producer	John Grierson
Direction, Scenario and Photography . . .	Basil Wright
Assistant	John Taylor
Music	Walter Leigh

SPANISH EARTH
1937 *(sound)*   AMERICAN

Production	Contemporary Historians, Inc.
Direction	Joris Ivens
Commentary and Narration	Ernest Hemingway
Photography . . .	John Ferno
Music	Marc Blitzstein
Editing	Helen Van Dongen

STALINGRAD
1943 *(sound)*   SOVIET

Production	Central Newsreel Studios
Photography . . .	Soviet cameramen on the Don and Stalingrad Fronts
Music	V. Smirnov
Editing	Leonid Varlamov

TARGET FOR TONIGHT

1941 *(sound)* BRITISH

Production	Crown Film Unit
Producer	Ian Dalrymple
Direction and Scenario .	Harry Watt
Photography . . .	Jonah Jones, Edward Catford
Design	Edward Carrick
Music	Leighton Lucas
Editing	Stewart McAllister

TEN DAYS THAT SHOOK THE WORLD
(OCTOBER)

1927-1928 *(silent)* SOVIET

Production	Sovkino
Direction and Scenario .	S. M. Eisenstein, G. V. Alexandrov
Assistant Direction .	M. Shtraukh, M. Gomorov, Ilya Trauberg
Photography . . .	Edouard Tissé
Design	Kovrigin
Musical Score . . .	Edmund Meisel

TRIUMPH OF THE WILL, THE

1936 *(sound)* GERMAN

Production	N.S.D.A.P.
Direction	Leni Riefenstahl
Direction of Photography .	Sepp Allgeier

TRUE GLORY, THE

1945 *(sound)* ANGLO-AMERICAN

Production	Ministry of Information and U.S. Office of War Information
Direction	Carol Reed, Capt. Garson Kanin
Scenario	Major Eric Maschwitz, Arthur MacRae, Flt/O. Jenny Nicholson, Gerald Kersh, Sgt. Guy Trosper
Research	Capt. Peter Cusick
Photography . . .	Army Film Unit and the American Army Pictorial Service
Music	William Alwyn
Editing Supervision . .	Lt. Robert Verrell

Editing	Sgt. Leiberwitz, Sgt. Bob Farrell, Sgt. Jerry Cowen, Sgt. Bob Carrick, Sgt. Bob Clarke
Administration . . .	Major Kentor
Production Manager . .	Lt. Patrick Jenkins

TURKSIB

1928 *(silent)* SOVIET

Production	Vostok Film
Direction and Scenario .	Victor Turin
Photography . . .	E. Slavinski, B. Srancisson

VERDUN

1926-1927 *(silent)* FRENCH

Direction	Léon Poirier
Assistant Direction . .	Thommy Bourdelle
Photography . . .	Robert Batton, Georges Million

With : Jeanne Marie-Laurent, Pierre Nay, Jean Dehelly, Antonin Artaud, Alfred Goddard, Albert Préjean, André Nox, Thommy Bourdelle, Hans Brausewetter, Maurice Schutz, José Davert, Suzanne Bianchetti, David Mendaille.

WESTERN APPROACHES

1944 *(sound)* BRITISH

Production	Crown Film Unit
Producer	Ian Dalrymple
Direction	Pat Jackson
Scenario	Pat Jackson, Gerry Bryant
Photography . . .	Jack Cardiff
Design	Edward Carrick
Music	Clifton Parker

III. TRICK, CARTOON, PUPPET AND OTHER KINDS OF SPECIALISED AND EXPERIMENTAL FILMS

A QUOI REVENT LES JEUNES FILMS

1924-1925 *(silent)* FRENCH

Production	Comte Etienne de Beaumont
Direction	Henri Chomette
Cinéportraits . . .	Man Ray
Orchestration . . .	Roger Désormières

With : Comtesse de Noailles, Princesse Bibesco, Mrs. Fellows, Lady Abdy.

CHIEN ANDALOU, Un

1929 *(silent)*   FRENCH
Production and Direction   .   Luis Bunuel
Scenario   .   .   .   .   Luis Bunuel, Salvador Dali

With : Pierre Batcheff, Simone Mareuil.

COLOURBOX

1935 *(sound)*   BRITISH
Production .   .   .   .   G.P.O. Film Unit
Devised and Made By   .   Len Lye

COQUILLE ET LE CLERGYMAN, La

1928 *(silent)*   FRENCH
Direction   .   .   .   .   Germaine Dulac
Scenario   .   .   .   .   Antonin Artaud
Photography   .   .   .   Paul Guichard

ENTR'ACTE

1924 *(silent)*   FRENCH
Production .   .   .   .   Ballets Suédoise de Rolf de Maré
Direction   .   .   .   .   René Clair
Assistant Direction   .   Caillard, Georges Lacombe
Scenario   .   .   .   .   Francis Picabia
Photography   .   .   .   Jimmy Berliet
Music .   .   .   .   .   Erik Satie
Story By   .   .   .   .   Arthur Rimbaud

With : Jean Borlin, Erik Satie, Marcel Duchamp, Man Ray.

LAMBETH WALK, The

1941 *(sound)*   BRITISH
Production .   .   .   .   British Council
Devised and Made By   .   Len Lye

MENILMONTANT

1926 *(silent)*   FRENCH
Production and Direction .   Dimitri Kirsanov
Photography   .   .   .   Léonce Crouan, Dimitri Kirsanov

With : Nadia Sibirskaia, Yolande Beaulieu.

169. THE TREASURE OF THE SIERRA MADRE, directed by John Huston. Humphrey Bogart.   [American, 1947]

170. LE DIABLE AU CORPS, directed by Claude Autant-Lara.   Micheline Presle, Gérard Philipe.   [French, 1947]

171. CROSSFIRE, directed by EDWARD DMYTRYK. ROBERT RYAN. [American, 1947]

172. BOOMERANG, directed by ELIA KAZAN. DANA ANDREWS, SAM LEVENE.
[American, 1947]

APPENDIX I

NEW GULLIVER, The

1935 (*sound*)   SOVIET

Production	Mosfilm
Direction	A. Ptushko
Scenario	A. Roshal, A. Ptushko
Puppet Design . . .	Sarra Mokil
Puppeteer	F. Krasny
Sculptor	O. Tayezhnaya
Music	Lev Schwartz
Photography . . .	N. Renkov
Voices by Artists of .	Moscow Kamerny Theatre
Based on	Jonathan Swift's *Gulliver's Travels*

With : V. Konstantinov.

RAINBOW DANCE

1936 (*sound*)   BRITISH

Production	G.P.O. Film Unit
Devised and Made By .	Len Lye

RELUCTANT DRAGON, The

1941 (*sound*)   AMERICAN

Production	Walt Disney
Direction	Alfred Werker
Based on Story By . .	Kenneth Grahame

With : Robert Benchley.

SANG D'UN POETE, Le

1930 (*sound*)   FRENCH

Production and Direction .	Jean Cocteau
Photography . . .	Georges Périnal
Music	Georges Auric

With: Enrique Rivero, Lee Miller, Odette Talazac.

SMILING MADAME BEUDET, The

1922 (*silent*)   FRENCH

Production	Vandal-Delac-Aubert
Direction	Germaine Dulac
Scenario	André Obey
Photography . . .	A. Morrin
From Play By . . .	André Obey and Denys Amiel

With : Germaine Dermoz, Alexander Arguillière, Madeleine Guitty, Jean d'Yd.

APPENDIX I
UEBERFALL
1929 *(silent)* GERMAN

Direction	.	.	.	Ernö Metzner
Scenario	.	.	.	Ernö Metzner, Grace Chaing
Photography	.	.	.	Hans Casparius

VOYAGE IMAGINAIRE, LE
1925 *(silent)* FRENCH

Direction and Scenario . René Clair
Photography . . . A. Morrin, J. Berliet
Design . . . . Robert Guys

With : Jean Borlin, Dolly Davis, Albert Préjean, Jim Gerald.

APPENDIX II

SOME TERMS USED IN THE FILM INDUSTRY

Abridged mainly from a Glossary of Film Terms prepared for the British Ministry of Information, Films Division, in 1943, and from the Glossary of the Arts Enquiry Report on Factual Films, 1947.

I. TECHNICAL TERMS USED MAINLY IN PRODUCTION

OUTLINE.—An *Outline*, or Synopsis, is a first brief written account of a film in general terms. The writer need not be a film expert.

TREATMENT.—A *Treatment* is an expansion of the outline, in sequence form, giving the filmic possibilities of the subject, characterisation, perhaps indications of dialogue. In a factual film, if there is a commentary, the treatment will give the . . .

COMMENTARY LINE.—An approximate draft, which will usually not be finalised until the picture has been shot, though occasionally a film can be shot to match a pre-existing final commentary.

SHOOTING-SCRIPT.—Where possible, and specially in studio-made films, or films under similar control, the final paper stage is the *Shooting-Script*, often shortened to *Script*, which should only be applied to the actual technical manuscript from which the film is shot. (' Scenario ' or ' Photoplay ' are alternative terms for the same thing.)

SCREENPLAY.—*Screenplay* is really an original story from which a treatment or script is prepared; when a treatment is taken from an existing work, say a novel or play, it is said to be *adapted* from.

BREAKDOWN : SHOTS.—In the shooting-script, the action is *broken down* into numbered *Shots*, each of which represents a change of camera set-up, although the same set-up can be used more than once. The description of these shots—i.e. *Close Up, Close Shot, Medium Close Shot, Mid Shot, Semi Long Shot* or *Medium Long Shot* and *Long Shot*, indicated by their initals, gives a guide to the desired size of the person or object in the frame of the screen.

CAMERA SET-UP: ANGLE.—Whatever its distance from the object or person being filmed, the camera is said to be *set-up* at an *angle* to it. This angle can vary from average eye-level to low-level or bird's-eye points of view, according to how the director thinks the set-up will express the dramatic content and pictorial qualities of the shot.

PANNING: TILTING: TRACK SHOT: CRANE SHOT.—Pivotal movement of the camera on its tripod horizontally from side to side is called *Panning*, derived from panorama. Pivotal camera movement vertically up and down is called *Tilting*. A camera can also be mounted on a mobile truck, dolley or 'velocilator' and the whole apparatus made to move towards or away from the object being filmed. This is called a *Track Shot*. *Panning, tilting,* and *tracking* can be made to happen simultaneously if desired. A camera can also be mounted on the arm of a crane and thus move through space, known as a *Crane Shot*.

CAMERA SPEED: FRAMES: SLOW MOTION: ACCELERATED MOTION.—In order that action and speech on the screen may be as exact to real life as possible, film runs through the camera, and later the projector, at a speed of 90 feet a minute, or 1½ feet a second. One thousand feet of film takes 11 minutes to show. Each foot of film contains 16 pictures or *Frames*. If the picture camera runs faster than this, the action being filmed will be slowed down producing the effect known as *Slow Motion*. Conversely, if the camera is run slower than normal speed, action is speeded up, known as *Accelerated Motion*. Both devices have potential dramatic uses, as well as being of scientific and record value.

FADES: DISSOLVE OR MIX: OPTICALS: WIPE.—*Fade In* and *Outs, Dissolves* or *Mixes* are normally made optically in the laboratory, on an 'optical printer' and hence are loosely called *Opticals*. Trick shots are also mainly optically done. (Note: 'mix' and 'dissolve' are synonymous, and denote a gradual transition from one scene to another, both scenes being visible in a superimposed state for a period during the middle of the transition.) A mix can vary in length from a short 1 ft. mix to a 10 or 12 feet long overlay, according to the director's intention. When a shot 'fades', the screen is a total black before the next shot appears. The next shot must then 'fade in'. *Wipes,* of which there are many fancy varieties, are used for more staccato film punctuation: in these, as one shot is obliterated, and the next one takes its place, the edge between (which may be a straight or diagonal line, or ' fancy ', such as a star developing from the centre or a wavy line from one corner) remains more or less sharp and traverses the screen until the old shot has been wiped off and the new one has taken its place.

TITLE : CREEPING TITLE.—*Title* is self-explanatory : when a lengthy title moves up the screen at reading pace it is called a *Creeping Title*.

MAIN TITLE.—Applied to the title which displays the name of the film.

CREDIT TITLES.—Carry the names of technicians, etc., and cast of actors, either at the beginning or end of a film.

SUB-TITLE : STRIP-TITLES.—In silent films, whether they be silent versions of sound films or silent films proper, titles used to tell the story are called *Sub-Titles*, but in practice ' title ' is often loosely used for all wording. *Strip-Titles* are translations of foreign dialogue superimposed at the bottom of the screen.

INSERT.—A slang term for any written (e.g. a letter) or printed (e.g. newspaper, poster) matter in a film, other than a title.

PRODUCER.—(*a*) In feature films the *Producer* is the guiding figure behind the production, acting as an intermediary between the financial investors and the film's director. Several feature films may be handled by a producer at one time. He is finally responsible for the film's entertainment value and therefore has the last word in casting, story treatment, etc.

(*b*) In documentary films the *Producer* is closer to day-to-day production and the creative shaping of the film than in story-films. Unlike the feature film producer, he always has firsthand experience of direction and editing. He co-ordinates personnel and has the final word in any disagreements between them, e.g. between writer and director. He may be head of his own unit of technicians, capable of producing three or more films at once, or he may divide his time among several units.

ASSOCIATE PRODUCER.—In a large organisation the Producer may appoint an *Associate Producer* to work to him and be responsible for a group of films.

DIRECTOR.—(*a*) In feature films the *Director* is usually the technician who directs the shooting of the film, that is, he tells the players what to do and the camerman what to shoot, and usually supervises the editing. Most feature films are directed from scripts written by the script department or by an independent script-writer. The editing is carried out by a department under a supervising editor working in consultation with the director and producer. Sometimes a director will write his own shooting-script and do his own editing; thus the film will tend much more to carry his individual mark. The screen credit ' Produced and Directed by . . . ' is thus a contradiction in terms. A director cannot very well ' produce ' himself in the technical sense.

(*b*) In documentary films the *Director* usually writes his own script after first-hand investigation of the subject, although sometimes he may employ a dialogue writer. He not only directs the action of the film, but controls it through all stages of editing, music, dubbing, etc. Wartime developments have tended to departmentalise documentary production as in story films.

PRODUCTION MANAGER : UNIT MANAGER.—The *Production Manager* is concerned with organisation and administration, and is especially responsible for expenditure, schedules and co-ordination of departments. The *Unit Manager* performs the same functions for one film only.

EDITOR : CUTTER.—The film *Editor* performs a creative function, sometimes as influential as that of the writer or director. (Some directors also edit their own films, usually in documentary.) An editor works to the producer and director and is usually assisted by *Cutters,* of various grades of skill. He may be offended if he is called a ' cutter,' even if he performs most of the manual labour himself, though it is common to ask ' Who cut such-and-such a film?' when one means—' Who edited it?' In big studios, it is customary to employ a *Supervising Editor* to oversee several productions.

SYNC. SHOOTING : SOUND CAMERA : MUTE : INTERLOCK : SOUND TRUCK.—In *Sync. Shooting* natural sound, whether dialogue or effects, is photographed synchronously by the *Sound Camera (Recording Camera)* while the picture camera takes the *Mute.* The two pieces of apparatus are *Interlocked* (usually electrically) to run at the same speed. For location shooting (away from studio) the sound camera is housed in a *Sound Truck* which contains its elaborate accessories (though sometimes a ' portable ' set is used).

(Normally sound and mute are recorded on separate strips of film, and are only combined at the end of production. But newsreels, for technical reasons connected with the need for speedy output, take sound and mute on *one* strip of film. Quality is here put second to speedy processing. Newsreel technique is not suitable for production where quality of sound and picture is of paramount importance.)

TAKES.—Each shot from each camera set-up may be taken several times. These *Takes* are noted down as *Print* or *N.G.* (no good) as an instruction to the laboratory. More than one take of a shot may be printed as a safeguard, or to provide a choice to the director and editor.

CLAPPER OR NUMBER BOARD.—In sync. shooting, the shot number in the script and take number chalked on a *Clapper Board* ('number board' in silent shooting) are photographed before each take. The sound made by the contact of two pieces of wood, called clappers, is photographed on the sound track—and, of course, the board with its chalked numbers is photographed on the mute.

MODULATIONS : IN SYNC.—The sound of the clappers can be identified by a characteristic pattern of *Modulations* on the sound track. By keeping in alignment the clapper marks on the sound track, and the corresponding picture of the clappers at point of impact on the mute, the film can be kept *In Sync.* during editing and at the laboratory. A maladjustment of only three frames (separate pictures) will throw a film just appreciably 'out of sync.'.

DOPE SHEET.—A detailed description of shots actually taken is called a *Dope Sheet* by a Unit working away from its base and can be used for identification. The term *Dopes* or *Dope Sheets* is also commonly applied to a description of a film taken down after its final assembly. It can also be used to describe the breakdown of a shooting-script into production requirements.

CONTINUITY SHEETS : PROGRESS REPORTS.—The shots taken on a given day are listed in detail, with dialogue, lens size, footage used on each take, and other particulars. This daily information is circulated in quadruplet to the Producer, Director, Production Manager and Editor. It also serves as a Report on Progress during production.

RATIO.—Film wastage inevitably occurs during shooting. Usually, at least 7,000 feet each of mute and sound film negative has to be exposed to yield 1,000 feet of sync. film on the screen. This *Ratio* may be reduced to a 5-1 allowance for mute shooting.

NEGATIVE: RUSHES: FIRST ASSEMBLY: CUTTING COPY.—The selected takes are printed from the developed *Negative*. The Negative is held at the laboratory and treated with great care because all the money and pains of production are locked up in this single piece of film. Sound and mute prints—*Rushes*—are examined daily by the director, etc., and can be replaced from the negative as often as required. Sound and mute are on separate rolls, of course, at this stage, and after being marked to keep in sync. the clapper marks are cut off for the *First Assembly* of the material, which has now become the *Cutting Copy*.

EDGE NUMBERS: NUMBERS.—Along the edges of the film can be seen *Edge Numbers,* which are part of the photographic base. Strips of film (perhaps re-prints) are ordered by referring to the edge numbers. (To assist him in keeping mute and sound track(s) in sync., the editor may have *Numbers* printed mechanically on sound and picture material: whenever the same numbers are opposite to each other the strips will be in sync.)

SOUND TRACK: VARIABLE AREA: VARIABLE DENSITY.—The *Sound Track* according to the system used is either a zig-zag line *(Variable Area)* or a band made up of bars of light and shade *(Variable Density)*. Mechanically, they can be used interchangeably, but there are certain patent regulations restricting this—these were partially waived only in wartime.

WILD TRACK.—A sound track of any sort which has not been taken in sync. with pictures (e.g. commentary, effects or music) is called a *Wild Track*. These may be freely inter-mixed or overlaid.

GUIDE TRACK.—During the shooting of the detail shots to a play-back, a *Guide Track* is sometimes taken. This will have on it all the sounds going on in the studio—i.e. the play-back plus any sound that may be made during the shooting of the detail action—probably the artists singing and playing with attention rather to what they *look* like than what they sound like. This guide track is *only* used to assist the editor in synching the detail shots with the original material: the sound used for the finished picture is, of course, that of the original track. A guide track may also be taken on location sound shooting when conditions are unfavourable for good sound reproduction. In this case, voices may be added later in more favourable conditions and cut in sync. with the guide track.

PRE-SCORING.—When the music is recorded *before* any mute action is photographed, it is called *Pre-scoring*.

PLAY-BACK.—A term from studio practice. In filming an orchestra or a dance number, a master-picture and master sound-track are taken of the whole operation. A copy of this sound track can be played-back in the studio, and the artists perform again, fitting their action to the play-back, while close-ups, etc., are taken for cutting into the basic picture. In order to avoid the delay that would be caused by waiting to process the track for play-back, a disc is often taken at the same time. This disc can be played-back immediately.

STOCK LIBRARY : COMPILATION FILM.—The editor may want to incorporate *Stock* or *Library Material* (pre-existing material from the libraries of newsreel or other companies). This will frequently lack sync. sound and the recordist may have to go out and shoot some wild tracks, if there is not a suitable sound track in stock. A film wholly, or almost wholly, edited from library material, or from footage of other films, is called a *Compilation Film*.

DISC.—Gramophone *discs* or records are sometimes used for sound and music, but their quality when transferred to film can leave much to be desired.

SYNCHRONISER.—The editor builds up his film on a *Synchroniser* which allows him to keep up to four rolls of film (normally one mute and three sound) in sync. Dissolves and other opticals are ordered from the laboratory at a later stage to replace the sections of film which have previously been marked with a rough (usually red) chalk line—this line is often noticeable when a cutting copy is screened.

CUT OUTS : OVERS.—Lengths of shots not used, *Cut Outs*, and whole shots or takes not used, *Overs*, are retained for library. Useless material is junked.

EDITING-MACHINE.—During editing the film is constantly run through an *Editing-Machine* for observation. This provides a kind of miniature peep show; it will take sound tracks as well.

EFFECTS TRACK.—*A Sound Effects* track must often be built up from a number of separately recorded sounds. It may contain voices and music, but only when these are casual or incidental.

MUSIC TRACK: PRE-MIXING.—Any large amout of music—the orchestration which runs through a film, for instance, has a separate *Music Track* at this stage. If effects tracks (for example) multiply beyond easy handling, they may be pre-recorded on to one film strip. This process is called *Pre-Mixing*. A track with all the sound and music, but excluding commentary and dialogue, is called a *Music and Effects track,* or ' M. and E.' track, usually needed for foreign versions of a film.

RE-RECORDING: DUBBING: MIXED TRACK:—*Re-Recording* or *Dubbing* is the process of adding any sound(s) whether already on a sound track, or newly created—(e.g. a commentary—in the recording studio) on to a strip of film. Re-recording can only refer to the dubbing of sounds already on film. At a typical dubbing or re-recording session one or more sound effects tracks, a separate music track, and perhaps the sound from a disc or from an endless loop of sound film, are mixed by the recordist, whose object it is to balance them as regards level. The result is a new track, a combined music and effects track (' M. and E.'). If this is further mixed with the dialogue and/or commentary track, the result is a *Mixed Track*.

LOOP.—A sound suitable for a *Loop* is one in which a repeated phrase (e.g. sound of engine) is required, or in the case of a persistent sound—for example, the blowing of wind—a strip in which an obvious repeat pattern does not become irritating or noticeable.

RE-VOICE: POST-SYNC: BI-MULTI-LINGUAL: A dialogue film in a foreign language may be *Re-Voiced* (synonymous with *Post-Sync.*). The term dubbing, which has a more universal use, is also used in this connection. One talks of a film *Dubbed into* . . . the language referred to. When a dialogue film is originally made in two languages with two sets of actors, it is called a *Bi-Lingual* . . . up to *Multi-Lingual*.

SOUND CHANNEL: DUBBING HEAD.—The term *Sound Channel* is commonly used to denote the course of the sound through all the various pieces of apparatus from microphone to sound camera. One thus says 'a sound channel is available'—meaning the whole set-up for recording sound. The course of the sound is, put simply, from its natural source through microphone and from a film track through a *Dubbing Head* or heads, and so through the mixing panel, where the sound recordist controls its balance, and so to the sound camera, where it is photographed on film.

ROUGH CUT.—At some period before the work is finally combined, the cutting copy of the mute and its one or two combined or uncombined sound tracks, is available as a *Rough Cut*. It remains in this stage until all concerned are satisfied.

FINE CUT.—A *Fine Cut* is merely a well-advanced rough cut. A rough cut can, of course, be re-viewed after alterations, but after the fine cut has been approved no alterations should be required, for after the O.K. has been given, the original negative, both sound and mute, still held at the laboratory, is cut to match the cutting-copy, and alterations thereafter endanger the quality of the film.

COMMENTARY TRACK.—The stage at which the commentary is recorded and the stage at which the *Commentary track* is mixed with the others depends upon circumstances. An average commentary, allowing for pauses, runs about 100 words a minute. A fully commentated one-reel film, therefore, runs to about 1,000 words, but there is a very wide latitude.

SCRATCH COMMENTARY.—It is common in factual films to record a *Scratch Commentary* at an early stage in editing to act as a guide for the visual assembly. This scratch commentary allows for revision before it is finally retaken with the right voices as will be heard in the final film.

MARRIED PRINT: COMBINED OR SYNCHRONISED SHOW COPY.— A *Married Print* is one on which both the visuals (mute) and the combined sound track have been printed from the cut negatives, and is the normal print for public exhibition. It may also be called a *Combined* or *Synchronised Print*. The combined print delivered for exhibition before release becomes a *Show Copy*.

GAUGE.—Standard film is 35mm. wide. Non-flam film for use by travelling projectors (to factories, halls, societies, etc., 'non-theatrical', i.e. for use outside the normal public theatres) is 16mm. wide. (Non-flam. 35mm. film is occasionally used.) Most professional films are shot on 35mm. even when their final destination is 16mm. Film made on 16mm. stock can, with difficulty, be blown up to 35mm.

STILLS.—*Stills* for publicity purposes can be blown up from a single frame if the definition is good. Stills for feature films are usually taken in the studio by a special still-camerman.

VAULTS : TRANSIT CASES.—Film is stored in *Vaults* licensed for the purpose and travels in metal *Transit Cases*.

REEL.—The term *Reel* is *not* an exact measure. It means a roll of film which can be contained in a normal ' 1,000 ft.' tin.

SPROCKET HOLES.—There are four perforations down each side of each 35mm. frame—*Sprocket Holes*. In 16mm. there is one on each side of each frame, but in 16mm. sound film there are only sprocket holes down one edge—those on the other edge having been removed to make way for the track.

SPOOL AND ROLL : REWINDER : LEADER.—It is convenient to confine the term Reel to the actual film, and the term *Spool* to the metal carrier on the projector etc. *Roll* is a convenient term for a quantity of film for projection so much shorter or longer than the normal reel of 1,000 feet that a wrong impression might be given by calling it a reel. After projection etc., film has to be run through a *Rewinder* to get the *Leader* of blank film on the outside of the reel again. Rewinders in cutting rooms are fitted with Footage Counters, by means of which reels and strips of film can be measured.

16MM. SPOOLS.—Sixteen mm. spools are made to take 400, 800, 1,600 feet of film. Four hundred feet of 16mm. film is equivalent to 1,000 feet of 35mm. *and takes the same time to show*. While 35mm. film is normally quoted in feet 16mm. is usually quoted in minutes.

PROJECTION BOX : CHANGE-OVER : OUT OF RACK.—The normal *Projection Box* contains two machines so that as the first spool runs out a *Change-over*, without any noticeable break, can be made to the second machine, where the next spool is ready threaded up. When the upper part of one frame and the lower part of another appear on the screen together the film is *Out of Rack*. This is easily corrected.

DOUBLE-HEADED.—An unmarried print—i.e. mute and sound track—can be shown *Double-Headed* by any projector fitted with double spools—one roll of film passing the picture illuminant, and the other roll passing the sound exciter lamp. Projectors in editing rooms and pre-view theatres are so fitted. On a married print the sound track is 19 frames ahead of the corresponding visuals, as the film passes the two sources of illumination in sequence. Thus, in any strip of married film the modulations of the sound track will not be opposite the corresponding picture-frame.

TRIPLE-HEADED.—When an unmarried print consists of three rolls—e.g. mute and two sound tracks (normally voice and music-and-effects) it can be shown *Triple-Headed* on two projectors, which should be interlocked to run in sync. As both projectors are being used for the three rolls, there must be a slight break after every 1,000 ft. reel. A third projector will allow for four separate rolls to be shown.

DUPE NEGATIVES.—From the original negative a large but limited number of prints can be made. It is therefore, usually necessary to make *Dupe Negs.* (i.e. duplicating negatives). To go from an original negative to a dupe neg., however, there is an intermediate positive stage.

LAVENDER : FINE GRAIN : DUPING PRINT.—This positive is made on special *Lavender* or *Fine Grain* stock. (Either type of duplicating positive is often, wrongly, called a lavender, or, rightly, a *Duping Print.*) Lavenders are so called from the characteristic colour of the dye used. From a duping print one can strike a number of dupe negs.

BLACKS AND WHITES.—Each dupe neg. will yield a further set of *Black and White* prints (up to 200-300 from each dupe neg. with care). B. and W. are so called to distinguish them from lavenders, and are the normal release prints as distributed for use in the cinemas. A lavender or duping positive can be projected like any other print, but as its destination is a matrix for dupe negs., and as every time it is handled there is danger of scratching, it should not be projected unless essential.

II. TERMS IN GENERAL USE IN THE TRADE AS A WHOLE.

'A' CERTIFICATE.—The British Board of Film Censors classifies films for public exhibition into three categories, of which an 'A' Certificate denotes that the film may not be seen by children under 16 years of age unless accompanied by a parent or guardian. (See 'U' and 'H' *Certificates* and *Censor.*)

'A' PICTURE.—A production intended to be booked as the

main feature in a cinema programme, thereby being allocated the largest share of the takings.

ATTENDANCES.—The number of seats sold per programme. It is often overlooked that the present figure of over 25,000,000 weekly attendance in Britain does not mean that 25,000,000 people go to the cinema each week, but that an unknown number of people together make that total of attendances.

ADVERTISING FILM.—A short film produced to advertise a branded product for the showing of which the cinema exhibitor gets paid.

'B' PICTURE.—A production intended to be booked as the second feature in a cinema programme and consequently budgeted in terms of those market potentialities.

BLIND BOOKING.—A term used to describe the practice of exhibitors booking a film before it has been trade-shown, or even before it has been made, on the strength of its star-value, or possibly because it is one of a series of which the exhibitor has seen and played the first. It is now illegal in Britain, by reason of the Cinematograph Films Act, 1938.

BLOCK BOOKING.—A term used to describe the practice of a renter requiring an exhibitor to book films other than the one he wants in order to secure the latter. Rendered illegal by the Cinematograph Films Act, 1938, it is nevertheless believed still to be in common practice.

BOX-OFFICE.—Actually the booking office in the cinema where seats are sold to the public, but more generally used to denote whether a film will show a profit on its capital production cost.

CARTOON.—A film mainly or wholly comprised of drawings animated into motion, often in colour.

CENSOR.—In Great Britain, the British Board of Film Censors a body without official status, set up by the Trade in 1912. Considerable obscurity surrounds its members and their appointment. They view films which, if acceptable, are classified under the categories of 'A', 'U', and 'H' certificates. (See '*A*' *Certificate*, etc.)

CIRCUIT.—A chain of cinemas in one town, in one region, or throughout the whole country, owned by one company, with its programmes booked centrally at head-office.

DISTRIBUTOR.—See *Renter*.

DOUBLE-FEATURE PROGRAMME.—Programme made up of two

feature-length films, usually one ' A ' picture, and one ' B ' picture.

EXHIBITOR.—The Cinematograph Films Act, 1938, defines an exhibitor as 'a person carrying on the business of exhibiting cinematograph films to the public and having licence to permit him to do so.' He books his films from the producer through a renter (or distributor). In practice, exhibitors can be subdivided into :

(a) Exhibitor-owners who book their films themselves.

(b) Those who own a number of cinemas (or circuit) for which films are booked by a booking manager; a circuit can range from 5 to 500 or more cinemas, and in some cases one booking manager may be responsible for the programmes of several hundred cinemas.

FEATURE FILM.—In Great Britain, the Cinematograph Films Act, 1938, defines a feature film as 'a film the length of which is not less than 3,000 feet' (33 mins.). Therefore it includes most story films, and occasional documentaries, cartoons, and newsreel compilations.

FEATURETTE.—A cheaply-made film of just over 3,000 feet, so as to rank as a feature film, which could well have been made as a short.

FICTION FILM.—Sometimes used to denote a story-film, made up from fictional characters, action, and events.

FILM SOCIETY.—Privately organised society formed to show films not considered generally commercial, by holding private performances to its members usually in a cinema hired specially for the purpose.

FIRST FEATURE.—The main film attraction in a cinema programme. See ' A ' picture.

GENERAL RELEASE.—The release of a film to cinema exhibitors in general after it has had its first pre-release run in a capital city.

' H ' CERTIFICATE.—Category allocated to films of a ' horrific ' nature by the British Board of Film Censors. (See *Censor*.)

INTEREST FILM.—Generally a short film dealing with a non-fictional subject, such as an industrial process, a nature study, or a travel or scenic film.

LABORATORY.—Plant where the developing, printing and other technical processes are undertaken for the Industry.

MANAGER.—Usually refers to the person employed to run the

management of a cinema; sometimes the employee of a large circuit or of an individual cinema owner.

MUSICAL.—Feature or short film mainly comprised of song and dance numbers, often in colour, usually spectacular in settings and lavishly produced.

NEWSREEL.—One-reel weekly report of current events.

NEWSREEL CINEMA.—Cinema purporting to show mainly newsreels of the week, but more often its programme has a majority of short interest, comedy, cartoon or travel films.

NON-THEATRICAL.—A term widely applied to all forms of film exhibition other than those in public cinemas for which admission has been paid, including sub-standard performances in schools, clubs, village halls, etc. It is also applied to production when the intention of the film is to appeal to specialised audiences not seeking entertainment.

OPERATOR.—Another word for a Projectionist who operates the cinema-projector.

PATRON.—Trade term for people who go to the cinema.

PRE-RELEASE.—Any advance booking given to a film before being issued on general release.

PRE-VIEW.—Try out of a film, unadvertised, before its first general showing, usually included without advance notice in a cinema programme in order to ascertain the public's reaction. Often called *Sneak-Preview.*

PROJECTIONIST.—See *Operator.*

PROJECTION THEATRE.—Small privately owned cinema, usually in a studio or laboratory, for the projection of films privately, or for seeing cutting-copies and rushes.

QUOTA.—The amount of British-made film footage which a renter or an exhibitor has to show over a given period as laid down by the Cinematograph Films Act, 1948, in order to import and exhibit imported films.

RE-ISSUE.—A film made available again by a renter for bookings after it has had a general release to cinemas.

RENTER.—The renter or distributor acts as middle-man between production company and exhibitor. The distribution rights of a film are acquired either on a sharing basis or, very occasionally, by outright purchase by the renter from the producer. The renter then gives a trade-show of the film to independent exhibitors and to the booking managers of the circuits. Contracts for hiring the film are

173. ODD MAN OUT, directed by CAROL REED.   [British, 1947]

174. OLIVER TWIST, directed by DAVID LEAN.   JOHN HOWARD DAVIES.
[British, 1947–48]

175. BICYCLE THIEVES, directed by VITTORIO DE SICA. LAMBERTO MAGGIORANI.
[Italian, 1948]

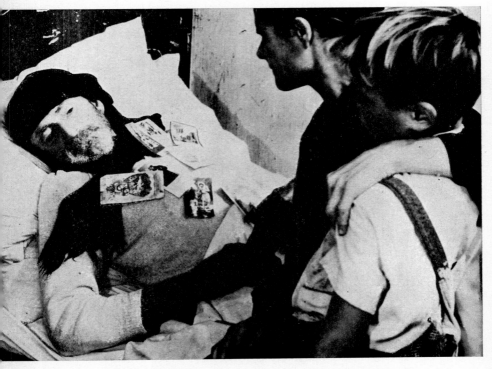

176. LA TERRA TREMA, directed by LUCHINO VISCONTI. [Italian, 1949]

subsequently arranged either on a flat rental basis or on a percentage of takings. As the industry has grown, producers, renters, and exhibitors have tended to become merged.

SALESMAN.—Renters maintain a staff of salesmen throughout the country to negotiate bookings for films. They customarily meet in London at regular times to be shown new product, and to be coached in new salemanship methods.

SHORT FILM.—The Cinematograph Films Act, 1938, defines a ' short ' film as ' a film the length of which is less than 3,000 feet ' (33 mins.). Therefore it includes newsreels, cartoons, and most documentary, instructional, and general interest films.

SLAPSTICK.—A type of comedy relying on fast action and broad knockabout humour, frequently embodying chases.

SNEAK PREVIEW.—*See Pre-view.*

STORY-FILM.—See *Fiction-film.*

TRADE-SHOW.—When offering a film for booking to exhibitors, trade-shows for viewers are held in London and the main provincial cities. A renter is legally obliged to hold a trade-show before he can book the film to exhibitors.

TRAILER.—A trailer is a short film, varying from 30-300 feet in length, specially made up of excerpts from a long film and shown in the ordinary cinema programme to whet the appetite of audiences for a coming programme. Their technique is elaborate, involving trick titles and optical devices, and their tempo very fast. The term is also used for Government informational short films, 130 feet or less in length, distributed and attached to the end of the news reel. ' Flashes ' of even shorter length, that is some 40-50 feet, are also used for the same purpose. Much originality has been used in their production.

TRAVELOGUE.—A short film of people and places, superficially described, sometimes set in Great Britain, but more often overseas.

' U ' CERTIFICATE.—A film classified by the British Board of Film Censors as being suitable for showing universally, including to unaccompanied children. (See *Censor.*)

WESTERN.—A type of American film devoted to cowboys and horses, usually set in real surroundings and containing chases and other thrills.

TFTN—45

705

APPENDIX III.

SELECTED BOOKLIST

I. BRITISH AND AMERICAN

America at the Movies. Margaret Farrand Thorp. 1939. (Yale University Press)

Anatomy of Motion Picture Art. Eric Elliott. 1928. (Pool)

Art in the Cinema. Edited by Frank Stauffacher. 1947. (San Francisco Museum of Art)

Art of the Film. Ernest Lindgren. 1948. (Allen and Unwin)

Art of the Moving Picture, The. Vachel Lindsay. 1922. (Macmillan)

British Film Year Book, 1946, 1947, and 1948. Compiled by Peter Noble. (British Year Books)

Celluloid: The Film To-day. Paul Rotha. 1931. (Longmans Green)

Cinema. C. A. Lejeune. 1931. (Maclehose)

Cinema as a Graphic Art, The. Vladimir Nilsen. 1936. (Newnes)

D. W. Griffith. Iris Barry. 1940. (Museum of Modern Art, New York)

Designing for Moving Pictures. Edward Carrick. 1941. (Studio Publications)

Documentary Film. Paul Rotha. 1936 and 1939. (Faber & Faber)

Douglas Fairbanks. Alistair Cooke. 1940. (Museum of Modern Art, New York)

Factual Film, The. Arts Enquiry Report. 1947. (Oxford University Press)

Fifty Years of German Film. H. H. Wollenberg. 1948. (Falcon Press)

Film. Roger Manvell. 1946. (Pelican)

Film. Rudolph Arnheim. 1933. (Faber & Faber)

Film Acting. V. I. Pudovkin. 1931. (Newnes)

Film in National Life, The. Report of the Educational and Cultural Films Commission. 1932. (Allen and Unwin)

Film Index, The. Vol. I., The Film as Art. 1940. (H. W. Wilson)

Film Sense, The. Sergei Eisenstein, trs. Jay Leyda. 1943. (Faber & Faber)

Films: Facts and Forecasts. L'Estrange Fawcett. 1927. (Bles)

Footnotes to the Film. Edited by Charles Davy. 1937. (Lovat Dickson)

706

For Filmgoers Only. Edited by R. S. Lambert. 1934. (Faber & Faber)

Freedom of the Movies, The. Ruth A. Inglis. 1947. (University of Chicago Press)

From Caligari to Hitler. Siegfried Kracauer. 1947. (Princeton University Press and Dennis Dobson)

Garbo and the Nightwatchmen. Edited by Alistair Cooke. 1937. (Cape)

Grammar of the Film, A. Raymond Spottiswoode. 1935. (Faber & Faber)

Grierson on Documentary. Edited by Forsyth Hardy. 1947. (Collins)

History of the Motion Pictures. Maurice Bardèche and Robert Brasillach. Trs. and edited by Iris Barry. 1938. (Norton)

History of the Movies, A. Benjamin Hampton. 1931. (Covici Friede)

Hollywood—The Movie Colony. Leo C. Rosten. 1941. (Harcourt Brace)

Hour with the Movies and the Talkies, An. Gilbert Seldes. 1929. (Lippincott)

Informational Film Year Book. 1947. 1948. (Albyn Press)

Let's go to the Pictures. Iris Barry. 1926. (Chatto and Windus)

Million and One Nights, A. Terry Ramsaye. 1926. (Simon and Schuster)

Money Behind the Screen. F. D. Klingender and Stuart Legg. 1937. (Lawrence and Wishart)

Motion Picture Industry, The. Howard T. Lewis. 1933. (Van Nostrand)

Movie Parade. Paul Rotha. 1936. (Studio Publications)

Movies for the Millions. Gilbert Seldes. 1937. (Batsford)

Movies on Trial, The. Edited by William J. Pearlman. 1936. (Macmillan)

Pudovkin on Film Technique. Trs. Ivor Montagu. 1929. (Gollancz)

Rise of the American Film, The. Lewis Jacobs. 1939. (Harcourt Brace)

Scrutiny of the Cinema. William Hunter. 1932. (Wishart)

Sociology of Film. J. P. Mayer. 1946. (Faber & Faber)

Soviet Cinema. Thorold Dickinson and Catherine de la Roche. 1948. (Falcon Press)

Twenty Years of British Films (1925-1947). Michael Balcon, Ernest Lindgren, Roger Manvell, and Forsyth Hardy. 1947. (Falcon Press)

Use of Film, The. Basil Wright. 1948. (John Lane, The Bodley Head)

We Make the Movies. Edited by Nancy Naumberg. 1938. (Faber & Faber)

Working For the Films. Edited by Oswell Blakeston. 1947. (Focal Press)

II. FOREIGN

Cinéma: Scénarios, Etudes et Chroniques. Abel Gance, Jean Epstein, René Clair, etc. 1928. (' Le Rouge et le Noir ', Paris)

Cinéma Russe, Le. René Marchand et Pierre Weinstein. 1927. (Paris)

Cinéma Soviétique, Le. Léon Moussinac. 1928. (Paris)

Cinéma Total. René Barjavel. 1944. (Denoël, Paris)

Der sichtbare Mensch. Béla Belázs. 1924. (Halle, Berlin)

Der Geist des Films. Béla Belázs. 1930. (Halle, Berlin)

Film. Theodor Christensen and Karl Roos. 1936. (Levin and Munksgaard, Copenhagen)

Film, Der. George Schmidt, Werner Schmalenbach and Peter Bachlin. 1947. (Holbein-Verlag, Basle)

Film, der kommende. Guido Bagier. 1928. (Berlin)

Filmen. (3 Vols.) Ove Brusendorff. 1940-47. (Universal Forlaget, Copenhagen)

Filmgegner von heute: Filmfreunde von morgen. Hans Richter. 1929. (Hermann Reckendorf, Berlin)

Film Photos wie noch nie. 1929 . (Kindt and Bucher, Berlin)

Histoire de l'Art Cinématographique. Carl Vincent. 1939. (Brussels)

Histoire Economique du Cinéma. Peter Bachlin. 1947. (La Nouvelle Edition, Paris)

Images du Cinéma Français. Nicole Vedrès. 1945. (Les Editions du Chêne, Paris)

Invention du Cinéma (1832-1897). Georges Sadoul. 1946 (Denoël, Paris)

Invitation to the Film. Liam O'Laoghaire. 1945. (Kerryman, Dublin)

Mezzo secolo di cinema. Francesco Pasinetti. 1946. (Biblioteca Cinematografica, Milan)

Panoramique du Cinéma. Léon Moussinac. 1929. (Au Sans Pareil, Paris)

Rôle Intellectuel du Cinéma. 1937. Institut International de Co-opération Intellectuelle. (Geneva)

Russische Filmkunst. Alfred Kerr. 1927. (Ernst Pollak, Berlin)

APPENDIX IV

EXTRACTS FROM A PROGRAMME ISSUED IN CONNECTION WITH A
MEMORIAL PERFORMANCE HELD OF CARL MAYER'S WORK,
SCALA THEATRE, LONDON, 13TH APRIL, 1947.

A NOTE ON THE GERMAN CINEMA—1919-1926

The memorable years of the German silent film may be said
to have begun in 1919 and 1920 with the appearance of *The
Cabinet of Dr. Caligari* and *The Golem*. There followed six
or seven years of intense production on a high artistic level,
which was unequalled by any other nation's contribution, until a
decline set in after 1926, after *Vaudeville* and *Faust*. This
Golden Period, as it is sometimes called, coincided with the post-
war flowering of German literature, drama and architecture;
the arts from which the cinema has so often borrowed.

Caligari came to a German public which was being shown
mainly spectacular films of the costume-period type, such as
Anne Boleyn, Madame Dubarry and *Caesar Borgia,* by directors
like Lubitsch and Buchowetski, possibly inspired to discredit the
successful Allies. It was probably not a popular success. The
films which followed it in using the expressionist technique
exploited the age-old German love for fantasy and the macabre,
which a hundred years before had surged through Romantic
literature. *Warning Shadows, Nosferatu (Dracula), The
Coffin Maker, Genuine, Waxworks, Destiny* and *The Stone
Rider*, all these displayed a growing technical and aesthetic
maturity in studio imaginativeness and pictorial design.

As the expressionist phase waned, the highly developed skill
of the set-designers and cameramen was applied increasingly to
films owing more allegiance to literary sources than before, for
example, adaptations of Hauptmann and Lessing. There was
still fantasy, as in *The Student of Prague*, but now it was
brought out from the sombre into the light of resplendent *décor*,
so well remembered in Lang's *Nibelungen*, Robison's *Manon
Lescaut*, Murnau's *Tartuffe* and Berger's *Cinderella*, films
unexcelled even to-day for their sheer architectural ingenuity
and the beauty of their design. It was a phase in cinema when
the craftsman, especially the set-designer and the cameraman,
really came into his own, which we have not seen since, except
perhaps recently in the English films *Gaslight* and
Great Expectations, and in the work of Carl Dreyer.

Von Gerlach's *Vanina,* in 1922, adapted from Stendhal, came out of context in this period to point the way to the future development of realist psychological German films, whose growth ran parallel with the decline of the 'art' film, culminating in *Westfront 1918* and *Kameradschaft.* To this new approach belonged Karl Grune's *The Street,* Jessner's *Hintertreppe,* Lupu Pick's *Scherben* and *Sylvester,* Pabst's *The Joyless Street* and *Jeanne Ney,* Murnau's *The Last Laugh,* Dupont's *Vaudeville,* and Bruno Rahn's *The Tragedy of the Street.* The makers of these well-remembered films, with their preoccupation for interpreting personal psychological problems, sought to express everyday experience and existence on the screen. In the same way that the earlier films had developed a mastery of set-design and light and shade, so these new films saw the camera take on a freedom of movement which was revolutionary. Their subjects and technique were as different from *Caligari* as is *Caesar and Cleopatra* from *The Day of Wrath;* but they had one thing in common with the earlier period, that dovetailed collaboration of director, writer, cameraman and set-designer needed to produce a unified work of film creation. Their films were the result of a pooling of talents, that genius for creative teamwork which has become recognised as an essential to the making of all great films, and which is all too rare in cinema.

Apart from the famous directors, we remember the writers like Carl Mayer and Henrik Galeen; the cameramen like Karl Freund, Günther Krampf, Fritz Arno Wagner, Guido Seeber and Karl Hoffmann; the designers like Walther Röhrig, Robert Herlth, Walther Reimann, Herman Warm, Paul Leni, Rudolph Bamberger and Albin Grau; the players like Wegener, Kortner, Jannings, Veidt, Lil Dagover, Asta Nielsen, Rudolf Klein-Rogge, Fritz Rasp and many others; and that producer of so many memorable films, Erich Pommer.

The economic depression at the end of the twenties hit Germany hard. Her film industry was crippled financially, and there had already begun the migration of her brilliant film creators to wealthier foreign studios who realised the value of this rich European talent. With the dispersal of these teams, mainly to America, inspiration largely left the German studios to the photoplays and melodramas that spun out the years till the sound film arrived. In Hollywood, these German and Austrian film creators, bewildered and dazed, settled down uneasily in the artificial atmosphere. Their love and devotion, sensitivity and knowledge, were not wanted by an industry which had already become debauched by attempting to appeal to the lowest average mentality of world markets. Only Lubitsch came through and prospered; nearly all the others are gone. Erich Pommer, the great producer of that period, has now returned to Germany and has the task of reorganising its film industry before him.

CARL MAYER'S DEBUT—BY ERICH POMMER

It was about a year after the end of the first World War. Within this year I had organised a small film studio, Decla, in Berlin and I was quite pleased with the way things were going —in spite of all the post-war restrictions on money and materials and electric power. Our most valuable assets were our enthusiasm and our ingenuity.

The enterprise didn't leave anyone much time for relaxation, so I used the lunch hour as my rest period. During this lunch hour, one day, there was a timid knock on my office door— which I didn't bother to answer. Nevertheless, the door was pushed open, and when the two young fellows there saw that someone was in the room, they knocked again, and asked for Mr. Pommer.

I said, 'I don't think you can see him to-day.'

They took turns speaking. 'We have a story that we're sure would interest him.'

'Mr. Pommer is a very busy man—leave your story—I'll see that it gets to him.'

'No, sir, we can't do that. We know that when we submit it officially, it just goes through a lot of secretaries (pardon!)—so we're determined to read it to him personally.'

'I'm *sorry*.'

But they weren't giving up yet. 'That's a shame. We have a lot of ideas, but we never seem able to reach the right man— and this idea is really something new—*different*.'

I tried another tack, to get rid of them. 'I'll let you into a secret. I'm Pommer, but I can't listen to any stories to-day. Can't you leave it with me?'

'Please give us just ten minutes—if you don't like what we've told you at the end of ten minutes, stop us, and we'll leave.'

They stayed three hours, and before they left I had written them a cheque for 800 marks. They called their story *The Cabinet of Dr. Caligari*. The two boys (I felt they were boys, even though I was only about five years older) were both from Prague. Carl Mayer was working as a *Dramaturg* (a combination play-reader and textual editor) at a small theatre on the Blumenstrasse. It was his collaborator, Hans Janowitz, who had had the idea for the story, after seeing a newspaper item about a Hamburg murderer. Janowitz and Mayer had developed the incident into a story that they insisted must be executed in a definite *style*. The artist whose style they wanted followed was Alfred Kubin, the hero of Prague's radical artists. While Mayer and Janowitz talked about art, I was thinking of rather different aspects of the script. The mystery and macabre atmosphere of the Grand Guignol was currently in vogue in German films, and this story fitted perfectly. They saw an ' experiment ' in the script—I saw a comparatively inexpensive production.

There was a pause of four or five months before the actual filming was planned. Wiene was considering directing it. The boys tried to get Kubin excited in their project. In the meantime I put them into work on another fantastic mystery idea, and put *Caligari* in the hands of the three artists who constituted Decla's designing staff—Warm, Herlth, and Röhrig, whom I had met as a soldier painting sets for a German military theatre in Braila, Rumania.

The studio had a very limited quota of power and light, and on the day when we were notified that we had exhausted the month's quota (several days before the end of the month), my three artists brought in a proposition that seemed to me absurd, and even reactionary—' Why not paint lights and shadows on the sets for this *Caligari* film? '

When I protested against this return to primitive film-making, Herlth (the quietest of the three) made his statement, ' Look here, Mr. Pommer, we are living in an age of expressionism, and in painting these sets in this style, we can do a great deal more in emphasising the important elements of the story.'

' Look here, boys, you're all crazy. It's impossible to put fantastic, unreal, flat sets behind real, solid people.'

The next day they brought me a series of drawings, which they probably had had all along, but hadn't wanted to frighten me with the day before. When I remained unconvinced, they coaxed me into letting Wiene make a test scene. When the test was screened, both Mayer and Janowitz were present. We were all convinced—and the writers dropped their efforts to engage Kubin. In fact, they were so impressed that they wrote their second script with this new method in mind, which may be the reason *Genuine* was so bad a film.

The Cabinet of Dr. Caligari cannot be called a typical Carl Mayer script, but it did serve to introduce him to his true medium. During its production the young writers saw each day's rushes, a habit that Mayer maintained throughout his screen-writing career. His powerful visual imagination was kept constantly stimulated by close contact with the entire production process—and from *Caligari* can be dated Mayer's well-known awareness of the camera and settings as vital dramatic elements.

Other writers wrote (and still write) scripts that have to be translated into film terms. Carl Mayer wrote true film-scripts and, in so doing, inspired all film artists who worked in that famous post-war period of German cinema.

CARL MAYER—
AN APPRECIATION BY PAUL ROTHA

Most writers who work in films are already writers of books and plays, or, at the least, they are journalists. Carl Mayer never wrote a play, a book or an article. He wrote only in film terms. He was an integral product of the medium he loved and understood so well.

Through Robert Flaherty, I first met Carl Mayer, in London, in 1936, but I had respected the name since the early '20s. It had been a script credit on some of the famous German films of what has been called the Golden Period. In Berlin in 1931, I had heard his name spoken with reverence; but it was only later, when I came to know him so well and after I talked with many famous contributors to early German cinema, that I realised the full extent of his influence.

He was born at Graz, Austria, in 1894, one of three brothers. He wanted to be an actor, then a painter, but became a kind of story-editor at a theatre. In Berlin in 1919 he conceived *The Cabinet of Dr. Caligari*. Of that conception I wrote in detail in *World Film News*, September, 1938.

Caligari and *Genuine* were the only two films to use expressionist painted backgrounds. This was not Mayer's idea, but that of the designers, Warm, Reimann, Röhrig. If you look at *Caligari* to-day, you respect it not so much for its sets or its formalised acting but for its conception, and the way the camera is used to present the madman's outlook on the world. For Carl Mayer saw everything through the camera. It was the flow of images, the creation of atmosphere by selected details, the expression of character by visual means, that compelled him to write films which refused to use printed subtitles to tell their story. With most other films, claim for this masterly technique would be given to the director, but because of his method of script-writing, Carl Mayer must take the major credit. His scripts were written in infinite detail, with meticulous instructions to director and cameraman. He frequently presided at the shooting and always had final say in the editing. His script of *Sunrise* is circulated to this day in

713

Hollywood as a model of structure and continuity. In the same way that he found himself logically writing scripts without sub-titles, so he came to suggest the moving camera. That was in *New Year's Eve*. The camera had, it is true, been put on motor cars and trains before that, but usually only for novelty's sake. Reminiscing, Carl told me many times how he fought with the problems of expressing time in that film. The clock in the town square dominated the story, which told the events minute by minute in the hour preceding midnight. 'Through the pages of my manuscript', he said, 'the face of the clock tower moved closer and closer towards me. It had to *move, to grow bigger*. So the camera had to move. Guido Seeber mounted it on a perambulator. It was so obvious.' The next year, he gave full vent to this new idea, and with the help of Karl Freund, *The Last Laugh* was a revolution in moving camera work. Its showing in America led to the ubiquitous use of the camera-dolly and the crane, now built with such elaborate mechanism and so often used without real cinematic reason.

From a story aspect, Mayer's great contribution was his choice of subject and characters. One must remember that the really popular German films in 1920-24 were the lavish spectacular pictures, imitations of the Italian *Salammbo*, and *Cabiria*. Successes of the day were *Anne Boleyn, Dubarry, Sumurun,* and *The Loves of Pharaoh,* some of them financed by Hugenberg as anti-allied propaganda. Set against this *kitsch*, Carl Mayer's simple, warm, human approach to the relationship of a few individuals—usually drawn from a lower middle-class environment, often concentrated on the story of a single character—was a new sociological use of cinema. *Berlin* was also his conception, but he disliked Ruttmann's inhuman handling of the idea and asked for his name to be removed from the credits. Few of these films were commercially successful if compared with the flamboyant romances, but they were the films that made Germany famous. It was to their creators that Hollywood offered big contracts: Murnau, Gliese, Lubitsch, Freund, Leni, Veidt, Jannings; most of them sacrificed themselves on the Hollywood machine. To Carl Mayer, whose script of *The Last Laugh* was studied so enviously in America, Fox made a handsome offer to write *Sunrise*. He wrote it, in his own good time; but he wrote it in Europe and stubbornly resisted going to Hollywood.

He was a careful, patient worker. He would take days over a few shots, a year or more over a script. He would wrestle and fight with his problems all day and all night. He would go long, lonely walks with them. He would never deliver a script until he was wholly satisfied that the problems were solved. He would rather cancel his contract and return the money than be forced to finish a script in the wrong way. He had iron principles arising from the film medium itself, and never once departed from them. His instinct and love for film dominated his way of living. Film mattered most and he gave everything, including his health, to it.

To Paris he went with Elisabeth Bergner and Czinner in the early sound-film days, and with them he worked on several films—*Der Träumende Mund* and *Ariane*. He came to England in 1932 and began a twelve-year period of helping others. He took no screen credits here, except only on the documentary film made of *The Times* newspaper in '38 and '39, but did advisory work on *Pygmalion* and *Major Barbara* among others. His script of the East End nobody would produce. His fascinating idea of translating Goldsmith's *She Stoops to Conquer* remained only an idea in script form. He gave much time to criticising scripts and cutting copies at my unit, and no technician can have failed to learn from him if they so wanted. To *World of Plenty* he contributed a great deal. Of the big commercial companies, only Two Cities recognised his talent and for them that last year, thanks to del Giudice, he acted as consultant. A few weeks before his death he received a letter from Dr. Siegfried Kracauer, from New York, who was writing for the Guggenheim Foundation a book on the social and political background of the great German films.[1] Kracauer had realised the great influence of Carl Mayer; almost every German film of the Golden Period leads back to his inspiration.

Such men in this mad, money-crazy industry of ours are rare. Had he craved a fortune, his name in tall letters, Carl could have had it at a price he was not prepared to pay—liberty to write as and how he believed. He loved life with a happiness you do not normally find among film-makers. He loved all films and could find something to talk about in the worst of pictures. Above all, he loved people—the people he met in cafés and trains and parks. He seldom read books, and possessed but a dozen connected with subjects on which he was working. He devoured newspapers. His little money he gave away to make others happy.

They are nearly all dead—that group which made German films so famous. Of them all, Carl Mayer's name will remain longest, for from him they drew their inspiration. He belonged to films like no man before him; his body died, July 1st, 1944, from cancer; his name and work will live on.

[1] *From Caligari to Hitler,* Siegfried Kracauer (Princeton University Press, 1947).

A FILM ARTIST—BY KARL FREUND

Carl Mayer was the only 100 per cent. screen-writer I've known. The film was the first and only medium in which he created, and the camera was the first artistic instrument he used.

It was not that he merely 'understood' the film medium. A script by Carl Mayer was already a film. The appearance of a Mayer script was that of a dramatic poem—a detailed recording of every shot and rhythm that he had formed in his imagination. And he was not content to sit down at a desk and imagine his scenes on paper; after repeatedly borrowing a 'finder' from me, I finally obtained one for his exclusive use, for it was with a camera-finder that Mayer experimented and rehearsed each shot of each sequence *at home*. He was so persistent in learning *more*, always *more* about the camera's possibilities, that he often came to my apartment in Berlin in the middle of the night, with a new problem that needed technical advice.

He was just as curious about every part of the many-sided job of film-making. With Emil Jannings, who lived on another floor of the same apartment house, Mayer would try out new ideas and sequences long before they were filmed. In the two and a half months of preparation on *The Last Laugh*, Mayer conferred every day with at least one of us—with Murnau, with the designers Herlth and Röhrig, with Pommer, with Jannings, or with me. It was out of this team-work that all the innovations in *The Last Laugh* evolved.

I remember the first words that set the camera into motion. Mayer asked me, 'Karl, is there any way to film a person's head first in a medium shot and then move in to a great close-up of the eyes alone?' This was for the moment when the aunt discovers that Jannings has been demoted to lavatory-attendant—and it was Jannings' reaction to her discovery that Mayer wanted to heighten. 'I guess you'd have to mount the whole camera apparatus on a wheeled platform of some sort.'

Carl Mayer immediately comprehended the possibilities of such a device, and the entire *Last Laugh* script was revised with camera movement. Actually, when we came to the shot that had started all this movement, wheels were useless, because the aunt looked down on Jannings from the top of a flight of steps. So we worked out this contraption for a descending approach to Jannings' face; taking a fire-ladder that was built in sections that were raised or lowered with a crank, we mounted the Debrie on its top, and chose our *smallest* camera assistant to sit by it to adjust the focus. We all began to look forward to new difficulties—as challenges that required completely original solutions. For the well-known trumpet shot, we suspended the camera in a basket from a bridge that ran the length of the courtyard, and when we found that our pulley couldn't manage the upward movement of the camera-basket, we made the shot downwards—and reversed the film in the camera. When the film had to be a drunken Jannings, I strapped the camera to my chest (with batteries on my back for balance), and played drunk! For the opening shot—down the elevator, across the lobby, and through the revolving-door, my camera and I sat on a bicycle in the descending elevator, and rode out through the opened elevator-door across the lobby, and through the huge revolving-doors. Mayer's imagination had convinced us that we could do anything!

He was extremely sensitive to the broad range of camera styles. He exploited contrasting camera styles in his version of *Tartuffe*—by demanding a cruelly realistic and unmade-up style for the modern sequences, and an unreal, diffuse, Watteau-esque style for the *Tartuffe* episodes. And it was in the modern sequences of *Tartuffe* that sets, for the first time, were lifted from the floor and ramped for the sake of the camera.

After Eisenstein's *Potemkin* exploded on the Berlin film-world in 1926, Carl Mayer's screen-writing career was abruptly altered. From this time on, he ceased writing screen-plays, and continued to function in films primarily as a production and script adviser—a very valuable function, but one far from the active, creative Carl Mayer with whom Murnau and I had worked. Apparently his concept of an increasingly fluid cinema had been shaken for ever by the new Russian principles of conflict and shock. The coming of sound seemed to send him even further away from active participation as a screen-writer. It seems almost ironical that this should have happened to the first consciously experimental writer of films.[1]

After this change in Mayer's career, the quality of his taste and intelligence remained as firm and pure as in his most active days. Even his slightest advice was precious—and evidence for this can be found in our film *Berlin*, whose only script was a single spoken question by Mayer—'Why don't you make a film about Berlin—without a story?'

If one man should ever be given credit for the best film-work to come from Germany, it would have to be Carl Mayer.

---

[1] It was *Potemkin*, Mayer told me, that opened his mind to the documentary approach as distinct from studio-made films, and which led him to work on the original conception of *Berlin*.—P.R.

EPILOGUE 1948–1958

177. RASHOMON, directed by Akira Kurosawa. Machiko Kyo, Toshiro Mifune.
[Japanese, 1950]

178. NO RESTING PLACE, directed by Paul Rotha. Brian O'Higgins, Jack McGowan,
Michael Gough, Noel Purcell. [British, 1950]

179. LOS OLVIDADOS, directed by Luis Buñuel. [Mexican, 1951]

180. UMBERTO D, directed by Vittorio de Sica. [Italian, 1952]

Introductory Note

Since 1948, when this world survey of the cinema was last revised, two vitally important events have made their impact, while a third lies in the immediate future. It is common knowledge that in all countries where television has become the new medium for mass-entertainment, cinema attendances have shrunk in number thereby affecting the whole economic structure of the film industry, especially in North America and the United Kingdom. Secondly, in an attempt to retain existing audiences and to re-attract lost audiences, the industry has resorted to various technical devices – notably cinema-screens of much bigger dimensions than heretofore as well as of different proportions and, less notably, processes which seek to create a three-dimensional illusion. Neither of these technological resources has had marked effect on the subjects chosen for film material, nor have they made any real impact on audiences. What they have done is to restrict the fluidity and selectivity of the film medium as we have known it for more than sixty years, especially in the use of the essential close-up, while at the same time they have heightened the appeal of the open-air picture, notably the American Western.

Of far greater importance is the fact that the American and British cinema-going habit of regular attendances, upon which the exhibition side of the industry based its economics for so many years, and which obviously in turn controlled the manufacturing process, has been broken for ever. In short, the whole distributing and exhibiting sides of the film industry are undergoing a complete reorganisation, although even as I write I do not believe that all those engaged in these undertakings fully understand the extent of what is happening. They cannot bring themselves to realise that the 'good old days' will not return.

The mass-production of motion pictures by departments, the weekly or twice-weekly unquestioning and gullible public lining up at cinemas which are organised into chains or circuits, showing often the same programmes, these have gone for good. Although the coming of mass-television hastened this change, I believe anyway that it would have taken place. When in the late twenties cinema audiences began to decline numerically as a result of the groove of mediocrity into which mass-production had lead motion picture making, the American and British industries were salvaged by turning silent films into talking ones. When in the fifties television in the home drained people away from the public cinemas, Hollywood again sought an innovation. But the phenomena of wider screens and three-dimensional effects were totally different in appeal from the introduction of a screen from which actors spoke.

Today, the shrewder leaders of the industry realise, I think, that the still vast cinemagoing audience can no longer be regarded as an amorphous mass. They perceive, I hope, that there is a large number of minority groups who want to go to see films for reasons other than soporific entertainment – maybe because of the kind of story, or because of the appeal of a name-star, or because they happen to like the cinema in its own artistic right as distinct from the theatre, television, radio, music-hall, opera, ballet or the concert.

It is unlikely that the cinema will be wholly supplanted as a mass-presenter of spectacle. There will always be a ready audience for lavish, crowd-filled productions projected onto a variety of multi-coloured wide-screens, immensely extravagant undertakings which will play to extended runs at selected specially equipped cinemas in key-cities, such as the jumbo-size re-make of *Ben-Hur* currently in hand. But there will also be, I believe, as the industry and its various publics settle down to the new state of affairs, room for a number of films a year which will really utilise the full resources of the cinema as a form of art. And it is obvious that such films will have to be made on an economic basis which is related to the size of the minority audiences to which they are intended to appeal.

In the present decade it is too early to assess the economic worth of these audiences and we find that producers (dependent on distribution-guarantees) are desperately trying to settle for a compromise with erratic and unpredictable results. Distributors have always shown a remarkable dislike for making judgements based on their own opinions; they prefer to mould their ideas on precedent. But with the steady growth of the specialist cinemas and 'art-houses' (as they are oddly named in the USA), backed by the gradual spreading of the film society movement in so many countries, the audience situation should become clearer in the next five years.

In addition, the method of financing film production itself is already undergoing radical change. Those who make a creative contribution to a film—producer, writer, director and main actors—are more and more prepared to be paid in part from the film's potential earnings. Thus, distinct from the very expensive spectacular pictures whose cost runs into millions—pounds not dollars—there should be a tendency for an increase in the number of moderate cost films which will be made because they are good films *per se* and not, as so often in the past, factory-made products.

The third event to which I refer, and which will greatly affect both production and distribution, will be the widescale use of magnetic tape for recording pictures as well as—what is already commonplace—sound. This may aesthetically influence technique by permitting the actual machinery of film-making—cameras and microphones and their operators —to be more distant physically from the actors and the action they are reproducing and thus make it easier for the film medium to be an interpreter of reality, even if that reality is creatively contrived.

*

For this survey of the past ten years, it is virtually impossible to give anything more than a brief and necessarily prejudiced account of the developments. I say 'prejudiced' because in the following country by country round-up I have only referred in the main to films which have appealed to me since 1948. It is, therefore, restricted to films which I have myself seen, either in Britain or during sundry visits abroad.[1] It is patently beyond the scope of any one person (unless he has unlimited travel resources) to embrace all the important films from so many countries in the world today.

One outstanding fact emerged, however, when I came to make this survey; that is the greater availability in Britain today of films from overseas countries other than America. This is due to the growth in the specialist cinema movement, and especially to the enterprise of the National Film Theatre in London, at first a temporary building during the Festival of Britain but since 1957 rebuilt on an adjacent and permanent site. Also, as the various international film festivals multiply—some 'recognised' by the International Federation of Film Producers and some not—more and more nations are sending their films to them. It has become a matter of national prestige.

There is, in addition, a much greater dissemination of information about world cinema today. Reliable journals like *Sight and Sound, Films and Filming, Film* (the English film societies' magazine), *Cahiers du Cinéma, Film Culture* and others did not exist in 1929, and did not operate even in 1948 on anything like the international scale that they do now. And I find that indispensable American trade-journal *Variety* of great help in the international field. For example, although I was remotely aware back in 1929, and again ten years later, that the Japanese produced several hundred films a year, it was impossible to see in Britain more than a very occasional example.

The war years, 1939–46, and the national restrictions hindering the interchange of films in the thirties, also hampered our access not only to films but even to information. So at least it is welcome to record that since 1946, there has been a big loosening up of both films and facts about them. This in turn has brought about a vast if gradual growth in the world interest in what we may call 'good cinema'.

During an all-too-brief visit to Australia in 1958, I was

[1]Countries to which I have been fortunate to have been asked are: Australia, Denmark, France, Germany, Ireland, Italy, Mexico, the Netherlands, Switzerland and the United States.

impressed by the display of interest in, and knowledge of, what constitutes the best in cinema. The vigorous film society movement in that Continent was stimulating and progressive. Never at any time in the past fifty years has there been so great and so serious an interest in the film as one of the major arts of our time as there is today, television notwithstanding. Television, in Britain at any rate, has aided this widening of film appreciation by itself transmitting films of specialised appeal.

As I said above, it is this increasingly selective and discriminating section of the huge general public which is going to be of major importance to the cinema of the future. Ten years ago I reluctantly wrote that the film-trade seldom missed a chance to deride film societies.[1] Today, it is glad of *any* audience. The shrewder operators realise that, with the halcyon days of the cinema-going addiction gone for ever, some fast thinking has got to be done about the likes and dislikes of minority audiences. Fewer films are being made by Britain and America and the disappearance of cinema-theatres will continue until the economic level has been reached appropriate to the different place that the cinema has now to fill in the world of mass-entertainment.

This survey is necessarily confined in the main to films and their makers; space does not permit any but the most cursory mention of the economic and industrial problems of the various national cinemas. Film titles are dated by their year of production and not, as is misleading in some film books, by the date of their release which can vary widely from country to country. The year in which a film is made is its historical importance.

[1] Cf. page 23.

I
United States

Apart from the crazy stampede to find gimmicks with which to fight the competition of television (including old movies) in the home, far and away the most powerful single factor affecting American films during the past decade has been the re-adjustment by Hollywood and Wall Street to meet the requirements of the anti-trust laws of 1948. It is now illegal for the same company to own both the means of production and exhibition of motion pictures.

In brief, an important result of this divorcement has been the big rise of American independent production. The major companies whose familiar names we know so well—M-G-M, Paramount, Warner Bros., Twentieth Century-Fox, Universal-International—can no longer release their films of varying quality through their own or associated circuits of theatres. One company, RKO-Radio, has disappeared entirely. The others are still in business but, like Columbia, making fewer films, preferring instead to finance, service and distribute films made by independent producers. In 1957, nearly half of Hollywood's output was independently made. Actors and directors have formed themselves into companies to produce. This has been beneficial to them tax-wise. The big organisation United Artists, set up it will be remembered in 1919 by Chaplin, Griffith, Mary Pickford and Douglas Fairbanks to distribute exclusively their own films, has now become the largest distributor and financier for many of the independents and has achieved a success without rival in recent years: but it does not itself produce films.

After the Red Menace scare in 1947, very few films for a time tackled any themes which could be conceivably labelled as controversial. Louis de Rochement's *Lost Boundaries* (1949), Kramer's *Home of the Brave* (1949), Clarence Brown's *Intruder in the Dust* (1949) and Joe Losey's *The Dividing Line* (in the USA, *The Lawless*, 1950), were exceptions in their brave attempt to spotlight the cancer of racial hatred and colour discrimination, Brown's film being especially notable. On these pictures and some which followed, both the documentary methods of filming which became conspicuous for their qualities of reality during the war, and the influence of the Italian post-war neo-realist films, had a strong effect.

Many Hollywood films of gangsterism, corruption, alcoholism, drug-addiction, perversion and delinquency of every kind plus mental upset were made in an adopted style of realism, with an emphasis on violence and the rights of physical force. Well-made technically, they seldom probed very deeply into the social and other causes of the sicknesses they portrayed. They set out to shock and stun and they succeeded.

One of the first, Jules Dassin's *Naked City* (1948) was largely shot on New York locations, and it was followed by Robert Wise's *The Set-Up* (1948), Ted Tetzlaff's *The Window* (1948), Nicholas Ray's *They Live by Night* (1948), Anatole Litvak's *The Snake-Pit* (1948), Fred Zinnemann's *Act of Violence* (1949) and *The Men* (1950), Elia Kazan's *Panic in the Streets* (1950), John Huston's *The Asphalt Jungle* (1950), Laszlo Benedek's *The Wild One* (1953), Kazan's *On the Waterfront* (1954) and Stanley Kubrick's *The Killing* (1956).

These films, and others like them, had an impact of vitality and an illusion of reality which made them seem convincing, but they mostly lacked any basic understanding of human relations. None had the compassion which inspired the Italian neo-realists. Their characters for the most part were bitter, violent, repressed, twisted, abnormal, neurotic, sadistic and anti-social. They reflected, maybe, a period of disquiet, of hysterical outbreak, of sullen protest and of violence for its own sake; a jagged wartime hangover and a harsh reminder that the frontier years of gun-law were not so far back.

It was not until the mid-fifties, with Paddy Chayevsky and Delbert Mann's *Marty*, that we find a warmer and more human approach to the American daily scene. A group of writers and directors had discovered a certain temporary freedom of treatment and subject-matter in American TV plays. Successful in an intimate, close-to-life way, some of this group turned from the midget's peepshow to the motion picture proper, and after several adaptations of their own television dramas, they began to create in terms of film itself.

Starting with *Marty* (1955), a number of socially-conscious,. realistically handled films emerged from New York as well as from Hollywood which made a considerable impact on critics and on some audiences. Among them were Martin Ritt's *A Man is Ten Feet Tall* (in USA, *The Edge of the City*, 1957), Robert Mulligan's *Fear Strikes Out* (1957), Chayevsky and Delbert Mann's *Bachelor Party* (1957), Frankenheimer's *The Young Stranger* (1957), Sidney Lumet's *Twelve Angry Men* (1957), and Chayevsky and Cromwell's *The Goddess* (1958), all films which had a common quality in being an interpretation of the contemporary scene in the United States but without unnecessary violence; all very well acted.

Two other characteristics of the period arising from the attempt to meet the competition from the little screen were a concentration of finance and a funnelling of talent into a few very costly and sometimes gigantically spectacular 'block-busters'—for example, *The Ten Commandments*—and a contagious rush to exploit foreign locations. In 1931, I had written, 'It would be the sanest thing in the sordid history of the cinema if every studio were to close down for the period of a year, if all the stars were given a vacation, and if production units . . . were to be sent to every part of the world. The resulting films would be the most thrilling entertainment that has ever been produced.'[1]

Well, the units have surely explored the world since then but entertainment of a mediocre kind has mostly resulted. Advantage has been taken of blocked earnings from American pictures abroad, of cheap local labour overseas, or of a star's wish to be absent from base for income-tax purposes. Much of Africa, India, Japan, Australia, the West Indies, and

[1] *Celluloid: The Film Today* (Longmans, 1931), page 34.

almost all of Europe west of the Curtain have been invaded. Unfortunately Hollywood methods and ways of thinking have been taken along too so that the resulting films may have had 'local' colour used much as a backdrop, but they have not had any quality other than that of Hollywood on holiday. *The Pride and the Passion, Kangaroo* and *Alexander the Great* were typical of their kind. In the continual striving for a world-market, which is essential today for such costly films, they have been ornamented with international casts of German, French, Italian, English and Swedish actors playing alongside Hollywood stars. Maybe this species of 'internationalism' has broadened a few minds among those involved, benefited the airlines, cable companies and hoteliers as well as giving well-paid casual labour to thousands of local inhabitants, but it gave us no films of any merit whatsoever, except perhaps that bonanza of entertainment which no one could possibly take seriously, the late Mike Todd's *Around the World in Eighty Days* (1956–57), directed largely by an Englishman, Michael Anderson.

As might be expected, Hollywood retained its unshakable superiority in the musical film over the decade. Of the many, my preferences were for Vincente Minnelli's *The Pirate* (1948), *Bandwagon* (1953) and *Gigi* (1957), together with Gene Kelly and Stanley Donen's *On the Town* (1949) and Donen's *Seven Brides for Seven Brothers* (1954). All of these displayed a scintillating amalgam of music, dancing, lyrics and design which echoed in the cinema America's unapproachable know-how of the stage-musical, which perhaps reached its top in *West Side Story*.

In another peculiarly Hollywood field, the Western, production never flagged. It became significant when Carl Foreman wrote and produced and Fred Zinnemann directed *High Noon* (1952), using the Western *genre* to interpret a wider theme of social comment—a 'democratic allegory' Richard Griffith called the film. A somewhat similar attempt was made by William Wyler in his sprawling *The Big Country* (1958) but without the same success. Among routine Westerns, John Ford's *Wagonmaster* (1950) was the only one by this maestro of the mythological American West to come anywhere near his memorable *My Darling Clementine* (1946). Mention should be made, too, of George Stevens's *Shane* (1953), the best film which, to me, this rather over-estimated director has to his credit. Today, perhaps as never before, the myth of the Western lives on in television as well as in cinema, a world in which each man is a law unto himself and the quickest on-the-draw is the self-appointed leader of the community.

Among other American films which rated well critically during the period, or at least merit place on the memory-record, were: Billy Wilder's macabre satire *Sunset Boulevard* (1948): Henry King's *Twelve O'Clock High* (1949), a half-successful study of wartime morale; Joseph Mankiewicz's *All About Eve* (1950), a clever social comedy; George Cukor's *Born Yesterday* (1950), from Kanin's brilliant satirical play and his admirable re-make of *A Star is Born* (1954); John Huston's inarticulated but very interesting *Red Badge of Courage* (1951) and his exhilarating adventure-comedy *The African Queen* (1952) ; Kazan's *Viva Zapata!* (1952), his best since *Boomerang!* (1947); Fred Zinnemann's explosive *From Here to Eternity* (1953); Walter Wanger and Don Siegal's dynamic *Riot in Cell Block 11* (1954); John Sturge's well-directed *Bad Day at Black Rock* (1954) ; Robert Aldrich's frank anti-war subject *Attack!* (1956); Orson Welles's European-made, oddly uneven and infuriating but at the same time essentially cinematic *Othello* (1956); Daniel Taradash's outspoken *Storm Centre* (1956); and, a picture which I admired a great deal both technically and for what it said, Stanley Kubrick's *Paths of Glory* (1957), an exposure of corruption in high military quarters and the resultant suffering by the rank-and-file in the French army of World War I. It should also be recorded that a young British director, Alexander McKendrick, made his best film to date in Hollywood in a savage exposure of the twilight world of the Broadway columnist, *The Sweet Smell of Success* (1957). Chaplin provided some of us with a nostalgic and most moving last American film, *Limelight* (1952). His

recent picture in England, *A King in New York* (1957), was
to many people a disappointment; to my regret, I found it
vulgar, bitter and singularly unfunny, but say so with
reluctance. I am sure that one day Chaplin will regret
having made it.

Among short and documentary films, there were far too
many to allow full comment. Those which particularly
rated mention were: Lerner's diverting and skilful *Muscle
Beach* (1950); Ashley and Engels' well-observed *Little
Fugitive* (1953); Roger Tilton's much imitated *Jazz Dance*
(1954); the Sanders brothers' now world-known *Time Out
of War* (1954); George Stoney's very human *All My Babies*
(1953); and Rogosin and partners' candid-camera study of
alcoholics on Skid Row, *On the Bowery* (1956). Disney's
'true-life' animal studies should also be remembered, perhaps the best being *The Vanishing Prairie* (1954).

In the huge field of animated cartoons, the most notable
event was the emergence of the UPA group, in which at
outset the director John Hubley had marked influence,
especially in the enchanting *Rooty-Toot-Toot* (1952), one of
the best cartoons I have ever seen and which I can re-see
times without number, and the amusing *Gerald McBoing-
Boing* (1953). Later, Hubley had his own unit called Storyboard, from which *The Tender Game* (1958) was outstanding
for its charm, good taste, design and music.

The American scene should not perhaps be left without
reference to the popular television series, *Victory at Sea*,
written and produced for NBC–TV by the late Henry
Salomon and brilliantly edited from wartime stock footage
by Isaac Kleineman. But to embark on comment about
films made for television is outside my scope; this series
justifies mention here because a single feature-length film
was compiled from the TV half-hour series for release in the
cinemas.

II

UNITED KINGDOM

The frustrating story of British films over the past ten years need not be retold in detail.[1] In spite of what must have been a total production expenditure of many million pounds, British films as a whole are now in much the same sterile position as they were in 1948, except that the mass-arrival of television into more than two-thirds of British homes has aggravated the constant crisis.

It is tempting to state that television alone is the cause of Britain's cinema decline but it is just not true. The monopolistic control by the circuits and distributors over production still obtains, unlike the changed situation referred to in the USA. Freedom for the genuine independent British producer remains as restricted as ever. Perhaps the only new portent is the appearance of what has been aptly named the Mid-Atlantic picture, but this is not really new if we remember back to the Anglo-American films made in the United Kingdom to meet the legal requirements of the various Cinematograph Films Acts.

In common with most production, these hybrids have been geared starwise and storywise to the hope of a world-market and have consequently become more and more costly and pseudo-cosmopolitan. *The Bridge on the River Kwai* (1956–57) and *The Key* (1957–58) were two recent examples; neither was really a British picture although made by British directors, and both suffered from attempts to introduce an American angle of approach. Co-production with European countries has been rare, not only because of inherent language problems and trade-union restrictions but also because, in my belief, there exists a wide difference in what might be called the psychological approach to film-making between British and Continental film minds. Seen in a European context, British film-makers are curiously paro-

---

[1] *Vide: Rotha on the Film* (Faber, 1958), Part IV. The Constant Crisis.

chial and uninformed about the world cinema. At the various international film festivals, for instance, British film contingents often produce the unconscious effect that they are on a day-trip to Boulogne.

For the record, and in perspective with the output of other nations, few British feature films deserve inclusion here, reluctant as I am to say it. The mediocre, the disappointments and the downright failures do not justify resurrection, any more than they do in other countries. Ealing Films, once the standby, have come and gone for reasons hard to explain, their studio lost in transit to television. Among their many pictures, singled out for the record, were: Robert Hamer's richly witty and sophisticated *Kind Hearts and Coronets* (1949); McKendrick's rollicking comedy *Whisky Galore* (1948) and his satirical *The Man in the White Suit* (1951); the late Henry Cornelius's engaging *Passport to Pimlico* (1949) and Charles Friend's sincere *The Cruel Sea* (1952). These films had two things in common: they had style and they reflected the imprint of their directors. That can seldom be said about British films, excepting always the work of David Lean and Carol Reed who have worked for American interests in recent years.

From Reed, only *The Third Man* (1949) fully demonstrated this director's superb technical skill, although other assessors might include *The Fallen Idol* (1948) and *The Key* (1958). From Britain's other 'top' director, David Lean, *The Bridge on the River Kwai* (1957) was a huge, popular success but was too confused storywise ever to be a good picture; *The Sound Barrier* (1952) was technically brilliant so long as it was airborne; while the Venetian escapade, *Summer Madness* (1955), was the best because the most human. But to be honest neither Lean nor Reed has fulfilled the expectancy that was implicit in *Brief Encounter* (1945) and *Odd Man Out* (1947). They both seem to be out of touch with common human experiences, to live in a world which has no contact with what is significant in life today.

Among Anthony Asquith's work, *Orders to Kill* (1958) attracted much critical acclaim (including mine) and showed that he had not lost, after all, his genuine feeling for cinema. Many would include his *The Browning Version* (1951), but one wishes that Asquith could be given more time away from making film versions of stage-plays, no matter how strongly he defends the process. The perennial *genre* of middle-class comedy, essentially suburban and always respectable and conformist, could boast Cornelius's *Genevieve* (1953) as its proudest example, while the equally perennial Boy Scout, war-heroics pictures of which there have been so many would no doubt have Lewis Gilbert's *The Dambusters* (1955) at its peak. To admirers of Olivier's particular style of cinema-cum-theatre acting, *Richard III* (1955) provided a surfeit of talent—histrionic and decorative; I found it preferable to the earlier Olivier-Shakespeares.

This leaves only a few unforeseen notables to record: Zoltan Korda's sincere and worthwhile *Cry, the Beloved Country* (1951); Havelock-Allan and Fergus McDonald's modest but excellent thriller *The Small Voice* (1948); Philip Leacock's honest *The Brave Don't Cry* (1952) (about the only Group III product worth recalling), and the same director's humble but commendable *The Kidnappers* (1953) and *Innocent Sinners* (1957). Other pictures worth mention were: Bernard Miles and Alan Osbiston's courageous independent effort *The Chance of a Lifetime* (1950); Jack Clayton's prize-winning and craftsmanlike short-story film *The Bespoke Overcoat* (1955); Thorold Dickinson's well-intentioned if uneven Israeli picture, *Hill 24 Does Not Answer* (1955); Peter Glenville's rather stagey but sincere *The Prisoner* (1955) and, more recently, Pat Jackson's fresh and charming *Virgin Island* (1957). As the period under review ended, Jack Clayton achieved high critical praise for *Room at the Top* (1958), which revealed him as a professionally-skilled director handling a subject which at least dealt with a serious aspect of contemporary England, while Ronald Neame's *The Horse's Mouth* (1958), lazily directed, allowed Alec Guinness to exploit the Ealing style comedy at the expense of 'modern art'. A last-minute surprise came from the film technicians union's own company, ACT Films; it was a modest enough psychological thriller, *The Man Upstairs* (1958), directed by Don Chaffey with skill and insight.

Is it conceivable that the commercial success of *Room at the Top* will mark a liberalising of attitude among British producers and provide them with the courage to make full use of the cinematic talent that exists in the frustrating climate of British film-making?

Few British documentaries, alas, made significant impact over the decade although many were technically proficient. John Eldridge's *Three Dawns to Sydney* (1949) was beautifully made, if a repeat of an old theme; Paul Dickson's *The Undefeated* (1950), a warmly observed film, was one of the Central Office of Information's last pictures to be of interest; Basil Wright's poetic but perhaps overstrained *Waters of Time* (1950) was not a step forward; Lindsay Anderson and Guy Brenton's *Thursday's Children* (1953) was an admirable study in observation and made with much feeling; Stuart Legg and Bert Haanstra's dynamic and purposeful *The Rival World* (1955) was one of the few socially important films; and James Hill's *The New Explorers* (1956) was a well-directed survey of world oil. Perhaps I may also be permitted to add *World Without End* (1952–53), produced and co-directed by Basil Wright for Unesco, which expressed the humanism of internationalism more than any other documentary since *The World is Rich*.

We also saw the emergence of what was styled Free Cinema, the work of a group of young film-makers, some of whose films were sponsored by the British Film Institute's experimental film fund. Although the pictures from this group have been over-praised—largely I suspect because so much orthodox British documentary has become pedestrian —Lindsay Anderson's *Every Day Except Christmas* (1957) had a lively style and a candid-camera technique which made it worthwhile and Karel Reisz's *We are the Lambeth Boys* (1958) had a vitality and an authenticity so badly lacking in the great majority of British feature productions.

The Shell Film Unit maintained its high standard of technical excellence with subjects mainly of specialised interest and the British Transport Unit continued with its conventionally competent output which lacks real creative inspiration. Little has been made which can even be remotely likened to the pre-war and wartime periods of British documentary. Since the abolition of the Crown Film Unit in 1952, Government sponsorship of films through its Central Office of Information has become ineffectual and negligible. Most industrial sponsorship, except for the Shell Film Unit, has become cautious and conformist. In fact, one of the few documentaries I have seen of late which had any kind of social significance and integrity was a BBC television film, *Night in the City* (1957), made by Denis Mitchell and the Corporation's Manchester Unit. A great deal of day-to-day reporting, some of which passes illegitimately under the name of documentary, is carried out by television, both by the BBC and the independent programme companies, but little of it has any lasting value. Only one genuine documentary (other than *We Are the Lambeth Boys*) emerged from Britain in 1958, Basil Wright's lyrical and very beautifully-made personal interpretation of ancient and modern Greece, *The Immortal Land*, and even this did not take its gifted director much further forward than his classic *Song of Ceylon* (1935).

In the animated cartoon field, the Halas Batchelor unit continued a steady stream of technically good work and tried its hand at a feature-length cartoon of George Orwell's *Animal Farm* (1954) with mixed results. A new name in this *genre* was Richard Williams, whose highly original, imaginative and courageous *The Little Island* (1957–58) rightly gained much critical applause. Another specialised form of film-making which has been well developed in the United Kingdom has been films made for child audiences, commissioned from the various short film-making companies by the Children's Film Foundation, now industry-aided. One of this series, *The Salvage Gang* (1958), directed by John Krish, was better in all ways than many feature films in the same year though made for about a tenth of the cost of an average feature picture.

181. CASQUE D'OR, directed by Jacques Becker. Simone Signoret, Serge Reggiani. [French, 1952]

182. LES JEUX INTERDITS, directed by René Clément. [French, 1952]

183. PATHER PANCHALI, directed by Satyajit Ray. [Indian, 1952–55]

184. UGETSU MONOGOTARI, directed by Kenji Mizoguchi. Machiko Kyo, Masayuki Mori. [Japanese, 1953]

III

FRANCE

If there is one thing that differentiates Britain from the main European film-making countries, it is that the latter believe in the cinema as an art as well as a commodity. Industrialised and commercialised as all film industries must be under the economic systems of the West, nevertheless it has been found possible to equate the art of film-making with the need for profit-return more successfully in Europe than in the English-speaking countries. In spite of under-going periodic crises, the French cinema especially—although frequently described as being in a state of *rigor mortis* by its own critics—contrives continuously to give forth important and seldom insignificant work. Since 1948, there has been in overall an inspiring revival in French cinema. There have been many disappointments and only half-fulfilled expectations but the French record of the past ten years—in the best work of Bresson, Renoir, Clément, Ophüls, Tati, Resnais, Lamorisse and Franju—is something not to be under-rated.

Various causes exist for this renaissance. The French have a tradition of good film-making and are conscious of it. They recognise that film-making is essentially an individualist activity, although the individual must depend on a team serving his needs. They appreciate the contribution of the writer to the final film. Jacques Prévert, Charles Spaak, Jean Aurenche and Pierre Bost, for example, are held in far higher esteem than any scriptwriters in Britain. It is not that we do not have as good writers as the French; it is that they are not given the respect which would be theirs in France. The French are less susceptible to compromise than the film-makers of Britain and the USA; feature film-makers are not ashamed to make short films or very modest budget pictures if they cannot achieve what they want in features. Short film production is more flexible and more generally imaginative than elsewhere, as well as being prolific and recently given Government financial encouragement. When the trade-body representing the whole French film industry, Unifrance, issues publicity, it includes and is proud of the work of its experimentalists and short film-makers. The British feature film industry couldn't care less about the short film-makers. It has no interest at all in experiment. It is this kind of attitude towards cinema as a whole that makes such a big difference between British and Continental films. In France, although there are frustrated film-makers like everywhere else, there is less antagonism to young talent in the creative field, especially recently. The national film school, the Institut des Hautes Etudes Cinématographiques, now 16 years old, has produced students whose work and ideas have had influence. Britain and America have no such national school of cinematography.

It is true that television has not as yet made its impact to anything like the degree that it has in the USA or the UK, but even if and when it does, it is most unlikely to have the effect which it has had in English-speaking countries because of what can only be called French film-consciousness. And, as Louis Marcorelles has pointed out, the influence of the French ciné-clubs has not been without some effect, although it must be remembered that Paris still traditionally sets the pace for the country as a whole.[1] He also makes the point that French film criticism of an intelligent kind has a far wider outlet than similar criticism in Britain or America. Groups of theorists have grown up around the two French film journals, *Cahiers du Cinéma* and *Positif*, who are not despised and jeered at by older professional film-makers as they would be in Britain.

To turn to films, it is often forgotten by critics today that the post-war Italian neo-realist movement had part of its roots in the French cinema of the thirties.[2] Jean Renoir's *Le Crime de Monsieur Lange* (1935), *Toni* (1935), *La Bête Humaine* (1938) and *La Règle du Jeu* (1939) represented an expression of social realism which was a forerunner of the later Italian work and was a true reflection of **its period.**

[1] *Sight & Sound*, Vol. 27. No. 4. Spring, 1948.
[2] Cf. page 532 *et seq.*

Some of the films of Feyder, Carné and Duvivier in the thirties almost pursued the same end but with less freedom of vitality; and we must not overlook Vigo's contribution to realism and poetry. After the constraints of the Occupation, the French cinema was for a long time struggling to reassert its economic independence and opportunities for creative freedom were rare. Nevertheless, as always happens in France, some notable films emerged, among them: Claude Autant-Lara's sensitive, finely-made and beautifully acted *Le Diable au Corps* (1947); Cocteau's (if you like Cocteau) fantasy *La Belle et la Bête* (1947); Clouzot's 'police-thriller' *Quai des Orfèvres* (1947); Cocteau's gloomy and powerful *Les Parents Terribles* (1948); and Grémillon's uneven but still fascinating *Pattes Blanches* (1948).

New names appeared, to be associated with films that showed a fresh feeling for the cinema after the repressed war years. Jacques Becker's *Antoine et Antoinette* (1948) and *Edouard et Caroline* (1951) were spontaneous and brilliant social comedies; but their director, after a superb excursion into a period-costume film, *Casque d'Or* (1952) became enmeshed in commercial entanglement. René Clément, whose *Bataille du Rail* (1945) and *Les Jeux Interdits* (1952) impressed so much, also became bogged down in bigger and costlier co-productions, of which *Gervaise* (1956) was the best. Some films which deserve the record from the first half of the decade were: Daquin's convincing and realistic *Le Point du Jour* (1949); Roger Leenhardt's talented *Les Dernières Vacances* (1949); Yves (brother to Marc) Allegret's depressing but sensitive *Une si jolie petite Plage* (1948); Cocteau's controversial and technically accomplished *Orphée* (1949); Clouzot's infuriating and all-too-clever *Manon* (1949) and his sadistic and violent *Salaire de la Peur* (1953); Renoir's rich *La Carosse d'Or* (1953); while the late Max Ophüls working in Paris gave us the never-to-be forgotten *La Ronde* (1950) and *Le Plaisir* (1952). Jacques Tati was revealed as a new director-comedian of immense versatility in *Jour de Fête* (1949) and *M. Hulot* (1953). Other new names included Cayatte, director of the grim but compelling *Nous sommes tous des Assassins* (1952) and, of course, Robert Bresson, already known by *Les Anges du Péché* (1943) and *Les Dames du Bois de Boulogne* (1944–46), whose *Journal d'un Curé de Campagne* (1951) brought him international fame but which to some critics (including this one) was far too literary in style to be true cinema.

Of these middle generation directors, only Tati and Bresson have maintained their uncompromising independence since the mid-fifties and then at the expense of making few films. In fact, Bresson has made only *Un Condamné à mort s'est échappé* (1957), to my mind his best film, and Tati's *Mon Oncle* (1956–57) has yet to be shown in England. Carné, Becker, Clément, Duvivier, Clouzot, Autant-Lara, Daquin, Allegret have all been disappointing in their recent assignments. And I personally found René Clair living on his past, an unquestionably distinguished past, in *La Beauté du Diable* (1949) and *Porte des Lilas* (1957), while *Les Belles de Nuit* (1952) was frankly a bore; he did, however, regain some of his impeccable good taste in *Les Grands Manoeuvres* (1955). Grémillon, the uncompromiser, has worked when at all mostly in documentary, and the same is true of Rouquier whose *Farrébique* (1944–46) is so well remembered.

An American emigré, Jules Dassin, prevented from working in Hollywood by the Red Menace fear, began with *Rififi* (1955) a whole cycle of black crime–thrillers or *policiers*, some of them as violent as anything thought up in Hollywood, but he himself went on to make a far more interesting film in *Celui qui doit mourir* (1957), which had no real claim to be called French. Clouzot, too, went on with the crime-thriller, making the cunningly clever if distasteful *Les Diaboliques* (1955). But, as Louis Marcorelles observes, few of these directors have either found fresh things to say in cinema in the way of subjects, or have rediscovered the inspiration which stimulated the French social realist school of the thirties, with the exception of Bresson. When considering the upheaval and restlessness of France over the period and its inclination to inversion, this is not surprising.

Among a host of new names which have cropped up lately,

Alexandre Astruc and Roger Vadim are best-known and are perhaps most representative of the current hopelessness of French intellectualism. Astruc's first film (after being a critic, theoretician and novelist), *Le Rideau Cramoisi* (1952) was to me greatly over-rated by the English critics and owed what virtues it had to the German cinema of the twenties. His second film, *Les Mauvaises Rencontres* (1955), I have unfortunately not seen but it aroused a storm of controversy and was said to be an accurate reflection of the cynical boredom and self-corruption of the young Paris intellectuals of the fifties. Vadim's talents have been partly obscured by the sex-exploitation of his star (and for a time wife) Brigitte Bardot, but *Et Dieu créa la Femme*(1956) and *Sait-on jamais?* (1957) both accurately interpreted the amoral, transient and all-too-cynical atmosphere of a certain strata of the young generation in Paris. Vadim has, too, a visual camera-sense that should not be dismissed.

Like Vadim, all other new names in French cinema are of young men—Louis Malle, assistant to Cousteau on the wonderful *Le Monde du Silence* (1956), whose *Ascenseur pour l'échafaud* (1957) has not been shown in England; Claude Bernard-Aubert, whose film of a French military patrol in the Vietnam jungle, *Patrouille de Choc* (1957) was an honest attempt to comment on French overseas policy, and the same is reported of Marcel Camus's *Mort en Fraude* (1958), about the Indo-China war, which I have not seen; and Norbert Carbonneaux, whose work again has not been shown in England but is said to have a 'truly personal sense of humour'.[1] Two recent films which, in spite of obvious faults, did strike me as revealing new exciting talent and approach were Claude Chabrol's *Le Beau Serge* (1958), an independently financed picture wholly shot on location in a village near Limoges, made with a raw integrity and human understanding; and François Truffaut's *Les Mistons* (1958), which had a freshness and youthful vitality which was stimulating. Meantime, we await the new Marcel Carné, *Les Tricheurs* (1958) which has created quite a storm in

[1] *International Film Annual*, No. 2 (Calder, 1958), article by Jean Queval and Gilbert Salachas.

France; Franju's first feature, *La Tête contre les Murs* (1958); Rouquier's feature *S.O.S. Noronha*; Louis Malle's *Les Amants*; and Alain Resnais's first full-length film in Japan.

By some ingenious financing not always stemming from sponsorship (as in Britain), but encouraged by a system of Government bonuses or *primes à la qualité*, French short and documentary film-making has maintained a wonderful and lively inspiration and a pleasurable versatility of subjects. Of the work of the many directors in this field, both established and new, mention must be made first of Alain Resnais, for his *Guernica* (1950), *Les Statues meurent aussi* (1954) and *Nuit et Brouillard* (1956). Resnais is one of the most brilliant cinematic and socially-critical minds in European cinema; all his films have a bite and a dynamic quality that make them unique and a challenge to the audience. They should be far more widely known and appreciated. Albert Lamorisse, with his *Crin Blanc* (1953) and *Le Ballon Rouge* (1956) is also in the front-rank of documentary makers, while the films of Georges Rouquier are always of first importance— *Le Sel de la Terre* (1950) and *Honegger* (1957). A new name to many during the decade will be Georges Franju, whose *Le Sang des Bêtes* (1949), *Hotel des Invalides* (1952) and *La Grand Méliès* (1953) were all notable. Commander Jacques Cousteau's *Le Monde du Silence* (1956), Nicole Védrès's *La Vie commence demain* (1950), Clouzot's *Le Mystère Picasso* (1956) and Joris Ivens's *La Seine a rencontré Paris* (1958) were equally of importance, while the work of Jacques Baratier, Agnes Varda, Pierre Kast, Jean Dewever, Louis Grospierre, Jean-Daniel Pollet, Edouard Molinaro, Jean-Jacques Langpain and Louis Bessieres is to be watched.

The French can also produce out-of-the-hat some captivating cartoons; among those I recall with pleasure were Jim Fabian's *Bouli Bouli: le Crocodil* (1957) and Jean Jabely's *Ballade Chromo* (1957).

IV

ITALY

By 1948 the first raw impact of the Italian neo-realists had made itself felt with memorable effect but it was only later that non-Italian critics were to find out that this powerful movement of social criticism in the cinema did not begin with *Roma Città aperta* (1945). It stemmed rather from Visconti's film *Ossessione* (1942) and De Sica's *I Bambini ci guardano*, with a script by Zavattini, in the same year. In 1948 Visconti gave us his magnificent and uncompromising study of the poverty-stricken fisher-people of Sicily, *La Terra trema*, although it was not seen abroad in its original version until some years later. It has been disappointing to some of us that Visconti like Rossellini has not developed further along this path. Whatever he may say to the contrary, his last film *Notti bianche* (1957) was a pale shadow in every way of his strong, warm and intensely human earlier work. It is hard for us to accept the statements made by some Italians in recent years that neo-realism is dead, or that it has been superseded by a cult of neo-romanticism. Such announcements suggest that those who utter them have no proper understanding of the purpose or meaning of neo-realism. As the decade progressed, it became clear that only a handful of film-makers in Italy faithfully subscribed to the neo-realist movement; of them De Sica and Cesar Zavattini were, and still remain, the outstanding.

So much has been written about De Sica's *Ladri di Biciclette* (1948) that it is almost redundant to reiterate here that it is among the great films of all time. Few films have matched it for its integrity, its profound humanism, its social comment on employment and unemployment, its portrayal of simple human relationships, its use of non-actors, its wholly successful interpretation of real life on the screen with a minimum of contrivance and great subtle technical skill. I am, however, in a minority, I believe, in liking De Sica's later film, *Umberto D* (1952) even more than I did

Bicycle Thieves. It is, in my considered opinion, one of the few complete masterpieces of the cinema—but I have written about it at length elsewhere and there is no sense in repetition.[1] De Sica's other works, *Miracolo a Milano* (1950) and *L'Oro di Napoli* (1954) were both full of wonderful humour and satire, but they were not up to his earlier work. To my regret, I have not seen his last film, *Il Tetto* (1956). De Sica and Zavattini have promised that they will resume their partnership in 1959 and I hope that the director's popular success as an actor in recent years has not blunted his supreme creative skill as a film-maker.

1948 also saw Alberto Lattuada make *Il Mulino del Po*, which brought him to the forefront for his acute cinematic sense and his expert handling of actors. His version of *Il Cappotto* (1951), from a Zavattini script, also had many admirable sequences, but his later work has tended to become more conformist to meet the commercial needs of the Italian cinema's striving for a world-market. Renato Castellani, whose *Due Soldi di Speranza* (1951) was so promising, is another director who has not lived up to first expectations and the same may be said of Luciano Emmer, the erstwhile maker of art-films, whose *Domenica d'Agosto* (1950) augured so well.

But I hesitate to criticise these Italian directors or their colleagues for desertion from the hard and difficult path of neo-realism. Three powerful factors opposed them. Firstly, the genuine neo-realist films were themselves never popular in the country in which they were made. After the depravations of the war and Occupation, the post-war Italian public wanted the glamour and glitter of the Hollywood way-of-life. The best of the neo-realist films had their success outside Italy.

Secondly, as the decade progressed, the Italian film industry gradually built up its economic stability, partly with the aid of American pictures made on Italian soil with blocked earnings, and set its eyes on the American market. Wanting to have the best of both worlds, Italian producers

[1] For full reviews of *Umberto D* and *Bicycle Thieves*, *vide: Rotha on the Film* (Faber, 1958), pp.144–147, 184–188.

744

tried to retain the earthy, actuality subjects for which De Sica and Rossellini had made the Italian cinema famous but sought to gloss them with a veneer of sensational sex and sadism. De Santis's *Riso Amaro* (1949) was one of the first examples and it was endlessly copied. The official, quarterly Italian film review, *Il film italiano*, published by Unitalia Film, is filled with articles by journalists who stand on their heads in order not to disparage true neo-realism but at the same time disown its validity, finally inventing a new and pathetic substitute—neo-romanticism!

Thirdly, Authority in the form of the Roman Catholic Church and Foreign Policy deprecated the export of true neo-realism as being 'unrepresentative' and dangerous to the tourist trade and politically unacceptable to Italy's post-war friends in economic circles.[1] Thus from the time of *Umberto* onwards it became increasingly difficult for the true Italian neo-realists to function while at the same time a phoney neo-realism was promoted. A new vogue in elaborate period costume pictures also flourished and more recently the European Common Market has opened the way for co-production, sometimes tripartite, with France, Spain, Germany and Yugoslavia, involving much bigger production costs which have inevitably caused a safer choice of subjects and casts selected with a world market in view.

One director, however, who has up to now avoided some of these pitfalls is Federico Fellini, at first a writer associated with Rossellini and Lattuada. With a sure sense of cinema, Fellini climbed to a world reputation with *I Vitelloni* (1953), *La Strada* (1954), *Il Bidone* (1955) and *Le Notti di Cabiria* (1957). His success has been coupled with that of his wife, the actress Giulietta Masina, who has played in most of his films. That Fellini has an understanding of neo-realism must, I think, be accepted but he has been able to invest it with a subtle kind of fantasy which no doubt makes it acceptable to the authorities, while his undeniable box-office success and critical prestige abroad have endeared him to the Italian producers. Personally, I do not believe that his work comes

[1] *Vide: Sight and Sound*, Vol. 24, No. 3, pp. 147–166.

near to approaching the raw, unvarnished, simple truth of De Sica at his best; it smacks too much of contrivance for that. But perhaps the real test of his integrity will be the star-studded co-production on which he is now working. Of his films to date, I liked *Cabiria* the best.

Numerous less important films over the period but worth the record were: Zavattini's omnibus project made by a clutch of directors, *Amore in Città* (1954); Pietro Germi's *Il Ferroviere* (1955); Franco Rossi's sensitive *Amici per la Pelle* (1955); and Francesco Masselli's unusual and most interesting *Gli sbandati* (1955). A film which is often overlooked among Italian work was *Donne senza Nome* (1950), made by the Hungarian director Geza Radvany, which had many excellent visual qualities and a considerable sense of social purpose.

'For some time Italy has produced several hundred documentaries every year, dozens of which demonstrate the striking personalities of the directors', wrote Vinicio Marinucci.[1] This official statement is, I am sure, numerically correct, but—as in British television today—any kind of travel-talk or snip-snap reportage is called 'documentary' by the Italians. In the same article, the writer coins the term 'neo-exoticism', than which no more apt label could be found to describe Italian globe-trottings to far-off lands during the fifties. Mostly well-photographed in colour, these films had little true documentary quality. Writing about that pretentious travelogue *Continente perduta* (1954), Mr Marinucci says, 'The spectacular narrative documentary in its present stage of development in Italy is the fruit of the evolution of the realistic current which, *lacking the dramatic themes offered by life after the war in its native country*, has looked abroad for the motives of an enquiry which is certainly less deep but rich in certain spectacular and emotional values, thus one is not wrong if one speaks of such works as a type of neo-realism'. (The italics are mine.)

Thus in one breath Mr Marinucci, speaking for the Italian film-trade, made it abundantly clear that he neither under-

---

[1] *Il film Italiano*, published by Unitalia Film, IX year, No. 24.

stands what is meant by neo-realism nor by documentary. Like the German, the Italian understanding of documentary is clearly quite different from the British, who after all coined the term. Of some 20 so-called documentaries submitted to the jury at the 1958 Venice Festival of Short and Documentary Films, only two had any distinction or were qualified for submission in the real meaning of the term. Those two were Cecilia Mangini's devastating exposure of child delinquency in Italian cities, *Ignoti alla Città* (1957), which was inexplicably withdrawn from being eligible for an award, and Luigi Gianni's study of dying folklore and superstition, *Magia Lucana* (1957), which was suitably rewarded. The remaining entries were mostly coloured picture postcards in motion, or examples of the new trend of 'neo-exoticism'. It is strange to note that whereas the French have a strong, imaginative and most worth-while documentary and short film movement, it scarcely exists to any purpose in Italy in spite of the hundreds of short films officially produced and encouraged.

V

SCANDINAVIA

Since Alf Sjöberg's *Frenzy* (1944), from a script by Ingmar Bergman, marked the revival of the cinema in SWEDEN, the picture from outside that country seems to be largely the Bergman story. True, Sjöberg's very beautiful and visually subtle *Miss Julie* (1950) placed him as a director of remarkable qualities and style, and Arne Sucksdorff's animal pictures, of which *The Great Adventure* (1953) was the most widely-known and liked, showed us that there was more to Swedish cinema than Ingmar Bergman, but the latter's uneven work, with its complex constructions and involved moral arguments, is what Swedish cinema has been best known for during the past ten years. We from the outside have only Mr Forsyth Hardy's reliable word that there are good directors called Hampe Faustman, Hasse Ekman, Ake Ohberg and Gosta Folke, all of whose work sounds of interest from Mr Hardy's descriptions.[1]

Few of us in England have seen all of the 23 films with which Bergman has been associated, or can trace his career in detail. My own criticism is based on his three by-now well-known works *Smiles of a Summer Night* (1955), *The Seventh Seal* (1956) and *Wild Strawberries* (1957).[2] He is without question a 'difficult' director. Much of the time I am led to think that he is as confused in his own mind as to what he is trying to say as we are trying to understand him. That he has a strong sense of the cinema, especially the use of the camera, is obvious from his three above-named films but I find his symbolism and his fondness for playing tricks with time, legitimate though they are, rather tedious. To be fair, Bergman's work deserves greater space than it can be given here. He is supremely an individualist but in nothing that I have seen of his is there any real warmth for humanity.

---

[1] *Scandinavian Film*, by H. Forsyth Hardy (Falcon Press, 1952).

[2] The 1959 Swedish season at the National Film Theatre will permit a fuller study of Bergman's work and also that of other Swedish directors.

His approach seems cold and detached, even in the handling of Victor Sjöström's fine performance as the Professor in *Wild Strawberries*. An early film, *Törst* (1949) is said to be his most 'human' work. I admire his craftsmanship and his sense of period, but I have never been moved by any of his work in the same way that most of the films of De Sica or Donskoi or Kurosawa move and hold me.

Of Swedish short films, one that I found admirable in style and in purpose was Gösta Werner's road-safety warning, *To Kill a Child* (1953).

In DENMARK the documentary movement in which this small country was prolific and imaginative in the immediate post-war years seems to have lost impetus as the decade progressed; it has certainly not kept abreast of the French or the Dutch. In feature films, the output is necessarily small in view of the limited language market. The fine qualities for which Bjärne Henning-Jensen's *Ditte—Menneskebarn* (1946) was notable do not seem to have been pursued, except in the delightful *Pal Alone in the World* (1949). This skilled director has mostly reverted to documentary, a charming work being *Ballet Girl* (1954). At last year's Berlin Festival, however, a clever and extremely humorous satirical comedy, *Guld og Grönne Skove* (1958), by Gabriel Axel, made a good impression. The most outstanding film internationally from Denmark was Carl Dreyer's *Ordet* (*The Word*, 1954). In spite of its slowness, it was a most sincerely made picture, extremely well acted and directed with all that love of the camera and lighting so long associated with this remarkable director; but it was not, to my mind, Dreyer at his best.

From FINLAND there came a rough-and-ready but surprisingly well-staged picture on an anti-war theme, *The Unknown Soldier* (1956), by Edvin Laine, adapted from a well-known book. From NORWAY, a few not especially notable documentaries have arrived and two features, *Suicide Mission* (1954), capably directed by Michael Forlong, of New Zealand, and *Nine Lives* (1956), by Arne Skouen, a quite well-made 'resistance' picture.

VI

Other European Countries

The overall picture of production in West Germany since the immediate post-war years of the so-called *Trümmerfilme* (films of the ruins) has been disappointing. In quantity, production has steadily increased but almost all of it has been evasive, escapist or retrogressive. Characteristic have been the ever-popular costume romances and films lauding pastoral life in the countryside, with a sprinkling of allegedly anti-Nazi films which depicted generals and admirals 'heroically' opposing Hitler. Re-makes of successful pre-war stories—such as *Mädchen in Uniform*, *Der Hauptmann von Köpenick* and *Der Letzte Mann*, have been plentiful but they were pale-imitations of their originals. On the whole, the product has been dull, unadventurous if painstakingly technically proficient. But one hears the complaint that production itself proceeds with too much haste, as if anxious to profit from the present high-level of German cinema attendances.

From the decade, few films really merit inclusion here and of these, Peter Lorre's deeply sincere and well-made *Der Verlorene* (1952), Robert Stemmle's satirical *Berliner Ballade* (1948) and Gerhard Lamprecht's honest *Irgendwo in Berlin* (1949) have prior claim. Some recent experimental work has been ingenious if rather aimless, smelling too strongly of the old *avant-garde* years. Two films well spoken of were Herbert Vesely's *Nicht mehr fliehen* (1955) and Hugo Niebeling's *Stählerne Adern* (1956). Dr Bernhard Grzimek's *Kein Platz für wilde Tiere* (1956) deserves inclusion for its courageous statement on the need for the protection of wild animal life in Central Africa and for its excellent satirical sequences of tourists on safari.

But West German production as a whole has lacked creative inspiration; directors and writers are badly needed. Two of the best films made on West German soil, *Nachts wenn der Teufel kam* (1958) and *Kinder, Mutter und ein*

General (1956) were directed by ex-European but mainly Hollywood-trained film-makers—Robert Siodmak and Laszlo Benedek respectively, a fact that speaks for itself.

From AUSTRIA, too, little has come our way that needs mention. Pabst's remarkable re-staging of the final days of the Hitler regime in Berlin, *Der Letzte Akt* (1955) showed that the master of earlier days had lost none of his cinematic skill, the flooding of the subways at the climax being amazingly well-handled. It was a film which, I suggest, was under-estimated by the English critics. In Austria, also, Cavalcanti made what is said to be his best film for many years, *Herr Puntila und sein Knecht Matti* (1955), adapted from Brecht, but it has not been seen in Britain.

In spite of a rigid political censorship, a few films have come from SPAIN which have shown a lively cinematic sense, notably the work of Juan Antonio Bardem. After a tentative start with *Comicos* (1953), he created international attention with *Muerte di un Ciclista* (1955) and *Gran' Rue* (1956). Both films carried considerable, if subtly implicit, social comment and had a dynamic camera-sense, if occasionally derivative. His last film, *La Venganza* (1957) is reported as being not of such interest. Bardem also wrote the script of Berlanga's *Welcome Mr Marshall* (1953), a satirical comedy about American aid to Spain, which was naive in execution but very funny. Ladislas Vajda is another director working in Spain whose *Marcelino Pan y Vino* (1955) had sincerity but was faulted by some ill-placed, crude symbolism of a Christ come alive from the Cross. Without an authoritarian, anti-liberal censorship, Spain could well produce stimulating work, other that is from some flashy co-productions and Hollywood and British location pictures which have been made there presumably because of cheap labour. They hardly do justice to the landscape.

Leopold Lindtberg, of SWITZERLAND, will be remembered for *The Last Chance* (1945); in *Four in a Jeep* (1950) he again dealt in a highly intelligent and objective way with an international problem, the four-power occupation of Vienna. The film was notable in that it lacked prejudice or propaganda and was very well directed and acted. I suggest that Lindtberg, his producer, L. Wechsler, and scriptwriter, Richard Schweizer, are an under-estimated European team who deserve more attention. They do not produce much—Switzerland is again a small country—but everything they do is internationally worth-while. Another Swiss picture which impressed me was *Es geschah am helllichten Tag* (*It Happened in Daylight*, 1958), from a book by Friedrich Dürrenmatt, also produced by Wechsler but this time directed by Ladislas Vajda, whose previous work was in Spain. This psychological study of a child-murderer was brilliantly unfolded detail by detail and extremely well acted, very largely made on real locations. I am surprised that it has not attracted wider attention. Although an elaborate piece of analysis, it was handled with commendable human warmth.

Like Denmark, the NETHERLANDS suffer from a limited language market and feature films are rare. But Dutch documentary is virile and internationally known, especially through the skilled work of Bert Haanstra and Herman van der Horst. In *Spiegel van Holland* (*Mirror of Holland*, 1950) Haanstra first revealed himself as an essentially poetic director in the true tradition of early Dutch cinema—Joris Ivens and John Ferno—and he followed this with a film on Dutch sculpture, then with *Panta Rhei* (1952), and later, for the Shell Film Unit in England, *The Rival World* (1955) and several films about oil in Sumatra. Next he made a fine picture about the Zuyder Zee, *En de Zee was niet meer* (*And Then There Was No More Sea*, 1955) and a superbly visualised film about the painter, *Rembrandt—The Man* (1957). His impressionist colour film *Glass* (1958) will become a classic of its *genre*. In 1958 he directed a charming and very funny, if overlong, rural comedy, *Fanfare*, one of the few Dutch feature pictures to be made. Van der Horst, after several try-outs, gave us *Het Schot is te Boord* (*Shoot the Nets*, 1951), *Houen Zo* (*Steady!*, 1952) about the devastation and rebuilding of Rotterdam, and *Lekko* (1954) in which he returned to fishermen and the sea with which he seems obsessed. He represents that rare but respected

185. UN CONDAMNE A MORT S'EST ECHAPPE, directed by ROBERT BRESSON.
FRANÇOIS LETERRIER. [French, 1956]

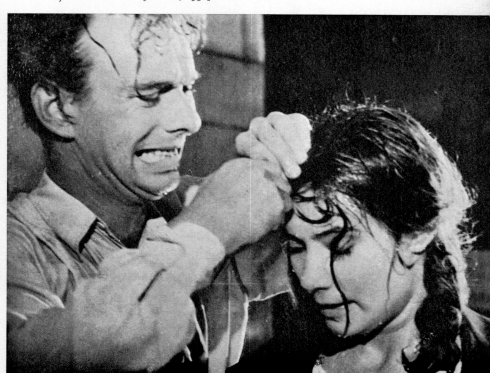

186. THE CRANES ARE FLYING, directed by MIKHAIL KALATOZOV. ALEXEI BATALOV,
TATYANA SAMOILOVA. [Soviet, 1957]

187. WILD STRAWBERRIES, directed by INGMAR BERGMAN. BIBI ANDERSON, VICTOR SEASTRÖM. [Swedish, 1957]

188. ASHES AND DIAMONDS, directed by ANDRZEJ WAJDA. ZBIGNIEW CYBULSKI. [Polish, 1958]

individual in film-making today who directs, photographs and edits his pictures—and each of them is a fine if sometimes pyrotechnical job of work. Others in Dutch documentary who should be listed are: Max de Haas, van der Linden, Ytzen Brusse, and the pair Varossieau and de Vogel for their scientific and medical films. The Dutch have also established a notable production of animated cartoon and puppet films; the work of the studios under Martin Troonder and Joop Geesink respectively have rightly attracted world attention. A feature film of note, but which I have not seen, was *De Dijk is Dicht* (*The Dyke is Sealed*, 1951), directed by A. Koohaas. One should also record that Wolfgang Staudte made one of his best features in Holland, *Ciske the Rat* (1957).

From neighbouring BELGIUM, the only work of value has again been in documentaries and films about the arts. Henri Storck, whose pre-war work is well-known, contributed among other films his solid study *Rubens* (1949), while a newcomer, Edmond Bernhard, directed the satirical and well-observed *Waterloo* (1958).

Up till now, except for Hollywood or British films on location, GREECE has meant the work of Michael Cacoyannis. His films to date have been: *Windfall in Athens* (1954), *Stella* (1955), *The Girl in Black* (1956) and *A Matter of Dignity* (1957). Each was undisciplined in script and uneven in direction but Cacoyannis has a strong feeling for atmosphere and uses his (to us) little-known actors with warmth. His style is as yet derivative but he has progressed with each film, shooting as much as possible on the real locations.

Much is read and heard about production in YUGO-SLAVIA but little has yet been screened in Britain, except for some nature-studies and travel pictures. Of the features which come to mind, Fedor Hanjekovitz's two historical films *Fra Brne* (1951) and *The Decline* (1954) were inclined to be slow but were imaginatively made, while *The Last Bridge* (1954), a co-production directed by the West German, Helmut Käutner, had a quality about it which was above this director's films in his own country.

VII

Soviet Union

The decade was ushered in by big spectacular and well-staged re-enactments of events of the war, such as Petrov's *Battle of Stalingrad* (1949) and Chiaureli's *Fall of Berlin* (1947), always of course with the slant on the Stalin father-image. They were ponderous, theatrical and fervently patriotic. One film, however, Sergei Gerasimov's *The Young Guard* (1948), about the partisan activities of a group of teenagers, marked a fresh interest in individuals as distinct from the mass although it centred mainly on their heroic exploits, but it was to be an exception. Up till about 1955, the dead hand of bureaucratic and political control frustrated what writing and directing talent there may have been waiting to flower. Peter Brinson has suggested that the subsequent loosening-up may partly have stemmed from the distinguished film-maker, Mikhail Romm's, outspoken article in *Sovietskaya Kultura* in 1954.[1]

Among several films made to celebrate the centenary of the birth of Tchekov, Sergei Samsonov's *The Grasshopper* (1955) had more sophistication, impeccable period taste and a concentration on individual characters than had been seen for many years in the Soviet cinema. In the same year, Yutkevich's *Othello* was deeply impressive and richly visual, freeing the play from stage-limitations but keeping to a closely-edited text. With a fluid camera, dramatic colour and magnificent acting, this was a fine piece of craftsmanship, preferable in my mind to the Olivier Shakespeare adaptations. Attempts to deal with contemporary life, however, were less successful and to Western eyes reminiscent of schoolboy yarns from *Chums*. Not until *Magdana's Donkey* (1956) by Harshiladze, set in a village in the south of the USSR, did we find a film which was not ashamed to express human feelings with poetic treatment. It was almost a harkback to the great Dovjenko. Kozintzev's

[1] *The Living Cinema*, Vol. 1, No. 1, 1956.

colourful *Don Quixote* (1957) was again in the romantic historical trend but at least it caught something of the spirit of Cervantes and was superbly mounted.

A new group of films, headed by Choukrai's *The Forty-First* (1957), indicated that the thaw was having an effect. Characters were no longer types epitomising idealised heroes and heroines but human beings of flesh and blood and, moreover, common feelings. For all its conventional story, this film was significant in that its hero, a White Army officer, was permitted to be presented with sympathy. Other films of this group—*The House Where I Live, Spring in Zaretchnaia Street* and *Our Court*—were said to explore the humanist line further. Kalatazov's much-discussed *The Cranes are Flying* (1957), however, firmly concentrated on the human relations and personal feelings of its protagonists as well as giving us, one imagines, a fairly authentic insight into Soviet home-life in the post-war years. On the whole very well directed and acted, with astonishing mobile camerawork, it was faulted only by some technical fireworks which would have been more appropriate to the French *avant-garde* of the twenties. Passages suggested that its director had discovered the freedom of the camera for the first time, but it was the most 'Westernised' film to come from the USSR since—since when?

Innumerable Soviet nature films, scientific films, travel films, culture films and children's films have come our way. They have mostly been well-made technically but lacking in imagination if compared with, say, French products of a similar kind. Many animated cartoons also have been exported; some have been charming.

VIII

Eastern Europe

The cinema of POLAND was literally born out of the devastation of the war, although some Polish technicians had worked in the USSR and the USA during the occupation of their own country. After the war, short film-making was quickly started, followed by such features as Wanda Jakubowska's *The Last Stage* (1948) and Aleksander Ford's *Border Street* (1947), well-made but not outstanding, both films looking back to the war for their inspiration. After 1953, output increased but an aggressive censorship by the State Film Board kept the subjects well to the line. Ford's *The Five Boys from Barksa Street* (1953) showed an improved technical excellence and the beginnings of handling characters as human beings and not stock figures. Ford's pre-war work will be remembered in *Sabra* (1933), a film made in Palestine with considerable qualities.[1]

In the autumn of 1956, with certain political restrictions relaxed, a number of self-contained production units were formed and it is from these, especially the experimental unit Kadr, that the recent stimulating Polish films have come. Jerzy Stawinski, scriptwriter, and the directors Andrzej Wajda (a pupil of Ford), Jerzy Kawalerowicz and Andrzej Munk have been responsible for a group of films which have aroused the admiration of many European critics and film-makers. *The Shadow* (1956) and *The Real End of the Great War* (1957), both by Kawalerowicz; *Man on the Tracks* (1956) and *Eroica* (1957) by Munk; *A Generation* (1954) and *Kanal* by Wajda, and the comedy *Eva Wants to Sleep* (1958) by Chmielewski—these represented a new force in European cinema which was exciting and provoking. Each film has gradually revealed a firmer independence of viewpoint combined with a sharpening of cinematic skill and experience.

Among many Polish short and experimental films,

[1] *Vide* page 616.

cartoons and documentaries, a high proportion has shown imagination and an urge for fresh ideas. Monk's *One Sunday Morning* (1955) suggested that he would develop into an important director, which indeed he has. Three recent films in particular have attracted world attention by their originality and skill: Raymond Polanski's *Two Men and a Wardrobe* (1957), made while he was still a student at Kadr, a satirical comment on modern social values which some regarded as a comedy but I found infinitely sad; Walerian Borowszyk and Jan Lenica's *Dom* (*House* 1957), an *avant-garde* picture of great inventiveness and subtle symbolism, perhaps the most exciting, truly experimental film of recent years; and the richly human, poetically sensitive, brilliantly directed *The Last Day of Summer* (1957) by Tadeusz Konwicki and Jan Laskowski, a short-story film which I rank among the best cinema seen for a long time.

This new revelation of what good cinema can really mean dates back, of course, to the careful training and groundwork in Poland after the war, which came to a full flowering with the wider freedom gained by creative artists after October, 1956. The Polish State Film School was first set up in 1949 and it has been developed under the wise guidance of Jerzy Toeplitz, the distinguished film historian and critic. From it have graduated such directors as Wajda, Munk, Lenartowicz and Polanski. New Polish films are awaited with the greatest expectancy. Ford's *The Eighth Day of the Week* (1957) and Lenartowicz's *Meetings* (1957) have not yet been seen in England. The news is heard with misgiving, however, that a new film by Zarzycki, *Lost Feelings*, and Wajda's *We Are Alone in the World*, have both been suspended, news which could suggest a tightening up of the freedom gained in 1956.

In EAST GERMANY all production since 1946 has been centred in the Defa Company (Deutsche Film Aktien Gesellschaft) and has, with very few exceptions, been rigorously designed to promote the socialist construction of the German Democratic Republic. Of varying technical quality, we may note Wolfgang Staudte's *Die Mörder sind unter uns*

(1946), *Rotation* (1949) and *Der Untertan* (1950; Erich Engels's *Affaire Blum* (1947); Slatan Dudow's *Stärker als die Nacht* (1954) and *Der Hauptmann von Köln* (1956); Vaclav Gajer's *Jahrgang* 21 (1957); Kurt Maetzig's *Rat der Götter* (1950); Konrad Wolf's *Lissy* (1957) and Kurt Jung-Alsen's *Betrogen bis zum Jüngsten Tag* (1957). Twisting events where necessary to suit political viewpoint, these films can be associated in trend with the output of the USSR over the same period. None of them was outstanding as a true interpretation of an individual's outlook, but none of them was meant to be so. No similar freedom of expression to that enjoyed in Poland occurred to let life and breath into the East German cinema.

A long tradition of film-making exists in CZECHOSLOVAKIA but, with rare exceptions, it has been a tradition of cultural and animated films. The cartoon and puppet productions by Jiri Trnka, Karel Zeman and Hermina Tyrlova Hofman have gained a deservedly wide reputation for their humour, technical skill and inventive powers. In this connection, it may be remembered that puppets have been a part of Czechoslovak theatrical tradition for at least two centuries and they have been logically adapted by the film medium. Solid, slow and well-costumed historical subjects of national pride and importance, such as Otaker Vavra's *Jan Huss* (1954) and *Against All* (1957), with vast battle panoramas, largely followed the pattern set by the Soviet cinema's massive historical biographies, well executed but deadly dull to outsiders. Among more recent contemporary subjects, Jiri Weiss's *The Wolf Trap* (1957) was said to be of much interest. The Czech State film industry also produces a large number of nature, travel and general interest films but of those which I have seen, none comes to mind for special note.[1]

Even during the war in HUNGARY, *The Men of the Mountain* (1942) by Ivan Szöts, heralded a more truly Hungarian cinema than the frothy pre-war product, although Georg Hoellering's *Hortobagy* (1936) should also go

[1] For a fuller survey of Czechoslovakian cinema, *vide* an article by Jiri Weiss in *Films and Filming*, Vol. 5, No. 6, 1959.

on the record. The influence of Béla Balázs, the internationally famous film theorist, had effect on the immediate post-war years and probably (thinks Marcorelles[1]) contributed to the renaissance of good film-making in Hungary. The first film to attract attention was Geza Radvany's *Somewhere in Europe* (1947), which tackled realistically one of the major social problems arising from the war—displaced children. Radvany's work has been referred to earlier in the Italian section and I am glad to do so again because of European directors he is often overlooked. A second film to be regarded highly was Frigyes Ban's *A Piece of Land* (1949), which dealt with the peasant revolt against rich landowners during the Horthy regime.

In the middle of the decade, Hungary emerged as a nation with a film industry worth considerable notice. Zoltan Fabri's *Merry-go-round* (1955) and Laszlo Ranody's *Discord* (1955) both revealed an honest and healthy understanding of the rural scene and were not afraid to handle social conflicts. They represented a big step forward in outlook from the stereotyped, propaganda-laden films of five years previously which had inevitably copied Soviet models. According to Marcorelles, an early film by Fabri, *Fourteen Lives in Danger* (1954), and Felix Mariassy's *Springtime in Budapest* (1955) contained scenes obviously dictated by official instructions. Mariassy's *A Little Glass of Beer* (1956) also ran into censor trouble. With the de-Stalinisation of the film industry, however, a greater freedom was found. As in Poland, there is a State Institute of Theatre and Film. Subsequently, several feature films have been much praised when seen abroad, among them: Fabri's *Professor Hannibal* (1956); Imre Feher's *A Sunday Romance* (1957); Mihaly Szemes's *Dani* (1957) Victor Goetler's *Fever* (1957); Karoly Makk's *Ward No. 9* (1957) and Zoltan Varkonyi's *The Bitter Truth* (1958) and, of those which have been screened in England, I add my praise. Like Poland, there has grown up a truly cinematic national industry with individual styles and a strong feeling for contemporary issues. After the revolution

[1] *Sight and Sound*, Vol. 26, No. 3, 1956. I am indebted to Louis Marcorelles for much of the information about the Hungarian cinema.

of 1956, however, the scene has again become clouded. Some of the 'free' pictures referred to above have met with official disapproval and been withdrawn, while directors it would seem are compelled to look back again to the pre-war years for inspiration.

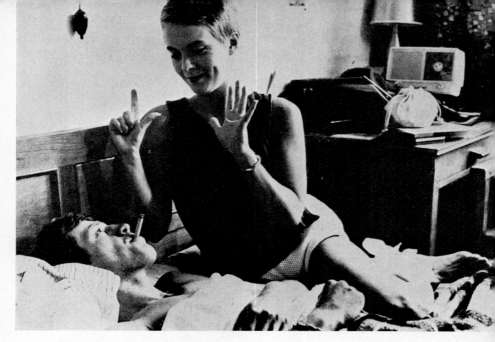

189. A BOUT DE SOUFFLE, directed by JEAN-LUC GODARD. JEAN-PAUL BELMONDO, JEAN SEBERG. [French, 1959]

190. HIROSHIMA MON AMOUR, directed by ALAIN RESNAIS. EMMANUELLE RIVA, EJI OKADA. [French-Japanese, 1959]

191. LES QUATRE CENTS COUPS, directed by FRANÇOIS TRUFFAUT. [French, 1959]

192. PSYCHO, directed by ALFRED HITCHCOCK. ANTHONY PERKINS, JANET LEIGH. [American, 1960]

193. THE LADY WITH THE LITTLE DOG, directed by Josif Heifitz. Ya Savina. [Soviet, 1960]

194. SATURDAY NIGHT, SUNDAY MORNING, directed by Karel Reisz. Albert Finney. [British, 1960]

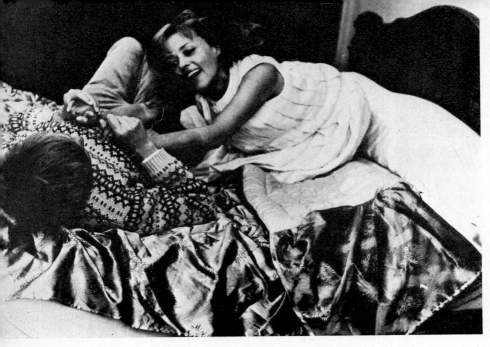

195. JULES ET JIM, directed by François Truffaut. Oscar Werner, Jeanne Moreau. [French, 1961]

196. VIRIDIANA, directed by Luis Buñuel. Silvia Pinal. [Spanish, 1961]

IX

BRITISH COMMONWEALTH

In the main, this has been a story of documentary and short film developments. Where there has been feature production, it has been mostly by visiting units from Britain or Hollywood with the usual hybrid results. In CANADA, the National Film Board has continued its steady output and in general maintained its high-level of quality. It is hard to single out individual successes in this brief survey but the work of Colin Low and Walter Koenig came right to the fore with the beautifully made, poetically conceived *Corral* (1954) and again with the imaginatively handled, highly cinematic *City of Gold* (1956), both films which I greatly liked. Colin Low had previously made, with Tom Daley, the diverting and widely successful animated cartoon, *The Romance of Transportation* (1953), one of the few examples of comedy mixed with straight information which came off. In the same *genre* as *Corral*, Julian Biggs's *The Shepherd* (1956) had some but not all of the former film's qualities. It might seem, however, that the time may have come when the NFB could with advantage step out into the world with at least one or two major projects. It cannot rest for all time on the well-deserved laurels for its short films. It has, of course, in Norman McClaren one of the most gifted and original of film artists; his animated experiments have continued to give immense pleasure all through the decade. One indigenous feature film came from Canada, Sidney Furie's *A Dangerous Age* (1957). As a first film by a very young man, it had courage and freshness in its study of adolescent love but it was, in my opinion, rated too high by our local critics.

In AUSTRALIA, the Commonwealth Film Unit has, like the NFB in Canada, kept up a steady flow of pictures but without anything like the same resources. It has suffered by having to operate as a sub-department of a sub-department and by not having sufficient encouragement at a top level. It deserves much credit for what it has been able to produce in these restricted circumstances. Of its many films, two especially come to mind: *Balloons and Spinifex* (1958) for which Shan Benson, Ian Dunlop and John Gray collectively deserved credit, and Malcolm Otton's *Paper-Run* (1957). The first was a home-spun, rough-and-ready picture of the building of a meteorological station in the remote outback, made with honest observation; the second was a wholly delightful but at the same time informative little picture of the Sunday morning delivery of newspapers. It should also be recorded that both the Australian and Canadian Government film units honorably acquitted themselves with sundry films of Royal visits, making more of such events than mere pomp and ceremony. The Shell Film Unit has also operated in Australia with distinction, notably with the work of John Heyer, who was a product of the Government unit. Heyer's three feature-length documentaries—*The Valley is Ours* (1949), *Back of Beyond* (1953) and *The Forerunner* (1957)— brought him deservedly wide recognition, even if in my opinion he owed a big debt to the early Pare Lorentz films, especially *The River*; but Heyer has a keen cinematic and visual sense though he lacks a constructive design to his scripts. Australia has made spasmodic attempts at its own feature production for many years but of them all, only Cecil Holmes's *Three in One* (1956) merits mention. Crude as it was, it had a certain earthy honesty which caught something of the Australian character, which is more than can be said for most of the films by visiting units to the Continent.

Official film-making was also continued in South Africa, Malaya, New Zealand, Pakistan and the Central African Federation but nothing stood out from the routine. From CEYLON, however, in addition to numerous shorts, there came the feature *Rekava* (1956–57), directed by Lester Peries, which though lacking in continuity and burdened with some naive characterisation, had sympathy for its subject of rural customs and superstition. Under the guidance of Sean Graham, the GHANA Film Unit (formerly the Gold Coast unit) kept bringing out wittily-made, locally-acted films, some in excellent colour, of which *The Boy Kumasenu* (1951), *Mr Mensa Builds a House* (1955) and *Jaguar* (1957) were memorable for their vitality and inventiveness.

It is well-known that INDIA produces nearly three hundred feature films a year but of this huge output, very few merit serious appraisal. India in the past ten years has meant first and foremost the astonishingly fine work of Satyajit Ray, whose first two films, *Pather Panchali* (1955) and *The Unvanquished* (1957) formed part of a trilogy yet to be completed. In the meantime, Ray has made a less important picture, *The Philosopher's Stone* (1958), almost a slapstick comedy. So much has been written by cinephiles and critics the world over about Ray's two major films that little remains to be said, except that it is one of the cinema's unpredictable facets for such a sudden discovery to be made.

Influenced clearly by the Italian neo-realists and by Renoir (when he made *The River* in India), Ray revealed himself as one of the true poets of the cinema, with a wonderfully sensitive understanding of simple human beings and a film sense which was remarkable in such a young and hitherto inexperienced film-maker. Neither film is without small blemishes but each has so many fine qualities that one overlooks such minor faults. The wide respect given to Satyajit Ray has tended to obscure the work of two other Indian directors who, although they do not achieve Ray's high poetic sense, still deserve our attention. The first is Bimal Roy, whose *Two Acres of Land* (1953) had a sincere and compassionate feeling for the poverty-stricken people of Calcutta; the second is K. K. Abbas, whose child-study *Munna* (1955) also showed a deep understanding for the problems and plight of India's poor. Both films, like those of Ray, revealed neo-realist inspirations but that was to their credit.

There has been much documentary and informational film activity in India during the period, but to a great extent it has been uncoordinated and without policy. An exception was the series made under the supervision of the Canadian, James Beveridge, for Burmah-Shell, of which *A Village in Travancore* (1956) was most notable. It is unfortunate that this project has now been discontinued. In a recent report from India,[1] a depressing picture is drawn of muddled censorship and bureaucratic interference with production. The Government itself would appear to have no line of imaginative policy towards its use of films, which is regrettable in a country which has so much to give to the world.

[1] Paul Zils in *The Living Cinema*, Vol. 2, No. 1, Summer, 1958.

X
ASIA

In spite of the many adverse criticisms that can be made of international film festivals, it was certainly the first presentation of *Rashomon* at Venice in 1951 which opened our eyes to the fact that JAPAN had at least one director of top world quality, whose work might not have been known to us but for that festival. For years, it was common knowledge that the Japanese, like the Indians, produced large quantities of films, that Japanese technicians had paid training visits to Hollywood, but only very rarely indeed did a Japanese film reach Europe.[1] In 1957, Japan topped the world in feature production with 443 films. Since 1951, a selection of Japanese work has arrived at the European festivals and a few specialist cinemas but even today it is clear that we have still to see many of the past films of directors whose recent work is now known to us, as well as of directors whose names remain only names. Unlike India where, until Satyajit Ray, there was no cinematic skill, it has come to light that there have been some really important films made in Japan way back in silent film days. It seems almost unbelievable that no one had written about the early work of directors such as the late Mizoguchi and Gosho until they have been recently 'discovered'. The tremendous impact made by *Rashomon* happily inspired a great deal of curiosity about the whole of Japanese cinema. Film journals like *Sight and Sound*, *Films and Filming* and the English film societies' *Film*, have carried much information in recent years, some of it by writers who have been fortunate enough to have been and seen for themselves. Apart from Japanese films shown in England and at some European festivals, therefore, I am indebted for some of my information to these sources: by the writers Jay Leyda, Donald Richie, J. L. Anderson, Lindsay Anderson, Marie Seton, R. E. Durgnat *et al*.[2]

[1] Cf. pp.324, 325.

[2] It was also to my regret that I was not in England all the time when the National Film Theatre screened a representative season of 15 Japanese films but I was able to catch some of them elsewhere.

Two directors who might have been called veterans, Kenji Mizoguchi and Heinosuke Gosho, both of whom are now dead, had been making films since the silent days. The former would appear to have made subjects of all kinds, historical or *jidai-geki*, as well as contemporary, or *gendai-geki*, but was best-known for his pictorially lovely mediaeval films, with an emphasis on fine settings and a preoccupation with the place of women in society in his later work. Among his most important pictures, according to report, were: *The Life of O-Haru* (1952), *Ugetsu Monogatari* (1953), *Sansho Dayu* (1954), *Chikamatzu Monogatari* (1955) amd *The Street of Shame* (1956). The second and last of these I saw and was deeply impressed, more by the last than by the first. It had a tremendous feeling for its characters and a simplicity of technique that was exemplary. Of Gosho's work, alas, I have seen none, but the highest praise has been given to *Drifting Clouds* (1951), *Four Chimneys* (1953) and *A Hotel at Osaka* (1955). He was nearly always, it seems, concerned with modern themes, even back in silent films, and with what are called 'the common people', of whose problems he had a profound understanding and sympathy.

Akira Kurosawa, whose films are the best-known outside Japan, alternates between mediaeval themes and modern subjects, and has made his own versions of Dostoievski, Gorki and Shakespeare. *The Lower Depths* (1951) was reputed to have been superb; *The Idiot* has not, I think, been screened outside Japan; while *Throne of Blood* (1957), from *Macbeth*, was in my opinion a magnificent piece of film-making gravely under estimated by our local critics, so sensitive are they to any foreigner who dares to play around with Shakespeare! It had a formal style, presumably based on traditional Japanese theatre, which was most impressive and passages of pure cinema, such as the two horsemen in the mountain mist, which revealed the hand of a master. Two modern films by Kurosawa which I much regret not having seen, *Drunken Angel* (1948), which was his seventh picture, and *Living* (1952) drew the warmest praise from two critics whose views I respect—Lindsay Anderson and

Jay Leyda. Kurosawa is, without dispute, a director of the highest talents with an astonishing control over and knowledge of the cinema's techniques and a superb sense of movement on the screen. Both *Rashomon* (1950) and *Seven Samurai* (1954) were among the most important and significant films of the decade under review.

Of the many other Japanese films and directors which must be recorded are: Yasujiro Ozu's leisurely and very human *Their First Trip to Tokio* (1953); Keisuke Kinoshita's *They Were Twelve* (1954); Hideo Sekigawa's charming *Trumpet Boy* (1955) and *The Boyhood of Dr. Noguchi* (1956); So Yamamura's *The Cannery Boat* (1953) and *The Black Tide* (1954); Shiro Toyoda's *Wild Geese* (1953) and *Love Never Fails* (1955); Kaneto Shindo's moving and socially most important *Children of Hiroshima* (1953), Hiroshi Shimizu's *Children of the Beehive* (1949); Kon Ichikawa's pacific argument *The Burmese Harp* (1956) and Tadashi Imai's *Squalor* (1954), *Shadows in the Sunlight* (1956) and the outspoken and topical *Story of a True Love* (1957). All these films dealt with contemporary subjects. If I do not include the popular mediaeval picture *Gate of Hell* (1954) by Teinosuke Kinugasa, it is because to me it was of importance only for its use of colour.

One aspect of Japanese production which is of great interest to the future of world cinema is that the cost of making films is relatively low. Nothing like the inflated salaries in Western cinema are paid to leading actors and directors and it would appear that a good deal more respect is paid by producers to the creative talent employed by them than is found in Britain or the USA.[1]

From CHINA there is unfortunately little to be recorded. There must have been considerable production but scarcely any of it has reached Europe. *The Letter with the Feathers* (1953) by Shih Hui, a story of the anti-Japanese war seen through its impact on a little boy's mind, had a freshness

[1] For a general picture of Japanese production and distribution, *vide: International Film Annual* (Calder), No. 2, 1958. *60 years of Japanese Cinema*, by David Robinson.

and simplicity that were engaging. *Liang Shan-Po and Chu Ying-Tai* (1953) by Sang Hu and Huang Sha was not much more than a photographed kind of opera, visually lovely if uneven in colour. A later film by Sang Hu, *New Year Sacrifice* (1956) also had a fascinating, distinctive quality. But we have yet to see in Britain any film that interprets or reflects the new People's China.

197. IL POSTO, directed by ERMANO OLMI. SANDRO PANZONI. [Italian, 1961]

198. DR. STRANGELOVE, directed by STANLEY KUBRICK. GEORGE C. SCOTT.
[Anglo-American, 1963]

199. HAMLET, directed by Grigor Kozintsev. Anastasia Vertinskaya. [Soviet, 1963]

200. THE RED DESERT, directed by Michelangelo Antonioni. Monica Vitti. [Italian, 1964]

XI

LATIN AMERICA

Bearing in mind the size of the Spanish-speaking territories, it is disappointing that more has not been developed in the way of good cinema. This is particularly true of MEXICO, a country rich in subject-matter, with a visually superb landscape, and equipped with efficient studios staffed by excellent technicians. Possibly it is the physical nearness of Hollywood and the habit of many American producers of using their neighbour country to the south as a popular location-source which have inhibited Mexican producers. The fact remains that although Mexican producers turn out a hundred or more feature films a year, very few indeed have commanded interest outside the Spanish-speaking market. Only the work of that unpredictable Spanish film-maker, Luis Buñuel, has really attracted attention. With his *Los Olvidados* (1950) Buñuel took the lid off the simmering juvenile delinquency problem. With his customary savagery, he presented a frightening picture of sadistic behaviour in the poverty-stricken back-streets of Mexico City and suggested possible palliatives to this grave social problem which is common to so many city communities in the world. This was an astonishingly fine piece of film-making, quite the best and most important film to come from Mexico. Among Buñuel's other films of the period were *El* (1952), *Robinson Crusoe* (1953) and *The Criminal Life of Archibaldo de la Cruz* (1955), all of which had moments of tremendous interest, as do all Buñuel's films, but in general they did not match up to the overall brilliance of *Los Olvidados*. Only two other Mexican directors deserve mention: Benito Alazraki for his *Raices* (1954), an over-rated but at least imaginative film; and Don Carlos Velo's *Torero* (1955), the best picture yet to be made about the life of a bull-fighter. Apart from this, prosperous Mexican producers have done nothing to develop or encourage their own script-writers and directors.

From other Latin-American countries, there is not much to record. Leopoldo Torre-Nilsson's two films made in the ARGENTINE, *La Casa del Angel* (1956) and *El Sequestrador* (1957) created much interest at the festivals, but I have not seen them. *The Strange Gods* (1957) directed by Roman Vinnoly Barreto, shot largely on location near the Bolivian Plateau with a story about archaeological discovery, had certain fascinating qualities and was excellent in its handling of local people. In PUERTO RICO, an interesting and ambitious project has been in progress for several years by the Division of Community Education of the Department of Education. In a highly-intelligent plan to take rural education into the villages of the people, a number of story-documentaries have been made of social problems, some of which I found stimulating and very human in their appeal. With a real social purpose to serve, I suspect that one of these days we shall find a film of stature coming from this worth-while experiment in fundamental education. The only other source of documentary in Latin-America to be included is the work of the Shell Film Unit in Venezuela.

CONCLUSION

As the cinema grows up, its human losses inevitably become more numerous. Some fine pioneers and distinguished exponents of the film died during the decade, artists for whom we had the deepest respect: the directors Erich von Stroheim, Robert J. Flaherty, V. I. Pudovkin, Alexander Dovjenko, Max Ophüls, Kenji Mizoguchi, Heinosuke Gosho, Humphrey Jennings, Jean Epstein, Val Lewton, Richard Massingham and Henry Cornelius; the writers and critics Richard Winnington, André Bazin and James Agee; Stephen Tallents, who fostered from start the British documentary movement whose example has spread so far and wide, and Jack Beddington who, first at Shell and later at the British Ministry of Information, did so much to promote the creative side of documentary; Alex Korda, colourful impresario and no mean film-maker himself; and that brilliant craftsman-cameraman, Gregg Toland, whose work influenced so many others. Each made his particular contribution and his name is on the record for the future.

What of the record? The increased size and activity of the International Federation of Film Archives demonstrate the need for the preservation of film history, but in most countries film museums are expected to operate on the flimsiest of funds. And as old films get scarcer, the tendency must be fought for archivists to sit tight on their possessions. Film libraries, museums and archives must not just concern themselves with dead cinema, they must not become cemeteries of celluloid rare and precious; they must be *living* museums. To have life, a film *must* have an audience. The cinema is far too young an art for its few masterpieces and its many minor masterpieces to become museum specimens for private inspection only. The film archives and the ever-growing film society movement both have progressive jobs to do which are directly related to the cinema's present and future, as well as its past. They should seek to work together in the closest collaboration. If the embryonic International

Federation of Film Societies ever becomes a real world force, which indeed it can, it must keep in the closest touch with the International Federation of Film Archives and *vice versa*. They have a common aim—the advancement of the cinema as the great interpretive art-form of the twentieth century.

From celluloid to the printed page. Of the various books in the English language about the cinema published during the past ten years, those which were of permanent value were: Richard Griffith and Arthur Mayer's monumental and gloriously illustrated *The Movies* (Simon & Schuster, 1957), its title being misleading because it deals only with the American film but that was the publisher's choice; the *National Cinema Series* (Falcon Press, 1947–1953) edited by Roger Manvell, the six volumes of which deal with the British, German, Soviet, Italian, French and Scandinavian cinemas and get increasingly better in that order; PEP's authoritative report on *The British Film Industry* (1952) and its Supplement (1958); Raymond Spottiswoode's invaluable and exhaustive *Film and Its Techniques* (Faber & Faber, 1951); and the first English edition of a famous book, Belá Balázs's *Theory of the Film* (Dobson, 1952). In the meantime, we await with high expectations the forthcoming publication of Dr. Siegfried Kracauer's volume on film aesthetics, upon which he has been at work for so long and which, from a privileged reading of the first draft MS, I forecast will be the most important treatise on the art of the film.

And so, looking back to 1948, it is seen to have been a decade rich in cinema, deserving of more detailed inspection than has been possible in this cursory survey. It has produced works of the highest artistic merit combined with social significance stemming from and reflecting the ideologies and tendencies and events of these troubled post-war times. When we think of the nervous exhaustion experienced by so many nations of the old world and the hysteria through which some of the so-called new nations are going, it is amazing that so much creative good has come from the

772

cinema. A medium which, in spite of all set-backs, political, economic and otherwise, can give birth to such works as— *Ladri di Biciclette, Nuit et Brouillard, La Terra Trema, The Last Day of Summer, Pather Panchali, Le Notti di Cabiria, Rashomon, Los Olvidados, Un Condamné à mort s'est échappé, Time Out of War, Umberto D* and *Les Jeux Interdits* (which are among my best-liked films of the decade)—has no reason to fear any allegedly competitive new medium. It has only to fear those in its midst who do not recognise the greatness of such films and who try to prevent others from being made.

What else have these years shown us? The steady growth of what is called neo-realism, notably in France, Italy, Poland, Japan and India. That is the outstanding trend— a striving to interpret life in dramatic and human terms through the film medium so that it can stimulate and enrich the lives of others among the audiences of the world. And implicit in that interpretation is an expression of social comment, blended with poetry and compassion, from the heart as well as from the mind of the film-maker. Even in hard-boiled America this trend has tentatively appeared, partly as a result of freer access to the means of film-making stemming from the increase in independent production. And in the search to fulfil this aim, there has been an attempt to make the actual technical process of filming less compli-cated, less apparent, more mobile and more intimate—even in the face of the big-screen onslaught.

At the same time, one notes a long-awaited expansion of the animated cartoon and model film. For too long the cartoon especially has been the slave of the style and tech-nique evolved by Disney, but in Europe and the USSR, as well as in the USA, there have been exciting and inventive new developments. In the use of the film as an educational medium, too, there has been a steady growth, notably in the fields of science and anthropology. On the user side, film society and specialised audiences are increasing in numbers and they will soon, if they do not already, comprise a minority audience for which films can be specifically produced.

CONCLUSION

Nevertheless, I feel that there is a need among the English-speaking peoples particularly for a deeper sense of dedication to the cinema and all that it should and could stand for in the world community. We all of us have a heavy responsibility for what we create in life because of its unpredictable effect on people everywhere; and this has never been more true but less appreciated about any medium than the cinema. But the artists of the cinema steadily grow in number and in stature, and function in more and more countries. As television' takes over the cinema's role as the world's provider of mass-entertainment, so I have every faith that the cinema itself will gain its freedom from the aims of its purely commercial and/or political exploiters and reach the adult status of a great art in its own right.

POSTSCRIPT

Since the foregoing Conclusion was written only a few years back, it has been increasingly difficult to write in terms of the world cinema. So many new names and so many new films, some from unexpected countries, have appeared. They have one thing in common. They confirm one's belief in films and film-making as the most vital and purposive art of the twentieth century. The ever-growing impact of television, with its constant vulgarity hand-in-hand with its stimulating instantaneous reporting, with its increasing dependence on filmed material, has done nothing to shake one's belief in the film *per se*.

When I first sat down in that little room in Hampstead to write this survey in 1928–29, not many people were writing about films from a serious viewpoint in the English language. Today, since the war, books and journals devoted to the film have multiplied. The spread of international film festivals has made festival-going almost a full-time job for those who can afford it. The most assiduous critic has the utmost difficulty to keep up with all that is good. Thus to update *The Film Till Now* again becomes an impossible task, but this new edition does permit me to add this Postscript.

The film is itself such a complex medium, such a synthesis of so many emotionally stimulating ingredients that I have always felt that it should be written or talked about in simple terms. My quarrel with a great deal of film criticism in recent years is that it has been choked by a desire on the part of critics to be complex and devious in their approach. Meanings, symbols, purposes and trends are found in films and in directors' work that have no existence in the original. Possibly it is inherent in our contemporary way of living to seek out elements in the arts that do not exist. It is for this reason that when making a round-up of some, but not all, critical writing about films during the past decade or so, I welcome the clear yet subtle, penetrating but not abstruse, criticism by an American writer, Pauline Kael, in *I Lost It at*

775

the Movies (1966). Although I deplore her too facile dismissal of Siegfried Kracauer and his passion for reality in film, overall I find Miss Kael much to my way of thinking. Like the lamented Richard Winnington or Otis Ferguson, she fast detects the slick, spurious and merely fashionable. She is calmly sane about such present-day idols as Fellini or Bergman or Antonioni.

*

When I wrote the original *Film Till Now* I had not myself made a film. Since that time, I have been fortunate enough to have either directed or produced more films than I care to remember. With each one I have realised how pleasurable but how difficult is this medium. *The World is Rich* (1947) and *The Life of Adolf Hitler* (1960–61) were both concerned with the *auteur* editing of already existing film material. Jay Leyda's book *Films Beget Films* (1964) and Karel Reisz's *The Technique of Film Editing* (1953) contain full notes about this fascinating kind of film-making. Both films will, I hope, remain as historical documents which had behind them strong convictions. Then again there were two feature films of the three I have made, *No Resting Place* (1950) and *De Overval* (*The Silent Raid*, 1962), in which I once more found experience of the medium. The former was the first English feature film to be made wholly without use of a studio. It had a modest budget, achieved critical acclaim, but lost money for no other reason than film-trade politics. When in 1950 studios in England were touting for clients, a feature film which showed that studios were redundant (for some kinds of film) was hardly welcome.

Apart from the great happiness I had in collaboration with Basil Wright on *World Without End* (1952–53), which I feel can be said with all due modesty was the only film of real international significance yet made by the United Nations —and then only after some feuds—making *De Overval* in the Netherlands for Rudolf Meyer, of Sapphire Film Productie, was my most exciting assignment. When we screened the film in Leeuwarden, Friesland, where the actual raid on the prison took place, and on which the film was based, to the men who took part in the actual event and received their acclaim, this indeed was a reward, not sentimental but deeply sincere. This is a basic reason for making a film. Its memorable premiere in Amsterdam and its subsequent enormous public success all over Holland contrasted oddly with the Rank Organisation's cavalier handling of its English distribution in a dubbed version.

*

Many differences clearly exist between the film scene of 1929 and that of today. Not just the obvious ones of the addition of sound and the available use of colour but in the internationalism of film-making. Who could have foreseen nearly forty years ago that two of the most gifted film artists of the 'sixties would be Japanese and Indian— Kurosawa and Satyajit Ray? France, Germany, the U.S.S.R. and the U.S.A. were at that time the countries from which one expected exciting new developments. Japan and India, one heard, produced a prodigious number of films, very few of which were shown in Europe or America. Nothing suggested that two film artists of such outstanding vision and technical talent would arise from, to us, far-off film industries.

I do not think either that the emergence of what has become known as neo-realism could have been easily foreseen as stemming from Italy. The partial decline of neo-realism was, however, predictable as a result of economic, political and religious pressures. Such a masterwork of film humanism and artistry as *Umberto D* (1952) had a lonely but wonderful descendant in *Il Posto* (1961). But the forging of vital purposes expressed through the observation and understanding that fired the early work of De Sica, Zavattini, Visconti and Rossellini have declined into the fashionable *chic* of *La Notte* (1961), *La Dolce Vita* (1960) and *8½* (1962). *L'Avventura* (1960) was the exception. How was it possible, one asks, that the maker of *Terra Trema* (1948), one of the cinema's major works, could be the maker of *The Leopard* (1963)? Much of the answer is, of course, economic.

The upsurge of the *nouvelle vague* in France should have been no surprise. The French have all the time had a deep understanding of the film. Unlike England, the film has been for a long time a part of French intellectual life—sometimes too intellectual. If the young French *cinéastes* could create an *avant-garde* movement out of nothing but ideas and a passion for *La Cinéma* in the 'twenties, then their descendants could create a new approach to films in the late 'fifties and 'sixties, especially with the flexibilities brought about by advances in technical equipment as foreseen and asked for earlier in this book. I do not share the cult of disrespect for knowing how properly to use the medium and its instruments, which some admirers and participants regard as inseparable from the *nouvelle vague*. Make-it-Yourself movie-kits have been on sale in photographers' shops for years. Nor do I share the idolatry of the abolition of narrative as in the work of Jean-Luc Godard and in some of Resnais. But I do thank this *Cahiers du Cinéma* clique for François Truffaut, whose compassionate sensitivity to life and whose use of the film medium to express it are very fine. *Les Mistons* (1957), *Quatre Cents Coups* (1958), *Jules et Jim* (1961) and *La Peau Douce* (1964) are diamonds of cinematic brilliance. André Bazin's influence has had rich rewards.

A number of important new books have been added to the cinema bookshelf. A long-overdue reprint, with additions, is John Grierson's collection of essays, lectures and criticisms, *Grierson on Documentary* (1966), as alive and purposeful today as at the time of its first publication (1946). Ivor Montagu's *Film World* (1964) is an expert survey and analysis, in fact a guide to cinema very worthwhile.

Penelope Houston, in her *The Contemporary Cinema* (1963), and Roger Manvell, in his *New Cinema in Europe* (1966), both gave a sensible and reliable survey of the last two decades, although the former did less than justice to the documentary tradition in Britain. John Russell Taylor's *Cinema Eye, Cinema Ear* (1964), in spite of its clumsy title, was a valuable study of some of the key directors of the 'sixties. All three singled out the move towards greater realism as the major characteristic of recent cinema, a move away from the contrived artificiality of the studios which one had asked for many years ago. In *Celluloid: The Film Today* (1931) I wrote: ' It would be the sanest thing in the sordid history of the cinema if every studio were to close down for the period of one year, if all the stars were given a vacation, and if production units (complete with cameras and recording equipment) were to be sent to every part of the world. The resulting films would be the most thrilling entertainment that has ever been produced.' What I did not foresee was that the studio-mind would be taken with them on location. To some extent this wishful thinking has come about. To a limited extent, some good has come from this emigration. Some tax obligations have no doubt been overcome. But in the mammoth spectaculars, *The Sound of Music*, *El Cid* and *King of Kings*, the studio-trained mind still obtains.

Even in conservative England this movement has found a place, notably with *This Sporting Life* (1962), *A Kind of Loving* (1962) and *Saturday Night, Sunday Morning* (1960), although we find the bizarre situation of much progressive film-making in England being made with American finance. New directors in this country—Lindsay Anderson, Karel Reisz, John Schlesinger—owe much to the documentary tradition. They have not wholly discarded the use of studios, as have some of the European film-makers, but they have used them only when essential. Such film-making in England is still, however, a struggle to find finance (in spite of the National Film Finance Corporation) for production (especially pre-production), and a struggle to find screen-outlet for the finished film due to the monopolistic machinery of distribution and exhibition. As I write, the British cinema is once again in the throes of a crisis. Has it ever, except during the war years of swollen audiences, not been in a crisis? At the moment we have the extraordinary situation of directors such as Kubrick, Antonioni, Truffaut, Losey, Polanski, Aldrich and even Chaplin—none of them English save perhaps the last—all working in England and mostly with American money.

779

Internationalism of production has in fact expanded to an extent which could not perhaps have been foreseen. In many ways it is to be welcomed. Co-production has for some years been an economic necessity in Europe. It is now under serious discussion in England. But if it materialises it will not solve the problems of lack of opportunity for creative film-making in England. The fact that non-British film-makers are working in England will certainly give employment to British technicians, but it will do nothing to create a healthy and indigenous film production.

With some liberalisation of censorship in the English-speaking cinema, there has been a move towards making subjects and themes of a more adult character than would have been possible a decade ago. They may not have been very good films, but at least Huston has made *Freud* and Orson Welles Kafka's *The Trial*, something unbelievable a few years ago.

In the East European countries, especially in Poland, there has also been some loosening up on subject material. Frankly, I have seen little from the U.S.S.R. which has been inspiring, except for a beautiful period piece, Josef Heifitz's *The Lady with the Little Dog* (1960) from Chekhov, and the monumental *Hamlet* (1963) by Kozintsev, which in some critics' opinion is the most successful film of Shakespeare yet to be made. With directors such as Wajda and the late Andrzej Munk, the Poles have made a deep impression in recent years. Thanks to an imaginative training school at Lodz under its gifted principal, Jerzy Toeplitz, these directors, and others such as Kawalerowicz and Polanski, have given us some of the most powerful films in Europe. Wajda's *Ashes and Diamonds* (1958) was outstanding. So also was Polanski's first feature picture, *Knife in the Water* (1962).

To give adequate space to much other interesting cinema to come recently from Europe is not possible, but mention must be made of Jacques Rivette's *Paris Nous Appartient* (1958), Robert Bresson's *Pickpocket* (1959), Pasolini's *Accatone* (1961), Resnais' three very controversial films

Hiroshima, Mon Amour (1959), *Last Year at Marienbad* (1963) and *Muriel* (1965), Milos Forman's *A Blonde in Love* (1965) and the first film by a young Italian director of much promise, Marco Bellocchio's *Fists in the Pocket* (1965). A film which unfortunately I have not seen, Dreyer's *Gertrud* (1964) is by all accounts a remarkable achievement by this veteran director. Bergman, of course, is a matter of taste; I do not share the cult which has grown up around him; the fault may be mine.

The American cinema has not brought forth much which has made a lasting impression on me. Parts of the dancing in Jerome Robbins' and Robert Wise's *West Side Story* (1961), Marlon Brando's underrated *One-Eyed Jacks* (1963), John Huston's also underrated *The Misfits* (1960), John Frankenheimer's *The Manchurian Candidate* (1962), Hitchcock's *Psycho* (1960) and *The Birds* (1963). There has been, we are told, some off-beat American film-making, mostly in New York. What I have seen of it is not impressive, but I liked Shirley Clarke's *The Connection* (1964), particularly Frank Perry's *David and Lisa* (1963) and also John Cassavetes' *Shadows* (1960). Richard Leacock and the group working with him in a pursuit of *cinéma vérité* has made some formidable *reportage* films, of which I liked *Primary* (1961) the best. There was also *Jazz on a Summer's Day* (1960) by Bert Stern, a must for all jazz-lovers but a brilliant piece of *reportage* as well. Overall, the American cinema has been notable for its disappointments.

Other films from various sources in the last few years have been: the British Jack Clayton's *The Innocents* (1961) from Henry James' novel *The Turn of a Screw*, Stanley Kubrick's Anglo-American *Dr. Strangelove, or How I Learned to Stop Worrying and Love the Bomb* (1963), Peter Brook's British *Lord of the Flies* (1963) and of course especially Buñuel's magnificent Spanish-made *Viridiana* (1961). Of particular importance in England was the making of Peter Watkins' *The War Game* (1966), originally commissioned by the BBC Television service but not screened by them. Thanks to the British Film Institute and with BBC agreement, the film has been given the public exhibition which it much deserves. As is well known, the film speculates as to what events might happen if there were a nuclear attack on southeast England. The Kevin Brownlow–Andrew Mollo film of what might have been the situation in England if the Nazis had succeeded in making occupation, *It Happened Here* (1960–65), finally achieved a long-delayed commercial showing by an American distributor. For what began as an amateur film it had much to recommend it. The Japanese *Tokyo Olympiad* was a magnificent piece of teamwork, cinematography at its best.

*

As they must be, all the foregoing represent a personal choice. For certain there will be omissions and disagreements.

Again inevitably there have been notable losses to the cinema. The distinguished French directors Jacques Becker, Jean Grémillon and Nicole Védrès; the memorable French actor Gérard Philipe; and the inimitable Buster Keaton, who in the last few years of his life was rightly paid much admiration and respect.

The film society audience continues to grow all over the world. So also does what we call in England specialist cinemas and the Americans call art-houses. It cannot be long before a modestly budgeted film will be able to recover its production cost and a surplus from such a kind of distribution and exhibition. What is needed is organisation and some kind of co-ordination between the cinemas. It is reported as I write that some attempt to organise a hundred such theatres is being made in America. In Britain there has been for years a project mooted for a new circuit of cinemas as an alternative to the circuits belonging to the Rank Organisation and ABC. This, however, can only happen with government backing. The present Labour Government has yet to make known its attitude to the cinema as a whole as a medium of creative expression. In no other country has the status of the independent film-maker become more precarious.

Film as a whole progresses in subject-matter and in purpose. The current flair for technical gimmicks will evaporate as quickly as Carnaby Street and Op Art. The film medium will always be the limitless and dynamic medium for the creative artist who wishes to use it—always provided he can solve the economic problems involved. The equation of the film as an art and the film as an industry remains to be solved by each user. All making of films that matter depends basically on the sincerity to truth of the maker. Money is spent on film stock, technicians' wages, on laboratory charges, on insurance, on copyrights, on actors, maybe on studio rental, on bank charges and on all the hangers-on and fringe types that suck off almost any production, but the only thing that comes clearly out is the sincerity of the film-maker himself. The magic is not in the techniques he uses but in his own vision and the filmic expression.

INDEX

(Page-numbers italicised indicate a reference to a film's production unit)

A

Aafa studios, 594
Abbas, K. K., 763
ABC, 782
Abdullah, Achmed, 207
Abel, Alfred, 258, 288, 309
Abetz, Otto, 584
Abraham Lincoln, 154, 447
Absolute film, the, 113-15
Abstract film, the, 113-15
Academy of Motion Picture Arts and Sciences, Eisenstein's address to, 1930, 562
Accatone, L', 780
Across the Pacific, 500
ACT Films, 734
Act of Violence, 727
Admiral Nakhimov, 574
Adventures in Bukhara, 579
Adventures of an Octoberite, The, 227, 237
Adventures of a Ten-Mark Note, 289
Adventures of Baron Münchhausen, The, 41, *621*
Adventures of Dolly, The, 150
Adventures of Mr. West Among the Bolsheviki, The, 227, 228
Adventures of Prince Achmed, The, 118
Aëlita, 98, 227n., 228, 248
Aerograd (Frontier), 574, *622*
Aesop's Fables, 119
Affaire Blum, 758
Affiche, L', 302
African Queen, The, 730
After the Verdict, 286, 317
Against All, 758
Age d'Or, L', 117n.
Agee, James, 573, 771
Ager, Cecelia, 496
Agony in the Garden, 330
Aigle à deux Têtes, L', 541
Alaskan, The, 209

Alazraki, Benito, 769
Albatross-Sequana, 298, 304
Aldrich, Robert, 730, 779
Alexander Hamilton, 447
Alexander Nevsky, 571-2
Alexander the Great, 729
Alexandrov, G. V., 230, 561, 564n., 575, 577
Algiers, 475, 531
All About Eve, 730
All-American, 441
Allan, Havelock A., *see* Havelock-Allan, Anthony
Allegret, Marc, 311
Allegret, Yves, 739, 740
Allen, Frederick Lewis, 145n.
Allgeier, Sepp, 272
All My Babies, 731
All Quiet on the Western Front, 340, 486, *622*
All That Money Can Buy, 493
Allvine, Glen, 384
Along Came Jones, 502
Alten, Ferdinand von, 282, 290
Amants, Les, 742
Ambler, Eric, 559
America, 149, 154
America at the Movies, 92n., 128n
American Biograph Company, 72
American Film Industry, Hollywood 'B' pictures, 27; and the world market, 30, 33, 40, 60, 73-6, 81, 83-5, 127; fails to sense after-effects of World War II, 32-3; restrictive methods, 33; Hollywood's mass dominance over producers and audiences, 34; Hollywood's reliance on audience surveys, 35, 137n.; documentary in, 47, 48, 458-64; standardised methods of, 57; Hollywood star-system, 74, 92, 126, 127, 128, 129-34, 334; European efforts to

break control of, 76-7, 78, 81;
hostility to European industry,
77; drift of directors and players
to Hollywood, 77, 78, 81, 82, 100,
133, 134-5, 177, 187, 710, 714;
effect of Hollywood on dirêctors
and players, 78-80, 141-3; quota
restrictions against, 81; exploits
the sound film, 82-3, 146; domestic comedies, 102-3; naturalistic
movement in, 103, 201, 203-8;
relationship of public to American
cinema, 128-33; feature films to
type, 133-4; German and Swedish
elements in, 134-6; organisation
of, 136-8; technical accomplishment, 139-40; 'committee-made
pictures', 140; sex in films of, 140,
144, 145, 209, 334; ingredients of
a Hollywood film, 140-1; characteristics of, 143-5; types of dialogue film, 146-7; comedies of,
214-15; ephemeral value of its
films, 215; some films of highest
merit, 216; beginning of sound
era, 429-32; in economic depression, 432-3, 438, 439; gangster
films, 433-7; the confession tale,
437-40, 442; the topical film,
440-2, 444, 454-6; the New Deal
phase, 443; musicals, 443-4; history and legend subjects, 446-9;
discovers Dickens, 448; 'fantasy of
good-will' finds film embodiment,
450-3; screwball comedy phase,
453-4; biographical films, 457;
trend towards realism, 457; U.S.
Film Service, 459; O.W.I. films,
460-1, 613; war-time documentary, 461-4; the war on the screen,
464-7; psychological films, 467-9;
religious films, 467-8; post-war
trends, 726, 728, 729, 731
American Madness, 441, *622*
American Motion Picture Association, 59, 74n.
American Prisoner, The, 316
American Romance, An, 473
American Telephone and Telegraph
Company, 84, 85
American Tragedy, An, 562
American Venus, The, 213, 270

American Western films, 729, 730
Amici per la Pelle, 746
Amidei, Sergio, 49, 50, 599
Amore, 601n.
Amore in Città, 746
Anatomy of Motion Picture Art, The,
110n., 330n., 358n., 399
Andersen, Hans, 118, 310
Anderson, J. L., 765
Anderson, Lindsay, 735, 765, 766,
779
Anderson, Michael, 729
Andreiev, Andrei, 98
And So They Live, 614
And Then There Was No More Sea,
752
Angel, 479
Angelina, 600-1
Angels with Dirty Faces, 455, 492
Anges du Péché, Les, 740
Angle, camera, 95, 368, 372
Anglo-American Film Agreement,
30, 552n.
Anglo-American Films, 732
Animal Farm, 736
Animated Cartoons, 731, 736, 753,
758, 761
Anna Karenina, 551
Anne Boleyn, 142, 177, 180, 287,
292, 547, 623, 709, 714
A Nous la Liberté, 36, 526-8, 529,
540, *623*
Anti-Trust Laws, 726
Antoine et Antoinette, 739
Antonioni, Michelangelo, 776, 779
Anything Goes, 487
Applause, 477
Appollinaire, Guillaume, 416
A quoi rêvent les jeunes films, 115,
295, 296, 369, *687*
Arab, The, 197
Arabella, 284
Arabesque, 312
Aran, Isle of, 520
Architectural Review, 407
Argent, L', 268, 309
Argentina, film-making in, 618, 770
Ariane, 715
Arizona, 173, 174
Arlen, Richard, 144, 207
Arliss, George, 447
Armageddon, 322

INDEX

Armat, Thomas, 69
Armenkino, 226
Army-Navy Screen Magazine, 463, 464
Arna, Lissi, 291
Arné's Treasure, see *Sir Arné's Treasure*
Arno, Siegfried, 283
Around the World in Eighty Days, 729
Arrowsmith, 482
Arsenal, 238, 239, 370, 532, 575, *623*
Arsenic and Old Lace, 452
Art film, the, 124
Arts Enquiry Report on the Factual Film, see *Factual Film*
Arzner, Dorothy, 212
Ascenseur pour l'Echafaud, 741
Ashes and Diamonds, 780
Ashley, Ray, 731
Asphalt, 101, 183, 255, 291
Asphalt Jungle, The, 727
Asquith, Anthony, 56, 314, 315, 320, 559, 733
Assembling of film, 341, 344. See also Montage
Association of Cine-Technicians, 549, 550
Astaire, Fred, 443
Asther, Nils, 135
Astruc, Alexandre, 741
Atalante, L', 117n., 541, *623*
Atlantic, 183, 322
Atlantide, 102, 307, 583
Atonement of Gösta Berling, The, 186, 187, 323, *624*
At the Edge of the World, 258, 268, 284
Attack, 730
Auberge en Folie, L', 289
Aubert, Claude Bernard, 741
Aubert Company, 311
Audience surveys, Hollywood's reliance on, 35, 137n.
Aurenche, Jean, 737
Australia, documentary in, 47, 48; censorship in, 83; film-making in, 619; National Film Board, 60, 619
Australian Film Industry, 724, 761
Austrian Film Industry, 751
Autant-Lara, Claude, 40, 541, 543, 739, 740

Avenging Conscience, The, 150
Avventura, L', 777
Awful Truth, The, 453
Axel, Gabriel, 749

B

Bachelor Party, 728
Back of Beyond, 762
Baclanova, Olga, 185, 195
Bad Company, 212
Bad Day at Black Rock, 730
Badger, Clarence, 212
Bad Girl, 490
Baggott, King, 212
Balaclava, 392
Balazs, Bela, 759, 772
Balcon, Sir Michael, 56, 548, 551, 554
Balfour, Betty, 309
Ballade Chromo, 742
Ballade du Canart, La, 116, 300
Ballad Film, the, 115-16
Ballet, analogy with cinema, 378
Ballet Girl, 749
Ballet Mécanique, Le, 115
Ball of Fire, 492, 503
Ballon Rouge, Le, 742
Balloons and Spinifex, 762
Baltic Deputy, 568, 576, *624*
Balzac, Honoré, 278
Bamberger, Rudolph, 118, 258, 281, 282, 710
Bambi, 518
Bambini ci guardano, I, 743
Ban, Frigyes, 759
Bancroft, George, 194, 294
Bandwagon, 729
Bankhead, Tallulah, 438, 479
Bank Holiday, 558
Baptism of Fire, 583
Baratier, Jacques, 742
Barbusse, Henri, 241
Barbed Wire, 183
Bardèche, H., 29, 99n., 312n.
Bardelys the Magnificent, 192
Bardem, Juan Antonio, 751
Bardot, Brigitte, 741
Barkas, Geoffrey, 322
Barnet, Boris, 116, 226, 247, 248, 370
Barrandov, studios at, 609
Barreto, Vinnoly, 770

Barrie, Sir James, 431
Barrière, La, 116
Barringer, Michael, 322
Barry, Iris, 29, 99n., 212n., 312n., 330n., 419, 590
Barrymore, John, 211, 428
Barrymore, Lionel, 209
Barski, —, 227
Barthelmess, Richard, 153, 200, 441, 583
Barty-King, Hugh, 51
Baruch, 292
Basement Room, The, 559
Bas-Fonds, Les, 624
Bataille du Rail, La, 541, 543, *674*, 759
Batalov, Nicolai, 241
Batcheff, Pierre, 117, 294
Bateson, Gregory, 586
Battle for the Ukraine, The, 579
Battles of Coronel and Falkland Islands, The, 123, 322
Battle of Midway, The, 485
Battle of Russia, The, 674
Battle of San Pietro, The, 48, 463, 500
Battle of Stalingrad, 754
Battle of the Sexes, The, 154
Battleship Potemkin, The, 36, 40, 94, 121, 129, 149n., 168, 226, 232, 255, 267, 406, 426, 534, 571; shown in London, 138; as an epic film, 221; theme of, 230, 231; influence on Grierson, 318; movement in, 379-80, 390, 394; Meisel's music for, 409; held up as model by Goebbels, 585; production unit of, *625*; influence on Mayer, 717n.
Baur, Harry, 531
Bavaria Film Company, 585, 587
Baxter, John, 551
Bazin, André, 771, 778
B.B.C.: The Voice of Britain, 675, 736
B.B.C. Television, 781
Beau Geste, 144, 209, 635
Beaumont, Harry, 135, 213, 493
Beau Serge, Le, 741
Beauté du Diable, La, 740
Beauty for Sale, 442
Be Big, 16
Becker, Jacques, 540, 543, 739, 740, 782

Becky Sharp, 477
Bed and Sofa, 144, 169, 240-1, 242, 333, 357-8, 364, 392, *625*
Beddington, Jack, 314n., 771
Bedlam, 508
Beery, Noah, 207
Beery, Wallace, 75, 212
Beggar on Horseback, The, 203, *625*
Behind the Screen, 73n.
Behrendt, Hans, 292
Belfrage, Cedric, 24
Belgian films, 615, 753
Belgoskino, 226
Bell, Monta, 135, 213, 263, 493
Belle Equipe, La, 531
Belle et la Bête, La, 541, 739
Belles de Nuit, Les, 740
Bell for Adano, A, 466
Bellocchio, Marco, 781
Beloved Rogue, The, 211, 213, 300
Belyaev, V., 579n.
Benedek, Laszlo, 727, 751
Ben-Hur, 73, 86, 125, 128, 139, 144, 211, 300, 399, *626*, 722
Bennett, Arnold, 329
Bennett, Belle, 200
Bennett, Compton, 555
Bennett, Constance, 438
Bennett, Joan, 481
Benoit-Lévy, Jean, 531, 542
Benson, Shan, 762
Berg, The, 321
Berger, Dr. Ludwig, 18, 135, 187, 258, 262, 280-1, 709
Bergman, Ingmar, 748, 776, 781
Berlin, 123, 261, 310, 378, 392, 409, *675*, 714, 717
Berliner Ballade, 750
Bern, Paul, 213
Bernard, Edmond, 753
Bernard-Aubert, Claude, see Aubert, Claude Bernard
Bernhardt, Kurt, 262, 289, 290, 292
Bernhardt, Sarah, 72
Bespoke Overcoat, The, 734
Bessières, Louis, 742
Bessy, Maurice, 70n.
Best Years of Our Lives, The, 22, 32, 35, 53, 468, 488, 508, *626*
·*Bête Humaine, La*, 534, *626*, 738
Betrayal, The, 142
Betrogen bis zum Jüngsten Tag, 758

INDEX

Bettauer, Hugo, 266
Beveridge, James, 764
Bezhin Meadow, 571
Bicycle Thieves, 743, 744, 744n., 773
Bidone, Il, 745
Bierce, Ambrose, 467
Big Broadcasts, 443
Big Country, The, 729
Biggs, Julian, 761
Big House, The, 434
Big Parade, The, 86, 128, 144, 189, 190-1, 335, 473, *626*
Big Sleep, The, 492
Bill Blewitt, 55, 56
Billboard, The, 95
Bilo, The, 603
Billy the Kid, 447, 471
Binyon, Claude, 507
Birds, The, 781
Biro, Lajos, 546
Birth of a Nation, The, 72, 128, 149, 150-1, 152, 367, 368, 534, *564*, *627*
Birth of the Hours, The, 121
Biscuit Eater, The, 502
Bitter Truth, The, 759
Blache, Herbert, 212
Blackbird, The, 211
Black Fury, 455, 492
Black Legion, 455, *627*
Blackmail, 83, 321, 382, 405
Black Narcissus, 553
Black Pirate, The, 144, 172, 175, 216, 399, *627*
Black Tide, The, 767
Blackton, Stuart, 399
Blakeston, Oswell, 115, 342n.
Blessed Event, 441
Blind Alleys, 213
Blind Husbands, 158, *627*
Blithe Spirit, 553
Blockade, 460, 493
Blonde Bombshell, 491
Blonde in Love, A, 781
Blondell, Joan, 436
Blonde or Brunette, 213
Blonde Venus, The, 438, 474
Blood and Sand, 478
Blood Money, 494
Blood on the Sun, 492
Blue, Monte, 141
Blue Angel, The, 474, 582, *628*
Bluebeard's Eighth Wife, 479

Bluebottles, 322
Blue Dahlia, The, 503
Blue Danube, The, 288
Blue Lagoon, The, 554
Bobbed Hair, 211
Body Snatcher, The, 508
Bogart, Humphrey, 500
Bohème, La, 192, 595
Bold Sea Rover, The, 262
Bolshevism, 105, 219
Bomber's Moon, 465
Bond, Ralph, 521n.
Bonheur, Le, 541
Boomerang, 33, 54, 56, 122n., 504, 628, 730
Border Legion, The, 208
Border Street, 756
Borinage, The, 611, *675*
Born Reckless, 505
Born to Love, 438
Born Yesterday, 730
Borowczyk, Walerian, 757
Borsky, Vladimir, 609
Borzage, Frank, 211, 489-90, 528
Bosch, Hieronymus, 339
Bost, Pierre, 737
Boucher, François, 280
Bought, 438
Bouli Bouli: le Crocodil, 742
Boulting, John and Roy, 56
Bovary, Geza von, 594
Bow, Clara, 75, 144, 207, 211, 389, 438
Box, Sydney, 555
Box of Pandora, The, 264, 270–1
Boyhood of Dr. Noguchi, The, 767
Boy Kumasenu, The, 763
Brabin, Charles, 212
Brackett, Charles, 503, 504, 506
Brady, M. B., 467
Brandes, Werner, 282, 317n., 321, 373
Brando, Marlon, 781
Brasillach, R., 29, 99n., 312n.
Brausewetter, Hans, 281
Brave Don't Cry, The, 734
Braverman, Barnet, 95
Brecht, Bertolt, 751
Breen, Joseph I., 446
Brenon, Herbert, 209, 340
Brenton, Guy, 735
Bresson, Robert, 543, 737, 740, 780

Bridge, The, 620
Bridge of San Luis Rey, The, 340
Bridge on the River Kwai, The, 732, 733
Brief Encounter, 560, *628*, 733
Brigade, The, 606
Bright, John, 434, 435
Bright Path, The, 576
Brinson, Peter, 754
Britain, feature films quota in, 30, 32; acceptance of U.S. films in, 73; American films taken by exhibitors in, 74, 75; percentage of screen-space occupied by Hollywood footage, 126n. See also British Film Industry
British and Colonial Kinematograph Company, 72
British Board of Film Censors, 86, 217
British Film Academy, 40, 59
British Film Industry, quota restrictions in favour of, 30, 32, 33, 59, 82; Anglo-American film agreement, 30, 552n.; feature film quota, 30, 32; boom and crash, 35; recent boom, 36; reception of its films in U.S.A., 36; and the American market, 36, 37, 552-3, 561; Rank and, 36, 552-3; realism in war-time films, 36, post-war films, 36-7; independent producers' position, 37-8, 58-9; increased production costs, 38; Trade Unions and, 38, 39; technicians in, 38-9; development of sponsored production, 42-5; documentary in, 43-6, 47, 322, 544, 555-6; documentary methods in commercially-made films, 56; need for experiment in, 57-8; effects of new Film Act, 58; prospects of, 58-9; early companies, 72; efforts to break U.S. domination, 76; loss of promising players to Hollywood, 78; campaign for British films, 81-2; collapse of small companies, 82; first dialogue film, 83; nature films, 122, 322; established on hollow foundation, 313-14; modernism in, 314; wealth of material at hand, 315; use of natural resources, 315; narrow-minded producing executives, 316-17; importation of foreign talent, 317-18; no clear phases of development, 318; reconstruction of war events, 322; factors hampering development, 544-6; revival after 1942, 552; crises since 1948, 728, 732, 733, 735, 772
British Film Institute, 23, 59, 735, 781
British Instructional Films, 82, 122, 322
British International Pictures, 82, 83, 283, 315, 321
British Lion Film Corporation, 76n.
British Movietone News, 123
British Transport Film Unit, 736
Broadway, 125
Broadway After Dark, 213
Broadway After Midnight, 136
Broadway Melody, The, 125, 144, 147, 213, 443
Broken Blossoms, 153, 216, *629*
Broken Dykes, 614
Broken Journey, 54
Broken Lullaby, 479
Brook, Clive, 207
Brook, Peter, 781
Brooks, Louise, 269, 270, 584n.
Brothers, The, 54, 555
Brothers Karamazov, The, 288
Brown, Clarence, 189, 197-8, 493, 726
Brown, Karl, 103, 206, 208, 216
Brown, Rowland, 493, 503
Browning, Tod, 211, 493
Browning Version, The, 734
Brownlow, Kevin, 782
Bruegel, Pieter, 280, 339
Bruguière, Francis, 115, 342n.
Brûmes d'Automne, 116, 297
Brunius, John, 186, 323
Brusse, Ytzen, 753
Bryher, Winifred, 111, 417, 422
Buchan, Sidney, 495, 506
Büchner, Georg, 594
Buchowetski, Dimitri, 135, 182, 187, 288, 709
Büchse der Pandora, Die, see *Pandora's Box*
Buczkovski, Leonard, 610

INDEX

Bulgaria, film industry in, 324
Bulldog Drummond, 147
Buñuel, Luis, 117, 333, 769, 781
Bureau of Foreign and Domestic Commerce (U.S.), Motion Picture Division, 30, 32
Burger, Hans, 608
Burke, Thómas, 153
Burmah-Shell, 764
Burma Victory, 56, *675*
Burmese Harp, The, 767
Burning Heart, The, 280, 282
Burning Question, The, 605
Burt, Struthers, 450

C

Cabinet of Dr. Caligari, The, 36, 100, 129, 148, 181, 254, 285, 365, 368, 376, 400, 421, 483, 615, 709, 710; importance and significance of, 93-8, 168, 256, 257; influence of, 99; use of psychology in, 292; expressionism of, 309; only one complete copy, 329n.; repetitive movement in, 380; production unit of, *629*; Pommer on, 711-13
Cabin in the Cotton, The, 441, 492
Cabiria, 323, 714
Cacoyannis, Michael, 753
Caesar and Cleopatra, 273, 553, 710
Caesar Borgia, 709
Cagliostro, 288
Cagney, James, 434, 435, 436
Cahiers du Cinéma, 724, 738, 778
Call Her Savage, 438
Calumny, 247
Camera, director's creative imagination expressed through, 89-90; angle of, 95, 368, 372; expressive capabilities of, 362, 366-75; position of, 366-8; distortion by, 366, 368-9, 383; movement of, 366, 370-5, 377-81; mobility, 367-9, 383; employment of gauzes with, 369; projection of negative film, 369-70; slow-motion, 370; ultra-rapid motion, 370; cessation of movement, 370; panning with, 373-4; rolling or travelling shots, 374; camera personification, 374-5
Cameraman, part in preparation of shooting-script, 348-9

Camille, 377n., 493
Campaign for a Crop, The, 251
Campeau, Frank, 199
Camus, Marcel, 741
Canada, film-making in, 618-19, 761; documentary in, 47, 618; National Film Board, 46-8, 60, 115n., 612, 618
Canary Murder Case, The, 270
Cannery Boat, The, 767
Canterbury Tale, The, 317n.
Cap, Frantisek, 609
Capablanca, José, 229
Cape, Jonathan, 15
Capitaine Fracasse, Le, 124, 310
Cappotto, Il, 744
Capra, Frank, 468, 480; his *Why We Fight* series, 17, 123n., 424, 461, 462, 482; attempt to exist as independent unit, 34; Riskin and, 49; work of, 450-4, 482; in command of U.S. Army's films, 460, 523, 612
Captain Hates the Sea, The, 487
Carbonneaux, Norbert, 741
Carewe, Edwin, 212
Cargo in Jamaica, 619
Carillon de Minuit, Le, 311
Carlyle, Thomas, 153
Carmen (*Gypsy Blood*), 134, 167, 307
Carnaby Street, 783
Carné, Marcel, 40, 49, 298n., 368n., 476n., 530, 538, 540, 543, 739, 740, 741
Carnegie Corporation, the, 459
Carnet de Bal, Un, 531
Carol, Sue, 133, 144, 294
Carosse d'Or, La, 739
Carroll, Madeleine, 319
Carroll, Nancy, 144
Cartoon Film, the, 118-20, 147. See also Disney, Walt
Carver, Richard P., 206
Casablanca, 492
Casa del Angel, La, 770
Casanova, 74, 102, 291, 300, 399
Casemate Blindée, La, 287
Case of Sergeant Grisha, The, 192, 340
Casque d'Or, 739
Cassavetes, John, 781
Castellani, Renato, 42, 744

791

INDEX

Cat and the Canary, The, 287
Catelain, Jacques, 309
Catherine the Great, 547n., 548
Catholic War Veterans, 512
Cat People, The, 507
Cava, Gregory la, 492
Cavalcanti, Alberto, 116, 193, 297, 299, 356; pictorial mind of, 301, 309-10; in England, 543
Cayatte, André, 739
Celluloid: The Film Today, 205n., 239n., 276n., 420n., 526n., 574n., 779
Celui qui doit mourir, 740
Censored, 86n.
Censorship, film, 85-7, 217, 446
Central African Film Industry, 762
Central Office of Information, 45, 47n., 48, 735
Centre, The, 55
Ceylon Film Industry, 762
Chabrol, Claude, 741
Chaffey, Don, 735
Chambers, J., 620
Champion Charlie, 167
Chance of a Lifetime, The, 734
Chandler, Raymond, 492, 503
Chaney, Lon, 185
Chang, 103, 122, 202, 204, 206, 207, 216, 384, *676*
Chants Populaires series, 618
Chaos and Order, 251
Chapaev, 566, 567, 575, *629*
Chapeau de Paille d'Italie, Le (The Italian Straw Hat), 297, 304, 305, 527, 529, *646*
Chaplin, Charles, 57, 102, 112, 125, 129, 135, 172, 178, 189, 193, 203, 214-16, 263, 420, 499, 517, 526, 557, 726, 730, 779; an independent film-maker, 33, 141; individualistic films of, 103; quoted, 111; early one-reelers of, 119; his understanding of human nature, 162, 335-6; his work, 163-70, 509-15; Clair's admiration for, 303, 305, 529; his view of the camera, 374
Chaplin, Sydney, 214
Chappell, Messrs., 85
Charles XII, 186
Charlie at the Bank, 167

Charlie at the Show, 167
Charlie the Perfect Lady, 167
Charming Sinners, 136, 147
Chasing Rainbows, 214
Chatterton, Ruth, 431
Chauve-Souris, 302
Chavannes, P. de., 299
Chayevsky, Paddy, 727, 728
Chekhov, Anton, 780
Chenal, Pierre, 475, 541
Cherkassov, Nikolai, 576
Cherviakov, Yevgeni, 243
Chess Fever, 228, 234
Chetniks, 465
Chevalier, Maurice, 147, 477, 529
Chiaureli, Mikhail, 754
Chien Andalou, Un, 117, 117n., 333
Chienne, La, 532, 535
Chikamatzu Monogatari, 766
Child, The, 605
Childhood of Maxim Gorki, The, 575, *629*
Children of Divorce, 605
Children of the Beehive, 767
Children of the Earth, 617
Children of Hiroshima, 767
Children on Trial, 556, *676*
Children's films, 58, 222, 577, 736
Children's Film Foundation, 736
China Seas, 444
Chinese Film Industry, 618, 767
Chinese Parrot, The, 287
Chmielewski, Tadeusz, 756
Chomette, Henri, 115, 295, 296
Choukrai, Grigori, 755
Christensen, Benjamin, 186, 187, 305, 605
Christensen, Theodore, 606
Christians, Mady, 260, 281, 282, 284, 289
Christmas in July, 498
Christ Stopped at Eboli, 600
Chronicle of the Grieshuus, 630
Chu Chin Chow, 448
Churchill, Sir Winston, 548
Chûte de la Maison Usher, La, 303
Cid, El, 779
Cigarette Merchant of Mosselprom, The, 227, 247
Cimarron, 447, 448, 492, *630*
Cinderella, 118, 187, 258, 280-2, *630*, 709

Cinema, The, **334, 396, 406n.**
Cine-Eye, the, **122-3, 363, 366**; theory of, **243-7**; manifesto, **244**
Cine-Fiction Film, kinds of, **124-5**
Cinema Eye, Cinema Ear, **778**
Cinema Quarterly, **521n., 543n., 547n., 583**
Cinemas, municipal, **23, 25, 28, 59**; nationalisation of, **25, 29**; need to investigate programmes of, **26**; for special films, **28-9**; early, **70-1**; new epoch in, **73**; producers' ownership of, **76**
Cinéma Soviétique, Le, **220n.**
Cinémathèque Française, Paris, **330n.**
Cinematograph Exhibitors Association, **23**
Cinematograph Film Acts (1927), **82, 544, 545**; (1938), **544, 551**; (1948), **25, 58, 552, 732**
Cine-Poem, the, **115-16**
Cine-Radio Film, the, **122-3**
Cine-Record Film, the, **123**
Cine-Surrealist Film, the, **116-17**
Cine-Technician, The, **35n., 507n.**
Circus, The, **164-6, 168, 172, 575, *631***
Ciske the Rat, **753**
Citadel, The, **472, 473, 551**
Citizen Kane, **382n., 495-7, *631***
City, The, **459, *676***
City for Conquest, **455**
City Lights, **509, 511, *631***
City of Gold, **761**
City Streets, **477, *631***
City that Never Sleeps, The, **203**
Clair, René, **40, 102-3, 111, 118, 263, 295-8, 302-5, 368, 477-8, 526-30, 540, 543, 546, 548, 740**
Clancey, V. J., **334, 406n.**
Clarke, Shirley, **781**
Clayton, Jack, **734, 781**
Clément, René, **40, 298n., 541, 543, 737, 739, 740**
Clift, Montgomery, **616**
Clive of India, **449**
Cloak, The, **237**
Clock, The, **502**
Close Quarters, **676**
Close-up, the, **90, 94-5, 107, 150, 367**
Close Up, **114, 217n., 231n., 355, 416-17, 422, 562, 564n., 584n.**

Clouzot, Henri-Georges, **540, 592, 739, 740, 742**
Cluny Brown, **479**
Coastal Command, **677**
Cob Film Company, **288**
Cocteau, Jean, **117n., 541, 601n., 739**
Coeur Fidèle, Le, **302**
Coeur Magnifique, Le, **311**
Coffin Maker, The, **257, 709**
College, **214**
College Days, **144, 215**
Collier de la Reine, Le, **125, 300**
Colonel Blimp, **317n., 553**
Colour, use of, **89, 110, 362, 398-401**
Colourbox, **115n., *688***
Columbia Broadcasting Company, **85, 726**
Columbia Gramophone Company, **84**
Columbia Pictures, **450, 475**
Come and Get It, **488**
Comet, **251**
Comicos, **751**
Committee of Enquiry into Exhibition, **25, 59**
Committee of Un-American Activities, **22, 455n., 466n., 503**
Common Clay, **438**
Common Law, The, **438**
Commonwealth Film Unit of Australia, **761**
Communism, **223-4**
Composition, see Visual Images
Compound Cinema, the, **360, 386**
Compson, Betty, **195**
Condamné à mort s'est échappé, Un, **740, 773**
Condition Humaine, La, **571**
Confessions of a Nazi Spy, **460**
Confessions of a Queen, **185**
Confession tale, the, **437-40, 442, 444**
Congress Dances, **632**
Conklin, Chester, **167**
Connection, The, **781**
Conquest of Europe on the Screen, The, **590**
Conrad, Joseph, **352**
Conscience, **291**
Contact, **397, 423, 619**
Contemporary Cinema, The, **778**
Continente perduta, **746**

Continuity, 351-2, 354-7
Contrast, use of, 107-8
Conway, Jack, 212, 493, 551
Cooke, Alistair, 24
Cooper, Diana, 399
Cooper, Merian C., 103, 206, 207, 216, 485
Co-optimists, The, 315
Coquette, 175, 176, 456
Coquille et le Clergyman, La, 86, 117, 297, 312, *688*
Corbeau, Le, 540, 592
Corda, Maria, 545
Cormack, Bartlett, 433
Cornelius, Henry, 733, 734, 771
Corral, 761
Cottage on Dartmoor, A, 314, 320, 377n., 384
Counsellor-at-Law, 488
Counterplan, 566, 569, *632*
Cousteau, Jacques, 741, 742
Cover to Cover, 423
Covered Wagon, The, 198, 202, 203, 208, 212, *632*
Coward, Noel, 560
Cradle, The, 245
Craigie, Jill, 55
Crainquebille, 307
Cranach, Lucas, 339
Crane, Stephen, 467
Cranes are Flying, The, 755
Crawford, Joan, 133, 144, 294, 439
Creativeness Cannot be Diffused, 508n.
Crighton, Charles, 555
Crime and Punishment, 98, 285, 475
Crime de Monsieur Lange, Le, 738
Crime et Chatiment, 541, *633*
Crime Without Passion, *633*
Criminal Life of Archibaldo de la Cruz, 769
Crimson Grill, The, 409
Crin Blanc, 742
Crisis, 262, 263, 266, 268, 460, 608, 677
Crisp, Donald, 210-11
Criticism, Trade's fear of, 23-4
Croisière Noire, La, 311
Cromwell, Richard, 728
Cronin, A. J., 472
Crosbie, Floyd, 617
Crosland, Alan, 211

Cross-cutting, 107; Pudovkin's use of, 235, 236
Crossfire, 20, 22, 32, 35, 37, 51, 140n., 369n., 468, 503, 507, *633*
Crowd, The, 124, 189-90, 191, 192, 295, 372, *634*
Crowd Roars, The, 492
Crown Film Unit, 43, 736
Crown of Lies, The, 78, 187
Cruel Sea, The, 733
Cruze, James, 103, 162, 178, 189, 201-3
Cry, the Beloved Country, 734
Cserèpy, Arzèn von, 123, 288
Cubism, 98, 256, 285
Cukor, George, 51, 493, 515, 730
Culver City, 205
Cummings, Irving, 212
Cure, The, 167, 322
Curse of the Cat People, The, 507
Curtiz, Michael, 187, 492, 572
Cutting, 352, 359, 386-95
Cyprus is an Island, 620
Cyrano de Bergerac, 399
Czarina, The, 178
Czech cultural films, 758
Czechoslovak Film Archive, Prague, 330n.
Czechoslovakia, nationalisation of films in, 25; film industry in, 41, 324, 607-10, 758n.; documentary in, 608-10
Czinner, Paul, 101, 276-8, 292, 537, 715

D

Daddy Long Legs, 176, 448
Dagover, Lil, 273, 279, 587, 710
Daley, T., 761
Dali, Salvador, 117n., 495
Dambusters, The, 734
Dames du Bois de Boulogne, Les, 740
Dana, Viola, 131
Dance Contest in Esira, 603
Dance Fever, 546
Dancing films, 125
Dangerous Age, A, 761
Dani, 759
Daniels, Bebe, 545
Danish Film Industry, 749
D'Annunzio, Gabriele, 324
Dansk-Kultur film, 606

Danton, 141, 180, 187, *634*
Daquin, Louis, 739, 740
Dark Angel, The, 211
Dark Horse, The, 440
D'Arrast, H. d'Abbadie, 213
Dassin, Jules, 54, 727, 740
Daughter of Destiny, A, 268, 286
Daughter of the Gods, The, 209
Daumier, Honoré, 339
David, Jacques Louis, 299
David Copperfield, 448
David and Lisa, 781
Davies, Marion, 192
Davis, Bette, 500
Davis, Harry, 70, 71
Davis, Joseph E., 465
Davis, Stuart, 106n., 293n.
Davy, Charles, 557n.
Dawn of Iran, 620
Daybreak, 54
Day Dreams, 322
Day of Wrath, The, 604-5, *634*,
    710
Days of Glory, 465
Day's Pleasure, A, 167
Dead End, 456, 488, *634*
Dead of Night, 555, 561
Death Bay, 241
Death Day, 563
Death Ray, The, 227, 228
De Baroncelli, Jacques, 304, 311
Decla-Bioskop, 94, 273
Decla film studio, 711
Decline, The, 753
Decorative Film, The, 124,
DEFA Company (Deutsche Film
    Aktien Gesellschaft), 594, 757
De Feraudy, Maurice, 294
De Forest, Lee, 428
Delannoy, Jean, 540
De la Roche, Catherine, 564n.
Del Giudice, Filippo, 554, 715
Delluc, Louis, 311
Del Rio, Dolores, 133, 618
Del Ruth, Roy, 135, 213
Delvaux, Paul, 615
De Mille, Cecil B., 152, 210, 340,
    490, 572
De Mille, W. C., 212, 430, 493
De Molina, Tirso, 277
Denham, 548, 549
Denmark, film industry in, 41, 78,

99n., 134, 603-7; documentary in,
    603, 605-7
De Pokkers Under, 605
Deppe, Hans, 594
De Putti, Lya, see Putti
Dernier Milliardaire, Le, 528
Dernières Vacances, Les, 739
De Rochemont, Louis, 54, 463, 492,
    504, 726
Deserter, 106, 565, 574, 597, *635*
Desert's Price, The, 205
Desert Victory, 44, 123n., 463, 556,
    579, *677*
De Sica, Vittorio, 599, 743, 744,
    746, 749, 777
Designer, part in preparation of
    shooting-script, 348, 349
Desire, 479
Deslav, Eugène, 114-15, 295, 297,
    300
Desmos, Robert, 116
Destiny, 101, 118, 124, 171, 258,
    272-3, 292, 329n., *635*, 709
Deux Timides, Les, 125, 304, 527
Devil is a Sissy, The, 494
Devil is a Woman, The, 474, 476
Devil's Circus, The, 187
Devil's Holiday, The, 491
Devil's Wheel, The, 237
De Vinna, Clyde, 205
Dewever, Jean, 742
Dharti ke Lal, 617
Diable au Coeur, Le, 309
Diable au Corps, Le, 541, *635*, 739
Diaboliques, Les, 740
Dialogue Film, introduction of, 82-3;
    effect on camera mobility, 370-1;
    a separate form of expression,
    404; characteristics of, 404-11;
    musical accompaniment, 408-9;
    impact of, 415; as photographic
    theatre, 417-18; *cinéastes'* view of,
    419, 422; hailed by Eisenstein and
    Pudovkin, 419; aesthetes' repug-
    nance to, 428; industry's repug-
    nance to, 428; Warners' gamble
    on, 428-9
Diana Productions, 481
Diary of a Chambermaid, The, 535
Diary of a Lost Girl, The, 264, 272
Dickens, Charles, films of his novels,
    448, 560, 561

Dickinson, Thorold, 551, 555, 564n., 734
Dickson, Paul, 735
Diesel, R., 592
Diessl, Gustav, 269
Dieterle, Wilhelm, 288, 290, 291, 493
Dietrich, Marlene, 438, 474, 476-7, 479, 529, 548
Dijk is Dicht, De, 753
Dinamov, —, 567
Diplomacy, 211
Director, difficulties of, 18; and technicians, 39; the main creative mind in film-making, 49-51; test of a, 50; capacities required of, 51-2; the central organiser, 344; and composition, 375
Director-scenarist, the, 347, 349, 351
Disappearing World, 608
Discord, 759
Dishonoured, 474
Disney, Walt, 33, 119-20, 420, 515-20, 610, 731, 773
Dissolve, the, 354-6, 395, 410
Distortion, camera, 92, 366, 368-9, 382
Distributors, control over production, 20-2, 37
Ditte-Menneskebarn, 605, *635*, 749
Divide and Conquer, 678
Dividing Line, The, 726
Divine Lady, The, 133
Divine Woman, The, 187
Division of Community Education, Puerto Rico, 770
Dix, Richard, 131
Dixième Symphonie, La, 311
Dmytryk, Edward, 35, 57, 368n., 369n., 426, 468, 503
Docks of New York, The, 159, 194-5, *636*
Doctor Mabuse, 101, 257, 274, 482, 582
Doctor's Secret, The, 147
Documentary Film, the, influence of methods on entertainment production, 41; sponsorship of, 42-5, 47; Trade's opposition to, 44-5; post-war loss of vitality in, 45; documentary movement, 45-6; standardisation of techniques and styles, 46; group production

dangers, 46, 51; use of term, 46-7; need for dramatic documentary, 47-8; fusion with fiction entertainment film, 53-6; British, 56, 122, 322, 422-5, 544, 555-6, 735; various forms of, 121-2; Soviet, 121, 667, 755; with story interest, 122; United States, 458-64, 731; Nazi, 590-1; Danish, 605-7, 749; Czech, 608-10; Canadian, 618-19; Austrian, 619; work of units sent overseas, 619-20; French, 742; Italian, 747; 1958 Venice Festival, 747; Dutch, 752; Belgian, 753; Indian, 763
Documentary Film, 122n., 242n., 422-3, 520n., 521n., 555n., 566n., 574n.
Documentary Film News, 595n.
Documentary, '47, 51
Documentary in Denmark, 603n.
Documentary News Letter, 106n., 559n.
Dodsworth, 488
Dog's Life, A, 167
Dolinov, —, 248
Dom, 757
Domenica d'Agosto, 744
Donen, Stanley, 729
Don Juan, 211, 428
Don Juan and Faust, 309
Donna Juana, 261, 277, 278
Donnelly, Ruth, 436
Don Q., 173, 174, 210, 357, 370
Don Quixote, 116n., 583, 755
Donne senza Nome, 746
Donskoi, Mark, 40, 575, 578, 749
Don't Play With Love, 264
Dood Wasser, 611
Doronin, —, 227
Dostoievski, F. M., 98, 104, 238, 285, 288, 475
'Double-feature' film programmes, 26-7
Double Indemnity, 503-4, 636
Douglas Melvyn, 454
Dovjenko, Alexander, 40, 105, 116, 118, 225-6, 229, 238-9, 370, 494, 532, 566, 574-5, 579n., 754, 771
Downhill, 321
Down to Earth, 174
Doyle, Conan, 212

Dracula (*Nosferatu*), 181, 278, 285, 303, 329n., 369, 370, *636*, 709
Dramaturg, 711
Drame du Shanghai, 583
Dr. Ehrlich's Magic Bullet, 457, 500
Dreigroschenoper, Die, 582
Dresser, Louise, 197, 198
Dressler, Marie, 167
Drew, Philip Yale, 91
Dreyer, Carl Theodore, 103, 123, 256, 263, 294, 295, 301, 302, 305-7, 339, 603-5, 638, 709
Dr. Fu Manchu, 147
Drifters, 49, 122, 314n., 315, 318, 378, *678*
Drifting Clouds, 766
Dr. Jekyll and Mr. Hyde, 477
Dr. Strangelove, 781
Drum, The, 548
Drums of Love, 154
Drunken Angel, 766
Dubarry (*Passion*), 78, 134, 142, 177, 274, 292, *651*, 709, 714
Duca, Lo, 70n.
Duchamp, Marcel, 115, 295
Duchesse de Langeais, 278
Duchess of Buffalo, The, 213
Dudow, Slatan, 594, 758
Due Soldi di Speranza, 744
Duel in the Sun, 473
Dulac, Germaine, 86, 117, 297, 311, 312
Dumbo, 120n., 518
Dunlop, Ian, 762
Dupont, E. A., 78, 135, 183, 260, 292, 317, 321, 373, 710
Dürer, Albrecht, 280, 339, 340
Durgnat, R. E., 765
Dürrenmatt, Friedrich, 752
Dutch Film Industry, 752
Duvivier, Julien, 298n., 311, 530-2, 538, 541, 608, 739, 740
Dwan, Allan, 211, 213, 493
Dyke is Sealed, The, 753
Dziga-Vertov, see Vertov

E

Eagle, N. H., 32
Eagle, The, 198
Ealing Films, 733, 734
Earth, 239n., 574, 575, *637*
Easiest Way, The, 438

Easter Island, 614
East German Film Industry, 757
East Lynne, 448
East of Suez, 210
Easy Living, 498
Easy Money, 555
Easy Street, 167
Easy Virtue, 321
Edeson, Arthur, 372n.
Edge of Darkness, 487
Edge of the City, The, 728
Edge of the World, The, 553, 556, 560
Edison, Thomas, A., 67-9
Editing, 105, 107; function of, 93; constructive, 362, 366-95; elementary principles, 387-8
Edouard et Caroline, 739
Educational films, 222, 240-1
Educational Foundation for Visual Aids, 59
Eggeling, Viking, 113-14, 381
Eggert, Konstantin, 226, 227
Egypt, film-making in, 618
Ehe im Schatten, 594
Ehrenburg, Ilya, 266
Eibenschütz, Lia, 289
Eichberg, Richard, 200
$8\frac{1}{2}$, 777
Eighth Day of the Week, The, 757
Eine Kleine Stadt, 592
Eisenstein, Sergei Mikhailovich, 331, 335, 357, 363, 368, 420, 470, 482, 565; Memorial Performance, London, 40, 562n.; devices used by, 92; ideas of 'intellectual cinematography', 105, 391; theories of montage construction, 108-9; Chaplin and, 162, 169; and the Soviet regime, 225; leaning towards the drama and comedy of Japanese theatre, 229; interest in Freud, 229; career of, 229-30; his films, 230-3; his spontaneity, 232; key to his direction, 232-3; his crowds, 248, 380; use of overlapping cutting, 267, 380; in England, 315; assembling and the intellectual process, 391; hails invention of sound, 419; his style betrays stigmata of bourgeois culture, 511; in California, 561-4;

returns to Moscow, 564; denounced by leaders of Central Committee, 566, 571; his aesthetic intellectualism, 567; later years, 570-3; death, 573
Ekelchik, Y., 575
Ekk, Nikolai, 564, 565
Ekman, Gösta, 280, 291
Ekman, Hasse, 748
El, 769
El Dorado, 309
Eldridge, J., 620, 785
Eleventh Year, The, 222, 245-6, 392
Elizabeth Bergner's Poetic Film Company, 276, 277
Elliott, Eric, 110, 114, 330, 358n., 399, 402
Elsom, Isobel, 311
Elstree, 138, 278, 315, 319, 549
Elstree Calling, 316
Elton, Sir Arthur, 595n., 606
Elvey, Maurice, 275, 314
Emak Bakia, 116
Emelka Films, 284
Emil and the Detectives, 594, 637
Emmer, Luciano, 744
Emperor Waltz, The, 504
Empire Marketing Board Film Unit, 15, 43, 229, 314n., 397
Enders, F. A., 227n.
En de Zee was niet meer, 752
End of St. Petersburg, The, 105, 107, 121, 221, 234-5, 337, 388, 392, 397, *637*
End of the World, The, 311
Enfants du Paradis, Les, 540, *638*
En Film instruktons Arbejde, 305n.
Engels, Erich, 758
Engels, Morris, 731
En Natt, 602
En Rade, 255, 294, 299, 301, 309-10, 384, *638*
Enthusiasm, 566
Entr'acte, 304, *688*
Epic Film, the, 120-1; Soviet, 222
Epstein, Jean, 102, 109, 208, 294-5, 297, 299, 301-3, 318, 363, 543, 771
Epstein, Marie, 542
Erdgeist, 270
Ermler, Frederic, 105, 225-6, 248-9, 353n., 566, 569
Ernst, Morris, 86n.

Eroica, 756
Erskine, John, 547
Es geschah am hellichten Tag, 752
Eskimo, 491
Espoir, 543
Esterhazy, Agnes, 265, 278, 288
Et Dieu créa la Femme, 741
Eternal Mask, The, 615
Eternel Retour, L', 540
Etoile de Mer, L', 116, 295
European Common Market, 745
Evasive Documentary, 521n.
Eva Wants to sleep, 756
Evening Clothes, 270
Eve of St. Mark, The, 465
Evergreen, 548
Every Day Except Christmas, 735
Executioners, The, 227
Exhibitors, influence over production, 20-1; reluctant to encourage thinking audiences, 21-2; hostility to film societies, 23; maximum returns sole motive of, 24; proposals to end control of, 25; longer programmes, policy, 27; and British films quota, 32, 82
Exiles, The, 323
Existentialism, 540
Experimental Cinema, 563n.
Expiation, The, 122, 228
Exposition des Arts Décoratifs, 294, 333
Expressionism, films and, 98, 101, 285, 287
Extase, 607, 608, 638
Exter, Alexandra, 228

F

Fabian, 594
Fabian, J., 742
Fabri, Zoltan, 759
Face on the Bar Room Floor, The, 167
Factual Film, The, 44n., 86n., 122n., 123n., 422n., 544n.
Fade-in, the, 354
Fade-out, the, 354
Fairbanks, Douglas, 103, 112, 115, 118, 124, 129, 141, 170-6, 215, 370, 399, 443, 726
Fait Divers, 295
Faithless, 438, 439

Falconetti, Maria, 307
Falkenstein, Julius, 258, 281
Fallen Idol, The, 51, 559n., 733
Fall of Berlin, 754
Fall of the House of Usher, The, 138, 638
Fall of Troy, The, 72
Fame is the Spur, 56
Famous-Players, 91
Famous-Players-Lasky Film Corporation, 91, 154, 165, 202, 208, 384
Fanck, Dr. Arnold, 272, 287, 587
Fanfare, 752
Fanny by Gaslight, 56
Fantasia, 519
Fantasy Film, the, 92, 117-18
Fantôme du Moulin Rouge, Le, 304
Farewell, My Lovely, 116n., 495, 503
Farewell to Arms, A, 490
Farmer's Wife, The, 321
Farnum, Dustin and William, 201
Farrébique, 678, 740
Fashions for Women, 212
Fatal Mallet, The, 167
Faust, 72, 78, 118, 135, 142, 181, 183, 258, 280, 288, 292, 339, 709
Faustman, Hampe, 748 .
Fawcett L'Estrange, 111n., 184
Fear Strikes Out, 728
Feeling of Rejection, The, 618
Feeling of Hostility, The, 618
Feher, Imre, 759
Fejos, Paul, 603, 615
Feldzug im Polen, 583, 592
Felix the Cat, 119
Fellini, Federico, 49, 745, 776
Fellow-Americans, 495
Femme de Nulle Part, La, 311
Femme du Boulanger, La, 532, 538
Ferber, Edna, 447
Ferghana Canal, 572
Ferguson, Otis, 420n., 564, 776
Ferno, John, 460, 611, 614, 615, 752
Ferroviere, Il, 746
Festival of Youth, 579, 591n.
Fête Espagnole, La, 311
Feu Mathias Pascal, Le, 309, *649*
Fever, 759
Fex group, 223

Feyder, Jacques, 102, 103, 187-8, 295, 297, 301-2, 307-9, 365, 368, 530, 536-7, 543, 546, 548, 739
Fields, Gracie, 549n.
Fièvre, 311
Fifty Years of German Film, 581n.
Fight for Life, The, 459, *678*
Fight for the Harvest, The, 251
Fighting Lady, The, 48, 463, *679*
Film, the: an art based on observation, 52-3; Rossellini and, 54-5; early experiments, 67-70; commercial development of, 67-87; early 'story-pictures', 70-1; longer story-films, 72; first Westerns, 72; early development in Europe, 72; feature films, 72; spectacle films, 72; development of as a means of expression, 87-112; an independent art form, 88, 109, 333; the 'absolute' film, 88, 113-14; slow aesthetic progress, 88, 90; realistic properties, 88-9; adaptation of subjects and persons for, 91; story-film, 91; modified stage technique, 91; 'acting' and, 91, 339; star-system, 92; slapstick comedy, 92-3; film fantasy, 92n., 117-18; melodramatic thrillers, 93; inherent assets of, 92-3; the first genuine imaginative film, 93; the break with realism, 96; established as an independent medium by *The Last Laugh*, 99; psychoanalysis in, 100; expressionism in, 101; individualism in, 101; naturalism in, 103; Soviet contribution a momentous advance, 103; tendency to find expression by climatic effect, 106; association of ideas in, 107; use of contrasts, 107-8; montage theories, 108; use of natural resources, 109; effect of advent of dialogue, 109-10; ballad film, 115-16; cine-surrealism, 116-17; cartoon film, 118-20; epic film, 120-1; difficulties of analysis, 329-31; scarcity of copies of important films, 329; misuse of technical resources, 331-2; nature and chief characteristics, 332-6, 339;

public and, **335**; dialogue in, **333-4**; definition of, **336**; two main aspects, **336**; director's creative impulse, **336-7**; themes in, **338-41**; stories written for, **340**; principles of movement in, **341**; the three acts of montage, **343-4**; construction of, **344-5**; expression of dramatic content of, **360, 361-412**; art experience of, **415**; cult of, **415-17, 419**; advent of sound, **415-19**; *cinéastes'* outlook, **420-2**; a popular creation, **420-1**; trends since 1948, **721-5, 772, 773**

Film, **724, 765**

Film and its Techniques, **772**

Film Booking Offices, London, **227n.**

Film Business is Big Business, **544n., 549n., 551**

Film Censors, British Board of, **288**

Film Culture, **724**

Film Industry, dominated by financial considerations, **18-20**; different branches merged, **20**; problems of individual expression in, **49**. See also under names of countries

Film italiano, Il, **745, 746n.**

Film Polski, **610**

Film Problems of Soviet Russia, **111**

Films: An Alternative to Rank, **544n.**

Films and Filming, **724, 765**

Films Beget Films, **776**

Film Sense, The, **571n.**

Films: Facts and Forecasts, **111n., 184**

Film Societies, **23, 27-8, 725**

Film Society, London, the, **87, 106, 117, 240, 293, 416, 422, 564n.**

Filmstudie, **115**

Film Today, The, **595n.**

Film Weekly, **15n., 389**

Film World, **778**

Fin du Jour, Le, **531**

Fin du Monde, **537**

Finis Terrae, **122, 208, 257, 294, 298, 299, 300, 301, 303, 318, 679**

Finnish Film Industry, **749**

Fire Brigade, The, **399**

Fireman, The, **167**

Fire Over England, **548**

Fires Were Started, **679**

First Born, The, **319**

First Kiss, The, **144**

First-National Company, **84, 167, 545**

Fischinger, Oscar, **115n.**

Fists in the Pocket, **781**

Fitzmaurice, George, **211**

Five Boys from Barksa Street, The, **756**

Five Graves to Cairo, **503**

Five Star Final, **441**

Flaherty, Robert, **33, 49, 51-2, 57-8, 103, 141, 183n., 203-5, 208, 216, 303, 316, 363, 421, 459, 515, 520-5, 532, 534, 613-14, 713, 771**

Flame, The, **78, 177, 181, 287**

Flame of New Orleans, The, **529**

Fleming, Victor, **103, 147, 201, 211, 491**

Flesh and Fantasy, **531**

Flesh and the Devil, **140, 198**

Flieger! Funker! Kanoniere!, **591**

Flood, James, **213**

Floorwalker, The, **167**

Florey, Robert, **124, 138**

Flowers and Trees, **516**

Flying camera, first use of, **332**

Flying Scotsman, The, **315**

Flynn, Errol, **572**

Fogel, Vladimir, **241**

Folke, Gosta, **748**

Fool, The, **275**

Foolish Wives, **124, 158, 212, *639***

Footnotes to the Film, **557n.**

Forbidden Paradise, **125, 160, 169, 178-9, 181, 216, 479, 639**

Forbidden Songs, **610**

Ford, Aleksander, **616, 756, 757**

Ford, John, **34, 49, 103, 198-9, 201, 318, 456, 460, 482-6, 558-9, 729**

Foreman, Carl, **729**

Foreman Went to France, The, **36, 55, 314n., 555**

Forerunner, The, **762**

Forgotten Faces, **212, 372**

Forgotten Village, The, **608, 679**

For Heaven's Sake, **215**

Forlong, Michael, **749**

Forman, Milos, **781**

Forty-First, The, 248, 755
Forty-Second Street, 443, *639*
Forty Thousand Horsemen, 619
For Whom the Bell Tolls, 505
For Wives Only, 213
Four Chimneys, 766
Four Devils, 78, 135, 182, 280
Four Feathers, The, 187, 202, 207, 384, 548
Four Horsemen of the Apocalypse, The, 128, 195, 196, *639*
Four Hundred Million, The, 460, 612, 614, *679*
Four in a Jeep, 751
Four Steps in the Clouds, 41
Fourteen Lives in Danger, 759
Fourth Estate, The, 394n.
Fox William, 76, 165, 181-3, 211, 714
Fox Film Company, 71, 84, 85, 433
Fox Film Corporation, 181
Fox Movietone Follies, 125, 147
Fox Movietone News, 123, 214
Fra Brne, 753
Fraenkel, Heinrich, 595n.
Fragment of an Empire, The, 222, 248, 353n.
France, Anatole, 307
France, film industry in, see French Film Industry
Francen, M., 114
Franco, General Francisco, 486
Franju, Georges, 737, 742
Frank, Leon, 340
Frank, Leonhard, 291
Frankenheimer, John, 728, 781
Franklin, Sidney, 213, 493
Fräulein Else, 278
Freaks, 493
Frederick, Pauline, 131, 198
Fredlos, 603
Free Cinema, 735
Freedom of the Movies, The, 80n., 86n., 446n.
French Film Industry, during the thirties, 39, 57-8, 530; Hollywood and, 40, 60, 294; early films of, 72, 252; directors' love of classical compositions, 102, 299-300; leaning towards spectacle, 102, 300; general ignorance about characteristics of, 293; individualistic approach, 295; experimental contribution of, 296-7; gulf between directors and producers, 298; decorative tendency, 301-2; postwar years, 311-12; early sound films, 526-7; revival in, 530-1, 538; cult of the French film, 530, 539; underworld films, 528-9; during the Occupation, 540-1; since 1945, 541-3, 737, 738, 740, 742
Frend, Charles, 555
Frenzy (Torment), 602, 748
Freshman, The, 500
Fresnay, Pierre, 533
Freud, 780
Freud, Sigmund, 229, 363, 496
Freund, Karl, 50, 99, 259, 272, 278-9, 280, 287, 332, 371, 710, 714; a note on Carl Mayer by, 716-17
Fric, Martin, 609
Friday the Thirteenth, 548
Fridericus Rex, 123, 288, 576n.
Friend, Charles, 733
Friese-Greene, H., 329
Friesennot, 589
Fritsch, Willy, 260, 272, 282
Fröhlich, Carl, 288
Fröhlich, Gustav, 281, 332
Frohman, Daniel, 72
From Caligari to Hitler, 17, 100n., 253n., 474n., 539n., 581, 585, 590n., 715n.
From Here to Eternity, 730
From Saturday to Sunday, 608
Frontier, 574, 575
Front Page, The, 441, 487, *640*
Fugitive, The, 485, 486
Fugitive Lover, The, 288
Furie, Sidney, 761
Furth, Jaro, 265
Für Uns, 591
Fütterer, Werner, 289
Future's in the Air, The, 620
Fury, 456, 480-1, *640*

G

Gabin, Jean, 533-4, 538
Gable, Clark, 435, 444
Gabriel Over the White House, 492
Gaiderov, Vladimir, 283
Gainsborough Films, 82, 321

INDEX

Galeen, Henrik, 285-6, 317, 531, 710
Gallup Audience Research Survey, 21
Gajer, Vaclav, 758
Gance, Abel, 121, 231, 297, 302, 310-11, 385, 537-8
Gangster films, 194, 433-7, 442
Garbo, Greta, 78, 135, 187-8, 198, 213, 265, 269, 439, 477, 479, 514
Garden of Allah, The, 195, 197
Gardin, V. R., 226, 227, 248
Gardner, Shayle, 197
Garrison, Robert, 265
Garson, Greer, 465
Gaslight, 493, 551, 709
Gate of Hell, 767
Gaucho, The, 171, 173, 175
Gauguin, Paul, 295
Gaumont-British, 76, 82, 85, 311, 315, 520, 549n., 552
Gaumont-British Picture Corporation, 548
Gautier, Théophile, 310
Gauzes, use of, 369
Gay Canary, The, 228
Gay Desperado, The, 477
Gaynor, Janet, 182, 432
Gebühr, Otto, 288, 289
Gee, Hugh, 333
Geesink, Joop, 753
Gendelstein, A., 569
General, The, 144, 214, *640*
General Crack, 125, 300
General Died at Dawn, The, 487, 505
General Electric Company, 84
General Line, The (*The Old and the New*), 109, 205, 222, 230, 233, 237, 340, 384, 390, 398, 567, 573, *680*
General Suvorov, 574
Generation, A, 756
Genevieve, 734
Gentleman of Paris, A, 213
Gentleman's Agreement, 22, 504
Gentlemen Prefer Blondes, 213
Gentle Sex, The, 55
Genuine, 98n., 292, *640*, 709, 712
Geographic films, 121-2, 250-1
George, Maude, 161
Gerald, Jim, 294
Gerald McBoing-Boing, 731
Gerasimov, Sergei, 576, 579n., 754
Gerlach, Arthur von, 710

German Film Industry, 709-11; studio creations, 37, 254-6, 258; in thirties, 40; Nazi control of, 40, 581, 585-94; after World War I, 77, 134; directors and players attracted to Hollywood, 77, 253; American influences, 78, 101-2, 261; decline after 1925, 100, 253, 260; decorative films, 100, 124, 258-9; Soviet influences, 102; in middle twenties, 252-3; financial difficulties, 253-4; help from Government for, 253; quota system, 253-4, 260; early period, 254-5, 287, 329; significance of Caligari, 256-7; psychology in its films, 257, 259; significant part played by architecture, 258-9; naturalism, 288-9; more pretentious productions, 290-1; photographic devices of, 371; 'accommodators' to Goebbels' scheme, 582-4; 'documentary', 590-1; post-war, 594-5
Germany Year Zero, 373, 601
Germi, Pietro, 746
Gershwin, George, 478
Gert, Valeska, 265
Gertrud, 781
Gervaise, 739
Gestapo, 559
Ghana Film Unit, 762
Ghost Goes West, The, 528, 548
Ghost That Never Returns, The, 241, *641*
Gianni, Luigi, 747
Gibbons, Cedric, 294, 333
Gibson, Hoot, 202
Gide, André, 311
Gigi, 729
Gilbert, John, 160, 198, 487
Gilbert, Lewis, 734
Gilliat, Sydney, 55, 56, 553, 554n., 651
Girl from Maxim's, The, 546
Girl in Black, The, 753
Girl with the Band-box, The, 222, 248
Gish, Dorothy, 131
Gish, Lillian, 131, 150, 152-4, 186, 417
Glace à Trois Faces, La, 302
Glasmon, Kubec, 434, 435

Glass, 752
Glass, Max, 291
Glass Houses, 213
Glass of Water, A, 280, 281
Glenville, Peter, 734
Gliese, Rochus, 182, 714
Gli sbandati, 746
Glorious Adventure, The, 399
Glory, Marie, 309
Glyn, Elinor, 91, 431
Godard, Jean-Luc, 778
Goddess, The, 728
Godless Girl, The, 144, 210
Goebbels, Joseph, 40, 585, 586, 587, 588, 590, 592, 593
Goering, Hermann, 591
Goetler, Victor, 759
Goetzke, Bernard, 258, 273, 291
Gogol, Nikolai, 104, 237, 238
Going My Way, 467
Gold Diggers, 213, 443
Golden Bed, The, 210
Golden Crown, The, 291
Golden, Nathan D., 30, 31, 32
Gold Rush, The, 164, 166, 168, 213, 216, *641*
Goldwyn, Samuel, 73n., 200, 456, 465, 483, 488, 494, 508
Golem, The, 125, 258, 285, 329n., 379, 531, 608, *641*, 709
Gone With the Wind, 491, *641*
Good and Naughty, 213
Good-bye, Mr. Chips, 551
Good Mothers, 606
Goodwill, fantasy of, 450-3
Goose Hangs High, The, 203
Goose Woman, The, 197
Gorki, Maxim, 104, 234, 568, 575
Gosho, Heinosuke, 765, 766, 771
Goskinprom, 226, 227
Goulding, Edmund, 162, 185, 491
Goupi-Mains-Rouges, 540
Government Girl, 505
Goya, Francisco José de, 339
Graham, Sean, 762
Grahame, Margot, 483
Granach, Alexander, 258, 282, 290
Grande Illusion, La, 532-3, 537, *642*
Grand Méliès, La, 742
Grands Manoeuvres, Les, 740
Gland Slam, 493
Gran' Rue, 751

Grant, Cary, 454
Grapes of Wrath, The, 122n., 140n., 381n., 484-5, 487, *642*
Grass, 103, 121, 204, 206-7, 216, *680*
Grasshopper, The, 754
Grau, Albin, 258, 282, 710
Graustark, 187
Graves, Robert, 475
Gray, Gilda, 318
Gray, John, 762
Great Adventure, The, 748
Great Bank Robbery, The, 70
Great Dictator, The, 510, 512
Great Expectations, 36, 51, 381n., 448, 553, 560, *642*, 709
Great Gabbo, The, 162, 203
Great McGinty, The, 498
Great Man Votes, The, 494
Great Moment, The, 499
Great Promise, The, 617
Great Train Robbery, The, 70, 91
Great Waltz, The, 531
Greco, El, 330, 339
Greed, 153-4, 156, 158-60, 168, 216, 264, 364, 365, 421, 426, 501, 512, 564, *643*
Greene, Graham, 486, 559
Green For Danger, 561
Greenwood, Walter, 551
Greek Film Industry, 753
Grein, Hans Baldung, 339
Grémillon, Jean, 40, 295, 297, 298n., 530, 543, 739, 740, 782
Greville, Edmond, 121, 611
Gribiche, 307
Grierson, John, 15, 47n., 109, 122, 229, 314n., 315, 318, 397, 422-3, 459, 520, 522, 555, 563, 565-6, 567-9, 580, 594, 618, 778
Grierson on Documentary, 122n., 555n., 563n., 566n., 594n., 778
Griffith, Corinne, 545
Griffith, David Wark, 29, 34, 36, 40, 48, 72, 73n., 94, 129, 148-55, 158, 176, 186-7, 189, 196-7, 200, 215, 231, 351, 358, 367, 398, 447, 476, 482, 511, 515, 599
Griffith, E. H., 212, 493
Griffith, Richard, 16-18, 29, 34, 36, 48, 726, 729, 772
Grimm, Jacob and Wilhelm, 118
Grospierre, Louis, 742

INDEX

Grounds for Divorce, 213
Grune, Karl, 101, 257-8, 260, 284, 289, 365, 710
Grzimek, Dr. Bernhard, 750
Guadalcanal Diary, 466
Guernica, 742
Guilbert, Yvette, 280
Guinness, Sir Alec, 734
Guitry, Sacha, 540n.
Guld og Grönne Skove, 749
Gülstorff, Max, 281, 282
Gypsy Blood, see *Carmen*

H

Haanstra, Bert, 735, 752
Haas, Max de, 753
Hackenschmied, Alexander, 608
Hackett, Albert, 506
Hackett, Frances, 506
Haid, Liane, 260, 284
Hail, James, 184
Hail the Conquering Hero, 499
Halas Batchelor unit, 736
Hale's Tours, 71
Half Naked Truth, The, 492
Hallelujah!, 147, 189, 192, 216, 419, 470-1, *643*
Halm, Harry, 260
Hameister, Willi, 95
Hamer, Robert, 733
Hamilton, James Shelley, 528
Hamlet, 37, 51, 124n., *643*, 780
Hammett, Dashiell, 500
Hands of Orlac, The, 285
Hangmen Also Die, 465, 481, 534
Hanjekovitz, Fedor, 753
Hanson, Einar, 265
Hanson, Lars, 135, 186, 198, 317
Hans Westmar, 585
Hardy, H. Forsyth, 122n., 555n., 563, 566n., 594n., 748, 748n.
Hardy, Oliver, 517
Harlan, Kenneth, 399
Harlow, Jean, 444, 491
Harshiladze, —, 754
Hart, William S., 129, 201
Hartmann, Paul, 259
Harvest, 538
Harvest Shall Come, The, *680*
Harvey, Lillian, 260
Hasselbuch, Hagen, 606
Hatfield, Hurd, 535

Hathaway, Henry, 492
Hatton, Raymond, 75
Hauptmann, Gerhart, 709
Hauptmann von Köln, Der, 758
Hauptmann von Köpenick, 750
Haver, Phyllis, 154
Havoc, 211
Havelock-Allan, Anthony, 734
Hawes, Stanley, 619, 620
Hawks, Howard, 492
Hawthorne, Nathaniel, 185
Hays, Will, 80, 429
Hays Organisation, the, 132, 435, 446, 449
Heading South, 173
Headlines, 212
Hearst, W. Randolph, 495
Heart of Asia, The, 251
Hearts and Spurs, 205
Hearts Are Trumps, 197
Heart's Desire, 305
Heaven Can Wait, 479
Heavenly Play, The, 602
He Comes Up Smiling, 129, 174
Heerman, Victor, 135, 213
Heifitz, Josef, 576, 579n., 780
Heir to Jenghiz Khan, The, 230n.
Heisler, Stuart, 502
Hellman, Lillian, 465, 506
Hello Sister, 490, 494
Hell's Highroad, 211
Hell's Highway, 494
Helm, Brigitte, 268-9, 284, 291, 309, 332
Hemingway, Ernest, 459, 490, 612
Henaberry, Joseph, 212
Henning-Jensen, Astrid, 606
Henning-Jensen, Bjärne, 605, 606, 749
Henry V, 125n., 553, 560, *643*
Hepburn, Katharine, 448
Hepworth Film Company, 72
Hériat, Phillipe, 294
Herlth, Robert, 97n., 258, 279-80, 283, 291, 710, 712, 716
Heroes for Sale, 441
Her Private Life, 546
Herr Puntila und sein Knecht Matli, 751
Hersholt, Jean, 154, 180, 200
Hessling, Catherine, 294, 310
Het shot is te Boord, 752

INDEX

He Who Gets Slapped, 185, 186
Heydrich, R., 481
Heyer, John, 762
Hey-Rup!, 608
High Noon, 729
High Sierra, 455, 492, 500
High Treason, 275, 314-15, 384
High, Wide and Handsome, 478
Hill, George, 434
Hill, James, 735
Hill 24 Does Not Answer, 734
Hindu Tomb, The, 291
Hintertreppe, 288, 710
Hiroshima, Mon Amour, 781
His Hour, 192
Histoire des Treize, L', 278
Historical romance, films of, 124
History, as film subject, 447-9
History of Charles XII, The, 323
History of Motion Pictures, The, 29, 99n., 312n.
Hitchcock, Alfred, 83, 320-1, 493, 548, 556-8, 561, 781
Hitler, A., 510, 511
Hitlerjunge Quex, 568
Hobson, Laura Z., 505
Hochbaum, Werner, 615
Hoellering, Georg, 615, 758
Hoffman, Karl, 272, 283, 291, 369, 371, 710
Hoffmann, E. T. W., 238
Höflich, Lucie, 281
Hofman, Hermina Tyrlova, 758
Holbein, Hans, 340
Hold Your Man, 444
Holiday Camp, 54, 555
Hollaman, Richard, 70
Holland, film industry in, 611-15
Hollywood, 'B' pictures of, 27; reliance on audience surveys, 35, 137n.; star-system, 74, 92, 126-34, 334; drift of directors and players to, 77-8, 81-2, 100, 133-5, 177, 187, 710, 714; effect on European directors and players, 78-80, 141-3; percentage of British screen-space occupied by footage of, 126n.; Eisenstein in 561-4; post-war trends, 726, 729. See also American Film Industry
Hollywood, 203

Hollywood on Trial, 22n., 455n, 466n.
Hollywood Quarterly, 508n.
Hollywood Revue, The, 125, 144, 147, 214
Hollywood Saga, 430
Holmes, Cecil, 762
Holmes, J. B., 55, 617
Holstenwal, 95
Homecoming, 101, 183, 255, 261, 291, 340
Home of the Brave, 726
Homme du large, L', 309
Honegger, Arthur, 408n., 742
Honzl, Jindrich, 608
Horn, Camilla, 135, 280
Horse Feathers, 644
Horse's Mouth, The, 734
Horst, Herman van der, 752
Hortobagy, 615, 758
Hose, Die, 292
Hotel at Osaka, A, 766
Hotel des Invalides, 742
Hotel Imperial, 131, 183, 184, 185, 256n., 644
Hotel Paradis, 603
Hot for Paris, 87
Houen Zo, 752
House, 757
Household, Geoffrey, 481
House in the Desert, The, 617
House in the Dragonerstrasse, The, 288
House in Trubnaya Square, The, 116, 248, 370
House on 92nd Street, The, 492
House Where I Live, The, 755
Houston, Penelope, 778
Howard, Leslie, 548
Howard, William K., 206, 208, 456, 548
How Green Was My Valley, 485
Hoyt, Harry, 212
Huang Sha, 768
Hubley, John, 731
Hue and Cry, 555
Huff, Theodore, 181
Hugenberg, A., 714
Hughes, Howard, 33, 500
Hughes, Lloyd, 212
Hugo, Victor, 311
Human Sparrows, 176

INDEX

Human Voice, The, 601n.
Hunchback of Notre Dame, The, 493
Hungarian Rhapsody, The, 101, 183, 290
Hungary, film industry in, 324, 615, 758
Hunt, J. Roy, 201, 369n.
Hunte, Otto, 258, 272
Hurrah! I'm Alive, 125, 262, 291
Hurricane, 483
Huston, John, 57, 368n., 372n., 426, 461, 463, 492, 500-2, 727, 730, 780, 781
Huston, Walter, 500
Hymer, Warren, 436

I

I Am a Fugitive from a Chain Gang, 441, 492, *644*
I, Claudius, 475, 548
Ichikawa, Kon, 767
Ideal Husband, An, 37, 560
Idiot, The, 766
Idle Class, The, 167
Ignoti alla Città, 747
I Lost it at the Movies, 775, 776
Image, L', 307
Imai, Tadashi, 767
I Married a Witch, 529
I Met Him in Paris, 492
Immigrant, The, 166
Immortal Land, The, 736
I'm No Angel, 444, 492
Imperial Airways, 620
Ince, Ralph, 212
Ince, Thomas H., 129, 212
Independent Frame method, 58
Independent Producers Ltd., 554
India, film-making in, 325, 617, 763
Indian People's Theatre Association, 617
Indonesia Calling!, 612
Industrial Britain, 520
Information Films of India, 617
Informer, The, 283, 284, 317, 483, 484, 485, 505, 559, *645*
In Former Days, 595
Inglis, Ruth, 80n., 446n.
Ingram, Rex, 189, 195-7, 272
Inhumaine, L', 309, 409, *645*
In Jenen Tagen, 595
Innemann, S., 608

Innocents, The, 781
Innocent Sinners, 734
Innocents of Paris, The, 147
In Old Arizona, 201
In Old Chicago, 491
Institut des Hautes Etudes Cinématographiques, 738
'Intellectual Cinematography', 105
Inter-cutting, 107
Interference, 136
International Federation of Film Archives, 330n., 771
International Federation of Film Producers, 724
International Federation of Film Societies, 771
International Film Annual, 741n., 767n.
In This Our Life, 500
Intolerance, 36, 73, 94n., 128, 150-2, 158, 495, 564, *645*
Intransigeant, L', 304
Intruder in the Dust, 726
In Which We Serve, 53, 122n., 560
Irgendwo in Berlin, 750
Iris-in, beginning sequences with, 95, 368, 380
Iris-out, ending sequences with, 95
Iron Horse, The, 198-9, 202, 318, 482, *646*
Islington, studios at, 315
Is My Face Red?, 441
Isn't Life Wonderful?, 149, 154
Italian Straw Hat, The, see *Chapeau de Paille d'Italie, Le*
Italy, film industry in, 41-2, 72, 323-4, 595-601, 727, 743-7
It Happened Here, 782
It Happened in Daylight, 752
It Happened One Night, 453, *646*
It Happened To-morrow, 529
It's a Wonderful Life, 32, 452, 468
It's Tough to be Famous, 442
Ivan, 566, 567
Ivanovski, —, 227
Ivan the Terrible, 242, 572-3, 574
Ivens, Joris, 49, 51, 114, 459, 611-14, 742, 752

J

Jabely, Jean, 742
J'Accuse, 311, 537

INDEX

Jackals, 291
Jackson, Charles, 504
Jackson, Pat, 734
Jack the Ripper, 79n.
Jacobs, Lewis, 18, 29, 92n., 128n., 212n., 453, 457, 469n., 479, 488, 494
Jaguar, 763
Jahrgang, 21, 758
Jakubowska, Wanda, 756
James, Forest, 208
James, Henry, 781
Jan Huss, 758
Jannings, Emil, 75, 99, 177, 179, 185, 187, 194, 211, 258-9, 276, 279-80, 282, 374, 381, 474, 531, 547, 587, 710, 714, 716-17; in Hollywood, 78, 135, 180; Americanisation of, 141-2; a great actor in theatrical manner, 180-1; early historical films, 180
Janowitz, Hans, 95n., 96, 711, 712
Janssen, Walther, 273
Japan, film industry in, 324-5, 765-7, low cost of, 767
Japanese Dagger, The, 291
Jaubert, Maurice, 614
Jazz, 203
Jazz Comedy, 575
Jazz Dance, 731
Jazz Fool, The, 120
Jazz on a Summer's Day, 781
Jazz Singer, The, 147, 429
Jealousy, 284
Jehanne, Edith, 269
Jenkins, Allen, 436
Jennings, Hilda, 289
Jennings, Humphrey, 620, 771
Jephcott, Pearl, 21n.
Jesse James, 491
Jessner, Leopold, 288, 710
Jeux Interdits, Les, 739, 773
Jew Süss, 448, 548, 549
Jezebel, 456, 488
Jocelyn, 311
Joffa studios, 594
Johnny in the Clouds, 559
Johnson, Mary, 291
Johnston, Eric, 35, 80n.
Jolson, Al, 147, 429
Jones, Buck, 205
Jones, Robert Edmond, 477

Joueur d'Echecs, Le, 300
Jour de Fête, 739
Journal d'un Curé de Campagne, 740
Journey into Fear, 497
Journey's End, 192
Journey Together, 56, 556, *680*
Jour se lève, Le, 476n., 534, 538-9, *646*
Joyce, James, 113
Joyless Street, The, 78, 86, 159, 260, 263, 264, 265, 266, 268, 292, 365, 583, *647*, 710
Juarez, 457, 500, 580
Judgement, 212
Jugo, Jenny, 260
Jules et Jim, 778
Julian, Rupert, 157, 211
Julius Caesar, 495
Jung-Alsen, Kurt, 758
Junge, Alfred, 317n., 321
Jungle Rhythm, 120

K

Kadr (Unit), 756
Kael, Pauline, 775, 776
Kafka, Franz, 780
Kahn, Gordon, 22n., 455n., 466n.
Kalatazov, Mikhail, 755
Kamata studios, 325
Kameradschaft, 36, 40, 558, 578n., 582-3, 602, *647*, 710
Kanal, 756
Kangaroo, 729
Kanin, Garson, 426, 462, 494-5, 502, 559, 730
Karl and Anna, 291, 340
Karloff, Boris, 508
Kast, Pierre, 742
Kästner, Erich, 594
Kauffmann, M., 122, 226, 245-6
Käutner, Helmut, 595, 753
Kavaléridze, —, 226
Kawalerowicz, Jerzy, 756, 780
Kazan, Elia, 504-5, 727, 730
Kean, 311, *647*
Keaton, Buster, 125, 135, 210, 214, 494, 499, 517, 782
Keene, Ralph, 620
Kein Platz für wilde Tiere, 750
Kelland, C. B., 450, 451
Kellerman, Annette, 209
Kelly, Gene, 729

Kennedy, Merna, 166
Kerensky, A., 230
Kermesse Héroïque, La, 536, *648*
Kerry, Norman, 158
Kessel, Adam, 166
Kettlehut, Erich, 258, 272
Key, The, 732, 733
Kid, The, 166, 167
Kidnappers, The, 734
Kid's Auto Races, The, 166
Kiessler, Hedy, 607
Killers, The, 502
Killing, The, 727
Kinder, Mutter und ein General, 750
Kind Hearts and Coronets, 733
Kind of Loving, A, 779
Kinematograph Renters Society, 23
Kinematograph Weekly, 23, 137n.
Kinetoscope, Edison's, 68-9
King, Henry, 103, 141, 199-200, 357, 491, 730
King in New York, A, 731
King of Kings, The, 121, 144, 210, 340, 779
King Who Was a King, The, 111
Kino-Sever, 227
Kinoshito, Keisuke, 767
Kinugasa, T., 767
Kipling, Rudyard, 522
Kipps, 559
Kirsanov, Dimitri, 116, 297
Kiss, The, 124, 140, 187-8
Kiss for Cinderella, A, 209
Kiss Me Again, 135, 178
Kiss of Death, 492
Klangfilm-Tobis-Siemen Company, 262
Kleine, George, 72
Kleineman, Isaac, 731
Klein-Rogge, Rudolf, 274, 710
Kleinstadtsunder, 289, 290
Kline, Herbert, 460, 608, 617
Klingender, F. D., 544n.
Klock, Karl, 289
Klöpfer, Eugen, 287, 288
Klos, Eugen, 609
Knickerbocker-Buckaroo, 173
Knife in the Water, 780
Knight, Arthur, 486
Knight, Castleton, 315
Knight, Eric, 16, 60, 424, 461
Knight in London, A, 287

Knight Without Armour, 548
Kobe, —, 527
Koenig, Walter, 761
Koenigsmark, 300
Kokoda Trail, 619
Kolin, Nikolai, 262, 291
Kolonne Stosstrupp, 594
Komsomol, 611
Konwicki, Tadeusz, 757
Koohaas, A., 753
Kopaline, I., 245
Kopf Hoch Charley, 291
Korda, Sir Alexander, 37, 51, 76n., 187, 475, 522, 523, 528, 531, 545-9, 552, 559-61, 771
Korda, Vincent, 560
Korda, Zoltan, 55, 734
Kortner, Fritz, 282, 288, 587, 710
Kozintzev, Grigori, 220, 225-7, 229, 237, 391, 567, 575, 754, 780
Kracauer, Dr. Siegfried, 17, 18, 100n., 253n., 469, 474, 476, 508, 539, 580-2, 585-6, 590, 592n., 593, 715, 772, 776
Kraly, Hans, 178
Kramer, Stanley, 726
Krampf, Günther, 285, 290, 371, 710
Krasna, Norman, 433, 456, 480
Kratky Film, 609
Krauss, Werner, 87, 258, 265-6, 279, 283-4, 286, 288, 310, 584, 587
Krish, John, 736
Kron, Walter, 133
Kubin, Alfred, 712
Kubrick, Stanley, 727, 730, 779, 781
Kuhle Wampe, 582, 594, *648*
Ku Klux Klan, the, 455
Kuleshov, Lev, 105, 226, 227, 228, 229, 234, 389, 411, 412
Kurosawa, Akira, 766, 767, 777
Kutuzov, 576
Kyser, Hans, 288

L

Laburnum Grove, 558
Lacombe, Georges, 297
Ladri di Biciclette, see *Bicycle Thieves*
Lady Eve, The, 498
Lady for a Day, 451
Lady Hamilton, 288
Lady in the Dark, 418n.
Lady in the Lake, 375n.

Lady in the Harem, The, 210
Lady Killer, 16
Lady of the Pavements, The, 154
Lady Vanishes, The, 557
Lady Windermere's Fan, 178
Lady With the Little Dog, The, 780
Laemmle, Carl, 71, 143
Laila, 603
Laine, Edvin, 749
Lamarr, Hedy, 475, 607
Lamb, The, 173, 174
Lambeth Walk, The, 688
Lamorisse, Albert, 737, 742
Lamprecht, Gerhard, 291, 594, 750
Lanchester, Elsa, 322
Land, The, 459, 523, 613, *681*
Land of Toys, 578
Landscapes, in pictorial composition, 375
Lane, Rose Wilder, 450
Lang, Fritz, 51, 101, 115, 124, 258, 261, 272-6, 292, 324, 382, 456, 464, 476, 480-2, 534, 587, 709
Langdon, Harry, 452n.
Langpain, Jean-Jacques, 742
La Rocque, Rod, see Rocque, Rod la
Laskowski, Jan, 757
Last Attraction, The, 243
Last Bridge, The, 753
Last Cab, The, 287
Last Chance, The, 602, 615, *648,* 751
Last Command, The, 140, 142, 194, *648*
Last Day of Summer, The, 757, 773
Last Laugh, The, 36, 78, 95n., 99-100, 135, 138, 142, 180-1, 183, 190, 252, 254, 255, 256, 257, 258, 259, 260, 278-9, 292, 356, 396, 477, *649,* 710, 714, 716
'Last-minute rescue', the, 148-50
Last of Mrs. Cheyney, The, 136, 147
Last Shot, The, 614
Last Stage, The, 756
Last Year at Marienbad, 781
Late Matthew Pascal, The, 309, *649*
Latham, Woodville, 69
Latin American Film Industry, 769
Lattuada, Alberto, 744, 745
Laughton, Charles, 546
Launder, Frank, 55, 56, 137n., 553, 554n., 561
Laurel, Stan, 517

Lautrec, see Toulouse-Lautrec
Lawless, The, 726
Lawrence, D. H., 472
Leacock, Philip, 734
Leacock, Richard, 781
Lean, David, 51, 368n., 554, 556n., 560, 733
Leander, Zarah, 587
Leaves from Satan's Book, 603
Lederer, Franz, 291
Lee, Rowland V., 211, 493
Leenhardt, Roger, 739
Lef, 244
Léger, Fernand, 115
Legg, Stuart, 544n., 618, 735
Legion of Decency, campaign of, 445-6
Legion of the Condemned, The, 144
Legoshin, Vladimir, 577
Leigh, Vivien, 531
Lejeune, C. A., 549n.
Lekko, 752
Leloir, Maurice, 171, 175
Lenartowicz, Stanislaw, 757
Lengyel, Melchior, 479
Leni, Paul, 78, 79, 124, 135, 283, 285-6, 573, 710, 714
Lenica, Jan, 757
Lenin, Nikolai, 103, 219, 230, 600
Lenin in 1918, 576
Lenin in October, 568, 576
Leontiev, —, 251
Leopard, The, 777
Lermontov, 569
Lerner, Irving, 731
Le Roy, Mervyn, 492
Lesser, Sol, 563
Lessing, Gotthold E., 709
Letter with the Feathers, The, 767
Let There Be Light, 48, 463n., 501
Letzte Akt, Der, 751
Letzte Mann, Der, 750
Levi, Carlo, 600
Levine, Meyer, 617
Lewton, Val, 507, 508, 771
Leyda, Jay, 571n., 573, 765, 767, 776
Leytes, Josef, 617
L'Herbier, Marcel, 309, 409, 541
Liang Shan-Po and Chu Ying-Tai, 768
Libraries, film, 330n.

Libre Amérique, La, 593
Liedtke, Harry, 260
Lieven, Albert, 602
Life and Loves of Beethoven, The, 537
Life of Adolf Hitler, The, 776
Lifeboat, 557
Life Goes to the Movies, 420n.
Life is Beautiful, 106, 234, 564
Life of an American Fireman, The, 149
Life of Buffalo Bill, The, 72
Life of Emile Zola, The, 457, 493, 580
Life of O-Haru, 766
Life's Roads, 222
Light, unity of, 383-4
Light and Shade, 115, 379
Light in the Dark, The, 198
Light of the Western Stars, 208
Light Rhythms, 115, 342
Lights Out in Europe, 460, 608
Limelight, 730
Linden, —, van der, 753
Linder, Max, 311
Lindsay, Vachel, 416
Lindtberg, Leopold, 751
Lissy, 758
Listen to Britain, 681
Little Annie Rooney, 176
Little Caesar, 434, *649*
Little Foxes, The, 488, 506
Little French Girl, The, 209
Little Friend, 548
Little Fugitive, 731
Little Glass of Beer, A, 759
Little Hunchbacked Horse, The, 578
Little Island, The, 736
Little Man What Now?, 490
Little Minister, The, 448
Little Women, 448
Litvak, Anatole, 460, 461, 727
Lives of a Bengal Lancer, The, 449, 492
Living, 766
Living Cinema, The, 764n.
Living Corpse, The, 235, 247, 355, 364, 377n., 395
Llewellyn, Richard, 485, 505
Lloyd, Frank, 212, 491-2
Lloyd, Harold, 125, 135, 211, 214-15, 303, 500

Lloyds of London, 491
Local Government Act, 23, 25, 59
Locomotive, 610
Lodger, The, 321, 548
Lods, Jean, 543
Loew, Marius, 71
Loew's International, 616
Lombard, Carole, 454
London Belongs to Me, 54, 56
London Film Company, 72
London Film Productions, 546, 552
London Film Society, the, 87, 106, 117, 240, 293, 416, 422, 564n.
London Polytechnic Institute, 71
London Town, 553
London Worker's Film Society, 250
Lonely Villa, The, 150
Lone White Sail, 577, *650*
Longstreet, Stephen, 502
Long Voyage Home, The, 485, 505
Lonsdale, Frederick, 136, 216, 421
Looking Forward, 443
Looping the Loop, 283
Lord Jim, 211
Lord of the Flies, 781
Lorentz, Pare, 86n., 458-9, 523, 612, 762
Lorre, Peter, 475, 750
Losey, Joseph, 726, 779
Lost Boundaries, 726
Lost Feelings, 757
Lost Horizon, 452
Lost Illusion, The, 559
Lost Patrol, The, 482, 483
Lost Week-End, The, 503, 504
Lost World, The, 212
Louis Blattner Film Corporation, 287
Louisiana Story, 524, 613, *681*
Lourie, Norman, 617
Love, Bessie, 212
Love Affair of the Dictator, The, 547n., 551
Love is a Racket, 442
Love Lies, 211
Love Me and the World is Mine, 78, 183
Love Me Tonight, 477
Love Never Fails, 767
Love on the Dole, 551
Love Parade, The, 102n., 478, *650*
Love's Crucible, 186

INDEX

Loves of Carmen, The, 210
Loves of Jeanne Ney, The, 124, 159, 174, 257, 261, 263-4, 266-8, 371, 390, 584, *650*, 710
Loves of Pharaoh, The, 141, 714
Loves of Zero, 124, 138
Love's Sacrifice, 262, 290
Low, Colin, 761
Lower Depths, The, 766
Lubitsch, Ernst, 78, 102-3, 134, 160, 176, 182, 203, 216, 274, 305, 337, 419, 477, 482, 526, 529, 557, 709, 710, 714; his films imitated by younger Hollywood directors, 135, 170, 317; his handling of Menjou, 169; goes to Hollywood, 177; his influence, 177; his European films, 177; his American period, 178-81; his first talkies, 478; his Dietrich films, 479; later films, 479-80; death, 480; observational use of camera in his early work, 515; private life films derived from, 547
Lucretia Borgia, 288
Lumet, Sidney, 728
Lumière, L. J. and A. M., 69, 329
Lunacharsky, A. V., 227
Lusk, Norbert, 436, 439, 487
Lye, Len, 155n., 138
Lynching at Cripple Creek, A, 70

M

M, 40, 475, 480, 482, 582, *651*
Macbeth, 495, 766
MacDonald, Farrell, 199
Macgowan, Kenneth, 481, 507
Macharet, Alexander, 566, 569
Machaty, Gustav, 607, 608
Machinery, as material basis for films, 114; in pictorial composition, 478
Mack, Max, 291
MacMurray, Fred, 454
Macpherson, Aimée, 91
Macpherson, Kenneth, 86, 417, 422
Madame Bovary, 532
Madame Dubarry, see Dubarry
Madame X, 147
Mädchen in Uniform, *651*, 750
Mad Wednesday, 500
Maetzig, Kurt, 594, 758

Magdana's Donkey, 754
Magia Lucana, 747
Magic Clock, The, 118
Magic Fish, The, 578
Magic Flame, The, 199
Magician, The, 197
Magnani, Anna, 600, 601n.
Magnascope, the, 206, 341, 384-5
Magnificent Ambersons, The, 497
Maisons de la Misère, Les, 615
Maître du Logis, Le, 305, 604
Major and the Minor, The, 503
Major Barbara, 715
Make Mine Music, 519
Makk, Karoly, 759
Malaria, 251
Malayan Film Industry, 762
Malraux, André, 543
Maltese Falcon, The, 372n., 500, 503, *652*
Mamoulian, Rouben, 476-8, 502
Man About Town, 529
Man and Maid, 212
Manchurian Candidate, The, 781
Mander, Miles, 319
Mandrake, 286
Manés, Gina, 188, 294, 307, 309
Man From Painted Post, The, 174
Man From the Restaurant, The, 248
Mangini, Cecilia, 747
Manhandled, 213
Man Hunt, 481
Man I Killed, The, 478
Man in the Box, The, 214
Man in the Forest, The, 247
Man in the Iron Mask, The, 171, 175
Man in the White Suit, The, 733
Man is Ten Feet Tall, A, 728
Mankiewicz, Joseph, 497, 730
Mann, Delbert, 727, 728
Mann, Thomas, 418
Man of Aran, 520, 521, 522, *681*
Manolescu, 261
Manon, 739
Manon Lescaut, 79, 283, 287, 317, 652, 709
Man on the Tracks, 756
Man's Past, A, 78
Man to Remember, A, 494
Mantrap, 211
Man Upstairs, The, 735

Manvell, Roger, 772, 778
Man Who Knew Too Much, The, 548, 557
Man Who Laughs, The, 78, 79, 143, 287
Man Without a Country, The, 211
Man With the Movie Camera, The, 245, 247, 366, *681*
Man, Woman and Sin, 136, 213
Manxman, The, 321
Marcelino Pan y Vino, 751
Marchand des Plaisirs, Le, 309
Marche des Machines, La, 114, 297, 369, 378, 394
March of Time, The, 26, 46, 123n., 425, 458, 460, 462, 464
Marcorelles, Louis, 738, 740, 759, 759n.
Mare Nostrum, 195, 197
Maria, Lia, 260
Maria Cantelaria, 618
Mariassy, Felix, 759
Marie, 615
Marie Antoinette, 491
Marie Chapdelaine, 531
Marie-Louise, 615
Marinucci, Vinicio, 746
Marius trilogy, 538
Mark of Zorro, The, 171, 173, 174, 175, 211
Marquis d'Eon, 262, 284
Marriage Circle, The, 102, 135, 169, 170, 178, 181, 212, 305, *652*
Marriage of Corbal, The, 551
Marriage of the Bear, The, 104, 227
Marriott, Charles, 90
Marseillaise, La, 125, 533
Martin Luther, 121, 262, 288, 380
Marty, 727, 728
Marx, Karl, 219
Marxism, 251
Mary Burns, Fugitive, 456
Masina, Giulietta, 745
Masking, 89
Mason, A. E. W., 207
Mason, James, 561
Massacre, 441
Masselli, Francesco, 746
Massingham, Richard, 771
Master of the House, The, 305, 605. See also *Le Maître du Logis.*
Masters of Nürnberg, The, 281

Maté, Rudolph, 604
Mater Dolorosa, 311, 537
Maternelle, La, 531, 542, *652*
Maternity, 288
Matrimaniac, The, 173
Matter of Dignity, A, 753
Matter of Life and Death, A, 317n., 553
Maugham, Somerset, 80, 136, 197, 209, 216, 421
Mauprat, 302
Maurus, Gerda, 272
Mauvaises Rencontres, Les, 741
May, Joe, 183, 260, 290, 291
Mayer, Arthur, 772
Mayer, Carl, 50, 60, 94n., 95n., 96, 98n., 98, 181, 259, 278, 356, 710; a note on by Erich Pommer, 711-13; an appreciation by Paul Rotha, 713-15; 'a film artist' by Karl Freund, 716-17
Mazzei, Andrew, 275
McClaren, Norman, 115n., 618, 761
McDonald, Fergus, 734
McKendrick, Alexander, 730, 733
McLaglen, Victor, 144, 294
McLean, Ross, 618
McMahon, Alice, 616
McTeague, 158
Mechanics of the Brain, The, 122
Medal for Beauty, A, 502
Meetings, 757
Meet John Doe, 452
Meet Me in Saint Louis, 502
Meierhold, V., 229
Meinert, Rudolf, 291
Mein Fräulein Frau, 594
Meisel, Edmund, 232, 409
Meistersingers, The, 262
Mejrabpom-Russ, 226, 227
Méliès, George, 70, 92, 114, 115, 529, 540n.
Meller, Racquel, 307
Melody of the World, 613
Melson, Soren, 606
Memphis Belle, 463, 488
Men, 187
Men, The, 727
Men and Jobs, 566, 569, *653*
Mendes, Lothar, 187, 207, 548
Menilmontant, 299, *688*
Menjou, Adolphe, 75, 169, 179, 213, 311

Men of the Mountain, The, 758
Men of the Woods, The, 251
Men Without Wings, 609
Men Without Women, 482
Menzies, William Cameron, 175, 548
Mercanton, Louis, 72
Merchant of Venice, 292
Merchant Seamen, 55, 682
Merry-Go-Round, The, 157-8, 211, 759
Merry Widow, The, 160, 399
Merton of the Movies, 203
Merveilleuse Vie de Jeanne d'Arc, La, 300
Messel, Rudolph, 87, 143, 367n.
Metro-Goldwyn-Mayer Film Company, 76, 84, 158, 179, 187, 191, 192, 195-6, 204-5, 340, 399, 421, 443, 472, 475, 485, 551, 616
Metropolis, 73, 261, 268, 272, 274-5, 324, 329, 332, 372, 476, 600, 653
Metzner, Ernö, 272, 333, 369
Mexico, Eisenstein films, 562; film-making in, 618
Meyer, Rudolf, 776
M-G-M, 726
M. Hulot, 739
Michael Strogoff, 102, 291, 300, 399
Mickey Mouse cartoons, 92, 119, 147, 515-17
Mickey's Choo-Choo, 120
Mid-Atlantic pictures, 732
Midnight Sun, The, 187
Midvinter Blott, 602
Miles, Bernard, 734
Milestone, Lewis, 211, 433, 456, 486-8
Milhaud, Darius, 409
Miller, Mary, 513
Millie, 438
Million, Le, 526, 527, 653
Million and One Nights, A, 73n.
Millions Like Us, 36, 53, 55-6, 122n., 314n., 553, 653
Ministeriernes Filmudvalg, 606
Ministry of Information, 44-5, 53, 221n.; Films Division, 314n.
Minkin, Adolf, 578
Minnelli, Vincente, 502, 729
Miracle, Silas, 208
Miracle, The, 20, 41, 51, 372, 601n.
Miracle at Verdun, 537

Miracle des Loups, Le, 300
Miracle of Morgan's Creek, The, 499
Miracolo a Milano, 744
Mirror of Holland, 752
Misérables, Les, 311
Misfits, The, 781
Mission to Moscow, 465, 492
Miss Julie, 748
Miss Mend, 247
Mistons, Les, 741, 778
Mitchell, Denis, 736
Mix, Tom, 202
Mix, see Dissolve
Mizoguchi, Kenji, 765-6, 771
Mme. Beudet, 312
Moana, 103, 122, 204-5, 208, 216, 303, 316, 372, 398, 520, 682
Moby Dick, 447
Modern Dubarry, A, 187, 546
Modern Hero, A, 583
Modern Musketeer, A, 172, 173
Modern Times, 509, 511, 526
Molander, Gustav, 307, 602
Molière, J. B., 280
Molinaro, Edouard, 742
Mollo, Andrew, 782
Monde du Silence, Le, 741, 742
Money Behind the Screen, 544n.
Money or Life, 608
Monkey Talks, The, 210
Mon Oncle, 740
Mons, 123, 322
Monsieur Verdoux, 36, 512-15, 654
Montage, Eisenstein's theories of, 108-9; defined, 343; forms of, 344; examination of the various acts of montage, 344-59
Montagu, Ivor, 86, 114, 322, 389, 561-2, 573, 778
Monte Carlo, 478
Monte Cristo, 300
Montgomery, Robert, 375n.
Montparnasse, 115, 295, 300
Moon is Down, The, 465
Moon of Israel, The, 187
Moontide, 531
Moore, Tom, 131
Moran, Lois, 200
Mörder Dimitri Karamazov, Der, 654
Morena, Erna, 278, 288
Morning of a Healthy Man, The, 251
Morning Post, The, 84

Morocco, film-making in, 618
Morocco, 474, 475
Morosko, 118, 227
Morris, Chester, 436
Mort en Fraude, 741
Moscow, 571
Moscow Art Theatre, 228
Moscow State School of Cinematography, 223
Moscow Strikes Back, 579
Moscow that Laughs and Weeps, 125
Mosjoukine, Ivan, 228, 309
Mother, 138, 221, 234, 235, 236, 329, 379, 396, 654
Mother and Child, 251
Motion Picture Association (U.S.), 30, 80n.
Motion Picture Board of Trade, New York, 80
Motion Picture Herald, 21, 22
Motion Picture Producers and Distributors of America Inc., 80
Motion Pictures in Denmark, 603n.
Moulin Rouge, 183
Mounting, 341
Mourning Becomes Electra, 505
Moussinac, Léon, 220n., 233, 313, 544
Mouthpiece, The, 441
Movement, of material, 341; of camera, 341, 366-9, 370-5, 377-81, 383; between one image and another, 341; of screen, 341
Movie Parade, 113n., 125n.
Movies, The, 772
Mr. Deeds Goes to Town, 451, 654
Mr. Fix It, 174
Mr. Mensa Builds a House, 763
Mrs. Miniver, 53, 465, 488
Mr. Smith Goes to Washington, 452, 453
Muerte di un Ciclista, 751
Mulino del Po, Il, 744
Mullally, Frederic, 544n.
Mulligan, Robert, 728
Munday, Helen, 208
Muni, Paul, 457
Munk, Andrzej, 756, 757, 780
Munna, 763
Murder, 655
Murderers Are Among Us, The, 41, 594, 757

Muriel, 781
Murnau, Fred W., 78, 99, 135, 181-3, 190, 258, 278, 280, 285, 288, 292, 303, 317, 339, 369, 379, 532, 709-10, 714, 716-17
Murphy, Dudley, 115
Murray, Mae, 131, 160, 187
Murray, Marie, 70
Muscle Beach, 731
Museum of Modern Art Film Library, New York, 16, 17, 212n., 330n., 591n.
Musical Film, the, 125, 147, 443-4, 729
Music Master, The, 211
Mussolini, Benito, 596
Mutiny on the Bounty, 491
Mutt and Jeff, 119
Mutual Film Corporation, 167
My Best Girl, 211
My Darling Clementine, 484, 485, 486, 730
My Father's House, 617
My Favourite Wife, 453
My Man Godfrey, 453, 492
Myrdal, Gunnar, 471
My Son, 243
Mystère Picasso, Le, 742
Mystères du Château du Dé, Les, 300, 369
Mystery of Edwin Drood, The, 448
Mystic, The, 211
Mystic Mirror, The, 329n.
My Universities, 575

N

Nachts wenn der Teufel kam, 750
Nagy, Kate von, 290
Naked City, 49n., 54, 727
Nalbandov, Sergei, 396
Naldi, Nita, 78, 131
Name the Man, 185
Nana, 310, 655
Nanook of the North, 36, 49, 103, 122, 204, 216, 491, 520, 524-5, 682
Napoléon, 121, 302, 310-11, 385, 537, 564
National Association of the Motion Picture Industry, 80
National Board of Review Magazine, 528

INDEX

National Board of Review of Motion Pictures, 16
National Cinema Series, 772
National Film Board of Canada, 761
National Film Finance Corporation, 20, 37, 58, 779
National Film Library (London), 320n.
National Film Theatre, 724
National Recovery Act, producers 'co-operation' with, 443
Native Land, 682
Naturalism in films, 103, 201-8, 237, 288, 452, 484
Nature films, British, 323
Navigator, The, 210, *655*
Nazis Strike, The, 682
NBC-TV, 731
Neame, Ronald, 734
Neergaard, Ebbe, 305n., 603n.
Negative film, projection of, 369-70
Negri, Pola, 78, 131, 134, 177, 179, 184-5, 187, 276, 288, 480, 587
Negro Soldier in World War II, The, 502
Neilan, Marshall, 211
Neo-Realism, 98, 727, 743, 745, 773
Neo-Romanticism, 743, 745
Neppach, A. D., 284
Netherlands Film Industry, see Dutch Film Industry
Neubabelsberg studios, 252
Neue Freie Presse, 266
Neumann, Alfred, 180
Neurath, Otto, 60
New Babylon, 125, 220-1, 237, 337n., 384, 391, 397, *655*
New Cinema in Europe, 778
New Earth, 611, 614, *683*
New Era Film Company, 322
New Explorers, The, 735
New Gulliver, The, 579, *689*
New Lot, The, 55
News-reels, 89, 123; Soviet, 222; use of dialogue in, 408
News Review Number Two, 461, 613
New Teacher, The, 576, 577
New Worlds for Old, 423
New Year's Eve (Sylvester), 101, 181, 260, 287, 292, 396, 710, 714
New Year Sacrifice, 768
New Yorker, The, 35

New Zealand Film Industry, 762
Next of Kin, 555, 556, *683*
Nibelungen Saga, The, 115, 124, 258, *656*, 709
Niblo, Fred, 211
Nichols, Dudley, 49, 486, 505, 534, 536
Nicht mehr fliehen, 750
'Nickelodeons', 70-1
Niebeling, Hugo, 750
Nielsen, Asta, 258, 259, 265, 269, 289, 290, 710
Night Angel, 491
Night Court, 441
Night in a London Club, A, 166
Night in Paradise, A, 507
Night in the City, The, 736
Night Mail, 56, *683*
Night Train to Munich, 558
Nikkatsu, 325
Nina Petrovna, 183, 255, 261, 291, 369
Nine Lives, 749
Nine Men, 55-6, 122n., 314n., 555, *683*
1905, 230
Ninotchka, 479, 503, *656*
Nissen, Greta, 135
Nitzschmann, Erich, 285
Nju, 101, 142, 276, 277, 292
Noa, Manfred, 291
Noah's Ark, 73, 125, 152, 187
None But the Lonely Heart, 505
No Place for Love, 594
Nora, 289
Nordisk Company, 603, 605, 607
No Resting Place, 776
Normand, Mabel, 167
Norris, Frank, 158
North Sea, 56, *684*
North Star, The, 465, 487, 506
Norwegian Film Industry, 25, 749
Nosferatu, see *Dracula*
Nothing Sacred, 453, 489, *656*
Notte, La, 777
Notti bianche, 743
Notti di Cabiria, Le, 745, 746, 773
Nous sommes tous des Assassins, 739, 740
Nouveaux Messieurs, Les, 124, 187, 307-8
Nouvelle Vague, 778, 779

815

Novarro, Ramon, 180, 196, 205
Novotna, Jarmila, 616
Nox, André, 309
Nuit du Carrefour, La, 532
Nuit et Brouillard, 742, 773
Nuits de Princes, 309
Nuits Electriques, Les, 115
Nuremberg Trial, film of, 579, 580
Nuri the Elephant, 325

O

Obelenski, V., 226
Oberammergau Passion Play, 70
Obratsov, —, 578
O'Brien, George, 182
Observer, The, 549n.
October, see Ten Days that Shook The
  World
Odd Man Out, 36, 51, 56, 116n.,
  381n., 553, 559, 657, 733
Odets, Clifford, 487, 505
Odyssey, 72
Office of War Information (U.S.),
  460, 461, 613
O'Flaherty, Liam, 284, 483
Of Mice and Men, 456, 487, 657
O'Fredericks, Alice, 605
Ohberg, Ake, 748
Okay, America, 441
Old and the New, The, see The
  General Line
Old Ironsides, 202, 384
Old Mill, The, 516
Oliver Twist, 37, 561, 657
Olivier, Sir Laurence, 124n., 548,
  560, 734, 754
Olvidados, Los, 769, 773
Olympiad, 591
Olympic Games, (1948), 591n.
Once Upon a Time, 604
One A.M., 167
One Exciting Night, 154
One-Eyed Jacks, 781
O'Neill, Eugene, 505
One of Our Aircraft is Missing, 53
One Sunday Morning, 757
Only Yesterday, 145n.
On the Bowery, 731
On the Mountains and in the Valleys,
  608
On the Red Front, 228
On the Town, 729

On the Waterfront, 727
On Trial, 48n.
On With the Show, 147
Oom Paul, 591
Op Art, 783
Open City, 41, 53, 56, 541, 547,
  596-7, 600, 684, 743
Operas, 113
Ophüls, Max, 737, 739, 771
Orders to Kill, 733
Ordet, 749
Oro di Napoli, L', 744
Orphans of the Storm, 150, 153, 196,
  357
Orphée, 739
Orwell, George, 736
Osbiston, Alan, 734
Ossessione, 743
Oswald, Richard, 288
Othello, 187, 292, 730, 754
Ott, Fred, 68
Otton, Malcolm, 762
Otzep, Fiodor, 226, 227, 247
Our Betters, 493
Our Court, 755
Our Daily Bread, 471, 472
Our Dancing Daughters, 87, 144,
  213, 294, 333
Out in the World, 575
Out of the Mist, 261, 289
Outsider, The, 211
Overlanders, The, 20, 56, 122n.,
  314n., 555, 619, 658
Over 21, 495
Overval, De, 776
Ox-Bow Incident, The, see Strange
  Incident
Ozu, Yasujiro, 767

P

Pabst, G. W., 85, 103, 112, 116n.,
  254, 261, 287, 289, 292, 368, 383,
  392, 501, 542, 565, 568, 587, 591,
  609, 710; interest in psycho-
  analysis, 101, 265, 336; quoted,
  111; and Stroheim, 159, 489; his
  importance, 263; unerring choice
  of camera angle, 263, 268; first
  films, 264; psychological understanding, 264; choice of melodramatic stories, 266; and Eisenstein, 267; reveals rare side of

Brigitte Helm, 268-9; concern with feminine character, 269-70; later films, 272; analytical approach, 489; bourgeois culture, 511; observational use of camera, 515; in Hollywood, 582; his recent work, 582-5, 751
Pacific 231, 408n.
Pagan, The, 205
Page, Anita, 144
Page, John, 620
Pagnol, Marcel, 532, 538
Paisan, 37, 41, 53, 597-8, 602, *658*
Pakistani Film Industry, 762
Pal, George, 118, 610
Pal Alone in the World, 749
Palace and Fortress, 227
Palace Hotel, 594
Palaver, 316
Palestine, film-making in, 616-17
Palestine Film Productions, 617
Pamyr, 121, 251
Pandora's Box, 264, 270-1
Pan Film Company, Austria, 285
Panic in the Streets, 727
Panique, 531, 541, *659*
Panning of camera, 341, 373-4
Panoramique du Cinéma, 544n.
Panta Rhei, 752
Pantelev, —, 227, 248
Pantomin Film Company, 290
Paper-Run, 762
Paracelsus, 584, 592, 609
Paradine Case, The, 557
Paramount Film Company, 80, 84, 85, 91n., 160-2, 180, 185, 194, 201, 207, 372, 384, 432, 443, 475, 479, 499, 546, 562, 726
Paramount-British Productions Ltd., 546
Paramount-Famous-Players, 193
Paramount News, 123
Parents Terribles, Les, 739
Parer, Damien, 619
Paris in Spring, 487
Paris Nous Appartient, 780
Paris qui Dort, 304
Paris Underground, 465
Parsons, Louella O., 133, 496
Partie du Campagne, La, 532
Pascal, Gabriel, 273, 560
Pasolini, Pier Paolo, 780

Passion, see *Dubarry*
Passion de Jeanne d'Arc, Le, 103, 123, 257, 298, 301, 305-6, 339, 372, 377, 398, 400, 419, 604, *659*
Passport to Pimlico, 733
Paterson, Isabel, 450
Pathé Film Company, 84, 311
Pather Panchali, 763, 773
Paths of Glory, 730
Patriot, The, 78, 124, 140, 142, 179, 180-1, 332, 374
Patris, Ludo, 583n.
Patrouille de Choc, 741
Pattes Blanches, 739
Paul, Robert, 69
Pavlov, Ivan Petrovich, 229, 234
Pawnshop, The, 167
Paxton, John, 503
Pay Day, 167
Pearl Harbour, 460, 461, 495
Peasants, 566, *659*
Peasant Woman of Riazan, The, 222, 242-3, 291, 329n., 381
Peau Douce, La, 778
Pêcheur d'Islande, 311
Pegler, Westbrook, 512
Peg O' My Heart, 192
Penguin Film Review, 540n., 543n., 544, 595n.
Pension Mimosas, 537
People on Sunday, 503
People's Holiday, 606
PEP, 772
Pépé Le Moko, 531, 538
Père Goriot, Le, 311
Perfect Alibi, The, 147
Peries, Lester, 762
Périnal, Georges, 560
Perry, Frank, 781
Personification, camera, 374-5
Peter Pan, 209
Peter the First, 576
Peter the Great, 141, 187
Petit Chaperon Rouge, Le, 310
Petite Marchande d'Allumettes, La, 118, 302, 310
Petrov, V., 576, 754
Phantom, 278
Phantom Carriage, The, 323, *659*
Phantom Lady, The, 502
Phantom President, The, 441
Phèdre, 91

Philadelphia Story, The, 493
Philbin, Mary, 158
Philipe, Gérard, 782
Philips Film Company, 94
Philips-Radio, 611
Philosopher's Stone, The, 763
Phoebus Film Company, 278, 281
Picabia, Francis, 296
Piccadilly, 124, 140, 183, 317, 321, 373
Pichel, Irving, 502, 505, 508n.
Pick, Lupu, 101, 259n., 260, 287, 289, 292, 710
Pickford, Mary, 129, 141, 147, 170, 172, 175-6, 178, 211, 477, 726
Pickpocket, 780
Piece of Land, A, 759
Pied Piper, The, 502
Pigskin Parade, 478
Pilgrim, The, 164, 167
Pinocchio, 518
Pioneer Pictures, 477
Pirandello, Luigi, 309
Pirate, The, 729
Pits, The, 241, 242
Pitts, Zasu, 160, 161
Plainsman, The, 491
Plaisir, Le, 739
Plicka, Karel, 608
Plough and the Stars, The, 483
Plow that Broke the Plains, The, 458
Pluie, 114
Poe, Edgar Allan, 303
Poil de Carotte, 530-1, *660*
Point du Jour, Le, 739
Poirier, Léon, 302, 311
Poland, film industry in, 41, 610, 756
Poland's West, 610
Polanski, Roman, 780
Polikushka, 227, 247
Polish State Film School, 757
Political Censorship of Films, The, 86
Politic Flapper, The, 189, 192
Pollet, Jean Daniel, 742
Pollock, Channing, 275
Pommer, Erich, 101, 112, 317, 548, 710, 716; on Carl Mayer, 50, 94n., 97n., 711-13; attempt to combine Hollywood commercialism with German school, 78, 261; in Hollywood, 135, 183, 260; supervision of other directors, 183-5, 290-1; his films damaged by studio-mind, 255; imports Josef von Sternberg for Ufa's talkies, 474; work in American zone of Germany, 594
Pont d'Acier, Le, 114
Pony Express, The, 203
Popov, —, 226
Poppies in Flanders, 335
Popular Sin, The, 213
Porgy and Bess, 478
Pori, 122
Porte des Lilas, 740
Porten, Henry, 258, 288
Porter, Edwin S., 70, 72
Portes de la Nuit, Les, 541
Portrait of a Woman, 537
Positif, 738
Postmaster, The, 104, 227, 247
Posto, Il, 777
Post Office Film Units, 43, 115n.
Potamkin, Harry Alan, 386
Potechina, Lydia, 258, 283
Powell, Michael, 553, 554n., 560
Powell, William, 49, 207
Power and the Glory, The, 486
Power and the Land, 459, 612
Pradot, Marcelle, 309
Praestev: Vejlby, 603
Prague Castle, 608
Pred Maturitou, 608
Prelude to War, 684
Premieres of films, 75-6
Preobrashenskaia, Olga, 226, 242, 291
President Vanishes, The, 489
Pressburger, Arnold, 49, 475
Pressburger, Emeric, 544n., 560
Pretty Ladies, 213
Prévert, Jacques, 49, 530, 737
Prévost, Abbé, 283
Pride and the Passion, The, 729
Primary, 781
Primrose Path, The, 492
Prince Cuckoo, 286
Princess Priscilla's Fortnight, 320
Prison, 248
Prisoner, The, 734
Prisoner of Zenda, The, 196, 197

Private Life of a Cat, 608
Private Life of Helen of Troy, The, 187, 545, 547
Private Life of Henry VIII, 546, 547, 548, *600*
Private Worlds, 492
Producers, maximum returns sole motive, 24, 87; attitude to public, 26
Production, exhibitor control of, 20, 24; proposals to separate exhibitors from, 25; effects of complex technological methods in, 49
Professional Sweetheart, 478
Professor Hannibal, 759
Professor Mamlock, 578, 594, *660*
Programmes, cinema, need to investigate, 26; double-feature, 26; treble-feature, 27; single-feature, 27
Proie du Vent, La, 304
Propaganda and the Nazi War Film, 590
Protozanov, Yakov A., 98, 226-8, 247-8, 579
Proud Flesh, 192
Provincial Cinematograph Theatres Ltd., 76
Psychiatry, Hollywood makes use of, 467
Psycho, 781
Psycho-analysis, effects on filmic treatment, 100-1, 274; Pabst and, 265-6, 336; part in conveying dramatic content of film, 363
Psychology, used in treatment of Swedish films, 323; of films, 362-6; flood of Hollywood films based on, 467-9
P'tite Lili, La, 116, 310
Ptushko, Alexander, 579
Public Enemy, The, 36, 434, 437, 489, 661
Public taste, 21, 22, 27-9, 436
Pudovkin, V. I., 40, 106, 121, 192, 225, 227, 239, 242n., 249, 322, 337, 357, 368, 381, 383, 410, 420, 470, 472, 532, 659n.; uses raw material as a foundation for filmic work, 105, 236-7; sense of reality, 162; and Kuleshov's experiments, 228-9, 234; his constructive editing, 229, 233, 388-9, 392-3; comparison with Eisenstein, 231-4; his principles, 233-7; his referential editing, 235-6, 358; quoted on filmic elements, 354; use of dissolves and direct cutting, 355-6; use of symbolism, 358, 477, 565; editing and cinematographic essence, 388-9; and placing of titles, 397-8; hails invention of sound, 419; sound films, 564-6; denounced by Central Committee of the C.P.S.U., 566; lost in aesthetic intellectualism, 567; his last work, 574, 771
Pudovkin on Film Technique, 354
Puerto Rican Film Industry, 770
Puerto Rico, 614
Puppets, Czech, 758
Purple Heart, The, 487
Purviance, Edna, 167, 169
Pushkin, Alexander, 227
Putti, Lya de, 78, 135, 283-4, 317
Pygmalion, 559, *661*, 715
Pyle, Ernie, 466

Q

'*Q' Ships*, 123, 322
Quai des Brûmes, Le, 538, 539, *661*
Quai des Orfèvres, 739
Quality Street, 448
Quatorze Juillet, Le, 527
Quatre Cent Coups, Les, 778
Queen Elizabeth, 72
Queen Kelly, 162
Queval, Jean, 741n.
Que Viva Mexico, 562, 563n., 564
Quick Millions, 434, 493, 504, *661*
Quo Vadis?, 72, 150

R

Rabinovitch, Isaac, 228
Racket, The, 212, 433, *662*
Rackety Rax, 441
Radio Corporation of America, the, 84
Radio-Keith Orpheum (R.K.O.), 35, 433, 483, 494-5, 497, 503, 507
Radio Pictures, 84

Radvany, Geza, 746, 759
Rahn, Bruno, 289, 290, 291, 292, 710
Raices, 769
Rail, The, 287
Raimu, 538
Rain, 80, 209, 487
Rainbow, 578
Rainbow Dance, 115n., *689*
Raizman, Yuli, 105, 226, 248, 249, 579n.
Ralston, Esther, 545
Rambeau, Marjorie, 436
Ramsaye, Terry, 22, 57, 73n.
Ranger of the Big Pines, 205
Rank, J. Arthur, 36-7, 58, 60, 124n., 273, 551-3, 561
Rank Organisation, 36-7, 122n., 503, 554, 777, 782
Ranody, Laszlo, 759
Rappaport, Herbert, 578
Rashomon, 765, 767, 773
Raskolnikov, 98, 285, 292
Rasp, Fritz, 282, 284, 584, 710
Rat der Götter, 758
Ravel, Gaston, 300
Ray, Man, 116, 295, 296, 297, 300
Ray, Nicholas, 727
Ray, Satyajit, 763, 765, 777
Razumni, A., 227
Reaching for the Moon, 129, 174
Real End of the Great War, The, 756
Rebecca, 557
Rebecca of Sunnybrook Farm, 448
Rector, Enoch, 70
Red Badge of Courage, 730
Red Dust, 444
Redgrave, Sir Michael, 558
Red Shoes, 37
Reed, Sir Carol, 51, 53, 55-6, 368n., 462, 495, 544, 553-4, 556n., 558, 733
Reed, John, 230n.
Règle du Jeu, La, 534, 738
Rehman, Hans, 278
Reiber, Willy, 291
Reid, Wallace, 131
Reimann, Walther, 94, 97n., 710, 713
Reinhardt, Gottfried, 589
Reinhardt, Max, 142, 177, 292, 493

Reiniger, Lotte, 116n., 118
Reisner, Charles, 213
Reisz, Karel, 735, 776, 779
Reka, 608
Rekava, 762
Religious films, 467-8
Reluctant Dragon, The, 120n., 519, *689*
Rembrandt, 560, *662*
Rembrandt—the Man, 752
Renoir, Jean, 54, 57, 118, 297, 298n., 302, 310, 456, 464, 530, 532-6, 543, 737-9, 763
Report from the Aleutians, 463, 500
Rescued from an Eagle's Nest, 150
Reserved for Ladies, 546
Resnais, Alain, 737, 742, 778, 780
Return of Frank James, The, 481
Return of Maxim, The, 575n.
Reuter's, 457
Réveil, 311
Révillon Frères, 204
Revolt in Kazan, 221, 248
Rhodes of Africa, 548
Rhythm of a City, 603
Rhythmus, 113
Richard, Frieda, 283
Richard III, 734
Richardson, Sir Ralph, 531
Rich and Strange, 557
Richie, Donald, 765
Richter, Ellen, 260, 291
Richter, Hans, 109, 112, 113, 114, 115
Richter, Paul, 260
Rideau Cramoisi, Le, 741
Riefenstahl, Leni, 591
Rien que les Heures, 309, 310, 356, *684*
Rififi, 740
Rilla, Walter, 278, 291
Rimax Film Company, 276
Ring, The, 321
Rink, The, 167
Rio Rita, 125
Riot in Cell Block 11, 730
Rise of the American Film, The, 18n., 29, 92n., 128n., 212n., 453n., 457n., 469n., 479n., 488n., 494n.
Rising Twenty, 21n.
Riskin, Robert, 49
Riso Amaro, 745

Ritt, Martin, 728
Rittau, Günther, 272, 291, 371
Rittner, Rudolph, 281
Rival World, The, 735, 752
River, The, 458, *685*, 762, 763
Rivette, Jacques, 780
RKO-Radio, 726
Roach, Hal, 487
Road to Life, The, 489, 564-5, *662*
Road to Yesterday, The, 210
Roaring Twenties, The, 455, 492
Robber Band, 292
Robbins, Jerome, 781
Roberts, Alice, 271n.
Robeson, Paul, 548
Robin Hood, 73, 172, 173, 174, *663*
Robinson, David, 767n.
Robinson, Edward G., 436, 457
Robinson Crusoe, 769
Robison, Arthur, 257-8, 282, 283, 284, 287, 317, 709
Rochemont, Louis de, see De Rochemont
Rocque, Rod la, 179
Rogers, Charles, 144
Rogers, Ginger, 443
Rogosin, Lionel, 731
Rogue Male, 481
Röhrig, Walther, 94, 258, 279, 280, 283, 291, 710, 713, 716
Rolling shots, 374
Romains, Jules, 307
Roman Catholic Church, 445, 446
Romance of Transportation, The, 761
Rome Express, 548
Romm, Mikhail, 576, 754
Romola, 199
Ronde, La, 739
Rookery Nook, 125
Room, Abram, 144, 169, 226, 239-42, 357
Room at the Top, 734, 735
Rooty Toot Toot, 731
Rosay, Françoise, 536, 537
Roscher, Charles, 182
Rosenkavalier, 125, 285
Rosita, 176, 178
Rossellini, Roberto, 42, 49, 50, 51, 52, 53, 54, 55, 57, 372, 426, 515, 532, 596-9, 600, 601, 743, 745, 777
Rossi, Franco, 746

Rostand, —, 478
Rotation, 758
Rotha, Paul, 419, 420n., 422-5, 545, 604, 607, 611, 619, 744n.; an appreciation of Carl Mayer, 713-15
Rou, Alexander, 578
Roue, La, 302, 311
Rougier, —, 297
Rouquier, Georges, 40, 543, 740, 742
Rovensky, —, 608
Roxie Hart, 489
Roy, Bimal, 763
Royal Remembrances, 92
Royal Scandal, A, 479
Rubens, 753
Rubens, Peter Paul, 615
Ruggles, Wesley, 447, 492
Runyon, Damon, 450, 451
Russell, William, 202
Russians at War, 613
Rutten, Gerard, 611
Ruttmann, Walther, 113-15, 123, 261, 273, 310, 392, 613, 714

S

Saalschutz, L., 355
Sable Cicada, 617
Sabra, 616, 756
Sabu, 523
Sack of Rome, The, 72
Sadie Thompson, 80, 209, *663*
Safety Last, 215, *663*
Sahara, 55
Sait-on-jamais?, 741
Salachas, Gilbert, 741n.
Salaire de la Peur, 739
Salammbo, 714
Sally, 125
Sally of the Sawdust Ring, 154
Salome, *663*
Salomon, Henry, 731
Salt Mines of Wielieczka, The, 610
Saludos Amigos, 519
Salvage Gang, The, 736
Salvation Hunters, The, 79, 159, 193
Samsonov, Sergei, 754
Sandberg, A. W., 291, 603
San Demetrio, 53
Sanders brothers, 731
Sanders of the River, 548

Sandy, —, 115, 491
San Francisco, 491
Sang des Bêtes, Le, 742
Sang d'un Poête, Le, 117n., *689*
Sang Hu, 768
Sansho Dayu, 766
Santis, Giuseppe de, 745
Santschi, Tom, 199
Sapphire Film Productie, 776
Sa Tête, 303
Saturday Evening Post, The, 450
Saturday Night, Sunday Morning, 779
Saville, Victor, 551
Say, Young Fellow, 174
Scandal Sheet, 441
Scandinavian Film, 748n.
Scaramouche, 125, 196-7
Scarface, 492, *664*
Scarlet Empress, The, 474
Scarlet Lady, The, 78
Scarlet Letter, The, 185, 186, 187
Scarlet Pimpernel, The, 548
Scarlet Street, 481
Scenario, assembling of, 344-9;
  drawing of, 348-9; importance of
  planning, 350-1; inefficient orga-
  nisation of in British Film Indus-
  try, 351n.
Scenarist, the, 344-9, 354, 359
Schach, Max, 551
Schary, Dore, 503, 507, 508
Scherben, 292, 710
Schertzinger, Victor, 212
Schiller, J. C. F. von, 592
Schinderhannes, 125, 262, 290
Schlesinger, John, 779
Schlettow, Hans von, 290, 291, 317
Schneevoigt, George, 603
Schnitzler, Arthur, 278
Schoedsack, Ernest B., 103, 206-7, 216
School in a Mail-Box, 619
Schrire, David, 521n.
Schub, Esther, 226
Schulberg, Budd, 506n.
Schwartz, Hans, 183, 262, 290
Schweizer, Richard, 752
Science Museum, South Kensington, 69n.
Scientific films, 122, 250-1; Soviet, 272

Scipio Africanus, 595
Scott, Adrian, 35, 503, 507n.
Screen, stereoscopic, 89, 110, 332,
  362, 398, 401-2; movement of,
  384-5; triptych, 385-6
Screen Directors' Guild, 470
Screen-writer, the, 49-50; as a direc-
  tor, 50
Screwball comedy, cycle of, 453-4
Sea Beast, The, 399
Search, The, 616
Seaström, Victor, 78, 135, 182,
  185-7, 317, 323, 532, 602, 749
Sea Warrens, 251
Secret Beyond the Door, The, 481
Secrets of Nature films, 322
Secrets of the East, 73, 118, 291
Secrets of the Soul, The, 261, 264,
  265, 269
Secret Six, The, 434
Sedgwick, Edward, 212
Seeber, Guido, 290, 371, 710, 714
Seine a rencontré Paris, La, 742
Sekigawa, Hideo, 767
Sel de la Terre, Le, 742
Selznick, David, O. 473
Semyonova, Ludmilla, 241
Sennett, Mack, 54, 129, 145, 166-7,
  303, 494, 517
Sensation Seekers, The, 212
Sequestrador, El, 770
Serenade, 213, 216
Sergeant Madden, 475
Service for Ladies, 213
Seton, Marie, 562, 765
Set-Up, The, 727
Seurat, Georges, 295
Seven Brides for Seven Brothers, 729
Seven Samurai, The, 767
Seventh Age, The, 606
Seventh Heaven, 211, 369
Seventh Seal, The, 748
Seventh Veil, The, 555
Severin-Mars, —, 311
Sevsapkino, 227
Sex in Fetters, 136
Shadow, The, 756
Shadow of a Doubt, 557
Shadows, 781
Shadows in the Sunlight, 767
Shakespeare, William, 175, 780

INDEX

Shakuntala, 617
Shane, 730
Shanghaied, 167
Shanghai Express, 474
Shanghai Gesture, The, 475, 476
Shape of Things to Come, The, 111n.
Shaw, Alexander, 617, 620
Shaw, George Bernard, 559, 560
Shearer, Norma, 180, 439
She Done Him Wrong, 444, *664*
Shell Film Unit, 735-6, 752, 762, 770
Shepherd, The, 761
Sheriff's Baby, The, 150
She Stoops to Conquer, 715
Shih Hui, 767
Shimizu, Hiroshi, 767
Shindo, Kaneto, 767
Shiraz, 325
Shoe-Shine, 599
Shooting-script, assembling of, 344, 346-50. See also Scenario
Shoot the Nets, 752
Shooting Stars, 320
Shors, 575, *664*
Shots, long, 95; medium, 95; travelling, 332, 341; duration of, 352. See also Close-up
Shoulder Arms, 166, 167
Show Off, The, 213
Show People, 192
Side-Show of Life, The, 209
Siegal, Don, 730
Siege of Leningrad, The, 579, *685*
Siegfried, 115, 118, 124, 171, 258, 272, 273, 292, 400
Sieg im Westen, 592
Siegmann, George, 184
Sight and Sound, 724, 738n., 745n., 759n., 765
Sign of the Cross, The, 491
Silence est d'Or, Le, 529
Silka, S., 116, 300
Silone, Ignazio, 600
Silver, Marcel, 214
Simenon, Georges, 531, 538
Simple Case, A, 564, 567
Sin, 307
Since Yesterday, 145n.
Sinclair, Upton, 562, 563
Sing and Like It, 478
Singing Fool, The, 71, 83, 147

Sing You Sinners, 492
Sin of Harold Diddlebock, The, 500
Sins of the Fathers, The, 142, 187, 282
Siodmak, Robert, 502, 751
Sir Arne's Treasure, 186, 323, *664*
Sister to Assist 'Er, A, 316
Six et Demi x Onze, 302
Sixth Part of the World, The, 245
60 years of Japanese Cinema, 767n.
Sjöberg, Alf, 602, 748
Skeleton Dance, The, 516, 518
Skot-Hansen, Morgens, 605
Skouen, Arne, 749
Sky Pilot, The, 192
Skyscraper Symphony, 394
Slapstick, 125
Slezak, Walther, 305
Small Town Idol, A, *665*
Small Voice, The, 734
Smart Money, 434, 436
Smash-Up, 507
Smiles of a Summer Night, 748
Smiling Lieutenant, The, 478
Smiling Madame Beudet, The, *689*
Smilin' Through, 448
Smouldering Fires, 198
Snake-Pit, The, 727
Snow White and the Seven Dwarfs, 518
Société Générale de Films, 298, 307
Societies, film, see Film societies
Society Scandal, A, 291
Sociological Film, the, 122, 240-2, 248-50
Sodom and Gomorrah, 152
Soetsiku, 325
Soil, The, 617
Sollen, Maurice, 115
Somewhere in Berlin, 594
Somewhere in Europe, 759
Somme, The, 123, 322
Song of Bernadette, The, 467
Song of Ceylon, The, *685*, 736
Song of Russia, 465
Song of the South, 519
Sons of the Sea, 202
Sorcery, 187
So Red the Rose, 472
Sorrell and Son, 209
Sorrows of Satan, 154
S.O.S. Noronha, 742

So This is Paris, 178, 216
Sound Barrier, The, 733
Sound films, see Dialogue Film
Sound of Music, The, 779
Sous les Toits de Paris, 526, 527, 528, 529, *665*
South African Film Industry, 762
Southerner, The, 456, 535, *665*
Soviet Cinema, 564n.
Soviet Cultural Relations, film section, 40
Soviet Film Industry, during the thirties, 40; early films, 104; sociological and political content of its films, 104-5, 218-24, 239-40, 248-50, 251; cult for Soviet films, 104, 217; films commissioned for tenth anniversary of regime, 105; Kuleshov's experiments, 105; most advanced forms of contemporary cinema in, 105; surrealism in, 116; epic mass films of, 121, 221; documentary in, 121, 222, 239-40, 250-1, 567; documentary films combined with story-interest, 122; Lenin and, 219; nationalisation of, 219; People's Cinema Commission, 219; historical distortion, 220; classes of films, 221-3; reconstruction films, 222; educational and cultural films, 222, 250-1; children's films, 222; training for, 223; antagonism between Government and production units, 224-5; restriction on liberty of directors, 224-6; producing companies, 226; advanced school of, 229-38; change of titles of films, 230n.; right-wing school, 239-43, 566-7; propaganda spoils, 241, 242; cine-eye group, 243-7; lesser directors, 247-8; its films appeal primarily to the mind, 334, 335; films dealing with five-year plans, 566; nationalist period, 574-6; contemporary life themes, 576-7; Stakhanovism and, 577; war films, 578-9; post-war, 754-5
Soviet Fordism, 251
Sovietskaya Kultura, 754
Sovkino, 220n., 226, 248
So Well Remembered, 503

Spaak, Charles, **536**, **737**
Space, filmic, **354**, **375**
Spain, film-making in, **323**, **751**
Spanish Earth, The, **459**, **612**, **614**, **685**
Spectacle films, **72**, **125**, **133**
Spellbound, 557
Speyer, Jaap, 291
Spiegal van Holland, 752
Spigelgass, Leonard, **461**, **462**, **506**
Spiral Staircase, The, **502**, **503**
Spite Marriage, 214
Splinters, 315
Sponsorship of films, **42-3**, **45-9**
Spoor-Bergen process, 401
Spottiswoode, Raymond, 772
Spring, **245**, **246**
Spring in Zaretchnaia Street, 755
Springtime, 120
Springtime in Budapest, 759
Spy, The, **124**, **261**, **272**, **274**, **382**, **665**
Squadron 992, 56
Squalor, 767
Squaw Man, The, 490
Staaken studios, 252
Stabavoi, Georgi, **226**, **247**
Stagecoach, **483**, **505**
Stage plays, adapted, **146**, **147**
Stählerne Adern, 750
Stakhanovism, 577
Stalingrad, **579**, **685**
Stalinism, 573
Stallings, Laurence, 191
Stampede, 316
Stand Up and Cheer, 443
Stanwyck, Barbara, 439
Starevitch, Stanislas, 118
Star is Born, A, **489**, *666*, **730**
Starke, Pauline, 179
Stärker als die Nacht, 758
Stark Love, **103**, **204**, **208**, **216**, *666*
Stars Look Down, The, 314n., **485**, **544**, **553**, **556**, **558**, **559**, *666*
State Fair, **491**, *666*
State Institute of Theatre and Film, Hungary, 759; Poland, 759
Statues meurent aussi, Les, 742
Staudte, Wolfgang, **594**, **753**, **757**
Stawinski, Jerzy, 756
Steady, 752
Steinbeck, John, **456**, **608**

INDEX

Steinrück, Albert, 258
Stekly, —, 609
Stella, 753
Stella Dallas, 199, 200, 472
Stemmle, Robert, 750
Sten, Anna, 477
Stendhal (Henri Beyle), 259, 710
Stereopticon, the, 84
Stereoscopic screen, 89, 110, 332, 362, 398, 401-2
Stern, Bert, 781
Sternberg, Josef von, 79, 80, 185, 189, 193-6, 294, 433, 473-6, 478, 479, 487, 548
Stevens, George, 34, 730
Stiller, Mauritz, 135, 183, 184, 185, 186, 323
Stoker, Bram, 278
Stolen Frontier, 609
Stone, Lewis, 180, 196, 212, 332
Stone Flower, The, 579, 609
Stone Rider, The, 292, *667*, 709
Stoney, George, 731
Storck, Henri, 612, 614, 615, 753
Storm Centre, 730
Storm Over Asia, 40, 122, 149n., 230n., 234, 236, 316, 322, 355, 377n., *667*
Story of a True Love, 767
Story of a Woman, The, 507
Story of G.I. Joe, The, 140n., 466, 467, 489, *667*
Story of Louis Pasteur, The, 457, 493, *668*
Story of Temple Drake, The, 456
Storyboard (unit), 731
Strada, La, 745
Stradling, Harry, 536
Strange Adventure of David Gray, The, 604
Strange Gods, The, 770
Strange Incident (The Ox-Bow Incident) 140n., 489, 507, *658*
Stranger, The, 498
Street, The, 101, 256, 257, 258, 284, 289, 290, 292, 365, 381, *668*, 710
Street Angel, The, 211
Street of Shame, The, 766
Street of Sin, The, 78, 142, 185, 193, 195
Street of Sorrow, The, 87
Street Scene, 471

Strictly Dishonourable, 498
Strike, 105, 221, 230
Strike, The, 609
Strindberg, August, 307
String of Beads, A, 620
Stroheim, Erich von, 103, 153, 155-62, 176, 189, 211, 215, 294, 421, 426, 489, 490, 494, 501, 511, 512, 520, 533, 537, 539, 542, 771
Struggle Under Czarism, The, 245
Stuart, Henry, 265
Student of Prague, The, 78, 125, 143, 179-80, 181, 254, 255, 257, 285, 317, 380, 587, *668*, 709
Student Prince, The, 179-80, 181
Studio, 28, 296
Studio des Ursulines, 296
Studio Diamant, 296
Studio-made films, 54, 55, 101, 102
Studio-settings, 376
Sturge, John, 730
Sturges, Preston, 498-500, 506
Sturmflut, 291
Stüwe, Hans, 288
Sucksdorff, Arne, 603, 748
Sudermann, Hermann, 182
Sue, Eugène, 230
Suicide Mission, 749
Sullivan's Travels, 498-9
Summer Madness, 733
Summers, Walter, 322
Sumurun, 171, 177, 181, 258, 288, *668*, 714
Sunday Romance, A, 756
Sunflower Industry, The, 251
Sunnyside, 166, 167
Sunrise, 78, 135, 182, 183, 280, *669*, 713, 714
Sunset Boulevard, 730
Sunshine Over Snow, 603
Surrealism, 98, 116-17
Susan Lennox, 439
Sutter's Gold, 562
S.V.D., 221, 237
Svendsen, Torben, 606
Swain, Mack, 167
Swamp Water, 505, 534
Swan, The, 187
Swanson, Gloria, 27, 130, 141, 147, 162, 185, 209, 210, 213
Sweden, film industry in, 41, 78, 99, 102, 134, 252, 323, 602-3, 748

Sweet Smell of Success, The, 730
Swift, Jonathan, 579
Switzerland, film industry in, 41, 615-16, 751
Sylvester, see *New Year's Eve*
Sylvie et la Fantôme, 543
Symphonie Diagonale, 113
Symphony of a City, see *Berlin*
Szemes, Mihaly, 759
Szöts, Ivan, 758

T

Tabu, 183n., 520
Tailor of Torjok, The, 227
Tales of Manhattan, 531
Talking films, see Dialogue Film
Tallents, Sir Stephen, 771
Talmadge, Constance, 131, 213
Talmadge, Norma, 131, 187
Taming of the Shrew, The, 147, 172, 174, 175, 176, 211
Tanya, 577
Taradash, Daniel, 730
Target for Tonight, 65, 556, *686*
Tarkington, Booth, 497
Tartuffe, 78, 91, 124, 142, 180, 181, 252, 256, 258, 278, 279, 280, 709, 717
Taste, public, 21, 22, 27-8, 29, 436
Tati, Jacques, 737, 739, 740
Taylor, John, 620
Taylor, John Russell, 778
Taylor, Sam, 211
Tchekov, Anton, 104
Technicolor process, 477
Technique of Film Editing, The, 776
Television, 725, 731-2, 738, 774
Tell England, 560
Temptress, The, 211
Ten Commandments, The, 73, 125, 152, 210
Ten Days That Shook the World (October), 92, 105, 121, 138, 220-1, 230-3, 331, 335, 337, 364, 377n., 390-1, 394, 397, 409, 572, *686*
Tendencies to Monopoly in the British Cinematograph Industry, 76n., 544n.
Tender Game, The, 731
Ten Little Indians, 529
Ten Years of Soviet Medicine, 251
Terra Firma, 41

Terra trema, La, 743, 773, 777
Terry, Alice, 195, 196
Tesha, 333
Tess of the d'Urbervilles, 211
Testament of Dr. Mabuse, The, 582. See also *Doctor Mabuse*
Tête contre les Murs, La, 742
Tetto, Il, 744
Tetzlaff, Ted, 727
Thalberg, Irving, 191
That They May Live, 537
That Uncertain Feeling, 479
Théâtre Robert Houdini, 70
Theatres, chains of, 76
Their First Trip to Tokio, 767
Theme, assembling of material for, 344, 345-50; expression of dramatic content of, 347-8
Theory of the Film, 772
Thérèse Raquin, 103, 124, 187, 294, 301, 307-8, 365, 384, 400, 536, *669*
These Three, 488, 506
They Live by Night, 727
They Were Expendable, 466, 485
They Were Twelve, 767
They Won't Forget, 455-6, 492, *669*
Thief of Bagdad, The, 115, 118, 124, 171, 173, 175, 210, 548, 579
Thiele, Wilhelm, 291, 478, 526
Thimig, Herman, 288
Thin Man, The, 453-4, 491
Third Man, The, 733
13 Rue Madeleine, 492
Thirty-Nine Steps, The, 548, 557
This Film Business, 87n., 143n., 367n.
This Happy Breed, 553, 560
This Land is Mine, 534
This Modern Age series, 26, 123n.
This Sporting Life, 779
Thomas, Helga, 281
Thorp, Margaret Farrand, 92n., 128n.
Those Confounded Children (De Pokkers Under), 605
Three Bad Men, 108, 199, 202, 482
Three Comrades, 490
Three Dawns to Sydney, 620
Three Hours, 213
Three in One, 762
Three Little Pigs, 517
Three Musketeers, The, 72, 172, 173

INDEX

Three Passions, The, 195, 197
Three-Soldiers, 467
Three Songs of Lenin, 566, 567
Three Thieves, The, 248
Three Weeks, 211
Three Women, 178
Thrillers, 147
Throne of Blood, The, 766
Throw of the Dice, A, 316, 325
Thunderbolt, 194
Thunder Mountain, 212
Thunder Over Mexico, 563
Thursday's Children, 735
Thy Soul Shall Bear Witness, 78, 186
Tillie's Punctured Romance, 167
Tilton, Roger, 731
Time, filmic, 352-6
Time and Tide, 547n.
Time in the Sun, 563
Time Out of War, 731, 773
Times, The, 715
Tin Gods, 211
Tiserands, Les, 288
Tisse, Edward, 230, 561
Titles, placing of, 362, 395-8
Today We Live, 423
Todd, Michael, 729
Toeplitz de Grand Ry, Count, 547n.,
  551
Toeplitz, Jerzy, 757, 780
To Kill a Child, 749
Tokyo Olympiad, 782
Tol'able David, 199, 200, 257, 357,
  669
Toland, Gregg, 382n., 771
To Live in Peace, 600
Toll of the Sea, 399
Tolstoi, Count Alexei, 228
Tolstoi, L. N., 227, 247
Tom, Dick and Harry, 494, *670*
Toni, 36, 54, 532, 533, 534, 536, 738
Toomai of the Elephants, 522
Topical Film, the, 440-2, 454-7
Torero, 769
Torgus, 257, 292
Torment (Frenzy), 602
Torments of the Night, 290
Torre-Nilsson, Leopoldo, 770
Torres, Raquel, 141
Törst, 749
Tosca, La, 150
To the Ladies, 203

Toulouse-Lautrec, Henri Marie,
  295
Tour, Le, 299, 304
Tour au Large, 299
Tourjanski, V., 261, 290, 291
Tourneur, Maurice, 493
Tournoi, Le, 310
Tower of Lies, The, 185, 186
Town, The, 475
Toyoda, Shiro, 767
Toy Wife, The, 456
Tracking, movement of camera, 374
Trader Horn, 204, 205n., 491
Trade Unions, in film industry, 38-9,
  51, 55
Tragédie de Lourdes, La, 311
Tragedy, 288
Tragedy of the Street, The, 289, 710
Tragic Ship, The, 323
Trail of the Meteorite, 251
Trail of '98, The, 198
Trapped by Bloodhounds, 70
Trauberg, L., 220, 225-7, 229, 237,
  391, 567, 575
Träumende Mund, Der, 715
Travelling shots, 332, 341, 374
Traven, B., 501
Treasure, The, 264
Treasure Island, 491
Treasure of the Sierra Madre, The,
  501, 670
Tree Grows in Brooklyn, A, 504
Trenker, Luis, 587
Trespasser, The, 147, 162, 185, 491
Trevor, Jack, 260
Trial, The, 584n., 780
Trial of Donald Westhof, The, 289
Tricheurs, Les, 741
Trifling Women, 197
Trip to the Moon, 70, 114
Trip to Tilsit, 182
Triptych screen, the, 341, 385-6
Triumph of the Will, 590, *686*
Trnka, Jiri, 758
Troonder, Martin, 753
Trotsky, L., 220
True Glory, The, 36, 44, 53, 56,
  123n., 462, 495, 559, 579, *686*
Truffaut, François, 741, 778
Trümmerfilme, 750
Trumpet Boy, 767
Trumpet Call, The, 211

827

Truth of Lenin, The, 245
Tschechowa, Olga, 291, 317, 615
Tunisian Victory, 463
Turgenev, Ivan S., 104
Turin, Victor, 105, 225, 229, 239, 248, 250, 340, 363, 388, 394
Turkmenkino, 226
Turksib, 122, 222, 248, 257, 316, 340, 377n., 388, 394, 397, *687*
Turn of the Screw, The, 781
Tusylava, 138
Tuttle, Frank, 135, 213, 493
Twelve Angry Men, 728
Twelve O'clock High, 730
Twelvetrees, Helen, 438
Twentieth Century-Fox, 481, 485, 489, 503, 534
Two Acres of Land, 763
Two Arabian Knights, 211
Two Brothers, The, 260, 284
2 Buldi 2, 228
Two Cities Films, 554, 715
Two Days, 247
Two Men and a Wardrobe, 757

U

Ueberfall, 272, 333, 369, *690*
Ufa (Universum Film, A.G.), 118, 253, 266, 277, 291, 305, 340, 474, 586, 591, 594
Ugetsu Monogatari, 766
Ulehla, Professor, 608
Umberto D., 743, 744n., 745, 773, 777
Um Das Menschen Recht, 589
Unconquered, 490
Undefeated, The, 735
Undercurrent, 502
Underground, 315, 320
Under the Lantern, 291
Under the Roman Sun, 41
Under Two Flags, 211
Underworld, 194, 433, 475, *670*
Une si jolie petite Plage, 739
Unholy Three, The, 211
Unifrance, 738
Union of a Great Cause, The, see S.V.D.
Unitalia Film, 745, 746n.
United Artists Corporation, 84, 168, 193, 210, 548-9, 726
United Nations, 34, 60

United Nations Educational Scien tific and Cultural Organisation (U.N.E.S.C.O.), 60
United Nations Film Board, 48
United States, importance of motion pictures in overseas markets, 30-2; see American Film Industry
United States Department of Commerce, 30
United States Film Service, 459, 523
United States Office of War Information, 460-1, 613
Universal, 76, 84, 143, 287, 340
Universal-International, 726
University of Life, The, 671
Universum Film, A.G., see Ufa
Unknown Soldier, The, 749
Untertan, Der, 758
Unvanquished, The, 763
UPA group, 731

V

Vadim, Roger, 741
Vadja, Ernst, 213
Vagabond King, The, 282
Vajda, Ladislas, 751, 752
Valencia, 187
Valentino, Rudolph, 131, 195-6, 198
Valley is Ours, The, 762
Valley of the Tennessee, 608
Vampyr, 604
Van Dongen, Helen, 461, 523, 606, 611, 613
Van Dyke, W. S., 141, 204, 205, 491
Van Eycks, the, 339
Van Gogh, Vincent, 52, 295
Vanina, 181, 254, 259, *671*, 710
Vanishing Prairie, The, 731
Van Leyden, Lucas, 339
Vansittart, Sir Robert, 548
Varda, Agnes, 742
Variety, see *Vaudeville*
Variety (trade journal), 724
Varkonyi, Zoltan, 759
Varossieau, —, 753
Vassiliev, G. and S., 567
Vaudeville, 124, 142, 183, 260, 277, 292, 315, 379, *671*, 709, 710
Vavra, Otaker, 758
Védrès, Nicole, 540, 543, 742, 782
Veidt, Conrad, 135, 143, 258, 276-7, 284-6, 380, 587, 710, 714

INDEX

Veiller, Anthony, 461, 506
Velez, Lupe, 133, 154, 294
Velo, Don Carlos, 769
Venezuelan Film Industry, 770
Venganza, La, 751
Venice Festival of Short and Documentary Films, 747
Venus of Venice, The, 211
Verdun, 302, 311, *687*
Verlorene, Der, 750
Verne, Jules, 70
Vertige, Le, 309
Vertov, Dziga, 122-3, 128, 222, 226, 243-8, 256, 337, 363, 392, 464, 566, 579n.
Vesely, Herbert, 750
Vice Versa, 553
Victor Gramophone Company, 84
Victory at Sea, 731
Victory in the West (Sieg im Westen), 592
Vidor, Florence, 294
Vidor, King, 103, 147, 155, 189-92, 216, 372, 419, 469, 470-3, 478, 532, 551
Vie commence demain, La, 742
Vie est à Nous, La, 539
Viertel, Berthold, 288, 289
Vigo, Jean, 177n., 530, 541, 542, 543
Viking, The, 125
Village in Travancore, A, 764
Violinist of Florence, The, 261, 277
Virginian, The, 124, 147, 201, 211, 671
Virgin Island, 734
Virgin Queen, The, 399
Viridiana, 781
Visages d'Enfants, 307
Visconti, Luchino, 42, 743, 777
Visiteurs du Soir, Les, 540
Viskovski, —, 227
Visual images, pictorial composition of, 362, 375-86
Vitaphone, the, 146
Vitascope, the, 69
Vitelloni, I, 745
Viva Zapata!, 730
Vogel, — de, 753
Voices of Malaya, 620
Vollbrecht, Karl, 258, 272
Volga Boatmen, The, 210
Volga-Volga, 140, 291

Volkoff, Nicolas, 290-1, 311, 380
Volksfilmverband, 464
Vormittagsspuk, 114
Vorticists, 101
Voskovec, —, 608
Vostok-Kino, 226
Vox Populi, 323
Voyage au Congo, 311
Voyage Imaginaire, Le, 118, 302, 304, *690*
Vufku-Kino, 220n., 226, 243, 245, 247
Vyborg Side, 575n.

W

Wagner, Elsa, 281
Wagner, Fritz Arno, 174, 267, 272, 274, 278, 282, 284, 371, 710
Wagonmaster, The, 729
Wajda, Andrzej, 756, 757, 780
Walking Down Broadway, 490
Walk in the Sun, A, 466, 487
Walküre, Die, 571
Wall Street, 32
Walsh, George, 178
Walsh, Raoul, 209-10, 492
Walthamstow studios, 315
Walther, Hertha von, 269
Waltz Dream, The, 280, 281
Wanderer, The, 210
Wanderer of the Wasteland, The, 399
Wangenheim, Gustav von, 282
Wanger, Walter, 460, 481, 507, 730
Waning Sex, The, 213
War against Mrs. Hadley, The, 465
War Game, The, 781
Ward No. 9, 759
Wardour Films, 266
Warm, Herman, 94, 97n., 258, 285, 710, 712, 713
Warner, Jack, 455n.
Warner Brothers, 83-4, 146, 165, 187, 428-9, 430, 440, 443, 454, 456-7, 460, 492, 500-1, 507, 726
Warning, The, 609
Warning Shadows, 256, 257, 258, 282, 317, 381, 396, 584, *672,* 709
War of the Worlds, The, 495
Warriors of Faith, 609
Washneck, Erich, 291
Wasmann, Hans, 290
Wassilevska, Wanda, 578

829

Watch on the Rhine, 506
Waterloo, 262, 284, 753
Waterloo Road, 314n.
Waters of Time, 735
Watkins, Maurine, 433
Watkins, Peter, 781
Watt, Harry, 55, 56, 555, 619
Watteau, J. A., 280
Watts, Stephen, 546
Waxworks, 78-9, 124, 142, 171, 257-8, 279, 285-6, 292, 573, *672*, 709
Way Ahead, The, 36, 53, 55, 122n., 314n., 556, 559, *672*
Way Down East, 149, 399, *672*
Way of All Flesh, The, 75, 142, 211, 216
Way to India, The, 251
Way to the Stars, 559
Way We Live, The, 55
We Are Alone in the World, 757
We Are the Lambeth Boys, 735, 736
Weber, Louis, 212
Wechsler, Lazar, 615, 752
We Dive at Dawn, 56, 560
Wedding March, The, 155, 156, 157, 160-2, 294, 369, 399
Wedding Night, The, 472
Wedding Rehearsal, 546
Wedekind, Frank, 270, 271
We From Kronstadt, 568, 673
Wegener, Paul, 197, 259, 285, 531, 586-7, 710
Weiss, Jiri, 609, 758, 758n.
Welcome Mr. Marshall, 751
Well-Digger's Daughter, The, 538
Welles, Orson, 476, 495-8, 502, 780
Wellman, William, 135, 213, 466-7, 489
Wells, H. G., 111, 275, 495, 548
Welwyn studios, 315
Wendhausen, Fritz, 288, 289
Werich, —, 608
Werndorff, Oscar, 272
Werner, Gösta, 602, 749
Werth, Alexander, 543
Wessel, Horst, 585
West, Mae, 444
Western Approaches, 44, 556, *687*
Western Electric Company, 85, 262, 430

Western films, 72, 103, 145, 198-201, 378, 447, 729, 730
Western Union, 481
Westfront 1918, 40, 467, 582, *673*, 710
West German Film Industry, 750
West Side Story, 729, 781
Weyher, Ruth, 282
What Every Woman Knows, 448
What Makes Sammy Run?, 506n.
What Price Glory?, 139, 144, 210, 335
What Price Hollywood?, 493
Wheel, The, 212
When the Movies Were Young, 73n.
Where the Pavement Ends, 197
Whisky Galore, 733
White Eagle, The, 248
White Gold, 103
White Hell of Pitz Palü, The, 264, 272, 287
White Shadows in the South Seas, 141, 190, 204-5, 294, 491, 522
White Sister, The, 199
Whitman, Walt, 152
Whitney, John Hay, 477
Why We Fight series, 17, 48, 123n., 353n., 424, 461-2, 482, 579, 606, 613
Wiene, Robert, 94-5, 98-9, 148, 256, 284-5, 712
Wife of the Centaur, The, 192
Wig, The, 289
Wild Boys of the Road, 489
Wild Duck, The, 101, 260, 287
Wilder, Billy, 503-4, 506, 730
Wild Geese, 767
Wild One, The, 727
Wild Orchids, 140, 213
Wild Strawberries, 748, 749
Will Day Collection, the, 69n.
Williams, Richard, 736
Wilson, 466
Wind, The, 186, *673*
Windfall in Athens, 753
Windmill in Barbados, 619
Window, The, 727
Wings, 144, 207, 213, 384
Wings Over Africa, 620
Winning of Barbara Worth, The, 199, 201
Winnington, Richard, 24, 771, 776

INDEX

'Wipe', the, 356
Wir Erobern Land, 591
Wise, Robert, 727, 781
With Cobham to the Cape, 121
Wolf, Konrad, 758
Wolff, Friederich, 594
Wolff, Willi, 260, 291
Wolf's Clothing, 213, 216
Wolf Trap, The, 758
Wolheim, Louis, 212
Wollenberg, H. H., 581n.
Woman Alone, The, 557
Woman Disputed, The, 199
Woman in the Moon, The, 272, 275
Woman in the Window, The, 481
Woman of Affairs, A, 78
Woman of Paris, A, 102, 124, 141, 166, 168-9, 170, 178, 213, 305, 529, *673*
Woman on the Beach, The, 535
Women Everywhere, 546
Wong, Anna May, 317, 399
Wood, Sam, 212, 493, 591
Woolfe, Bruce, 322
Word, The, 749
World Changes, The, 448
World Film News, 156n., 522n., 713
World in Action, The, series, 618
World is Rich, The, 353n., 556, 611, 735, 776
World Moves On, The, 448
World of Plenty, 353n., 424, 556, 611, 715
World Union of Documentary, 45
World Without End, 735, 776
Wozzeck, 594
Wrath of the Gods, The, 272, 287
Wray, Fay, 144, 185, 207
Wright, Basil, 49, 619, 735, 736, 776
Writers, as directors, 50
Wuthering Heights, 488
Wyler, William, 35, 52, 53, 57, 463, 465, 468, 488-9, 729

Y

Yamamura, Sartoru, 767
Yank at Oxford, The, 551

Yellow Pass, The, 247
Yolanda and the Thief, 502
You and Me, 456, 480, 481
You Can't Take It With You, 452
You Never Know Women, 213
Young Guard, The, 754
Young Mr. Lincoln, 484
Young Mr. Pitt, 559
Young Stranger, The, 728
You Only Live Once, 456, 480
Your Freedom is at Stake, 606
Youth of Maxim, The, 575n.
Youth of Queen Louise, The, 284
Youth Railway, 610
Youth Runs Wild, 507
Yugoslavia, 41; film industry in, 41, 610-11, 753
Yuri-Tarich, —, 226-7, 247-8
Yutkevich, Sergei, 566, 569, 579n., 754
Yvette, 309

Z

Zampa, Luigi, 600
Zanuck, Darryl, 440, 485, 534
Zarkhi, Nathan A., 227
Zarzycki, Jerzy, 757
Zavattini, Cesar, 743-4, 746, 777
Zeebrugge, 123, 322
Zeller, Wolfgang, 308
Zelnig, Frederick, 288
Zeman, Darel, 758
Zéro de Conduite, 117n., 541, *674*
Zharki, Alexander, 576, 579n.
Zheliabuzhski, —, 226, 227
Ziegfeld Follies, 502
Zils, Paul, 764n.
Zinnemann, Fred, 616, 727, 729, 730
Zola, Emile, 187, 188, 307, 308, 309, 310, 534
Zola, 457, 493, 580
Zone, La, 229
Zone de la Mort, La, 311
Zoo in Budapest, 381n.
Zukor, Adolf, 71-2, 91, 165
Zvenigora, 116, 118, 238, 239, 370